Communication and Culture

READINGS IN THE CODES OF HUMAN INTERACTION

Communication and Culture

READINGS IN THE CODES OF HUMAN INTERACTION

ALFRED G. SMITH
University of Oregon

HOLT, RINEHART AND WINSTON
New York   Chicago   San Francisco   Toronto   London

Preface

This book is broad in scope. It reaches freely across many different fields of study. But all of its range converges and focuses on a single point—the heart and core of human communication.

Human communication is a subtle and ingenious set of processes. It is always thick with a thousand ingredients—signals, codes, meanings—no matter how simple the message or the transaction. Human communication is also a varied set of processes. It can use any one of a hundred different means, either words or gestures or punched cards, either intimate conversations or mass media and world-wide audiences. And human communication is an ever present set of processes. Whenever people interact, they communicate. To live in societies and to maintain their culture they have to communicate. When people control one another, they do so primarily through communication.

This book aims to present the basic features, the common denominators that are the underpinnings of all the subtlety, variety, and ubiquity of the processes of communication. It aims to present the common threads between verbal and nonverbal signals, between signals and meanings, and between face to face networks and national networks. This book aims to show how the findings of the various kinds of communication studies are related to one another, and how they elucidate and support one another. The unity of this book and its broad scope are two sides of the same coin.

The first part of the book presents the theory of human communication. This is based on three scientific approaches: the mathematical theory of communication; social psychology; and linguistic anthropology. The other three parts of this book use this theory to analyze the three major dimensions of human communication: syntactics; semantics; and pragmatics. These three approaches and three dimensions cut across one another, creating a matrix of three rows and three columns. These are the fundamental axes and parameters of the book. They create a heady interaction, a creative synthesis of many exciting fields of inquiry. The Introduction and the introductions to each of the chapters will explain further how each part of the book fits into the design of the book as a whole.

This synthesis is presented through fifty-five selections. Each of these was chosen after weighing many factors and many alternatives. For any one selection included in this book, a dozen or more were excluded. These choices were made using five primary criteria. First, each selection had to be essential in the over-all plan of the book. Second, all selections had to be written after the publication of Shannon and of Wiener. Third, all the selections had to be tied to one another internally. The goal was for each selection to be a development of the preceding one and a springboard for the next one. Fourth, each selection had to be grounded in empirical tests—or in testability in any event. And fifth, each had to meet the test of the classroom. In my classes this has meant that it had to be fully understandable by nonspecialists. Were the social psychology majors able to understand the selection on morphemes, after they had read the preceding selections? With a little appropriate effort, were the linguistic anthropology majors able to understand the selections on feedback? Were the journalism majors able to understand the selections on equilibrium theory and relate them to mass communication? In every case the answer had to be yes.

In order to meet these five criteria many of the selections were also edited. This editing removed redundancy from one selection to the next. The editing also filtered out the noise of irrelevancy, deleting parts that did not fit the function of the selection in the book. Footnotes and references were deleted from individual selections because they were highly repetitious from one selection to the next, and because many of the studies they referred to are themselves reprinted here. In the place of references for each selection there is a carefully selected bibliography for the book as a whole at the end. The editing also aimed to make the selections more readable, uniform, and inviting.

All of the editing was done with the approval of the authors, and generally with their active participation and help. The cooperation of all the authors in this enterprise has been a wonderful and happy experience for me. I am deeply grateful to each one of them.

I am also indebted to the copyright holders for permitting the selections to be reprinted. And I acknowledge with real satisfaction all the good offices of the staff of Holt, Rinehart and Winston, Inc. My gratitude to my wife, Britta, is beyond measure.

Eugene, Oregon
January 1966

ALFRED G. SMITH

Contents

Communication and Culture

READINGS IN THE CODES OF HUMAN INTERACTION

CHAPTER I

Introduction: Communication and Culture

Living is largely a matter of communicating. The husband kisses his wife; the customer looks at the price tag; the pupil raises his hand; the little girl smiles. They are all communicating. People communicate from morning to night, particularly in the modern world, where most people make their living communicating. Authors and actors, preachers and teachers are professional communicators. Most other people also make their living communicating, as salesmen, policemen, secretaries, or psychiatrists. In modern society few people farm, hunt, or draw water for a living; most people transmit information. When communication is not their principal line of work, it is still a principal part of their life. The coal miner attends a union meeting, the carpenter bids for a contract, the father teaches his son. They communicate through language and through other codes of human interaction.

In modern society different people communicate in different ways, as do people in different societies around the world; and the way people communicate is the way they live. It is their culture. Who talks with whom? How? And about what? These are questions of communication and culture. A Japanese geisha and a New England librarian send and receive different messages on different channels and in different networks. When the elements of communication differ or change, the elements of culture differ or change. Communication and culture are inseparable.

Three kinds of investigators have made most of the empirical studies of human communication: mathematicians, social psychologists, and linguistic anthropologists. Human communication has also been divided into three principal parts: syntactics, semantics, and pragmatics. These investigators and these parts cut across one another, creating a matrix of three rows and three columns in which to formulate and answer most questions about human communication.

The first kind of investigator is a special kind of mathematician, like Claude E. Shannon and Norbert Wiener. They are partly electronic engineers, partly theoretical physicists, and partly communications analysts. Their studies stem from two sources. The first is from technical developments in telecommunications engineering, that is, from innovations in telephone, computer, and television circuitry. The mathematical formulations of these developments have had implications that go far beyond the wires and switches of these circuits. They have, for example, introduced new concepts for studying face-to-face communication and for studying the social organization of human groups. The mathematicians have had this influence because they developed fruitful models of communication processes in general.

The basic concern of these mathematical studies is the transmission of messages, either exactly or approximately, from one point to another. This linear transmission involves many problems, and the mathematical answers to these problems developed such new concepts as noise and redundancy, channels and equilibrium. These kinds of concepts help to answer such electronic questions as: (1) How much of the living quality of the human voice does a telephone have to transmit for the message to be intelligible? (2) What is the relation between the speed of transmission and the fidelity of transmission, as in playing a phonograph or tape recorder at different speeds? These are mathematical questions before they are questions of human hearing. The mathematical concepts used to answer these questions have led to a linear model of communication that has helped to illuminate many other aspects of human behavior.

The mathematical studies also stem from the concept of feedback. This refers to a circular process rather than a linear one, and it is the basis of automatic control devices. When a guided missile is launched, such as a rocket to the moon, it is set a course. It is given a set of instructions or messages that says: "Do X until Y happens and then do Z." If the missile swerves from its course by doing $X + 1$ instead of X, its deviation is fed back to change the original instructions automatically, from Z to $Z - 1$. The study of such automatic control systems is cybernetics. Among other things, cybernetics has stimulated automation in industry, led to new studies of automatic changes in our physiological system, such as changes of blood pressure and endocrine output, and it has produced new studies of the social controls that are a part of our social systems. In all these servomechanisms, feedback is a matter of communication, of transmitting information. Since the response to one message often controls the next message to be sent, feedback and cybernetics are keystones for understanding human communication generally.

Through communication people control one another's behavior and unite themselves into groups. It is the social psychologist who studies how people interact in these ways. In his studies of human communication the social psychologist adopts and adapts many concepts of the mathematical theory of communication, concepts like channels and networks, feedback and equilibrium. The social psychologist may be trained as an anthropologist, communications analyst, political scientist, or as some other behavioral scientist, but whatever his training, he studies group dynamics—in a juvenile gang, in a business conference, in a combat unit, or in a whole society. What are the lines of communication within the group? Do leaders use the same channels that the other members use? Are some kinds of communicational organizations more efficient than others? The social psychologist also studies how social interaction affects the attitudes of individuals within the group. When are rumors accepted and when are they rejected? In a mass society, how do the media of mass interaction such as newspapers and television affect an individual's opinion?

As the mathematical theory of communication is related to electronic engineering but is also distinct from it, so the social psychology of communication is related to the sociology and the psychology of language, but it is also quite distinct from them. Language is one of many forms of human communication. It is basically a matter of talking and listening, of "How are you?" and "I am fine." Language is a form of behavior, of actions such as speaking and of reactions such as understanding what was said. Linguistic behavior is a part of the full web of human interaction. People interact not only through words but also through spatial relations, as when a boy sidles up to a girl. They interact through temporal relations, as when the girl keeps the boy waiting. And people interact through gesture and touch and many other media. They not only send and receive information in these many different ways; they use each of these ways for participating in a communal dialogue, for reciprocating and mediating one another's meanings. Communication is far more comprehensive than language.

The sociology and the psychology of language have a narrower scope than the social psychology of communication. Sociological linguistics studies different kinds of speech situations, like whispering in church and shouting at a ball game. It also studies differences in speech communities, like different dialect areas and the jargons of different occupations. The related field of psychological linguistics studies speech behavior. This includes among other things: how we learn to speak, the relation between speaking and thinking, and deviations in speech behavior like stuttering and aphasia. The social psychology of communication, with which we are concerned, differs from these studies by focusing not so much on speech as on all the forms of communal interaction among individuals and groups.

The linguistic anthropologist is the third kind of investigator. He may be trained as an anthropologist or as a linguist or as both, or in communications or foreign languages. The linguistic anthropologist, like the cultural and the physical anthropologist, studies the various peoples of the world: how they resemble and differ from one another, and how they have changed and developed. The linguistic anthropologist differs from the other anthropologists in being less concerned with human biology and technology—with variations in hat size and in ways of chipping arrowheads—and being more concerned with the languages of the peoples of the world. Each language is a code of human interaction. Some of these codes are verbal and involve words and sentences. Some of these codes are vocal but nonverbal and involve tones of voice. Still other codes are nonverbal and nonvocal and involve gestures and other kinds of action and conduct.

While the mathematician is concerned with electronic signals, the linguistic anthropologist studies human signals. While the social psychologist is generally concerned with human communication in his own culture in his own time, the linguistic anthropologist works with a world-wide range of data, with all the codes of the Greeks, the Bantu, and the Samoans. This broad range of data provides a necessary test of generalizations that may have been derived from too small a sample, from studying only one's own way of behavior. Most important, the linguistic anthropologist contributes a rigorous methodology and a set of theoretical concepts. These procedures and concepts identify minimal or emic units in the codes. Although these units were originally established in the analysis of speech, they can guide the analysis of other codes of human interaction. The linguistic anthropologist is the third leg of the tripod; the analysis of human communication is a free-standing enterprise.

These three approaches—the mathematical, the social psychological, and the linguistic anthropological—join to form a theoretical orientation. Part 1 of this book presents this theoretical background. The other three parts of the book use that theory to analyze the three major divisions of human communication: the syntactic, the semantic, and the pragmatic. These terms were first used by philosophers, such as C. S. Peirce and C. W. Morris, and they are now used by telecommunications engineers, such as Colin Cherry, and by psychologists, such as S. S. Stevens. These divisions are definable in different ways, and with some shift in meaning they are sometimes given different names, such as the technical, the semantic, and the influential. For our purposes, however, syntactics studies how signs are related to each other. Semantics studies how these signs are related to things. And pragmatics studies how they are related to people. These three divisions study different kinds of relationships, not different kinds of substances or entities.

These divisions have many doors and windows for communicating among one another; they are not sealed compartments. No act of communication is purely syntactic or semantic or pragmatic. No act is even pure communication. Teaching a class, for example, is not only an act of communicating; it is also an adjunct for fielding a football team; it is a symbol of pure and disinterested truth supported by a society that often sweats and schemes for money; teaching is many things and has many functions. So is every act that we call communication. In the same way no aspect of communication is purely syntactic, semantic, or pragmatic. These divisions simply help to organize our analyses. Moreover, these three divisions are cross-cut by the approaches of the three kinds of investigators. Together the divisions and the approaches form a single organizational matrix.

Syntactics studies the relations of signs to signs, and most empirical studies of human communication have been devoted to syntactics. In a sentence, for example, each word is related to the other words. This is the syntax of that sentence. One way these words are related is in their position or arrangement; another way is in their inflection or grammatical form. In "Nancy kisses the boys," the words are arranged in one way; in "The boys kiss Nancy," the position of the words is changed, and the grammatical form of the verb is also changed. Every message consists of words, or of gestures like bowing or kneeling, or of other forms of symbolic behavior. Every message consists of signs and these signs are related to one another. This is the syntactic relationship.

Mathematicians and linguistic anthropologists are primarily concerned with syntactics. The mathematicians find that signs are related to each other in being too predictable, which is redundancy, or in being unpredictable, which is entropy, or in being other things. The linguistic anthropologist finds other kinds of relationships in the syntax of German or Swahili. He finds, for example, that adjectives must agree with nouns, as in *liebe Frau* but *lieber Mann*. This repetition of the gender is a kind of redundancy. It is a matter of syntax, of the relation between signs and signs.

While the mathematicians and the linguistic anthropologists have analyzed the syntactics within messages, the social psychologists have analyzed the syntactics between messages. Redundancy is a relation not only within messages like, "I love you. I love you," but it also exists between messages as in the dialogue: "Good morning." "Good morning." For people to communicate with one another they must not only have a common set of signs, but also a common set of relations among these signs. We must have a certain amount of redundancy, a certain amount of entropy, and other determinate relations. We need these relations not only within messages but also between messages.

Space forms one important relation between messages. Messages are sent across space, from point *A* to point *B*. When people communicate with one another they organize this space into communication networks. Social psychologists have found that different groups organize their social distances into different syntactic structures, just as different languages have different grammars. These social networks represent who talks with whom. In a bureaucracy, for example, social distances and lines of communication are organized into various hierarchies. The messages that travel up the echelons of any one hierarchy are not the same as those that travel down, yet the ones going one way elicit those going the other way. These relations between messages are the grammar of interaction in the human group. There is redundancy, entropy, and other syntactic relations among these messages and in these networks. It is both logical and fruitful to extend the traditional meaning of syntactics in this way to include the relation between message and message as well as the relation between sign and sign.

These syntactic relations are vehicles for communicating meaning. The syntactic structure in "The boys kiss Nancy" communicates one meaning; changing the syntax to "Nancy kisses the boys" changes the meaning. In the same way, the message, "We are going to work only thirty hours a week," means one thing when it is sent up the echelons, and it means something else when it is sent down. Meaning depends largely on structure, and there is a logical development from syntactics to semantics. The relation between sign and sign is, however, only a first dimension of semantics. Besides structural meaning, there is also assigned meaning. This is the relation between a sign and an object, between the name "Nancy" and the girl who is called by that name.

The three kinds of investigators are not equally concerned with semantics. The mathematicians are generally concerned with the transmission of messages and not with the meaning of these messages. "These semantic aspects of communication," Claude E. Shannon said, "are irrelevant to the engineering problem." In the mathematical theory of communication, meaning is a part of the processes of encoding and decoding. These are cultural processes beyond the scope of mathematical theory. In some mathematical theories, particularly those of logical syntax, semantics deals with the truth of a proposition, but that is beyond the scope of communication theory. It is the social psychologists and the linguistic anthropologists who are concerned with semantics, because they are concerned with learned, shared, and symbolic behavior.

Meaning is a product of coding, and coding is a form of behavior that is learned and shared by the members of a communicating group. A

Burmese learns to code like other Burmese and a Bushman learns to code like other Bushmen. This is how his words, gestures, and other forms of communication can carry any meaning. Coding is learned and shared, and any behavior that is learned and shared is cultural. Making an arrowhead, tying one's shoelaces, calling a man your brother, believing and denying, these are all cultural forms of behavior. Breathing is also a form of behavior, but ordinarily we do not learn to breathe; we just do it automatically. Some Hindu ascetics, however, do learn to breathe in special ways. Their forms of breathing are no longer automatic and direct. Ideas have intervened. Their behavior is learned and standardized and mediated by symbols. To look at the world around us is a form of behavior. Each of us learns to look at it in the way that other members of our communicating group have learned to look at it. We learn to see it as more than the buzzing blooming confusion we saw when we were first born. We look at it now through learned concepts, categories, and labels: animal, vegetable, and mineral; eatable, drinkable, and desirable; good, bad, and indifferent. Our perception is behavior that is learned and shared, and it is mediated by symbols. Culture is a code we learn and share, and learning and sharing require communication. And communication requires coding and symbols, which must be learned and shared. Communication and culture are inseparable.

The social psychologists and the linguistic anthropologists are concerned with the semantics of communication. They are concerned with coding in general, and also with whether different peoples organize their perceptions into different categories of meaning. Does the Bantu word for "blue" refer to the same part of the spectrum as the Pushtu word? This is a perennial issue for semantics. It is also an issue for pragmatics.

Pragmatics studies how people react to signs. This follows from the way they decode those signs. Pragmatics follows semantics. How do these people react to cuff shooting and Bible thumping in a sermon? How do those people interpret the news of the war? How do signs affect behavior? The social psychologist, rather than the mathematician or the linguistic anthropologist, has made most of the studies in pragmatics. By and large he has studied the reactions to signs in two kinds of communicating groups: small experimental face-to-face groups of about five people each; and the large groups of mass communication and public opinion studies. Pragmatics in small groups is a direct by-product of small group structures and is therefore treated with syntactics. The last part of this book emphasizes pragmatics in large groups.

The three investigators—mathematicians, social psychologists, and linguistic anthropologists—and the three divisions—syntactics, semantics, and pragmatics—form an organizational matrix for the study of human communication. It is possible to approach the subject in other ways and with other categories. It is possible, for example, to follow the parts of the mathematical model of communication, or perhaps reorganize them into: senders and receivers, encoding and decoding, signs and messages. It is possible to follow the pentad of Kenneth Burke: act, scene, agent, agency, and purpose. I have found, however, that the organizational matrix developed here best integrates the various aspects and the various empirical studies into a single picture. This matrix also defines the field most clearly and gives that picture its sharpest focus. Within this framework of integration and focus, this matrix provides the broadest coverage, the biggest picture. It is also based on familiar or readily understood concepts and, most important, it is fruitful. It leads to the development of new hypotheses and theories.

The primary aim of this book is to build a theoretical framework for empirical research. Our organizational matrix gives the outlines of such a theory. This theoretical organization is important because the way a field is organized helps determine whether that field is accepted for research, and accepted for what kind of research. This is particularly important in the field of human communication because that is a teeming wilderness of facts and notions, instances and generalizations, proofs and surmises. Many explorers have beaten paths through these jungles, not only mathematicians, social psychologists, and linguistic anthropologists, but other kinds of anthropologists, linguists, psychologists, and sociologists as well, and also ethologists, journalists, management engineers, philosophers, semanticists, and many more. Some of these paths cross, some go in circles, and some lead into other jungles. These pathways have seldom been planned as parts of an over-all network. Without such a plan or map, without some reference points, we cannot identify and interpret the contributions of old research, nor can we orient ourselves in new research. The organizational matrix used in this book is devised to provide such a map.

This map is also devised by the principles used to winnow and sift the selections and readings. This book is a mosaic: many carefully selected pieces are fitted together to create a single picture. The mathematical theory of communication is the point of departure for this theoretical framework. Therefore all the selections in this book were written after the publication of the mathematical theory, and they were directly or indirectly informed by it. The mathematical theory is based on empirical data and is designed to promote further inquiry. Each selection in this book is also based on empirical data and serves to develop a heuristic theory. We particularly need empirical data when using electronic theories as points of departure for human theories because the translations from one theory to the other are otherwise questionable analogies. In the mathematical theory, for example, redundancy yields no new information. In human communication, however, redundancy may be impossible: each successive reception of the same signal changes the decoding of that signal. To some extent the same signal cannot be received more than once. This is not a matter for Heraclitean conjecture, but for empirical research. This research has, in fact, led to that tautology in advertising, to the controlled repetition of the name of the sponsor in the message from your sponsor. In the same way, human feedback is often quite different from electronic feedback; it may not only be delayed and discontinuous, but also positive and negative at the same time. A third concept, entropy, is already a kind of analogy from thermodynamics in the mathematical theory. When the analogy is stretched further to human communication, it generally leads to more confusion than enlightenment. This concept has not led to new empirical data about human communication. Therefore, although there are chapters on redundancy and on feedback in this book, there is no chapter on entropy.

To the theory of electronic communication we add the idea of culture. Here again we have winnowed and sifted the selections. Communication and culture are learned, and there is a large body of research on how they are learned. Those learning studies are beyond the scope of this book, which considers how people communicate rather than how they learn to communicate. Also beyond the scope of this book is how the human species learned to communicate. Many different kinds of scholars, from anthropology to zoology, ride under the banners of ethology and study communication among monkeys and apes, and among bees and dolphins. These studies often provide a suggestive perspective for understanding human communication, but they are not broached here. The learning process sometimes goes astray, and this leads to pathologies of communication, such as aphasia or the disarticulation of schizophrenia. All studies of pathology are also winnowed out. The theoretical framework of this book is limited to the acts of human communication: what they are; what they mean; and what effects they have.

The various selections were originally written for their own various purposes. Each selection was not written to be a piece in the mosaic of this book. To make these pieces fit together into a single picture, they were carefully selected, and then many of the pieces were edited by cutting off parts that do not fit into the context in this book. If each selection were a poem or a short story such deletions would destroy the literary form, but editing scientific reports serves to sharpen their focus on the issue at hand and to integrate them into a coherent pattern.

And so this book strives for a theoretical integration. It means to unite things that belong together but that are often seen separately. They are often seen, therefore, as insignificant and meaningless, for nothing has meaning in itself. There are separate headlines in this morning's newspaper about a battle in Asia, a rise in the market, and a victory for Springfield. No one of these headlines has any meaning by itself. Each item becomes meaningful only when it is related to some other item. Did the market go up because Springfield won? Or is it significant that the market went up because this is the first time in six weeks? By the same token, no one aspect of human communication, such as speech, is really understandable apart from all the other codes of human interaction. Things only have meaning in their relation to other things. The solitary and isolated thing, all alone, is unintelligible.

Nor is there any more meaning in a random plurality of facts. All the data on human communication are like a sky full of stars on a winter's night. They form an irrational jumble, a chaos, senseless and incomprehensible—unless we arrange the plurality of stars into constellations, and organize the random facts of human interaction into some comparable outline. Our facts become meaningful by being related to each other. All things are not necessarily meaningful. Some things may be unrelated and at loose ends. But we can aim to fit as many facts together as possible.

Only then do they become useful and practical. Only when we see the stars as constellations can any one star keep us on our course. Only when we see our communicational facts and experiments in a theoretical configuration can they serve as guides in our research and in our daily lives. This book is not directly concerned with the utility of these facts. It describes and explains how people interact, not how they should interact for greater effectiveness or enjoyment. This book is descriptive rather than prescriptive. But although it does not lead us on any specific line of flight, it does give us a chart from which we can take our bearings.

PART 1

The Theory of
Human Communication

CHAPTER II

The Mathematical Theory

INTRODUCTION   We begin with an introduction to communication theory. There are three principal traditions in this theory: the mathematical; the social psychological; and the linguistic. The mathematical theory stems from the work of mathematicians and engineers who helped create the modern radio, telephone, and television as means of electronic communication. These mathematicians and engineers also created the electronic computers and the other instruments of modern automation.

Warren Weaver's "The Mathematics of Communication" introduces the theory of telecommunications engineering. It presents the general model that these mathematicians have constructed of the communication process. It involves a *source* selecting a *message* that is *encoded* into *signals* by a *transmitter*; a *receiver decodes* the signals so that the *destination* can recover the original message. This is a linear process because it has a beginning and an end, a source and a destination. The messages that are received, however, also affect the messages that are sent. Norbert Wiener adds the concept of feedback which introduces circular processes into the model. Wiener's "Cybernetics" reports on the studies of these feedback controls that are used to guide missiles and to automate mass production in factories. These same feedback controls also regulate the physiological and mental processes of the body, and they are equally important in regulating our social relations. "In short, the newer study of automata, whether in the metal or in the flesh, is a branch of communications engineering, and its cardinal ideas are those of the message, of the amount of disturbance or 'noise' (a term taken from the telephone engineer), of the quantity of information to be transmitted, of coding technique, and so on."

The next two selections restate this general model of communication and develop some of the specific concepts, such as noise, redundancy, entropy, and feedback. Colin Cherry's "The Communication of Information" shows the relation between communication theory and cybernetics, the relation in fact between the Weaver and Wiener selections. Parts of the selection by Cherry also serve to indicate the technicality of the subject. Thus it provides a necessary brake on too glib a use of such technical terms as information, feedback, and channel capacity when speaking of human communication. Anatol Rapoport's "What is Information?" is also a restatement and amplification of the concepts of information, signal, code, and entropy. He shows how these concepts are definable mathematically in terms of probability and statistics. Communication requires some regularity and orderliness, some structure in the code, or grammar in the language; it also requires some disorder and the unexpected, some surprise value in a message. Probability and statistics express these degrees of disorder and order in communication. Rapoport also extends these concepts beyond the realm of communication proper. "Life, therefore, depends essentially on an ordering process. . . ."

While Weaver's selection started with a broad meaning of the word "communication," which included "all of the procedures by which one mind can affect another," the last selection of this group reexamines the definition of communication. In "A Rationale for a Definition of Communication," John B. Newman demonstrates that we need "*a* meaning *for* communication" rather than "*the* meaning *of* communication." He gives the parameters of such a definition, giving the form that a satisfactory definition of the term must have, and he supplies some of the content also.

1 | The Mathematics of Communication
WARREN WEAVER

How do men communicate, one with another? The spoken word, either direct or by telephone or radio; the written or printed word, transmitted by hand, by post, by telegraph, or in any other way—these are obvious and common forms of communication. But there are many others. A nod or a wink, a drumbeat in the jungle, a gesture pictured on a television screen, the blinking of a signal light, a bit of music that reminds one of an event in the past, puffs of smoke in the desert air, the movements and posturing in a ballet—all of these are means men use to convey ideas.

The word communication, in fact, will be used here in a very broad sense to include all of the procedures by which one mind can affect another. Although the language used will often refer specifically to the communication of speech, practically everything said applies equally to music, to pictures, to a variety of other methods of conveying information.

In communication there seem to be problems at three levels: 1) technical, 2) semantic, and 3) influential.

The technical problems are concerned with the accuracy of transference of information from sender to receiver. They are inherent in all forms of communication, whether by sets of discrete symbols (written speech), or by a varying signal (telephonic or radio transmission of voice or music), or by a varying two-dimensional pattern (television).

The semantic problems are concerned with the interpretation of meaning by the receiver, as compared with the intended meaning of the sender. This is a very deep and involved situation, even when one deals only with the relatively simple problems of communicating through speech. For example, if Mr. X is suspected not to understand what Mr. Y says, then it is not possible, by having Mr. Y do nothing but talk further with Mr. X, completely to clarify this situation in any finite time. If Mr. Y says "Do you now understand me?" and Mr. X says "Certainly I do," this is not necessarily a certification that understanding has been achieved. It may just be that Mr. X did not understand the question. If this sounds silly, try it again as "Czy pan mnie rozumie?" with the answer "Hai wakkate imasu." In the restricted field of speech communication, the difficulty may be reduced to a tolerable size, but never completely eliminated, by "explanations." They are presumably never more than approximations to the ideas being explained, but are understandable when phrased in language that has previously been made reasonably clear by usage. For example, it does not take long to make the symbol for "yes" in any language understandable.

The problems of influence or effectiveness are concerned with the success with which the meaning conveyed to the receiver leads to the desired conduct of his part. It may seem at first glance undesirably narrow to imply that the purpose of all communication is to influence the conduct of the receiver. But with any reasonably broad definition of conduct, it is clear that communication either affects conduct or is without any discernible and provable effect at all.

One might be inclined to think that the technical problems involve only the engineering details of good design of a communication system, while the semantic and the effectiveness problems contain most if not all of the philosophical content of the general problem of communication. To see that this is not the case, we must now examine some important recent work in the mathematical theory of communication.

This is by no means a wholly new theory. As the mathematician John von Neumann has pointed out, the 19th-century Austrian physicist Ludwig Boltzmann suggested that some concepts of statistical mechanics were applicable to the concept of information. Other scientists, notably Norbert Wiener of the Massachusetts Institute of Technology, have made profound contributions. The work which will be here reported is that of Claude Shannon of the Bell Telephone Laboratories, which was preceded by that of H. Nyquist and R. V. L. Hartley in the same organization. This work applies in the first instance only to the technical problem, but the theory has broader significance. To begin with, meaning and effectiveness are inevitably restricted by the theoretical limits of accuracy in symbol transmission. Even more significant, a theoretical analysis of the technical problem reveals that it overlaps the semantic and the effectiveness problems more than one might suspect.

A communication system is symbolically represented in the drawing in Figure 1. The information source selects a desired message out of

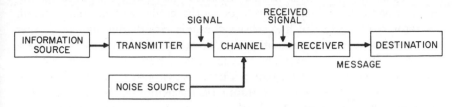

Figure 1. A communication system may be reduced to these fundamental elements. In telephony the signal is a varying electric current, and the channel is a wire. In speech the signal is varying sound pressure, and the channel the air. Frequently things not intended by the information source are impressed on the signal. The static of radio is one example; distortion in telephony is another. All these additions may be called noise.

a set of possible messages. (As will be shown, this is a particularly important function.) The transmitter changes this message into a signal which is sent over the communication channel to the receiver.

The receiver is a sort of inverse transmitter, changing the transmitted signal back into a message, and handing this message on to the destination. When I talk to you, my brain is the information source, yours the destination; my vocal system is the transmitter, and your ear with the eighth nerve is the receiver.

In the process of transmitting the signal, it is unfortunately characteristic that certain things not intended by the information source are added to the signal. These unwanted additions may be distortions of sound (in telephony, for example), or static (in radio), or distortions in the shape or shading of a picture (television), or errors in transmission (telegraphy or facsimile). All these changes in the signal may be called noise.

The questions to be studied in a communication system have to do with the amount of information, the capacity of the communication channel, the coding process that may be used to change a message into a signal and the effects of noise.

First off, we have to be clear about the rather strange way in which, in this theory, the word "information" is used; for it has a special sense which, among other things, must not be confused at all with meaning. It is surprising but true that, from the present viewpoint, two messages, one heavily loaded with meaning and the other pure nonsense, can be equivalent as regards information.

In fact, in this new theory the word information relates not so much to what you *do* say, as to what you *could* say. That is, information is a measure of your freedom of choice when you select a message. If you are confronted with a very elementary situation where you have to choose one of two alternative messages, then it is arbitrarily said that the information associated with this situation is unity. The concept of information applies not to the individual messages, as the concept of meaning would, but rather to the situation as a whole, the unit information indicating that in this situation one has an amount of freedom of choice, in selecting a message, which it is convenient to regard as a standard or unit amount. The two messages between which one must choose in such a selection can be anything one likes. One might be the King James version of the Bible, and the other might be "Yes."

The remarks thus far relate to artificially simple situations where the information source is free to choose only among several definite messages —like a man picking out one of a set of standard birthday-greeting tele- grams. A more natural and more important situation is that in which the information source makes a sequence of choices from some set of ele- mentary symbols, the selected sequence then forming the message. Thus a man may pick out one word after another, these individually selected words then adding up to the message.

Obviously probability plays a major role in the generation of the mes- sage, and the choices of the successive symbols depend upon the preced- ing choices. Thus, if we are concerned with English speech, and if the last symbol chosen is "the," then the probability that the next word will be an article, or a verb form other than a verbal, is very small. After the three words "in the event," the probability for "that" as the next word is fairly high, and for "elephant" as the next word is very low. Similarly, the probability is low for such a sequence of words as "Constantinople fishing nasty pink." Incidentally, it is low, but not zero, for it is perfectly possible to think of a passage in which one sentence closes with "Con- stantinople fishing," and the next begins with "Nasty pink." (We might observe in passing that the sequence under discussion *has* occurred in a single good English sentence, namely the one second preceding.)

As a matter of fact, Shannon has shown that when letters or words chosen at random are set down in sequences dictated by probability con- siderations alone, they tend to arrange themselves in meaningful words and phrases.

Now let us return to the idea of information. The quantity which uniquely meets the natural requirements that one sets up for a measure of information turns out to be exactly that which is known in thermo- dynamics as entropy, or the degree of randomness, or of "shuffledness" if you will, in a situation. It is expressed in terms of the various probabilities involved.

To those who have studied the physical sciences, it is most significant that an entropy-like expression appears in communication theory as a measure of information. The concept of entropy, introduced by the

German physicist Rudolf Clausius nearly 100 years ago, closely associated with the name of Boltzmann, and given deep meaning by Willard
Gibbs of Yale in his classic work on statistical mechanics, has become so
basic and pervasive a concept that Sir Arthur Eddington remarked:
"The law that entropy always increases—the second law of thermodynamics—holds, I think, the supreme position among the laws of Nature."

Thus when one meets the concept of entropy in communication theory,
he has a right to be rather excited. That information should be measured
by entropy is, after all, natural when we remember that information is
associated with the amount of freedom of choice we have in constructing
messages. Thus one can say of a communication source, just as he would
also say of a thermodynamic ensemble: "This situation is highly organized; it is not characterized by a large degree of randomness or of choice
—that is to say, the information, or the entropy, is low."

We must keep in mind that in the mathematical theory of communication we are concerned not with the meaning of individual messages but
with the whole statistical nature of the information source. Thus one is
not surprised that the capacity of a channel of communication is to be
described in terms of the amount of information it can transmit, or better,
in terms of its ability to transmit what is produced out of a source of a
given information.

The transmitter may take a written message and use some code to en-
cipher this message into, say, a sequence of numbers, these numbers then
being sent over the channel as the signal. Thus one says, in general, that
the function of the transmitter is to encode, and that of the receiver to
decode, the message. The theory provides for very sophisticated transmitters and receivers—such, for example, as possess "memories," so that
the way they encode a certain symbol of the message depends not only
upon this one symbol but also upon previous symbols of the message and
the way they have been encoded.

We are now in a position to state the fundamental theorem for a noiseless channel transmitting discrete symbols. This theorem relates to a
communication channel which has a capacity of C units per second, accepting signals from an information source of H units per second. The
theorem states that by devising proper coding procedures for the transmitter it is possible to transmit symbols over the channel at an average rate
which is nearly C/H, but which, no matter how clever the coding, can
never be made to exceed C/H.

Viewed superficially, say in rough analogy to the use of transformers to
match impedances in electrical circuits, it seems very natural, although
certainly pretty neat, to have this theorem which says that efficient coding
is that which matches the statistical characteristics of information source

and channel. But when it is examined in detail for any one of the vast array of situations to which this result applies, one realizes how deep and powerful this theory is.

How does noise affect information? Information, we must steadily remember, is a measure of one's freedom of choice in selecting a message. The greater this freedom of choice, the greater is the uncertainty that the message actually selected is some particular one. Thus greater freedom of choice, greater uncertainty and greater information all go hand in hand.

If noise is introduced, then the received message contains certain distortions, certain errors, certain extraneous material, that would certainly lead to increased uncertainty. But if the uncertainty is increased, the information is increased, and this sounds as though the noise were beneficial!

It is true that when there is noise, the received signal is selected out of a more varied set of signals than was intended by the sender. This situation beautifully illustrates the semantic trap into which one can fall if he does not remember that "information" is used here with a special meaning that measures freedom of choice and hence uncertainty as to what choice has been made. Uncertainty that arises by virtue of freedom of choice on the part of the sender is desirable uncertainty. Uncertainty that arises because of errors or because of the influence of noise is undesirable uncertainty. To get the useful information in the received signal we must subtract the spurious portion. This is accomplished, in the theory, by establishing a quantity known as the "equivocation," meaning the amount of ambiguity introduced by noise. One then refines or extends the previous definition of the capacity of a noiseless channel, and states that the capacity of a noisy channel is defined to be equal to the maximum rate at which useful information (*i.e.*, total uncertainty minus noise uncertainty) can be transmitted over the channel.

Now, finally, we can state the great central theorem of this whole communication theory. Suppose a noisy channel of capacity C is accepting information from a source of entropy H, entropy corresponding to the number of possible messages from the source. If the channel capacity C is equal to or larger than H, then by devising appropriate coding systems the output of the source can be transmitted over the channel with as little error as one pleases. But if the channel capacity C is less than H, the entropy of the source, then it is impossible to devise codes which reduce the error frequency as low as one may please.

However clever one is with the coding process, it will always be true that after the signal is received there remains some undesirable uncertainty about what the message was; and this undesirable uncertainty—this noise or equivocation—will always be equal to or greater than H minus C. But there is always at least one code capable of reducing this undesirable uncertainty down to a value that exceeds H minus C by a small amount.

This powerful theorem gives a precise and almost startlingly simple description of the utmost dependability one can ever obtain from a communication channel which operates in the presense of noise. One must think a long time, and consider many applications, before he fully realizes how powerful and general this amazingly compact theorem really is. One single application can be indicated here, but in order to do so, we must go back for a moment to the idea of the information of a source.

Having calculated the entropy (or the information, or the freedom of choice) of a certain information source, one can compare it to the maximum value this entropy could have, subject only to the condition that the source continue to employ the same symbols. The ratio of the actual to the maximum entropy is called the relative entropy of the source. If the relative entropy of a certain source is, say, eight-tenths, this means roughly that this source is, in its choice of symbols to form a message, about 80 percent as free as it could possibly be with these same symbols. One minus the relative entropy is called the "redundancy." That is to say, this fraction of the message is unnecessary in the sense that if it were missing the message would still be essentially complete, or at least could be completed.

It is most interesting to note that the redundancy of English is just about 50 percent. In other words, about half of the letters or words we choose in writing or speaking are under our free choice, and about half are really controlled by the statistical structure of the language, although we are not ordinarily aware of it. Incidentally, this is just about the minimum of freedom (or relative entropy) in the choice of letters that one must have to be able to construct satisfactory crossword puzzles. In a language that had only 20 percent of freedom, or 80 percent redundancy, it would be impossible to construct crossword puzzles in sufficient complexity and number to make the game popular.

Now since English is about 50 percent redundant, it would be impossible to save about one-half the time of ordinary telegraphy by a proper encoding process, provided one transmitted over a noiseless channel. When there is noise on a channel, however, there is some real advantage in not using a coding process that eliminates all of the redundancy. For the remaining redundancy helps combat the noise. It is the high redundancy of English, for example, that makes it easy to correct errors in spelling that have arisen during transmission.

The communication systems dealt with so far involve the use of a discrete set of symbols—say letters—only moderately numerous. One might well expect that the theory would become almost indefinitely more complicated when it seeks to deal with continuous messages such as those of the speaking voice, with its continuous variation of pitch and energy. As is often the case, however, a very interesting mathematical theorem comes to the rescue. As a practical matter, one is always interested in a continuous signal which is built up of simple harmonic constituents, not of all frequencies but only of those that lie wholly within a band from zero to, say, W cycles per second. Thus very satisfactory communication can be achieved over a telephone channel that handles frequencies up to about 4,000, although the human voice does contain higher frequencies. With frequencies up to 10,000 or 12,000, high-fidelity radio transmission of symphonic music is possible.

The theorem that helps us is one which states that a continuous signal, T seconds in duration and band-limited in frequency to the range from zero to W, can be completely specified by stating 2TW numbers. This is really a remarkable theorem. Ordinarily a continuous curve can be defined only approximately by a finite number of points. But if the curve is built up out of simple harmonic constituents of a limited number of frequencies, as a complex sound is built up out of a limited number of pure tones, then a finite number of quantities is all that is necessary to define the curve completely.

Thanks partly to this theorem, and partly to the essential nature of the situation, it turns out that the extended theory of continuous communication is somewhat more difficult and complicated mathematically, but not essentially different from the theory for discrete symbols. Many of the statements for the discrete case require no modification for the continuous case, and others require only minor change.

The mathematical theory of communication is so general that one does not need to say what kinds of symbols are being considered—whether written letters or words, or musical notes, or spoken words, or symphonic music, or pictures. The relationships it reveals apply to all these and to other forms of comunication. The theory is so imaginatively motivated that it deals with the real inner core of the communication problem.

One evidence of its generality is that the theory contributes importantly to, and in fact is really the basic theory of, cryptography, which is of course a form of coding. In a similar way, the theory contributes to the problem of translation from one language to another, although the complete story here clearly requires consideration of meaning, as well as of information. Similarly, the ideas developed in this work connect so closely with the problem of the logical design of computing machines that it is no surprise that Shannon has written a paper on the design of a computer that would be capable of playing a skillful game of chess. And it is of further pertinence to the present contention that his paper closes with the remark that either one must say that such a computer "thinks," or one must substantially modify the conventional implication of the verb "to think."

The theory goes further. Though ostensibly applicable only to problems at the technical level, it is helpful and suggestive at the levels of semantics and effectiveness as well. The formal diagram of a communication system in Figure 1 can, in all likelihood, be extended to include the central issues of meaning and effectiveness.

Thus when one moves to those levels it may prove to be essential to take account of the statistical characteristics of the destination. One can imagine, as an addition to the diagram, another box labeled "Semantic Receiver" interposed between the engineering receiver (which changes signals to messages) and the destination. This semantic receiver subjects the message to a second decoding, the demand on this one being that it must match the statistical semantic characteristics of the message to the statistical semantic capacities of the totality of receivers, or of that subset of receivers which constitutes the audience one wishes to affect.

Similarly one can imagine another box in the diagram which, inserted between the information source and the transmitter, would be labeled "Semantic Noise" (not to be confused with "engineering noise"). This would represent distortions of meaning introduced by the information source, such as a speaker, which are not intentional but nevertheless affect the destination, or listener. And the problem of semantic decoding must take this semantic noise into account. It is also possible to think of a treatment or adjustment of the original message that would make the sum of message meaning plus semantic noise equal to the desired total message meaning at the destination.

Another way in which the theory can be helpful in improving communication is suggested by the fact that error and confusion arise and fidelity decreases when, no matter how good the coding, one tries to crowd too much over a channel. A general theory at all levels will surely have to take into account not only the capacity of the channel but also (even the words are right!) the capacity of the audience. If you overcrowd the capacity of the audience, it is probably true, by direct analogy, that you do not fill the audience up and then waste only the remainder by spilling. More likely, and again by direct analogy, you force a general error and confusion.

The concept of information developed in this theory at first seems disappointing and bizarre—disappointing because it has nothing to do with meaning, and bizarre because it deals not with a single message but rather with the statistical character of a whole ensemble of messages, bizarre also because in these statistical terms the words information and uncertainty find themselves partners.

But we have seen upon further examination of the theory that this analysis has so penetratingly cleared the air that one is now perhaps for the first time ready for a real theory of meaning. An engineering communication theory is just like a very proper and discreet girl at the telegraph office accepting your telegram. She pays no attention to the meaning, whether it be sad or joyous or embarrassing. But she must be prepared to deal intelligently with all messages that come to her desk. This idea that a communication system ought to try to deal with all possible messages, and that the intelligent way to try is to base design on the statistical character of the source, is surely not without significance for communication in general. Language must be designed, or developed, with a view to the totality of things that man may wish to say; but not being able to accomplish everything, it should do as well as possible as often as possible. That is to say, it too should deal with its task statistically.

This study reveals facts about the statistical structure of the English language, as an example, which must seem significant to students of every phase of language and communication. It suggests, as a particularly promising lead, the application of probability theory to semantic studies. Especially pertinent is the powerful body of probability theory dealing with what mathematicians call the Markoff processes, whereby past events influence present probabilities, since this theory is specifically adapted to handle one of the most significant but difficult aspects of meaning, namely the influence of context. One has the vague feeling that information and meaning may prove to be something like a pair of canonically conjugate variables in quantum theory, that is, that information and meaning may be subject to some joint restriction that compels the sacrifice of one if you insist on having much of the other.

Or perhaps meaning may be shown to be analogous to one of the quantities on which the entropy of a thermodynamic ensemble depends. Here Eddington has another apt comment:

Suppose that we were asked to arrange the following in two categories—
distance, mass, electric force, entropy, beauty, melody.
I think there are the strongest grounds for placing entropy alongside beauty and melody, and not with the first three. Entropy is only found when the parts are viewed in association, and it is by viewing or hearing the parts in association that beauty and melody are discerned. All three are features of arrangement. It is a pregnant thought that one of these three associates should be able to figure as a commonplace quantity of science. The reason why this stranger can pass itself off among the aborigines of the physical world is that it is able to speak their language, *viz.,* the language of arithmetic.

One feels sure that Eddington would have been willing to include the word meaning along with beauty and melody; and one suspects he would have been thrilled to see, in this theory, that entropy not only speaks the language of arithmetic; it also speaks the language of language.

2 Cybernetics
NORBERT WIENER

Cybernetics is a word invented to define a new field in science. It combines under one heading the study of what in a human context is sometimes loosely described as thinking and in engineering is known as control and communication. In other words, cybernetics attempts to find the common elements in the functioning of automatic machines and of the human nervous system, and to develop a theory which will cover the entire field of control and communication in machines and in living organisms.

It is well known that between the most complex activities of the human brain and the operations of a simple adding machine there is a wide area where brain and machine overlap. In their more elaborate forms, modern computing machines are capable of memory, association, choice and many other brain functions. Indeed, the experts have gone so far in the elaboration of such machines that we can say the human brain behaves very much like the machines. The construction of more and more complex mechanisms actually is bringing us closer to an understanding of how the brain itself operates.

The word cybernetics is taken from the Greek *kybernetes*, meaning steersman. From the same Greek word, through the Latin corruption *gubernator*, came the term governor, which has been used for a long time to designate a certain type of control mechanism, and was the title of a brilliant study written by the Scottish physicist James Clerk Maxwell 80 years ago. The basic concept which both Maxwell and the investigators of cybernetics mean to describe by the choice of this term is that of a feedback mechanism, which is especially well represented by the steering engine of a ship. Its meaning is made clear by the following example.

Suppose that I pick up a pencil. To do this I have to move certain muscles. Only an expert anatomist knows what all these muscles are, and even an anatomist could hardly perform the act by a conscious exertion of the will to contract each muscle concerned in succession. Actually what we will is not to move individual muscles but to pick up the pencil.

Once we have determined on this, the motion of the arm and hand proceeds in such a way that we may say that the amount by which the pencil is not yet picked up is decreased at each stage. This part of the action is not in full consciousness.

To perform an action in such a manner, there must be a report to the nervous system, conscious or unconscious, of the amount by which we have failed to pick up the pencil at each instant. The report may be visual, at least in part, but it is more generally kinesthetic, or to use a term now in vogue, proprioceptive. If the proprioceptive sensations are wanting, and we do not replace them by a visual or other substitute, we are unable to perform the act of picking up the pencil, and find ourselves in a state known as ataxia. On the other hand, an excessive feedback is likely to be just as serious a handicap. In the latter case the muscles overshoot the mark and go into an uncontrollable oscillation. This condition, often associated with injury to the cerebellum, is known as purpose tremor.

Here, then, is a significant parallel between the workings of the nervous system and of certain machines. The feedback principle introduces an important new idea in nerve physiology. The central nervous system no longer appears to be a self-contained organ receiving signals from the senses and discharging into the muscles. On the contrary, some its most characteristic activities are explainable only as circular processes, traveling from the nervous system into the muscles and re-entering the nervous system through the sense organs. This finding seems to mark a step forward in the study of the nervous system as an integrated whole.

The new approach represented by cybernetics—an integration of studies which is not strictly biological or strictly physical, but a combination of the two—has already given evidence that it may help to solve many problems in engineering, in physiology and very likely in psychiatry.

This work represents the outcome of a program undertaken jointly several years ago by the writer and Arturo Rosenblueth, then of the Harvard Medical School and now of the National Institute of Cardiology of Mexico. Dr. Rosenblueth is a physiologist; I am a mathematician. For many years Dr. Rosenblueth and I had shared the conviction that the most fruitful areas for the growth of the sciences were those which had been neglected as no-man's lands between the various established fields. Dr. Rosenblueth always insisted that a proper exploration of these blank spaces on the map of science could be made only by a team of scientists, each a specialist but each possessing a thoroughly sound acquaintance with the fields of his fellows.

Our collaboration began as the result of a wartime project. I had been assigned, with a partner, Julian H. Bigelow, to the problem of working out a fire-control apparatus for anti-aircraft artillery which would be capable of tracking the curving course of a plane and predicting its future position. We soon came to the conclusion that any solution of the problem must depend heavily on the feedback principle, as it operated not only in the apparatus but in the human operators of the gun and of the plane. We approached Dr. Rosenblueth with a specific question concerning oscillations in the nervous system, and his reply, which cited the phenomenon of purpose tremor, confirmed our hypothesis about the importance of feedback in voluntary activity.

The ideas suggested by this discussion led to several joint experiments, one of which was a study of feedback in the muscles of cats. The scope of our investigations steadily widened, and as it did so scientists from widely diverse fields joined our group. Among them were the mathematicians John von Neumann of the Institute for Advanced Study and Walter Pitts of Massachusetts Institute of Technology; the physiologists Warren McCulloch of the University of Pennsylvania and Lorente de No of the Rockefeller Institute; the late Kurt Lewin, psychologist, of M.I.T.; the anthropologists Gregory Bateson and Margaret Mead; the economist Oskar Morgenstern of the Institute for Advanced Study; and others in psychology, sociology, engineering, anatomy, neurophysiology, physics, and so on.

The study of cybernetics is likely to have fruitful applications in many fields, from the design of control mechanisms for artificial limbs to the almost complete mechanization of industry. But in our view it encompasses much wider horizons. If the 17th and early 18th centuries were the age of clocks, and the latter 18th and 19th centuries the age of steam engines, the present time is the age of communication and control. There is in electical engineering a division which is known as the split between the technique of strong currents and the technique of weak currents; it is this split which separates the age just passed from that in which we are living. What distinguishes communication engineering from power engineering is that the main interest of the former is not the economy of energy but the accurate reproduction of a signal.

At every stage of technique since Daedalus, the ability of the artificer to produce a working simulacrum of a living organism has always intrigued people. In the days of magic, there was the bizarre and sinister concept of the Golem, that figure of clay into which the rabbi of Prague breathed life. In Isaac Newton's time the automation became the clockwork music box. In the 19th century, the automation was a glorified heat engine, burning a combustible fuel instead of the glycogen of human muscles. The automation of our day opens doors by means of photocells, or points guns to the place at which a radar beam picks up a hostile airplane, or computes the solution of a differential equation.

Under the influence of the prevailing view in the science of the 19th century, the engineering of the body was naturally considered to be a branch of power engineering. Even today this is the predominant point of view among classically minded, conservative physiologists. But we are now coming to realize that the body is very far from a conservative system, and that the power available to it is much less limited than was formerly believed. We are beginning to see that such important elements as the neurones—the units of the nervous complex of our bodies—do their work under much the same conditions as vacuum tubes, their relatively small power being supplied from outside by the body's circulation, and that the bookkeeping which is most essential to describe their function is not one of energy.

In short, the newer study of automata, whether in the metal or in the flesh, is a branch of communications engineering, and its cardinal ideas are those of the message, of the amount of disturbance or "noise" (a term taken from the telephone engineer), of the quantity of information to be transmitted, of coding technique, and so on.

This view obviously has implications which affect many branches of science. Let us consider here the application of cybernetics to the problem of mental disorders. The realization that the brain and computing machines have much in common may suggest new and valid approaches to psychopathology, and even to psychiatry.

These begin with perhaps the simplest question of all: how the brain avoids gross blunders or gross miscarriages of activity due to the malfunction of individual parts. Similar questions referring to the computing machine are of great practical importance, for here a chain of operations, each of which covers only a fraction of a millionth of a second, may last a matter of hours or days. It is quite possible for a chain of computational operations to involve a billion separate steps. Under these circumstances, the chance that at least one operation will go amiss is far from negligible, even though the reliability of modern electronic apparatus has exceeded the most sanguine expectations.

In ordinary computational practice by hand or by desk machines, it is the custom to check every step of the computation and, when an error is found, to localize it by a backward process starting from the first point where the error is noted. To do this with a high-speed machine, the check must proceed at the pace of the original machine, or the whole effective order of speed of the machine will conform to that of the slower process of checking.

A much better method of checking, and in fact the one generally used in practice, is to refer every operation simultaneously to two or three separate mechanisms. When two such mechanisms are used, their answers are automatically collated against each other; and if there is a discrepancy, all data are transferred to permanent storage, the machine stops and a signal is sent to the operator that something is wrong. The operator then compares the results, and is guided by them in his search for the malfunctioning part, perhaps a tube which has burned out and needs replacement. If three separate mechanisms are used for each stage, there will practically always be agreement between two of the three mechanisms, and this agreement will give the required result. In this case the collation mechanism accepts the majority report, and the machine need not stop. There is a signal, however, indicating where and how the minority report differs from the majority report. If this occurs at the first moment of discrepancy, the indication of the position of the error may be very precise.

It is conceivable, and not implausible, that at least two of the elements of this process are also represented in the nervous system. It is hardly to be expected that any important message is entrusted for transmission to a single neurone, or that an important operation is entrusted to a single neuronal mechanism. Like the computing machine, the brain probably works on a variant of the famous principle expounded by Lewis Carroll in *The Hunting of the Snark:* "What I tell you three times is true."

It is also improbable that the various channels available for the transfer of information generally go from one end of their course to the other without connecting with one another. It is much more probable that when a message reaches a certain level of the nervous system, it may leave that point and proceed to the next by one or more alternative routes. There may be parts of the nervous system, especially in the cortex, where this interchangeability is much limited or abolished. Still, the principle holds, and it probably holds most clearly for the relatively unspecialized cortical areas which serve the purpose of association and of what we call the higher mental functions.

So far we have been considering errors in performance that are normal and pathological only in an extended sense. Let us now turn to those that are much more clearly pathological. Psychopathology has been rather a disappointment to the instinctive materialism of the doctors, who have taken the view that every disorder must be accompanied by actual lesions of some specific tissue involved. It is true that specific brain lesions, such as injuries, tumors, clots and the like, may be accompanied by psychic symptoms, and that certain mental diseases, such as paresis, are the sequelae of general bodily disease and show a pathological condition of the brain tissue. But there is no way of identifying the brain of a schizophrenic of one of the strict Kraepelin types, nor of a manic-depressive patient, nor of a paranoiac. These we call functional disorders.

This distinction between functional and organic disorders is illuminated by the consideration of the computing machine. It is not the empty physical structure of the computing machine that corresponds to the brain—to the adult brain, at least—but the combination of this structure with the instructions given it at the beginning of a chain of operations and with all the additional information stored and gained from outside in the course of its operation. This information is stored in some physical form —in the form of memory. But part of it is in the form of circulating memories, with a physical basis that vanishes when the machine is shut down or the brain dies, and part is in the form of long-time memories, which are stored in a way at which we can only guess, but probably also in a form with a physical basis that vanishes at death.

There is therefore nothing surprising in considering the functional mental disorders fundamentally as diseases of memory, of the circulating information kept by the brain in active state and of the long-time permeability of synapses. Even the grosser disorders such as paresis may produce a large part of their effects not so much by the destruction of tissue which they involve and the alteration of synaptic thresholds as by the secondary disturbances of traffic, the overload of what remains of the nervous system and the rerouting of messages which must follow such primary injuries.

In a system containing a large number of neurones, circular processes can hardly be stable for long periods of time. Either they run their course, dissipate themselves and die out, as in the case of memories belonging to the specious present, or they embrace more and more neurones in their system, until they occupy an inordinate part of the neurone pool. This is what we should expect to be the case in the malignant worry that accompanies anxiety neuroses. In such a case, it is possible that the patient simply does not have the room—*i.e.*, a sufficient number of neurones— to carry out his normal processes of thought. Under such conditions, there may be less going on in the brain to occupy the neurones not yet affected, so that they are all the more readily involved in the expanding process. Furthermore, the permanent memory becomes more and more deeply involved, and the pathological process which began at the level of the circulating memories may repeat itself in a more untractable form at the level of the permanent memories. Thus what started as a relatively trivial and accidental disturbance of stability may build itself up into a process totally destructive to the normal mental life.

Pathological processes of a somewhat similar nature are not unknown in the case of mechanical or electrical computing machines. A tooth of a wheel may slip under such conditions that no tooth with which it engages can pull it back into its normal relations, or a high-speed electrical computing machine may go into a circular process that seems impossible to stop.

How do we deal with these accidents in the case of the machine? We first try to clear the machine of all information, in the hope that when it starts again with different data the difficulty will not recur. If this fails and the difficulty is inaccessible to the clearing mechanism, we shake the machine or, if it is electrical, subject it to an abnormally large electrical impulse in the hope that we may jolt the inaccessible part into a position where the false cycle of its activities will be interrupted. If even this fails, we may disconnect an erring part of the apparatus, for it is possible that what remains may be adequate for our purpose.

In the case of the brain, there is no normal process, except death, that can clear it of all past impressions. Of the normal non-fatal processes, sleep comes closest to clearing the brain. How often we find that the best way to handle a complicated worry or an intellectual muddle is to sleep on it! Sleep, however, does not clear away the deeper memories, nor indeed is a malignant state of worry compatible with adequate sleep.

Thus we are often forced to resort to more violent types of intervention in the memory cycle. The most violent of these involve surgery on the brain, leaving behind permanent damage, mutilation and the abridgement of the powers of the victim, for the mammalian central nervous system seems to possess no power of regeneration. The principal type of surgical intervention that has been practiced is known as prefrontal lobotomy, or leucotomy. It consists in the removal or isolation of a portion of the prefrontal lobe of the cortex. It is currently having a certain vogue, probably not unconnected with the fact that it makes the custodial care of many patients easier. (Let me remark in passing that killing them makes their custodial care still easier.) Prefrontal lobotomy does seem to have a genuine effect on malignant worry, not by bringing the patient nearer to a solution of his problem, but by damaging or destroying the capacity for maintained worry, known in the terminology of another profession as the conscience. It appears to impair the circulating memory, i.e., the ability to keep in mind a situation not actually presented.

The various forms of shock treatment—electric, insulin, metrazol—are less drastic methods of doing a very similar thing. They do not destroy brain tissue, or at least are not intended to destroy it, but they do have a decidedly damaging effect on the memory. In so far as the shock treatment affects recent disordered memories, which are probably scarcely worth preserving anyhow, it has something to recommend it as against lobotomy, but it is sometimes followed by deleterious effects on the permanent memory and the personality. As it is used at present, it is another violent, imperfectly understood, imperfectly controlled method to interrupt a mental vicious circle.

In long-established cases of mental disorder, the permanent memory is as badly deranged as the circulating memory. We do not seem to possess any purely pharmaceutical or surgical weapon for intervening selectively in the permanent memory. This is where psychoanalysis and the other psychotherapeutic measures come in.

Whether psychoanalysis is taken in the orthodox Freudian sense or in the modified senses of Jung and of Adler, or whether the psychotherapy is not strictly psychoanalytic at all, the treatment is clearly based on the concept that the stored information of the mind lies on many levels of accessibility. The effect and accessibility of this stored information are vitally conditioned by affective experiences that we cannot always uncover by introspection. The technique of the psychoanalyst consists in a series of means to discover and interpret these hidden memories, to make the patient accept them for what they are, and thus to modify, if not their content, at least the affective tone they carry, and make them less harmful.

All this is perfectly consistent with the cybernetic point of view. Our theory perhaps explains, too, why there are circumstances in which a joint use of shock treatment and psychotherapy is indicated, combining a physical or pharmacological therapy for the malignant reverberations in the nervous system and a psychological therapy for the damaging long-time memories which might re-establish the vicious circle broken up by the shock treatments.

We have already mentioned the traffic problem of the nervous system. It has been noted by many writers that each form of organization has an upper limit of size beyond which it will not function. Thus insect organization is limited by the length of tubing over which the spiracle method of bringing air by diffusion directly to the breathing tissues will function; a land animal cannot be so big that the legs or other portions in contact with the ground will be crushed by its weight, and so on. The same sort of thing is observed in engineering structures. Skyscrapers are limited in size by the fact that when they exceed a certain height, the elevator space needed for the upper stories consumes an excessive part of the cross section of the lower floors. Beyond a certain span, the best possible suspension bridge will collapse under its own weight. Similarly, the size of a single telephone exchange is limited.

In a telephone system, the important limiting factor is the fraction of the time during which a subscriber will find it impossible to put a call through. A 90 percent chance of completing calls is probably good enough to permit business to be carried on with reasonable facility. A success of 75 percent is annoying but will permit business to be carried on after a fashion; if half the calls are not completed, subscribers will begin to ask to have their telephones taken out. Now, these represent all-over figures. If the calls go through a number of distinct stages of switching, and the probability of failure is independent and equal for each stage, in order to get a high probability of final success the probability of success at each stage must be higher than the final one. Thus to obtain a 75 percent chance for the completion of the call after five stages, we must have about 95 percent chance of success at each stage. The more stages there are, the more rapidly the service becomes extremely bad when a critical level of failure for the individual call is exceeded, and extremely good when this critical level of failure is not quite reached. Thus a switching service involving many stages and designed for a certain level of failure shows no obvious signs of failure until the traffic comes up to the edge of the critical point, when it goes completely to pieces and we have a catastrophic traffic jam.

So many, with the best developed nervous system of all the animals, probably involving the longest chains of effectively operated neurones, is likely to perform a complicated type of behavior efficiently very close to the edge of an overload, when he will give way in a serious and catastrophic manner. This overload may take place in several ways: by an excess in the amount of traffic to be carried; by a physical removal of channels for the carrying of traffic; or by the excessive occupation of such channels by undesirable systems of traffic, such as circulating memories that have accumulated to the extent of becoming pathological worries. In all these cases, a point is reached—quite suddenly—when the normal traffic does not have space enough allotted to it, and we have a form of mental breakdown, very possibly amounting to insanity.

This will first affect the faculties or operations involving the longest chains of neurones. There is appreciable evidence, of various kinds, that these are precisely the processes recognized as the highest in our ordinary scale of valuation.

If we compare the human brain with that of a lower mammal, we find that it is much more convoluted. The relative thickness of the gray matter is much the same, but it is spread over a far more involved system of grooves and ridges. The effect of this is to increase the amount of gray matter at the expense of the amount of white matter. Within a ridge, this decrease of the white matter is largely a decrease in length rather than in number of fibers, as the opposing folds are nearer together than the same areas would be on a smooth-surfaced brain of the same size. On the other hand, when it comes to connectors between different ridges, the distance they have to run is increased by the convolution of the brain.

Thus the human brain would seem to be fairly efficient in the matter of the short-distance connectors, but defective in the matter of long-distance trunk lines. This means that in the case of a traffic jam, the processes involving parts of the brain quite remote from one another should suffer first. That is, processes involving several centers, a number of different motor processes and a considerable number of association areas should be among the least stable in cases of insanity. These are precisely the processes which we should normally class as higher, thereby confirming our theory, as experience does also, that the higher processes deteriorate first in insanity.

The phenomena of handedness and of hemispheric dominance suggest other interesting speculations. Right-handedness, as is well known, is generally associated with left-brainedness, and left-handedness with right-brainedness. The dominant hemisphere has the lion's share of the higher cerebral functions. In the adult, the effect of an extensive injury in the secondary hemisphere is far less serious than the effect of a similar injury in the dominant hemisphere. At a relatively early stage in his career, Louis Pasteur suffered a cerebral hemorrhage on the right side which left him with a moderate degree of one-sided paralysis. When he died, his brain was examined and the damage to its right side was found to be so extensive that it has been said that after his injury "he had only half a brain." Nevertheless, after this injury he did some of his best work. A similar injury to the left side of the brain in a right-handed adult would almost certainly have been fatal; at the least it would have reduced the patient to an animal condition.

In the first six months of life, an extensive injury to the dominant hemisphere may compel the normally secondary hemisphere to take its place, so that the patient appears far more nearly normal than he would have been had the injury occurred at a later stage. This is quite in accordance with the great flexibility shown by the nervous system in the early weeks of life. It is possible that, short of very serious injuries, handedness is reasonably flexible in the very young child. Long before the child is of school age, however, the natural handedness and cerebral dominance are established for life. Many people have changed the handedness of their children by education, though of course they could not change its physiological basis in hemispheric dominance. These hemispheric changelings often become stutterers and develop other defects of speech, reading and writing.

We now see at least one possible explanation for this phenomenon. With the education of the secondary hand, there has been a partial education of that part of the secondary hemisphere which deals with skilled motions such as writing. Since these motions are carried out in the closest possible association with reading, and with speech and other activities which are inseparably connected with the dominant hemisphere, the neurone chains involved in these processes must cross over from hemisphere to hemisphere, and in any complex activity they must do this again and again. But the direct connectors between the hemispheres in a brain as large as that of man are so few in number that they are of very little help. Consequently the interhemispheric traffic must go by round-about routes through the brain stem. We know little about these routes, but they are certainly long, scanty and subject to interruption. As a consequence, the processes associated with speech and writing are very likely to be involved in a traffic jam, and stuttering is the most natural thing in the world.

The human brain is probably too large already to use in an efficient manner all the facilities which seem to be present. In a cat, the destruction of the dominant hemisphere seems to produce relatively less damage than in man, while the destruction of the secondary hemisphere probably produces more damage. At any rate, the apportionment of function in the two hemispheres is more nearly equal. In man, the gain achieved by the increase in the size and complexity of the brain is partly nullified by the fact that less of the organ can be used effectively at one time.

It is interesting to reflect that we may be facing one of those limitations of nature in which highly specialized organs reach a level of declining efficiency and ultimately lead to the extinction of the species. The human brain may be as far along on its road to destructive specialization as the great nose horns of the last of the titanotheres.

3 | The Communication of Information
E. COLIN CHERRY

The science of communication is of vital importance nowadays, and its ramifications reach into fields of human interest of great diversity. Man is essentially a communicating animal; communication is one of his oldest activities.

In modern times a great deal of analysis has been made, directed toward the improvement of certain technical communication apparatus, in particular the telephone and radio systems. Much of this work is of a specialized mathematical character, but the implications are broad and have attracted the attentions of a wide audience. It is the purpose of this

This material has been extracted from the article by Colin Cherry entitled "The Communication of Information," *American Scientist*, 40:640–663 (1952), and is published here with their permission and that of the Institution of Electrical Engineers, London. The material also forms part of Chapter 2 of the same author's book *On Human Communication*, The MIT Press, Cambridge, Mass., and John Wiley & Sons, Inc., New York (1957).

article to illustrate the early historic origins of this theoretical work, but with little use of mathematical notation, and to show the relationships between the diverse interpretations of the word "communication."

Perhaps the simplest and broadest definition of the word "communication" is afforded by this statement: "It is that which links any organism together." Here "organism" may mean two friends in conversation, newspapers and their reading public, a country and its postal service and telephone system. At another level it may refer to the nervous system of an animal, while at another it may relate to a civilization and its culture. When communication ceases, the organism breaks up.

But what is the commodity which is communicated? What is there truly in common between these scattered examples? These questions are extremely difficult to answer with precision, yet recent mathematical work is enabling such questions to be discussed in a scientific manner, quantitatively. It must be emphasized, however, that this mathematical "theory of communication" is by no means complete and that, although it has proved to be particularly relevant to technical communication channels such as the telephone, radio, radar, and television, its interpretation in broader fields of interest is relatively undeveloped and controversial, yet at the same time intensely interesting.

Perhaps the most important technical development which has assisted in the birth of communication theory is that of telegraphy. With its introduction, the idea of speed of transmission arose, and when its economic value was fully realized, the problems of compressing signals exercised many minds, leading eventually to the concept of "quantity of information" and to theories on times and speed of signalling.

Related techniques which have greatly urged the development of general communication theory are those of telephony and television. Alexander Graham Bell's invention of the telephone in 1876 has particular significance in relation to the physiologist's interest in communication theory; otherwise it is, from our present point of view, purely a technological development, setting up problems similar to those of telegraphy. However, early in the history of television, 1925–27, the very great channel capacity required for detailed "instantaneous" picture transmission was appreciated, and this was brought to a head with the introduction of the techniques of cathode-ray tubes, mosaic cameras and other electronic equipment rendering high-definition practicable. Great masses of information had to be read off at high speed at the camera end, transmitted and reassembled at the receiver. Major theoretical studies were forced by the great capacity required for television; in particular the "noise" problem received much attention. In this technical sense, "noise" refers to any disturbances or interference, apart from the wanted signal or message. This factor is always present to some degree, in every type of communication link whether electrical or not. "Noise" is the ultimate limiter of communication. The physical form of it which has most been studied is the *random* motion of the electrons in the various conductors and tubes in electrical apparatus.

In 1924, Nyquist in the United States and Küpfmüller in Germany simultaneously stated the law that, in order to transmit telegraph signals at a certain rate, a definite bandwidth is required, a law which was expressed more generally by Hartley in 1928. This work of Hartley's has a very modern ring about it; he defined *information* as the successive *selection* of symbols or words, repecting all "meaning" as a mere subjective factor, and showed that a message of N symbols chosen from an alphabet or code of S symbols has S^N possibilities and that the "quantity of information" H is most reasonably defined as the logarithm, that is, $H = N \log S$. Hartley also showed that in order to transmit a given "quantity of information" a definite product (bandwidth $\times$ time), is required. We shall later be considering the more modern aspects of this theory of Hartley's, which may be regarded as the genesis of the modern theory of the communication of information. This factor we call bandwidth $\times$ time is a fundamental one which has some analogous counterpart in all systems of communication, whether electrical or not. It may be loosely interpreted to mean "the more elements of a message we transmit simultaneously, the shorter the time required for transmission."

The earliest suggestion for the simultaneous transmission of two messages, over one line without frequency separation, seems to have come from Edison, who introduced the "duplex" and "quadruplex" systems in 1874. With this system one message, sent in Morse code, was read at the receiving end by a polarized relay; the second message was transmitted by an amplitude modulation of the first signal and was read by an unpolarized relay, the first message merely acting as a carrier wave and so being ignored by this unpolarized relay. The important principle was employed here that two messages can be sent simultaneously, over the same bandwidth that is required for one, if the power is increased. Although not explicitly stated in this form in his paper, Hartley has implied that the quantity of information which can be transmitted in a frequency band of width B and time t is proportional to the product: $2Bt \log S$, where S is the number of "distinguishable amplitude levels." Hartley has considered messages consisting of discrete symbols, *e.g.*, letters or Morse code, and also messages consisting of continuous waveforms, such as speech and music. He observes that the latter signals do not contain infinite information since "the sender is unable to control the waveform with complete accuracy." He approximates the waveform by a series of steps, each one representing a *selection* of an amplitude level. Such a representation is nowadays referred to as *amplitude quantization* of the waveform.

Any quantitative description of the information in a message must be given in statistical terms; the information conveyed by a symbol must decrease as its probability of occurrence increases. With probabilities attached to the various symbols $P_1 P_2 \ldots P_i \ldots$ in a message, or to the various "states" of a waveform, Hartley's law may be reinterpreted so as to define the average information in a long sequence of n symbols as

$$H_n = - \Sigma P_i \log P_i$$

an expression which has been evolved in various ways by several different authors, in particular Shannon and Wiener during the last few years.

This expression for the information is similar to that for the entropy of a system with states of probabilities $P_1, P_2 \ldots P_i \ldots P_n$, using the term in the Boltzmann statistical sense. Probably the first detailed discussion of the identity between information and entropy was made by Szilard as early as 1929, who, in a discussion on the problem of "Maxwell's demon," pointed out that the entropy lost by the gas, due to the separation of the high- and low-energy particles, was equal to the information gained by the "demon" and passed on to the observer of the "experiment." In his recent publications, Shannon has developed this view of communication of information into a coherent theory, using the Boltzmann statistical definition of entropy as a basis. Now the use of the entropy concept here is a perfectly valid one. Boltzmann's order-disorder notion is directly applicable to the process of communicating information. In the next section some discussion will be made concerning the intervention of an "intelligent being" into a natural process—also of the being as a "source of information."

One of Shannon's principal contributions to communication theory is his expression for the maximum capacity of a channel. This gives the greatest quantity of information which may be communicated in a time t over bandwidth B, in the presence of white Gaussian noise (i.e. random) as

$$Bt \log \left(1 + \frac{P}{N} \right)$$

where P and N are the signal and noise powers.

The operating of a computing machine is of the same nature as that of any electrical communication channel; information is supplied from a "source," suitably coded, transmitted, operated on in various ways, and passed to the output. From the information theory point of view there are, however, certain differences. First, a computing machine is usually "noiseless" in that it cannot be allowed to make a single mistake, since this mistake would render all subsequent calculations invalid; it may, however, possess a limiting accuracy, set by the limited digital capacity. Secondly, the machine comprises many individual communication channels. Thirdly, the questions of the language statistics and coding such as arise in electrical communication are replaced by problems of "programming"; the development of the more recent digital computing machines, such as the Eniac and the Edsac, and the Ace in Great Britain, the so-called "electronic brains," primarily for application to problems in mathematical physics and in pure mathematics, has raised complex problems in "programming," i.e., the breaking down of mathematical operations into the most elementary steps and the logical feeding of these steps into the machine together with *a priori* data referring to the particular calculation. The surprising thing is that, once the mathematical processes have so been broken down, both these fundamental steps and the actions required of the machine are few in number and elementary in principle; being merely such simple processes as adding, subtracting, moving-up one, etc. It is the automatic feeding-in of the sequence of instructions which distinguishes these modern machines from the manually operated desk types, and especially the facility of changing the sequence according to criteria evaluated during the course of calculation.

It was apparent during the years immediately preceding the Second World War that the ideas, basic concepts, and methods of communication engineering were of wide applicability to other specialized branches of science. The lead was taken by Norbert Wiener who, with Rosenbleuth, named this field of applicability *cybernetics*, from the Greek κυβερνητης meaning "steersman." The word *cybernétique* was originally coined by Ampère (1834) in "Essai sur la Philosophie des Sciences," to mean the "science of government." The needs of the war brought matters to a head, with the urgency of developing not only highspeed computing machines, but automatic predictors, automatic gun-laying mechanisms and other automatic following or "self-controlling" systems, and to these two scientists should be given the credit for calling attention to the need for a general study to include, not only these automatic mechanisms, but certain aspects of physiology, the central nervous system and the operation of the brain, and even certain problems in economics concerning the theory of booms and slumps. The common thread here, linking these topics, whether mechanical, biological, or mathematical, is the idea of the communication of information and the production of self-stabilizing control action. Apart from a study of the mechanical governor by Maxwell, in 1868, the first mathematical treatment of the stabilization of a dynamic system by feeding information back from the output or "receiver" end to the input or "transmitter" end was made by H. S. Black, in a study of electrical feedback amplifiers in 1934, and later developed, largely due to the efforts of Nyquist and of Bode into an exact mathematical method and a system of design. The extension of the principles to electromechanical or to purely mechanical systems was a logical and natural one, and the design of automatic following systems, such as those for anti-aircraft guns, for automatic pilots in aircraft, etc., need no longer proceed entirely on a trial-and-error basis.

For these automatic control systems, the term "servo mechanism" has been coined. The existence of numerous controls in the body accounts partly for a common interest with physiology. For example, there is homeostasis, or the involuntary control of body temperature, of heart rate, blood pressure, and other essentials for life, while voluntary control is involved in muscular actions, such as those required for walking along a narrow plank; the simplest movement of a limb may involve multiple feedback actions. If a stabilized servo mechanism has its feedback path open-circuited, so that the magnitude of its error cannot be measured at the input end and so automatically corrected, it is liable to violent oscillation; an analogous state of affairs in the human body has been mentioned by Wiener, called ataxia, corresponding to a nervous disorder which affects the control of muscular actions. The analogies in physiology are countless; Wiener even goes so far, in developing the analogy between the operations of a digital computing machine and of the brain and central nervous system, as to compare certain mental functional disorders (the layman's "nervous breakdowns") to the breakdown of the machine when overloaded with an excess of input instructions as, for example, when the storage or "memory circuits" cannot store enough instructions to be able to tackle the situation. Note again, the emphasis is on the operation of the machine together with its instructions; no material damage may have occurred.

One is led instinctively to ask whether such analogies are not modern examples of a kind of animism, though these analogies do not imply any attempt to "explain" life on a mechanistic basis or to explain the body as a machine in the sense of Descartes, who observed that the action of the body, apart from the guidance of the will, "does not appear at all strange to those who are acquainted with the variety of movements performed by the different automata, or moving machines fabricated by human industry. . . . Such persons will look upon this body as a machine made by the hand of God."

4 | What Is Information?
ANATOL RAPOPORT

Suppose some one tosses a penny, and you try to guess "heads" or "tails." Every time you guess correctly you win the penny, and every time you guess wrong you pay your opponent a penny. You have a fifty-fifty chance to win on each throw. If you keep playing long enough, unless you are extremely lucky or unlucky, your winnings will about equal your losses.

Now suppose some character comes along and tells you he has a crystal ball through which he can see how the penny falls, and that for a price, he will signal this information to you, so that you can win every time. You have no scruples about playing the game fairly (you are the "economic man" that classical theoreticians of economics keep talking about). What is the information offered worth to you?

A common sense argument shows that if the crystal ball really works, the information is worth to you anywhere up to a penny a reading. If you pay a whole penny, you will win all of your opponent's money and pay it all to the crystal ball reader. Then you can expect to be no better or no worse off than if you played the game trusting to your own guesses (or if you didn't play the game at all: the fun of playing the game doesn't count here, because the "economic man" doesn't have any fun anyway). It follows that if you pay your informant anything less than a penny a guess, you are sure to be ahead in the long run.

Now suppose the man with the crystal ball is a charlatan. He can't guess the throws any better than you can. He knows, of course, that very soon he will give you wrong information and that when he does, you may balk at paying him for further "tip offs." So he proposes what seems like a fair deal: you give him a percentage of your winnings *only* when you win and pay him nothing if his information proves false. Is it now worth while to employ him? This time a common sense argument says that it is worth nothing to have him around. If he is no better guesser than you are, you may as well make the guesses yourself and not pay anything.

But now consider the intermediate case, where the crystal ball is good but not perfect. In other words, your informant can guess better than

Reprinted with permission of the publisher and the author. From *ETC*, 10:247–260 (1953).

you, but he makes mistakes. Now is it worthwhile to pay him? Yes, it is worthwhile. And it is the more worthwhile the greater the *difference* between his guessing ability and yours. Certainly if you are as good as he is, there is no point in paying him. In other words, if your chances of guessing are as good as his, he is *giving you no information in the long run.* If he is better than you are, even if he is not a perfect guesser, your guessing record will be improved by the information he gives you, and the amount of improvement is, in a way, a measure of the information you receive from him. If he is a worse guesser than you are, you *lose* information if you follow his advice. This situation hints at a possibility of defining information *quantitatively* as the improvement of one's chances of making the right guess.

In *any* situation, information about something we already know is worthless as information. The keen competition among newspapers for "scoops" reflects this attitude. A "scoop" carries more information than a re-write story. Any kind of a message carries more or less information in it depending on the state of knowledge of the recipients. This much has been known ever since messages were invented. In our own day of precise formulation of problems, however, an altogether new way of measuring the amount of information in a message is being developed.

In the example just cited a measure of the amount of information contained in a message is indicated in terms of how much such information is worth in a gambling situation. It is not necessary, however, to measure information in terms of its monetary value any more than it is necessary to depict chance events in terms of gambling situations. Such examples are often chosen because gambling has long served as a link between commonplace situations and sophisticated probabilistic arguments. There is more to the mathematical theory of information than a computation of how much we are willing to pay for the privilege of cheating in games or how the novelty of stories is reflected in the circulation of the newspapers that print them.

THE MATHEMATICAL THEORY OF INFORMATION

The mathematical theory of information was born among communication engineers and is commanding ever greater attention among mathematically inclined biologists and semanticists. The reason for this increasing interest lies, I think, in the fact that the mathematical theory of information has been recognized as another successful instance of making *precise* and *quantitative* an extremely important concept which had been talked about only vaguely before. I believe that the notion of the "quantity of information" is a Big Idea in science, similar in scope to the precise definition of "the amount of matter" as registered on a balance or the "amount of energy" as derived from potentials, velocities, and heat, or the "amount of entropy" as derived from the probabilities of the states of a system. The vast importance of this new big idea is in its potential applications to the fundamental biological and general semantics problems. We will touch on some of these below. Let us first take a closer look at some basic notions contained in the definition of the "amount of information."

As Warren Weaver has remarked, the amount of information in your message is related not to what you are saying but to what you *could* say. This relation links the amount of information in a message with the amount of *pre-conceived* knowledge about its content (recall the intuitive relation between the amount of information and how much we already know or can guess).

Let us suppose that all you can say is "yes" and "no" (in other words, you are as either-or-ish as you can possibly be). Then all you are ever *expected* to say is "yes" or "no," so that one already has a 50 percent "knowledge" of your potential pronouncements. Thus, if you are entirely two-valued, you cannot give as much information in your one-word speeches as you could if you were "multivalued." If you selected your messages from *ten* possible ones, all equally likely, then one could hope to guess what you are going to say only once in ten times, instead of every other time, and your information giving capacity would be considerably increased.

The "canned" messages offered by Western Union (birthday greetings, etc.) carry far less information (and therefore are cheaper to send) than individually composed messages, because there are far fewer canned messages to choose from.

In order to define the amount of information in a message, then, we must know the total number of messages in the *repertoire of the source* from which the message is chosen. Let us take a concrete case.

For simplicity, we will assume that all messages are in code and consist of combinations of two signals "1" and "0" (just as all Morse code messages are combinations of two signals "dit" and "dah"). We ask: how many different messages can we send? Obviously if the length of the message is unlimited, we can send an unlimited number of messages. Let us, therefore, consider only messages of a certain length, say n signals long. We can easily see that there can be exactly 2^n distinct messages n signals long. This follows, because we have 2 choices for the first signal ("1" or "0"), 2 for the second, which makes $2^2 = 4$ choices for a message of two signals. To each of these, we can again add either of two signals to make a message three signals long, etc., so that to make a message n signals long, we have $2 \times 2 \times 2 \ldots 2$ a product of n 2's or 2^n choices.

Therefore if you know that a certain message is n "binary" signals long, you know you have one chance in 2^n to guess its contents exactly, provided all the messages are equally likely. We could therefore take the number 2^n as a measure of the amount of information such a message carries. But we don't have to take 2^n. We can take some other number *derived* from 2^n, if it is more convenient to do so. The choice of a quantity with which we measure something is not unique. For example, to measure the "size" of a circle, we can take its diameter, but we are equally justified in taking its area, which is a quantity derived from the diameter in a certain way. There is good reason for taking as the measure of the amount of information, carried by a message n binary signals long, not 2^n (which is the reciprocal of the probability of guessing it, or, if you like, the "unlikelihood" of guessing it) but the *logarithm* of that number.

If you remember your high school algebra, you will recall that the logarithm of a number is the power to which a certain fixed number, called the "base" must be raised to get that number. If we conveniently take 2 as our base, then $\log_2(2^n)$ (read "the logarithm to the base of two to the n-th) is just n. Thus, by the convention we have just established, a message n binary signals long contains n "binary units" of information, or one binary unit per signal. This binary unit is called a "bit" for short. Now we see the advantage of taking the logarithm of the unlikelihood of guessing (2^n) for our measure, since we can now say that a message twice as long (one $2n$ signals long) will contain just twice the amount of information. This is a very convenient way of talking.

It may have occurred to the reader that we have gone around in a circle. Would it not have been simpler to skip the argument about "probabilities of guessing" altogether and start out by a "natural" definition of the amount of information as simply a number proportional to the length of the message?

It would, if we confined ourselves to messages from a single source. However the interesting part of information theory deals with determining the amount of information in a message in terms of the character of its *source*, not merely in terms of its length (it isn't what you say; it's what you *could* say). It is the amount of information per *signal* that we are interested in, in other words, the rate at which information is coming at us as we are receiving the message. This rate is one bit per signal in the case of a source with two equally likely signals. Where there are more signals in the source, and especially where the signals are not equally likely or where they are not independent, the amount of information per signal is not nearly so easy to compute. For this purpose, the "round about" definition is necessary. Furthermore, the "round about" definition points up the connection between information theory and the possibility of mathematicizing psychological and semantic concepts, as we shall see.

Let us again suppose that we speak a language composed of two binary signals "1" and "0." But let us now suppose that the "1" occurs far more frequently than the "0." Such is actually the case with the symbols of the languages we ordinarily use. For example, good English can be written with some 30 symbols (the 26 letters, a "space" and some punctuation marks). We can say definitely that some signals occur in English far more frequently than others. Or suppose that "1" and "0" are signals given out by a machine which is inspecting mass-produced parts, where "1" means "O.K." and "0" means "reject." If on the average only one item in a hundred is defective, the "1'" will register ninety-nine times more frequently than the "0." How much information is now contained in a message n units long?

In view of what we have said about the meaning of information, we must conclude that in this case the amount of information contained in a message n units long must be less than n bits, because we already have a good chance of guessing what a message will say. If n is, say 10, we have better than nine chances out of ten to guess the message if we guess it to be all "1's." Since the message does not add as much to our knowledge as it would if the signals were equally likely, we must conclude that it carries less than n bits of information. But how much less?

Suppose a message n units long has n_1 "1's" and n_2 "0's," so that $n_1 + n_2 = n$. What is the probability of occurrence of such a message? If the occurrence of one signal does not influence that of another, it doesn't matter in what order the signals occur. Since in our example the probability of a "1" is .99, and that of a "0" is .01, the probability of n_1 "1's" and n_2 "0's" *arranged in a particular way* (that is, the probability of a particular message) will be $(.99)$ n_1 $(.01) n_2$. The logarithm of the reciprocal of this number to the base 2, as we have agreed, will be a measure of the amount of information in such a message. This logarithm is equal to $- n_1 \log_2(.99) - n_2 \log_2(.01)$.

Now we have the amount of information in a particular message with n_1 "1's" and n_2 "0's." But we don't want to measure the information of particular messages. We want to measure the information of an *average* message n signals long coming from the source we have described. We will get this average if we substitute for n_1 and n_2 their average values, averaged over a great many messages coming from the source. Since the frequencies of the "1's" and the "0's" are in the ratio of 99 to 1, it follows that the average value of n_1 will be 99 times that of n_2. Furthermore, $n_1 + n_2$ must equal n. Therefore $n_1 = .99n$ and $n_2 = .01n$ on the average. Then the amount of information in an average message n signals long will be $- .99_n \log_2(.99) - .01n \log_2(.01)$. If we wish to express the amount of information per signal, we divide by n and get $- .99 \log (.99) - .01$ $\log (.01)$. If we calculate this number, we find it to be equal to about .11 bits or only one-ninth of what it would be if the "O.K." and "reject" signals were equally likely.

The method here described can be extended to compute the amount of information per signal from any source in which the occurrence of one signal does not influence the occurrence or non-occurrence of another. If the source has a repertoire of signals numbered 1 to N, and if they occur with relative frequencies (probabilities) $p_1, p_2 \ldots p_N$, then the amount of information per signal, usually denoted by H, is expressed in the following formula:

$$H = - p_1 \log p_1 - p_2 \log p_2 - p_3 \log p_3 \ldots - p_N \log p_N.$$

In the example we solved there were only two signals, whose p_1 and p_2 were respectively .99 and .01.

APPLICATIONS TO TECHNOLOGICAL COMMUNICATION THEORY

So far we really did nothing but define terms and draw consequences from our definitions. We said nothing concrete about why we should want to make these particular definitions or draw these particular consequences. We did mention the looming importance of the information concept in semantics, psychology, and biology, but to some one who encounters this concept for the first time, the connection between it and what is generally thought to be the subject matter of biology, etc., is anything but clear.

It is not easy to make such connections clear. In fact, the strenuous work of highly skilled specialists goes almost entirely into uncovering such connections. They cannot be therefore obvious or intuitively evident or even easy to understand when explained. All we can do within the scope of this article is give hints about the sort of reasoning which leads to uncovering the possibilities of applying the quantification of information to several scientific fields.

The first step in solving a problem is to state it. The statement usually involves a description of an existing state and a desirable state of affairs where the factors involved in the discrepancy are explicitly pointed out. The success with which any problem is solved depends to a great extent on the clarity with which it is stated. In fact, the solution of the problem is, in a sense, a clarification (or concretization) of the objectives. Take the problem of curing disease. For ages, it had been implicitly stated thus:

> A is sick.
> This is bad.
> Let us find ways to make A well.

Vague statements lead to vague methods, where success is erratic and questionable. With the classification of diseases (as initiated, say, by Hippocrates), the problem is re-stated:

> A has a fever.
> This is bad.
> Let us look for ways to rid A of fever.

Here there is more promise of success, because the events which make up sickness are somewhat extensionalized. Still further extensionalization appears with the discovery of events *concomitant* with the symptoms, for example the presence of micro-organisms. Now the problem is

> A is infected with tuberculosis bacilli.
> They make A sick.
> Let us find ways to get rid of the bacilli.

Further extensionalization could be, for example, a description of the bio-chemical processes characteristic of the tuberculosis bacilli which interfere with A's bio-chemical processes, etc. The more a given problem is extensionalized, the greater promise there is in finding a solution.

The problems of communication hygiene are now assuming an importance equal to those of physiological hygiene. A naïve statement of a communication problem dates back to antiquity.

> A talks to B.
> B does not understand A.
> Let us explain to B what A means.

However "attempts to explain" *themselves* depend on the proper functioning of the communication process. If this process is not understood, attempts to explain cannot be expected to have more success than the original attempt to communicate. The first steps in communication hygiene are therefore aimed at the understanding of the communication process. Hence the emergence of communication science.

In examining instances of "failure to understand," we see that it can occur on different levels. A most obvious cause of such failure can be laid to the imperfect transmission of signals. B can fail to understand A simply because A talks with a heavy accent, or is a small child who has not learned to pronounce the words clearly or is talking over a telephone with a bad connection or over a radio with too much static.

Communication problems on this level may deal with acoustics or electronics but also with physiological functions such as hearing and sight and their psychological correlates, the perception of "gestalts" and recognition. Obviously no transmission and no reception of any signal is perfect. An important class of questions in communication theory concerns with the *thresholds* of intelligibility. One wishes to know, for example, how bad static has to be before it begins seriously to interfere with the transmission of spoken information over a radio channel of given characteristics. Evidently both the characteristics of transmission and reception and those of the subject matter broadcast are important in the problem. Information theory provides a measure of these variables. It provides, for example, a measure of the complexity involved in "fidelity" of reproduction. It provides a method of estimating quantitatively the effects of "noise" on reception, since the effects of noise are equivalent to loss of information. It provides theoretical limits for the performance of a channel of given characteristics, somewhat in the way thermodynamics indicates the limits of efficiency of a heat engine.

APPLICATIONS TO SEMANTICS

The semanticist is usually unconcerned with these purely "technical" problems of communication and leaves them to the communication engineer. Division of labor is entirely proper in approaching any complicated set of problems; but it is a mistake to take too seriously the dichotomies we set up in parceling out the jobs. These dichotomies lead not only to the persistence of elementalistic notions but also delay the discovery of analogous *methods* fruitful in the various aspects of the problem. It may be true that the technical problems of long range communication (radio, television, etc.) can be treated entirely independently of the semantic content of the messages or the semantic reactions of the audience. But it may also be true that the methods involved in treating those problems (for example, the mathematical theory of information) can be applied in the seemingly different context of the events which interest general semanticists, psychologists, and others.

Such possibilities are already apparent. To point them out, we will examine a little more closely the formula given above which describes the amount of information in terms of the repertoire of the source and the relative frequencies of the signals employed. As we said, the formula holds if the signals are independent of each other. But what if this is not the case? What if the occurrence of one signal influences the chances of the occurrence of another? This is certainly true in the case where the source is the English alphabet, and the messages consist of English sentences. In this case, it is almost certain that the letter *q* will be followed by a *u* (barring comparatively rare words like Iraqi). It is practically impossible for the letter z to be followed by a consonant, etc.

Under these conditions, the formula for the amount of information per signal must be modified. We will not go into the details of this modification here. We will only point out that the problem of computing the amount of information under various conditions of communication has led to a number of important *concepts*, in terms of which the technical problems of communication are described. One important characteristic of those concepts is that they are often stated in mathematical language *and therefore the techniques of mathematical deduction can be applied to them.* This circumstance makes the problems of communication much more explicit and the solutions to such problems easier to find.

Another important advantage of those concepts is that they give hints on how the precise methods of dealing with communication in the (comparatively) uncomplicated area of technology could be extended to the more complicated areas of psychology, semantics, and general semantics. For example, the modification of our formula on page 46 to take into account the interdependence of signals gives rise to the concept of "redundancy" of the source output, and if the source is an entire language, this concept can be extended to mean the "redundancy" of a language. In information theory, redundancy is a measure of the interdependence of the signals. But redundancy has also an intuitive component, and the precise definition makes possible the extensionalization of this intuitive component.

The connection between the precise and the intuitive notions of redundancy is dramatically illustrated in C. Shannon's monograph, *The Mathematical Theory of Communication.* Suppose we put all the letters of the English alphabet into a hat in equal amounts and pull them out one by one "at random." What would they spell? Here is a sample of such a "language."

XFOML RXKHRJFFJUJ ZLPWCFWKCYJ FFUEYVKCQSGHYD
QPAAMKBZAACIBZLHJQD

In anyone's estimation this sample does not "make sense." Now suppose that instead of putting the letters into the hat in equal numbers, we put them in proportionally to the frequency with which they actually occur in English and again pull them out at random. The resulting sample now looks like this.

OCRO HLI RGWR NMIELWIS EU LL NBNESEBYA TH EEI ALHENHTTPA
OOBTTVA NAH BRL.

This still doesn't make "sense." But there is no question that it makes *somewhat* more "sense" than before. It *looks* more like English. It does not bristle quite so much with J's and Z's. Somehow we feel that a "gradation" of sense can be established even among random samples of letters. The feeling is strengthened when we perform the next experiment. We now put into our hat not single letters but *pairs*, taking care of keeping their numbers proportional to their actual occurrence in English. Now we get the following sample.

> ON IE ANTSOUTINYS ARE T INCTORE ST BE S DEAMY ACHIN D ILONASIVE
> TUCOOWE AT TEASONARE FUSO TIZIN ANDY TOBE SEACE CTISBE.

Now there is no doubt that we are approaching "English." The sample contains two or three real English words and several "near-words" like DEAMY and TEASONARE. A sample of "triples" looks even better.

> IN NO IST LAT WHEY CRATICT FROURE BIRS GROCID PONDENOME OF
> DEMONSTURES OF THE REPTAGIN IS REGOACTION OF CRE.

Perhaps this sample reminds us of Jabberwocky. It should, because Jabberwocky too is an "approximation" to English, a very good approximation that almost makes real sense.

What can be done with letters can be done with words. Compare, for example, the sample of randomly selected words,

> REPRESENTING AND SPEEDILY IS AN GOOD APT OR COME CAN DIFFERENT
> NATURAL HERE HE THE A IN CAME THE TO OF TO EXPERT GRAY COME
> TO FURNISHES THE LINE MESSAGE HAD BE THESE

with a sample of randomly selected *pairs* of words,

> THE HEAD AND IN FRONTAL ATTACK ON AN ENGLISH WRITER THAT THE
> CHARACTER OF THIS POINT IS THEREFORE ANOTHER METHOD FOR THE
> LETTERS THAT THE TIME OF WHO EVER TOLD THE PROBLEM FOR AN
> UNEXPECTED,

and see how much more "sense" there is in the second, although it still doesn't "mean" anything.

These "approximations" to English are examples of how the intuitive feeling that one piece of gibberish is somehow closer to the English language than another is a reflection of a precisely and quantitatively defined situation. The situation has to do with the characteristic linkages used in

English. The extent of these linkages is also a measure of the *redundancy* of the English language. Redundancy can also be taken as a measure of the fraction of letters which can be randomly deleted from a reasonably long message without making the message unintelligible. FR EXMPLE WENTYIVE PRCET OF HE LTTERS I TIS SENTENCE HVEBEN DLETED AT RANM. The redundancy of English is said to be over 50 percent.

Redundancy is thus both a linguistic and a mathematical term. The more redundancy there is in a source, the more tolerance there is for noise and other imperfections of transmission without serious interference with intelligibility. The importance of the redundancy concept in crytography is likewise apparent. The more redundant the source of messages, the easier it is to break a code. In stenography redundancy is a measure of the amount of drastic abbreviation that can be introduced without danger of confusion. All these linguistic matters are contiguous to the field of interest of semanticists and of general semanticists. A manner of expression full of clichés is, of course, high in redundancy. It turns out in the mathematical theory of information that messages from a cliché-ridden source (such as the oratorical repertoire of a run-of-the-mill politician) are also poor in information. This is something semanticists have known all along, but it is gratifying to have this knowledge formulated precisely. Precisely formulated knowledge is valuable not only for its own sake but also as a jumping-off place to new knowledge.

CONNECTION WITH PHYSICS

The mathematicians who derived the formula for the amount of information soon noticed that it looks exactly like the formula for *entropy* in statistical mechanics. Mathematicians are often excited by such analogies. There is an important difference between a mathematical analogy and an ordinary "metaphorical" one. Arguments based on ordinary analogies are seldom conclusive. For example, just because it is true that natural selection benefits the survival of a species, it does not follow that economic competition is indispensable for the vigor of a nation. Nor is the justification of capital punishment convincing on the basis of its analogy with surgery applied to a diseased part of the body. A mathematical analogy, however, is a quite different matter. Such analogy is evidence of similar *structure* in two or more classes of events, and a great deal can be deduced from such similarity. For example, because both electrical and mechanical oscillators can be described by the same kinds of equations, it follows that a great deal of reasoning which applies to one applies also to the other. Since the analogy between information and entropy is a mathematical analogy, it too may be symptomatic of a structure similarity in the events involved in the determination of physical entropy and those involved in the measurement of information. It seems worthwhile, therefore, to look at this analogy more closely.

The concept of entropy was first introduced into thermodynamics as a measure of the *unavailability* of heat energy for transformation into useful work. The principle of conservation of energy (the First Law of thermodynamics) says that a given amount of heat is equivalent in terms of its energy content to a given amount of work. For example, the heat energy of a slice of bread (about 100 "large" calories) is theoretically convertible into about 300,000 foot pounds of work. But this equivalence of heat and work does not mean that we can take heat from any source and convert it all into work. If this were true, there would be no need of fuels. We could take the practically inexhaustible heat of the oceans and drive all our machinery with it, with only a slight cooling of the oceans as the result. But this cannot be done. In any engine, where heat is converted into work, this can be done only if heat is allowed to flow from a source at higher temperature to a sink at lower temperature. Thus a difference in temperature is indispensable for turning heat into work. The boiler and the cooler of a steam engine illustrate this principle. The less the difference in temperatures, the smaller is the fraction of the amount of heat which can be transformed into work, i.e., the smaller the efficiency of the engine.

Now entropy is, among other things, a measure of the equalization of temperature throughout a system. If the temperature is constant throughout a system, the entropy is greatest in it, and none of the heat is available for work.

In classical thermodynamics, entropy was expressed in terms of the heat and the temperature of the system. With the advent of the kinetic theory of matter, an entirely new approach to thermodynamics was developed. Temperature and heat are now pictured in terms of the kinetic energy of the molecules comprising the system, and entropy becomes a measure of the *probability* that the velocities of the molecules and other variables of a system are distributed in a certain way. The reason the entropy of a system is greatest when its temperature is constant throughout is because this distribution of temperature is the *most probable*. Increase of entropy was thus interpreted as the passage of a system from less probable to more probable states.

A similar process occurs when we shuffle a deck of cards. If we start with an orderly arrangement, say the cards of each suit following each other according to their value, the shuffling will tend to make the arrangement disorderly. But if we start with a disorderly arrangement, it is very unlikely that through shuffling the cards will come into an orderly one.

This is so, because there are many more "disorderly" than orderly arrangements, and so the disorderly state of a deck of cards is more probable.

Thus, the "amount of order" is connected with probabilistic concepts and through them with entropy (the less order, the more entropy). But it is also connected with the "amount of information." For example, far less information is required to describe an orderly arrangement of the cards than a disorderly one. If I say "Starting with ace, deuce, etc., to king; hearts, diamonds, clubs, spades," I have determined the position of every card in the deck. But to describe an arbitrary random arrangement, I have to specify every one of the fifty-two cards.

It is through these notions of probability, order, and disorder that entropy is related to information. The formal equivalence of their mathematical expressions indicates that both concepts describe similarly structured events.

APPLICATIONS TO BIOLOGY

Both entropy and information can be defined in terms of the same kinds of variables, namely probabilities of events. Now entropy plays an important part in chemistry and in biochemistry. For example, the knowledge of the entropies of two states of a system indicates whether the system can pass from one state to the other *spontaneously*, say whether a certain chemical reaction can take place *without outside interference*. The interesting thing about chemical reactions in living organisms is that many of them are such that they do not ordinarily take place without interference. Such are, for example, the synthesis of sugars from water and carbon dioxide by green plants and the synthesis of complicated proteins from amino-acids by animals. In these reactions, the ordinary processes (oxidation of sugars and the decomposition of proteins) are reversed. Therefore there must be interference. Early thinkers on this subject postulated the operations of "vital forces" within living things which made these "up-hill" reactions possible.

No evidence of any phenomenon explicitly violating known physical and chemical laws has ever been observed in any organism. True, "up-hill" reactions seem to contradict the law of thermodynamics which demands a continuous increase in entropy (the Second Law of thermodynamics), but there is nothing in the laws that says that it cannot be circumvented *locally*. In other words, what living things seem to do is create little "islands of order" in themselves at the expense of increased disorder elsewhere. This is the meaning of Schroedinger's famous remark that "life feeds on negative entropy."

Life, therefore, depends essentially on an ordering process, on fighting off the general trend toward chaos, which is always present in the non-living world. But to increase the order of anything means to make it describable with less information (less effort). And is this process not the very essence of knowledge, of science itself? Or of any behavior where complex skills are involved? When a chess genius plays a dozen games simultaneously from memory, or when a musician masters the intricate complexity of muscular movements which go into the rendition of a musical creation, or when a scientist weaves a mass of seemingly unrelated data into a monolithic theory, they are all contributing to the process of decreasing the "entropy" of a portion of the world, of making it more comprehensible with less effort.

Organisms, geneticists tell us, evolve by suffering random genetic variations, which in the process of many generations are selected for their survival value. If these variations were independent of each other, nothing would ever come of evolution. God alone knows how many mutations it took to enable our pre-human ancestor to speak and to make him *want* to speak. Single mutations are improbable enough. But when many have to combine to give rise to some complex patterns of behavior, such as speech, the probability of their being so combined would be infinitesimally small, if the futations were accumulated independently of each other. But they are not accumulated independently. Rather they seem to be "hoarded" like pieces of a jigsaw puzzle, so that in the process of accumulation *gaps* arise, which are later filled by the proper mutations.

Thus evolution itself is an ordering process. Gross changes of structure, of physiology, and of behavior are made possible because structures, physiological processes, and behavior patterns are always being organized into assemblies. The promise which information theory holds for biology is the same that it holds for linguistics and semantics—the promise to make possible a precise language for talking about the structure of assemblies and the fundamental processes involving the emergence of order from chaos and chaos from order.

Korzybski and others maintained that structure is the only content of knowledge. Korzybski also emphasized the "false-to-factness" of the two-valued orientation. It is therefore futile to suppose that a portion of the world either is or is not "structured." It may be *partially* structured. Therefore a measure of structure or of the amount of organization is required. We have seen how through the entropy concept "amount of information" can be equated to the "amount of disorder." That is not to say that information is a carrier of disorder. On the contrary, information is the carrier of order. What is meant by the equivalence is that the more disordered a portion of the world is, the more information is *required* to describe it completely, that is, to make it known. Thus the process of obtaining knowledge is quantitatively equated to the process of ordering portions of the world.

Significantly, attempts are made to define the life process itself in terms of the creation of order. It has been proposed, for example, to define the amount of entropy in an organism as equal to the amount of entropy it would have if it were completely disorganized minus the amount of information necessary to construct it from its disorganized state. It follows that the more complex an organism is, the more ordered it is, the less entropy it contains. One also suspects from this definition that it is easier to construct a dead organism than a live one. But one also conjectures that the only difficulty in constructing an actual living thing is that an immense amount of information is required to do so.

Living things, therefore, appear in the light of information theory as the carriers of knowledge (i.e., of structure). Man's unique place in the universe is in that he not only carries this "physiological knowledge" within him but has also developed a "second order knowledge," a knowledge of what knowledge consists of and has thus added a new dimension to the life process.

5

A Rationale for a Definition of Communication
JOHN B. NEWMAN

A respected scholar recently observed in the pages of this *Journal* that "considering that communication is one of the oldest human activities, it is somewhat astonishing that no generally accepted definition exists." It is the present writer's contention that the reasons for this apparent anomaly can be identified and that a lack of a definition is not as serious as it seems: for just as Einstein did not change "the laws of the universe," so no definition can change "the laws of communication."

It is the purpose of this paper, therefore, to explicate the problems of defining communication—not to create a definition. In the following pages, we propose to show that:

(1) The reason that no generally accepted definition exists is not because of a lack of knowledge of communication, whether as a process, a

Reprinted with permission of the National Society for the Study of Communication and the author. From *Journal of Communication*, 10:115–124 (1960).

body of knowledge, or a field of study, but because of a lack of understanding of the nature, the scope, and the function of a definition.

√ (2) The epistemological notion that a definition must account completely for that which it defines is impractical and should be rejected.

(3) Communication is so diverse and discursive that the attempt to create a generally accepted definition becomes so profoundly involved that it hinders rather than helps further thought on the subject.

Since the present writer regards an espistemological definition of communication as impractical, his purpose in these pages is to present a rationale for a pragmatic definition. Thus, he does not seek *the* meaning *of* communication—something that everyone must use if he is to be deemed "rational" or "logical" in his consideration of ideas or problems that may pertain to this field. Instead, the present writer proposes that scholars should seek *a* meaning *for* communication—one which will permit all persons concerned with communication, regardless of their background, their professional area, or their immediate purposes, to speak intelligibly to one another.

PROBLEMS OF DEFINITION

One appropriate point for beginning an analysis of the problems of definition is the realization that basically any definition involves the use of words about words. This brings up the problem of distinguishing words that are *used* in a given context as contrasted with words that are simply *mentioned* in the same instance; for example, "Say, Tom!" (in which the word "Tom" is *used* as part of the statement) and "Say *Tom!*" —i.e., "Say [the word] *Tom!*" (in which the word "Tom" is *mentioned* in the course of the statement). Punctuation (or inflection of voice) frequently helps in distinguishing the two, but not always. Rules need, therefore, to be established regarding the use of words about words.

The rules for pragmatic definition should be distinguished from those for an epistemological definition. For one thing, the rules for a pragmatic definition do not pertain to the *definiendum* (that element of the definition whose meaning is explained in the definition—in the present case, the *definiendum* is *communication*), to the *definiens* (that element of the definition which indicates the meaning of the *definiendum*), or to the structure of either or both. Our rules may be said to be the "ground rules" or "house rules" for any pragmatic definition which some future scholar may evolve.

First, a pragmatic definition is not "simply a matter of 'definition.' " This is to say that a pragmatic definition is based upon more than simply mutual agreement. A pragmatic definition must consist of terms which act, as Ludwig Wittgenstein insists, "as a symbolism used in an exact calculus." General acceptance and widespread use—the popular criteria for definitions—therefore do not necessarily render a given definition satisfactory; and argumentative opportunism and rhetorical expediency, needless to say, are poor reasons indeed for one to be satisfied with a verbal rendering. If such "nonce-forms" are spurious, they are to be rejected. A satisfactory definition, however, need not be finally, universally, and eternally "complete"; though a pragmatic definition should be a calculus that is validly derived, it may, and perhaps should, remain "in process."

Second, a pragmatic definition circumscribes a concept or referent; hence it is more than a simple lexical explication. Whereas the transliteration of an entry in a lexicon or the annotation of an item in a glossary expresses a relationship between *a name* or *a word* and certain verbal territory, a definition which circumscribes a concept avoids the pitfall "between *meaning* and *naming* even in the case of a singular term which *is* genuinely a name of an object." Gottlob Frege's classic example serves to illustrate the difference between *meaning* and *naming*:

The phrase "Evening Star" names a certain large physical object of spherical form, which is hurtling through space some scores of millions of miles from here. The phrase "Morning Star" names the same thing, as was probably first established by some observant Babylonian. But the two phrases cannot be regarded as having the same meaning; otherwise that Babylonian could have dispensed with his observations and contented himself with reflecting on the meanings of his words. The meanings, then, being different from one another, must be other than the named object, which is one and the same in both cases.

The bastion of lexical explanation, of course, is the dictionary; and although its usefulness is beyond question, its function is generally misunderstood. Actually, it records past practices in using a word, be those practices right or wrong by an absolute standard. It is a form of history and not a set of mathematical tables. Unfortunately, this characteristic is not generally known:

[Many persons] look upon a dictionary not as they look upon a book of history but rather as they look upon a book of mathematical tables. . . . As the square root of 1,369 is and always must be 37, no matter what any human may have thought or said or done, and this fact is pretty sure to be accurately stated in one's book of mathematical tables, so, men think, the meaning of a word is and always must be such and such, no matter how men have actually spoken and written, and this eternal and independent meaning is pretty sure to be accurately stated in one's dictionary. As the engineer who goes against the mathematical tables comes to grief, they think, the writer or speaker who goes against the dictionary comes to grief.

Lest the present writer be interpreted as making a rash attack upon a basic characteristic of language as a communicative medium, permit him to make his position clear. He agrees with the principle that mutual agreement upon the meaning of a term provides a workable basis for communication and that dictionaries provide a service in recording with a reasonable degree of accuracy the nature of the agreement. If the concept is simple, perhaps no serious harm occurs even if that agreement is basically illogical. On the other hand, if the concept is complex (as *communication* certainly is), recording the agreed-upon meaning can render a serious disservice if that meaning is basically illogical and/or false. The problems of reasoning with and about complex concepts are great enuogh without adding the further difficulty of a term whose definition is inconsistent with reality. The writer, therefore, takes the position that the criterion of general acceptance is inadequate for complex terms and that specialists can be satisfied with nothing less than a definition which is validly derived. Whether dictionaries which seek to serve the general public should concern themselves with this second criterion is beyond the scope of the present paper.

Third, a satisfactory definition is not tautological. Some persons find tautology attractive. For example, Louis MacNeice says, "In the beginning and in the end the only decent/ Definition is tautology; man is man,/ Woman woman, and tree tree, and world world." Wendell Johnson, however, makes short shrift of this idea:

> To a mouse, cheese is cheese. That is why mouse traps are effective. To many human beings Right is Right, Wrong is Wrong, Capital is Capital, and Labor is Labor. That is why propaganda is effective. . . . If you call the hogs and then give them corn they will, after a few feedings, come even if you don't give them corn, provided you call them. For the pigs, . . . "the farmer's call is corn." The stupidity of a pig is to be measured in terms of the number of times he comes in response to your call after you have discontinued the corn—and in terms of the promptness and speed, the lack of delay, with which he continues to come.

Thinking which is based upon tautological definitions is as unsound for people as it is for animals. The response to the call "Capital is Capital" or "Labor is Labor" continues long after the original stimuli have been discontinued. Man's stupidity, like that of the pig, may be measured in terms of the promptness, the speed, and the number of times he continues to come to calls which have long since "stopped producing corn." If "cheese is cheese" and we happen to be hungry, we may find a metal spring crashing down on the back of our necks. Tautology has its shortcomings.

THEORETICAL CONSIDERATIONS

Does a pragmatic definition need to be "complete" in the sense that "a complete definition" is prescribed epistemologically? The viewpoint of the present writer, as was stated earlier, is that the concept of communication is inherently so diverse and discursive that (a) any attempt "completely to determine" the meaning of communication will not be generally accepted (*Q.E.D.!*) and (b) any attempt "completely to explain" its meaning can only result in a map so specifically detailed as to be the equivalent of the territory it is intended to represent. Thus, it would not serve the purpose of a map!

To argue the possible merits of an "incomplete definition" in these special circumstances as compared to the merits of a "complete" one is to argue the number of angels that can dance on the head of a pin. The issue is not what is ideal but what is possible. "Completeness" and "incompleteness"· would seem, therefore, not to pertain to a pragmatic definition of communication.

Another theoretical problem, derived perhaps from the Aristotelian doctrines of first principles and prime movers, is whether defining words in terms of other words does not lead ultimately to an undefined term in each field of human knowledge. The present writer agrees with Cohen and Nagel that "it is a mistake to suppose that there are *intrinsically* undefinable terms." Such rationalized, though verbally diversified, justifications as "primitive terms," "primal facts," "*Urphänomen*," and "eternally precalibrated monads" serve only to cause confusion, and the implication of mysticism in these cases is a useless diversion. *Phlogiston* is an example of a term whose definition was thus rendered meaningless:

[*Phlogiston* was a term in the old chemistry] designating an element supposed to be weightless, odorless, and intangible and the cause of fire. If we think, we see that the term either means nothing at all or simply means "the unknown cause of fire."

ANALYSIS OF REPRESENTATIVE DEFINITIONS OF COMMUNICATION

The preceding section developed in some detail various points pertaining to the process of definition as it relates to defining the term *communication*. The following paragraphs seek to illuminate further the problem of defining this term by analyzing critically definitions by a philosopher, a psychologist, and a psychiatrist. Scores of additional published definitions also exist, but these three are sufficiently representative to serve the purposes of this paper.

Woodrow W. Sayre posits communication as "a first principle in philosophy," a principle "whose denial is impossible because it is reinvolved in the very denial." This argument, however, is simply a restatement of "the old Platonic riddle of non-being." Willard Quine has refuted it as follows:

When a statement of being or non-being is analyzed by Russell's theory of descriptions, it ceases to contain any expression which even purports to name the alleged entity whose being is in question, so that the meaningfulness of the statement no longer can be thought to presuppose that there be such an entity. . . . So the old notion that statements of non-being defeat themselves goes by the board.

Furthermore, even if it is a first principle of philosophy, such a postulation rather than being a definition of communication is actually the avoidance of one.

Almost as though to avoid such philosophical entanglements, a famous psychologist has approached the problem behavioristically. His widely (though not generally) accepted definition is presented as follows:

Although no phenomenon is more familiar to us than communication, the fact of the matter is that this magic word means many things to many people. A definition broad enough to encompass all these meanings may risk finding itself dissipated in generalities, but for [present] purposes . . . a broad operational definition of communication is, I believe, both appropriate and possible. I should like, therefore, to venture the following: *Communication is the discriminatory response of an organism to a stimulus.*

This definition says that communication occurs when some environmental disturbance (the stimulus) impinges on an organism and the organism does something about it (makes a discriminatory response). If the stimulus is ignored by the organism, there has been no communication. The test is differential reaction of some sort. The message that gets no response is not a communication.

This definition is broad, operational, and behavioristic.

This definition is open to two points of criticism, the first of which is that Stevens confuses the "reality" of *communication* with the *name* "communication." Although he criticizes a definition of the *word*, which would "risk finding itself dissipated in generalities," he advocates his own "broad, operational, and behavioristic" definition of specific, concrete acts or events.

As was mentioned earlier, a definition must not confuse a referent and the name for it. In classical terms, unless a distinction is made between a "real" definition, which circumscribes a concept or referent, and a "nominal" definition, which transliterates the lexical "name" of that referent, unnecessary vagueness results. Such definitions "serve as little more than foci for discussion."

A second criticism is that the definition is not based upon a sensible interpretation of empirical data. Colin Cherry points out that "communication is not the response itself but is essentially the *relationship* set up by the transmission of stimuli and the evocation of responses." Furthermore, the arbitrary rule that "the message that gets no response is not a communication" forces a longer look both at the notion of a stimulus and at the notion of a response to "it," in "languages, codes, and logical sign systems, at least."

In an earlier article, the present writer presented his own analysis of the rule that "the message that gets no response is not a communication." Space will not be consumed here by a repetition of that argument.

A third definition originally appeared in a well-known book with a psychiatric context:

Communication does not refer to verbal, explicit, and intentional transmission of messages alone. . . . The concept of communication would include all those processes by which people influence one another. . . . This definition is based upon the premise that all actions and events have communicative aspects, as soon as they are perceived by a human being; it implies, furthermore, that such perception changes the information which an individual possesses and therefore influences him.

The essential difference between this definition and Stevens' is the difference between perception *qua* perception and perception as the "trigger" for response; whereas Ruesch and Bateson posit perception as changing an individual's "store" of information, Stevens implies that perception "triggers" the response, which he conceives to be communication.

The shortcoming in this definition, however, is its limitation to human beings. This restriction not only rules out communicative interactions between men and machines and between machines and machines but also those yet intuited circumstances known variously by such names as revelation, epiphany, satori, etc.

DIVERSITY AS A FACTOR MAKING DEFINITION DIFFICULT

That the definitions of even some of the ablest thinkers in their respective academic areas are unsatisfactory is proof of the difficulty of the task. The following paragraphs on the diverse nature of communication not only help to explain the problems of these scholars but also suggest that the pragmatic approach which the present writer recommends also will be hard to follow.

Simply to enumerate some of the aspects of the communication process makes one question both the justification for the present-day consideration of such a diversity as a unified concept and the feasibility of positing "communication" as the unifying symbol for such discursiveness. Such was not always the case, however.

In 1935, when [Kenneth] Burke proposed to call his book *Treatise on Communication*, the publishers assured him that the title would suggest a book on telephone wires. So Burke was persuaded to accept the title *Permanence and Change*.

By 1956, Richard L. Meier indicated that "communication" suggested the following categories:

a. *face to face* conferences, meetings, gossip, etc.
b. *reading* newspapers, magazines, books, billboards, etc.
c. *man-machine*, reading instruments, gauges, microscopes, radar, etc.
d. *person-person* (*machine interposed*) telephone, radio, TV, films.
e. *machine-machine*, feedbacks, interlocks, automatism.

In 1960, "communication" is not even restricted to processes! Today "communication" also encompasses a body of knowledge and a field of study, including listening.

Messages that are communicated are verbal and nonverbal, with the latter including paralanguage and kinesics as well as nonlinguistic contextual cultural messages involving association, subsistence, sexuality, territoriality, temporality, learning, play, defense, and exploitation. Myths and dreams also constitute "languages."

That *communication* includes diverse ideas becomes still more evident if the nature of messages is analyzed: (a) directed messages, such as those transmitted in a telephone system as well as those transmitted in a face-to-face discussion system, are in contrast with undirected messages, such as those transmitted in a broadcasting system or in a public address to a multitude; (b) messages of primary information or content are in contrast with messages of secondary information (consisting of the reflexive awareness of who knows what); (c) consummatory messages, such as the expression of emotion (which does not depend upon feedback from the recipient) are in contrast with instrumental messages, which require feedback or secondary information about the effect of the message on the recipient; (d) the attenuation of primary information in "phatic communion" is in contrast with the density of information in the compressed tower talk of airport operations. Even this much of an itemization (and no claim to completeness is made) makes the possibility of a single or unified definition—even an incomplete one—appear to be little more than wishful thinking, well-intentioned though it may be.

CONCLUSION

If any definition is possible, it must be descriptive and pragmatic. Prescriptivists will no doubt complain, for to them a definition is expected to state what *should* take place. The creation of a satisfactory definition is going to be extremely difficult, but this writer hopes that his analysis of the nature of definition and his critiques of some of the preceding attempts will be helpful to others. Of one thing he is sure: no acceptable definition is possible unless its creator has an understanding of the broad theory of definition-making.

CHAPTER III

The Social Psychological Theory

INTRODUCTION   While the key orientation for the mathematical theory of communication is the analysis of information is terms of probability and statistics, the key orientation for the social psychological theory of communication is the analysis of human codes and networks. Social psychologists observe people interacting in groups. This interaction is communication. It involves some kind of behavior such as speech or gestures into which any member of the group can encode a message that any other member of the group can then decode. Social interaction also involves some kinds of rules as to who in the group encodes which messages and who decodes them. This is the basis of social organization and communication networks. Among the social psychologists some have given greater emphasis to the social aspects of communication while others have emphasized the psychological aspects.

Theodore M. Newcomb's "An Approach to the Study of Communicative Acts" introduces the concept of coorientation as the basis of human communication. Coorientation means that people in communication with each other "maintain simultaneous orientation toward one another as communicators *and* toward objects of communication." These coorientations form the psychological basis of group behavior. For us this social psychological concept is a human analog of the concept of coding in the mathematical theory of communication. If two people or two radio stations or any two systems are to communicate, they must be able to respond in corresponding ways to the same things. Electronic engineers often say that the two systems must be coupled or matched to one another. Newcomb recognized this in human terms. Moreover, he recognizes that these coorientations are changeable, and thus he develops a dynamic picture of human communication.

Bruce H. Westley and Malcolm S. MacLean, Jr., in "A Conceptual Model for Communications Research" begin with Newcomb's social psychological coorientations. Then they add such concepts as coding, channels, and feedback from the mathematical theory of communication. The composite model they present is based essentially on the concepts of roles, messages, channels, and codes. Although their model is general and theoretical, it is oriented toward the social psychology of the mass media: radio, television, and the press. Other social psychologists are more concerned with small groups.

The next two selections present a slightly different approach. They are somewhat more concerned with the social aspects than the psychological ones, with the social cohesiveness of the group rather than the psychological coorientations of its members. A. Paul Hare in "The Dimensions of Social Interaction" presents a model of social interaction in face-to-face groups. Essentially this model is a paradigm for the analysis of communication, and it is based on four variables: form and content; and personal and interpersonal behavior. Robert F. Bales uses the same kind of approach in "How People Interact in Conferences." Bales gives a concrete illustration of the general theory of interaction by making formal observations and analyses of conferences, which are one kind of the face-to-face groups that Hare analyzed. Bales discovered that different kinds of leadership emerge at different stages in the work of the group. Leadership is a part of the social structure of the group, and this structure changes. Like Newcomb's approach, therefore, this one is also dynamic and concerned with change.

Erving Goffman maintains that face-to-face communication between two people involves a mutual involvement between them, a "socialized trance." This mutual involvement is like Newcomb's concept of coorientation. Goffman, in "Alienation from Interaction," presents informal observations and analyses of social communication in terms of the appropriateness, spontaneity, intentionality, and involvement obligations of these interactions. These terms help to explain "the generic properties of spoken interaction" within any group of people.

6 | An Approach to the Study of Communicative Acts
THEODORE M. NEWCOMB

This paper points toward the possibility that many of those phenomena of social behavior which have been somewhat loosely assembled under the label of "interaction" can be more adequately studied as communicative acts. It further points to the possibility that, just as the observable forms of certain solids are macroscopic outcomes of molecular structure, so certain observable group properties are predetermined by the conditions and consequences of communicative acts.

The initial assumption is that communication among humans performs the essential function of enabling two or more individuals to maintain simultaneous orientation toward one another as communicators *and* toward objects of communication. After presenting a rationale for this assumption, we shall attempt to show that a set of propositions derived from or consistent with it seems to be supported by empirical findings.

CO-ORIENTATION AND THE A-B-X SYSTEM

Every communicative act is viewed as a transmission of information, consisting of discriminative stimuli, from a source to a recipient. For present purposes it is assumed that the discriminative stimuli have a discriminable object as referent. Thus in the simplest possible communicative act one person (A) transmits information to another person (B) about something (X). Such an act is symbolized here as AtoBreX.

The term "orientation" is used as equivalent to "attitude" in its more inclusive sense of referring to both cathectic and cognitive tendencies. The phrase "simultaneous orientation" (hereinafter abbreviated to "co-orientation") itself represents an assumption; namely, that A's orientation

Reprinted with permission of the American Psychological Association and the author. From *Psychological Review*, 60:393–404 (1953).

toward B and toward X are interdependent. A-B-X is therefore regarded as constituting a system. That is, certain definable relationships between A and B, between A and X, and between B and X are all viewed as interdependent. For some purposes the system may be regarded as a phenomenal one within the life space of A or B, for other purposes as an "objective" system including all of the possible relationships as inferred from observations of A's and B's behavior. It is presumed that a given state of the system exists when a given instance of AtoBreX occurs, and that as a result of this occurrence the system undergoes some change (even though the change be regarded as only a reinforcement of the pre-existing state).

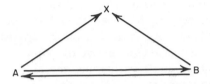

Figure 1. Schematic illustration of the minimal A-B-X system.

The minimal components of the A-B-X system, as schematically illustrated in Figure 1, are as follows:

1. A's orientation toward X, including both attitude toward X as an object to be approached or avoided (characterized by sign and intensity) and cognitive attributes (beliefs and cognitive structuring).
2. A's orientations toward B, in exactly the same sense. (For purposes of avoiding confusing terms, we shall speak of positive and negative *attraction* toward A or B as persons, and of favorable and unfavorable *attitudes* toward X.)
3. B's orientation toward X.
4. B's orientation toward A.

In order to examine the possible relationships of similarity and difference between A and B, we shall make use of simple dichotomies in regard to these four relationships. That is, with respect to a given X at a given time, A and B will be regarded as cathectically alike (++ or --) or different (+- or -+) in attitude and in attraction; and as cognitively alike or different. We shall also make use of simple dichotomies of degree —i.e., more alike, less alike. We shall refer to lateral similarities of A's and B's orientations to X as *symmetrical* relationships.

This very simple system is designed to fit two-person communication. In the following discussion these additional limitations will be imposed, for simplicity's sake: (*a*) communicative acts will be treated as verbal ones, in face-to-face situations; (*b*) initiation of the communicative act is considered to be intentional (i.e., such acts are excluded as those which the actor assumes to be unobserved); (*c*) it is assumed that the "message" is received—i.e., that the communicative act is attended to by an intended recipient, though not necessarily with any particular degree of accuracy; and (d) A and B are assumed to be group members, characterized by continued association.

The assumption that co-orientation is essential to human life is based upon two considerations of complementary nature. First, the orientation of any A toward any B (assuming that they are capable of verbal communication) is rarely, if ever, made in an environmental vacuum. Even in what seems the maximally "pure" case of two lovers oblivious to all but each other, both singly and both jointly are dependent upon a common environment; and their continued attachment is notoriously contingent upon the discovery or development of common interests beyond themselves. It is not certain that even their most person-oriented communications (e.g., "I love you") are devoid of environmental reference. The more intense one person's concern for another the more sensitive he is likely to be to the other's orientations to objects in the environment.

Second, the orientation of any A capable of verbal communication about almost any conceivable X is rarely, if ever, made in a social vacuum. There are few if any objects so private that one's orientations toward them are uninfluenced by others' orientations. This is particularly true with regard to what has been termed "social reality"; i.e., the less the possibility of testing one's assumptions by observing the physical consequences of those assumptions, the greater the reliance upon social confirmation as the test of what is true and valid. And even when assumptions can be put to the direct test (e.g., the child can find out for himself about the stove which he has been told is hot), social reality is often accepted as the quicker or the safer test. As various linguists have pointed out, moreover, a good deal of social reality is built into the very language with which we communicate about things. Under the conditions of continued association which we are assuming, A and B as they communicate about X are dependent upon each other, not only because the other's eyes and ears provide an additional source of information about X, but also because the other's judgment provides a testing ground for social reality. And to be dependent upon the other, in so far as such dependence influences behavior, is to be oriented toward him.

In short, it is an almost constant human necessity to orient oneself toward objects in the environment and also toward other persons oriented toward those same objects. To the degree that A's orientation either toward X or toward B is contingent upon B's orientation toward X, A is motivated to influence and/or to inform himself about B's orientation toward X. Communication is the most common and usually the most effective means by which he does so.

SYMMETRY OF ORIENTATION

Much of the remainder of this paper will deal with the relationships between A's and B's orientations toward X, within the postulated A-B-X system. The implications of this model are: (*a*) that while at any given moment the system may be conceived of as being "at rest," it is characterized not by the absence but by the balance of forces; and (*b*) that a change in any part of the system (any of the four relationships portrayed in Figure 1) may lead to changes in any of the others. We shall also make the assumption (not inherent in the model) that certain forces impinging upon the system are relatively strong and persistent, and that thus there are "strains" toward preferred states of equilibrium.

This assumption, related to the initial one concerning the co-orientation function of communication, is as follows. To the degree that A's orientation toward X is contingent upon B's orientation toward X, A's co-orientation will be facilitated by similarity of his own and B's orientation toward X. The first advantage of symmetry—particularly of cognitive symmetry—is that of ready calculability of the other's behavior; the more similar A's and B's cognitive orientations, the less the necessity for either of them to "translate" X in terms of the other's orientations, the less the likelihood of failure or error in such "translations," and thus the less different and/or the less erroneous the co-orientation of either. Second, there is the advantage of validation of one's own orientation toward X; the more similar A's and B's orientations, either cognitive or cathectic (particularly in the many areas where validation is heavily dependent upon "social reality"), the more confident each of them can be of his own cognitive and evaluative orientations. Co-orientation is of course possible with little or no symmetry, but the facilitative value of symmetry, for co-orientation is considerable.

If these advantages are commonly experienced as such, communicative acts resulting in increased symmetry are likely to be rewarded, and symmetry is likely to acquire secondary reward value. This is the basis of our assumption of a persistent "strain toward symmetry," under the conditions noted.

These assumptions may now be brought together in terms of the following inclusive postulate: *The stronger the forces toward A's co-orientation in respect to B and X, (a) the greater A's strain toward symmetry with B in respect to X; and (b) the greater the likelihood of increased symmetry as a consequence of one or more communicative acts.* The latter part of the postulate assumes the possibility of modified orientations toward X on the part of both A and B, who over a period of time exchange roles as transmitters and receivers of information.

Several testable propositions are derivable from this postulate. First, if the likelihood of instigation to and achievement of symmetry varies as a function of forces toward co-orientation, the latter varies, presumably, with valence of the objects of co-orientation—i.e., of intensity of attitude toward X and of attraction toward B. That is, under conditions such that orientation toward either B or X also demands orientation toward the other, the greater the valence of B or of X the greater the induced force toward co-orientation, and thus the greater the likelihood of both instigation toward and achievement of symmetry.

Such research findings as are known to the writer are in support of these predictions. Experimental results reported by Festinger and Thibaut, by Schachter, and by Back indicate that attempts to influence another toward one's own point of view vary as a function of attraction. In the second of these studies it is shown that communications within a cohesive group are directed most frequently toward those perceived as deviates, up to a point where the deviate is sociometrically rejected (i.e., attraction decreases or becomes negative), beyond which point communication to them becomes less frequent. It is also shown in this study that frequency of influence-attempting communication varies with degree of interest in the topic of group discussion.

Some of these same studies, and some others, present data concerning symmetry as a consequence of communication. Thus Festinger and Thibaut, varying "pressure toward uniformity" and "perception of homogeneous group composition," found actual change toward uniformity following a discussion to be a function of both these variables, but some change toward uniformity took place in every group, under all conditions. Back found that subjects who started with different interpretations of the same material and who were given an opportunity to discuss the matter were influenced by each other as a direct function of attraction.

Findings from two community studies may also be cited, as consistent with these laboratory studies. Newcomb, in a replicated study of friendship choices as related to political attitudes in a small college community, found on both occasions that students at each extreme of the attitude continuum tended to have as friends those like themselves in attitude. Festinger, Schachter, and Back, in their study of a housing project, found a correlation of +.72 between a measure of attraction and a measure of "conformity in attitude." No direct observations of communication are made in these two studies; the relevance of their findings for the present point depends upon the assumption that frequency of communication is a function of attraction. This assumption is clearly justified in these two particular investigations, since in both communities there was complete freedom of association. As noted below, this assumption is not justified in all situations.

Other testable propositions derivable from the general postulate have to do with A's judgments of existing symmetry between himself and B with respect to X. Such judgments (to which the writer has for some time applied the term "perceived consensus") are represented by the symbol B-X, within A's phenomenal A-B-X system. Such a judgment, under given conditions of demand for co-orientation with respect to a given B and a given X, is a major determinant of the likelihood of a given AtoBreX, since strain toward symmetry is influenced by perception of existing symmetry. Such a judgment, moreover, is either confirmed or modified by whatever response B makes to AtoBreX. The continuity of an A-B-X system thus depends upon perceived consensus, which may be viewed either as an independent or as a dependent variable.

According to the previous proposition, the likelihood of increased symmetry (objectively observed) as a consequence of communicative acts increases with attraction and with intensity of attitude. The likelihood of perceived symmetry presumably increases with the same variables. Judgments of symmetry, like other judgments, are influenced both by "reality" and by "autistic" factors, both of which tend, as a function of attraction and intensity of attitude, to increase the likelihood of perceived consensus. Frequency of communication with B about X is the most important of the "reality" factors, and this, as we have seen, tends to vary with valence toward B and toward X. As for the "autistic" factors, the greater the positive attraction toward B and the more intense the attitude toward X, the greater the likelihood of cognitive distortion toward symmetry. Hypothetically, then, perceived symmetry with regard to X varies as a function of intensity of attitude toward X and of attraction toward B.

A considerable number of research studies, published and unpublished, are known to the writer in which subjects' own attitudes are related to their estimates of majority or modal position of specified groups. Only a minority of the studies systematically relate these judgments to attraction, and still fewer to intensity of attitude. Among this minority, however, the writer knows of no exceptions to the above proposition. The most striking of the known findings were obtained from students in several university classes in April of 1951, in a questionnaire dealing with the very recent dismissal of General MacArthur by President Truman:

	pro-Truman Ss who . . .	anti-Truman Ss who . . .
attribute to "most of my closest friends"		
pro-Truman attitudes	48	2
anti-Truman attitudes	0	34
neither	4	4
attribute to "most uninformed people"		
pro-Truman attitudes	6	13
anti-Truman attitudes	32	14
neither	14	13

If we assume that "closest friends" are more attractive to university students than "uninformed people," these data provide support for the attraction hypothesis. Comparisons of those who own attitudes are more and less intense also provide support, though less strikingly, for the hypothesis concerning attitude intensity.

Perceived symmetry, viewed as an independent variable, is obviously a determinant of instigation to symmetry-directed communication. Festinger, with specific reference to groups characterized by "pressures toward uniformity," hypothesizes that "pressure on members to communicate to others in the group concerning item x increases monotonically with increase in the perceived discrepancy in opinion concerning item x among members of the group," as well as with "relevance of item x to the functioning of the group," and with "cohesiveness of the group." And, with reference to the choice of recipient for communications, "The force to communicate about item x to a particular member of the group will increase as the discrepancy in opinion between that member and the communicator increases [and] will decrease to the extent that he is perceived as not a member of the group or to the extent that he is not wanted as a member of the group." Support for all of these hypotheses is to be found in one or more of his and his associates' studies. They are consistent with the following proposition: the likelihood of a symmetry-directed Ato-BreX varies as a multiple function of perceived discrepancy (i.e., inversely with perceived symmetry), with valence toward B and with valence toward X.

Common sense and selected observations from everyday behavior may also be adduced in support of these propositions. For example, A observes that an attractive B differs with him on an important issue and seeks symmetry by trying to persuade B to his own point of view; or A seeks to reassure himself that B does not disagree with him; or A gives information to B about X or asks B for information about X. From all these acts we may infer perception of asymmetry and direction of communication toward symmetry. Selected observations concerning symmetry as a consequence of communication are equally plentiful; there is, in fact, no social phenomenon which can be more commonly observed than the tendency for freely communicating persons to resemble one another in orientation toward objects of common concern. The very nature of the communicative act as a transmission of information would, on a priori grounds alone, lead to the prediction of increased symmetry, since following the communication both A and B possess the information which was only A's before. B will not necessarily accept or believe all information transmitted by A, of course, but the likelihood of his doing so presumably varies not only with attraction toward A but also with intensity of attitude toward X, since in the long run the more important X is to him the more likely it is that he will avoid communicating with B about X if he cannot believe him. Thus the propositions have a considerable degree of face validity.

But everyday observation also provides instances to the contrary. Not all communications are directed toward symmetry, nor is symmetry an inevitable consequence of communication, even when attraction is strong and attitudes are intense. A devoted husband may refrain from discussing important business matters with his wife, or two close friends may "agree to disagree" in silence about matters of importance to both. People who are attracted toward one another often continue to communicate about subjects on which they continue to disagree—and this is particularly apt to happen with regard to attitudes which are intense, contrary to our theoretical prediction.

In sum, the available research findings and a considerable body of everyday observation support our predictions that instigation toward, perception of, and actual achievement of symmetry vary with intensity of attitude toward X and attraction toward B. The readiness with which exceptions can be adduced, however, indicates that these are not the only variables involved. The propositions, at best, rest upon the assumption of *ceteris paribus;* they cannot account for the fact that the probabilities of A's instigation to communicate about a given X are not the same for all potential B's of equal attraction for him, nor the fact that his instigation to communicate to a given B are not the same for all X's of equal valence to him. We shall therefore attempt to derive certain further propositions from our basic assumption that both instigation to and achievement of symmetry vary with strength of forces toward co-orientation in the given situation.

DYNAMICS OF CO-ORIENTATION

The foregoing propositions represent only a slight extrapolation of Heider's general principle of "balanced states" in the absence of which "unit relations will be changed through action or through cognitive reorganization." In a later paper devoted specifically to the implications of Heider's hypotheses for interrelationships among attitudes toward a person and toward his acts, Horowitz *et al.* note the following possible resolutions to states of imbalance: (*a*) the sign-valence of the act is changed to agree with that of the actor; (*b*) the reverse of this; and (*c*) the act is cognitively divorced from the actor; in addition, of course, the disharmony may be tolerated.

Orientations as attributed by A to B are here considered as equivalent to acts so attributed, in Heider's sense, and symmetry is taken as a special case of balance. Assume, for example, the following asymmetry in A's phenomenal system: $+A:X$, $+A:B$, $-B:X$, $+B:A$ (i.e., A has positive attitude toward X, positive attraction toward B, perceives B's attitude toward X as negative, and B's attraction toward A as positive). Any of the following attempts at "resolution," analogous to those mentioned by Heider, are possible: (*a*) $-A:X$; (*b*) $-A:B$; or (*c*) cognitive dissociation. These can occur in the absence of any communication with B. Attempts at harmony (symmetry) may also be made via communications directed toward $+B:X$. And, if such attempts fail, the three alternatives mentioned as possible without communication are still available. Finally, there is the possibility of compromise, following communication (e.g., agreement on some midpoint), and the possibility of "agreeing to disagree."

Such acts of resolution are made necessary, according to the present theory, by the situational demands of co-orientation on the one hand and by the psychological strain toward symmetry on the other. But symmetry is only a facilitating condition for co-orientation, not a necessary one. While (as maintained in the preceding propositions) the probabilities of symmetry vary, *ceteris paribus,* with demand for co-orientation, the theory does not demand that a symmetry-directed AtoBreX occur in every instance of strong demand for co-orientation. On the contrary, the theory demands that it occur only if, as, and when co-orientation is facilitated thereby. We must therefore inquire more closely into the nature of the forces toward co-orientation as related to possible forces against symmetry.

One kind of situational variable has to do with the nature of the forces which result in association between A and B. Of particular importance are constrained (enforced) vs. voluntary association, and association based upon broad as contrasted with narrow common interests. The range of X's with regard to which there is demand for co-orientation is presumably influenced by such forces. The relevant generalization seems to be as follows: *The less the attraction between A and B, the more nearly strain toward symmetry is limited to those particular X's co-orientation toward which is required by the conditions of association.* This would mean, for example, that as attraction between two spouses decreases, strain toward symmetry would increasingly narrow to such X's as are required by personal comfort and conformity with external propriety; similarly, the range of X's with regard to which there is strain toward symmetry is greater for two friendly than for two hostile members of a chess club.

The problem of constraint has already been noted. In some of the studies cited above it was assumed that frequency of communication varies with attraction, but this is not necessarily true under conditions of forced association. Two recent theoretical treatises deal with this problem.

Homans, one of whose group variables is "frequency of interaction" (though not communication, specifically), includes the following among his other propositions: "If the frequency of interaction between two or more persons increases, the degree of their liking for one another will increase, and vice versa"; and "The more frequently persons interact with one another, the more alike in some respects both their activities and their sentiments tend to become." (The latter proposition, which closely resembles the one here under consideration, apparently takes a much less important place in Homans' system than the former.) Almost immediately, however, the latter proposition is qualified by the statement, "It is only when people interact as social equals and their jobs are not sharply differentiated that our hypothesis comes fully into its own." In nearly every chapter, moreover, Homans (whose propositions are drawn *post hoc* from various community, industrial, and ethnological studies) points to the limitations which are imposed by constraining forces—particularly those of rank and hierarchy—upon the relations among attraction, similarity of attitude, and communication.

Blake manages to incorporate these considerations in a more rigorous proposition. Noting that hostility cannot be considered as the simple psychological opposite of positive attraction, he proposes to substitute a curvilinear for Homans' linear hypothesis: ". . . when pressures operate to keep members of a group together, the stresses that drive toward interaction will be stronger in *both* positive and negative feeling states than in neutral ones." This proposition seems consistent with the present argument to the effect that demands for co-orientation are likely to vary with the nature and degree of constraints upon association; hence communicative acts, together with their consequences, will also vary with such constraints.

Another situational variable deals with the fact that, under conditions of prescribed role differentiation, symmetry may take the form of "complementarity" rather than sameness. For example, both a man and his small son may (following a certain amount of communication of a certain nature) subscribe to the *same norms* which prescribe *differentiated behavior* for man and boy with respect to a whiskey and soda. If the father drinks in the son's presence, there are demands upon both of them for co-orientation; but there is strain toward symmetry only with respect to "the code," and not with respect to personal orientation toward the whiskey and soda. The code becomes the X with regard to which there is strain toward symmetry. In more general terms, *under conditions of differentiation of A's and B's role prescriptions with regard to X, the greater the demand for co-orientation the greater the likelihood of strain toward symmetry with respect to the role system* (rather than with respect to X itself).

A third situational variable has to do with the possibility that symmetry may be threatening. Particularly under circumstances of shame, guilt, or fear of punishment there are apt to be strong forces against a symmetry-directed AtoBreX, even though—in fact, especially when—attitude toward X (the guilty act) and attraction toward B (a person from whom it is to be concealed) are strong. Under these conditions it is the demand for co-orientation which creates the problem; if A could utterly divorce X (his own act) from B, he would not feel guilty. Forces toward symmetry, however, are opposed by counterforces. Demand for co-orientation induces strain toward symmetry, but does not necessarily lead to a symmetry-directed AtoBreX.

A theoretically analogous situation may result from the omnipresent fact of multiple membership groups. That is, strains toward symmetry with B_1 in regard to X may be outweighed by strains toward symmetry with B_2, whose orientations toward X are viewed as contradictory with those of B_1. This is often the case when, for example, two good friends "agree to disagree" about something of importance to both. Thus in one study it was found that those members least influenced by reported information concerning their own group norms were those most attracted to groups whose norms were perceived as highly divergent from those of the group in question.

Communicative acts, like others, are thus subject to inhibition. Such "resolutions" as "agreement to disagree," however, represent relatively stressful states of equilibrium. It is therefore to be expected, in ways analogous to those noted by Lewin in his discussion of the quasi-stationary equilibrium, that A-B-X systems characterized by such stress will be particularly susceptible to change. Such change need not necessarily occur in the particular region of the system characterized by maximal strain.

The dynamics of such a system are by no means limited to those of strains toward symmetry, but must include changes resulting from acceptance of existing asymmetry. The possible range of dynamic changes is illustrated in Figure 2. (In this figure, the A and B at either side repre-

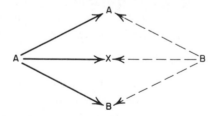

Figure 2.   Schematic illustration of A's phenomenal A-B-X system.

sent persons as communicators; the A and B in the center represent the same persons as objects of co-orientation. The broken lines represent A's judgments of B's orientations.) Given perceived asymmetry with regard to X, and demand for co-orientation toward B and X, the possibilities for A are such that he can:

1. achieve, or attempt to achieve, symmetry with regard to X
   a. by influencing B toward own orientation,
   b. by changing own orientation toward B's,
   c. by cognitively distorting B's orientation;
2. introduce changes in other parts of the system
   a. modify his attraction toward B,
   b. modify his judgment of own attraction for B,
   c. modify evaluation of (attraction toward) himself (A),
   d. modify his judgment of B's evaluation of himself (B);
3. tolerate the asymmetry, without change.

As suggested by this listing of possible "solutions," the perception of asymmetry, under conditions of demand for co-orientation, confronts A with a problem which he can attempt to solve behaviorally (i.e., by communicative acts) and/or cognitively (i.e., by changing either his own orientations or his perception of B's orientations). Whatever his chosen "solution," it has some effect upon A's phenomenal A-B-X system—either to reinforce it or to modify it. As a result of repeatedly facing and "solving" problems of co-orientation with regard to a given B and a given X, a relatively stable equilibrium is established. If A is free either to continue or not to continue his association with B, one or the other of two eventual outcomes is likely: (*a*) he achieves an equilibrium characterized by relatively great attraction toward B and by relatively high perceived symmetry, and the association is continued; or (*b*) he achieves an equilibrium characterized by relatively little attraction toward B and by relatively low perceived symmetry, and the association is discontinued. This "either-or" assumption under conditions of low constraint presupposes a circular relationship between attraction and the perception of symmetry. The present theory demands this assumption of circularity, and empirical evidence (under conditions of relative freedom from constraint) seems to support it.

Under conditions of little or no freedom to discontinue association, no such circularity is assumed. The conditions which dictate continued association also dictate the requirements for co-orientation, which are independent of attraction. The empirical data suggest that the degree to which attraction is independent of symmetry varies with the degree of *perceived* (rather than the degree of objectively observed) constraint.

GROUP PROPERTIES

It follows from the preceding assumptions and propositions that there should be predictable relationships between certain properties of any group and variables having to do with communicative behavior within that group. A group's structural properties, for example, viewed as in-- dependent variables, may create problems and may provide solutions to other problems of communication. Viewed the other way around, many properties of a group are outcomes of its communicative practices. Evidence from many sources points to distinctive properties of groups which are precisely those which the foregoing considerations would lead us to expect, either as conditions for or as consequences of a given kind and frequency of communicative acts.

Three kinds of properties are briefly noted. Each of them is hypothetically related (either as dependent or as independent variable) to the probabilities of the occurrence of a given kind of communicative act.

1. *Homogeneity of orientation* toward certain objects. All descriptive accounts of interacting groups note this property, in one way or another and by one label or another. As applied to behavior, it does not necessarily refer to similarity of action on the part of all group members, but only of demand or expectation; e.g., all expect each to take his own differentiated role. In order to account for the observed facts it is necessary to make the assumptions (not previously made in this paper) that information may be transmitted in non-verbal ways, and with or without intention to do so—e.g., a person's behavior with regard to a given object informs observers about his orientation to it.

If communication is thus broadly defined, then the degrees of homogeneity of orientation of a given group with respect to specified objects are presumably related to communication variables with respect to those objects. It is not hypothesized that homogeneity is an invariable function of any single index of communication (frequency, for example), but rather that it varies in accordance with the dynamics of A-B-X systems. While there are often extragroup determinants of homogeneity of orientation, it seems reasonable to view this very important group property as an outcome of the conditions and consequences of communicative acts.

2. *Homogeneity of perceived consensus* (i.e., homogeneity of judgments of homogeneity of orientation). This property, though not often specifically mentioned in the literature on groups, is usually implicitly assumed. Most communication presupposes a considerable degree of perceived as well as objective homogeneity of orientation. The very fact of using language or gesture presupposes the assumption of consensus among communicants as to the information transmitted by the use of symbols.

Homogeneity of orientation and of perceived consensus do not, in spite of implicit assumptions to the contrary, have an invariant relationship; judgments of homogeneity may be of any degree of accuracy. If, as in the village reported by Schanck, each of many dissenters from a supposed norm believes himself the only dissenter, this state of pluralistic ignorance is an important group property, and is plausibly described by the author as an outcome of certain practices of communication. Any degree of homogeneity of perceived consensus, representing any degree of accuracy, is hypothetically an outcome of previous communicative acts and a determinant of future ones.

3. *Attraction among members.* Relationships of positive attraction of some degree invariably characterize continuing groups under conditions of minimal constraint, and are commonly found even under conditions of considerable constraint. This is so commonly the case that Homans ventures the almost unqualified hypothesis that "liking" increases with frequency of interaction, and vice versa. Viewed in the light of the hypothetical dynamics of A-B-X systems, Homans' proposition would be amended to the effect that interpersonal attraction varies with the degree to which the demands of co-orientation are met by communicative acts.

These are not, of course, the only group properties of significance, nor are these properties outcomes exclusively of intragroup communication. (Some properties of almost any group, particularly at early stages of its history, derive largely from individual characteristics which its members bring to it.) It appears to be the case, nevertheless, that the hypothetical conditions and consequences of communicative acts are not limited to groups of two, and that some of the important properties of observed groups are consistent with the hypothetical dynamics of A-B-X systems.

SUMMARY

Communicative acts, like other molar behaviors, may be viewed as outcomes of changes in organism-environment relationships, actual and/or anticipated. Communicative acts are distinctive in that they may be aroused by and may result in changes anywhere within the system of relations between two or more communicators and the objects of their communication. It seems likely that the dynamics of such a system are such that from an adequate understanding of its properties at a given moment there can be predicted both the likelihood of occurrence of a given act of communication and the nature of changes in those properties which will result from that act.

Some of the most significant of group properties are those which, hypothetically, vary with intragroup communicative acts. It should therefore be rewarding to discover whether support for the present hypotheses, as apparently provided by the scattered evidence now available, can be confirmed in more systematic ways. If so, there are promising possibilities of investigating the phenomena of social interaction by viewing them as events within communication systems.

7 | A Conceptual Model for Communications Research
BRUCE H. WESTLEY
and MALCOLM S. MacLEAN, JR.

Communications research and theory have blossomed from a variety of disciplinary sources in recent years. People probing the communications area have here focused on theoretical issues and there on "practical" concerns. Thus, one finds today a jungle of unrelated concepts and systems of concepts on the one hand and a mass of undigested, often sterile empirical data on the other.

In this paper, we are trying to develop a single communications model which may help to order existing findings. It also may provide a system of concepts which will evoke new and interrelated research directions, compose old theoretical and disciplinary differences, and in general bring some order out of a chaotic situation. Clearly, we do not propose here a full-blown theory of mass communications, but rather a paradigm or model as a preliminary orientation to a theoretical system.

Can a simple, parsimonious model be built capable of drawing together many of the existing approaches to mass communications without serious loss in utility?

FROM FACE-TO-FACE TO MASS

First, let us look at a simple act of communication. Person A transmits something about an object X to person B. Newcomb has found this simple model of interpersonal communications useful in the study of roles and norms. He says that, when A communicates to B about X (other things being equal), systematic changes in the condition of the system can be predicted. For example, if B likes A (or, at least, does not dislike him), B's perception of X will be more similar to A's after than before the communicative act.

This model frees one from the limitations of either the personality or social systems as such. Can it serve as a guide to both face-to-face and mass communications? Need the extension from the simple communicative act to the mass communicative act destroy its system character?

Reprinted with permission of the publisher and the authors. From *Journalism Quarterly*, 34:31–38 (1957).

Two basic distinctions between face-to-face and mass communications are suggested: Face-to-face communication involves more sense modalities. It also provides immediate "feedback"—that is, information from B back to A about the change condition of B. In other words, more senses (and kinds of stimuli) can come into play in the person-person act than in any other situation. Thus, B has a "cross-modality" check. He can clear impressions he gets through one sense with those he gets through another. And A has the advantage of learning B's response almost immediately— for instance, "message received."

Mass communications, then, differ from face-to-face communications to the extent that (a) the number of modalities tends to be minimized and (b) "orientative" feedback is minimized or delayed.

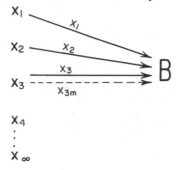

Figure 1. Objects of orientation (X_1 . . . X_∞) in the sensory field of the receiver (B) are transmitted directly to him in abstracted form (X_1 . . . X_3) after a process of selection from among all Xs, such selection being based at least in part on the needs and problems of B. Some or all are transmitted in more than one sense (X_{3m}, for example).

Now for a look at X, which may be taken as an "object of orientation." From the standpoint of B, the world consists of a confusion of X's. And these Xs may include As. B has within his sensory field an infinity of potential Xs. He has learned that in order to maximize satisfactions and solve security problems he must orient toward Xs selectively. But the mature B, Newcomb emphasizes, does not orient toward X alone, but tends, in the presence of an A, to orient simultaneously toward both A and X. This means that he comes to orient toward an X not alone on the basis of its intrinsic capacity to provide satisfactions and help solve problems but also with respect to the relationship between A and X. This also means that A and X relate systematically to B.

Let us assume that an X is any object (or event) that has characteristics capable of being transmitted in some abstracted form. Let us assume further that a system has a need for transmissible messages as a means of orienting itself in its environment and as a means of securing problem solutions and need satisfactions. The significant things is that Xs have stimulus characteristics that can be responded to in the absence of an *A*.

For instance, *B* looks out his window and sees flames in the house of his neighbor. This event as surely transmits information to him as would the shouts of his neighbor *about* the fire.

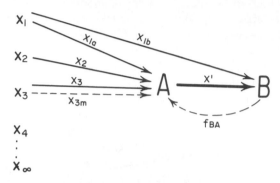

Figure 2.   The same Xs are selected and abstracted by communicator (A) and transmitted as a message (X') to B, who may or may not have part or all of the Xs in his own sensory field (X_{1b}). Either purposively or non-purposively B transmits feedback (f_{BA}) to A.

With respect to the *A*s and *X*s in his own immediate sensory field, *B* is capable of receiving and acting upon information thus transmitted to him and must do so if he is to maintain an adequate orientation to his immediate environment. But what of *A*s and *X*s relevant to such orientation but lying outside his immediate reach? If these are to impinge on him, there is need for another role, which we will call *C*.

C is conceived of as one who can (a) select the abstractions of object *X* appropriate to *B*'s need satisfactions or problem solutions, (b) transform them into some form of symbol containing meanings shared with *B*, and finally (c) transmit such symbols by means of some channel or medium to *B*.

The added element *C* will be recognized as the "gatekeeper" of Lewin as adapted to mass communications by White. It is also recognizable as the "encoder" suggested by Bush as an adaptation of the encoding process in information theory.

It may be asked why *C* would choose *X*s "appropriate" to the requirements of *B*. The answer would appear to be that the *C* role can survive only to the extent that this is true. For *B* is still a selector among the offerings of various *C*s and this means that *C*s are in effect competitors for the attention of *B*s (and for that matter competitors with *A*s and *X*s in *B*'s immediate field). *C*s therefore survive as *C*s to the extent that they satisfy needs for *B*s. And *B*s, on the basis of the most obvious propositions of learning theory, will tend to return to those Cs which have provided past need satisfactions and problem solutions.

C, then, is capable of serving as an agent for B in selecting and transmitting information about an X (or an A-X relationship). He does so by

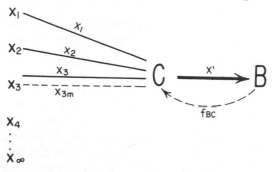

Figure 3.   What Xs B receives may be owing to selected abstractions transmitted by a non-purposive encoder (C), acting for B and thus extending B's environment. C's selections are necessarily based in part on feedback (f_{BC}) from B.

means of symbols expressing shared meanings about Xs through channels that provide connection between X and B. And he does so in circumstances where such a connection is otherwise impossible for B. Thus B has a basis for increasing his security in the larger environment and for gaining increased need satisfactions. In other words, *the effect of the addition of the C role is to provide B with a more extended environment.*

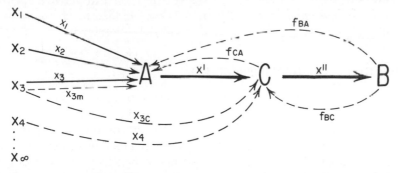

Figure 4.   The messages C transmits to B (X″) represent his selections from both messages to him from A's (X′) and C's selections and abstractions from Xs in his own sensory field (X_{3c}, X_4), which may or may not be Xs in A's field. Feedback not only moves from B to A (f_{BA}) and from B to C (f_{BC}) but also from C to A (f_{CA}). Clearly, in the mass communication situation, a large number of Cs receive from a very large number of As and transmit to a vastly larger number of Bs, who simultaneously receive from other Cs.

For Newcomb, *A* and *B* can only be persons. While we have tended to imply persons in these roles, it should now be made clear that we do not intend to confine the model to the level of the individual personality. The role of *B*, for instance, may be that of a person, or a primary group, or a total social system.

In stating that any "system" has need for transmissible messages as a means of orienting itself in its environment, it is meant that this statement be applied to a person, a primary group, or even a social system. Any of these levels can be plugged into the role of *B*. At the personality level, *B* can be the housewife, too busy to rush around the neighborhood in order to observe the details of her surroundings; in such a case the *C* function can be attributed to the neighborhood gossip, and transmits a limited portion of all possible messages supplying the information needs of *B*. At something like the primary group level, one can think of the relatively isolated frontier colony, which posted sentinels as *C*s to observe and report the condition of the environment by means of a special code such as a rifle shot and greeted eagerly another kind of *C*, the information-bearing circuit rider. At the social system level, a national state requires and maintains an elaborate network of *C*s performing such special information functions as that of the diplomatic service.

It might even be possible that the model holds for even "lower" levels than that of the personality. For instance, at the physiological level, it would appear that homeostasis requires some sort of "transmission" of "information" with respect to states of parts of the body.

Not only is the model highly general with respect to levels, it is highly general with respect to kinds of messages. Messages can be seen as either *purposive* or *non-purposive*. Other models have tended to obscure one or the other.

"PURPOSIVE" OR "NON-PURPOSIVE"?

A purpose message is one *A* originates for the purpose of modifying *B*'s perception of an *X*. A non-purposive message is one which is transmitted to *B* directly or by means of a *C* and in the absence of any communicator's intent to influence him. The absence of a communicator's intent to influence *B* transforms his act into an *X*. When a person says something he hopes will reach another person's ears, he is an *A*; but if he says it without such intent and it nevertheless is transmitted to *B*, his act must be conceived of as an *X*, the selection and transmission having been performed by a *C*. The reasons we consider this distinction to be crucial for mass communications theory will be discussed below.

Messages are transmitted in codes (symbol systems). But this model is by no means limited to the most obvious ones—linguistic systems. In fact, as Newcomb has already emphasized, the crucial characteristic is the shared meanings associated with symbols. Such symbols can take virtually any form, so long as and to the extent that there exist shared meanings and that they are transmissible. Such shared meanings surrounding symbols can be either *affective* or *cognitive*. Language has both affective and cognitive elements. Poetry, for instance, emphasizes the former. This emphasis is, of course, characteristic of all the arts. For instance, modern artist A in communicating with a series of Bs casts his message in a symbol system which is shared, even though with only a few of them; those Bs who share it or part of it will attain satisfaction from the communication of an affective state; those who cannot decode the message but attempt to do so will probably be frustrated in the attempt and express hostility toward the message, or the communicator, or conceivably even the gatekeeper.

The example above leads into further illustration of how the model deals with "special publics." These are illustrated by the immense segment of the media consisting of trade publications, scholarly journals, hobby and craft media, house organs, and the like. These are often defined out of the area of mass communications, usually on the grounds of audience size; and this in spite of the fact that some of these special interest publications media shade off from the specificity of the *Turkey Grower's Gazette* to attain circulations in the millions. The fact would seem to be that these the generality of *Holiday*, suggesting that decisions as to what is "mass" and what is not mass must necessarily be arbitrary.

The present model requires no such distinction. Our Bs vary in the degree to which they share common problems. Common problems imply the necessity of attaining communication with common Xs. Media serving to bring such Xs to such Bs arise out of the perceptions by Cs of the existence of just such a need. Special symbol systems are developed to maximize transmission.

It will be noted that we have consistently referred to both "need satisfactions" and "problem solutions." These concepts relate directly to the "immediate" and "delayed" rewards of Schramm which seem to us to be provocative and potentially fruitful. Building on the two-factor learning theory of Mowrer, Schramm proposed a "reader reward" basis for characterizing the content of news stories. The correspondence is, of course, between his "immediate reward" and our "need satisfactions" and between his "delayed reward" and our "problem solutions."

FEEDBACK

Another concept crucial to the model is that of "feedback." In the first place it should be clear from the foregoing that it is feedback that assures the system character of the ABX (or $ABCX$) relationship. If A is to utilize his experience in influencing *B*, he must have information about any changes in the condition of *B* attributable to his communications. *C* is equally concerned with effects on *B* if he is to make realistic adjustments in his role as *B*'s "agent." Such *A*s as advertisers facilitate feedback by means of elaborate market research; public relations men obtain feedback by means of public-opinion polls and other devices for determining the effects of their messages. Such *C*s as newspaper publishers sponsor readership surveys and, more recently, reader motivation studies to estimate and predict reader response. Radio's concern with "fan mail" and popularity ratings is well known.

Although feedback originates with *B* under most circumstances, it need not be assumed that *B* is necessarily trying to communicate back to *C* or *A*. When he does try to do so, we may think of this as *purposive* feedback. This is the case when an angry reader writes a letter "straightening out" the editor on some favorite issue. But there are also many ways *B* can feed back without intending to. These we will call *non-purposive* feedback. When a television fan decides to try a well-advertised detergent, his purchase becomes part of the data of a market survey, even though he may not have intended to let the sponsor know he had won a convert.

OTHER MODELS

In the final analysis the worth of such a model as this lies in its heuristic value. In view of the fact that several other models already exist in this field, it is reasonable to ask why another is necessary. A brief look at some others may be in order.

Perhaps the most pervasive of existing "models" is that of Lasswell: "*Who* says *what* through *what channels* to *whom* with *what effect*." The difficulty here is that the model seems to demand the presence of a communicator—the *who*—and to imply that his communication is a purposive one. It is no accident that our model has included the non-purposive case, transmitting *X*s to *B*s by the way of *C*s in the total absence of *A*s. The fortuitous origination of a great deal of the news material transmitted in all media seems to demand a place in the model. There is also an unidirectional implication in the Lasswellian formulation that ignores feedback phenomena.

The information theory-cybernetics paradigm has excited some interesting theoretical contributions but would appear to have certain drawbacks. It, too, appears to require the presence of a communicator, although not necessarily a purposive one. In addition it poses all the problems of a "borrowed" model. Taylor's use of the redundancy concept would appear to be an example of an exact mapping from mass communications phenomena to an element in the model. But such precise correspondences appear to be rare, and mappings become contrived and tenuous. The model strains common knowledge, for instance, in assuming perfect correspondence of symbol systems encoded and decoded.

SUMMARY

A conceptual model of the total communication process has been presented in the belief that such a model will prove useful in ordering existing data in mass communications research, point to areas of strength and weakness in our knowledge, and stimulate further efforts. The model is intended to be sufficiently general to treat all kinds of human communication from two-person face-to-face interaction to international and intercultural communications. It assumes that a minimum number of roles and processes are needed in any general theory of communications and attempts to isolate and tentatively define them. It must not be viewed as a theory but as a preliminary step to the construction of a general theory.

The principal elements in the model are these:

As (Advocacy roles). This is what is usually meant by "the communicator"—a personality or social system engaged in selecting and transmitting messages *purposively*.

Bs. (Behavioral system roles). This is what is usually meant by "the receiver," "the public," etc.—a personality or social system requiring and using communications about the condition of its environment for the satisfaction of its needs and solution of its problems.

Cs. (Channel roles). Often confounded with As, Cs serve as the agents of Bs in selecting and transmitting non-purposively the information Bs require, especially when the information is beyond the immediate reach of B.

X. The totality of objects and events "out there." X^1 is these objects and events as abstracted into transmissible form: "*messages*" about Xs and A-X relationships (such as "opinions").

Channels. The means by which Xs are moved by way of As and/or Cs to Bs. Channels include "gates" manned by Cs who in various ways alter messages.

Encoding. The process by which As and Cs transform Xs into X^1s. *Decoding* is the process by which Bs interiorize messages.

Feedback. The means by which As and Cs obtain information about the effects of messages on Bs.

The Dimensions of Social Interaction
A. PAUL HARE

8

In reviewing the literature on social interaction in small groups which has been published during the past 50 years, it became apparent that many of the authors were talking about the same things but with different vocabularies and from different points of view. A conceptual scheme was developed to include the dimensions of social interaction that appeared most frequently in the literature.

The literature on social interaction covers three general classes of observations. In some cases, the focus is on *inter*personal behavior such as cooperative problem solving; in other cases, it is on *intra*personal behavior as evidenced in tension or anxiety. In still other cases, the focus is on aspects of *individual performance*, which may characterize an individual whether he is alone or in a group. In this paper, intrapersonal behavior and individual performance will be combined, leaving two very general categories—*interpersonal behavior* and *personal behavior*.

Although many different category systems have been used in describing interpersonal behavior, the categories of interaction given in Figure 1 appear to represent the major "dimensions" of observed behavior. These dimensions refer to both the form and the content of interaction.

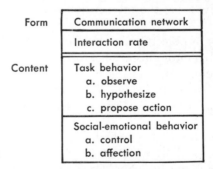

Figure 1. A paradigm for the analysis of interaction.

The form of interaction is less specific than content and is more easily recorded. As one approaches a group from the "outside," the first aspect

Reprinted with permission of the Mental Health Research Institute and the author. From *Behavioral Science*, 5:211–215 (1960).

of interaction which becomes apparent is the communication network (i.e., who speaks to whom) and next the amount of interaction carried by each of the channels. For a closer analysis of what is going on in the group, one needs some content categories. Here the most frequent division is between content directed primarily towards the solution of task problems vs. content directed primarily towards the solution of social-emotional problems. Within the social-emotional area, the categories of control and affection represent the predominant types of behavior, while in the task area there is less consensus on the "typical" problem-solving categories. The minimum set of categories parallels the steps in the scientific method, namely of observation, hypothesis formation, and the testing of hypotheses.

Each of the major categories in Figure 1 can be identified as follows:

Form: *Communication network*. The channels of communication between group members. *Interaction rate*. The frequency of interactions, sometimes represented by the number of contributions, sometimes by the relationship between the number and duration of contributions, i.e., action and silence, and sometimes by the number of contributions times the average duration of each, i.e., total talking time.

Content: *Task behavior*. Interaction directed toward the completion of group or individual tasks. The minimum number of categories would include observing, hypothesizing, and formulating action. *Social-emotional behavior*. Interaction directed primarily toward the relationships between group members which form the basis for problem solving. The minimum number of categories would include control and affection.

Each of these categories can be used at the level of personality, behavior, and role. At the level of personality they represent *tendencies to act* and at the level of role they represent *expectations for behavior*.

OUTPUT AND INPUT: FORM

The description of a person from the interaction point of view includes not only how he acts toward others (output), but also how others respond to him (input). For this reason, the minimum number of actors in a unit of interaction is two, the minimum number of acts is two (one action and one reaction), and the minimum number of time periods in which interaction occurs is two.

The output and input characteristics for both form and content of interaction can be considered with varying degrees of complexity. For the communication network one can record simply the total number of channels for outgoing messages and incoming messages. At the other extreme, one can specify the extent to which each channel from a subject to every other member of the group is open for output or input. Similarly, the interaction rate can be described simply as the total number of acts an individual gives and the total number he receives, or the output and input rate can be given for each channel in the communication network.

Although it is possible to differentiate output and input for the communication network, particularly in experiments in which the communication network is the major variable, the correlation between output and input for a given channel in most situations is very high. The person who speaks most often in a group is usually the one who is spoken to most often. In those cases where the correlation is high, specification of the input characteristics may add little to the description of the interaction process.

This type of reduction in the number of experimental "variables" occurs over and over again in those experiments which use comprehensive category systems for recording the interaction process. Since relatively few categories of behavior are appropriate in any given situation, most of the interaction tends to take place within two or three categories. As a result the remaining categories are either correlated with those or appear too infrequently to yield reliable measures.

OUTPUT AND INPUT: CONTENT

For the analysis of behavior where one may wish to consider several categories of content simultaneously, the characteristics of an individual's interaction for either output or input may be described by a set of *interaction profiles* similar to those used by Bales. If only one dimension or area of content is to be considered at a time, a graphic plot may be used to advantage, with one axis representing output and the other input (see Figure 2). The explicit recognition of the distinction between input and output may help to clarify some theoretical issues, especially in the construction of typologies.

In the description of behavior tendencies in the area of control, for example, the vertical axis might represent the behavior desired from others ranging from *yes* he wants to be controlled by others to *no* he does not want to be controlled by others. The horizontal axis could then represent the desired behavior towards other ranging from *yes* he wants to control others to *no* he does not want to control others.

The individual who wants strongly either to control or be controlled has been called *authoritarian*. On the other hand, the individual who wants neither to control nor to be controlled may be said to desire a situation in which there is distance between group members. In the extreme, this kind of independence has been called *anarchism*.

On the opposite diagonal are individuals who vary from wanting to control but not be controlled, the *dominators*, to those who want to be controlled but do not want to control, the *submitters*. In the center are those individuals who want to both control and be controlled in a moderate degree, a type of behavior which tends to be called *democratic*. All other combinations of tendencies to give or receive control can be represented as points in this two dimensional space.

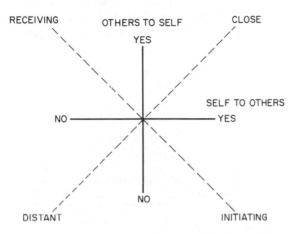

Figure 2. Representation of input and output in a two-dimensional plot.

In the description of personality, the two axes in Figure 2 would represent the tendencies to give and receive which the individual brings to the situation. In the description of *role*, the axes would represent expected behavior, the duties (output) and the rights (input) associated with each role. The expectations for behavior would vary along each axis from behavior which is required to that which is prohibited.

PERSONAL BEHAVIOR

In addition to the interpersonal categories, there are dimensions of personal behavior which also play a part in the activity of a group. The personal categories include those dimensions usually associated with personality such as intelligence, social sensitivity, and adjustment, as well as aspects of the individual's biological nature such as age, sex, and physical strength. These categories, like the previously discussed interpersonal categories, can also be used to describe "tendencies" within the individual and "expectations" for the role he is to perform.

Although the mean or average behavior in each category of personal and interpersonal behavior is stressed in the present formulation, this should not obscure the fact that the mean may not be as important for the prediction of behavior in a particular instance as some measure of the extent of variation and the conditions under which the variation occurs.

PREDICTING BEHAVIOR FROM PERSONALITY AND ROLE

To predict an individual's behavior in one of the form or content areas, one could first indicate on the plane a point representing the tendency in the personality (see Figure 3) and also a point representing the expected behavior called for by the individual's role in the group. The actual behavior would then lie somewhere along the line between the personality and role.

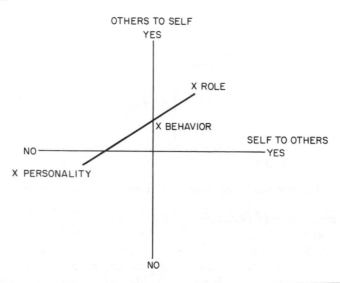

Figure 3. The relationship between personality, behavior, and role on one dimension.

In a ceremony, such as a marriage, the actual behavior would be very close to the role. At the other extreme, when role is not well defined, for example, the role for a patient in a mental hospital ward, the behavior would be close to the tendencies in the personality. Since in many personalities and in many roles one of the content areas may be more salient than the others, an individual's behavior may be predominantly in *one* of the content areas.

VARIATIONS IN INTERACTION RATE

The characteristic of an individual's interactive behavior most frequently reported in the literature is his interaction rate. An individual's interaction rate can vary while the content of interaction remains relatively stable. In most situations, the interaction rate of a single group member is related to the rates of other members of the group as well as to his own personality.

An increase in the interaction rate of an individual may be associated with activity in any one of the content areas. In some experiments, an increase in interaction has been found to be associated with attempts to control a deviant member. In other research, a high interaction rate is correlated with task success (Strodtbeck). In still other studies, as for example in the observation of working girls doing piece work which does not require control, the interaction rate is highly correlated with affection (Homans).

CHOICE BEHAVIOR AND COHESIVENESS

The criteria which individuals use in making interpersonal choices may fall into any of the content areas. However, in social research, subjects are often asked to designate group members whom they would like to work with (a criterion which appears to combine task ability and control), and whom they would like to play with (a criterion which appears to be primarily affection). Since individuals who desire to be close to people will choose others who prefer closeness, there is evidence that "birds of a feather flock together." However, individuals who like to initiate tend to choose those who like to receive so that it is also true that "opposites attract."

Groups containing a large number of mutual choices on either "work" or "play" criterion are often said to be highly "cohesive" in that they will "stick together" longer than groups in which there are few mutual choices. Although groups are often referred to as being highly "cohesive" without specifying the basis on which the choices were made, the criterion is important. Subjects who have chosen each other because they like to "work with" each other should be more productive than those who have chosen each other because they like to play together, provided, of course, that the task calls for the type of control relationships they prefer. A group composed of anarchists who had chosen each other could not be expected to do well on a task requiring authoritarian relationships.

The importance of the criterion on which choice is based is not always evident in the literature since many subjects will make the same choices regardless of the criterion which the experimenter suggests. In some cases, the multiple choice is justified since there are "great men" who are actually high on all criteria (Borgatta, Couch, and Bales), but in other cases it appears that the subject has his own preferred criterion for choice and will use the same one no matter what the experimenter suggests (French). That is, a subject with a salient need for affection would always choose others whom he expected to satisfy his affectional need whether the situation called for affection, or some other predominant category of behavior.

The approach to the analysis of interaction in small groups outlined in this paper is suggested as a framework for organizing ideas. The elements included in the theory have been found to be important sources of variation in social behavior in a variety of situations. However, the prediction of behavior in any specific situation may require knowledge of only a few of these elements or, on the other hand, an elaboration and differentiation of these concepts well beyond the present level of analysis.

9

How People Interact in Conferences
ROBERT F. BALES

Social interaction is made up largely of the talking that people do when they get together. Talk is an elusive object of study in spite of the fact that a good deal of it exists. It is also a rather sensitive subject. Even a friend might find it hard to put up with a dissection of the following kind: "I was just noticing how much you talk. In the last 10 minutes I noticed that you made a total of 114 remarks, while I made a total of 86. According to my count you gave about twice as many opinions as facts. Although I agreed with you 15 times and didn't disagree at all, I noticed that you stammered once and blushed twice."

I first began to develop a systematic procedure for analyzing social interaction when I became interested in trying to account for the success of Alcoholics Anonymous in helping apparently hopeless drinkers to stop drinking. Although I attended meetings and talked with many members, I did not feel free to ask all the questions I wished. Consequently I fell back on observation and began to develop crude methods for recording who did what, who spoke to whom, and how. Eventually even this quiet occupation began to appear sinister and the effort was abandoned. But by this time my fascination with the process of social interaction had developed to the point of no return. I decided that I must pursue my studies in the more favorable conditions of a laboratory.

A number of laboratories for the study of social interaction within small

Reprinted with permission of the publisher and the author. Copyright © 1955 by Scientific American, Inc. All rights reserved. From *Scientific American*, 192:31–55 (1955).

groups and organizations have been started in the last 10 years—in hospitals, clinics, special research centers and military installations. The studies and experiments I shall describe were conducted in one of the earliest laboratories, established in 1947 at Harvard University.

The laboratory consists of a large, well-lighted room for the group under study and an adjoining room for observers, who listen and watch from behind windows and one-way vision. The subjects are told at the beginning that the room has been constructed for the special purpose of studying group discussion, that a complete sound recording will be made and that there are observers behind the one-way mirrors. The purpose of the separation is not to deceive the subjects but to minimize interaction between them and the observing team.

After much research we developed a standardized task from which significant generalizations could be drawn. A group of persons (ranging from two to seven in number) is asked to discuss the complex human relations problem of the sort typically faced by an administrator. Each member of the group first reads a five-page presentation of facts about the case to be discussed, but each is left uncertain as to whether he has been given exactly the same range of facts as the others in the group. The members are not introduced to one another or coached in any way; they must develop their own organization and procedure. They are to consider the facts and report to an administrator, as if they were his staff, their joint conclusions concerning the problem and what should be done about it. They are allowed 40 minutes for the discussion. The group is observed for four such sessions.

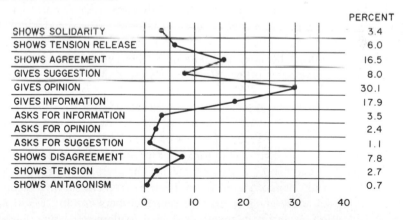

Figure 1. *Types of acts* in social interaction may be classed in four main categories: positive reactions, problem-solving attempts, questions, and negative reactions. The averages for 96 group sessions show that 56 percent of the acts fall into the problem-solving category.

On the other side of the one-way screen the observers systematically record every step of the interaction, not omitting such items as nods and frowns. Each observer has a small machine with a moving paper tape on which he writes in code a description of every act—an act being defined essentially as a single statement, question or gesture. Acts ordinarily occur at the rate of 15 to 20 per minute. The recorded information on each includes identification of the person speaking and the person spoken to and classification of the act according to predetermined categories. There are 12 categories, covering positive and negative reactions, questions and attempts to solve the problem by the offering of information, opinion or suggestions (see Figure 1).

As this figure shows, on the average about half (56 percent) of the acts during a group session fall into the categories of problem-solving attempts; the remaining 44 percent are distributed among positive reactions, negative reactions and questions. In other words, the process tends to be two-sided, with the reactions acting as a more or less constant feedback on the acceptability of the problem-solving attempts. The following is a typical example of the pattern of interchange:

Member 1: "I wonder if we have the same facts about the problem? [Asks for opinion.] Perhaps we should take some time in the beginning to find out." [Gives suggestions.]
Member 2: "Yes. [Agrees.] We may be able to fill in some gaps in our information. [Gives opinion.] Let's go around the table and each tell what the report said in his case." [Gives suggestion.]

This example illustrates that a speaker's first remark is likely to be a reaction, and if he continues speaking, the probability is very high that his second act will be a problem-solving attempt. Figure 2 sums up this finding statistically: about 50 percent of the time a member's first remark in a series is a reaction; if he continues, about 80 percent of the succeeding comments are opinions or other offerings classed as attempts to solve the problem.

When we examine the reactions, we find that positive reactions commonly outnumber negative ones about two to one during a session. It is as if after every negative reaction, the members of the group feel they must make another problem-solving attempt which meets with a positive reaction "just to catch up," and net forward progress is felt to be sufficiently secure only when a repetition of the problem-solving attempt meets unopposed acceptance. It may be that members employ repetition, or near repetition, as an error-checking device to determine whether the others "really agree." Social interaction, in common with many other goal-seeking control mechanisms, seems to depend upon error and correction of error for guidance.

The process of attempting to arrive at a group decision through discussion is in many ways very like the operation of a large-scale communication and control system such as an air-defense network. I recently compared the two processes in collaboration with John Kennedy of the Systems Research Laboratory at the Rand Corporation.

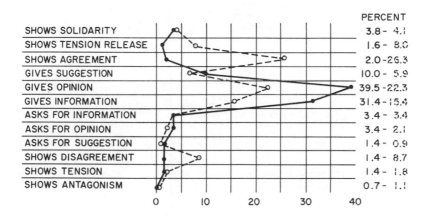

	PERCENT
SHOWS SOLIDARITY	3.8 - 4.1
SHOWS TENSION RELEASE	1.6 - 8.0
SHOWS AGREEMENT	2.0 - 26.3
GIVES SUGGESTION	10.0 - 5.9
GIVES OPINION	39.5 - 22.3
GIVES INFORMATION	31.4 - 15.4
ASKS FOR INFORMATION	3.4 - 3.4
ASKS FOR OPINION	3.4 - 2.1
ASKS FOR SUGGESTION	1.4 - 0.9
SHOWS DISAGREEMENT	1.4 - 8.7
SHOWS TENSION	1.4 - 1.8
SHOWS ANTAGONISM	0.7 - 1.1

Figure 2. *Pattern of action* of individuals in a discussion is illustrated statistically. When a member takes the floor, his first remark (*broken curve*) is likely to be a reaction to the preceding speaker. His next remarks (*black curve*) tend to be problem-solving attempts.

In the military case there are three functions to be performed: surveillance of the air by radar, identification of planes as friendly or unknown and direction of fighters sent out to intercept unknown planes. These are something like the three problems confronting our groups in the standard interaction task: assembling the given information on the case, evaluating it and proceeding toward a solution as the goal. Now the stepwise operations involved in the air-defense system may be tolerably well described as an interlocking series of seven types of information-processing operations. Here X stands for the path of a plane tracked by radar, and O represents the class of objects unknown. If no known flight plan of a friendly plane coincides with x—a fact represented by the symbol y—then x must belong to the class O. Since there is a general rule, W, that all unknown planes are to be intercepted, the conclusion is that a specific order, w, should be given to intercept x.

Such a decision, involving many groups and interlocking processes, is obviously a very complicated affair, socially as well as technically. The job of the decision-making organization is essentially to build and maintain through means of communication and evaluation a sufficiently complex and commonly accepted symbolic structure to guide or control the stages

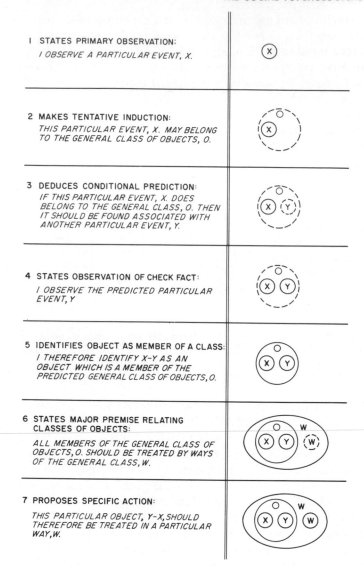

1 STATES PRIMARY OBSERVATION:
   I OBSERVE A PARTICULAR EVENT, X.

2 MAKES TENTATIVE INDUCTION:
   *THIS PARTICULAR EVENT, X. MAY BELONG
   TO THE GENERAL CLASS OF OBJECTS, O.*

3 DEDUCES CONDITIONAL PREDICTION:
   *IF THIS PARTICULAR EVENT, X. DOES
   BELONG TO THE GENERAL CLASS, O. THEN
   IT SHOULD BE FOUND ASSOCIATED WITH
   ANOTHER PARTICULAR EVENT, Y.*

4 STATES OBSERVATION OF CHECK FACT:
   *I OBSERVE THE PREDICTED PARTICULAR
   EVENT, Y*

5 IDENTIFIES OBJECT AS MEMBER OF A CLASS:
   *I THEREFORE IDENTIFY X-Y AS AN
   OBJECT WHICH IS A MEMBER OF THE
   PREDICTED GENERAL CLASS OF OBJECTS, O.*

6 STATES MAJOR PREMISE RELATING
   CLASSES OF OBJECTS:
   *ALL MEMBERS OF THE GENERAL CLASS OF
   OBJECTS, O. SHOULD BE TREATED BY WAYS
   OF THE GENERAL CLASS, W.*

7 PROPOSES SPECIFIC ACTION:
   *THIS PARTICULAR OBJECT, Y-X, SHOULD
   THEREFORE BE TREATED IN A PARTICULAR
   WAY, W.*

Figure 3. *Process in reaching a group decision* is analogous to the operation of a large-scale communication and control system such as the air-defense network. The steps consist of observing an object or event, comparing it with several possible identifications, considering the associated facts and, once its nature is understood, taking the appropriate action.

of behavior of all the operating units. Effective decision making is basically a continuous process of building and maintaining a structure of cultural objects which in their totality constitute the common culture of the organization affected.

The seven types of acts, or stages, just described are very general: they apply quite as well to the interaction of five experimental subjects in the laboratory group, trying to decide in 40 minutes what the administrator in their case should do about his problem, as to the large-scale operations of an air-defense network. Not all of the elements in the process are primarily logical in character. They involve elements of perception, memory, association and perhaps inductive insight. All sorts of motivational and evaluative pressures affect the process. The steps make sense not as a formally perfect chain of logic, but rather as a set of symbol transformations which help to guide, although in an imperfect way, a process of decision-making behavior. Error checking is an integral part of this fallible process.

The reason for calling attention to the seven-step structure of the process is that it may help to explain the unequal ratios of suggestions, opinions and information offered in the problem-solving attempts of the groups in our tests. As the first table shows, of every seven problem-solving attempts on the average four are opinions, two are offers of information and one is a suggestion. It seems significant that in the idealized seven-step outline of the air-defense operation two steps have the interaction form of giving information, four intermediate steps have the interaction form of giving opinion and only one step, the final one, has the form of giving a suggestion.

From the transcription of a group discussion it is often possible to reconstruct complete seven-step chains leading to agreement on specific points and the final conclusion. In a general way there is even a tendency for the steps to proceed in a regular order in time. During a session the rates of giving information tend to be highest in the first third of the meeting and to decline in the next two thirds (see Figure 4). Rates of giving opinion are usually highest in the middle portion of the meeting. Rates of giving suggestion are generally low in the early period and reach their high point in the last third of the meeting.

Rates of both positive and negative reactions tend to rise from the first third of the meeting to the last third. These increases may be connected mainly with social and emotional problems of the group process itself. The ratio of negative to positive reactions tends to be higher in response to suggestions than in response to factual statements. The decision point is a critical bottleneck in the process. Once the decision point has been passed, however, the rates of negative reaction usually fall off and the rates of positive reaction rise sharply. Joking and laughter, indicating solidarity and tension release, become more frequent. With the problems of the task and common values stabilized for the time being by the decision, the interaction process apparently turns to restabilizing the emotional states of the individuals and their social relations to one another.

There is a good deal of evidence that the process of social interaction, like other processes involving feedback, tends to fall into oscillation as it "hunts" around a hypothetical steady state. Over a small time span the action tends to alternate every few acts between the problem-solving attempts of one person and the social-emotional reaction of some other. But this rapid oscillation is not quite rapid enough to keep all elements of the process in perfect balance. There is a drift toward inequality of participation, which in time has cumulative effects on the social relationships of the members. The reason for this drift may be seen fairly easily. When a person has completed one act, the chances are a little better than even that he will continue for another act. After each succeeding act his probability of continuing drops, but never as far as if he simply flipped a coin at each point to determine whether to continue or to yield the floor.

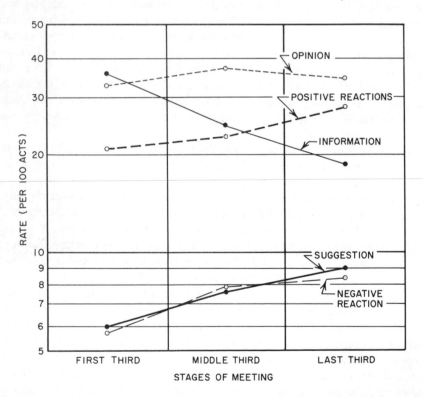

Figure 4. *Group progress* toward a decision is characterized by a change in the frequency of different types of social acts as the meeting wears on. Information-giving decreases while suggestions and positive and negative reactions increase.

In fact, relatively speaking, he exceeds this chance probability by a larger and larger fraction with each succeeding act.

We have already noted that when a person continues several acts in succession the probability is very high that he is giving information, opinion or suggestion—in other words, specializing in problem-solving attempts. We may also infer from the seven step theory of problem-solving attempts that the tendency to continue for several acts in succession is probably due in part to a felt need on the part of the speaker to provide inferences and check facts which will result in the acceptance of a more advanced step in the series, with an accepted suggestion as the goal.

This tendency toward inequality of participation over the short run has cumulative side effects on the social organization of the group. The man who gets his speech in first begins to build a reputation. Success in obtaining acceptance of problem-solving attempts seems to lead the successful person to do more of the same, with the result that eventually the members come to assume a rank order by task ability. In some groups the members reach a high degree of consensus on their ranking of "who had the best ideas." (The members are interviewed by questionnaire after each meeting.) Usually the persons so ranked also did the most talking and had higher than average rates of giving suggestions and opinion.

While one person becomes a specialist in advancing ideas another is apt to be developing a specialization on the reactive side. The men most commonly rated "best liked" typically have higher than average rates of showing tension release (mainly smiling and laughing) and showing agreement. It is not impossible for the men ranked at the top in ideas also to be best liked, but apparently it is difficult. In one set of experiments the top idea man had about an even chance of also being best liked at the end of the first meeting, but by the end of the fourth meeting his chances were only about one in 10. The best-liked man is usually second or third in the participation hierarchy.

The task specialist seems to "lock onto" the person who is most responsive to what he is saying and address more remarks to him than to the others. In turn, the best-liked man talks more and agrees more with the top-ranking idea specialist than with any other member. The idea specialist and the best-liked man often form a mutually supporting pair. However, the best-liked man may attract the idea specialist even though they are not always in agreement. Indeed in order for a person to become established in the minds of other members as a social-emotional specialist, it is probably more important that he be representative of their reactions, both positive and negative, than that he should ardently support everything the task specialist says. Apparently reactions that are emotionally gratifying to other members tend to be generalized by them into liking for the person who expresses the reactions.

Giving suggestions, necessary as it may be for accomplishment of the task, is more likely to arouse negative reactions than is giving information or opinions. This tends to put the task specialist in a vulnerable position. The group commonly develops a certain amount of negative feeling toward him. Not only is he likely to lose the status of being best liked, but he may lose his position as task leader unless he is sensitive to the problem and is well supported by other members. Even in a group which ends its first meeting with a high consensus on who has the best ideas, the second meeting is apt to see a challenge to his leadership, with a rise in rates of disagreement and antagonism and a precipitous-drop in his popularity. But then, in a group where the original consensus was high, a peculiar thing seems to happen. Apparently as progress toward accomplishment of the task slows down, some members rally around the leader again and his popularity tends to rise. By the third meeting the rates of disagreement and antagonism go down. The task leader may not retain all the liking that was transferred to him in his time of need, but the net effect of the hunting kind of oscillation that takes place is a tendency to maintain the original rank order of task ability.

In a group that starts with a low degree of consensus on who has the best ideas, the developments usually are more dismal. There tends to be a high turnover in the top ranks throughout the four meetings, with one would-be leader replacing another. In such a group the man ranked as having the best ideas is less apt to be best liked. Furthermore an additional specialist is likely to appear—a man who talks more than anybody else but is neither best liked nor most highly respected for his task ability.

It appears probable that whether the members will agree on who has the best ideas depends to a large degree on how well they agree on basic premises or norms—what we may call the "common culture." If such consensus is not present, at least implicitly, at the beginning, it may take a long time to build. While consensus on major values does not solve all the problems of arriving at a stable social organization, probably no stable organization is possible without this control factor. If it is lacking, the interaction process becomes primarily a means for the expression of individual emotional states.

Our studies have made clear that social stability is an extremely complex achievement: it takes time and patience to arrive at a common culture extensive enough and sensitive enough to regulate strong counter motives, to promote task accomplishment, to harmonize social relationships and to rejuvenate itself whenever the conditions demand. A clear recognition of the complexity of cultural control of behavior should encourage us to believe that interminable series of meetings around the conference table, international and otherwise, are perhaps worth while after all.

10 | Alienation from Interaction
ERVING GOFFMAN

I. INTRODUCTION

When the individual in our Anglo-American society engages in a conversational encounter with others he may become spontaneously involved in it. He can become unthinkingly and impulsively immersed in the talk and carried away by it, oblivious to other things, including himself. Whether his involvement is intense and not easily disrupted, or meager and easily distracted, the topic of talk can form the main focus of his cognitive attention and the current talker can form the main focus of his visual attention. The binding and hypnotic effect of such involvement is illustrated by the fact that while thus involved the individual can simultaneously engage in other goal-directed activities (chewing gum, smoking, finding a comfortable sitting position, performing repetitive tasks, etc.) yet manage such side-involvements in an abstracted, fugue-like fashion so as not to be distracted from his main focus of attention by them.

The individual, like an infant or an animal, can of course become spontaneously involved in unsociable solitary tasks. When this occurs the task takes on at once a weight and a lightness, affording the performer a firm sense of reality. As a main focus of attention talk is unique, however, for talk creates for the participant a world and a reality that has other participants in it. Conjoint spontaneous involvement is a *unio mystico*, a socialized trance. We must also see that a conversation has a life of its own and makes demands on its own behalf. It is a little social system with its own boundary-maintaining tendencies; it is a little patch of commitment and loyalty with its own heroes and its own villains.

Taking conjoint spontaneous involvement as a point of reference, I want to discuss how this involvement can fail to occur and the consequence of this failure. I want to consider the ways in which the individual can become alienated from a conversational encounter, the uneasiness that arises with this, and the consequence of this alienation and uneasiness upon the

Reprinted with permission of Tavistock Publications and the author. From *Human Relations*, 10:47–60 (1957).

interaction. Since alienation can occur in regard to any imaginable talk, we may be able to learn from it something about the generic properties of spoken interaction.

II. INVOLVEMENT OBLIGATIONS

When individuals are in one another's immediate presence, a multitude of words, gestures, acts, and minor events become available, whether desired or not, through which one who is present can intentionally or unintentionally symbolize his character and his attitudes. In our society a system of etiquette obtains that enjoins the individual to handle these expressive events fittingly, projecting through them a proper image of himself, an appropriate respect for the others present, and a suitable regard for the setting. When the individual intentionally or unintentionally breaks a rule of etiquette, others present may mobilize themselves to restore the ceremonial order, somewhat as they do when other types of social order are transgressed.

Through the ceremonial order that is maintained by a system of etiquette, the capacity of the individual to be carried away by a talk becomes socialized, taking on a burden of ritual value and social function. Choice of main focus of attention, choice of side-involvements and of intensity of involvement, become hedged in with social constraints, so that some allocations of attention become socially proper and other allocations improper.

There are many occasions when the individual participant in a conversation finds that he and the others are locked together by involvement obligations with respect to it. He comes to feel it is defined as appropriate (and hence either desirable in itself or prudent) to give his main focus of attention to the talk, and to become spontaneously involved in it, while at the same time he feels that each of the other participants has the same obligation. Due to the ceremonial order in which his actions are embedded, he may find that any alternate allocation of involvement on his part will be taken as a discourtesy and cast an uncalled-for reflection upon the others, the setting, or himself. And he will find that his offense has been committed in the very presence of those who are offended by it. Those who break the rules of interaction commit their crimes in jail.

The task of becoming spontaneously involved in something, when it is a duty to oneself or others to do so, is a ticklish thing, as we all know from experience with dull chores or threatening ones. The individual's actions must happen to satisfy his involvement obligations, but in a certain sense he cannot act *in order* to satisfy these obligations, for such an effort would require him to shift his attention from the topic of conversation to the problem of being spontaneously involved in it. Here, in a component of non-rational impulsiveness—not only tolerated but actually demanded—we find an important way in which the interactional order differs from other kinds of social order.

The individual's obligation to maintain spontaneous involvement in the conversation and the difficulty of doing so place him in a delicate position. He is rescued by his co-participants, who control their own actions so that he will not be forced from appropriate involvement. But the moment he is rescued he will have to rescue someone else, and so his job as interactant is only complicated the more. Here, then, is one of the fundamental aspects of social control in conversation: the individual must not only maintain proper involvement himself but also act so as to ensure that others will maintain theirs. This is what the individual owes the others in their capacity as interactants, regardless of what is owed them in whatever other capacities they participate, and it is this obligation that tells us that, whatever social role the individual plays during a conversational encounter, he will in addition have to fill the role of interactant.

The individual will have approved and unapproved reasons for fulfilling his obligation *qua* interactant, but in all cases to do so he must be able rapidly and delicately to take the role of the others and sense the qualifications their situation ought to bring to his conduct if they are not to be brought up short by it. He must be sympathetically aware of the kinds of things in which the others present can become spontaneously and properly involved, and then attempt to modulate his expression of attitudes, feelings, and opinions according to the company.

Thus, as Adam Smith argued in his *Theory of the Moral Sentiments*, the individual must phrase his own concerns and feelings and interests in such a way as to make these maximally usable by the others as a source of appropriate involvement; and this major obligation of the individual *qua* interactant is balanced by his right to expect that others present will make some effort to stir up their sympathies and place them at his command. These two tendencies, that of the speaker to scale down his expressions and that of the listeners to scale up their interests, each in the light of the other's capacities and demands, form the bridge that people build to one another, allowing them to meet for a moment of talk in a communion of reciprocally sustained involvement. It is this spark, not the more obvious kinds of love, that lights up the world.

III. THE FORMS OF ALIENATION

If we take conjoint spontaneous involvement in a topic of conversation as a point of reference, we shall find that alienation from it is common indeed. Conjoint involvement appears to be a fragile thing, with standard points of weakness and decay, a precariously unsteady state that is likely at any time to lead the individual into some form of alienation. Since we

are dealing with obligatory involvement, forms of alienation will constitute misbehavior of a kind that can be called "misinvolvement." Some of
the standard forms of alienative misinvolvement may be considered now.

1. EXTERNAL PREOCCUPATION. The individual may neglect the prescribed
focus of attention and give his main concern to something that is unconnected with what is being talked about at the time and even unconnected with the other persons present, at least in their capacity as fellow-
participants. The object of the individual's preoccupation may be one that
he ought to have ceased considering upon entering the interaction, or one
that is to be appropriately considered only later in the encounter or after
the encounter has terminated. The preoccupation may also take the form
of furtive by-play between the individual and one or two other participants. The individual may even be preoccupied with a vague standard of
work-activity, which he cannot maintain because of his obligation to participate in the interaction.

The offensiveness of the individual's preoccupation varies according to
the kind of excuse the others feel he has for it. At one extreme there is
preoccupation that is felt to be quite voluntary, the offender giving the
impression that he could easily give his attention to the conversation but is
wilfully refusing to do so. At the other extreme there is "involuntary"
preoccupation, a consequence of the offender's understandably deep involvement in vital matters outside the interaction.

Individuals who could excusably withdraw involvement from a conversation often remain loyal and decline to do so. Through this they show
a nice respect for fellow-participants and affirm the moral rules that transform socially responsible people into people who are interactively responsible as well. It is of course through such rules, and through such reaffirming gestures, that society is made safe for the little worlds sustained in
face-to-face encounters. No culture, in fact, seems to be without exem-
plary tales for illustrating the dignity and weight that might be given to
these passing realities; everywhere we find enshrined a Drake who
gallantly finishes some kind of game before going out to battle some kind
of Armada, and everywhere an outlaw who is engagingly civil to those he
robs and to those who later hang him for it.

2. SELF-CONCIOUSNESS. At the cost of his involvement in the prescribed
focus of attention, the individual may focus his attention more than he
ought upon himself—himself as someone who is faring well or badly, as
someone calling forth a desirable or undesirable response from others. It is
possible, of course, for the individual to dwell upon himself as a topic of
conversation—to be self-centered in this way—and yet not to be self-
conscious. Self-consciousness for the individual does not, it seems, result
from his deep interest in the topic of conversation, which may happen to

be himself, but rather from his giving attention to himself as an interactant at a time when he ought to be free to involve himself in the content of the conversation.

A general statement about sources of self-consciousness ought to be added. During interaction the individual is often accorded by others and by impersonal events in the situation an image and appraisal of self that is at least temporarily acceptable to him. He is then free to turn his attention to matters less close to home. When this definition of self is threatened, the individual typically withdraws attention from the interaction in a hurried effort to correct for the incident that has occurred. If the incident threatens to raise his standing in the interaction, his flight into self-consciousness may be a way of rejoicing; if the incident threatens to lower his standing and damage or discredit his self-image in some way, then flight into self-consciousness may be a way of protecting the self and licking its wounds. As a source of self-consciousness, threat of loss seems more common and important than threat of gain.

Whatever the cause of self-consciousness, we are all familiar with the vacillation of action and the flusterings through which self-consciousness is expressed; we are all familiar with the phenomenon of embarrassment.

Self-consciousness can be thought of as a kind of preoccupation with matters internal to the interactive social system, and as such has received more common-sense consideration than other kinds of internal preoccupation. In fact we do not have common-sense words to refer to these other kinds of improper involvement. Two forms of these I shall refer to as "interaction-consciousness" and "other-consciousness" to emphasize a similarity to self-consciousness.

3. INTERACTION-CONSCIOUSNESS. A participant in talk may become consciously concerned to an improper degree with the way in which the interaction, *qua* interaction, is proceeding, instead of becoming spontaneously involved in the official topic of conversation. Since interaction-consciousness is not as famous as self-consciousness, some sources of it may be cited by way of illustration.

A common source of interaction-consciousness is related to the special responsibility that an individual may have for the interaction "going well," i.e. calling forth the proper kind of involvement from those present. Thus, at a small social gathering the hostess may be expected to join in with her guests and become spontaneously involved in the conversation they are maintaining, and yet at the same time if the occasion does not go well she, more than others, will be held responsible for the failure. In consequence, she sometimes becomes so much concerned with the social machinery of the occasion and with how the evening is going as a whole that she finds it impossible to give herself up to her own party.

Another common source of interaction-consciousness may be mentioned. Once individuals enter a conversation they are obliged to continue it until they have the kind of basis for withdrawing that will neutralize the potentially offensive implications of taking leave of others. While engaged in the interaction it will be necessary for them to have subjects at hand to talk about that fit the occasion and yet provide content enough to keep the talk going; in other words, safe supplies are needed. What we call "small talk" serves this purpose. When individuals use up their small talk, they find themselves officially lodged in a state of talk but with nothing to talk about; interaction-consciousness experienced as a "painful silence" is the typical consequence.

4. OTHER-CONSCIOUSNESS. During interaction, the individual may become distracted by another participant as an object of attention—exactly as in the case of self-consciousness he can become distracted by concern over himself.

If the individual finds that whenever he is in the conversational presence of specific others they cause him to be overly conscious of them at the expense of the prescribed involvement in the topic of conversation, then they may acquire the reputation in his eyes of being faulty interactants, especially if he feels he is not alone in the trouble he has with them. He is then likely to impute certain characteristics to those who are thus perceived, doing so in order to explain and account for the distraction they cause him. It will be useful to our understanding of interaction to list a few of the attributes imputed in this way.

By the terms "affectation" and "insincerity" the individual tends to identify those who seem to feign through gestures what they expect him to accept as an uncontrived expressive overflow of their behavior. Affectation, as Cooley suggests,

. . . exists when the passion to influence others seems to overbalance the established character and give it an obvious twist or pose.

Thus there are persons who in the simplest conversation do not seem to forget themselves, and enter frankly and disinterestedly into the subject, but are felt to be always preoccupied with the thought of the impression they are making, imagining praise or depreciation, and usually posing a little to avoid the one or gain the other.

Affected individuals seem chiefly concerned with controlling the evaluation an observer will make of them, and seem partly taken in by their own pose; insincere individuals seem chiefly concerned with controlling the impression the observer will form of their attitude toward certain things or persons, especially toward him, and seem not to be taken in by their own pose. It may be added that while those who are felt to be self-conscious give the impression of being overly concerned with what will happen or has happened to them, those who are felt to be insincere or affected give the impression that they are overly concerned with what they can achieve in what is to follow and are willing to put on an act in order to achieve it. When the individual senses that others are insincere or affected he tends to feel they have taken unfair advantage of their communication position to promote their own interests; he feels they have broken the ground rules of interaction. His hostility to their unfair play leads him to focus his attention upon them and their misdemeanor at the price of his own involvement in the conversation.

In considering the attributes imputed to those who cause another to be conscious of them, we must give importance to the factor of immodesty. On analytical grounds over-modesty should equally count as a source of other-consciousness, but, empirically, immodesty seems much the more important of the two. What the individual takes to be immodesty in others may present itself in many forms: immodest individuals may seem to praise themselves verbally; they may talk about themselves and their activity in a way that assumes greater interest in and familiarity with their personal life than the individual actually possesses; they may speak more frequently and at greater length than the individual feels is fitting; they may take a more prominent "ecological" position than he thinks they warrant, etc.

One interesting source of other-consciousness is to be found in the phenomenon of "over-involvement." During any conversation, standards are established as to how much the individual is to allow himself to be carried away by the talk, how thoroughly he is to permit himself to be caught up in it. He will be obliged to prevent himself from becoming so swollen with feelings and a readiness to act that he threatens the bounds regarding affect that have been established for him in the interaction. He will be obliged to express a margin of disinvolvement, although of course this margin will differ in extent according to the socially recognized importance of the occasion and his official role in it. When the individual does become over-involved in the topic of conversation, and gives others the impression that he does not have a necessary measure of self-control over his feelings and actions, when, in short, the interactive world becomes too real for him, then the others are likely to be drawn from involvement in the talk to an involvement in the talker. What is one man's over-eagerness will become another's alienation. In any case we are to see that over-involvement has the effect of momentarily incapacitating the individual as an interactant; others have to adjust to his state while he becomes incapable of adjusting to theirs. Interestingly enough, when the impulse of the over-involved individual has ebbed a little, he may come to sense his impropriety and become self-conscious, illustrating again the fact that the alienative effect the individual has on others is usually one he cannot escape having upon himself. Regardless of this, we must see that a readiness to become over-involved is a form of tyranny practised by children, *prima donnas*, and lords of all kinds, who momentarily put their own feelings above the moral rules that ought to have made society safe for interaction.

A final source of other-consciousness may be mentioned. If the individual is to become involved in a topic of conversation, then, as a listener, he will have to give his aural and usually his visual attention to the source of communication, that is, to the speaker, and especially to the speaker's voice and face. (This physical requirement is underlined by social rules that often define inattention to the speaker as an affront to him.) If the speaker's communication apparatus itself conveys additional information all during the time that transmission is occurring, then the listener is likely to be distracted by competing sources of stimuli, becoming over-aware of the speaker at the expense of what is being said. The sources of this distraction are well known: the speaker may be very ugly or very beautiful; he may have a speech defect such as a lisp or a stutter; he may have inadequate familiarity with the language, dialect, or jargon that the listeners expect to hear; he may have a slight facial peculiarity, such as a hare lip, eye twitch, crossed or wall eyes; he may have temporary communication difficulties such as a stiff neck, a hoarse voice, etc. Apparently the closer the defect is to the communication equipment upon which the listener must focus his attention, the smaller the defect need be to throw the listener off balance. (It should be added that in so far as a speaker is required to direct his attention to his listener and yet not be overly conscious of him, defects in the appearance of the listener can cause the speaker to be uneasy.) These minor defects in the apparatus of communication tend to shut off the afflicted individual from the stream of daily contacts, transforming him into a faulty interactant, either in his own eyes or in the eyes of others.

In concluding this discussion of sources of alienating distraction, I should like to state an obvious caution. When the individual senses that others are unsuitably involved, it will always be relative to the standards of his group that he will sense the others have behaved improperly. Similarly, an individual who would cause certain others to be unduly conscious of him because of his apparent insincerity, affectation, or immodesty would pass unnoticed in a subculture where conversational discipline was less strict. Hence, when members of different groups interact with one another, it is quite likely that at least one of the participants will be distracted from spontaneous involvement in the topic of conversation because of what appears to him to be unsuitable behavior on the part of the others. It is to these differences in expressive customs that we ought to look first in trying to account for the improper behavior of those with whom we happen to be participating and not try, initially at least, to find some source of blame within the personalities of the offenders.

IV. ON THE REPERCUSSIVE CHARACTER OF INVOLVEMENT OFFENSES

I have suggested that disenchantment with an interaction may take the form of preoccupation, self-consciousness, other-consciousness, and interaction-consciousness. These forms of alienation have been separated for purposes of identification. In actual conversation, when one kind occurs the others will not be far behind.

When the individual senses that he or other participants are failing to allocate their involvement according to standards that he approves, and in consequence that they are conveying an improper attitude toward the interaction and the participants, then his sentiments are likely to be roused by the impropriety—much as they would be were any other obligations of the ceremonial order broken. But matters do not stop here. The witnessing of an offense against involvement obligations, as against other ceremonial obligations, causes the witness to turn his attention from the conversation at hand to the offense that has occurred during it. If the individual feels responsible for the offense that has occurred, he is likely to be led to feel shamefully self-conscious. If others seem responsible for the offense, then he is likely to be led to feel indignantly other-conscious in regard to them. But to be self-conscious or other-conscious is in itself an offense against involvement obligations. The mere witnessing of an involvement offense, let alone its punishment, can cause a crime against the interaction, the victim of the first crime himself being made a criminal. Thus, during spoken interaction, when one individual is stricken with uneasiness, others often come down with the disease.

A note of qualification should be added. The individual may become misinvolved and yet neither he nor others may become aware that this is the case, let alone become improperly involved because of this awareness. He commits a latent offense that only awaits someone's perception of it to make it manifest. When others come to see that he is misinvolved, and convey the fact of this judgment to him, he may become self-consciously flustered in consequence, as he may also do when he discovers this fact for himself. Thus an individual may "come to" from a brown study and embarrassingly find himself in the midst of an interaction but patently alienated from it.

V. THE AFFECTATION OF INVOLVEMENT

When a conversation fails to capture the spontaneous involvement of an individual who is obliged to participate in it, he is likely to contrive an appearance of being really involved. This he must do to save the feelings of the other participants and their good opinion of him, regardless of his motives for wanting to effect this saving. In doing so he has a damping effect upon the repercussive consequences of misinvolvement, ensuring that while he may be disaffected his disaffection will not contaminate others. At the same time, however, he drives a wedge between himself and the world that could become real for him. And the gap that is created in this way he fills with that special kind of uneasiness that is characteristically found during conversation; the kind of uneasiness that occurs when involvement obligations can neither be laid aside nor spontaneously realized; the kind that occurs when the individual is separated from the reality of interaction, yet at a time when interaction is all around him.

As a form of contrivance, affected involvement will be differently judged according to the motive the alienated individual has for contriving it. Some shows of involvement are felt to be cynical because the individual seems to be interested ultimately not in the feelings of the others but rather in what can be gained by deluding the others into a belief that they have captured his attention. He gives the impression that he is occupied with the talk but proves to be really occupied with the task of giving this impression.

On the other hand, if the alienated individual is genuinely concerned with the feelings of the others, as important matters in their own right, then any act that protects these feelings may be considered a form of tact and approved on this ground.

It should be noted that often the show of involvement given by the tactful interactant is not as good a show as he is capable of giving. Some power that is almost beyond him will force him to demonstrate to others and to himself that this kind of interaction with these participants is not the sort of thing that can capture his attention; someone must see that he is perhaps above or beyond it. Here we find a form of insubordination carried on by those who may not really be in a position to rebel.

The ways of not quite concealing tactfully concealed misinvolvement constitute, then, the symptoms of boredom. Some symptoms of boredom suggest that the individual will make no effort to terminate the encounter or his official participation in it but that he will no longer give as much to it. The initiation of side-involvements, such as leafing through a magazine or lighting a cigarette, are instances. Other symptoms of boredom suggest that the individual is about to terminate official participation and function as a tactful warning of this.

To manifest signs of boredom is an inconsiderate thing. But in a certain way he who does so assures the others that he is not affecting something that is not felt; they at least know where they stand with him. To suppress these signs completely is suspect, for this prevents others from obtaining the benefit of feed-back cues that might tell them what the situation really is. Thus, while there is one obligation to affect involvement, there is another one inducing the individual not to affect it too well. It is an interesting fact that when the self of the boring individual is deeply committed to the proceedings, as it may be, for example, during leave-takings and avowals of affection, then the bored individual is likely to feel a strong compunction to conceal signs of alienation and thoroughly affect involvement. It is thus at the most poignant and crucial moments of life that the individual is often forced to be the most contriving; these, too, will be the times when the boring individual will be in greatest need of candor from others and least able to bear receiving it.

I have suggested that a show of involvement may be affected by cynical participants and by tactful ones; the same show may also be affected by those who feel self-consciously embarrassed. They may even add to their production by affecting signs of boredom. A condition that casts doubt upon the individual himself is thus exchanged, he hopes, for one that casts doubt upon the others. There is a psychological doctrine that carries this observation one step further and argues that when the individual is himself convinced that he is bored, he may be trying to conceal from himself that he is actually embarrassed.

Conversational encounters in which participants feel obligated to maintain spontaneous involvement and yet cannot manage to do so are ones in which they feel uneasy, and ones in which they may well generate uneasiness in others. The individual recognizes that certain situations will produce this alienation in him and others, and that other situations are quite unlikely to do so. He recognizes that certain individuals are faulty interactants because they are never ready to become spontaneously involved in social encounters and he will have folk-terms such as "cold fish," "kill-joy," "drag," "wet blanket" to refer to these refractory participants. Those who fail to support conversations with their social betters he may call gauche; while those who disdain involvement with their inferiors he may call snobs; in either case condemning these persons for putting rank before interaction. As previously suggested, the individual will also know some persons who are faulty because their manner and social attributes make it difficult for others to become properly involved. It is apparent, too, that in any interaction a role-function develops, that of ensuring that everyone becomes and remains spontaneously involved. This sparking function may be fulfilled by different participants at different times in the interaction. Should one participant fail to help keep the interaction going, other participants will have to do his share of work. An

individual may acquire a reputation for this kind of labor, creating gratitude or resentment as one who is always the life of the encounter.

VI. GENERALIZING THE FRAMEWORK

1. THE CONTEXT OF INVOLVEMENT OBLIGATIONS. One limitation we have
set ourselves is to deal with situations where all those present to one
another are officially obliged to maintain themselves as participants in
conversation and to maintain spontaneous involvement in the conversation. This is a frequent enough condition to serve as a reference point, but
there is no need to be ultimately bound by it. Involvement obligations are
in fact defined in terms of the total context in which the individual finds
himself. Thus there will be some situations where the main involvement
of those present is supposed to be invested in a physical task; conversation,
if carried on at all, will have to be treated as a side-involvement to be
picked up or dropped, depending on the current demands of the task at
hand. There will be other situations where the role and status of a particular participant will be nicely expressed by his right to treat a conversation in a cavalier fashion, participating in it or not, depending on his
inclination at the moment. A father sometimes has this right regarding the
mealtime conversation maintained by lesser members of the family, while
they do not.

I should like to cite another way in which the individual may accept a
different allocation of involvement for himself from that expected of
others. In the teasing that the young receive from the old, or in the
interrogations that employees receive from employers, loss of composure
on the subordinate's part may be accepted by the superordinate as an
expected and proper part of the involvement pattern. At such times the
subordinate may feel he would like to be spontaneously involved in the
talk but is in too much of a panic to do so, while the superordinate may
feel that for him the appropriate focus of attention, and one he can sustain
with comfort, is not the actual talk but the wider situation created by the
humorous plight of the inferior as he struggles in the conversation. In
fact, if the subordinate shows composure on these occasions, the superior
may feel affronted and embarrassed. Similarly there will be occasions when
we feel an individual ought, out of respect for the difficulties he is in, to
be preoccupied or over-involved. This misinvolvement may somewhat
disrupt the interaction, but perfect poise on his part might so scandalize
those present as to disrupt the interaction even more. Thus while it is true
that sometimes an individual will be thought an interaction hero if he
remains involved in a conversation under difficult conditions, at other
times such loyalty will be thought foolhardy.

Differential obligations regarding the same spoken interaction may be seen most clearly in large-scale interactions, such as public speeches, where we are likely to find specialization and segregation of involvement roles, with a division between full participants, who are expected to talk or listen, and non-participating specialists, whose job is to move unobtrusively about and look after some of the mechanics of the occasion. Examples of these non-participants are domestics, ushers, doormen, stenographers, and microphone men. The special alignment these officials have to the interaction is their particular right and obligation; it is accepted openly by them and for them, and they would in fact cause uneasiness were they to become manifestly involved in the content of the talk. They show respect for the occasion by treating it as a side-involvement.

Participants, themselves, in large-scale interaction can have a license in regard to involvement that could not be afforded them in two- or three-person talk, perhaps because the more participants there are to sustain the proceedings, the less dependent the occasion will be on any one participant. In any case, we often find in large-scale interaction that it is permissible for a few participants to enter for a moment into by-plays and side-discussions, providing they modulate their voice and manner to show respect for the official proceedings. In fact, a participant may even leave the room for a moment and do this in such a way as to convey the impression that his main focus of attention is still held by the talk, even though his body is not present. On such occasions, main involvement and side-involvements may become fictions maintained officially in form while alternate involvement patterns are actually maintained in practice.

2. PSEUDO-CONVERSATIONS. We have so far restricted our attention to interactions that have as their constituent communicative acts the turns at talking taken by participants. We can extend our view and consider conversation-like interactions in which the token exchanged is not speeches but stylized gestures, as in the interchange of non-verbal greetings, or moves of some kind, as in card games. These unspoken yet conversation-like interactions seem to be similar, structurally, to spoken interaction, except that the capacities that must be mobilized in order to carry on such interaction seem to have more to do with muscular control of limbs than in the case of spoken interaction.

3. UNFOCUSED INTERACTION. I have suggested that speech-, gesture-, and game-interactions are characterized by a single official focus of cognitive and visual attention that all full-fledged participants help to sustain. (The focus of visual attention may move, of course, from one participant to another as one speaker gives up his speaking-role and returns to the role of listener.) With this focused kind of interaction we must contrast the

unfocused kind, where individuals in one another's visual and aural range go on about their respective business unconnected by a shared focus of attention. Street behavior and conduct at a large social party are instances.

When we examine unfocused interactions we find that involvement obligations are defined not in relation to a conjoint focus of cognitive and visual attention but in relation to a role that can be suggested by the phrase "decorous individual non-interferingly going about his proper business." Once we shift to this point of reference, however, we find that all the kinds of misinvolvement that occur during focused interaction also occur during unfocused interaction, though sometimes under a different name. Just as an adolescent may become self-consciously uneasy when talking to his teacher, so, in walking into a full classroom, he may feel that he is being critically observed and that his way of walking, which he feels is stiff and wooden, reveals his social anxiety. Just as we can have preoccupied persons in conversational interaction, so in unfocused inter-action we can have "absent-minded" participants, who by their posture, facial expression, and physical movements suggest that they are momen-tarily "away," that they have momentarily let fall the expressive costume that individuals are expected to wear whenever they are in the immediate presence of others. And, of course, boredom, too, can occur during un-focused interaction, as we may observe in almost any queue of individuals waiting to buy a ticket. And just as agencies such as alcohol and mari-juana may be employed to transform a conversation into something that is not embarrassing or boring, so these may function to put individuals at ease in the wider scene provided by unfocused interaction. Just as a witticism may do honor to the conversational moment, so the wearing of new or special clothing, the serving of rare or costly food, and the use of perishable flowers can draw attention to the unique value of a wider social occasion. Clearly, then, there are ways in which the perspective employed in this paper can be used for studying unfocused interaction.

We must not, however, expect the similarity between the two kinds of interaction to be too complete. For example, it appears that individuals are more frequently unself-conscious in their capacity as participants in unfocused interaction than they are as participants in focused interaction, especially focused interaction of the spoken kind. In fact, in spoken interaction, spontaneous "normal" involvement seems to be the exception and alienation of some kind the statistical rule. This is understandable. On the one hand, participants are required to be spontaneously carried away by the topic of conversation; on the other hand, they are obliged to con-trol themselves so that they will always be ready to stay within the role of communicator and stay alive to the touchy issues that might cause the others to become ill at ease. On the one hand they are obliged to adhere to all applicable rules of conduct, on the other they are obliged to take enough liberties to ensure a minimum level of involving excitement. These obligations seem to be in opposition to each other, requiring a balance of conduct that is so delicate and precarious that alienation and uneasiness for someone in the interaction are the typical result. Unfocused interaction does not seem to require the same delicacy of adjustment.

VII. CONCLUSION

Many social encounters of the conversational type seem to share a fundamental requirement: the spontaneous involvement of the participants in an official focus of attention must be called forth and sustained. When this requirement exists and is fulfilled, the interaction "comes off" or is euphoric as an interaction. When the encounter fails to capture the attention of the participants, but does not release them from the obligation of involving themselves in it, then persons present are likely to feel uneasy; for them the interaction fails to come off. A person who chronically makes himself or others uneasy in conversation and perpetually kills encounters is a faulty interactant; he is likely to have such a baleful effect upon the social life around him that he may just as well be called a faulty person.

Of any individual, then, it will be significant to know whether his status and manner tend to hinder the maintenance of spontaneous involvement in the interaction, or to help it along. It should be noted that this information pertains to the individual in his capacity as interactant, and that, regardless of the other capacities in which he may be active at the time, the role of interactant is something he will be obliged to maintain.

Social encounters differ a great deal in the importance that participants give to them but, whether crucial or picayune, all encounters represent occasions when the individual can become spontaneously involved in the proceedings and derive from this a firm sense of reality. And this kind of feeling is not a trivial thing, regardless of the package in which it comes. When an incident occurs and spontaneous involvement is threatened, then reality is threatened. Unless the disturbance is checked, unless the interactants regain their proper involvement, the illusion of reality will be shattered, the minute social system that is brought into being with each encounter will be disorganized, and the participants will feel unruled, unreal, and anomic.

Aside from the sense of reality it offers, a particular encounter may be of little consequence, yet we must see that the rules of conduct that oblige individuals to be able and ready to give themselves up to such moments are of transcendent importance. Men who are held by these rules are held ready for spoken interaction, and spoken interaction between many kinds of people on many kinds of occasion is necessary if society's work is to be done.

The sense of reality that has been discussed in this paper takes its form in opposition to modes of alienation, to states like preoccupation, self-consciousness, and boredom. In turn, these modes of disengagement are to be understood by reference to the central issue of spontaneous involvement. When we have seen the way in which a spoken encounter can succeed or fail in bringing its participants to it, and have seen that unfocused interaction can be looked at in the same way, we have a lead to follow in the understanding of other kinds of commitments—the individual's occupational career, his political involvements, his family membership—for there will be a sense in which these wider matters consist in recurrent occasions of focused and unfocused interaction. By looking at the ways in which the individual can be thrown out of step with the sociable moment, perhaps we can learn something about the way in which he can become alienated from things that take much more of his time.

CHAPTER IV

The Linguistic Theory

INTRODUCTION   While mathematicians and social psychologists developed the first two parts of the theory of human communication, anthropologists and linguists developed the third. Linguistic theory is primarily concerned with the analysis of speech, but speech is more than just another form of signaling: it is also a form of human behavior in general. This form of behavior has been analyzed more completely and precisely than any other. The aim of linguistic theory is to develop a model and a procedure for making a complete, concise, and objective description of the speech of a people: the phonology, the grammar, and the other parts of English and of all other languages. This linguistic theory has been developed so far that it is often considered as a potential model for the other behavioral sciences.

"The Linguistic Approach" by Joseph H. Greenberg introduces this theory with a description of a description of verbal behavior. It gives the general characteristics of a modern analysis of any language. The linguistic descriptions emphasize patterns and structures. They do this by isolating structural units, such as phonemes and morphemes. This is in some ways comparable to the isolation of genes in the analysis of biological structures or of electrons in physical structures. Phonemes and morphemes are basic elements in the sound system and the grammatical system of any language. The speakers and hearers of a language perceive these units as units, consciously or unconsciously. Ernst Pulgram's "Phoneme and Grapheme: A Parallel" goes on to show how readers and writers perceive basic visual units as well. Any "-eme" is a class of things, a class of auditory sounds (phoneme) or visual marks (grapheme), and communication requires a process of abstraction whereby we recognize the class in a specimen of the class.

119

"The Morpheme" by H. A. Gleason, Jr., shows how this basic unit—which is often equivalent to a "word"—is also a class of things, a configuration of meaning. The way morphemes are combined and distributed in a language is the grammar of that language; but the complete listing of all combinations and distributions of a good number of morphemes in any one language would be a most unwieldy grammar. Moreover, as Noam Chomsky shows in "Three Models for the Description of Language," this would not explain how anyone can use the available words and grammar and say something new, meaningful, and grammatically correct. Languages are not finite because we can generally make new sentences that have never been made before. A grammar, therefore, must describe and systematize not only what has been said, or what is said, but what can be said. This entails a broader grammar, a generative grammar.

The mathematical theory and the social psychological theory have been applied to the analysis of all human behavior. Kenneth L. Pike does the same thing with the linguistic theory. In his "Emic and Etic Standpoints for the Description of Behavior" he extends the use of basic structural units beyond language and applies them to human behavior in general. Pike goes beyond phonemic and morphemic structures to the study of emics as a whole. Using linguistically based concepts he describes not only what a people say or have said, but how they act.

11 | The Linguistic Approach
JOSEPH H. GREENBERG

As distinct from psychology, which is concerned with verbal behavior in the context of events occurring within the organism, and from the other social sciences, which analyze the contents of verbal behavior insofar as it consists of shared cultural beliefs and actions (e.g., religion, philosophy, economic and political norms), linguistic science has as its traditional subject matter the signal system as such. Its orientation tends to be social rather than individual, since the use of speech in communication presupposes a group of inter-communicating people, a speech community. In general, therefore, it has dealt with the speech of individuals merely as representative of the speech of a community. The interest in an individual's speech as such, his *idiolect*, in relation to his personality structure constitutes a relatively new, marginal, and little explored area. The distinction between language as a system and its actual employment has been variously phrased as *langue* vs. *parole* (de Saussure), syntactic vs. pragmatic (Morris) or code vs. message (information theory). However stated, it marks in general the boundary between what has traditionally been considered the province of linguistic science and what lies outside it.

THE FIELD OF LINGUISTICS

The primary subject matter of the linguist is spoken language. Writing and other systems partly or wholly isomorphic with speech are viewed by most linguists as secondary systems. Speech has both ontogenetic and phylogentic priority. There are even now peoples with spoken but not written languages (so-called primitives), but the reverse situation has

Reprinted with permission of the publisher and the author. From *Psycholinguistics: Survey of Theory and Research Problems*, C. E. Osgood, ed. and T. A. Sebeok, assoc. ed., Indiana University Publications in Anthropology and Linguistics, *International Journal of American Linguistics*, Memoir 10, pp. 8–16 (1954).

never been obtained. Moreover, written systems are relatively stable while spoken language, by and large, changes more rapidly. It is always the written language which must make the readaptation, when it is made, by way of a new orthography. The effect of, say, alphabetic writing on speech, in the form of spelling pronunciations, is a real but quite minor factor in the change of spoken language. The linguist views writing, then, as a derivative system whose symbols stand for units of the spoken language.

Linguistic science is divided into two main branches, the *descriptive* and the *historical*. Historical interests presided at the inception of modern linguistic science (*ca.* 1800) and have predominated until fairly recently. Within the last few decades the focal point of linguistics has shifted to problems of description. These two chief areas of study complement each other. The degree of success of historical inquiry is largely dependent on the adequacy of descriptive data. On the other hand any particular stage of a language, while it can be completely described without reference to its past, can be more fully understood if the time axis is also taken into account. A cardinal and generally accepted methodological principle, however, is the clear distinction between synchronic and diachronic investigations. In particular, descriptive grammars were, and sometimes are, so replete with historical interpretations, that the locus in time of individual linguistic facts is obscured and observed phenomena are not distinguished from inferences, so that no clear picture of the structure of the language at any one time emerges.

The aim of a scientific language description is to state as accurately, exhaustively, concisely, and elegantly as possible, the facts concerning a particular language at a particular time. It is assumed that the changes which are inevitably proceeding during the period in which the linguistic informant's speech is being studied are negligible and can be safely disregarded. It is also assumed that the speech of the informant is an adequate sample of some speech community. This concept is applied rather vaguely to any group within which linguistic communication takes place regularly. Minor cleavages within a group of mutually intelligible speech forms are called *dialects*. The maximal mutually intelligible group is a *language community*, as defined by scientific linguistics, but the term is often loosely applied on a political basis. Thus Norwegian is usually called a language although it is mutually intelligible with Danish, while Low German is considered a form of German, although objectively the difference between Low and High German is greater than that between Danish and Norwegian. The phrase "mutually intelligible" is itself vague.

The speech of an informant is normally characteristic of that of a dialect community along with some idiosyncrasies. Language is so standardized an aspect of culture, particularly in regard to those structural aspects which are of chief concern to the linguist, that a very small number of informants usually proves to be adequate. If necessary, the linguist will even be satisfied with a single informant in the belief that systematic divergence from the shared habits of the community as a whole are likely to be of minimal significance. However, the sampling problem must eventually be faced in a less makeshift manner. The systematic mapping of speech differences on a geographic basis, through sampling at selected points, is known as *linguistic geography* and is a well-established sub-discipline of linguistics. Far more remains to be done with non-geographic factors of cleavage within the language community, on sex, occupational and class lines. Such study is a prerequisite for adequate sampling.

UNITS OF LINGUISTIC ANALYSIS

Linguistic description is carried out in terms of certain fundamental units which can be isolated by analytic procedures. The two key units are the *phoneme* and the *morpheme*, of which the phoneme has a somewhat more assured status. The phoneme is the unit of description of the sound system (phonology) of a language. Many widely differing definitions have been offered, some of which are objects of doctrinal differences between various linguistic "schools." Fortunately, the actual results in practice of the applications of these divergent approaches are surprisingly similar.

The *phoneme* was foreshadowed by the pre-scientific invention of alphabetic writing. An adequate orthography of this kind disregards differences in sound which have no potential for the discrimination of meaning. Moreover, unlike syllabic writing, alphabetic writing selects the minimal unit capable of such differential contrast. The naive speaker is generally unaware of sound variations which do not carry this function of distinguishing different forms. For example, speakers of English have usually never noticed that the sound spelled t in "stop" is unaspirated as contrasted with the aspirated t of "top." Yet this difference is sufficient to differentiate forms in Chinese, Hindustani, and many other languages. Phonemic theory is necessary because if we approach other languages naively we will only respond to those cues as different which are significant in our own languge. On the other hand, we will attribute significance, and consider as indicative of separate elements, those differences which have a function in our own language, although they may not have such a function in the language we are describing.

For example, in Algonquian languages distinctions of voicing are not significant. A naive observer with an English linguistic background will carefully mark all p's as different from b's. The reaction of an Algonquian would be similar to that of an English speaker if he were presented with an orthography devised by a Hindu in which the *t* of "top" was represented by a different symbol from the *t* of "stop." The arbitrariness of such a procedure comes out when we realize that an untrained Frenchman would describe the sound system of a particular language in different terms than a naive Englishman or German. As a matter of fact, this has often occurred. Equally unsatisfactory results are obtained by a phonetically trained observer, unaware of the phonemic principle, who indicates all kinds of non-essential variants because his training permits him to distinguish them. Here also there is a certain arbitrariness based on the particular phonetic training of the observer. The logical outcome of such a phonetic approach would be to carry discriminations even further by instrumental means, and the results would be that every utterance of a language would be completely unique, for no two utterances of the "same" sequence of phonemes is ever acoustically identical with any other.

The procedure of the descriptive linguist, then, is a process of discovering the basic contrasts which are significant in a language. Since he cannot know *a priori* which particular features of an utterance will prove to be significant, he must be prepared to indicate them all at the beginning by a phonetic transcription. Instrumental aids, though useful, are not essential to the preliminary research. The linguist gradually eliminates those sound differences from his transcription which prove to be non-significant so that the phonetic transcription becomes a phonemic one. In doing this, he makes use of the two principles of *conditioned* and *non-conditioned variation*. If the occurrence of one or another of a set of sounds may be predicted in terms of other sounds in the environment, this variation is said to be conditioned. If either of two sounds may be used for the other and still produce a meaningful utterance, the variation is called free, or non-conditioned. Such variant sounds grouped within the same phoneme are called allophones. In English, k, a front velar sound is found before *i, I, e, E* and other front vowels (e.g., the initial sound of "key"). A sound different enough to be a separate phoneme in many languages, k, a back velar sound, is found before *u, v, o, ɔ* and other back vowels (e.g., the initial sound of "coat"). Since the particular variant can be predicted by reference to the following vowel sound, k and k are in conditioned allophonic variation and are members of the same English /k/ phoneme.

The number of potential phones (sounds) in a language approaches infinity. The great virtue of the phonemic principle is that it enables the linguist to effect a powerful reduction from this complexity to a limited number of signals that constitute the code, and this represents a great economy in description. For languages so far investigated, the number of phonemes runs about 25 to 30 (the English system tending toward the higher figure). It is possible to effect a still greater economy in description. This is achieved by the analysis of phonemes into concurrent sets of *distinctive features*. Since the features which distinguish certain pairs of phonemes are found to be identical with the features which distinguish certain other pairs, the number of entities necessary to describe the significant aspects of the sound matter is thus further reduced. For example, in English /p/ is distinguished from /b/, /t/ from /d/, /k/ from /g/, and /s/ from /z/ on the basis of the same feature, the former being unvoiced and the latter voiced. Other distinctive features, such as tongue position or nasalization, produce other sets of contrasts. By contrasting every phoneme in the language with every other phoneme, each phoneme comes to be uniquely identified in terms of the set of contrasts into which it enters, this "bundle of distinctive features" being the definition of that phoneme. The distinctive oppositions that occur in languages studied so far run about 6 to 8. These are perhaps the minimal discriminanda in language codes.

Analysis into distinctive features is a development within the past two decades, associated with the Prague School but not universally accepted. Jakobson and his associates go one step further still, by imposing upon the entire phonemic material *binary opposition* as a consistent patterning principle, but this needs much further exploration. Whereas American linguists usually say that sounds must be phonetically similar to be classed as members of the same phoneme, members of the Prague School state that members of the same phoneme class must share the same set of distinctive features. These criteria will generally lead to the same classificatory structure.

For example, k̯ and k̯ would be said by members of the Prague School to share the following features in common: velar articulation, non-nasality and lack of voicing. These would be the relevant features shared by all varieties of the /k/ phoneme while, in this instance, back or forward articulation is irrelevant. The /g/ phoneme shares velarity and non-nasality with /k/ but not lack of voicing. The /n/ phoneme (as in "sing") shares velar articulation but not non-nasality or lack of voicing. The /t/ phoneme shares non-nasality and lack of voicing with /k/ but not velar articulation. Thus /k/ is uniquely determined by these three relevant features. Certain recent American analyses employ a methodology nearly identical with that just described.

Phonemes are sometimes distinguished as being either *segmental* or *prosodic*. The former proceed in one dimensional time succession without gap. The latter are intermittent and necessarily simultaneous with segmental phonemes or successions of segmental phonemes. Examples of prosodic phonemes are phonemes of tone (sometimes called tonemes), stress, etc. In principle, we should sharply distinguish prosodic phonemes simultaneous with a single segmental phoneme from those which are distributed over a grammatically defined unit such as a phrase or sentence. The former can always be dispensed with in analysis, though they often prove convenient. For example, in a language with three vowel phonemes /a, i, u/ and two tone levels high /'/ and low /`/ we might analyze /à/, /á/, /ì/, /í/, /ù/ and /ú/ as six separate segmental phonemes or we might make /a/, /i/ and /u/ segmental and /'/ and /`/ prosodic. This particular analysis has no doubt been largely determined by our traditional orthography which uses separate marks for pitch. The carrying through of this procedure to its logical conclusion is called *componential analysis* and results in the resolution of each phoneme into a set of simultaneous elements equivalent to the distinctive features mentioned above. The other type of prosodic element is illustrated by question or statement intonation in English. Unlike the elements just discussed, it cannot be dispensed with.

Still another type of phoneme is the juncture or significant boundary, whose status is much disputed in contemporary linguistics. The conditioning factor for phonemic variation is sometimes found to be the initial or final position in some grammatical unit such as a word, rather than a neighboring sound. For example, unreleased stops *p, t, k* are found in English in final morpheme or word position. Unless we indicate the boundary in some fashion we must nearly double the number of phonemes in English. Spaces, hyphens and other devices are employed to indicate the presence of these modifications. For example, the *n* of "syntax" is shorter than the *n* in "sin-tax." Either we posit two different *n* phonemes or we describe the longer *n* as *n* plus juncture, transcribing /sintaks/ and /sin-taks/ respectively (or we deny the existence of the phenomenon altogether). The agreement as to the boundaries of grammatical elements is almost never perfect, and some linguists assume that if such boundary modifications exist in some cases they must exist in all, even though they have not actually been observed to occur.

In addition to the enumeration of phonemes and their allophonic variants, the phonological section of a description usually contains a set of statements regarding permitted and non-permitted sequences of phonemes, frequently in terms of the structure of the syllable. In this as in other aspects of linguistic description it is not usual to give text or lexicon frequencies. Statements are limited to those of simple occurrence or nonoccurrence. Only such quantifiers as some, none and all occur in most linguistic description.

Corresponding to the minimal unit of phonology, the phoneme, we have a unit of somewhat less certain status, the *morpheme*, which is basic for grammatical description. Bloomfield states as the fundamental assumption of linguistic science that in a given speech community some utterances show partial formal-semantic similarity. For example, in the English-speaking community the utterances "the dog is eating meat" and "the dog is eating biscuits" are partially similar in their sequence of phonemes and refer to partially similar situations. The linguist, through the analysis of these partial similarities, arrives at the division of utterances into meaningful parts. The analytical procedure as applied to individual utterances must eventually reach a point beyond which analysis becomes arbitrary and futile. The minimum sequence of phonemes thus isolated, which has a meaning, is called a morpheme. The morpheme is a smaller unit than the word. Some words are monomorphemic, e.g., "house." Others are multi-morphemic, e.g., "un-child-like." There is some uncertainty as to the point up to which such divisions are justified and the rules of procedure may be stated in several alternate ways. Thus all would concur in analyzing "singing" as having two morphemes "sing-" and "-ing" and there would likewise be general agreement that to analyze "chair" as containing two morphemes, say "ch-" meaning "wooden object" and "-air" meaning "something to sit on" is not acceptable. But there is an intermediate area in which opinions differ. For example, "deceive" contains two morphemes "de" and "ceive" according to some but not according to others. In such borderline cases it becomes impossible to specify the meaning of each morpheme without some arbitrariness.

MORPHOLOGY AND SYNTAX

The work of the descriptive linguists in this area is not exhausted by the analytic task just described. Having arrived at his units he must describe the rules according to which they are synthesized into words, phrases, and sentences. In somewhat parallel fashion to the situation in phonology, having isolated minimal units, he must describe their variation and their rules of combination.

In regard to the first of these problems, it is not sufficient to consider each sequence of phonemes which differs either in form or meaning as a different unit from every other. For example, the sequence "leaf" /lijf/ is different in form from "leav-" of the plural "leaves" /lijv-z/ but we cannot consider them as units without relation to each other. We call /lijf/ and /lijv-/ morphs rather than morphemes and consider them allomorphs of the same morpheme because: (1) they are in complementary distribution /lijv-/ occuring only with /-z/ of the plural and /lijf/ under all other conditions; (2) they have the same meaning; (3) there are other sequences which do not vary in form and which have the same type of distribution, e.g., "cliff" for which we have /klif/ and /klif-s/. Such variation in the phonemic composition of allomorphs of the same morpheme is called morphophonemic alternation, and systematic statements of such alternations comprise the portion of grammar known as *morphophonemics*. Some alternations occur in all instances in a language regardless of the particular morphemes in which the phonemes occur. Such alternations are called automatic. There are others which are unique. These are called irregular. Others are intermediate in that they apply to classes of morphemes of various sizes. In English, morphemes which have *s*, *z* and *əz* as variants exhibit automatic alternation, *əz* occurring after sibilants (and affricates), *s* after unvoiced non-sibilants and *z* after voiced non-sibilants. Thus the same rule applies both for the third person singular present of the verb and the nominative plural. On the other hand, the variation between /čajld/ "child" and /čildr-/ of the plural "childr-en" is a unique irregularity. Psychologically, there would seem to be a real difference between these extremes.

Having distinguished morphemic units, there remains the basic task of grammatical description—the setting up of rules of permitted combinations of morphemes to form sentences. Generality of statement is here obviously a prime requirement. Languages vary widely in number of morphemes, from some hundreds to many thousands. Their possible sequences in constructions can only be stated in practice by the setting up of classes whose members have the same privilege of occurrence. In setting up such classes, modern linguistics characteristically uses a formal, rather than semantic approach. Classes of morphemes or classes of sequences of morphemes (word classes, phrase types, etc.) are defined in terms of mutual substitutability in a given frame. Any utterance and the morpheme or morpheme sequence within it, for which substitutions are made, defines a class. Thus, in English, among other criteria, substitution of single words for *house* in the frame "I see the house" determines the class of nouns. This contrasts with the traditional *a priori* semantic approach according to which all languages have the same basic grammatical categories (actually based on Latin grammar) and a noun, for example is defined as the name of a person, place, or thing. Actually, formal criteria have always been used in grammars, although often tacitly. "Lightning" is a noun in traditional English grammar also, although it names an event, because it functions in the same constructions as other nouns.

It is customary to regard sentences as the largest normalized units, and these are successively decomposed into clauses, phrases, words, and morphemes. These units constitute a hierarchy which is also reflected in the speech event by *configurational features*, which, like the distinctive features of phonemic analysis, are assumed to operate on a strictly binary, "yes-no" basis. Configurational features include such distinctions as those of pitch, stress, rhythm, and juncture, and provide appropriate signals as to construction. The sentence is so complex a unit that it cannot be described directly in terms of morpheme constructions. Rather, the description is built up in layers. On any particular level, the combinations are practically always accounted for in terms of *immediate constituents*. In the sentence "unlikely events may actually occur," the morpheme *un-* and the morpheme sequence *-likely* are the two immediate constituents which make up the word *unlikely*. In turn, *likely* has as immediate binary constituents the morphemes "*like-*" and "*ly*." On a higher level *unlikely* enters as a whole in a construction with *events* while *events* itself has *event-* and *-s* as immediate constituents.

It is usual to distinguish as primary divisions of grammar all constructions of morphemes to form words as *morphology* and all constructions using words as units to form phrases, clauses, and sentences as *syntax*. Although no generally accepted definition of the word-unit exists, in fact very nearly every grammar written makes use of the word as a fundamental unit and describes morphological and syntactic constructions separately. In spite of traditional differences of terminology in morphology and syntax, it is generally agreed that the same fundamental principles of analysis apply.

PROBLEM OF MEANING IN LINGUISTICS

Besides specifying meaningful units and their constructions, a complete linguistic description must state the meanings of these units and of the constructions into which they enter. The status of meaning has been a crucial point in contemporary linguistic theory. The statements of Bloomfield concerning meaning in his influential book have sometimes been interpreted both by followers and opponents as indicating that the field of linguistic science only includes a logical syntax of language without reference to meanings. The definition of meanings, on this view, rests with other sciences which deal with the subject matters which speakers talk about. Thus, the definition of "moon" is the business of the astronomer, not the linguist. The actual practice of linguists both here and in Europe, however, indicates that semantic problems are in fact dealt with and cannot well be excluded from scientific linguistics.

Without entering into the exegetical problem of what Bloomfield meant, which is irrelevant to the present purpose, it may be pointed out that Bloomfield coined the technical terms "sememe" for the meaning of a morpheme and "episememe" for the meaning of a construction, both of which are current in American linguistics. Moreover, problems of historical meaning change are discussed at length in his book. This would imply that scientific linguistics does not exclude semantics. It is evident that historical linguistics draws conclusions regarding relationships by comparisons of cognates, that is, forms with both formal and semantic resemblances, so that in this branch, at least, meanings must be dealt with. It is likewise clear that the compiling of dictionaries has traditionally fallen within the linguist's province and continues to do so. No linguist has ever written a grammar in which the forms cited were not accompanied by translations.

The linguist deals with meaning by the bilingual method of translation or the unilingual method of paraphrase, that is, by the apparatus of traditional lexicography. In keeping with the general orientation of linguistics as a social science, the linguist defines the socially shared denotative meanings. Avoiding as far as possible controversial issues in the domain of epistemology, it may perhaps be ventured that a distinction may be, and in practice is, drawn between definitions which embody our scientific knowledge about a thing and nominal definitions which are observed rules of use in a given speech community. The linguist practices the latter type of definition. His methods up to now have been the more less rough and ready methods of lexicography based on the traditional logical concepts of definition. The difficulties involved in the vagueness of actual usage of all linguistic terms in a speech community (if we exclude some scientific discourse in a few societies) are in practice circumvented by the not altogether happy devices of translation and paraphrase, which, involving as they do, language in its everyday use, are equally as vague as the terms which are to be defined. Ambiguity is dealt with by multiple listings of separate meanings based primarily on common-sense analysis. The boundary between the same form with synonymous meanings and separate homonymous forms has never been clearly determined, since it has not been possible to specify *how* different meanings must be in order to justify treatment as homonyms. Nor, in this instance, does an approach in terms of purely formal differences in distribution prove more successful.

12 | Phoneme and Grapheme: A Parallel
ERNST PULGRAM

Phoneme is a class name, hence a phoneme cannot occur.

What does occur are phones, that is, phonetic realizations, articulated sounds. All phones identifiable as members of a phoneme are its allophones. Phonemes are distinctive classes of speech sounds, hence phonemic differences make semantic distinctions possible. Differences less than phonemic produce forms that cannot be meaningfully distinguished. We are, then, dealing with a linguistic performance, oral and aural, whereby individual, local and social differences in enunciation, pronunciation, style are abstracted and only the essential features with distinctive value made functional.

Reprinted with permission of The Linguistic Circle of New York and the author. From *Word*, 7:15–20 (1951).

The same situation prevails, mutatis mutandis, with regard to writing. Just as we speak of speech communities using different languages or dialects, so we also have writing communities using various alphabets with their varieties: Greek, Roman, Cyrillic, etc. Each alphabet has a certain fixed number of distinctively shaped classes of symbols, usually called letters, which are graphemes. They correspond to phonemes in that they are classes serving to provide the function of distinctiveness. No matter how a person's handwriting realizes the graphemes of, say, the Latin alphabet, no matter what style or font a printer employs, each hic et nunc realization of a grapheme, which may be called graph, can be recognized as belonging to a certain class and therefore deciphered by the reader. All graphs so identifiable are allographs of a given grapheme. Putting statements on the phoneme and the grapheme side by side in two columns, the parallelism becomes obvious.

P1 The smallest distinctive audible units of a dialect are its phonemes.

G1 The smallest distinctive visual units of an alphabet are its graphemes.

P2 A phoneme is a class of articulated speech sounds pertaining to one dialect.

G2 A grapheme is a class of written characters pertaining to one alphabet.

P3 The hic et nunc spoken realization of a phoneme is an articulated speech sound or phone.

G3 The hic et nunc written realization of a grapheme is a written alphabetic character or graph.

P4 The number of phonemes in each dialect must be limited, the number of phones cannot be.

G4 The number of graphemes in each alphabet must be limited, the number of graphs cannot be.

P5 By definition, all phones identifiable as members of one phoneme are its allophones.

G5 By definition, all graphs identifiable as members of one grapheme are its allographs.

P6 The phonetic shape of an allophone is dependent on its producer and on its phonetic surroundings.

G6 The graphic shape of an allograph is dependent on its producer and on its graphic surroundings.

P7 Phones which are not immediately and correctly identifiable as belonging to a certain phoneme when occurring in isolation, may be identified through their meaningful position in a tion of graphemes varies from context.

G7 Graphs which are not immediately and correctly identifiable as belonging to a certain grapheme when occurring in isolation, may be identified through their meaningful position in a context.

P8 Dialects are subject to phonemic change and substitution.

G8 Alphabets are subject to graphemic change and substitution.

P9 The number, kind, and distribution of phonemes varies from dialect to dialect.

G9 The number, kind, and distribution of graphemes varies from alphabet to alphabet.

Now a few remarks elaborating and commenting on the points cited.

P1, P2. These are not meant, singly or in combination, as *the* definition of the phoneme. But they are good enough working formulae.

P5, G5. Identifiable refers both to the performer (speaker, writer) and the receiver (hearer, reader). Both must possess certain scales of standards in order to communicate. The phonemic and graphemic scales of no two persons ever coincide exactly. In other words, no two persons talk alike or write alike. If communication takes place, acoustically or optically, then this is due to the faculty of abstraction of the auditory and visual centers in the brain, that is, to the ability of the brain to recognize the class in a specimen of the class, regardless of the individual features of the specimen. This intellectual process is of greatest linguistic and epistemological importance, because thanks to it human beings can devise and use common nouns, which are class names, and not merely proper names for each individual of a species of beings or class of things. Phoneme and grapheme are precisely such class abstractions. In the absence of classes of phones, or phonemes, valid for all members of a linguistic community, all oral communication would cease, for every individual could talk intelligibly only to himself, because he could meaningfully use, actively and passively, only one set of phones, namely his own. Even animals can do better than that, since they react to phonemes (hardly to the intellectual, semantic content) of a human command regardless of the speaker's allophonic habits. Once a dog has learned to obey the order "Down," he will behave accordingly no matter who pronounces the word. Similarly, lack of graphemes would stop communication by writing, since no one could decipher, that is, classify graphemically, anyone else's graphs.

P6, G6. Let us first consider the factors inherent in the performer which determine certain properties of his allophones. We can recognize a person by his speech quite apart from the intelligence or the intelligibility of his utterance. The mere physical features of his speech, conditioned anatomically and by habits, suffice for identification. If, in addition, what he says and how he says it, in other words, his style, provide further clues, all the better. The what and how are socially conditioned, however, by the speaker's education, surroundings, profession, etc. Directors and actors of radio plays, who cannot convey any part of the contents of the performance visually, are very skillful in the art of voice characterization. Even the psyche, the temperament of a person finds expression in his speech, to say nothing of his temporary moods, and every hearer makes a certain value judgment of a speaker simply on the basis of "what he talks like." Is this true of writing also? It seems to be. A heavy untrained hand is at once visible (and "heavy" may have more than metaphorical meaning). The stiff fingers of a laborer who wields a pick axe all day, will obviously grasp and guide a pen in a different way from those of a surgeon or a professor. Again the intellectual contents of the written piece are not of essence, only the shape of the graphs. As for the appearance of the psyche, the mental and psychological rather than social personality in a person's handwriting, graphologists tell us, surely with a good deal of justification, though in absence of a truly scientific procedure and system, that no man can deny or dissimulate his soul in his handwriting. There are, to my knowledge, no analyzers of speech performing a job similar to that of the graphologists.

Concerning the shape of allophones conditioned by their surroundings, the phenomenon of positional variants is too well known to need comment. It simply means that, within the stream of speech, phones are not produced singly and in isolation, each with a certain fixed articulation, like the separate tones on the keyboard of a piano. Instead, every sound is, as it were, a glide, obtaining part of the articulatory shape from its predecessor and preparing that of its successor. Is this true of allographs also? I daresay it is, though it may be difficult to make precise statements. But I do know from my own habits that, for example, a capital *T* before an *i* is different from one before *h;* that an initial *d* does not look exactly like a final *d*. Handwriting experts know this well, and they can identify a writer by his allographic habits.

P7, G7. An allophone in isolation is not necessarily identified as member of the same class by two speakers, even though they may belong to the same speech community. The reason for this is again the non-congruence of individual scales. What to one speaker may be a very open low [i] may belong to the /e/ phoneme of another. However, since the phone [i] occurs in a form in which it must be understood as an allophone of /i/ rather than /e/, say in *bit* as opposed to *bet,* the listener can immediately so recognize it on the basis of the context. The meaning of the whole utterance will facilitate correct classification of a single phone. This will hold true especially if the phone is very far from being allophonic, for instance in the speech of a foreigner with a strong accent who says actually "Please [fil] out this paper" instead of [fIl]. But the unphonemically pronounced form will be understood phonemically as /fil/ rather than /fijl/, even though in English [i] is not a permissible allophone of /i/, because the statement makes sense only with /fil/. In other words, we listen not just for phones but for larger units.

Everyone knows that the reading of handwriting is based to a great extent on the reading of context. The eye of the proficient reader, though not that of the learner, seizes upon a whole word or a series of words at once. It does not move in little hops from letter to letter, but in leaps from word to word, or even over larger units. Since the eye does not tarry on each graph any more than the ear does on each phone, allographic variations, like allophonic ones, will not be felt as disturbing, and even truly ungraphemic performance on the part of the writer (misspelling, miswriting) will automatically be adjusted and understood thanks to the context, as was done in the case of the unphonemic pronunciation of the foreigner. Indeed one could talk also of writing with a "foreign accent": French, Italian, English, American children, while learning the same Latin graphemes, do acquire certain national writing characteristics in school, which show in letters as well as in figures. An untrained eye may then have to proceed, like the eye of the beginner, from graph to graph. And does not the untrained ear that is not yet accustomed to a foreign phonemic system grope its way from phone to phone, taking care to identify each as the allophone of a certain phoneme? ("Talk more slowly, please, I can't follow you!") And does not the untrained tongue take more time for enunciating foreign phonemes?

P8, G8. Let us suppose that we have designed and imposed, by force or persuasion, a strictly phonemic system of writing for a certain dialect. This dialect will, as all human language must, change its phonetic and phonemic appearance. Unless our phonemic alphabet keeps pace with the changes in speech, the one to one ratio between phoneme and grapheme will be upset. It seems then that, in order to retain that ideal ratio, spelling would have to be constantly revised. That is, of course, impractical. The organizational problem of divulging each orthographic change to all teachers and users of writing, and the educational task of reteaching everyone would be staggering. The result would be confusion thrice confounded. Worse even, since much sound change is gradual, it would be difficult to determine just when the time had come to align the writing with a new speech habit, especially as synchronically there is no awareness of change.

Instead of changing spelling piece by piece at the same rate as speech changes, it might be more feasible to take stock of the phonemes of a dialect, say, once every hundred years, and to entrust to linguists of that period the task of legislating the new phonemic writing. I rather doubt that all linguists could agree on a unique solution (in fact, there is no reason why they should have to). Perhaps the majority opinion should prevail—whereupon, naturally, the dissenting experts will secede in a huff and write as they see fit. Then we shall have the Professor X Alphabet, the Professor Y Phonemic System, the American National Orthography, the Royal Society of Yorkshire for the Preservation of English, and the Mississippi Reformed Southern Speller. And that does not seem much of an advance over what we have got today.

A third possibility is to abolish all rules of spelling and writing. Why be undemocratic? Let every man be his own Webster and NED. This movement will be fathered by the work of a progressive linguistician, entitled *Leave Your Spelling Alone,* or LYSA, whence the name of the

Lysanders: men who don't much care how they spell as long as they get the meaning across. This is a pretty good system, especially for many practicing and producing Lysanders, but the rest of the people, including a number of Lysanders who are mainly consumers, will find the labor of reading greatly increased. For it is a fact, as we just saw, that one does not simply pick out one letter after the other but rather takes in a whole word or even more, at one glance; one perceives these larger-than-graph units as composite *Gestalten*, not as series of graphs. One reads CITY, not C, I, T, Y. And if anyone prefers to write SITI without forewarning us, we shall be much disturbed and impeded. We have just barely become accustomed to nite, thru, and tho, and if we have to expect arbitrary and capricious spellings like nait, noit, thruw, throo, thow, thou etc. we shall have not a bit of fun reading. And I should hate particularly to be type-setter for a Lysandrian manuscript—unless I should be free to respell everything to suit my own fancy. The best solution is then to have the author record his opus on a disk or wire or tape. There will be no trouble about understanding his allophones and classifying them properly as phonemes so that they will be meaningful, for no one can change arbitrarily his phonemes (there can be no LYPA) if he wants to be understood.

Fantastic? Perhaps; but it does throw some light on the perennial problem of spelling reform and on the practical value and virtue of reasonable permanence of a reasonable agreement.

It is precisely that parallelism of phonemics and graphemics which renders feasible a phonemic transcription, that is, a transcription in which each grapheme represents one phoneme, and in which no phoneme can be rendered by more than one grapheme. In such a writing the function and properties of the phoneme and grapheme are exactly equivalent, except that different processes of production and different perceptive senses are involved: the hand and the eyes for the grapheme, the vocal apparatus and the ears for the phoneme. In such an alphabet "letter" and "sound" are synonymous. If today we distinguish between letter (or better grapheme) and speech sound (or better phoneme), the reason is that there has hardly ever existed in any language with some tradition of writing a strictly one to one ratio between the two. While grammarians and "phoneticians" of past centuries, of the Middle Ages and antiquity, had cognizance of that lack of congruence, they nonetheless based whatever phonetic systems they presented on the written letter. But in so doing they did concede that the letter possessed, beyond its appearance, certain attributes which we associate now with the sound, especially the phoneme. However, ". . . the application of the word 'letter' exclusively to the written character is a recent limitation of its sense. As a technical term of traditional grammar, it originally stood for an entity possessing three attributes or aspects: *nomen,* *figura,* and *potestas.* Early writers may be misinterpreted if the implications of this concept are not realized." No doubt the distinction of phonemes and graphemes is valid enough, even in truly phonemic alphabets and transcriptions, because we are really dealing with two fundamentally different phenomena. Nonetheless, ". . . it may be questioned whether, if *letter* had been retained in something like its traditional functional sense, the need for a phoneme theory would never have arisen—though we should, certainly, have subtle theories of the letter in its place."

The basic phenomenon in phonemics and graphemics, as well as in semantics and in non-linguistic human activities, seems to be the faculty of the brain to classify numerous single items as members of a much smaller number of species. Ultimately this labor of sorting and classing is a device of economy, designed to crystallize the relevant features and abstract them from a mass of non-distinctive individual details. Epistemologically and linguistically (are the two identical?) this may well be the most humanly intelligent performance of the human intellect.

13 | The Morpheme
H. A. GLEASON, JR.

If the morpheme is to be described as the smallest meaningful unit in the structure of a language, care must be taken not to misconstrue the words "meaningful" or "meaning." "Meaning" is intended to represent the relationship which exists between morphemes as part of the expression system of a language and comparable units in the content system of the same language. A morpheme is the smallest unit in the expression system which can be correlated directly with any part of the content system.

Using the term *meaning* in its ordinary familiar sense without careful control will in some cases be quite misleading. In many instances, however, it will serve as a workable approximation, if used with caution. For example, *cat* may be said to have a meaning since it refers, among other

Reprinted with permission of the publisher and the author. From H. A. Gleason, Jr., *An Introduction to Descriptive Linguistics,* rev. ed., pp. 54–58. Copyright © 1961 by Holt, Rinehart and Winston, Inc.

things, to a specific kind of animal. But it is also used of humans with certain personality characteristics. In a like sense, *go* may be said to have a similar kind of meaning, since it refers (among other things) to a motion of an object. But it is difficult, even fruitless, to attempt to specify exactly what motions are indicated. Compare *He goes home. John goes with Mary.* and *The watch goes.* Indeed, it may be used of a quite immobile subject as in *This road goes to Weston.* These variations of reference to the outside world can in part be accounted for by the assumption that a speaker of English has learned to structure content in such a way as to bring these diverse elements of experience together into a single category. The meaning of *go* rests in the interrelationship between the morpheme /gow/ and the point within the content system where these things are brought together.

The content system of a language is not directly observable, so that we can only with great difficulty check any such statement as that just made. It does, however, serve this useful function: It should be a distinct warning against relying on translations to get access to meanings. If the structure of content imposes a filter between the expression system and human experience, translation must impose two such. Translation can only be accurate where the content structures of the two languages coincide. Such places are too infrequent to be depended upon. Where translation must be used (and there are many such instances in practical language work) the user must be constantly alert against its pitfalls.

With some morphemes, meaning in the sense of reference to human experience outside language is wholly or largely lacking. Consider *to* in *I want to go.* The elements *I, want,* and *go* are referable, through the intermediary of English content structure, to aspects of human experience. But it is impossible to find a specific factor in the situation which can be considered as the "meaning" of *to*. Nevertheless, *to* does have a function, since without it **I want go.* means nothing. (The symbol * is used to indicate that a form cited is either unattested or known to be impossible.) *To* merely fulfills a requirement of English structure, in that *want* cannot be followed by *go* without *to*. Such a function cannot be included within the traditional meaning of "meaning," but in the sense in which we are using it (the interrelationship between expression and content), "meaning"—with a little stretching, perhaps—can comprehend it.

The meaning of *cat* might be explained (partially, to be sure) to a non-English speaking person by pointing out the animal to which it refers. It would not be possible to explain *to* in this way. Instead, it would be necessary to cite a number of cases of its use, and thereby point out the contexts in which it occurs regularly, those in which it may occur, and those in which it cannot occur (e.g., **I can to go.*). That is to say, *to* has a characteristic distribution. For the foreigner, this distribution is the most easily observable feature of such a morpheme, and hence the chief clue to its meaning.

Morphemes like *to* are not alone in having a characteristic distribution. Every morpheme has. *Cat* may occur in *I saw the* ——. but not in *I will* —— *home. Go* can occur in the second, but not in the first. The distribution of the morpheme is the sum of all the contexts in which it can occur in contrast to all those in which it cannot occur. A full understanding of any morpheme involves understanding its distribution as well as its meaning in the familiar sense. It is partly for this reason that a good dictionary always cites instances illustrative of usage. One that does not is of very restricted usefulness, or even very misleading.

Morphemes can be identified only by comparing various samples of a language. If two or more samples can be found in which there is some feature of expression which all share and some feature of content which all hold in common, then one requirement is met, and these samples may be tentatively identified as a morpheme and its meaning. Thus *boys* /bɔ́yz/, *girls* /gɔ́rlz/, *roads* /rówdz/, etc., are all alike in containing *s* /z/ and meaning "two or more." We therefore identify *s* /z/ as a morpheme meaning "plural." This is not actually sufficient. In addition there must be some contrast between samples with similar meaning and content, some of which have the tentative morpheme and some of which do not. Comparison of *boy* /bɔ́y/ will serve to confirm the example we have just discussed. That such a condition is necessary is shown by the following words: *bug* /bɔ́g/, *bee* /bíy/, *beetle* /bíytil/, *butterfly* /bɔ́təflày/. It seems ridiculous to suggest that since these all include /b/ and all mean some kind of insect, /b/ must be a morpheme. But this is only because, as native speakers, we know that /əg/, /iy/, /iytil/, and /ətərflay/ do not exist as morphemes that can be associated with these words. Finally, it is necessary to ascertain that what we have isolated are actually single morphemes rather than combinations.

When a person is dealing with his own native language, much of this seems superfluous. This is simply because such comparisons have been made repeatedly and subconsciously, if not consciously, in the past. We can identify English morphemes without detailed comparison because we have already identified most of them. That this is true, even of young children, can be seen from a common type of mistake. The child hears and learns to associate *show* /šów/ with *showed* /šówd/, *tow* /tów/ with *towed* /tówd/, etc. Then he assumes *go* /gów/ must be associated in the same way with /gówd/. He is, of course, wrong in detail, but right in principle, and has obviously made a morphemic analysis. He must merely learn the limits within which the pattern he has discovered is valid.

Certain constructions composed of morphemes have a rigidly fixed order. For example *re-con-vene* (the hyphens merely separate the morphemes) is a familiar English word. But *con-re-vene or *re-vene-con are not. They are not only unfamiliar in sound and appearance, but also are actually meaningless to a native speaker. The meaning of a word depends not only upon the morphemes that are present but also on the order of their occurrence.

Other constructions allow some, but only partial, freedom of order. *Then I went.* and *I went then.* are both possible and have at most only slight difference of meaning. But *Went then I.* is unintelligible because it departs from established English structure. In general, the more intimate constructions, like words, have the most rigidly fixed order, and the less closely knit constructions, like sentences, allow more freedom. But even longer sequences have some definite restrictions on order, sometimes of a subtle sort. For example, *John came. He went away.* might imply that John did both. But *He came. John went away.* certainly could not have that meaning. A specific reference to a person must precede a pronoun reference to the same person, unless some special device is used. This is a peculiarity of English structure, not of logic, nor of the general nature of speech, since some other languages have quite different rules.

The fixed order of morphemes in certain constructions, and the definable degree of freedom, are basic to language. They are expressions of the systematic structure which is the real essence of speech. It is the business of linguistic science to describe these principles of arrangement in the most comprehensive and concise way possible. Such a description is the grammar of the language. The term is in poor repute with some, largely because of lack of precision in its use, and because it has frequently served as a label for legislation as to how a language should be used, rather than as a description of how it actually is used. These implications are not, of course, inherent in the term, but it is necessary to take care to avoid them. As used in this book, grammar will comprehend two convenient, but not precisely delimitable, subdivisions: morphology, the description of the more intimate combinations of morphemes, roughly what are familiarly called "words"; and syntax, the description of larger combinations involving as basic units the combinations described under the morphology of the language. Some linguists use the term morphology to cover both subdivisions, in which case it is equivalent to grammar as used here.

The grammar of a given language cannot conveniently be stated in terms of the arrangement of specific morphemes, because the total number of morphemes in any language is far too large to permit this. However, it is always found that the morphemes can be grouped into certain classes, each with a characteristic distribution. The structure of utterances in the language can then be stated in terms of these classes of morphemes. In this way the material which must be described is reduced to manageable proportions.

For example, *walk, talk, follow, call,* etc., form an extensive class of morphemes. So likewise *s* (marking the third person singular), *ed* and *ing* form a smaller class. The latter can occur only immediately following one of the former (or some equivalent construction). The members of the first group can be found immediately preceding one of the second group, or they may be found alone. That is, *walks, walked, walking,* and *walk* all occur. But in **swalk* or **ingwalk* the order is wrong and the forms are accordingly impossible. **Walkeding* is unintelligible because *ing* cannot follow *ed*. **Shelfed* is not found because *shelf* belongs to another class which never precedes *ed*. All such facts, and many more like them, can be comprehended in a relatively few simple statements about the classes of morphemes. The complete listing of all possible and impossible sequences, on the other hand, even within a closely restricted sample of English, would be cumbersome and rapidly becomes utterly impossible as the number of morphemes treated increases.

14 | Three Models for the Description of Language
NOAM CHOMSKY

1. INTRODUCTION

There are two central problems in the descriptive study of language. One primary concern of the linguist is to discover simple and "revealing" grammars for natural languages. At the same time, by studying the properties of such successful grammars and clarifying the basic conceptions that underlie them, he hopes to arrive at a general theory of linguistic structure. We shall examine certain features of these related inquiries.

Reprinted with permission of The Institute of Electrical Engineers and the author. From *I.R.E. Transactions on Information Theory,* Vol. IT–2:113–124 (1956). A later, expanded, and more technical development of the analysis that is here presented in a simplified form appears in Noam Chomsky and George A. Miller, "Introduction to the Formal Analysis of Natural Languages"; Noam Chomsky, "Formal Properties of Grammar"; and George A. Miller and Noam Chomsky, "Finitary Models of Language Users," all in *Handbook of Mathematical Psychology,* Volume II, edited by R. Duncan Luce, Robert R. Busch, and Eugene Galanter. John Wiley & Sons, Inc., New York (1963).

The grammar of a language can be viewed as a theory of the structure of this language. Any scientific theory is based on a certain finite set of observations and, by establishing general laws stated in terms of certain hypothetical constructs, it attempts to account for these observations, to show how they are interrelated, and to predict an indefinite number of new phenomena. A mathematical theory has the additional property that predictions follow rigorously from the body of theory. Similarly, a grammar is based on a finite number of observed sentences (the linguist's corpus) and it "projects" this set to an infinite set of grammatical sentences by establishing general "laws" (grammatical rules) framed in terms of such hypothetical constructs as the particular phonemes, words, phrases, and so on, of the language under analysis. A properly formulated grammar should determine unambiguously the set of grammatical sentences.

General linguistic theory can be viewed as a metatheory which is concerned with the problem of how to choose such a grammar in the case of each particular language on the basis of a finite corpus of sentences. In particular, it will consider and attempt to explicate the relation between the set of grammatical sentences and the set of observed sentences. In other words, linguistic theory attempts to explain the ability of a speaker to produce and understand new sentences, and to reject as ungrammatical other new sequences, on the basis of his limited linguistic experience.

Suppose that for many languages there are certain clear cases of grammatical sentences and certain clear cases of ungrammatical sequences, e.g., (1) and (2), respectively, in English.

(1) John ate a sandwich.
(2) Sandwich a ate John.

In this case, we can test the adequacy of a proposed linguistic theory by determining, for each language, whether or not the clear cases are handled properly by the grammars constructed in accordance with this theory. For example, if a large corpus of English does not happen to contain either (1) or (2), we ask whether the grammar that is determined for this corpus will project the corpus to include (1) and exclude (2). Even though such clear cases may provide only a weak test of adequacy for the grammar of a given language taken in isolation, they provide a very strong test for any general linguistic theory and for the set of grammars to which it leads, since we insist that in the case of each language the clear cases be handled properly in a fixed and predetermined manner. We can take certain steps towards the construction of an operational characterization of "grammatical sentence" that will provide us with the clear cases required to set the task of linguistics significantly. Observe, for example, that (1) will be read by an English speaker with the normal intonation of a sentence of the corpus, while (2) will be read with a falling intonation on each word, as will any sequence of unrelated words. Other distinguishing criteria of the same sort can be described.

Before we can hope to provide a satisfactory account of the general relation between observed sentences and grammatical sentences, we must learn a great deal more about the formal properties of each of these sets. This paper is concerned with the formal structure of the set of grammatical sentences. We shall limit ourselves to English, and shall assume intuitive knowledge of English sentences and nonsentences. We then ask what sort of linguistic theory is required as a basis for an English grammar that will describe the set of English sentences in an interesting and satisfactory manner.

The first step in the linguistic analysis of a language is to provide a finite system of representation for its sentences. We shall assume that this step has been carried out, and we shall deal with languages only in phonemic or alphabetic transcription. By a *language* then, we shall mean a set (finite or infinite) of sentences, each of finite length, all constructed from a finite alphabet of symbols. If A is an alphabet, we shall say that anything formed by concatenating the symbols of A is a *string* in A. By a *grammar* of the language L we mean a device of some sort that produces all of the strings that are sentences of L and only these.

No matter how we ultimately decide to construct linguistic theory, we shall surely require that the grammar of any language must be finite. It follows that only a countable set of grammars is made available by any linguistic theory; hence that uncountably many languages, in our general sense, are literally not describable in terms of the conception of linguistic structure provided by any particular theory. Given a proposed theory of linguistic structure, then, it is always appropriate to ask the following question:

(3) Are there interesting languages that are simply outside the range of description of the proposed type?

In particular, we shall ask whether English is such a language. If it is, then the proposed conception of linguistic structure must be judged inadequate. If the answer to (3) is negative, we go on to ask such questions as the following:

(4) Can we construct reasonably simple grammars for all interesting languages?

(5) Are such grammars "revealing" in the sense that the syntactic structure that they exhibit can support semantic analysis, can provide insight into the use and understanding of language, etc.?

We shall first examine various conceptions of linguistic structure in terms of the possibility and complexity of description (questions (3), (4)). Then, in § 6, we shall briefly consider the same theories in terms of (5), and shall see that we are independently led to the same conclusions as to relative adequacy for the purposes of linguistics.

2. FINITE STATE MARKOV PROCESSES

2.1 The most elementary grammars which, with a finite amount of apparatus, will generate an infinite number of sentences, are those based on a familiar conception of language as a particularly simple type of information source, namely, a finite-state Markov process.

We say that a language L is a *finite-state language* if L is the set of sentences generated by some finite-state grammar G.

2.2. Suppose that we take the set A of transition symbols to be the set of English phonemes. We can attempt to construct a finite state grammar G which will generate every string of English phonemes which is a grammatical sentence of English, and only such strings. It is immediately evident that the task of constructing a finite-state grammar for English can be considerably simplified if we take A as the set of English morphemes or words, and construct G so that it will generate exactly the grammatical strings of these units. We can then complete the grammar by giving a finite set of rules that give the phonemic spelling of each word or morpheme in each context in which it occurs.

2.3. Turning now to English, we find that there are infinite sets of sentences that have dependency sets with more than any fixed number of terms. For example, let $S_1, S_2, \ldots$ be declarative sentences. Then the following are all English sentences:

(6) (i) If S_1, then S_2.
     (ii) Either S_3, or S_4.
     (iii) The man who said that S_5, is arriving today.

These sentences have dependencies between "if"-"then," "either"-"or," "man"-"is." But we can choose S_1, S_3, S_5 which appear between the interdependent words, as (6i), (6ii), or (6iii) themselves. Proceeding to construct sentences in this way we arrive at subparts of English. Consequently, English is not a finite-state language, and we are forced to reject the theory of language under discussion as failing condition (3).

2.4. Although we have found that no finite-state Markov process that produces sentences from left to right can serve as an English grammar, we might inquire into the possibility of constructing a sequence of such devices that, in some nontrivial way, come closer and closer to matching the output of a satisfactory English grammar. Suppose, for example, that for fixed n we construct a finite-state grammar in the following manner: one state of the grammar is associated with each sequence of English words of length n and the probability that the word X will be produced when the system is in the state S_i is equal to the conditional probability of X, given the sequence of n words which defines S_i. The output of such grammar is customarily called an n + 1st order approximation to English. Evidently, as n increases, the output of such grammars will come to look more and more like English, since longer and longer sequences have a high probability of being taken directly from the sample of English in which the probabilities were determined. This fact has occasionally led to the suggestion that a theory of linguistic structure might be fashioned on such a model.

Whatever the other interest of statistical approximation in this sense may be, it is clear that it can shed no light on the problems of grammar. There is no general relation between the frequency of a string (or its component parts) and its grammaticalness. We can see this most clearly by considering such strings as

(7) colorless green ideas sleep furiously

which is a grammatical sentence, even though it is fair to assume that no pair of its words may ever have occurred together in the past. Notice that a speaker of English will read (7) with the ordinary intonation pattern of an English sentence, while he will read the equally unfamiliar string

(8) furiously sleep ideas green colorless

with a falling intonation on each word, as in the case of any ungrammatical string. Thus (7) differs from (8) exactly as (1) differs from (2); our tentative operational criterion for grammaticalness supports our intuitive feeling that (7) is a grammatical sentence and that (8) is not. We might state the problem of grammar, in part, as that of explaining and reconstructing the ability of an English speaker to recognize (1), (7), etc., as grammatical, while rejecting (2), (8), etc. But no order of approximation model can distinguish (7) from (8) (or an indefinite number of similar pairs). As n increases, an nth order approximation to English will exclude (as more and more improbable) an ever-increasing number of grammatical sentences, while it still contains vast numbers of completely un-grammatical strings. We are forced to conclude that there is apparently no significant approach to the problems of grammar in this direction.

In § 2.4 we argued that there is no significant correlation between order of approximation and grammaticalness. If we order the strings of a given length in terms of order of approximation to English, we shall find both grammatical and ungrammatical strings scattered throughout the list, from top to bottom. Hence the notion of statistical approximation appears to be irrelevant to grammar. In § 2.3 we pointed out that a much broader class of processes, namely, all finite-state Markov processes that produce transition symbols, does not include an English grammar. That is, if we construct a finite-state grammar that produces only English sentences, we know that it will fail to produce an infinite number of these sentences; in particular, it will fail to produce an infinite number of true sentences, false sentences, reasonable questions that could be intelligibly asked, and the like. Below, we shall investigate a still broader class of processes that might provide us with an English grammar.

3. PHRASE STRUCTURE

3.1   Customarily, syntactic description is given in terms of what is called "immediate constituent analysis." In description of this sort the words of a sentence are grouped into phrases, these are grouped into smaller con-stituent phrases and so on, until the ultimate constituents (generally mor-phemes) are reached. These phrases are then classified as noun phrases (NP), verb phrases (VP), etc. For example, the sentence (9) might be analyzed as in the accompanying diagram.

(9)

the man	took	the book
NP	Verb	NP
	VP	
Sentence		

Evidently, description of sentences in such terms permits considerable simplification over the word-by-word model, since the composition of a complex class of expressions such as NP can be stated just once in the grammar, and this class can be used as a building block at various points in the construction of sentences. We now ask what form of grammar cor-responds to this conception of linguistic structure.

3.2   We say that L is a *derivable language* if L is the set of strings that are derivable from some [Σ,F] grammar, and we say that L is a *terminal language* if it is the set of terminal strings from some system [Σ,F].

3.3   As a simple example consider the following small part of English grammar:

(10) Σ: #^Sentence^#
      F: Sentence → NP^VP
              VP → Verb^NP
              NP → the^man, the^book
              Verb → took

Among the derivations from (10) we have, in particular:

(11) D_1: #^Sentence^#
            #^NP^VP^#
            #^NP^Verb^NP^#
            #^the^man^Verb^NP^#
            #^the^man^Verb^the^book^#
            #^the^man^took^the^book^#

      D_2: #^Sentence^#
            #^NP^VP^#
            #^the^man^VP^#
            #^the^man^Verb^NP^#
            #^the^man^took^NP^#
            #^the^man^took^the^book^#

These derivations are evidently equivalent; they differ only in the order in which the rules are applied. We can represent this equivalence graphically by constructing diagrams that correspond, in an obvious way, to derivations. Both D_1 and D_2 reduce to the diagram:

(12)

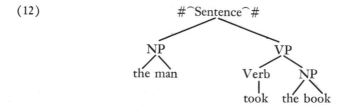

The diagram (12) gives the phrase structure of the terminal sentence "the man took the book," just as in (9). In general, given a derivation D of a string S, we say that a substring s of S is an X if in the diagram corresponding to D, s is traceable back to a single node, and this node is labelled X. Thus given D_1 or D_2, corresponding to (12), we say that "the^man" is an

NP, "took^the^book" is a VP, "the^book" is an NP, "the^man^took^the^book" is a Sentence. "man^took," however, is not a phrase of this string at all, since it is not traceable back to any node.

When we attempt to construct the simplest possible $[\Sigma,\mathrm{F}]$ grammar for English we find that certain sentences automatically receive non-equivalent derivations. Along with (10), the grammar of English will certainly have to contain such rules as

(13) Verb → are^flying
     Verb → are
     NP → they
     NP → planes
     NP → flying^planes

in order to account for such sentences as "they are flying—a plane" (NP–Verb–NP), "(flying) planes—are—noisy" (NP–Verb–Adjective), etc. But this set of rules provides us with two non-equivalent derivations of the sentence "they are flying planes," reducing to the diagrams:

(14)

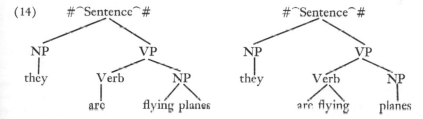

Hence this sentence will have two phrase structures assigned to it; it can be analyzed as "they—are—flying planes" or "they—are flying—planes." And in fact, this sentence is ambiguous in just this way; we can understand it as meaning that "those specks on the horizon—are—flying planes" or "those pilots—are flying—planes." When the simplest grammar automatically provides nonequivalent derivations for some sentence, we say that we have a case of *constructional homonymity*, and we can suggest this formal property as an explanation for the semantic ambiguity of the sentence in question. In §1 we posed the requirement that grammars offer insight into the use and understanding of language. One way to test the adequacy of a grammar is by determining whether or not the cases of constructional homonymity are actually cases of semantic ambiguity, as in (14).

4. INADEQUACIES OF PHRASE-STRUCTURE GRAMMAR

4.1   In the first paragraph of §2.2 we intended that a grammar will contain a set of rules (called morphophonemic rules) which convert strings of morphemes into strings of phonemes. In the morphophonemics of English, we shall have such rules as the following (we use conventional, rather than phonemic orthography):

(15) have⌢past → had
       be⌢en → been
       take⌢ing → taking
       will⌢past → would
       can⌢past → could
       M⌢present → M
       walk⌢past → walked
       take⌢past → took
       etc.

This very simple analysis, however, goes beyond the bounds of [Σ,F] grammars in several respects.

4.2.   The fact that this simple analysis of the verb phrase as a sequence of independently chosen units goes beyond the bounds of [Σ,F] grammars, suggests that such grammars are too limited to give a true picture of linguistic structure. Further study of the verb phrase lends additional support to this conclusion. If we choose an intransitive verb (e.g., "come," "occur," etc.), we cannot select be⌢en as an auxiliary. We cannot have such phrases as "John has been come," "John is occurred," and the like. Furthermore, the element be⌢en cannot be chosen independently of the context of the phrase "Verb." If we have the element "Verb" in the context "the man—the food," we can have "the man is eating the food," "the man would have been eating the food," etc., but not "the man is eaten the food," "the man would have been eaten the food," etc. On the other hand, if the context of the phrase "Verb" is, e.g., "the food—by the man," we are *required* to select be⌢en. We can have "the food is eaten by the man," but not "the food is eating by the man," etc.

There is, in fact, a very simple way to incorporate sentences with be⌢en (i.e., passives) into the grammar. Notice that for every active sentence such as "the man ate the food" we have a corresponding passive "the food was eaten by the man" and conversely. Suppose then that we add to the grammar the following rule:

(16) If S is a sentence of the form NP₁-Auxiliary-V-NP₂, then the corresponding string of the form NP₂-Auxiliary⌢be⌢en-V-by⌢NP₁ is also a sentence.

For example, if "the man—past—eat the food" (NP₁-Auxiliary-V-NP₂) is a sentence, then "the food—past be en—eat—by the man" (NP₂-Auxiliary⌢be⌢en-V-by⌢NP₁) is also a sentence.

The advantages of this analysis of passives are unmistakable. The fact that be⌢en can occur only with transitive verbs, that it is excluded in the context "the man—the food" and that it is required in the context "the food—by the man," is now, in each case, an automatic consequence of the analysis we have just given.

A rule of the form (16), however, is well beyond the limits of phrase-structure grammars. It rearranges the elements of the string to which it applies, and it requires considerable information about the constituent structure of this string. When we carry the detailed study of English syntax further, we find that there are many other cases in which the grammar can be simplified if the [Σ,F] system is supplemented by rules of the same general form as (16). Let us call each such rule a *grammatical transformation*. As our third model for the description of linguistic structure, we now consider briefly the formal properties of a transformational grammar that can be adjoined to the [Σ,F] grammar of phrase structure.

5. TRANSFORMATIONAL GRAMMAR

5.1. Each grammatical transformation T will essentially be a rule that converts every sentence with a given constituent structure into a new sentence with derived constituent structure. The transform and its derived structure must be related in a fixed and constant way to the structure of the transformed string, for each T. We can characterize T by stating, in structural terms, the domain of strings to which it applies and the change that it effects on any such string.

Let us suppose in the following discussion that we have a [Σ,F] grammar with a vocabulary V_P and a terminal vocabulary $V_T \subset V_P$, as in §3.2.

In §3.3 we showed that a [Σ,F] grammar permits the derivation of terminal strings, and we pointed out that in general a given terminal string will have several equivalent derivations. Two derivations were said to be equivalent if they reduce to the same diagram of the form (12), etc. Suppose that D_1 , . . . , D_n constitute a maximal set of equivalent derivations of a terminal string S. Then we define a *phrase marker* of S as the set of strings that occur as lines in the derivations D_1 , . . . , D_n. A string will have more than one phrase marker if and only if it has nonequivalent derivations (cf. (12)).

5.2. In this way, we can describe in structural terms the set of strings (with phrase markers) to which any transformation applies.

5.3. In §3.4 we noted that it is advantageous to order the rules of phrase structure into a sequence, and to distinguish obligatory from optional rules. The same is true of the transformational part of the grammar. In § 4 we discussed the transformation which converts a sequence affix-verb into the sequence verb-affix, and the passive transformation. The passive transformation, however, may or may not be applied; either way we have a sentence. The passive is thus an optional transformation. This distinction between optional and obligatory transformations leads us to distinguish between two classes of sentences of the language. We have, on the one hand, a *kernel* of basic sentences that are derived from the terminal strings of the phrase-structure grammar by application of only obligatory transformations. We then have a set of derived sentences that are generated by applying optional transformations to the strings underlying kernel sentences.

When we actually carry out a detailed study of English structure, we find that the grammar can be greatly simplified if we limit the kernel to a very small set of simple, active, declarative sentences (in fact, probably a finite set) such as "the man ate the food," etc. We then derive questions, passives, sentences with conjunction, sentences with compound noun phrases (e.g., "proving that theorem was difficult," with the NP "proving that theorem"), etc., by transformations. Since the result of a transformation is a sentence with derived constituent structure, transformations can be compounded, and we can form questions from passives (e.g., "was the food eaten by the man"), etc. The actual sentences of real life are usually not kernel sentences, but rather complicated transforms of these. We find, however, that the transformations are, by and large, meaning-preserving, so that we can view the kernel sentences underlying a given sentence as being, in some sense, the elementary "content elements" in terms of which the actual transform is "understood."

6. EXPLANATORY POWER OF LINGUISTIC THEORIES

We have thus far considered the relative adequacy of theories of linguistic structure only in terms of such essentially formal criteria as simplicity. In §1 we suggested that there are other relevant considerations of adequacy for such theories. We can ask whether or not the syntactic structure revealed by these theories provides insight into the use and understanding of language. We can barely touch on this problem here, but even this brief discussion will suggest that this criterion provides the same order of relative adequacy for the three models we have considered.

If the grammar of a language is to provide insight into the way the language is understood, it must be true, in particular, that if a sentence is ambiguous (understood in more than one way), then this sentence is provided with alternative analyses by the grammar. In other words, if a certain sentence S is ambiguous, we can test the adequacy of a given linguistic theory by asking whether or not the simplest grammar constructible in terms of this theory for the language in question automatically provides distinct ways of generating the sentence S. It is instructive to compare the Markov process, phrase-structure, and transformational models in the light of this test.

In §3.3 we pointed out that the simplest $[\Sigma,\text{F}]$ grammar for English happens to provide nonequivalent derivations for the sentence "they are flying planes," which is, in fact, ambiguous. This reasoning does not appear to carry over for finite-state grammars, however. That is, there is no obvious motivation for assigning two different paths to this ambiguous sentence in any finite-state grammar that might be proposed for a part of English. Such examples of constructional homonymity (there are many others) constitute independent evidence for the superiority of the phrase-structure model over finite-state grammars.

Further investigation of English brings to light examples that are not easily explained in terms of phrase structure. Consider the phrase

(17) the shooting of the hunters.

We can understand this phrase with "hunters" as the subject, analogously to (18), or as the object, analogously to (19).

(18) the growling of lions
(19) the raising of flowers.

Phrases (18) and (19), however, are not similarly ambiguous. Yet in terms of phrase structure, each of these phrases is represented as: the—V⌒ing—of⌒NP.

Careful analysis of English shows that we can simplify the grammar if we strike the phrases (17)–(19) out of the kernel and reintroduce them transformationally by a transformation T_1 that carries such sentences as "lions growl" into (18), and a transformation T_2 that carries such sentences as "they raise flowers" into (19). T_1 and T_2 will be similar to the nominalizing transformation, when they are correctly constructed. But both "hunters shoot" and "they shoot the hunters" are kernel sentences; and application of T_1 to the former and T_2 to the latter yields the result (17). Hence (17) has two distinct transformational origins. It is a case of constructional homonymity on the transformational level. The ambiguity of the grammatical relation in (17) is a consequence of the fact that the relation of "shoot" to "hunters" differs in the two underlying kernel sentences. We do not have this ambiguity in the case of (18), (19), since neither "they growl lions" nor "flowers raise" is a grammatical kernel sentence.

There are many other examples of the same general kind and to my mind, they provide quite convincing evidence not only for the greater adequacy of the transformational conception of linguistic structure, but also for the view that transformational analysis enables us to reduce partially the problem of explaining how we understand a sentence to that of explaining how we understand a kernel sentence.

In summary, then, we picture a language as having a small, possibly finite kernel of basic sentences with phrase structure in the sense of § 3, along with a set of transformations which can be applied to kernel sentences or to earlier transforms to produce new and more complicated sentences from elementary components. We have seen certain indications that this approach may enable us to reduce the immense complexity of actual language to manageable proportions and, in addition, that it may provide considerable insight into the actual use and understanding of language.

15 | Etic and Emic Standpoints for the Description of Behavior
KENNETH L. PIKE

It proves convenient—though partially arbitrary—to describe behavior from two different standpoints, which lead to results which shade into one another. The etic viewpoint studies behavior as from outside of a particular system, and as an essential initial approach to an alien system. The emic viewpoint results from studying behavior as from inside the system. (I coined the words etic and emic from the words phonetic and phonemic, following the conventional linguistic usage of these latter terms. The short terms are used in an analogous manner, but for more general purposes.)

CHARACTERISTICS OF THE TWO STANDPOINTS

The principal differences between the etic and emic approaches to language and culture can be summarized as follows:

Reprinted with permission of the publisher and author. From *Language in Relation to a Unified Theory of the Structure of Human Behavior*, Chapter 2. N. V. Uitgeverij Mouton en Co., The Hague (1966).

CROSS-CULTURAL VERSUS SPECIFIC. The etic approach treats all cultures or languages—or a selected group of them—at one time. It might well be called "comparative" in the anthropological sense were it not for the fact that the phrase "comparative linguistics" has a quite different usage already current in linguistic circles, in reference to comparing related languages with a view to reconstructing parent forms. The emic approach is, on the contrary, culturally specific, applied to one language or culture at a time.

UNITS AVAILABLE IN ADVANCE VERSUS DETERMINED DURING ANALYSIS. Etic units and classifications, based on prior broad sampling or surveys (and studied in training courses) may be available before one begins the analysis of a further particular language or culture. Regardless of how much training one has however, emic units of a language must be determined during the analysis of that language; they must be discovered, not predicted—even though the range of kinds of components of language has restrictions placed upon it by the physiology of the human organism, and these restrictions are to some degree reflected in the events of the observed range of language phenomena.

CREATION VERSUS DISCOVERY OF A SYSTEM. The etic organization of a world-wide cross-cultural scheme may be created by the analyst. The emic structure of a particular system must, I hold, be discovered. (But here I am assuming a philosophy of science which grants that in the universe some structures occur other than in the mind of the analyst himself. If one adopts a view that no structure of language or culture is present in the universe, except as a theoretical construct created by the analyst, then the paragraph must be restated in a different way, to preserve its usefulness in such a context. Specifically, the linguist who denies structure to a naïve sentence or to a sonnet must settle for having his own statements, descriptions, or rules about these phenomena as also being without a publically available structure or ordering. Linguistic statement comprises a subvariety of language utterance, and hence can have no structure if language has no structure.)

EXTERNAL VERSUS INTERNAL VIEW. Descriptions or analyses from the etic standpoint are "alien" in view, with criteria external to the system. Emic descriptions provide an internal view, with criteria chosen from within the system. They represent to us the view of one familiar with the system and who knows how to function within it himself.

EXTERNAL VERSUS INTERNAL PLAN. An etic system may be set up by criteria or "logical" plan whose relevance is external to the system being studied. The discovery or setting up of the emic system requires the inclusion of criteria relevant to the internal functioning of the system itself.

ABSOLUTE VERSUS RELATIVE CRITERIA. The etic criteria may often be considered absolute, or measurable directly. Emic criteria are relative to the internal characteristics of the system, and can be usefully described or measured relative to each other.

NON-INTEGRATION VERSUS INTEGRATION. The etic view does not require that every unit be viewed as part of a larger setting. The emic view, however, insists that every unit be seen as somehow distributed and functioning within a larger structural unit or setting, in a hierarchy of units and hierarchy of settings as units.

SAMENESS AND DIFFERENCE AS MEASURED VERSUS SYSTEMIC. Two units are different etically when instrumental measurements can show them to be so. Units are different emically only when they elicit different responses from people acting within the system.

PARTIAL VERSUS TOTAL DATA. Etic data are obtainable early in analysis with partial information. In principle, on the contrary, emic criteria require a knowledge of the total system to which they are relative and from which they ultimately draw their significance.

PRELIMINARY VERSUS FINAL PRESENTATION. Hence, etic data provide access into the system—the starting point of analysis. They give tentative results, tentative units. The final analysis or presentation, however, would be in emic units. In the total analysis, the initial etic description gradually is refined, and is ultimately—in principle, but probably never in practice—replaced by one which is totally emic.

If, furthermore, it is desired to present the emic—structural—units not only as algebraic points relative to a system, but also as elements physically described, the emic notation must be supplemented by etic, physical description.

The penalty for ignoring the etic-emic distinction, and of attempting to utilize (without knowing it) an etic description when an emic one is needed, is best stated in the words of Sapir, who anticipated this position years ago:

It is impossible to say what an individual is doing unless we have tacitly accepted the essentially arbitrary modes of interpretation that social tradition is constantly suggesting to us from the very moment of our birth. Let anyone who doubts this try the experiment of making a painstaking report [i.e., an etic one] of the actions of a group of natives engaged in some activity, say religious, to which he has not the cultural key [i.e., a knowledge of the emic system]. If he is a skillful writer, he may succeed in giving a picturesque account of what he sees and hears, or thinks he sees and hears, but the chances of his being able to give a relation of what happens, in terms that would be intelligible and acceptable to the natives themselves, are practically nil. He will be guilty of all manner of distortion; his emphasis will be constantly askew. He will find interesting what the natives take for granted as a casual kind of behavior worthy of no particular comment, and he will utterly fail to observe the crucial turning points in the course of action that give formal significance to the whole in the minds of those who do possess the key to its understanding.

An illustration remote from human behavior may be helpful: in an emic approach, the analyst might describe the structural functioning of a particular car as a whole, and might include charts showing the parts of the whole car as they function in relation one to another; in an etic approach he might describe the elements one at a time as they are found in a stock room, where bolts, screws, rims, fenders and complex parts, such as generators and motors from various models and makes of cars, have been systematically "filed" according to general criteria.

PHYSICAL NATURE, RESPONSE, AND DISTRIBUTION

Certain physical events must be kept in mind for an emic analysis of verbal materials. They include at least two types, neither of which, in the view presented here, can be ignored at any level of language structure without ultimate loss of some relevant data, or distortion of the system being studied. These two types of events are (a) linguistic—i.e., verbal, and (b) extralinguistic—i.e., nonverbal. Every emic unit of language behavior must be studied in reference to its distribution—distribution in reference to verbal behavior, and distribution in reference to nonverbal cultural behavior. Within the study of the distribution of language units in nonverbal contexts is included the consideration of the nonverbal responses of individuals to speech addressed to them. Just as the verbal replies of a speaker help one determine meanings of elements of communication, so the nonverbal ones do likewise. To attempt to analyze or describe language without reference to its function in eliciting responses —verbal and nonverbal—is to ignore one of the crucial kinds of evidence which is essential if the emic structure of language is to be determined, whether one is dealing with the larger units of that structure, such as the sentence, or smaller ones, such as some of the emic units of the sound system.

This analytical dependence can be in part ignored at the presentation of the material after the language structure has been analyzed. But this theory maintains that in the analytical process there is tacit or explicit reference to cultural distribution, nonverbal as well as verbal. If one is working through a second language, by interpretation, it is easy to succumb to the illusion that there is no such dependence, since one may appear to be using "words," only, to get data and to determine its function and structure. With a monolingual approach, the direct dependence upon nonverbal contexts is more easily seen. In either case, once the analyst notes his ultimate reliance upon cultural distribution of nonverbal as well as verbal types, he is ready to appreciate, in further detail, the insistence of a unified theory that a theory of language is needed which is not discontinuous with a theory of other phases of human activity.

VALUE OF STANDPOINTS

Both etic and emic approaches are of great value for special phases of behavioral analysis. The etic approach to behavior is of especial value, first, in giving to a beginning student a broad training as to the kinds of behavior occurring around the world, so that he may be the more prepared to recognize quickly the different kinds of events observed, and to help him see slight differences between similar events. Second, during this process he may obtain a technique and symbolism (say a phonetic alphabet) for recording the events of a culture. Third, even the specialist, coming from one culture to a sharply different one, has no other way to begin its analysis than by starting with a rough, tentative (and inaccurate) etic description of it. No matter how skilful an emicist he may be, he can complete his emic description only after the analysis is complete—not before—and that analysis must be begun by recording data etically in terms of his prior experience (systematic training, or unclassified knowledge gained in terms of his own culture). Fourth, in studies of the geographical occurrence or diffusion of single kinds of activity, or of a pre-selected list of activities within an area, the analyst may not choose (because of financial limitations, pressure of time, and so on), to make a complete emic study of each local culture or dialect; under such circumstances an etic comparison may be used—or, better, a widespread etic sampling of many local areas with additional intensive emic studies of a few strategically located areas.

The value of emic study is, first, that it leads to an understanding of the way in which a language or culture is constructed, not as a series of miscellaneous parts, but as a working whole. Second, it helps one to appreciate not only the culture or language as an ordered whole, but it helps one to understand the individual actors in such a life drama—their attitudes, motives, interests, responses, conflicts, and personality development. In addition, it provides the only basis upon which a predictive science of behavior can be expected to make some of its greatest progress, since even statistical predictive studies will in many instances ultimately prove invalid, except as they reflect samplings and classifications which are homogeneous—but homogeneity in behavior must for many of these purposes be emically defined.

CAUTION—NOT A DICHOTOMY

A caution needs to be given at this point: in many instances, an etic and an emic description may appear to be almost alike—so much so, in fact, that the unwary reader may say that there is "no difference," say, between the phonetic and phonemic descriptions of the system of sounds of a language, or that the difference is so slight as not to warrant the extra effort an emic description requires.

To be sure, much of the data is the same, and the general content looks much alike. Yet this is also true of the two separate pictures which go into a stereoscopic viewer; an untrained person usually sees them as identical, but the three-dimensional effect evoked by seeing simultaneously through the stereoscope the two views of the same scene—taken at the same time, under the same lighting conditions, but with viewpoints scant inches apart —makes this added perception startling indeed. And so it can be with the two viewpoints of etics and emics. Through the etic "lens" the analyst views the data in tacit reference to a perspective oriented to all comparable events (whether sounds, ceremonies, activities), of all peoples, of all parts of the earth; through the other lens, the emic one, he views the same events, at the same time, in the same context, in reference to a perspective oriented to the particular function of those particular events in that particular culture, as it and it alone is structured. The result is a kind of "tri-dimensional understanding" of human behavior instead of a "flat" etic one.

It must be further emphasized that etic and emic data do not constitute a rigid dichotomy of bits of data, but often present the same data from two points of view. Specifically, for example, the emic units of a language, once discovered by emic procedures, may be listed for comparative purposes with the similar emic units from other languages so studied. The moment that this has been done, however, the emic units have changed into etic units, since they are divorced from the context of the structure of the language from which they have come, and are viewed as generalized instances of abstract stereotypes, rather than as living parts of an actual sequence of behavior events within a particular culture. Similarly, if a person working in one dialect moves to a very similar neighboring dialect, his first transcription is an etic one, perforce, because he is alien to that dialect, but it may actually be very close to the final emic transcription which he will produce; many of his tentative etic units will turn out to be emic units as well.

We turn, now, to illustrations of differences in outlook on particular events where a camera recording of the physical event would not be enough—but where other data must also be used.

ILLUSTRATIONS OF PURPOSIVE EMIC DIFFERENCES WITHIN A CULTURE

Within a particular culture there are many events which on the surface appear to be similar or identical, but which function very differently. This difference often consists in the different purpose of the actors. This purpose is frequently obvious to the outside observer or other participants; at other times it is obscure both to the outside observer and to the participant. When the difference of purpose is easily seen, it is detected in terms of the kind of observable larger sequence of events within which the smaller event occurs (i.e., its distribution)—and in terms of the response which it immediately receives. When the purpose is temporarily hidden from the other participants, the choice of alternate responses may be delayed until after other events have made the purposive difference clear, or a response may be given which the participants may later judge to have been inappropriate.

In the United States Senate a camera and recorder on different occasions might register two speeches which were physically similar. The first, let us say, is intended to affect the attitude of listeners, such as to convince them of the necessity of the course of action being presented. The second is discussing the same course of action, with the same words, but without any such purpose. It is a filibuster designed not to affect that irrelevant issue which happens to provide the words, but is calculated so to delay the course of business as to force the speaker's opponents to give up the attempt to pass a measure unpalatable to him. Some of the immediate reactions to a filibuster (such as inattention by the audience) may be quite different from that of the same data given as part of a different address.

A partial small-scale parallel with such an instance would be the speaking of any pair of homophones such as *pare, pair; rite, write; seal* (animal, noun), *seal* (of wax, noun), *seal* (verb). Here, too, the outward visible form may be the same, whereas the words as a whole must be considered different because of the responses which they elicit from the hearers, and the kind of verbal sequences into which they enter.

Units of size intermediate between a filibuster and single words may occur which must be similarly differentiated. Note such items as mimicry, where a child is trying to learn to speak by repeating sentences after adults; the homonymous repeated sentence is often inappropriate to normal conversation since the child may fail, for example, to change *you* to *I*, or to replace question with answer. A lie is homophonous with a parallel normal sentence, but they must be considered different emically, in spite of the identity of their internal structures. Even the immediate responses—and hence its then apparent meanings—may be the same. In order to detect the essential difference between them, the observer must be prepared to notice reactions (say, a spanking) delayed for a much longer time. In lying, therefore, we have an illustration of an emic difference, where the natives themselves cannot immediately detect that difference—or it may go permanently undetected by the hearers. Here, then, there is some temporary or permanent indeterminacy of meaning.

Irony brings us a different type of homophony which includes, usually, the intention of having at least part of the audience to so detect it; if that purpose fails, the irony will be "lost on" the receiver of it—though it may cause the amusement of onlookers. Mimicry of the lisping character of someone's speech is similar to such irony—and quite different from the mimicry of an adult by a child learning to talk. An adult in learning a foreign language may be badly inhibited from adequate mimcry by reacting to his own learning process as if it were the kind of socially inacceptable mimcry rather than the other.

Nonverbal mimicry shows a similar patterning: a child utilizes small-scale implements to *do like Daddy*, in raking the lawn, digging a hole, or fishing. With his father gone from the scene, and the mimicry purpose removed, the child may not finish raking the lawn.

On an adult scale, the working activity may be quite similar, whether the regular workers or strike breakers are performing it, but the reaction to the first is one of normal community relations, whereas reaction to the second may include violent attempts by the strikers to interrupt the work of the strike breakers. The killing of a single fly by a Western adult might be an act of cleanliness, but by a Hindu might have implications of profound religious significance, because of their beliefs concerning the possibility of the reincarnation of human souls into animal bodies. Tea drinking at 4:30 P.M. in some parts of the U.S.A. would imply a somewhat formal social gathering; in Australia it often means little more than quenching one's thirst. In meetings of the United Nations, the circumstances (i.e. distribution) and purpose of activities affect the reaction of people—to seeing one of, e.g., the participants "walk out" as a political measure to indicate disapproval (rather than to go to the toilet).

In our culture there are, furthermore, specific legal procedures which are used in an attempt to differentiate between events which are physically similar but emically different, with sharply different cultural penalties: Was the man carrying a pistol when he robbed the house? Did the driver run through a red light when he hit the man? Was the violence premeditated or the result of sudden anger? Was the author of it insane or was he deliberately cruel? Was the prisoner really trying to escape, or did the guard misunderstand, or pretend to do so, or even stage the event under orders? Nonlegal activity similarly attempts to apply criteria to determine such matters: Is this explanation the real reason, or is it just an excuse to mask laziness or irresponsibility or viciousness? Was the plate really cracked?

In nonverbal activity as in verbal activity there may be temporary ambiguities which can only be resolved by a study of a larger context. For example: Do the people of Country X know the issues which lead to their activity and choose that activity deliberately, or are they following the lead of someone else blindly or under compulsion?

Perhaps the illustration of such emic differences best known to linguistic circles is one given by Sapir. A candle-blowing *wh*, though physically similar to the *wh* of *which, why* in some dialects of English is, nevertheless, "entirely distinct" from it in the series of kinds of events to which it belongs. For both of them the lips are puckered up, and air is blown out of the mouth with a slight friction sound. In the first, the purpose is to blow out a candle, and the event is part of a series, such as "going to bed"; in the second, the sound becomes part of a word, and the word becomes part of a sentence, and the sentence becomes part of a conversation.

An emic approach would treat as significantly different the preceding pairs of events. One kind of etic approach—one which ignored meaning or purpose—might treat them as nearly identical pairs. In between these two approaches would be a different etic classification of these emic types, listing them in relation to differential purpose, meaning, or response, but not in relation to the full systems from which they were abstracted.

VARIANTS OF EMIC UNITS

Sapir says:

Every typical human action has a certain range of variation and, properly speaking, no such reaction can be understood except as a series of variants distributed about a norm or type.

In the preceding section we illustrated events which were physically same, or approximately so, but emically different. Now we show how events may be physically different but emically same.

It proves impossible for a person to repeat any movement so that it is *exactly* duplicated. Delicate measuring instruments will show some variation, a "scatter" or "spread" of slight differences when a person tries to do so. Whether it be shaking the head to signal *no*, or moving the lips, tongue, and vocal cords to say *no*, or jumping out of the way to refuse to catch a ball—none of these movement types can be repeated without deviation; minor differences are certain to appear.

There will be such minor physical variants of any unit of purposeful activity. Etically, each repetition of such a unit may be considered to be distinct, within that variety of etic study which is looking for absolute physical differences. Emically, such a scatter of variation would be irrelevant.

Often, however, the physical variation between repetitions of the same emic event is much greater than the physiological characteristics of man impose on his activity. Although, in some instances, the variation may be so small that the eye cannot see it—nor the ear hear the resultant acoustic differences, for speech—the variation in other instances may be large enough for trained alien observers to notice it very clearly and easily, even while untrained native participants do not ordinarily notice it at all, or may fail to see it or hear it even when one attempts to point it out to them. Following the last sound in the phrase, *Here is a cup*, spoken in a matter-of-fact manner, for example, the lips sometimes remain closed; at other times they open slightly, allowing a puff of breath to escape. Such pronunciations of English are etically (here, absolutely) different but emically the same.

Any other kind of activity may have comparable variants. In hopscotch, for example, it is irrelevant to the progress of the game whether a child hops high on one foot, with the other wildly swinging, or whether the hop is low, with relatively steady opposite foot; relevant—emic—factors are rather the success in reaching the next square without stepping on a line or letting both feet touch ground, and so on.

Etic, non-emic differences occur elsewhere than in sheer repetition of emically same events: the variants may be caused by inevitable, minimal changes of movement accompanying the slurring of one emic movement into a following (or preceding) movement. Every movement is so modified. The movements of the tongue in forming *s* differ etically in *missile* from what the movements can be in forming *s* in *task;* starting from a position during the pronunciation of the *i* of *missile*, the tongue glides by degrees into movements which in part constitute *s*. The border between *i* and *s* cannot, in fact, be determined. The first part of the *s* is inevitably modified by the movements which produce the last part of the *i;* similarly, in *task*, the first part of *s* is modified by the end of *a;* likewise, *s* differs before *l* and *k*. To some extent, no matter how small (even if below the threshold of perception), every sound differs etically according to the sequences of comparable movements within which it occurs.

Every movement, including nonvocal ones, is so affected. The movements of the first hop of a child playing hopscotch differ considerably from the others. The first hop starts from a standing position, whereas the middle ones may have movements slurred together from the momentum of earlier movements, and the last hop into the center must (lest the child receive a penalty) have the movements checked from going too far and throwing the child off balance.

As with repeated movements, however, so with those in sequence, the observed difference between emically same movements may be considerably greater than is necessitated by the physiological mechanisms involved. Like the repeated types, also, the etic difference may be so great as to be easily noted by an alien observer even while the native actor, reacting emically, fails to see any difference between them. I clearly remember, for example, the surprise—almost incredulity—with which I first received the information that the two *p* sounds in *paper* were not the same—that a puff of breath followed the first one, but no breath, or a weak puff only, followed the second; it was probably two years before I heard the difference easily.

These types of etic differences occur simultaneously in sequences. Thus, every repetition of *missile* by itself finds the *s* different each time, and every repetition of *past* has each *s* different. This scatter of differences in repetition is in addition to the etic differences caused by (or accompanying) the differences in environment when, say, *s* slurs from or to *i*, *l*, *a*, or *k*.

It should also be observed that the first *p* of *paper* differs not only in movement type but in movement sequence from the second. Whereas, perceptually, the second seems etically to be a "single" sound, the first may seem etically to be two—the *p* plus the puff.

The type of variant seen in sheer repetition may be called FREE; that resultant from or accompanying a slur into or from neighboring movements, CONDITIONED; that from a sequence of movements acting in some way as a single unit, COMPLEX. Free, conditioned, and complex variants occur in all general types of behavior; the analyst must be prepared to find them at any stage in the analysis.

In addition to being simple or complex, variants may also be fused, such that a single etic segment is a fused composite of two emic segments.

DIFFERENCES IN ETIC OBSERVERS

In the alien reporting of observations, the human element brings in great differences. One observer may have much more etic training than another; one may have keener hearing of pitch differences, or of intensity, duration, rhythm, or timbre; or one may have a longer memory span than the other. The one observer may fix his attention on one set of etic details through accident, or intention, or training, and hence "see" and record them; the other may not notice these details, though watching the same event. Likewise, the one observer may be interested temporarily or permanently in one component of behavior and fail to report other components.

Each observer will also have some bias in terms of the behavior events most familiar to him—those which are emic in his own activity. These he tends to take as his point of departure, as his norms, so that cultural background may affect an etic report.

Adequate etic training lessens these differences a great deal, so that individual phonetic reports of the sounds of a language tend to be similar. Nevertheless, the differences in the etic reports of different observers frequently cause confusion.

In order to refer to certain etic types we may label as an INSTRUMENTAL etic report one which records details as absolute, i.e., as accurately as some particular measuring machine is capable of recording. A THRESHOLD etic report will be one which attempts to give differentiations as fine as the physiological limits of a particular individual—or, the average of a group of such individuals—permits. A PERCEPTUAL etic report would be the report of a particular observer at a particular time, reflecting within it the variables and idiosyncrasies of individual ability, training, and momentary focus of attention.

Emic reports of a particular phase or component of behavior of a particular culture should be much more uniform than etic ones, however, since the emic procedures are specifically designed to help *any* observer report the data from an internal structured standpoint.

PART 2

Syntactics

CHAPTER V

Signals: Verbal and Nonverbal

INTRODUCTION   Communication involves the transmission of information by signals. The best known form of human communication is speech, which involves the best known kinds of human signals—the sounds that make up words. These sounds, however, carry only a small part of the information that people convey among one another in everyday interaction. The full range of human communication is based on many more signals than these phones and phonemes. At least as important are such less fully analyzed signals as tones of voice, gestures, and other nonverbal and nonvocal information carriers.

Robert E. Pittenger and Henry Lee Smith, Jr., in "A Basis for Some Contributions of Linguistics to Psychiatry" consider the segmental sounds of everyday speech, sounds like the consonants and vowels that make up words. They also show the importance of three kinds of nonverbal signals. They first analyze suprasegmentals, that is, the stresses, pitches, and junctures that form the intonation patterns of our speech. They then analyze the paralinguistic modifiers and qualifiers that we use, that is, the transmission of information by tones of voice, like rasping, clipping, and squeezing. And thirdly, they consider nonvocal signals, such as a raised eyebrow or a raised fist. Speech transmits information not only through what we say but also through how we say it.

Kinesics refers to the way people communicate through body movements and gestures, such as a raised eyebrow, a medial brow pinch, or a shift in posture. While the phonetic signals of speech are sounds we hear, kinesic signals are motions we see and feel. We can analyze both kinds of signals from both etic and emic points of view. While meaningfully different vocal signals are different phonemes and morphemes, meaning-

167

fully different movements and gestures are different kinemes and kinemor-phemes. Ray L. Birdwhistell in "Some Relationships between American Kinesics and Spoken American English" shows how the structure of gestures parallels the structure of vocal signals in that kinesics also has its suprasegmentals and paralinguistics. Our gestures even have a grammar with plural markers, verboid markers, pronominal markers, and many other syntactic forms.

John H. Starkweather investigated "Content-Free Speech as a Source of Information about the Speaker" by filtering out the verbal com-ponents of speech so that people could only hear a mumble. In this mumble people could still decode the semantics of voice quality, decode the still available nonverbal signals such as the pitches, stresses, and rates of speech. Starkweather found, in fact, that content-free speech provides some kinds of meanings more clearly than speech with full content.

Lawrence K. Frank considers an even more pervasive and primitive sensory process in "Tactile Communication." Nuzzling, cuddling, pet-ting, kissing, and sexual behavior are important forms of tactile signaling that have great influence in the early growth of infants and in the de-velopment of social interaction generally. We have barely begun to investigate the communicative role of such other senses as smell and taste.

Jurgen Ruesch's "Nonverbal Language and Therapy" reports that verbal and nonverbal signals differ primarily in the way digital computers differ from analog computers, and in the continuity of the signals, their redundancy, and their variability. Clinical psychologists initiated most studies of nonverbal communication.

16

A Basis for Some Contributions of Linguistics to Psychiatry

ROBERT E. PITTENGER
and HENRY LEE SMITH, JR.

In this paper we shall describe briefly some of the developments of scientific linguistics and kinesics—the systematic study of gestures and motions—which now afford more accurate descriptive tools for the study of interpersonal communication than have previously been available.

LANGUAGE

Language, then, may be described as an arbitrary system of vocal symbols by which human beings, as members of a social group and participants in a given culture, interact and communicate. Language, however, does not involve all the possible sounds and sound qualities involved in communication. The following discussion of language is a brief systematic describing and classifying the minimal discernible sound-units of a lansystem, analyzed in ascending levels of complexity.

The Phonological Level of Language

A spoken language is composed of combinations of sounds. The gross analysis of these sounds as vowels and consonants is common knowledge. Scientific linguists, however, have made progress in more systematically describing and classifying the minimal discernible sound-units of a language. These units are the vowels, consonants, stresses, pitches, and pauses that the person learns as significant *structure points* in the inventory of sounds he uses in speech. Each one of these structure points, technically termed phonemes, has a range of predictable variations (*allophones*) which are automatic and which are reacted to as the "same

Reprinted with permission of the authors and by special permission of The William Alanson White Psychiatric Foundation, Inc. Copyright © 1957. From *Psychiatry*, 20:61–78 (1957).

sound" by the native speaker of the language. For example, if one listens carefully, the *p* sounds heard in *pin, upper,* and *cup* are noticeably different, and *different in the same way* each time one says them; yet one reacts to them as the "same" in contrast to the *b*'s in *bin, lubber,* and *sub.* Thus *p* and *b* represent *phonemes*—contrasting structure points—and the automatic variations we have tried to bring into awareness are the principal allophones of the phonemes. The classifications of sounds in the stream of speech (*phones*) into the allophones of phonemes is the business of *phonology.*

The Morphological Level of Language

In the analysis of language, the next level of organization after the phoneme is the *morpheme.* The patterning of the phonemes into words within any one language can systematically be described and constitutes the *morphology.* This includes in addition to *words,* the *suffixes,* patterns of *stress,* patterns of *intonation,* and the *syntax* or *constructions.*

The items analyzed as the words and suffixes of language structure are found to be put together in certain statable arrangements, and the words can then be seen to form into phrases and other constructions—clauses and sentences. As an example, the item *boy* recurs in English by itself and in *boy-s, boy-ish, boy-hood;* similarly *-s* recurs in *boy-s, girl-s,* and so on, and *-ish* and *-hood* likewise recur. These are orthographic representations of *morphemes.* The arrangement is always in a fixed order to form words —*boy-s* and not *s-boy, boy-ish* and not *ish-boy,* and so on. In English sentences, one says *The man goes home,* or occasionally *Home goes the man,* but not *Man the home goes.*

The choice of a word among synonyms is important in respect to its fitting the over-all style of the discourse. In a discourse which is relatively formal in its tone, *evil,* for example, may well be selected rather than *bad.* The selection of *evil* in informal discourse may be made for stylistic effect precisely because it would *not* be the expected choice. The momentary disruption of congruence and the study of the selection of words in various contexts is obviously one of the main concerns of stylistics. Compare "The evil that men do lives after them" and "I'll have to warn you about the evil the little boys in this neighborhood are liable to do on Halloween." It is a significant signal in the communication situation when a person strives with great regularity to use precise, literary words and constructions despite quite different standard colloquial usage in his environment.

From the linguistic scientist's point of view, the systematic analysis of this area of language is far from complete, with more study and research needed. Parallel to this knowledge from language study as a cultural phenomenon, psychoanalytic psychiatry has added significantly to the knowledge about the selection of words and the meanings such selections have within the personality and in the interaction of a personality with others.

An area of morphology in which systematic patterns have recently been described in English is that of the use of *stress*. Stress has to do with the structured degrees of relative loudness with which syllables are uttered. Certain syllables are said louder than others in many different contexts; an example is seen in such contrasting noun-verb pairs as *cóntract* and *contráct*. Most dictionaries indicate three degree of stress but more rigorous analysis of the language shows that there are four. They are not systematically treated in school, are not represented in the writing system, and are learned *out of awareness*. Nevertheless, all English speakers have learned to react to these four degrees of stress and to their patterned occurrences. Three words repeated with different stress arrangements can be shown to refer to three different things in experience:

(1) Light house keeper
(2) Light house keeper
(3) Light house keeper

If number 1 is read to mean "a person who keeps a lighthouse," the *light* is said with the loudest stress, *keep-* is said next loudest, *-er* is said weakest and *house* is said not so loud as *keep-* but louder than *-er*. To symbolize and name these four stresses the loudest, *primary*, is symbolized by an acute accent, ´; the next loudest, *secondary*, by a circumflex accent, ˆ; the third loudest, *tertiary*, by a grave accent, `; and the least loud, *weak*, by a breve, ˘. The stress degrees could be called by any other names or symbolized in any desired way just so long as it is realized that they are four significant structure-points or phonemes in the sound-system of English.

Number 1, then, would be marked:

(1) Líght hòuse kêepĕr.

The different arrangement of stresses that accompanies these same words to make the whole mean "a person who does light-housekeeping" for number 2, then, would be marked:

(2) Lìght hóuse kèepĕr.

The contrast between this and number 3 is achieved by saying the first word, *light*, not on *tertiary* stress but on *secondary* as follows:

(3) Lîght hóuse kèepĕr.

The last group of three words means, in contradistinction to the other two, "a housekeeper who doesn't weigh very much." These examples establish the fact that English has four stresses and begins to show a very slight variation in loudness can be extremely important in the way language works. Other examples of the contrast between secondary and tertiary can be heard in such a sentence as "Lòng Ísland is a lông ísland" or "A Nèw Yórker is not a nêw Yórker."

Immediately it becomes apparent that an item under secondary stress which precedes an item under primary stress is of secondary *syntactic rank* to the primary-stressed item, or, to put it in more conventional terms, this order and stress arrangement signals that the first item *modifies* the second. But note here no recourse to referential meaning is required. Perfectly automatically it can be said that *lîght* in *light hóusekèepĕr* is of *secondary* rank to *hóusekèeper*, and if it is intended to refer to a "light-housekeeper" who doesn't weigh very much, *lîght* can be put in front of "light-housekeeper" with the result Lîght lìght hóusekèepĕr. The real *structural signals* received by the hearer in determining "what goes with what and how" is to a large extent dependent in English on *order* and *stress patterns*. The adjectival-nominal relationship in English is most frequently signaled as just shown by an item under secondary stress preceding an item under primary stress.

But there are other patterns of stresses that can be seen systematically. An arrangement of primary followed by tertiary signals a unit-grouping or *construct* as in *hóuse-kèepĕr, líghthòuse, máke-ùp, bláck bìrd*, and *lístĕn tò*. Also, a *tertiary* followed by a *primary* signals a *construct* as in *Lòng Ísland, Nèw Yórker, màke úp, lìght hóusekéepĕr*. Then, too, as in number 1 example above, an over-all arrangement of *primary* and *secondary* holds words together to form a *construct* as in *líght-hòuse kêepĕr, élĕvàtŏr-ôpĕràtŏr.*

A foreign language may structure in a somewhat similar way, or may lack a stress system on the word level entirely, as in the case of French. It is well to take a moment to describe the similarities and differences in the operation of stress between German and English. In the first place, German has four levels of stress as does English, and they may be named and symbolized in the same way. German uses stress patterns similar to those of English: primary and tertiary as in Whíte Hòuse and Báhnhòf; primary and secondary as in líght-hòuse kêepĕr and Stúrm bànn Fûhrĕr. But tertiary and primary, and secondary and primary are used in opposite ways in the two languages. German puts *tertiary* stress over an adjective and uses *secondary* stress with primary stress to signal a unit construct. Compare the difference in the stresses in the following examples:

The "Nèw Yórker" is a nêw mágazine.
Die "Nêue Zeítung" ist eine neùe Zéitung (The newspaper "Neue Zeitung" is a new newspaper).

The use of English stress patterns in German, with a tertiary for a secondary and a secondary for a tertiary, does not make sense to the speaker of German, any more than reversing the secondary and tertiary stresses in "Long Island is a lòng ísland"—to get "Lông Ísland is a lòng ísland"—would make sense to a speaker of English.

Stress (differing degrees of relative loudness) is analyzable as a separate system from *intonation* (differing degrees of pitch and pausal phenomena). However, they are interrelated and simultaneous in the spoken language. Intonation as commonly used refers to the general "tone of voice" of an utterance. Scientific linguists are now able to analyze this level of language structure systematically, as evident in the following discussion.

English uses four significant levels of pitch. These *relative* pitch levels are part of the sound-structure of the language in a way analogous to the four significant levels of relative loudness or stress treated above. The pitch levels are symbolized by the numbers 1, 2, 3, 4, with 1 standing for the lowest level and 4 for the highest. Consider an ordinary sentence, "He's going to Paris." As a statement of fact, this is said with the highest level of pitch on the syllable that bears the primary stress, the first syllable of *Paris*. This is pitch 3. The sentence starts on pitch 2, as do most English sentences, and pitch 2 continues over all the syllables before the primary stress on *Paris*, when it rises to 3. After that syllable, there is a sharp drop to pitch 1. The sentence can be marked thus:

²He's going to ³Páris.¹

What takes place after the fall in pitch from level 3 to level 1 is a gradual diminution of intensity and a slight continuing fall in pitch until silence is reached. This is a structural signal in English, symbolized by #, and called by the technical name, *double-cross juncture*. A *juncture* is a signal of *transition* in a language—of the way of getting from one stretch of utterance to another or of completing utterances and starting others. The double-cross juncture is an example of what is called a *terminal* juncture. Intonation patterns are composed of pitches and terminal junctures, so that the intonation pattern of the above sentence is transcribed

231#. The period is used, although not consistently, to symbolize the double-cross juncture in ordinary writing.

In response to such a sentence as that above, a speaker might say, with surprise or incredulity, "He's going to Paris?" Here the sentence starts on pitch 2, as in the previous case, rises to pitch 3 at the same point, but *stays* on 3 throughout the whole word *Paris*, and then *rises* in pitch slightly at the end. A third speaker, who heard perfectly what the first speaker had said, might ask, "Why's he going to Paris?" in such a way as to imply "and not London or Cairo or Berlin?" Here the pitch on the primary stressed syllable of *Paris* is an example of pitch 4, and English speakers can easily hear the greater height of 4 as compared to the rise from 3 at the end of the second speaker's question. After the 4, the pitch falls rapidly to level 1 and trails off into silence as the original sentence did. The rise at the end of the second speaker's question is an example of another terminal juncture, one characterized by a rise in pitch, but not up to the level of the next highest significant pitch point. This is symbolized by a double bar, ||, and is called *double-bar juncture.*

The entire interchange may be transcribed thus:

(1) ^{2}He's going to ^{3}Páris^1#
(2) ^{2}He's going to ^{3}Páris^3||
(3) ^{2}Why's he going to ^{4}Páris^1#

These are examples of all four significant pitch levels and two *terminal junctures.* They are also examples of the following *intonation patterns:* 231#, 233||, 241#.

Consider now the following sentence:

What're we having for dinner, Mother?

If this is said in the ordinary way by a dutiful son or daughter, it starts on pitch 2 with a rise to 3 on the stressed syllable of *dinner.* The pitch then falls to 2, *not* to 1, at the point where the writing system puts a comma, and what then takes place can be described as a slight pause, or break. Then pitch 2 is heard again on the primary stress on *Mother*, with a continuation on 2 over the weak-stressed syllable, ending with the slight rise in pitch symbolized by ||. The slight pause, or break, which is characterized neither by a fading off nor by a rise in pitch, is another terminal juncture, in contrast to the other two. This one is termed single-bar juncture, symbolized by |. The sentence would be transcribed as follows:

^{2}What're we having for ^{3}dínner^2|^{2}Móther^2||

This gives examples of two more intonation patterns—232| and 222||.

Pitch and stress are *independent* systems in English, although *interde-*

pendent. Most frequently the primary stress coincides with pitches 3 or 4, but there are numerous occasions when this is not the case. Take the sentence above and use the intonation pattern 111# instead of the pattern 222|| on *Mother*, as follows:

²What're we having for ³dínner²|²Móther²||

When the *primary* stress occurs with pitch 1, which continues throughout the word *mother*, terminating with a #, it gives the impression that the speaker is not being nearly so polite to his mother as this culture says is right and proper. If pitch 1 is used on the stressed syllable of *dinner*, continued on 1 throughout the remainder of the sentence, the effect is even more pronounced, and the impression is that the speaker does not have much regard for his mother as a person *or* a cook.

²What're we having for ¹dínner¹|¹Móther¹#

This gives another *intonation pattern*, 211|.

Intonation patterns have no referential meaning as such. They, *plus* the words, the *vocal qualifiers*, and the *kinesics*, taken together furnish the *totality* to which meaning can be assigned. Speakers of English have been brought up to be extremely sensitive to the difference in meaning associated with the selection of different intonation patterns. It is the *totality of the interrelation* of the various components of language and of the other communication systems which is the basis for referential meaning. Altering one isolate in an *intonation pattern—a pitch* or a *terminal juncture*—can register significantly on the hearer who has learned the structure of the communication systems and its relationship to the other cultural systems.

Another series of sentences will illustrate this. A asks B how he likes his new boss. B pauses noticeably before replying and says:

²He has a ⁴véry pleasant²|²perso³nálity²#

Here note that B does *not* fall to pitch 1 at the end of his reply but remains on 2 followed by #, giving another *intonation pattern—232#*. In the actual speech situation from which this example was recorded, A laughed when he heard B's reply because the inference was obvious—the only *good* thing the boss had to recommend him was his outward pleasantness; everything else he had was, to say the least, disqualifying. After laughing, A asked B whether he'd put a period or a semicolon after the sentence, B replied, "I'm afraid I put a period after it." If A and B had learned the analysis being presented here and had been familiar with this system of symbolization, A would have said, "I'm sure I heard you right, but I'm asking did you end your intonation pattern with a double cross or a double bar?" If B had used a 232|| intonation pattern, this would be represented as:

^{2}He has a ^{4}véry pleasant^2|^{2}perso^{3}nálity^2||

The inference would have been, "He's a very nice person *but* I don't like the way he talks to his wife at the bridge table," or some other relatively minor pejorative statement. If B had used a 231# intonation pattern on *personality*, the statement would have been entirely complimentary, and some additional statement would have to be added if anything uncomplimentary were to be communicated.

^{2}He has a ^{4}véry pleasant^2|^{2}perso^{3}nálity^1#

Thus a change of only one pitch or juncture can bring about a change of intonation pattern which, when used with the same words, can alter the entire message from an extremely complimentary one to a mildly disqualifying one, or even to what amounts to an insult, though couched in diplomatic words. This is an excellent example of what is meant by, "It wasn't his words I objected to, but his tone of voice." But "tone of voice" is not just a matter of intonation patterns; what people thus refer to covers phenomena that are analyzed also in other systems, the vocal modifiers and *kinesics*, which go along with language in order to form the total context of communication.

OTHER VOCAL PHENOMENA

The other vocal phenomena which accompany language can be systematically analyzed as qualities and noises separable from language itself. Informally, the recognition of these elements of communication has long been stated as, "It wasn't what he said, it was how he said it." As with all scientific statements, the descriptions amount to hypotheses which seem best able at the moment to describe and explain the phenomena.[1]

Although the vocal modifiers are quite clearly separable phenomena, many of them are not yet systematically describable and are in need of

[1] These vocal phenomena are now generally called "paralanguage." See George L. Trager, "Paralanguage: A First Approximation," *Studies in Linguistics* 13:1–12 (1958), and George L. Trager, "The Typology of Paralanguage," *Anthropological Linguistics* 3(1):17–21 (1961).

much further research. However, information can be given which is suggestive of the kinds of elements observable.

In considering all of the phenomena discussed below, it is important to realize that, like intonation patterns, these events *in and of themselves* have no referential meaning—they *contribute* to the total meaning of the communication. What one usually refers to as meaning derives first from the structured interrelation of *all* the communication systems and then from the interrelation of the communication systems as a whole to the other systems which comprise the total culture.

Vocal qualifiers is a term applied to one kind of these phenomena which has been more systematically described than the others. These phenomena, usually thought of as "tone of voice," seem to be composed of events that may be arranged as polar pairs, each component of which is identifiable in terms of a single auditory impression, but which is the result of a combination of readily determinable physiological occurrences.

In general, any spoken communication will be established on a level or base line of (1) intensity, (2) pitch range over-all, (3) pitch intervals between the four pitch levels of the intonation patterns, (4) degree of tension or laxness of the vocal organs, (5) tempo for the uttering of the multiple sound elements within single words, and (6) tempo for the sequential march of words within the context. These concurrent base lines within a communication depend on the speaker's adjusting to a variety of factors, including among other things the size of the room, the spacing of those who are communicating, the acoustic properties of the room, personal habits, and the assessment of the social situation. The following pairs of vocal qualifiers which have been identified indicate variations in each of two directions from the base line involved and are qualities which are imposed over whole stretches within utterances and are not dependent upon the particular language elements involved. But combinations of certain vocal qualifiers with each other and with certain intonation patterns recur with great frequency. The discussion of each is only suggestive of some of the numerous contextual uses, and is *not* to be considered as giving an exhaustive inventory of the 'meanings' of the events.

There is some evidence in hand already that the pairs of vocal qualifiers may actually be the positive and negative intensities, to at least three degrees, of phenomena that might be covered by a single term. For instance, three degrees each of *drawl* and *clipping* have been noted, starting from what may be called the absence of either.

(1) *Increasing loudness* and *increasing softness*. The part of the utterance having the increasing loudness or softness may be a single syllable or a whole sentence or more.

(2) *Raised pitch* and *lowered pitch*. The physiological and acoustic basis is obvious. Increasing loudness may be used in contexts of alarm, annoyance, and so on, particularly in combination with intonation patterns of 241#. Occasionally, increasing loudness and *raised pitch* may be used together, also in contexts of alarm, annoyance, and so on. Increasing softness, particularly with the vocative, signals displeasure and disappointment. *Raised pitch* is quite frequently used when adults talk to infants. *Lowered pitch* is seldom used by itself, but is often used with openness and/or drawl (which are discussed below) for various kinds of emphasis including incredulity.

(3) *Spread register* and *squeezed register*. These are respectively the "stretching" and compressing of the usual interval between the pitch phonemes in the utterance. Spread register is accompanied automatically by a kind of drawling which is, however, distinct from the drawl described below, since spread register and drawl can be used in combination and isolated in description as two features. Spread register is most frequently heard when names of people are used vocatively, when the person spoken to is not within easy touching distance. If the person is not visible, spread register is used with increasing loudness. (*John*-ny, are you *home* yet?) Squeezed register is the opposite of spread register in that the intervals between the pitches are "squeezed down" to give a monotone effect. Squeezed register used with rasp, particularly with the vocative said with the intonation pattern 222#, signals lack of interest or weariness.

(4) *Rasp* and *openness*. These have to do physiologically with the amount of muscular tension under which the laryngeal apparatus is held. Under tension the strained or rasping quality is heard. With openness a sort of hollow or booming acoustic impression is added to the communication. This open quality is associated with the "tone of voice" of clergymen, politicians, and undertakers. Most Americans get the impression that there is a lack of sincerity connected with its use. It signals that the speaker is of superordinate status and has the answers to one's problems. From mother to child, openness is used to signal security, but reminds the child of his dependent state. Rasp often accompanies increasing loudness in contexts of extreme annoyance, but with squeezed register it generally helps give the impression of lack of interest or weariness.

(5) *Drawl* and *clipping*. These have to do with the tempo of individual syllables in contrast to the terms *increased* and *decreased tempo* used below to describe longer utterances. The sentence, "Yeah, he's a nice guy," said with drawl contradicts the meaning of the words, but with decreased tempo and a different intonation pattern it tends to emphasize the meaning. Clipping is the exact opposite of drawl, in that the syllable is checked or squeezed into a far shorter time interval. Quite frequently

so-called interjections such as "Well," "Yep," and "Nope" are heard with this vocal qualifier, usually signaling, "It's my turn to talk now." "No" or "Nope" so interjected will often be found not to have the meaning of negation; for example, in "No, you're exactly right," basic agreement with the previous speaker is being signaled, along with the strong opinion that the previous speaker has not gone anywhere near far enough.

(6) *Increased tempo* and *decreased tempo*. Again the physiological acoustic basis is clear. These qualifiers are frequently used for emphasis. Increased tempo in many contexts signals annoyance; in others it may show anxiety about being heard or about being interrupted. Decreased tempo allows each separate phrase or even each word of a sentence to sink in. Uncertainty is also often signaled in this way.

Normally in communications these elements are interspersed as useful and needed. Most of the time, when they are successfully integrated by the speaker into the utterance, the listener will be unaware of the "tone of voice." When they are used in unusual contexts or in differing amounts than 'normal,' the listener becomes aware of something, although without this frame of reference he may be unable to locate the source of his impression. Many psychiatrists and others skilled in communication have learned to value the information received from these kinds of phenomena and trust its validity, even though they consider the source to be experience, or intuition, or a third ear.

Laughing, crying, and *breaking* used for communication purposes are parts of another set of these vocalization phenomena, termed *vocal differentiators*. People learn the culturally accepted uses of crying. After the age of about twelve, boys in this culture are strongly discouraged from crying except for severe pain, in a process started much earlier by frowns, admonitions, "Big boys don't cry," and the like. Women have more leeway in this; in many circumstances they may continue to use crying for communication all through their lives. To be reminded that this is a quite arbitrary communication pattern of a particular culture, it is only necessary to recall that in Persia, *men* are allowed to weep all their lives and, in some cases, even expected to—as in the case of Premier Mossadegh. Laughing and crying may 'mean' quite different things from culture to culture. Who can laugh or cry at what, how much, in what way, and what will be signaled thereby is a part of each person's cultural learning about these elements of communication.

Another vocal differentiator is termed *breaking*. *Breaking*, like rasp and openness, is characterized by special muscular phenomena of the laryngeal machinery, especially the vocal cords. There is a rigid and intermittent tension and relaxation of the vocal cords so that the voice is broken, resulting in a sort of tremulousness, with interruption of the tone. The nervous giggle is a frequently occurring example of breaking, but the use of breaking accompanied by overloudness, openness, and *overslow tempo* in the style of orators and preachers to signal deep emotional involvement is perhaps its most characteristic occurrence. The quavering voice of great emotion frequently precedes tears, anger, or excitement. It signals uncertain control in this context. Laughing and breaking get confused across cultural lines; for instance, Japanese breaking which communicates insecurity—as giggling does in this culture sometimes—is so much more pronounced and differently uttered that the Western hearer mistakes it for laughing.

Vocal identifiers is a term applied to another very significant cluster of vocal phenomena. So far, only one has been described in the communication systems. In the utterance "uh-huh" or "ah-hah" meaning affirmation, *yes,* there is a smooth transition between the syllables, whereas in "uh-uh" or "ah-ah" meaning *no,* there is a glottal closure. No significant difference in meaning is noted whether these vocalizations are uttered with the lips closed and full nasalization (a vocal differentiator), or with partial nasalization with the lips apart, or with the lips apart and no accompanying nasalization. It is the glottal catch in contrast to its absence which makes the difference between the meaning of agreement and disagreement. These utterances, whether they occur as single syllables or as dissyllabic utterances, are always accompanied by stress and intonation patterns. They may also be augmented by vocal qualifiers. In the flow of other utterances the interruption of a word by a glottal stop and pause is frequently a signal that all or part of the utterance is negated or changed by a suddenly perceived contrasting thought.

Certain other phenomena may be usefully termed *voice quality* and *voice set.* These phenomena are at present not included in the communication systems proper, but seem to be in a close supporting role to language, vocal modifiers, and kinesics. Although quite clearly separable phenomena, they are not yet so systematically describable as the vocal modifiers and are even more in need of further research. Information can be given which is suggestive of the kinds of elements observable, but more definitive statements will of necessity await further advances in linguistic science. Probably a great many of the impressions that psychiatrists receive in terms of "general emotional state" are to be handled in these areas —the voice as anxious, the voice as hostile, and so forth (voice quality); thin voice, immature voice, aged voice, dispirited voice (voice set). In all cases, phenomena to be classified here are separable from the vocal modifiers and are, so to speak, left over after these other phenomena have been accounted for and analyzed. Or they may be termed more persistent, in the sense that they continue over the whole communication or at least large sections of it, in contrast to the more transient occurrence of vocal modifiers.

The patterns of use of the various elements of all the vocal phenomena so far treated, singly or in combinations, are recognizable as culturally, personally, and institutionally determined. Variations on the group and individual level can be systematically studied. It is readily evident that, as in language, the patterns used have cultural meaning, so that many of the impressions and evaluations one makes about such things as rank, social status, flexibility, and so on have to do with observations of the occurrence and use of these communication elements in patterns.

KINESICS

Kinesics, or gestures and motions, are not instinctive human nature but are learned systems of behavior differing markedly from culture to culture. Like language and the vocalizations they are learned *informally*—that is, by imitation of others with little or no awareness on the part of the learner that he is learning or the teacher that he is teaching. Because most of this behavior is learned out of awareness, people remain unaware of their participation in an elaborate system of bodily gestures and motions, and most groups tend to think of members of other groups as "using their hands" and making "funny faces." Most people have heard such statements as, "If the Frenchman's hands were tied behind his back, he'd be tongue tied." Those who point with the index finger consider it a matter of course and are startled to encounter people who point with the lower lip or with the chin. In a study of kinesics, it is necessary to be aware that one's gestures differ from those of others, and to become aware of these differences in a systematic way.

Although the scientific study of this area of communication is in its infancy, real growth has taken place. Just as in language and vocalizations, it is necessary to analyze this system in terms of its own minimal units. Over-all patterns of movement can be subdivided into component sets of movement in various body areas,—for instance, the face, arms, legs. The minimal discernible isolate which can be significantly differentiated from other, though similar, isolates is seen as the basic building block from which the sets are composed in combination with other isolates.

Language with its vocalizations is marked by frequent obvious cessations. The communications of kinesics are a flow of patterns without such obvious interruptions.

The environment shows one, and less often tells one, how to walk, sit, stand, hold one's hands, scratch, and so on, and also the way in which these things are done—for instance, how close one stands to another person and for how long. The differentiation of movement patterns for boys and girls starts early. Although there is very little systematic teaching of these behavioral patterns, everyone learns to react to these phenomena of communication and to rely on their consistent symbolic value. For a full study of communications it is imperative to achieve a systematic analysis of these nonverbal components. Ray L. Birdwhistell has made the beginnings of such an analysis, upon which these comments on kinesics are based.

17 | Some Relations between American Kinesics and Spoken American English
RAY L. BIRDWHISTELL

Two classes of phenomena thus appear in the kinesically analyzable stream concurrent with vocalic behavior. First, there are the kinesic phenomena which appear in interactional sequences whether there is speech present or not. This data has been assigned to macro-kinesics proper. This includes all of the material which is structured into the complex kinemorphic constructions: the words, the phrases, the sentences and paragraphs, if you will, of the kinesic communicative stream.

Surrounding, or rather, associated with these highly structured forms is the range of parakinesic behaviors which cross-reference, in a variety of ways, the kinesic or linguistic messages emitted or received. These cross-referencing signals may emphasize or modify the constructions themselves, or they may make statements about the *context* of the message situation. In the latter instance, they may help to define the context of the interaction by identifying the actor or his audience, and, furthermore, they may identify the larger context in which the interaction takes place. However, the cross-referencing signals differ systematically from those included in the discussion to follow in that while they occur with speech, they also appear in inaudible interaction.

At this point let me underline the point made elsewhere that signals may appear either in the behavior of a single individual or may be shared in

This is part of a paper that was originally presented at the annual meeting of the American Association for the Advancement of Science, Section H, December 27, 1963. It is printed here for the first time with the permission of the author. The analysis is further developed in the author's "Communication Without Words," *L'Aventure Humaine,* Paris: Societé d'Etudes Litteraires et Artistiques (1965); "Body Behavior and Communication" and "Communication as a Multichannel System," *International Encyclopedia of the Social Sciences,* New York (1965).

performance by a group of communicants. In fact, it is customary in an interactional situation for the membership to share the message transmission system. Only in highly stylized stage forms do we get the alternating receiver-sender system so often depicted in the dialogue or the attorney-witness representation. To say it simply, the examination of the behavior of a single individual (while it always contains items of kinesic behavior and, usually, will contain full constructions), does not exhaust the kinesic behavior of the interactive scene. The behavior of all participants is significant to the final analysis of the message content of the scene.

Second, there is the major class of behaviors which seems exclusively related to the speech stream. One set of these, with which we are concerned in this present discussion, includes a group which, parallel to the stress and pitch structuring of American English, I call the supra-segmental kinemorphemes. American kinesics has definitely three and perhaps four kinemes of stress which combine to specially mark certain aspects of American English phrase and clause structure. These, and the kinesic terminal junctures appear to be intimately related to the task of organizing groups of lexemes into larger coherent streams. They identify phrases, clauses, sentences, "paragraphs" and other major sequences which have special internal connectedness.

THE KINESIC MARKERS

The kinesic markers differ systematically from these supra-segmental kinemorphemes in that the markers seem to have a special relationship to the behavior of particular classes of lexical and syntactic items. It is with the presentation of these that our discussion here is concerned. However, before I can make these comprehensible to an audience unconversant with general kinesics, one more item must be discussed. Early in the investigation of body movement patterning, I had had to deal with that deceptively transparent set of phenomena commonly called *gestures*. A considerable body of ethnographic data was extant demonstrating that these varied from culture to culture. An even larger body of philosophical and psychological literature maintained that these could be understood as "signs" as distinct from less transparent or easily translatable "symbols." Examination of these phenomena in context, however, soon revealed that this was at best a dubious interpretation of their activity or function.

Under kinesic analysis, once I had gotten some idea of how items of the stream are systematically linked to other items of the stream, it became clear that so-called gestures are really *bound* morphs. That is, gestures are forms which are incapable of standing alone—except, of course, where the context is provided by the questioner. Just as there is no "cept" in isolation in American English, an informant may be taught how to produce it together with "pro-" or "con-" or ". . . tion." As bound morphs, as stem forms, gestures require infixual, suffixual, prefixual or transfixual kinesic behavior to achieve identity.

Gestures are characterized by the fact that informants can easily recall them and attach a general order of meaning to them as recognized. However, this easy access to their form or meaning proves illusory when they are examined in the actual interactional flow. Although they have an apparent unitary and discrete quality, they prove under examination to consistently carry the instruction to look elsewhere in the body behavioral stream for their modification or interpretation. A "salute," for example, depending upon the integrally associated total body or facial behavior, may convey a range of messages from ridicule and rebellion to subservience or respect. A "smile" can have at least this range, as can a "wink," a "wave," or a "bow." To call these "signals" is to indicate a specificity such behavior lacks in actual practice.

To return to the kinesic markers: Regularly around certain kinds of audible syntactic items appear kinic behavior which looks like the gestural bound morph except that these behaviors appear also to be linguistic. The term "kinesic marker" represents a tentative compromise between a position which would definitively designate such behavior as macrokinesic and that of prematurely (in terms of kinesic methodology) assigning them some kind of supra-linguistic and supra-kinesic position in the semiotic system. For purely heuristic purposes I have made the admittedly questionable decision to classify them according to the classes of lexical items ("words") with which they are regularly associated. I say "questionable" because such a designation may signal an unintended priority to the linguistic form. Since these data have thus far resisted placement in the kinesiological structure *per se*, their isolation dictates a differential procedure than that customary in kinesiological analysis. (However, and this is essential to all kinesic research, before I was willing to present the data in the form described below, I ran hundreds of tests to make sure that they were units which did not enter into discretely kinesic structuring.)

MARKER QUALITIES

The units abstracted below have four characteristics.

1. They have articulatory properties which are abstractable into *contrastive* behavioral classes. However, the articulations themselves are not distinctively and exclusively related to specific functions. The articulatory behaviors may in other environments have other functions, e.g. a lid closure articulation may be, at one level, a kineme in a kinemorpheme; at another, a stress kineme in a supra-segmental organization. Here we locate it as a marker.

2. These units appear in distinctive syntactic environments, i.e. the lexemes with which they appear belong to distinctive syntactic classes.

3. The articulatory behavior, if two or more of these units appear in series, are always sufficiently varied to reduce signal confusion, i.e. we have situational articulatory contrast.

4. Since the articulatory behavior is not definitively distinctive, in and of itself, the abstraction of the unit depends upon the isolation of contrastive sequences of behavior in contrastive syntactic neighborhoods.

Thus, a marker is a *contrastable* range of behavior in a *particular* neighborhood.

KINESIC PRONOMINAL MARKERS

First, and most easily recognizable, were what I called the K^p group, so identified because they are normally associated with or may in certain environments, be substituted for pronominals.

In address or reference, the head, a finger, the hand or a glance may be moved so that a *distal* extension of the movement can be interpreted as leading toward, actually or symbolically, the object or event referred to. These K^p's may be found in association with the verbalizations, "he," "she," "it," "those," "they," "that," "then," "there," "any," and "some."

The *proximal* movement of these same body parts are used in association with "I," "me," "us," "we," "this," and "now."

In recording, I originally ignored the distalproximal distinction and listed the behavior associated with "I," "me," "he," "she," "it," "we," "they," "here," "there," "now," and "then" as K^p's *pronominal markers*. It soon became evident that the more complex patterning of the K^p distinguished kinesic marker behavior from kinesic stress behavior. As the investigation of larger and varied corpora of data proceeded and the methods for tieing the body motion and the vocalic behavior improved, it was clear that what had at first been seen as an indicator over a single lexeme was more complex both at the articulatory level and as a functioning structural unit. First of all, a lateral sweep often appeared at either the proximal or the distal end of the act. This sweep distinguished *pluralization*.

PLURALIZATION MARKER

Pluralization is indicated by a slight sweep of the moved member over "we," "we'uns," "they," "these," "those," "them," "our," "you" (plural), "you all," "you'uns," "youse," "their," and "us." "Any" and "some" show the same contrast from the singular as do "many," and "several," etc. Since, however, a similar sweep often takes place in association with name forms which are ambiguous ("fish," "sheep," "deer," and "bear," etc.), or over-pluralized name forms, it seems necessary to make a double annotation over plural pronominals of K^p followed by a *marker of pluralization* (K^{pp}).

In association with a phrase like "all of them" or "none of them," "all" or "none" may have a head-sweep or lid-close (K^{pp}) in association. "None" is a particularly interesting form as kinesically marked. It varies in articulation (perhaps dialectically) from a K^p of a single lower nod to a sweep K^{pp}. When the hand or the foot is involved a single (S) may alternate with a single (n).

I have never seen (S), thus K^{pp} parallel to the spoken "none is" but (S) as K^{pp} is common in the environment of "none are." Depending upon stress in the sentence, "them" in either of the phrases (none of them) (all of them) may or may not be marked. Examination of several hundred examples of this phrase has indicated that we will find, if the phrases "all of them" or "none of them" do not have a primary vocalic over "all" or "them" or "none" or "them," the entire phrase is covered by the behavior of the (K^{pp}) pluralization marker.

VERBOID MARKERS

The distal and proximal aspect of the movement became increasingly important after the *pluralization* sweep was isolated. At this point the micro-kinesic recording indicated that such a proximal or distal movement was not limited to the sound stretch of the pronoun but, rather linked the subject form to the verb form. Thus "I went" has a proximal movement over "I" which, *without interruption* moves distally over "went." "I went to the house" may well be marked by a proximal movement over "I" which moves, *without interruption*, over "went." Then the movement combines *with a change of direction*, over "to the house." These movements are clearly distinguishable from the kinesic stress markers which take place in either the same or other body parts.

In a form like "I gave it to him" the marker movement is very much the same as in "I went to the house." "He gave it to me" reverses the action, the movement terminating in a proximal position. The demand, "Give it to me," logically enough, has the same shape as "You give it to me."

Such sentences stand in sharp contrast to sentences of the form "The book is red" in which there are no markers. "The dog is barking" requires no markers, while "He's barking" has the characteristic distal movement followed by a continuous move. On the other hand, "The dog barked," or "The dog was barking" are customarily accompanied by a distal movement to the rear of the body, whereas "The dog will bark" has a distal movement toward the front of the body. This indicates the presence of *tense markers*.

Let us attempt to diagram our articulations and see whether we can abstract certain regularities (see Figure 1).

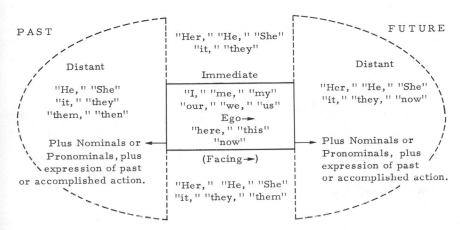

Figure 1.

With the application of this chart to my data it was possible to now distinguish the first person pronouns K^{p1} from all other pronouns K^{p2}. By extending the K^{nn} convention of pluralization K^{pp1} and K^{pp2} could be distinguished. Tense is clearly signalled here. Futurity is signalled by an anterior progression of the movement; the past, in general is signalled by a posterior movement. Thus, "He will give it to me" involves: 1. A distal extension K^p over "he"; 2. a K^v (verboid marker) of continuous movement over "will give it;" 3. a K^t of tense supplied by the direction of the movement over "will give it;" 4. a K^p, the proximal movement, over "to me." Exhaustive repetitions with parallel forms demonstrate that these operate apart from the kinesic stress system.

By contrast "He gave it to me" utilizes position and proximal movements to carry the parallel message. In all cases a sweep over the K^p changes it to a K^{pp}. These rules seem to hold for all actor → action sentences although they are most easily detected in actor-action-object sentences. However, in forms like "He *was* a red" or "She *was* crazy" in which the emphasis is on completed action, a K^t may be the only marker. Comparably, "*She* is crazy" usually has only a K^p. Under certain circumstances "*She* is crazy" may have both a K^p and a K^v. In both of the former cases there is, of course, a kinesic primary stress concurrent with the K^t or the K^p.

AREA MARKERS

Besides these we have the *area markers*. "On," "over," "under," "by," "through," "behind," "in front of," and the like, which, when accompanied by verbs of action, usually take a K^a. The articulations are particularly noticeable when these items are under primary linguistic stress. I am indebted to Harvey Sarles and his associates at Western Psychiatric Institute for pointing out the distinction in this regard between sentences like— "Put it behind the stove" which requires a K^a over "behind" and "He arrived behind time," in which "behind" requires no marker. Or, "He arrived in the nick of time" where the "in" requires no marking in contrast to, "Put it in the can" where "in" is customarily marked. When the Western Psychiatric group completes its analyses of American English prepositional phrases, we shall have excellent data for the final isolation of this type of marker.

MANNER MARKERS

In parallel fashion, I mark the behavior which is associated with such phrases as "a short time" or "a longtime," and with "slowly" and "swiftly." These I annotate as K^m for *kinesic manner markers*. Also as K^m's are listed the behaviors associated with forms like "roughly," "jerkily," "smoothly," and so on.

This delineation may seem to imply that kinesic markers are moved adjectivals or adverbials or pronominals or verbals. Even if such a description seems satisfactory, we should take care to avoid assuming that this *proves* that kinesic markers are derived from spoken language. There is no more evidence for this than there is that syntactic activity is not ultimately a derivation from body movement. From my point of view, it is premature at this stage in analysis to conjecture about origins. Our central concern is how such behaviors operate, not where they come from.

Before concluding, let us take up one point of general theoretical interest. Our discussion has led us to the point that we need to ask whether there is a qualitative difference between such behavior as we have been describing here and the elaborately descriptive behavior that accompanies certain kinds of story telling and technical instructions.

There will be a temptation, when the kinesic markers are first examined, to somehow feel that all of these markers are no more than gestures which designate or modify the morphemes, the lexemes, (the words) with which they are associated. At one level of description this is a supportable, if a not very productive, contention. However, such description may well lure the student into the kind of assumptions about universal symbolism in body motion that earlier thinking about onomatopoeia led to in language description. Even the most cursory cross-cultural examination reveals that such behavior varies from group to group at least as much as does the spoken language of these groups.

ARE THERE MARKERS OF DEMONSTRATION?

How can we best analyze the behavior of a woman telling another woman about the intricacies of dressmaking? Her apparently imitative demonstrative movements, like those of a man discussing his exploits in playing and landing a trout, seem qualitatively different than do the behavior which surrounds the orders of discourse discussed above. Earlier, I used a cover marker which I termed a K^d or marker of demonstration for such extended and elaborate gesticulation. Analysis of these, however, revealed that this convention would over-extend the concept of marker. For while such demonstrative behavior is clearly distinguishable, it is not unitary; it is made up of complex kinemorphic constructions, kinesic markers and parakinesic behavior. At the moment I am inclined to regard such behavior as examples of derived communicational systems. As such, they are not the primary subject matter of kinesics at the present.

18 | Content-Free Speech as a Source of Information about the Speaker
JOHN A. STARKWEATHER

A distinction often made with regard to speech behavior is that between the verbal and the vocal aspects of speech. The verbal component is the pattern of sound which results in words, phrases, and other linguistic units making up the content of speech. The vocal components are all the remaining characteristics of sound which may be called tonal variation or voice quality. Soskin has presented these two aspects in communication terms as the simultaneous operation of two communication channels, the verbal channel carrying potential semantic information and the vocal channel carrying potential affective information. He has also spoken of the vocal channel as the carrier upon which the content is superimposed.

Reprinted with permission of the American Psychological Association and the author. From *Journal of Abnormal and Social Psychology*, 52:394–402 (1956).

When interest is primarily in the personality of the speaker, some consider the vocal component of speech more important than the verbal component. Both are, of course, present in normal undifferentiated speech, and one might expect a loss of some pertinent information with the removal of either component. A summary of studies since 1931 which have dealt with the reliability of judgments of personality from normal voice, with both kinds of information available at once, points out that a number of the studies found difficulty in this type of judgment.

It is possible that the inaccuracy of judging in these studies may be due in part to confusion arising between verbal and vocal aspects of speech. If one is primarily interested in the personality of the speaker, perhaps the isolated vocal aspect would be a better basis for judgment than normal speech. There are apparently only two studies which bear on this point, both of which indicate the presence of affective information in speech rendered content-free by electronic removal of high frequencies.

One of these studies also demonstrates the possibility of confusion between verbal and vocal components by showing less agreement among judges listening to the normal voice when its verbal and vocal components have been arranged to be incongruent.

Soskin has presented the argument that a difference in meaning carried by the verbal and vocal components (incongruence) is produced when the speaker is in conflict, because the vocal channel is under less conscious control than the verbal channel. Verbal-vocal incongruence should then be characteristic of Ss who are in conflict and have difficulty in control of their emotions. Normal, undisturbed speech, on the other hand, is presumed to be congruent, with appropriate similarity between meanings conveyed by verbal and vocal components. Following this suggestion, the general purpose in the present study is to compare judgments of the verbal and vocal aspects of speech with special reference to Ss who may be expected to have some difficulty in controlling their emotions.

One group of Ss who fit this description are those diagnosed as having essential hypertension. It has not been unusual for clinicians to propose that personality factors are associated with essential hypertension. In particular these writers have stressed a constant struggle for control of hostile impulses.

Harris obtained a personality measure related to high blood pressure. Because of the association with high blood pressure, Harris has called the scale the hypertensive personality syndrome (HPS). He summarized the content of the items of Ss with high blood pressure as involving dominance, assertiveness, initiative, and a lack of awareness or concern about other people. Though the HPS scale was derived from a relationship with blood pressure, this is far from a perfect correlation. He further compared two groups with equally high scores on the HPS scale but differing in blood pressure. Interviewers rated Ss with high blood pressure as having more pathogenic childhoods and as significantly less at ease in interpersonal relations than Ss with low blood pressure. The possibility was raised that whereas both groups were self-assertive, there was a harsher quality to the assertiveness of those with high blood pressure, perhaps bordering on hostility.

This difference suggests that it may be important to separate the variables of HPS and blood pressure. Voices of Ss with high blood pressure should show evidence of aggressiveness and assertiveness when compared with Ss having low blood pressure. In addition, assertive (high HPS) Ss with high blood pressure should show a harsher, less acceptable quality in their voices when compared to assertive Ss with low blood pressure.

The purpose of the present study is twofold. First, judgments of isolated verbal and vocal aspects of speech are compared with judgments of the same speech in its normal form. Second, the judgments are compared with respect to their relative usefulness for describing the personalities of Ss who are likely to show verbal-vocal incongruence.

METHOD

Subjects

The Ss were selected from 100 U.S. Air Force captains studied at the University of California Institute of Personality Assessment and Research.

Speech Samples

ORIGINAL RECORDINGS OF ROLE-PLAYING SESSIONS. The Ss were seen in groups of ten for three days of living-in assessment. As one assessment procedure, they were studied one at a time in two interpersonal role-playing situations. A situation, a plot outline, and a role, were described to each S, as well as the role of the standard role-player, a staff member who played opposite him. The standard role-player guided the interaction in accordance with a prearranged outline and forced the initiative on the S at prearranged points. Observers of these situations were unanimous in asserting that the Ss were obviously under stress, showing evidence of autonomic and skeletal tension, and indications that they were experiencing real emotion.

In the first situation S was asked to play the role of a spokesman for his fellow salesmen to protest the firing of a salesmanager whom they all respected. In this situation the standard role-player acted the part of the vice-president. He evaded any explanations of the firing of the salesmanager, but offered the same position to S, making it as attractive as possible.

In the second situation, S was assigned the role of a young man who has recently inherited his father's business. He was told that he had had adequate training and experience for the position, but that he had been away in the service; that he now finds many practices of the company to be out of date, but his plans are blocked by the general manager. He has been debating whether or not to fire the general manager and has called him in to see him. In this situation the standard role-player played the general manager.

SELECTION OF VOICE SAMPLES. For each S whose voice was to be used, three 20-second voice samples were chosen from the recordings of these two situations. In the first situation, the vice-president began by saying "I understand you wanted to see me." The S was then expected to explain his role as a spokesman for the other salesmen. One 20-second sample (Context A) was taken from this point. A second 20-second sample (Context B) was taken immediately after the vice-president offered the sales-manager's position. In the second situation the general manager who has been called in said "I understand you wish to see me," and a 20-second sample (Context C) was taken from the initial remarks of S. Although these three equivalent points in time were used to obtain comparable voice samples, there was of course no guarantee that they were equivalent in their implications to the Ss.

The 20-second samples varied from 22 to 77 words, with a mean of 40. An attempt to relate the number of words used to any of the variables in this study was unsuccessful.

Derived recordings. The selected voice samples (a total of 90) were copied on recording tape in a random order with a ten-second silence between them. Four similar voice samples from other Ss not in the experimental groups were placed at the beginning to be used as introductory samples in judging. When numbers were later inserted between voice samples, this tape became the normal material to be played back for judging. Another copy was made through an electronic filter in order to produce content-free material. The content of speech without vocal cues was reproduced in typescript. Thus, the stimulus materials were in three forms, each consisting of four introductory 20-second voice samples and 90 20-second experimental voice samples. The three forms of material differed in the *information* available to the judges: a filtered *content-free* recording, presented aurally with a ten-second space between voice samples; a *normal* recording, presented as above; and *content-only*, presented in typewritten form.

Judging

The judges were 75 students from an elementary psychology course at Northwestern University, divided into three groups of 25. One group judged the filtered, content-free speech samples; a second group judged the normal voice samples; and the third group judged the content-only samples from the typescript. Immediately following presentation of each voice sample, the judges wrote a scale value from one to six to indicate their judgment on each of two scales. One scale was labeled "submissive" at position one and "aggressive" at position six. The other was labeled "unpleasant" at position one and "pleasant" at position six.

Apparatus

ELECTRONIC FILTER. The isolation of vocal speech components for the presentation of content-free speech samples was accomplished by an electronic filter passing the frequencies from 100 to 450 cycles per second with a 60-decibel per octave attenuation at the upper limit.

Voices filtered in this way are reduced to a kind of mumble as though heard through a wall. One still hears indications of pitch, rate, and loudness, though probably a good deal of what is usually called voice quality is lost along with the high frequencies.

RESULTS

Analysis with Regard to Information Available for Judging

It will be recalled that data were gathered simultaneously on both "aggressive" and "pleasant" scales (the judges marked both scales in the intervals between voice samples).

Reliability estimates of judgments on the two scales are presented in Table 1. These estimates are based on the total 90 experimental voice samples, with independent groups of 25 judges for each type of information. Although all of these correlations are significant, it is obvious that the coefficients for interjudge reliability (r_i) are not particularly high.

Table 1

Reliability Estimates of "Aggressive" and "Pleasant" Judgments

Information	r_i	r_n		r_i	r_n
"Aggressive" Judgments			"Pleasant" Judgments		
Content-free	.42	.95	Content-free	.12	.77
Content-only	.21	.87	Content-only	.14	.80
Normal	.42	.95	Normal	.26	.90

Note.—All the above correlations are significant beyond the .01 level. r_i is the intraclass correlation estimate of interjudge reliability. r_n is an estimate of the reliability of the pooled measure obtained from 25 judges (based on r_i).

However, the pooled reliability for a group of judges (r_n) is quite satis-factory. These estimates are somewhat lower for "pleasant" than for "aggressive" judgments.

Since each judge rated all 90 voice samples, the 90 scores from one judge are not independent. The data were therefore analyzed by an analysis of variance of repeated measures. Thus, there are three types of information, each judged by separate groups, each of whom yielded 90 scores. Since the 90 voice samples represent only 30 different voices each appearing in three different contexts, the analysis also included a breakdown for the voice variable and its interactions.

"AGGRESSIVE" JUDGMENTS. The analysis of "aggressive" judgments is significant at well beyond the .01 level.

There is thus a significant difference between the three kinds of infor-mation. There is a significant difference between the voices of the 30 Ss, as well as between the three voice samples of each S. This latter difference can be interpreted as the variation among the three contexts, pooled for the 30 Ss. There are significant interactions both between information and voices, and between information and the pooled context variation.

"PLEASANT" JUDGMENTS. The results of analysis of "pleasant" judgments, analyzed in the same way as the "aggressive" judgments, are much the same as for the "aggressive" judgments.

Relation between "aggressive" and "pleasant" judgments. Product-moment correlations were computed between judgments on the "aggres-sive" scale and on the "pleasant" scale. The correlation for content-free judgments was .62, for content-only judgments it was $-.04$, and for nor-mal it was .82. It is clear that "aggressive" and "pleasant" judgments are related in the audible material, but that this is not true for judgments of the typescript.

Analysis with Regard to Voice Sample Variables

"AGGRESSIVE" JUDGMENTS. Since each S spoke in three contexts, the three mean judgments for each S are not independent. The method of analysis of variance of repeated measures was again used for each of the three types of information separately. Thus, in the analysis for each type of information there are independent groups of Ss who differ on HPS and BP scores, and each S yielded three mean judgment scores. (Group I has high HPS and high BP; Group II has high HPS and low BP; Group III has low HPS and low BP.)

One of these analyses, that computed for content-free information shows the only significant difference found in any of the three analyses:

the three groups differ on "aggressive" judgments of content-free information.

The groups may also be compared in another way, appropriate because they differ on two variables, BP and HPS. Two groups, I and II, differ in BP and pairs of Ss in these groups are matched on HPS. Groups II and III differ on HPS and pairs of Ss in these groups are matched on BP. The third possible comparison, between Groups I and III, is not meaningful since these groups differ on both variables.

Comparisons were carried out in this way, i.e., between Groups I and II, and II and III, for the three types of information and for each context separately, resulting in 18 comparisons of "aggressive" judgments. The results may be summarized as follows, without presenting detailed tables of the other comparisons. There were no significant differences between groups in the B or C contexts (the second and third role-playing situations). Results for the A context amplify the previous over-all difference found for content-free information. In this context, the first psychodrama situation, judgments of content-free information differentiated both variables of BP and HPS (both Groups I and II, and II and III, were significantly different). Judgments of normal information differentiated the HPS variable but not BP (Groups II and III were significantly different, but I and II were not).

"PLEASANT" JUDGMENTS. All analyses that have been described for the "aggressive" judgments were also carried out for the "pleasant" judgments. They may be easily summarized: no differences were found to be significant. The correlations measuring congruence between "pleasant" judgments of content-free and content-only information were found to be as follows: $-.18$ for Group I, .21 for Group II, and .07 for Group III. These correlations are in the same relative order as those based on the "aggressive" judgments, but none here are significant, since again an r of .355 is required ($df = 29$) at the .05 level for a significant difference from zero.

Agreement among judges was again used as an inverse measure of ambiguity for the "pleasant" judgments. The correlations were as follows: .27 for Group I, .22 for Group II, and .27 for Group III. These are again all significant beyond the .01 level, but with little difference between groups. Contrary to expectation, judgments of Group II were slightly less reliable.

DISCUSSION

The Information Available for Judging

Results have been presented indicating acceptable reliability of judging for all types of information: content-free, content-only, and normal. The reliabilities were somewhat higher for the "aggressive" judgments than for the "pleasant" judgments. It was expected that confusion might arise between vocal and verbal information and affect the reliability of normal judgments. Significant differences in reliability were not present to bear out this expectation. The possibility remains that judging stereotypes may have more effect on normal information than on isolated aspects, leaving the latter more useful as personality measures.

Since there is an overlap of information between the normal voice and either isolated aspect of voice, a higher correlation was to be expected between normal information and either isolated aspect than between the two isolated aspects themselves. The results from both scales bear out this expectation. In addition, judges seem to have paid more attention to the vocal than to the verbal component when listening to the normal voice; that is, there was a higher correlation between the normal and the vocal than between the normal and the verbal judgments. The finding is in keeping with the expectation that vocal aspects of speech are more important for making expressive judgments, and that judges of personality characteristics will therefore tend to pay more attention to the vocal aspects when listening to a normal recording. To offset this finding, however, it should be pointed out that content was severely restricted in range in the speech samples used since subject matter was controlled by the role-playing situations.

The data give little evidence to justify the use of both "aggressive" and "pleasant" scales. For both kinds of audible information, judgments on the two scales were highly related, with a higher correlation for normal than for content-free speech. A similar finding for normal speech was reported by Eisenberg and Zalowitz, who investigated judgments of "dominance feeling" from normal recordings. They found judgments of dominance generally correlated with favorable qualities, concluding that this was evidence of judging stereotypes and that judgments of voice could not be relied on for personality description.

The high relationship between "aggressive" and "pleasant" judgments suggests that the judges interpreted the "aggressive" scale as "dominant" or "assertive," rather than as "hostile." Labeling the other extreme of this scale as "submissive" was perhaps unfortunate in suggesting this interpretation. If some Ss were heard as "assertive," however, in a negative, hostile way, a difference would be expected between them and others in judgments of "pleasantness." The Harris finding previously mentioned suggested a less acceptable quality in the assertiveness of high HPS Ss with high blood pressure when compared to high HPS Ss with low blood pressure. But the expected difference in "pleasantness" between Groups I and II in this study was not found.

Application of the Combined Judgments to Selected S Groups

It will be recalled that one purpose of the present study was to investigate the possibility that inaccuracy in judgments of normal speech might be due to confusion between verbal and vocal aspects. This confusion is expected to be especially severe if verbal and vocal aspects are incongruent. A reason for choosing prehypertensive Ss for this study was the possibility that they might show verbal-vocal incongruence, which would be shown by a lack of correlation between the isolated verbal and vocal aspects of speech. There was in fact no correlation found between the two aspects of speech of the prehypertensive Ss (Group I). In contrast, the normal expectation of significant congruence was found for the assertive (high HPS) Ss with low blood pressure (Group II). An unexpected finding was a lack of congruence for the unassertive (low HPS) Ss with low blood pressure (Group III).

The measure of congruence does not seem related to the measure of ambiguity as defined by a lack of agreement in judgments of normal speech. This may seem to contradict the results of Kauffman who found a relation between congruence and ambiguity, but it should be remembered that the judging scales and methods of measuring both congruence and ambiguity differ from his, and in addition, his voice samples were contrived to differ greatly in congruence.

"Aggressive" judgments of content-free and normal information differentiated the three groups. Voices of Group II were judged most "aggressive," voices of Group I intermediate, and voices of Group III least "aggressive." Judgments of content-free information were slightly more efficient in this differentiation. This finding is in line with the expectation that the presence of content may be a distraction for judges making expressive judgments. It should be pointed out that there is an element of contamination in the relationship between "aggressive" judgments and HPS scores, since the same voice information available to judges in this study was also available to the original observers from whose Q sorts the HPS score was derived. It is surprising, however, that the aggressive-HPS relationship reappeared in an unequivocal way from 90 short speech samples, presented in a completely scrambled order to judges who knew nothing of the original situations.

An unexpected difference was that of "aggressive" judgments between the two groups with equally high HPS scores but differing in blood pressure. The voices of those with high blood pressure were judged less "aggressive" than those with low blood pressure. The lack of an expected difference between these same two groups on "pleasantness" has already been mentioned. One speculation about the difference found might be that both these groups of Ss were trying to appear assertive, and that prehypertensive Ss succeeded in convincing Q-sort observers of the original situations with many cues, but could not control the vocal aspect of speech rated by judges of their filtered voices. The Ss with low blood pressure and low HPS were not judged as assertive from either many or few cues.

The finding of better group separation for judgments of content-free information adds evidence to the contention that the vocal aspect of speech is of particular importance when interest is focused on the personality of the speaker.

SUMMARY

The present study was designed for two purposes. The first was a comparison of judgments of isolated verbal and vocal aspects of speech to judgments of the same speech in its normal form where both aspects are present. The second was to compare the relative usefulness of the judgments for personality descriptions of Ss likely to develop essential hypertension, who are sometimes said to have difficulty in controlling the expression of emotion and whose speech may therefore show verbal-vocal incongruence.

Three groups of ten Ss each were selected on the basis of their scores both on blood-pressure recordings and on a personality score related to high blood pressure. For each of the Ss, three speech recordings, each 20 seconds long, were selected from the Ss' responses at particular points in role-playing sessions. These 90 speech samples were used as stimulus material for judging in three forms which differed in the information available to the judges: a filtered content-free recording, a normal recording, and content only, presented in typewritten form. For each type of information a separate group of 25 undergraduates judged all 90 voice samples on scales labeled "aggressive," and "pleasant."

It was found that reliability of judging was acceptable, with somewhat higher reliability for "aggressive" than for "pleasant" judgments. The judgments for all types of information significantly differentiated the voices of the 30 Ss, as well as the three voice samples of each S. In addition there were significant interactions of voices and voice samples with information.

The group with high blood-pressure scores showed a lack of significant verbal-vocal congruence. However, a measure of ambiguity of judgments of the normal information did not significantly differentiate the groups, and no relationship was found between the measures of congruence and ambiguity.

When the combined judgment of 25 judges was used as a measure, significant differences were found between groups for "aggressive" judgments of both content-free and normal information of speech samples from the first role-playing situation. Judgments of content-free information were related to both the blood-pressure measure and the personality measure associated with high blood pressure. Judgments of normal information were related only to the personality measure.

The finding of greater relative usefulness of content-free speech is evidence for the importance of the vocal aspect of speech regarding the personality of the speaker.

19 | Tactile Communication
LAWRENCE K. FRANK

I. INTRODUCTION

The skin is the outer boundary, the envelope which contains the human organism and provides its earliest and most elemental mode of communication. Despite its often crucial rôle in human behavior, touch or tactile experiences have been largely neglected, especially by those concerned with personality development and expression. In view of their pervasive rôle in human communication, this statement of what tactile experiences involve may offer clues to further study and provide some insights into the large significance of tactile communications.

Tactile experiences considered as messages and responses are exceedingly diverse and capable of an amazing variety of transformations in human communication, where, as in language, we must recognize both the cultural patterning and the idiosyncratic deviations and elaborations.

The skin, according to the textbooks, is sensitive to warm-cold, pain, and pressure, with varying thresholds to stimulation. The awareness or perception of warmth or cold is, however, relative to the state of the organism, including emotional reactions, immediately prior experience and earlier experience, such as habituation (e.g., "chemical fingers"), also impairment of homeostasis. Pain likewise may be elicited in varying de-

Reprinted with permission of The Journal Press. From *Genetic Psychology Monographs*, 56:209–255 (1957).

grees, although Hardy *et al.* assert a constant threshold to pain produced by a heat lamp upon the forehead. An altered awareness of pain has been observed in individuals under different circumstances, such as fighting, and especially strong sexual or emotional disturbances (which may be exhibited in higher or lower thresholds to pain). And as indicated later (Pathology), there may be acute hyper-sensitivity as well as anesthesias to pain or any tactile stimulation, a masochistic enjoyment of pain, and a variety of aberrant responses to experiences exhibited in and through the skin (stigmata).

Head suggested the two terms: protopathic and epicritic sensory awareness: protopathic being the awareness of the undifferentiated, more or less massive, impacts of noxious, harmful or painful stimuli, and epicritic being the capacity for discriminating through tactile contacts, especially in purposive seeking or skillful manipulations. This distinction, whether or not structurally present in the nerves, calls attention to the two phases or stages in tactile experiences which may be received as gross undifferentiated tactile contacts or pressures, and the finely differentiated contacts of varying intensity and tempo. The first often evokes avoidance although in some cultures close tactile contacts are frequently sought and, of course, are present in sexual intercourse. The second involves not only discrimination of textures, shapes, elasticity, etc., but also manipulations of what is perceived tactually. Tactile perception always involves some kind of contact or impact and may be increased by training or decreased by habituation.

The skin is the largest organ of the body with a variety of functions including the crucial function of acting as a thermostat for regulating the homeostatic processes. Being exposed to the world it receives the direct impacts of the environment which it mediates to the organism. Also, the human skin is being continually renewed in the epidermis and is richly provided with sweat glands, except for a few surfaces, and with apocrine glands under the arm (which do not function until puberty), and with sebaceous glands at the roots of hair. The skin has both a taste and an odor. Thus sweat is salt and secretions from various areas of the body, especially the apocrine glands and the genital areas, may be considered as messages which have a highly stimulating effect on others. Unlike many other mammals, the human body has only vestigial body hair and therefore the human skin is more exposed to the world and is probably more sensitive. Moreover, movements of the hair of the body stimulate various cutaneous sensations by greater or less follicular displacements. Thus, stroking the hair "against the grain" may tickle or be painful, while "with the grain," as the hair lays naturally, may be pleasant, soothing and reassuring.

There are sympathetic connections to the sweat glands and to the capillaries just under the skin, but until recently these have not been considered as conducting tactile stimuli. As is well known, the sweat glands function not only in response to heat, but also as the human subject undergoes stress and emotional reactions of greater or less magnitude—the so-called psycho-galvanic reflex. The capillaries also dilate and contract under similar stimulation of heat-cold and of emotional reaction, as shown by blushing and pallor in various psychosomatic disorders, like Reynaud's disease.

Rats which have been gentled are better able to metabolize food and are less susceptible to surgical shock (Hammett), and various forms of experimentally produced convulsions, etc. (Bovard). Licking, nuzzling, cuddling of young mammals by the mother is a form of tactual stimulation that apparently has an important function in the care and rearing of the young. Kittens cannot urinate or defecate unless the mother licks the anus or urethra and thereby elicits evacuation (Reyniers). Rats raised from birth with a cardboard ruff around their necks to prevent licking their bodies were less capable as adults of caring for their own young by licking them (Birch). Pavlov is reported to have induced sleep in dogs by applying rhythmic electrical stimuli of low intensity to the skin of the animal.

While we think of the skin as the outer integument exposed to the world, the gut, from the mouth to the anus, is exposed to material from the environment and is lined with epithelial cells not unrelated to the skin and derived from the same embryological layer as skin and nervous system. It is also significant that end organs for tactile stimuli are richly provided in and around the mouth and anus, in the male and female genitals, and are apparently more numerous or sensitive in the skin adjacent to these parts, the so-called erogenous zones or areas. Apparently the human female is actually sensitive all over her body (M. Mead).

Tactual sensitivity is probably the most primitive sensory process appearing as a tropism, thigmotaxis, in lower organisms. Many infra-human organisms are oriented by their feelers or antennae by which they feel their way through life. It is also the primary mode of orientation to the world in organisms living underground, in fish and probably many reptiles. Tactual sensitivity operates before the appearance of other sensory processes, except perhaps the chemical sensitivity of organisms to alterations in their fluid medium (reaction to heat-cold, acidity-alkalinity), presence or absence of specific chemical substances, and later to odors. Even smell may be considered as a refined tactual response—the airborne particles impinging upon the olfactory organs.

Being such a primitive mode of reception and orientation, tactual sensitivity is of large significance in the early development of the infant, both as an embryo and as a foetus, and in the early years of life. Also, being the primary mode of infantile communication, tactile experiences are crucial in later learning, providing much of the basic experiences for developing symbolic recognition and response, as will be discussed later. In view of this, it is noteworthy that many theories of personality development have generally ignored or neglected tactile experiences to focus upon the sphincters and orifices—mouth, anus, urethra, which, however, operate largely by tactual stimulation and the variations therein induced by experiences, largely tactile. The various orifices and sphincters, such as the mouth and lips, the anus and perineum, the genitals, the nose and eyelids, are all richly supplied with end organs for tactile reception with low thresholds normally.

II. TACTILE EXPERIENCES IN PERSONALITY DEVELOPMENT

During the nine months of gestation, the embryo and foetus is continuously receiving the rhythmic impacts of the maternal heart beat, transmitted through the amniotic fluid (and therefore magnified), impinging upon the skin of his whole body. His own heart beats will later synchronize or be out of tune with the maternal heart beats and so provide either a series of coordinated or dissimilar impacts upon his skin to which he develops a continuous response, as a physiological resonance. Thus at birth the infant comes from a rhythmically pulsating environment into an atmosphere where he has to exist as a discrete organism and relate himself through a variety of modes of communication. Probably the infants who are carried close to the mother on her back or hip receive some continuation of these rhythmic impacts upon the skin.

At birth the foetus passing through the birth canal undergoes a series of pressures and constrictions which involve sometimes intense tactual experiences. Moreover, the newborn is more or less suddenly exposed to the atmospheric pressures and altered temperature, evoking respiratory activity and presumably a number of tactile responses. The skin of the newborn is covered with a creamy substance which, if not interfered with, will be absorbed like a vanishing cream. Usually the newborn is bathed, dried, and often oiled, greased, or powdered.

The infant's need for contacts, for nuzzling, cuddling, patting, and his usually quick and accepting response to these tactile messages may be largely derived from his uterine experiences which have exercised his tactuality. Each infant differs in his "needs," his susceptibility and response and in the time when he will relinquish these infantile experiences and accept alienation from close contact with the mother. Putting fingers, thumb, food, objects or parts of another person's body in the mouth is a tactual experience. It may lead to chewing and swallowing or it may be retained and used as a source of gratification. Parental care and love may be largely tactual contacts and comforting, reassuring tactile experiences which give the infant encouragement and the confidence in the world as well as physiological assistance in achieving a more effective homeostasis, especially when under stress. Thus the kind and duration of early tactile experiences wherein the infant can send and receive messages outside his body have a large significance in early personality development as his first so-called "object-relations." "No new external element gives rise to perceptive, motor or intelligent adaptation without being related to earlier activities."

It is well recognized that the newborn mammal "needs" to be nuzzled, and licked, by the mother who, among infra-human species, performs these functions after biting the cord and often eating the placenta. The young remain close to the mother's body, receiving warmth and close tactual contacts, plus frequent licking and nursing. The human infant may receive a variety of treatments that conforms to this mammalian pattern or departs drastically therefrom. Some infants are kept close to the mother, may be given the colostrum (as do infra-human babies), allowed to nurse freely and as long as desired. Other infants may be isolated from the mother, as in most hospitals, fed at intervals and given a minimum of bodily contacts. The opossum young are extreme cases of pups born prematurely who can survive only by attaching themselves to a teat and remaining there close to the mother for the time necessary for maturation. Tactile experience is immediate, and transitory, operating only as long as contact is maintained. It is also a reciprocal experience in the sense that what a person touches also touches him, and often evokes emotional reactions of greater or less magnitude. Tactile experience is ordinarily limited to two persons, a means to intimacy and expression of affection or hostility and anger.

In his earliest experiences, the infant has a number of tactile experiences: close bodily contacts, being cuddled or patted rhythmically, touching the lips to the mother's body and more specifically to the nipple, increasingly fingering or handling the mother, especially the breast. These experiences may be viewed as early tactile communications which are carried on as transactional processes. The infant evokes from the mother the tactile stimulation which he "needs" and to which he responds in his own individual fashion as in sucking; the mother solicits from the infant this touching and sucking, which evokes milk from the breast. Babies seem to differ widely in their "needs" for tactile experiences and in their acceptance and response to tactile ministrations. They are dependent upon the mother person who may provide these generously or may deny or largely deprive the infant of these experiences. A baby may become attached to a blanket, soft cuddly animal, a rattle and begin to enjoy the tactile contacts, especially of textures. These early-found sources of satisfaction may serve as surrogates for contact with the mother's person.

It may not be unwarranted to assume that the infant initially has a primitive tactual sensitivity and capacity for response which is acute at birth in varying degrees in individual infants and which needs to be functionally operative and fulfilled as an essential stage in his development. Denial or deprivation of these early tactile experiences may compromise his future learning, such as speech, cognition, and symbolic recognition, and his capacity for more mature tactile communication, as we will discuss later. This initial or primary tactual sensitivity and need for tactile experiences may then diminish, or be incorporated in larger patterns as do the early reflexes (Babinski diminishing but retained in walking).

In these early tactile experiences we may see more clearly how the infant begins to communicate tactually and gradually enlarges his communications as he develops his capacities for other sensory awareness and perception and for other forms of response. Here the suggestion made earlier about signals, signs, and symbols finds application since in infant development, and indeed in personality development generally, we may observe this progression from signal to sign to symbol.

The baby begins to communicate with himself by feeling his own body, exploring its shape and textures, discovering its orifices and thereby begins to establish his body image which, of course, is reinforced or often negated by pleasurable or painful tactile experiences with other human beings. It seems highly probable that the continual physiological alterations internally, some of which he has such as colic or stomach ache or a full bladder or rectum, also enter into this evolving image of the body. Later on various visual cues may be established as he focuses his vision upon his fingers and feet and so begins to build up a visual image to supplement and to reinforce his tactile experiences.

As indicated in the section on "Cultural Patterning of Tactile Processes," one of the basic experiences of a child is learning to respect the inviolability of things, animals, places, and persons which occurs when the child becomes mobile and explores the world. This involves the curtailment and prohibition of tactile experiences, forbidding the child to touch whatever is defined by adults as inviolable (property, sacred places, forbidden objects, persons). His naïve approach to these inviting object-persons is blocked and prohibited, often with painful punishment, until they are perceived as not-touchable except when he has permission or has performed the necessary rituals, negotiations, buying, etc. Not only are these tactile experiences of crucial significance for social order, but the transformation of the child's naïve impulsive response to the world into the learned observance of inviolability, usually involves emotional disturbances, conflicts with parents and often over-learning, so that the child may become inhibited and less capable of making tactile contacts, even those which he or she may seek as occasions for interpersonal relations, as in intercourse.

Here we see how tactile experiences undergo a second critical phase. Early, he has experienced primary tactile fulfillment or denial as a baby, and developed his idiosyncratic mode of tactile communication and its elaboration into other modes. Now he must undergo an often severe restriction upon tactile experiences in which the world around him is alienated from his touch so that he must learn to recognize almost everything visually and auditorially, as a symbol of inviolability which he must recognize, inhibiting his spontaneous impulse to touch or strike. His own body, especially the genitals, may be defined as inviolable, not to be touched under penalty of punishment. This means the child must learn to impute inviolability to what was previously accessible and thereby he is inducted into the social world of respect for property and persons and of sex morals, according to the often highly elaborate codes of custom and law. Needless to say, children may learn to observe these inviolabilities through punishment, and exhibit law-abiding conduct when watched or fearful of detection and punishment, but not develop the self-administered inhibitions for social order. Or, they undergo continual conflicts between the impulsive response to forbidden things and persons and the partially learned, but not fully accepted, prohibitions. A recognition of the basic tactile experiences in learning socially-prescribed conduct and respect for the law offers clues to the genetic study of socialization and its vicissitudes.

Tactile communications are also involved in interpersonal relations in a more direct manner, as we may observe in the infant and child. Through the earliest bodily contacts and other tactile experiences, the baby communicates in a reciprocal way, mother to baby, and baby to mother, one evoking from the other what will in turn evoke his or her response in a tactile dialectic. These experiences establish the individual's early pattern of intimacy and affection, his first interpersonal relations which apparently persist as a sort of template by which he establishes and conducts his subsequent interpersonal relations, using verbal and kinesic patterns, especially in more intimate sexual relations. The baby develops confidence in the world, trust in people, through these early tactile relations which reciprocally establish the meaning of the world for him and also his expectations and feelings toward that world.

If the baby is limited in his tactile experiences, denied much opportunity to send or receive tactile communications, he presumably must wait until his capacity for visual and auditory recognition and reception have developed sufficiently to permit him to enter into communication with others. Thus, such a child will not only have little of the primary tactile experiences upon which to develop his sign and symbolic communication, but will be expected to rely upon more or less arbitrary visual and auditory symbols and to accept their meanings, not as experientially learned, but as prescribed by others. This suggests that while children so reared can and do learn sign and symbol recognition and response, they may be more dependent than other children upon the authority of parents who define and impose these signs and symbols. These children, also being limited in early motor activities and manipulation therefore may be more willing to abide by authoritative pronouncements or more ready to rebel.

In adolescence we see the increasing frequency of tactile communication, at first between members of the same sex, as boys walk together with arms on each others' shoulders, girls with arms around each others' waists, and then the first tentative heterosexual explorations of caressing, petting, "necking" and frequently attempts at intercourse. Tactile communication in adult mating, both as foreplay and in intercourse, has been elaborated and refined by some cultures into the most amazing array of erotic patterns which through a variety of tactual stimulation of various parts of the body serve to arouse, prolong, intensify, and evoke communication. Here we see tactile communication, reinforced and elaborated by motor activities and language, by concomitant stimulation, visual, auditory, olfactory, gustatory, and the deeper muscle senses, combined to provide an organic-personality relationship which may be one of the most intense human experiences. It is, or can be, considered an esthetic experience in that there be little or no instrumental, purposive or cognitive elements, with greater or less loss of space-time orientation. But the elementary sexual processes of the human organism may be transformed and focused into an interpersonal love relationship with an identified person to whom each is seeking to communicate, using sex not for procreation, as in the mating of a female in heat ready to be fertilized, but as "another language" for interpersonal communication. Here we see how the primary tactile mode of communication, which has been largely overlaid and superseded by auditory and visual signs and symbols, is reinstated to function with elementary organic intensity, provided the individuals have not lost the capacity for communication with the self through tactile experiences.

III. CULTURAL PATTERNING OF TACTILE EXPERIENCES

As pointed out in the discussion of personality development, cultures differ in the kind, amount, and duration of tactile experiences people give the infant. Thus the parents in each culture activate or limit initial tactile communication with the infant and provide such tactile communication in and through the patterns and relationships which are prescribed or permitted by tradition.

Grooming the skin, bathing of all kinds, anointing, oiling, perfuming the skin, plucking hair, shaving, are patterns for modifying communication by the skin, again relying upon visual cues to indicate tactual readiness for communication (actual or symbolic). Such grooming and decorating may also serve as signs of rank, caste, prestige, authority which others recognize and respond to with appropriate conduct. Indeed, these skin decorations and coverings are of large significance in the assumption and performance of the various rôles when not only the individual assuming a rôle must act in a prescribed manner, but others must respond appropriately if the rôle performance is to be completed. Here the skin serves like a carrier wave upon which the particular message is imposed as a modification or patterning of that wave, as in telephoning.

Thus admiring glances, indicating approval of the individual's clothing, body arts, and grooming, serve as surrogates for invitations to actual tactile contacts. This is often elaborated in the customary public exhibition of the self through which courtship is conducted openly and directly, or indirectly as in public strolling or dancing.

The masculine and feminine rôles are defined in large part by these different patterns of exposure of skin, body arts, clothing, grooming, and the kinds of tactile approaches and contacts allowed or forbidden to the male and female. Since masculinity and femininity are more or less polarized positions and relations which the boy and girl must learn, each may develop a kind of complementary tactile communication in which the intent may be, not primarily to transmit a message, but to evoke a response by a variety of tactual approaches or exhibition of signs and symbols of tactile significance. If these responses are evoked, then the initiator may offer more direct tactile communication as in flirting or seduction. There is usually a well-established code for these communications, with degree of intimacy of direct tactual contacts.

Each culture fosters or specifically trains its young as children and as adolescents to develop different kinds of thresholds to tactile contacts and stimulation so that their organic, constitutional, temperamental characteristics are accentuated or reduced. As adults they are more susceptible and vulnerable, or are anesthetic and indifferent to various kinds of tactile communications, as is evidenced by the clinical material on the number and variety of tactual idiosyncrasies, including sexual. Moreover, each culture builds upon the early tactile experience of the infant and child a more or less elaborate series of patterns of adult conduct in which tactile surrogates and symbolic fulfillments are provided.

We may say, therefore, that tactile experiences seem to be basic to many of the crucially important patterns of a culture, that tactile communication takes place on the level of signals, direct tactual stimulation, and on the level of signs and symbols which have been established as surrogates for tactile communications, both for sending and receiving. As in other forms of communication, tactile communication is highly susceptible to interference by noise (any kind of disturbance in transmission, or confusion and conflict in sender or receiver) is peculiarly ambiguous, often redundant and liable to frequent errors in coding and decoding. Without tactile communication, interpersonal relations would be bare and largely meaningless, with a minimum of affective coloring or emotional provocation, since linguistic and much of kinetic communication are signs and symbols which become operative only by evoking some of the responses which were initially stimulated by the tactile stimuli for which these signs and symbols are surrogates. Tactile communications are largely reciprocal transactions between two persons, each of whom in responding to the other, provides the stimulus for a response to him that will in turn initiate his response in a tactile dialectic of greater or less duration. These interpersonal communications may become increasingly symbolic as individuals learn to use words and gestures for sending and receiving such messages as culturally patterned.

Severing tactile communications, especially those which have involved intimacy, often creates a crisis for one or both participants for which some cultures provide rituals, ceremonies, and special sanctions (such as legal separation or divorce), or puberty rites. Likewise, as indicated earlier, specific rituals, like betrothal and marriage, are provided in some cultures as public sanction for establishing tactile communications, while others permit premarital relations which eventually lead to marriage.

In ritual and ceremonial activities, the tactile communications play a large rôle, but often on a symbolic level where there is no actual tactile contact, but every action implies or indicates as in the dance some tactile communication, a threat or invitation, and its patterned response. This is apparent in much of the kinesic activity and communication and in linguistic communication where the message may originate in a tactile context, be coded in verbal symbols, and decoded into tactile experiences.

The elaboration and refinement of cultures may be interpreted in part as the provision of signs and symbols as surrogates for tactile communications which, being more elementary and ambiguous, are superseded by more discriminatory symbols, just as writing offers more scope and subtlety than hieroglyphics or a rebus. Abstractions, concepts, generalizations would seem to be impossible through tactile communication, but tactile experiences transformed into signs and symbols may become abstracted and conceptualized as in finger language used by the blind, as Helen Keller has shown.

It should be emphasized that the establishment of signs and symbols has been a very difficult and often precarious undertaking. Every culture has been dependent upon gifted individuals who could perceive the world in new ways and imaginatively create the symbols which then were accepted and utilized by others. Since this is the kind of world in which many events are occurring more or less simultaneously, and every event, object, and animal appears in a context of greater or less complexity that is, with many other existents, it is not at all easy or simple to recognize which particular signal belongs to or is emitted by a specific event, object, or animal to be identified. We speak of data, which literally means that which is given, but the whole history of science shows that these so-called data or signals are rarely or ever given; they must be laboriously and often painfully discovered, isolated, and established as unequivocal indicators of whatever is the focus of inquiry. Indeed, we might say that the progress of science takes place in large part through the recognition that what have been considered as valid data are not reliable and unequivocal indicators and must be replaced by other indicators that seem to be more nearly reliable signals.

20 | Nonverbal Language and Therapy
JURGEN RUESCH

Specifically I shall be concerned with the following facts: First, that mental disease is intimately associated with disturbances in sign behavior, language, and communication. Second, that disturbances in nonverbal sign behavior, language, and communication are associated with more severe and often longer lasting mental and nervous conditions, while disturbances in verbal sign behavior, language, and communication are associated with less severe psychiatric conditions. And third, that the way is now open for the development of new and more effective methods of therapy.

Broadly speaking, nonverbal forms of language fall into three distinct categories: *Sign language* includes all those forms of codification in which words, numbers, and punctuation signs have been supplanted by gestures; these vary from the 'monosyllabic' gesture of the hitchhiker to such complete systems as the language of the deaf. *Action language* embraces all movements that are not used exclusively as signals. Such acts as walking and drinking, for instance, have a dual function; on the one hand, they serve personal needs, and on the other, they constitute statements to

Reprinted with permission of the author and by special permission of the William Alanson White Psychiatric Foundation, Inc. Copyright © 1957. From *Psychiatry*, 18:323–330 (1955).

those who may perceive them. *Object language* comprises all intentional and nonintentional display of material things such as implements, machines, art objects, architectural structures, and last but not least, the human body and whatever clothes it. The embodiment of letters in books and on signs has a material substance, and this aspect of words also has to be considered as object language.

Although these various forms of nonverbal codification differ somewhat from each other, they can nevertheless be considered together for comparison with verbal codifications. From the evidence presented in Table I and the experience gained in the construction of computers, in the study of interpersonal communication, and in the study of neuroanatomy, neurophysiology, and speech pathology, one can presume the existence of at least two principles of human symbolization, the analogic and the verbal or digital, which apply to both intraorganismic and interpersonal codifications. Since these two kinds of codification yield different types of information, the human being is faced with the task of exploiting the resulting attenuations, reinforcements, repetitions, or contradictions, in order to obtain additional knowledge about the events he is trying to understand. Indeed, the problem of coordinating information based upon different codifications—not to mention the difficulties involved in coordinating information which is contradictory because of other factors —becomes a major task. But unfortunately not all people are capable of mastering these difficulties inherent in language and human communication. The defects encountered may reflect primarily lack of mastery of nonverbal codifications, lack of mastery of verbal codifications, or deficient synchronization between the two methods of codification. But none of these disturbances is really pure and isolated; in accepting the genetic principle as a factor in the development of psychopathology one is in fact saying that earlier, nonverbal events determine later verbal and general communicative behavior.

In language development, the gradual shift from nonverbal to verbal codifications occurs in three distinct steps: The earliest forms of codification involve action signals, mediated predominantly through contraction of the smooth muscles, which appear in changes in the color and temperature of the skin, the consistency of bowel movements, the rate of breathing, and other movements, such as sucking, which are subordinated to those autonomic functions. Although such statements as can be made in early infancy usually are unintentional, they are language in the sense that the signals are understandable to both mother and child. Later on, when the child is learning to move, such somatic language is supplemented by action signals mediated through contraction of the striped muscles. The external expression of inner events through bodily manifestations of the intestinal, respiratory, and vascular systems recedes and is replaced by movements of the face and the extremities. Finally, when social action has been learned, verbal, gestural, and other symbolic forms of denotation replace some of the previously employed methods of action codification.

The consideration of language development and the relationship of nonverbal to verbal codifications sheds some light upon the shortcomings

Table 1

Similarities and Differences between Verbal and Nonverbal Codification

Nonverbal Codification	Verbal Codification
General Characteristics	
The nonverbal denotation unit is a Gestalt, the appreciation of which is based on analogies.	The verbal denotation unit—either sound or its written representation—is based on phonetics.
The nonverbal denotation unit can be broken down further—for example, parts of a unit such as a photograph can be cut out and the details are meaningful in themselves.	The verbal denotation unit—spoken or written —cannot be broken down further; for example, there does not exist a meaningful fraction of the letter, word, or sound A.
Nonverbal denotation is based on continuous functions; for example, the hand is continuously involved in movement as long as the organism lives.	Verbal denotation is based on discontinuous functions; for example, sounds and letters have a discrete beginning and end.
Nonverbal denotation is governed by principles and rules which depend largely upon biological necessities—for example, the signals which indicate alarm.	Verbal denotation is governed by arbitrary, man made principles; for example, grammatical and language rules differ in various cultural groups
Nonverbal denotation is used as an international, intercultural, interracial, and interspecies language; it is adapted to communication with an out-group.	Verbal denotation is used as a culturally specific language; it is adapted to communication with the in-group.
Spatiotemporal Characteristics	
Nonverbal denotation can indicate successive events simultaneously; for example, come and go signals can be given at the same time.	Verbal denotation must indicate simultaneous events successively; for example, a spoken or written report consists of words which are aligned serially.
Nonverbal denotation is temporally flexible; for example, a movement can be carried out slowly or quickly.	Verbal denotation is temporally rather inflexible; for example, words when spoken too slowly or too quickly become unintelligible.
Nonverbal denotation is spatially inflexible; movements and objects require a known but inflexible amount of space.	Verbal denotation is spatially flexible; print may be large or small.
Methods of nonverbal denotation such as sketches, photographs, or three-dimensional models can represent space superbly.	Verbal denotation cannot indicate space successfully except for description of boundaries.
Nonverbal denotation is poor for indicating elapsed time, but good for indicating timing and coordination.	Verbal denotation is good for indicating elapsed time, but poor for indicating timing and coordination.

Characteristics Referring to Perception, Evaluation, and Transmission

Nonverbal denotation can be perceived by distance and proximity receivers alike; for example, action may be not only seen and heard, but may also produce physical impact.

Verbal denotation can be perceived by distance receivers only; that is, it can only be heard or read.

Nonverbal language influences perception, co-ordination, and integration, and leads to the acquisition of skills.

Verbal language influences thinking and leads to the acquisition of information.

In nonverbal language, evaluation is tied to appreciation of similarities and differences.

In verbal language, evaluation is governed by principles of logic.

In nonverbal language, expression may be skilled or unskilled, but regardless of its quality, it is usually understandable.

In verbal language, expression must be skilled; otherwise it is unintelligible.

The understanding of nonverbal denotation is based upon the participant's empathic assessment of biological similarity; no explanation is needed for understanding what pain is.

The understanding of verbal denotation is based on prior verbal agreement; the word *pain* differs from the Geman word *Schmerz* or the French word *douleur*, and the understanding of the significance of these words is bound to such previous arrangements.

Neurophysiological and Developmental Characteristics

Nonverbal denotation is tied to phylogenetically old structures of the central and autonomic nervous systems.

Verbal denotation is tied to phylogenetically younger structures, particularly the cortex.

Nonverbal denotation is learned early in life.

Verbal denotation is learned later in life.

In the presence of brain lesions, analogic understanding may be affected, while repetition of words or ability to read is retained; for example, disturbances such as aphasic alexia or transcortical sensory aphasia indicate separate neural pathways for nonverbal as opposed to verbal codification.

In the presence of brain lesions, understanding may be retained while verbal ability is impaired; for example, verbal agnosia or alexia indicate again separate neural pathways for verbal as opposed to nonverbal codification.

Nonverbal codification involves complicated networks and includes the effector organs; for example, athletes and musicians go through certain warming-up motions prior to a performance.

Verbal codification involves the central nervous system only; for example, no movements and no external perceptions are necessary in order to recall a name.

Semantic Characteristics

Actions and objects exist in their own right and usually fulfill not only symbolic but also practical functions.

Words do not exist in their own right; they are only symbols. Words, therefore, represent abstractions of aspects of events, the accuracy of which is a function of the human observer.

Nonverbal codifications permit redundancies.

Verbal codification produces fatigue when redundant.

Nonverbal codifications permit brief and succinct statements.

Verbal codification necessitates somewhat long-winded statements.

Nonverbal codifications are subject-oriented.

Verbal codification is predicate-oriented.

Nonverbal codifications have emotional appeal.

Verbal codification exerts an intellectual appeal.

Nonverbal, analogic codifications are suitable for understanding.

Verbal codification is suitable for reaching agreements.

Nonverbal codifications represent an intimate language.

Verbal codification represents a distant language.

of psychotherapeutic methods. For example, when a patient verbalizes his memories or relates his dreams, a psychiatrist who attempts to reconstruct earlier events usually obtains a one-sided view. Those aspects that lend themselves most readily to verbal treatment—names of persons and places, labels of situations, and designations of stereotyped actions and unusual events—usually make up the bulk of these accounts. Every good therapist eventually arrives at the inescapable conclusion that verbal accounts cannot adequately represent analogically codified events. Furthermore, verbal denotation cannot adequately represent experiences and skills which are accessible in terms of action only. However, society, including the majority of psychiatrists, looks askance at re-enactment, action therapy, stimulation of the proximity receivers, or nonverbal exchange. When the patient has to deny himself or is denied by others nonverbal modes of exchange and analogic expression, the only solution left is a psychosis. And strangely enough, in a psychosis the nonverbal needs of a patient are acknowledged. The successful communicative therapies for acute mental illness are designed to further nonverbal expression and to stimulate the proximity receivers; among them are music therapy, psychodrama, dancing, play and occupational therapy, and such treatment methods as wet packs, continuous baths, and massage. One of the aims of therapy is to provide mentally sick patients with tasks which may develop their analogic codifications into a language which can be shared with others, but no such provisions have been made for prepsychotic conditions. Actually, by his fear that the patient may repress, the psychiatrist is likely to indicate to the patient that he does not understand the problem. He will not seem to appreciate that the patient has to gain communicative experience in the nonverbal mode before he can engage in verbal exchange.

CHAPTER VI

Networks: Directions and Distances

INTRODUCTION   All communication can be represented as transmission through space, as dispatching from one point to another. These points can be organized into networks—by highways and railways, or telephone lines and coaxial cables. In human communication the signals of the preceding section are transmitted through human space, across social and psychological distances. This human space is also organized into networks. The study of these human networks is most advanced in the analysis of small social groups, and these studies are generally based on the social psychological theory that was presented earlier.

Alex Bavelas in "A Mathematical Model for Group Structures" presents a general approach to the communication structures of psychological situations. As five points can be organized in different ways, into pentagons or into crosses, so groups of five people can be organized into different communicational networks. The lines of these networks represent who talks to whom. Bavelas develops a geometry of these human networks, spaces, and cells.

Harold J. Leavitt, following Bavelas' approach, conducts experiments with small groups to determine "Some Effects of Certain Communicational Patterns on Group Performance." In these experiments, the members of the group are dealt cards with different symbols on them. The task of the group is to find the symbol that is common to all the hands. Leavitt finds that different kinds of communicational networks lead to differences in the accuracy of accomplishing the task, differences in the satisfaction that members of the group have in working in a particular network, and differences in the leadership positions that develop within the group. Leavitt's experiments are replicated by Harold Guetzkow and Herbert A. Simon in "The Impact of Certain Communication Nets upon Organization and Performance in Task-Oriented Groups." They show that different communicational networks make a difference primarily in how small groups can organize. In turn, this procedural difference in ability to organize leads to the substantive differences in the accuracy and speed with which a task is accomplished.

Thus it is evident that if two different groups are given the same task but different communicational networks, one network can be more efficient than the other. But what if two different groups are given the same network but different kinds of tasks? Leavitt, Guetzkow, and Simon gave their groups tasks that had explicit and logical solutions. Marvin E. Shaw, Gerard H. Rothschild, and John F. Strickland in "Decision Processes in Communication Nets" give their groups a task that "does not have a generally agreed upon solution, e.g., a problem requiring agreement among the group members about the proper way to deal with an issue involving interpersonal relations." Their results indicate that different tasks call for different networks.

Mauk Mulder in "The Power Variable in Communicative Experiments" adds another dimension to the social psychological distances that are organized into human networks. We often ignore the power dimension in social relations (in accordance with a cultural taboo), but Mulder's experiments show that people tend to reduce their distance from more powerful group members, and increase their distance from less powerful members—in a European military setting. These increases and decreases are preferences and rejections, and they too determine who communicates with whom. The studies in this section have had a significant impact in industrial management.

A Mathematical Model for Group Structures

21

ALEX BAVELAS

INTRODUCTION

At the time of the first world war psychologists in Germany were splitting roughly into these two camps: One group followed the path of breaking down the person and the situation into elements and attempting to explain behavior in terms of simple causal relationships. The other group attempted to explain behavior as a function of groups of factors constituting a dynamic whole—the psychological field. This field consisted essentially of the person himself and his environment as he saw it. In these terms, the problem was no longer conceived as one of relationships between isolated elements, but one of dynamic interplay of all the factors of the situation.

At this time Kurt Lewin began to formulate a method of analysis of psychological situations which rested upon their restatement in mathematical terms: geometry for the expression of the positional relationships between parts of the life space, and vectors for the expression of strength, direction, and point of application of psychological forces. The use of geometry was natural in a psychological approach which insisted upon a world "as the person himself sees it," since human beings tend to picture the contextual field as existing in a "space" around them. Also, the geometric approach offered a convenient means for diagramatic representation of many psychological situations.

Concepts of pattern and communication are the heart of this paper. They are developed with the deliberate purpose of application to psychological situations. Although no rigid coordination of these ideas with psychological or social situations is attempted, general areas within which

Reprinted with permission of the Society for Applied Anthropology and the author. From *Applied Anthropology*, 7:16–30 (1948).

application might be fruitful are suggested. For instance, in the realm of social groups, there would seem to be two outstanding aspects of communication deserving attention: that of communication between individuals (or between groups), and that of communication between ideas and attitudes. The spread of rumor is a good example of the close relationship between these aspects. While the rapidity, direction, and extent of the spread depends partly upon the patterns of connection between individuals and groups, they also depend—especially with respect to the growth and bias of the rumor, and the readiness to hear and transmit—upon the connection of the content of the rumor with other ideas and attitudes.

BASIC ASSUMPTION

1. The space being dealt with consists of collections of cells.
2. A cell is equivalent to a point or position in the space.
3. A given cell may or may not be touching another cell.
4. If a cell A_1 is touching another cell A_2, then cell A_2 is said to be touching cell A_1.
5. A cell cannot touch itself.

DEFINITIONS

1. Boundary of a cell: the boundary of a cell A consists of all cells touching A.
2. Region: a region is any class or collection of cells.
3. Open cell: cell A is open relative to region g if the boundary of A is not contained in g.
4. Closed cell: cell A is closed relative to region g if the boundary of A is contained in g.
5. Boundary of a region: the boundary of the region g is the class of all cells not in g and touching at least one cell in g.
6. Chain: cells A_1, A_2, ..., A_n are said to form a chain if A_1 is touching A_2, A_2 is touching A_3, ..., A_{n-1} is touching A_n. A_n may or may not be equivalent to A_1.
    a) Simple chain: cells A_1, A_2, ..., A_n are said to form a simple chain if A_1 touches cell A_2 and no other cell, if A_2 touches A_1 and A_3 and no other cell, if A_3 touches A_2 and A_4 and no other cell, etc., ...and cell A_n touches cell A_{n-1} and either does or does not touch cell A_1.
7. Length of a chain: the length of a chain is equal to the number of cells contained in the chain less one.
8. Structure: a region g is said to be a structure if for any pair of cell A_1, A_2 contained in g, there exists a chain contained in g and connecting A_1 and A_2.
9. Distance between two cells: the distance between any two cells A_1, $A_2(\overline{A_1 A_2})$ in a structure w is the minimum length chain contained in w and connecting A_1 and A_2.
10. Distance between a cell and a region: when cell A and region g are both included in w, and when A is not in g two distances are distinguished.
    a) Maximum distance: the longest distance of all distances from A to every cell in g.

b) Minimum distance: the shortest of all distances from cell A to any cell in g.

11. The outermost region of a structure: the outermost region of a structure is the class of all cells which are open relative to the structure.

12. The innermost region of a structure: the innermost region of a structure is the class of all cells with the largest minimum distance from the outermost region of the structure.

13. The largest of the maximum distances between the outermost and innermost regions of a structure is denoted by the letter r.

14. The largest of all distances between a cell A_1 and any other cell in the structure is denoted by p.

15. The diameter of a structure: the diameter of a structure (d) is equal to the largest p that can be found in the structure.

16. The central region of a structure: the central region of a structure is the class of all cells with the smallest p to be found in the structure.

17. The peripheral region of a structure: the peripheral region of a structure is the class of all cells having the greatest maximum distance from the central region. This distance will be denoted as c.

A DISCUSSION OF THE DISTANCES d, c, and r.

A Method of Illustration

In a discussion of patterns of communication within a structure, three structural distances are distinguished: d, c, and r (see Definitions 12, 14, & 17). Although not strictly necessary, and often undesirable, some kind of picture of a structure is helpful in illustrating certain relationships between these distances. The pictures will be constructed in the following way: a structure of three cells all of which touch each other would be shown as in Figure 1. If in this structure cell A was an open cell (see Definition 3), the structure would be shown as in Figure 2. The picture shown in Figure 3 would mean (1) that A, C, F were open cells and that B, D, E were closed cells; (2) that A (with respect to this structure) touched only B, and F touched only E; that B touched A and D, D touched B, C, and E, and E touched D and F.

The reason for this change from the kind of pictures used by Lewin is that certain types of structures are very difficult or impossible to draw in that manner. For instance, it is impossible to represent, Lewin-wise, a structure in which A touches B, B touches C, and A and C are open cells and B is closed. (See Figure 4.) The distance d (Definition 14: The largest of all distances between a cell A_1 and any other cell in the structure is denoted by p; Definition 15: The diameter of a structure (d) is equal to the largest p that can be found in the structure.)

The way in which the distance d may vary in a structure with a constant number of cells can be shown by the use of several pictures.

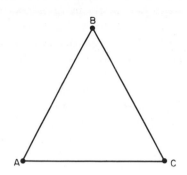

Figure 1.

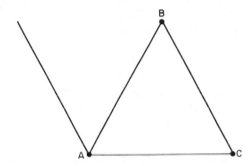

Figure 2.

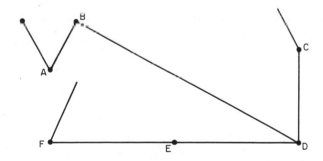

Figure 3.

Figure 4.

It may be seen from the foregoing illustrations that the limits of the distance d may be expressed in terms of n (the number of cells in the structure). The value of d will be at its minimum when the longest distance which may be found between any two cells is equal to n-(n-1) or simply 1, as in Figure 5c. The value of d will be at a maximum when the longest distance to be found between any two cells is equal to n-1— which means that the structure will take the form of a simple chain in which the first cell does not touch the last one. The distance c (Definition 17:) (The peripheral region of structure is the class of all cells having the greatest maximum distance from the central region. This distance will be denoted as c.)

The way in which the distance c may vary in a structure with a constant number of cells is shown in Figure 6.

In Figure 6c the peripheral region (see Definition 16) would consist of cells A and F. Lewin defines the peripheral region of a structure as all cells A for which a cell B may be found so that the shortest distance from A to B is equal to d. In some cases, such as that shown in Figure 6c, both definitions distinguish the same region. In other cases, such as that shown in Figure 6d, the regions distinguished are different.

According to Lewin's definition the peripheral region consists of cells A, B, C, D, E, F, G, H. According to the definition in this paper the peripheral region consists of cells A, B, C, D.

The distance r (Definition 13: The largest of the maximum distances between the outermost and innermost regions of a structure is denoted by the letter r.)

The way in which the distance r may vary in a structure with a constant number of cells is shown in the following pictures.

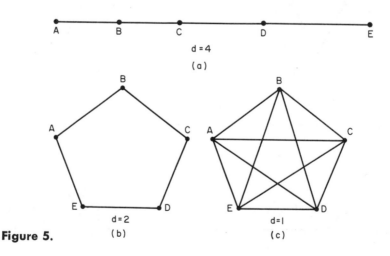

Figure 5.

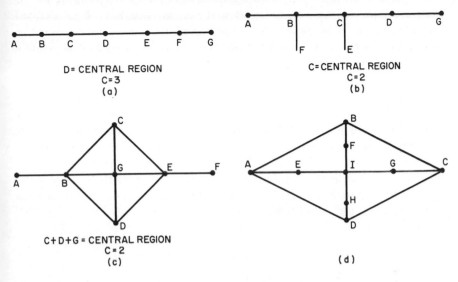

Figure 6.

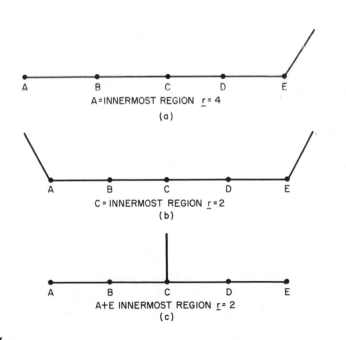

Figure 7.

In addition to showing how the distance c may vary, Figures 7a, 7b, 7c illustrate some of the properties of a region as they have been defined (see Definition 2). In Figure 7c, for instance, the region distinguished as innermost consists of two non-connected cells as far apart as it is possible for them to be.

CONCLUSION

The mathematical model presented here is admittedly in an early state of development, and the problem of coordinating the mathematical concepts to psychological data is still to be met. The main objective of this paper is to define a possible geometry for dealing with psychological space, and to explore in a limited way the consequences of a particular set of assumptions and definitions.

22 | Some Effects of Certain Communication Patterns on Group Performance
HAROLD J. LEAVITT

INTRODUCTION

Cooperative action by a group of individuals having a common objective requires, as a necessary condition, a certain minimum of communication. This does not mean that all the individuals must be able to communicate with one another. It is enough, in some cases, if they are each touched by some part of a network of communication which also touches each of the others at some point. The ways in which the members of a group may be linked together by such a network of communication are numerous; very possibly only a few of the many ways have any usefulness in terms of effective performance. Which of all feasible patterns are "good" patterns from this point of view? Will different patterns give different results in the performance of group tasks?

In a free group, the kind of network that evolves may be determined by a multitude of variables. The job to be done by the group may be a

Reprinted with permission of the American Psychological Association and the author. From *Journal of Abnormal and Social Psychology*, 46:38–50 (1951).

determinant, or the particular abilities or social ranks of the group members, or other cultural factors may be involved.

Even in a group in which some parent organization defines the network of communication, as in most military or industrial situations, the networks themselves may differ along a variety of dimensions. There may be differences in number of connections, in the symmetry of the pattern of connections, in "channel capacity" (how much and what kind of information), and in many other ways.

It was the purpose of this investigation to explore experimentally the relationship between the behavior of small groups and the patterns of communication in which the groups operate. It was our further purpose to consider the psychological conditions that are imposed on group members by various communication patterns, and the effects of these conditions on the organization and the behavior of its members. We tried to do this for small groups of a constant size, using two-way written communication and a task that required the simple collection of information.

Some Characteristics of Communication Structures

The stimulus for this research lies primarily in the work of Bavelas, who considered the problem of defining some of the dimensions of group structures. In his study, the structures analyzed consist of cells connected to one another. If we make persons analogous to "cells" and communication channels analogous to "connections," we find that some of the dimensions that Bavelas defines are directly applicable to the description of communication patterns. Thus, one way in which communication patterns vary can be described by the sum of the neighbors that each individual member has, neighbors being defined as individuals to whom a member has communicative access. So, too, the concept of *centrality*, as defined by Bavelas, is of value in describing differences within and between structures. The most central position in a pattern is the position closest to all other positions. Distance is measured by number of communicative links which must be utilized to get, by the shortest route, from one position to another.

Bavelas also introduced a *sum of neighbors* measure—sum of neighbors being a summation, for the entire pattern, of the number of positions one link away from each position. Similarly, *sum of distances* is the summation, for all positions, of the shortest distances (in links) from every position to every other one.

Unfortunately, these dimensions we have mentioned do not in themselves uniquely define a pattern of communication. What defines a pattern is the *way* the cells are connected, regardless of how they are represented on paper. In essence, our criterion is this: if two patterns cannot be "bent" into the same shape without breaking a link, they are different patterns. A more precise definition of unique patterns would require the use of complex topological concepts.

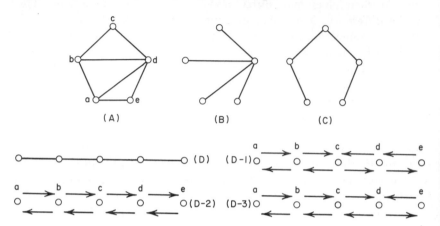

Figure 1. Communication patterns.

Some Operational Characteristics of Communication Patterns

Consider the pattern depicted as A in Figure 1. If at each dot or cell (lettered *a*, *b*, etc.) we place a person; if each link (line between dots) represents a two-way channel for written communications; and if we assign to the five participants a task requiring that *every* member get an answer to a problem which can be solved only by pooling segments of information originally held separately by each member, then it is possible a priori to consider the ways in which the problem can be solved.

PATTERN FLEXIBILITY. First we note that the subject (*Ss*) need not always use all the channels potentially available to them in order to reach an adequate solution of the problem. Although pattern A (Figure 1) contains potentially seven links or channels of communication, it can be solved as follows with three of the seven channels ignored.

Step 1: *a* and *e* each send their separate items of information to *b* and *d* respectively.
Step 2: *b* and *d* each send their separate items of information, along with those from *a* and *b* respectively, to *c*.
Step 3: *c* organizes all the items of information, arrives at an answer, and sends the answer to *b* and then to *d*.
Step 4: *b* and *d* then send the answer to *a* and *e* respectively.

The use of these particular four channels yields pattern C (Figure 1). The original seven-link pattern (A) can be used as a four-link pattern in various ways. For instance, each of the four *Ss* diagrammatically labeled *c*, *b*, *a*, and *e* might send his item of information to *d* who would organize the items, arrive at the answer, and send it back to each respectively. Use of these particular four channels would yield the pattern B in Figure 1. The problem could also be solved by the *Ss* using five, six, or all of the seven potential channels.

OPERATIONAL FLEXIBILITY. Secondly, with the specification that a given number of links be used, any pattern can be operated in a variety of ways. Thus the pattern D (Figure 1), which has no pattern flexibility, can be used as shown in D-1, with information funnelled in to C and the answer sent out from C. It is also possible to use it, as in D-2, with E as the key position; or as in D-3. These are operational differences that can be characterized in terms of the roles taken by the various positions. Thus in D-1, C is the decision-making position. In D-2, it is E or A. Some patterns can be operated with two or three decision-makers.

The Definition of Maximum Theoretical Efficiency

Before going further it may be helpful to state the task used in this research. To each *S* in an experiment (see Figure 2), was given a card on which there appeared a set of five (out of six possible) symbols. Each *S*'s

SIX SYMBOLS USED: ○ △ ◇ □ + ✳						
TRIAL NO.	SYMBOL MISSING FROM: WHITE	RED	BROWN	YELLOW	BLUE	COMMON SYMBOL
1	△	◇	✳	○	□	+
2	◇	○	□	△	+	✳
3	+	✳	□	△	◇	○
4	□	◇	△	✳	+	○
5	○	✳	+	△	□	◇
6	△	○	□	✳	◇	+
7	□	+	○	◇	△	✳
8	◇	✳	□	+	○	△
9	✳	◇	□	△	○	+
10	+	○	□	✳	◇	△
11	○	+	△	◇	✳	□
12	✳	○	□	△	+	◇
13	△	○	◇	□	+	✳
14	□	◇	+	✳	△	○
15	+	○	□	◇	✳	△

Figure 2. Symbol distribution by trial.

card was different from all the others in that the symbol lacking, the sixth one, was a different symbol in each case.

Thus, in any set of five cards there was only one symbol in common. The problem was for every member to find the common symbol. To accomplish this each member was allowed to communicate, by means of written messages, with those other members of the group to whom he had an open channel (a link in our diagrams). Every separate written communication from one S (A) to another (B) was considered one message. An S who had discovered the answer was allowed to pass the answer along.

MINIMUM NUMBER OF COMMUNICATIONS. For any pattern of n Ss, the minimum number of communications, C, is given by $C = 2(n\text{-}1)$.

Theoretically, then, with *number of messages as the sole criterion*, any pattern of n Ss is as efficient as any other n-sized pattern.

THE MINIMUM TIME REQUIRED FOR SOLUTION. If we assume "standard" S's, all of whom work, think, and write at the same speed, it is possible to calculate the limit set by the communication pattern on the speed with which the problem can be solved. Toward this end, we can arbitrarily define a *time unit* as the time required to complete any message, from its inception by any S to its reception by any other.

For any n not a power of 2 and *with unrestricted linkage*, when $2^x < n < 2^{x+1}$ and x is a power of 2, $x + 1$ equals the minimum possible time units for solution of the problem. Thus, for a five-man group we have $2^x < 5 < 2^{x+1}$ becoming $2^2 > 5 > 2^3$, and $x + 1 = 3$ time units. *No* five-man pattern can be done in less than three time units, although several require more than three time units. When n is an even power of 2, the formula $2^x = n$ holds, and $x =$ minimum time.

It will be noted that, although some patterns require fewer time units than others, they may also require more message (m) units. This phenomenon, effectively the generalization that it requires increased messages to save time units, holds for all the patterns we have examined. It is, however, true that certain patterns requiring different times can be solved in the same number of message units.

Some Possible Effects of Various Patterns on the Performance of Individuals

There are two general kinds of reasons which dictate against our theoretically perfect performance from real people. The first of these is the obvious one that people are not standardized. There are also the forces set up by the patterns themselves to be considered. The problem becomes one of analyzing the forces operating on an individual in any particular position in a communication pattern and then predicting how the effects of these forces will be translated into behavior.

It is our belief that the primary source of differential forces will be *centrality*. Centrality will be the chief (though perhaps not the sole) determinant of behavioral differences because centrality reflects the extent to which one position is strategically located relative to other positions in the pattern.

Our selection of centrality derives from the belief that availability of information necessary for the solution of the problem will be of prime importance in affecting one's behavior. Centrality is a measure of one's closeness to all other group members and, hence, is a measure of the availability of the information necessary for solving the problem.

Availability of information should affect behavior, in turn, by determining one's role in the group. An individual who can rapidly collect information should see himself and be seen by others in a different way from an individual to whom vital information is not accessible. Such roles should be different in the extent to which they permit independence of action, in the responsibility they entail, and in the monotony they impose. Finally, differences in independence, in responsibility, and in monotony should affect the speed, the accuracy, the aggressiveness, and the flexibility of behavior.

METHOD

The Problem To Be Solved

We have already described the task to be given our Ss—a task of discovering the single common symbol from among several symbols. When *all five* men indicated that they knew the common symbol, a trial was ended. Another set of cards, with another common symbol, was then given to the Ss, and another trial was begun.

Each group of Ss was given 15 consecutive trials. The composition of the standard sets of cards, used for all groups, is indicated in Figure 2, which indicates the symbol *not* on each person's card for each trial. By referring this missing symbol to the set of six symbols at the top, the reader may reconstruct the symbols actually on each man's card. The common symbol (the right answer) is also shown in Figure 2.

The Apparatus

The Ss were seated around a circular table (Figure 3) so that each was separated from the next by a vertical partition from the center to six

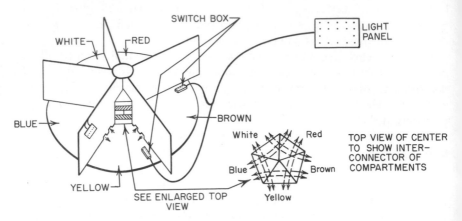

Figure 3. Apparatus.

inches beyond the table's edge. The partitions had slots permitting subjects to push written message cards to the men on either side of them.

To allow for communication to the other men in the group, a five-
layered pentagonal box was built and placed at the center of the table.
The box was placed so that the partitions just touched each of the five
points of the pentagon. Each of the five resulting wedge-shaped work-
spaces was then painted a different color. The Ss were supplied with
blank message cards whose colors matched that of their work spaces. Any
message sent from a booth had to be on a card of the booth's color. On
the left wall of each partition, 16 large symbol cards, representing 16
trials, were hung in loose-leaf fashion. The cards were placed in order
with numbered backs to S. At the starting signal, S could pull down the
first card and go to work.

In addition, each work space was provided with a board on which were
mounted six switches. Above each switch appeared one of the six symbols.
When S got an answer to the problem, he was to throw the proper switch,
which would turn on an appropriate light on a master board of 30 lights
in the observer's room. When five lights (whether or not they were under
the correct symbol), representing five different Ss, were lit, the observer
called a halt to the trial. The observer could tell by a glance at the light
panel whether (a) five different Ss had thrown their switches, (b)
whether all five had decided on the same answer, and (c) whether the
answer decided on was right or wrong. The same detailed instructions
were given to all Ss.

A preliminary series of four problems, in which each S was given all
the information required for solution, was used. This was done to note
the extent of differences among Ss in the time required to solve such
problems.

The Procedure

One hundred male undergraduates of M.I.T., drawn from various classes at the Institute, served as *S*s for these experiments. These 100 were split up into 20 groups of five men each. These 20 groups were then further subdivided so that five groups could be tested on each of four experimental patterns.

Each group was given 15 consecutive trials on *one* pattern, a process which required one session of about fifty minutes. These *S*s were *not used again*. The order in which we used our patterns was also randomized. Just in case the color or geographical position of one's work-space might affect one's behavior, we shifted positions for each new group. After a group had completed its 15 trials, and before members were permitted to talk with one another, each member was asked to fill out a questionnaire.

The Patterns Selected

The four five-man patterns selected for this research are shown in Figure 4.

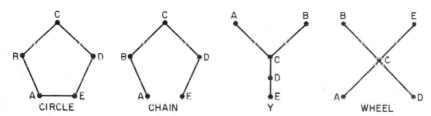

Figure 4. The experimental patterns.

These four patterns represented extremes in centrality (as in the circle vs. the wheel), as well as considerable differences in other characteristics (Table 1).

Table I

Characteristics of the Experimental Patterns

Pattern	No. of Links	Most Central Position	Sum of Neighbors	Sum of Distances	Min. Time Units	Min. Messages
Chain	4	C(6.7)	8	40	5(8m)	8(5t)
Y	4	C(7.2)	8	36	4(8m)	8(4t)
Wheel	4	C(8.0)	8	32	5(8m)	8(5t)
Circle	5	All(5.0)	10	30	3(14m)	8(5t)

RESULTS

The data which have been accumulated are broken down in the pages that follow into (a) a comparison of total patterns and (b) a comparison of positions within patterns.

A. Differences among Patterns

It was possible to reconstruct a picture of the operational methods actually used by means of: (a) direct observations, (b) postexperimental analysis of messages, and (c) postexperimental talks with Ss.

The *wheel* operated in the same way in all five cases. The peripheral men funnelled information to the center where an answer decision was made and the answer sent out. This organization had usually evolved by the fourth or fifth trial and remained in use throughout.

The *Y* operated so as to give the most central position, C (see Figure 4 and Table 1), complete decision-making authority. The next-most-central position, D (see Figure 4), served only as a transmitter of information and of answers. In at least one case, C transmitted answers first to A and B and only then to D. Organization for the Y evolved a little more slowly than for the wheel, but, once achieved, it was just as stable.

In the *chain* information was usually funnelled in from both ends to C, whence the answer was sent out in both directions. There were several cases, however, in which B or D reached an answer decision and passed it to C. The organization was slower in emerging than the Y's or the wheel's, but consistent once reached.

The *circle* showed no consistent operational organization. Most commonly messages were just sent in both directions until any S received an answer or worked one out. In every case, all available links were used at some time during the course of each trial.

Direct Measures of Differences among Patterns

TIME. The curves in Figure 5 are for *correct* trials only, that is, for trials in which all five switches represented the correct common symbols. In most cases, the medians shown are for distributions of five groups, but in no case do they represent less than three groups.

The variability of the distributions represented by these medians is considerable. In the fifteenth trial, the distribution for the circle has a range of 50–96 seconds; for the chain, 28–220 seconds; for the Y, 24–52 seconds; and for the wheel, 21–46 seconds. Moreover, much of the time that went to make up each trial was a constant consisting of writing and

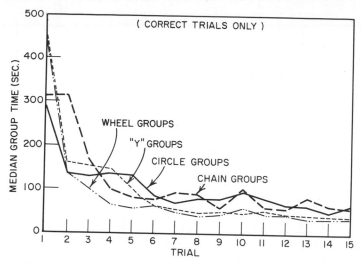

Figure 5.   Median group-times per trial.

passing time. Any differences attributable to pattern would be a small fraction of this large constant and would be easily obscured by accidents of misplacing or dropping of messages.

Despite all these factors, one measure of speed did give statistically significant differences. A measure of the *fastest single trial* of each group indicates that the wheel was considerably faster (at its fastest) than the circle (Table 2).

Table 2

Fastest Single Correct Trial

	Circle	Chain	Y	Wheel	Diff.	p*
Mean	50.4	53.2	35.4	32.0	Ci–W	<.01
Median	55.0	57.0	32.0	36.0	Ch–W	<.10
Range	44–59	19–87	22–53	20–41	Ci–Y	<.05
					Ch–Y	<.20

* Significance of differences between means were measured throughout by *t*-tests. The *p*-values are based on distributions of *t* which include both tails of the distribution. Where differences are between proportions, *p* is derived from the usual measure of significance of differences between proportions. Ci-W means the circle-wheel difference, and so on.

MESSAGES. The medians in Figure 6 represent a count of the number of messages sent by each group during a given (correct) trial. It seems clear that the circle pattern used more messages to solve the problem than the others.

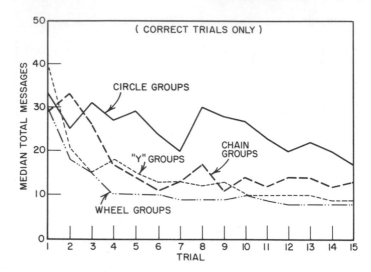

Figure 6.   Median messages per trial.

ERRORS. An error was defined as the throwing of any incorrect switch by an *S* during a trial. Errors that were *not* corrected before the end of a trial are labelled "final errors"; the others are referred to as "corrected errors."

It should be pointed out that the error figures for the *wheel* in Table 3

Table 3

Errors

Pattern	Total Errors (15 Trials)		Total Errors (Last 8 Trials)		Final Errors		Mean No. of Trials with at Least One Final Error
	Mean	Range	Mean	Range	Mean	Range	
Circle	16.6	9–33	7.6	1–18	6.4	2–14	3.4
Chain	9.8	3–19	2.8	0–11	6.2	1–19	1.8
Y	2.6	1–8	0	0	1.6	0–5	.8
Wheel	9.8	0–34	0.6	0–2	2.2	0–7	1.2

p Values Ci–Y $< .02$

are distorted by the peculiar behavior of one of the five wheel groups. The center man in this group took the messages which he received to be *answers* rather than simple information, and, in addition to throwing his own switch, passed the information on *as an answer*. This difficulty was cleared up after a few trials, and the figures for the last eight trials are probably more representative than the figures for the full 15 trials.

In addition to the differences in errors, there are differences in the proportion of total errors that were corrected. Although more errors were made in the circle pattern than any other, a greater proportion of them (61 percent) were corrected than in any other pattern. Too, the frequency of unanimous five-man final errors is lower, both absolutely and percentage-wise, for the circle than for the chain.

Questionnaire Results

1. *"Did your group have a leader? If so, who?"*
Only 13 of 25 people who worked in the circle named a leader, and those named were scattered among all the positions in the circle. For all patterns, the total frequency of people named increased in the order *circle, chain, Y, wheel.* Similarly, the unanimity of opinion increased in the same order so that, for the wheel pattern, all 23 members who recognized any leader agreed that position C was that leader.

2. *"Describe briefly the organization of your group."*
The word "organization" in this question was ambiguous. Some of the Ss understood the word to mean pattern of communication, while others equated it with their own duties or with status difference.

These differences in interpretation were not random, however. Sixteen people in the wheel groups fully reproduced the wheel structure in answer to this question, while only one circle member reproduced the circle pattern.

3. *"How did you like your job in the group?"*
In this question Ss were asked to place a check on a rating scale marked "disliked it" at one end and "liked it" at the other. For purposes of analysis, the scale was translated into numerical scores from 0 at the dislike end to 100. Each rating was estimated only to the closest decile.

Again, we find the order circle, chain, Y, wheel, with circle members enjoying their jobs significantly more than the wheel members.

4. *"See if you can recall how you felt about the job as you went along. Draw the curve below."*
The Ss were asked to sketch a curve into a space provided for it. We measured the height of these curves on a six-point scale at trials 1, 5, 10, and 15. These heights were averaged for each group, and the averages of the group averages were plotted.

Although the differences between groups are not statistically significant, trends of increasing satisfaction in the circle and decreasing satisfaction in the wheel seem to corroborate the findings in the question on satisfaction with one's job. Except for a modest Y-chain reversal, the order is, as usual, from circle to wheel.

5. *"Was there anything, at any time, that kept your group from per-forming at its best? If so, what?"*

The answers to this question were categorized as far as possible into several classes.

None of the circle members feels that "nothing" was wrong with his group; a fact that is suggestive of an attitude different from that held by members of the other patterns. So, too, is the finding that insufficient knowledge of the pattern does not appear as an obstacle to the circle member but is mentioned at least five times in each of the other patterns.

6. *"Do you think your group could improve its efficiency? If so, how?"*

Circle members place great emphasis on *organizing* their groups, on working out a "system" (mentioned 17 times). Members of the other patterns, if they felt that any improvement at all was possible, emphasized a great variety of possibilities.

7. *"Rate your group on the scale below."*

For purposes of analysis, these ratings (along a straight line) were transposed into numbers from 0, for "poor," to 100.

The same progression of differences that we have already encountered, the progression *circle, chain, Y, wheel,* holds for this question. Once again the circle group thinks less well of itself (Mean $= 56$) than do the other patterns ($M_{ch} = 60$; $M_y = 70$; $M_w = 71$).

Message Analysis

The messages sent by all Ss were collected at the end of each experimental run and their contents coded and categorized. Some of these categories overlapped with others, and hence some messages were counted in more than one category.

The now familiar progression, *circle, chain, Y, wheel,* continues into this area. Circle members send many more informational messages than members of the other patterns ($M_{ci} = 283$; $M_w = 101$). Circle members also send more answers ($M_{ci} = 91$; $M_w = 65$).

The same tendency remains in proportion to total errors as well as absolutely. The circle has a mean of 4.8 recognition-of-error messages for a mean of 16.6 errors; the chain has a mean of 1 recognition-of-error messages for a mean of 9.8 errors.

We were concerned, before beginning these experiments, lest Ss find short cuts for solving the problem, thus making certain comparisons among patterns difficult. One such short cut we have called "elimination." Instead of taking time to write their five symbols, many Ss, after discovering that only six symbols existed in all, wrote just the missing symbol, thus saving considerable time. This method was used by at least one member in two of the circle groups, in all the chain groups, in three of the

Y groups, and in four of the wheel groups. In *both* the circle cases, the method was used by *all five members* during final trials. In the chain, though present in every group, elimination was used only once by all five members, twice by three members, and twice by just one member. In the Y, the method was adopted once by four members (the fifth man was *not* the center) and twice by two members. There was at least one case (in the wheel) in which a member who suggested the use of elimination was ordered by another member not to use it.

The questions raised here are two. Is the idea of elimination more likely to occur in some patterns than in others? Is an innovation like elimination likely to be more readily accepted in some patterns than in others? To neither of these questions do we have an adequate answer.

B. A Positional Analysis of the Data

Observation of the experimental patterns indicates that every position in the circle is indistinguishable from every other one. No one has more neighbors, is more central, or is closer to anyone than anyone else. In the wheel, the four peripheral positions are alike, and so on. Despite our inability to differentiate these positions from one another, we have set up the data in the following sections as if all positions in each pattern were actually different from one another.

Direct Observations

MESSAGES. The most central positions, it will be seen from Table 4, send the greatest number of messages; the least central ones send the fewest.

Table 4

Number of Messages Sent by Each Position

		A	B	C	D	E	Diff.	p
Circle	Mean	78.4	90.0	83.6	86.2	81.0	A–B	<.30
	Range	64–101	63–102	60–98	60–122	72–90		
Chain	Mean	24.8	70.8	82.4	71.8	27.6	C–E	<.01
	Range	20–34	43–112	45–113	42–101	22–43		
Y	Mean	28.0	23.8	79.8	63.8	25.6	A–C	<.01
							D–C	<.20
	Range	20–44	21–28	65–104	43–78	21–37	D–E	<.01
Wheel	Mean	29.4	26.2	102.8	26.6	30.2	C–E	<.01
	Range	19–48	17–40	78–138	17–39	22–43		

ERRORS. The analysis of total errors made in each position showed nothing of significance.

Questionnaire Results by Position

1. "How much did you enjoy your job?"

The most central positions in other patterns enjoy their jobs more than any circle position. Peripheral positions, on the other hand, enjoy the job less than any circle position (Table 5).

Table 5

Enjoyment of the Job

		A	B	C	D	E	Diff.	p
Circle	Mean	58.0	64.0	70.0	65.0	71.0	A–E	<.70
	Range	0–100	0–100	20–100	40–100	25–100		
Chain	Mean	45.0	82.5	78.0	70.0	24.0	C–E	<.02
	Range	25–55	50–100	50–100	40–100	0–70	C–AE	<.01
Y	Mean	46.0	49.0	95.0	71.0	31.0	C–A	<.02
							C–AB	<.01
	Range	0–100	25–100	75–100	30–100	0–75	D–E	<.10
Wheel	Mean	37.5	20.0	97.0	25.0	42.5	B–C	<.01
							C–E	<.02
	Range	0–50	0–40	85–100	0–75	0–100	ABED–C	<.01

2. "See if you can recall how you felt about the job as you went along. Draw the curve below."

The data for this question are gathered after all most-peripheral and all most-central positions are combined. Peripheral positions were: positions A and E, in the chain; position E in the Y; and positions A, B, D, and E in the wheel. Central positions were all C positions with the exception of C in the circle. The data thus combined highlight the trend toward higher satisfaction with increasing centrality. The central positions progress from a mean of 2.1 at trial 1 to a mean of 3.9 at trial 15. Peripheral positions decline from 3.9 to 2.3.

Message Analysis by Position

One of the things that immediately stands out from an examination of the messages is an apparent peculiarity in the *informational message* category. Although the most central man in the chain sends more informational messages (52) than the other positions in that pattern, the same is not true of the most central men in the Y and the wheel. In the Y, it is position D, the next-most-central position, that sends most; while in the wheel all positions are about equal. This peculiarity becomes quite understandable if we take into account (a) the kind of organization used in each pattern and (b) the fact that these figures represent the entire 15 trials, some of which occurred before the group got itself stably organized. In the wheel, the Y, and the chain, the center man really needed to send *no* informational messages, only answers; but in the *early* trials, before his role was clarified, he apparently sent enough to bring his total up to or higher than the level of the rest.

It can also be noted that the number of *organizational messages* (messages which seek to establish some plan of action for future trials) is negatively correlated with positional centrality. The most peripheral men send the greatest numbers of organizational messages, the most central men least.

DISCUSSION

Patternwise, the picture formed by the results is of differences almost always in the order *circle, chain, Y, wheel.*

We may grossly characterize the kinds of differences that occur in this way: the circle, one extreme, is active, leaderless, unorganized, erratic, and yet is enjoyed by its members. The wheel, at the other extreme, is less active, has a distinct leader, is well and stably organized, is less erratic, and yet is unsatisfying to most of its members.

There are two questions raised by these behavioral differences. First, what was wrong with our a priori time-unit analysis? The results measured in clock time do not at all match the time-unit figures. And second, to what extent are behavioral differences matched by centrality differences?

The Time Unit

It was hypothesized earlier that the time taken to solve a problem should be limited at the lower end by the structure of the pattern of communication. If pattern does set such a limitation on speed, the limitation is not in the direction we would have predicted. Our analysis (Table 1), based on a theoretical time unit, led us falsely to expect greatest speed from the circle pattern.

There are three outstanding reasons for the failure of the time-unit analysis to predict clock time. First, the time unit, itself, was too gross a measure. We defined the time unit as the time required for the transmission of one message from its inception to its reception. In actuality, different kinds of messages required very different clock times for transmission. *S*s could send two messages simultaneously. They could also lay out and write several messages before sending any.

A second reason for the failure of the time-unit analysis was the assumption that *S*s would gravitate to the theoretically "best" operating organization. Only the wheel groups used the theoretically "best" method (the minimum time method) consistently.

Finally, it should be pointed out that differences in speed between patterns were subject to major fluctuations for reasons of differences in writing speed, dexterity in passing messages, and other extraneous factors.

The Relation of the Centrality Measure to Behavior

Our second and more important question is: Are the behavioral differences among patterns and among positions related consistently to the centrality index? An examination of Table 1 indicates that the centrality index shows the same progression, *circle, chain, Y, wheel*, as do most of the behavioral differences. On a positional basis, centrality also differentiates members of a pattern in the same order that their behavior does.

Because such a relationship does exist between behavior and centrality, a more detailed consideration of the centrality concept is in order.

The central region of a structure is defined by Bavelas as "the class of all cells with the smallest p to be found in the structure." The quantity, p, in turn, is defined as the largest distance between one cell and any other cell in the structure. Distance is measured in link units. Thus the distance from A to B in the chain is one link; from A to C the distance is two links. The most central position in a pattern is the position that is closest to all other positions. Quantitatively, an index of the centrality of position A in any pattern can be found by (a) summing the shortest distances from *each* position to every other one and (b) dividing this summation by the total of the shortest distances from position A to every other position.

Centrality, then, is a function of the size of a pattern as well as of its structure. Thus, in a five-man circle, the centrality of each man is 5.0. In a six-man circle, the centrality of each man jumps to 6.0. The two most peripheral men in a five-man chain each have a centrality of 4.0. But in a seven-man chain, the two most peripheral men have centralities of 5.3.

In Figure 7 are given the centralities of each position in each of our four test patterns. The sum of centralities is also given. Both total centrality and distribution of centralities fall in the order *circle, chain, Y, wheel*.

These centrality figures correlate with the behavior we have observed. But it seems unreasonable to assume that the correlation would hold for larger n's. Certainly we would not expect *more* message activity or *more*

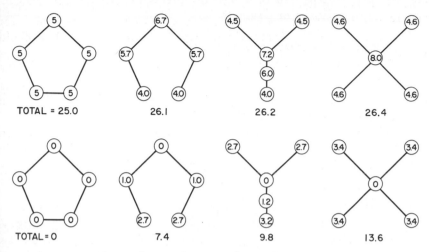

Figure 7.   Centrality indices (*above*) and peripherality indices (*below*).

satisfaction from peripheral positions in a chain of a larger n than from a five-man chain.

To obviate this difficulty, a measure we have called "relative peripherality" may be established. The relative peripherality of any position in a pattern is the difference between the centrality of that position and the centrality of the most central position in that pattern. Thus, for the two end men in a five-man chain, the peripherality index is 2.7 (the difference between their centralities of 4.0 and the centrality of the most central position, 6.7). For a total pattern, the peripherality index may be taken by summating all the peripherality indices in the pattern (Figure 7).

Examination of the data will show that observed differences in behavior correlate positively with these peripherality measures. By *total pattern*, messages, satisfaction, and errors (except for the wheel) vary consistently with total peripherality index. Similarly, by position, messages and satisfaction vary with peripherality. Errors, however, show no clear relationship with peripherality of position, a finding which is discussed in detail later in this section.

Recognition of a leader also seems to be a function of peripherality, but in a somewhat different way. A review of our leadership findings will show that leadership becomes more clear-cut as the differences in peripherality *within a pattern become greater*. Recognition of a leader seems to be determined by the extent of the difference in centrality between the most central and next-most-central man.

There arises next the question: What is the mechanism by which the peripherality of a pattern or a position affects the behavior of persons occupying that pattern or position?

A reconstruction of the experimental situation leads us to this analysis of the peripherality-behavior relationship:

First, let us assume standard Ss, motivated to try to solve our experimental problem as quickly as possible. Let them be "intelligent" Ss who do not send the same information more than once to any neighbor. Let them also be Ss who, given several neighbors, will send, with equal probability, their first message to any one of those neighbors.

Given such standard Ss, certain specific positions will probably get an answer to the problem before other positions. In the chain, position C will be most likely to get the answer first, but, in the circle, all positions have an equal opportunity.

To illustrate, consider the chain pattern (see Figure 4): During time unit 1, A may send only to B. B may send either to C or to A. C may send either to B or to D. D may send either to C or to E. E may send only to D. No matter where B, C, and D send their messages, B and D will have, at the end of one time unit, A's and E's information. During the second time unit, if B and/or D had sent to C the first time, they will now send to A and E. If they sent to A and E the first time, they will send to C, and C will have the answer. Even if B and D do not send to C until the third time unit, C will either get the answer before or simultaneously with B and D. In *no* case can any other position beat C to the answer. In the wheel, C cannot even be tied in getting an answer. He will *always* get it first.

Our second concern is with Ss' perceptions of these answer-getting potentials. We suggest that these random differences in answer-getting potentials rapidly structure members' perceptions of their own roles in the group. These differences affect one's independence from, or dependence on, the other members of the group. In the wheel, for example, a peripheral S perceives, at first, only that he gets the answer and information from C and can send only to C. C perceives that he gets information from everyone and must send the answer to everyone. The recognition of roles is easy. The peripheral men are dependent on C. C is autonomous and controls the organization.

In the circle, an S's perception must be very different. He gets information from both sides; sometimes he gets the answer, sometimes he sends it. He has two channels of communication. He is exclusively dependent on no one. His role is not clearly different from anyone else's.

Thirdly, having closed the gap between structural pattern and Ss' perceptions of their roles in the group, the problem reduces to one purely psychological. The question becomes: How do differences in one's perception of one's own dependence or independence bring about specific behavior differences of the sort we have observed?

Differences in satisfaction level are relatively easy to relate to independence. In our culture, in which needs for autonomy, recognition, and achievement are strong, it is to be expected that positions which limit independence of action (peripheral positions) would be unsatisfying.

A fairly direct relationship between centrality (and, hence, independence) and the speed with which a group gets organized is also perceptible. In the wheel, unless Ss act "unintelligently," an organization, with C as center, is forced on the wheel groups by the structural pattern. In the circle, no such differences in role and, hence, in organization are forced on the group.

Message-activity can also be related to centrality by means of the independence-of-action concept. A peripheral person in any pattern can send messages to only one other position. Only one informational message is called for. Extra messages would be repetitious. Central positions, however, are free to send more than one non-repetitious informational message until an organization evolves. Once the most central man perceives that he is most central, he need send *no* informational messages. But so long as the most central man does not perceive his own position, it is intelligent to send informational messages to whomever he feels may require some information. It is in keeping with this analysis that the circle should yield maximum messages and the wheel minimum messages.

If the behavior of one of the wheel groups can be discounted, then an explanation, in terms of peripherality, is also possible for both differences in tendencies to correct errors and total error differences.

If peripherality determines one's independence of action, it seems very likely that positions most limited in independence should begin to perceive themselves as subordinates whose sole function is to send information and await an answer. That they should then uncritically accept whatever answer they receive is perfectly in keeping with their subordinate, relatively unresponsible positions—hence, very little correction of errors in the patterns in which there are great differences in peripherality.

Total errors, it will be recalled, were correlated with total peripherality indices but showed no clear relationship with the relative peripherality of particular positions. A consideration of our definition of error may shed some light on this apparent anomaly.

The "errors" that we recorded were signals from the S that indicated a wrong answer. But these wrong answers derived from a variety of sources. First, Ss might wrongly interpret the correct information they received. They might also make errors in throwing switches; and they might also *correctly* interpret *wrong* information. In all three cases, "errors" were recorded.

We submit that this broad definition of error should yield a total pattern relationship with peripherality, but no positional relationship. Our reasoning can be illustrated by an example. Suppose that the central man in the wheel wrongly interprets information sent to him and, hence, throws an incorrect switch. This is a "real" error. He then funnels out the wrong answer to the other members. At least three of these intelligently conclude that the answer sent them is correct and also throw the wrong switches. We then have three "false" errors consequent to our single "real" one. When several independent answer decisions are made (as in the circle), we should expect several real errors, multiplication of these by a factor of about 3, and a larger total of errors. This process should lead to a correlation between total pattern behavior and peripherality but not to a correlation between positional behavior and peripherality. The process simply multiplies real errors more or less constantly for a whole pattern but obscures positional differences because the "real" and the "false" errors are indistinguishable in our data.

We submit, further, that pattern differences in real errors, if such there be, may be attributable to "over-information"; too much information to too many members which, under pressure, leads to errors. Central positions or positions which are no less central than others in the pattern should be the ones to yield the greatest number of real errors, while peripheral positions, which require no such rapid collation of information, should be the false error sources. Such an hypothesis would be in keeping with our total pattern findings and might also clarify our positional findings. Only an experiment designed to differentiate real from false errors can answer this question.

It is in keeping with this peripherality-independence analysis, also, that we should find the recognition of a single leader occurring most frequently in the wheel and Y groups. It is also to be expected that we should find circle members emphasizing need for organization and planning and seldom giving a complete picture of their pattern. Perhaps, too, it is reasonable to expect that the whole group should be considered good in the highly organized wheel (and not so good in the unorganized circle) even though one's own job is considered poor.

In summary, then, it is our feeling that centrality determines behavior by limiting independence of action, thus producing differences in activity, accuracy, satisfaction, leadership, recognition of pattern, and other behavioral characteristics.

SUMMARY AND CONCLUSIONS

Within the limits set by the experimental conditions—group size, type of problem, source of Ss—these conclusions seem warranted:

1. The communication patterns within which our groups worked affected their behavior. The major behavioral differences attributable to communication patterns were differences in accuracy, total activity, satis-

faction of group members, emergence of a leader, and organization of the group. There may also be differences among patterns in speed of problem solving, self-correcting tendencies, and durability of the group as a group.

2. The positions which individuals occupied in a communication pattern affected their behavior while occupying those positions. One's position in the group affected the chances of becoming a leader of the group, one's satisfaction with one's job and with the group, the quantity of one's activity, and the extent to which one contributed to the group's functional organization.

3. The characteristic of communication patterns that was most clearly correlated with behavioral differences was *centrality*. Total pattern differences in behavior seemed to be correlated with a measure of centrality we have labelled the *peripherality index*. Positional differences in behavior seemed to be correlated with the positional peripherality indices of the various positions within patterns.

4. It is tentatively suggested that centrality affects behavior via the limits that centrality imposes upon independent action. Independence of action, relative to other members of the group is, in turn, held to be the primary determinant of the definition of who shall take the leadership role, total activity, satisfaction with one's lot, and other specific behaviors.

More precisely, it is felt that where centrality and, hence, independence are evenly distributed, there will be no leader, many errors, high activity, slow organization, and high satisfaction. Whatever frustration occurs will occur as a result of the inadequacy of the group, not the inadequacy of the environment.

Where one position is low in centrality relative to other members of the group, that position will be a follower position, dependent on the leader, accepting his dictates, falling into a role that allows little opportunity for prestige, activity, or self-expression.

23 The Impact of Certain Communication Nets Upon Organization and Performance in Task-Oriented Groups
HAROLD GUETZKOW
and HERBERT A. SIMON

Bavelas, Smith and Leavitt have posed the problem: What effect do communication patterns have upon the operation of groups? To study this problem they designed a laboratory situation that is a prototype of those occurring in "natural" organizations existing in government and business. Each member of the group is given certain information. Their task is to assemble this information, use it to make a decision, and then issue orders based on the decision. This design provides a situation stripped of the complexities of large-scale social groups but retaining some essential characteristics of the organizational communication problem. In it we can examine how the communication net affects simultaneously (a) the development of the organization's internal structure, and (b) the group's performance of its operating task.

Leavitt made certain deductions from Bavelas' model of communication nets, but his empirical studies did not confirm the derivations. Leavitt explains the discrepancies in terms of such concepts as "different kinds of messages require very different clock times," and the failure of his subjects "to gravitate to the theoretically 'best' operating organization." It is the purpose of this paper to present an alternative theory of these miniature organizations, and to test this theory by new empirical data and by comparison with Leavitt's original empirical findings.

The proposed explanation requires that a sharp distinction be made between: (a) the effects of communication restrictions upon performance of the operating task; and (b) the effects of the restrictions upon a group's ability to organize itself for such performance. That is, instead of regarding the group's problem as unitary, it appears essential to separate the operating or "substantive" task from the organizational or "procedural" problem. Our hypothesis may be stated thus: Imposition of certain restrictions on the communication channels available to a group affects the efficiency of the group's performance, not *directly* by limiting the potential efficiency of task performance with optimal organization in the given net, *but indirectly* by handicapping their ability to organize themselves for efficient task performance.

Reprinted with permission of The Institute of Management Sciences and the authors. From *Management Science*, 1:233–250 (1955).

Our empirical study involves basically a replication of Leavitt's work, but with essential modifications to permit us to study separately the group's performance of its operating task and its organizational task. Except for the explicit separation of trial and intertrial periods, our procedures paralleled those used by Leavitt and Smith. As will be indicated later, our results substantially replicate their findings.

In Section I, we shall set forth the theory from which our central hypothesis is derived. In Section II, we shall test the hypothesis with the new empirical data we have obtained. In Section III, we shall compare our findings with those of Leavitt.

I. SEPARATION OF OPERATING TASK FROM ORGANIZATIONAL PROBLEM: THEORETICAL CONSIDERATIONS

Description and Analysis of the Operating Task

Simon, Smithburg and Thompson argue that communication in a decision-making organization is two-fold:

Communications must flow to the decision center to provide the basis for decision, and the decision must be communicated from the decision center in order to influence other members of the organizations whose cooperation must be secured to carry out the decision.

The Bavelas-Leavitt-Smith problem requires both processes. In the operating task each person must record which one symbol of six is held in common by the five members of the group. The same six symbols are used on each trial. At the beginning of each trial, each person is given a card on which is printed five symbols; the other symbol is missing. Each individual is lacking a different symbol. The problem on a given trial is to have the group discover and record the one symbol that no one is lacking. The variation in distribution of the symbols from trial to trial in this investigation followed the schedule used by Leavitt.

Note the two-fold communication process involved in this line task:

(a) Information Flow: At the beginning of a trial each participant knows only one of the missing symbols—his own. The participant need not know all of the missing symbols for solution of the problem. Each group member needs to know only the answer to record it, or to "carry out the decision." There must, however, be sufficient exchange of information so that one or more persons can form the solution, or "make the decision."

(b) Decision Flow: Once an answer is formed by one or more persons in the group, it must be communicated to those who are unable to, or do not, make the decision themselves.

Before proceeding with the analysis, let us explain the mechanics of the experiment. The subjects, seated around a circular table, were separated from each other by five vertical wooden partitions. They were able to pass messages to each other through interconnecting slots. During the operating trials, they interchanged messages written on pre-coded cards which contained places for information and answers. During the intertrials the subjects were free to write to each other uncoded messages on blank cards about their organizational arrangements. This meant the group could determine who would send information to whom, who would make the problem-decision, who would send the decision-order to whom.

When a subject had recorded the problem-decision, this fact was immediately conveyed to the experimenter. When all five persons had recorded the solution, the trial automatically ended and the intertrial period began. The subjects were silent throughout the experiment, communicating only through pre-coded cards during the operating task trial and by written "free" messages during the intertrial periods. This enabled us to obtain a complete record of their communications.

Two hundred and eighty male freshmen engineering students at Carnegie Institute of Technology served as subjects for the experiment. The two hours devoted to the experiment were a required substitute for one class and an out-of-class assignment in a required freshman course. Most subjects were not very well acquainted with each other. Each group was composed of one man from each of the Carnegie Tech quintiles of the American Council on Education Psychological Examination; scores were available on all subjects. This insured an equating of groups with respect to intellective ability.

Given this task, how will a five-man group divide the labor involved in completing it? (1) It is possible either for everyone to *exchange information* with everyone else, or to have the missing symbol information collected by a single person. (2) It is possible either for everyone to *form the solution*, or to specialize to the extent that only one person forms the solution. (3) It is possible either to complete the problem without *circulation of answers* (since each may form the solution by himself), or to have the answer relayed from a single central source. But which organizational arrangement will be adopted? To what extent does the choice depend upon communication restrictions?

In replicating Leavitt's experiment, we have used two of his restrictions —those constituting his extreme cases: the "Wheel" and "Circle." In addition, we established groups that were entirely free of restrictions, using an "All-Channel" pattern. The three communication nets are illustrated in Figure 1. Our initial problem is to discover how the net restrictions imposed upon the various groups determined the organizational patterns used in performing the operating task.

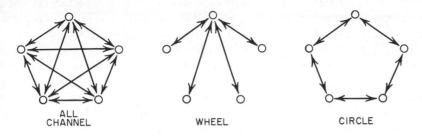

Figure 1. Open channels used in the three nets.

Consider first the Wheel net: If the task is divided so that the "spokes" send their information to the "hub," the latter can make the decision and in turn return answers to the spokes. We will call this pattern a "two-level hierarchy." Next, consider the Circle net: If two neighbors send their information to their opposite neighbors, who in turn relay this information with their own to the fifth member of the circle, this "keyman" can make the decision and relay the answer back through the "relayers" to the "endmen." We will call this pattern a "three-level hierarchy." In the All-Channel nets, either one of these procedures—or others—may be used. It can be shown that the arrangements just described are the most efficient of those available. Although the use of the relays in the three-level hierarchy involves time delays, the minimum number of messages required by the two- and three-level hierarchies is the same—eight.

A channel-usage analysis, as suggested by Bavelas' model, misleads one into supposing that the two-level hierarchy is twice as efficient as the three-level hierarchy; for the two-level arrangement obviates the need for relaying, both when sending information and when sending answers. But the task is more than one of merely sending messages—messages must also be received, collated, and prepared. To compare efficiencies we need an estimate of the time required to perform *all* these task elements, and in proper sequence.

Description and Analysis of the Organizational Problem

The theoretical discussion to this point supports our hypothesis that the communication restrictions affect the task performance of the groups not directly, but only indirectly by influencing the ability of the members to organize themselves for optimum performance in their line operation. Now let us examine in more detail the way in which the nets pose organizational problems.

Twenty of our 56 groups were allowed to operate without any imposed restrictions on their internal communication. The other groups operated within communication restrictions that reduced the number of channels for communication to approximately half of those available in the un-restricted groups. The two sets of restrictions differed from each other, however, in their effects upon the ease with which the groups might develop interaction patterns. The 15 wheel groups were restricted in such a way that their organizational problems should be minimal. The 20 circle groups were restricted with almost the same degree of severity (in terms of number of open channels), but in a way that made their organizing tasks comparatively difficult.

The three variations in the nets had different relationships to the organizational problem:

(a) *The "All-Channel" Net:* The organizational problem for an All-Channel group is not simple. The group has an advantage in that each member can communicate with the others, so that no relaying of messages through a "second party" is required. Yet the lack of communication restrictions means an open field with almost too many opportunities—a total of 20 one-way channels. Accordingly, each All-Channel group has the difficult job of developing its own restrictions—deciding that certain available channels will *not* be used. In addition, each of the members is equipotential with respect to his place in the communication net; no one member has initial advantages from his place in the net with respect to the functional requirements of the task.

(b) *The "Wheel" Net:* The Wheel groups are in a net in which the communication restrictions reduce the difficulty of the organizational problems to a minimum, yet hold the requirements of the operating prob-lem constant. If the task is divided so that the spokes send their informa-tion to the hub, the latter can solve the problem and in turn send answers to the spokes. There would be no need for relay through a "second party." All the "unnecessary" channels have been blocked, so that their elimination is no longer part of the organizational problem. This reduces the number of open channels from 20 to 8, some 60 percent. The existence of a hub means that the positions in the net are not equipotential—the four spokes are disadvantageously situated. Should a spoke attempt to become the solution former, he would need to depend upon the hub for relaying both information and answers. In addition, in such a situation, the or-ganizational problem as to which of the four equipotential spokes would become problem-solver would need to be handled. But, if the hub be-comes the solution-former, the wheel requires a minimum of organizing effort for solving the operating task.

(c) *The "Circle" Net:* This net retains the symmetry of the positions in the free situation but restricts drastically the number of communication opportunities. Simultaneously it makes imperative the use of a relay sys-tem, or three-level hierarchy, within the organization. No potential solution-former has immediate access to the other four missing symbols. His two neighbors need to relay their information and that of their other neighbors to him. Along with this impediment to organizing, there is the added difficulty that no one position is more or less advantageously situated for handling the solution-forming requirement. The reduction of available channels in this net is from 20 to 10, just 50 percent.

A comparison of the way in which the three characteristics of the net differ from net to net is diagrammed in Table 1. From this display it is possible to make rough estimates of the difficulty of the organizational problem for groups in each type of net. The Wheel groups would have the least difficulty, for they have no channels to eliminate, no relays to establish, and already have one person occupying a dominant position in the net. The All-Channel groups would have the next grade of difficulty, since the elimination of excess channels and the evolution of one person as solution-former are both required, yet relays need not be established. The Circle groups should have the most difficulty, for they need both to establish relays and to evolve an asymmetrical arrangement among the positions. They also must do some eliminating of unneeded channels, although this last requirement is minimal. The difficulty of the organizational problem in the different nets varies as follows:

Wheel < All-Channel < Circle

This analysis of the organizational difficulty yields a surprising outcome in indicating that an unrestricted net (All Channel) in itself involves difficulties, and that restrictions in communication may be helpful (Wheel) or harmful (Circle) in the evolution of organizational structures, depending upon the nature of the relation of the restriction to the organizing and operating tasks.

Table 1

Comparison of the Three Nets
Characteristic Differences among the Three Nets

Characteristics	All-Channel	Wheel	Circle
Number of Open Channels	20	8*	10*
Number of Symmetric Positions	5	4*	5
Minimum Number of Relays Necessary	0	0	2*

* The italic entries indicate the points at which the Wheel and Circle nets contrast with the All-Channel net.

This concludes our theoretical analysis. It develops our basic hypothesis by arguing that the communication restrictions have no direct effect upon performance of the operating task. It argues that the communication pattern has important effects upon the difficulty the group will encounter in organizing itself—but that the restricted patterns do not necessarily make for more difficulties than the unrestricted patterns. Now let us examine the empirical data to determine whether they support or refute our theoretical analysis.

II. THE EMPIRICAL FINDINGS

Performance Times in Operating Task Trials

As far as the subjects were concerned, the time required for each trial was the central focus of the experiment. In the instructions they were told, "Your team is competing with the other five-man groups to see which group is fastest at getting the answer. The shorter the time, the better your team score."

The average time per trial for the three types of groups is presented in Figure 2. The Circle groups are clearly slower than the Wheel groups after the first trial. The All-Channel groups occupy an intermediate position. A statistical check of the differences between the types of groups was made on the cumulative time required for the 20 trials. This table also includes the averages for the three fastest trials within each type of group. Although the Circle groups are significantly different from the Wheel and All-Channel groups for both measures, there was a significant difference between the Wheel and All-Channel groups on only the "total time" measure.

The effects of the communication nets upon the time criteria were marked. During the 8th trial, the Wheel groups had already reached the levels eventually attained by the All-Channel groups in their last few trials. At the end of the 20 trials, the Circle groups were using some 60 percent more time than the Wheel groups in performing their operations. During the course of the twenty trials, there were performance differences between the All-Channel and Wheel groups that eventually disappeared.

These findings hint that the Wheel groups, with the least difficult organizational problem, organized earliest; that the All-Channel groups, with a more difficult job, organized more slowly, but were eventually performing as well as the Wheel groups; that the Circle groups had difficulty in organizing, not reaching optimum performance within the 20 trials allowed. These differences correspond to the variations in organizational difficulty imposed by each net. The more difficult the organizational job, the less rapid was the evolution toward efficient task performance.

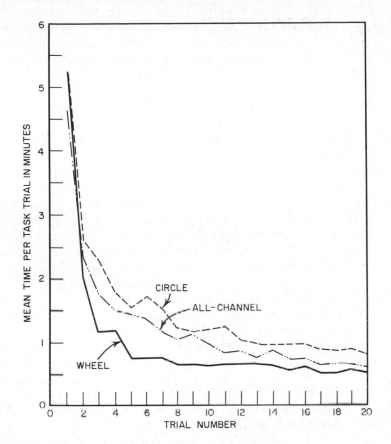

Figure 2. Average time per group for task trials.

III. REPLICATION OF LEAVITT'S EXPERIMENT

Our experimental procedure used the Wheel and Circle nets in common with Leavitt. We ran our groups 20 trials, in contrast with his 15 trials. He did not match his groups on the basis of intellective ability. In his experiment, the task and non-task messages were written contemporaneously during the operating trial itself, without benefit of a pre-coded task message card; we had the non-task messages written during an inter-trial period.

Despite these differences, our empirical results in the main are a forth-right confirmation of the work that was replicated. Leavitt found the fastest trial in his Wheel and Circle groups to average .53 and .83 minutes respectively. The Wheel groups in both his and our experiments took a little more than 60 percent of the time taken by the Circle groups for completion of their fastest task runs. The absolute differences in times between the two experiments may be artifacts produced by apparatus dissimilarities and by the fact that Leavitt's data include the time used for sending non-task messages.

Leavitt's figures on volume of messages are comparable to the sum of our task *and* intertrial messages. In the Wheel nets our groups sent an average of 177 messages per group during the first 15 trials compared with Leavitt's 166, our average being about 7 percent greater. In the Circle nets our groups sent an average of 389 messages over the first 15 trials and intertrials compared with Leavitt's 372, ours being about 2 percent greater. These differences are not statistically significant. The ratio of information messages to answer messages in the two experiments is similar. Thus, our use of an intertrial period seems not to have disturbed the situation as originally designed by Bavelas, Leavitt, and Smith.

Despite our ability to replicate Leavitt's results as far as the time and volume of messages are concerned, there is a striking difference with regard to the extent to which our Circles organized. Leavitt says, "The *circle* showed no consistent operational organization. Most commonly messages were just sent in both directions until any *S*(ubject) received an answer or worked one out." Although our Circle groups were much less differentiated than groups in the other two nets, many consistent patterns evolved. The latter difference between our results and Leavitt's cannot be ascribed to the fact that we ran twenty rather than fifteen trials. At the end of the 15 trials some 48 percent of the segments had already differentiated into stable or semi-stable interaction structures. We cannot explain these differences.

Our results on the Wheel groups are identical with those obtained by Leavitt. All of his groups, like ours, used the same interaction structure, the information pattern being the inverse of the answer pattern. Like our groups, his evolved the organization by the fourth or fifth trials.

IV. SUMMARY

This replication and extension of the work of Bavelas, Leavitt, and Smith on communication patterns in task-oriented groups enabled us to separate the effect of communication nets upon the performance of an operating task by the group, and upon the ability of the group to organize itself for this operating task. The particular nets we explored did not create differences among the groups with respect to the time needed for handling the operating task when an optimal organization was used. These same nets did introduce important differences in the organizing difficulties encountered. In this way we obtained an estimate, which can be refined through further experimentation, of the relative difficulties introduced by demanding the establishment of non-symmetric "keyman" roles, the organization of relay points, and the elimination of unnecessary channels.

The current management literature on the topic of communication leaves one with the expectation that certainly a reduction in communication restrictions should lead to a more adequately functioning organization. Yet, our findings in this experiment indicate that assertion of a one-to-one relationship between effective functioning and freedom in communication is unwarranted. Had our analysis not separated the organizational problem from the operating problem, it would have seemed paradoxical that complete freedom of communication is at times more limiting than restricted communication. The findings warn the practical communications expert working in industry or government that a change in communications structure may have quite different consequences for the efficiency of immediate day-to-day operations, and for the ability of the organization to handle changes in its own structure.

24 | Decision Processes in Communication Nets
MARVIN E. SHAW, GERARD H. ROTHSCHILD, and JOHN F. STRICKLAND

There is ample experimental evidence that the communication structure of a group influences the performance and satisfaction of the group when the task is to solve problems having logically imperative solutions. However, there seems to be no evidence that the same kinds of effects obtain when the problem to be solved does not have a generally agreed upon solution, e.g., a problem requiring agreement among the group members about the proper way to deal with an issue involving interpersonal relations.

EXPERIMENT

METHOD. The apparatus used in this experiment consists of four cubicles, each of which has a worktable, work materials, and a switch which controls a light and timer located at E's position. The cubicles are inter-

Reprinted with permission of the American Psychological Association and the authors. From *Journal of Abnormal and Social Psychology*, 54:323–330 (1957).

connected by means of slots through the walls separating them. Group members can communicate with each other by writing messages on cards and passing these cards through the slots. Various communication nets can be arranged by closing the necessary slots. The communication nets investigated in this study are shown in Figure 1.

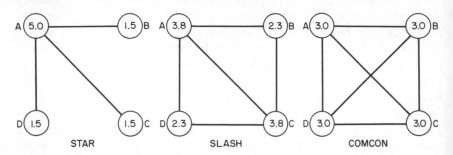

Figure 1. The experimental nets. Circles represent persons and the lines represent two-way communication channels between persons. Numbers within circles are the independence scores for the positions within the net.

The Ss for this experiment were students (all male) at the Johns Hopkins University. All were highly experienced, having served previously as Ss in this kind of experimental situation for a total of 12 sessions during which they solved a total of 24 problems involving simple arithmetical manipulations. For purposes of counterbalancing, the experimental design required that eight groups of four Ss be assigned to each of the three communication nets. One group which had been assigned to the "slash" failed to report for the experimental session, and since no other experienced Ss were available the data reported here are for eight groups in the "star," eight in the "comcon," and seven in the "slash." It appears highly unlikely that failure to fill this one cell in the design resulted in any serious bias in the final results.

Two human relations problems were used. One was a modified version of Deutsch's "The World War II Veteran" problem. As presented to the Ss in this experiment, the central figure in the story was an executive who had had an affair with his secretary. The secretary had subsequently resigned to get married. The executive's wife is intelligent but suffers from a traumatic childhood experience which made her especially sensitive to this kind of unfaithfulness. The question: What should the executive do, assuming that for his own peace of mind he cannot just forget the matter?

The other problem was essentially the same as that used by Festinger and Hutte. The central figure in this story is Henry, the son of a physician, who has a friend, Jim, who is incurably ill. Both are in love with the same girl. Just as Henry has decided to ask the girl to marry him, she announces her engagement to Jim. The girl does not know that Jim is incurably ill, although Henry does. The question: What should Henry do and say?

Except for the communication net and the order in which the problems were presented, the procedure was the same for all groups. The Ss were seated in their cubicles and handed a mimeographed set of instructions. The E then read the instructions while the Ss followed along on the printed page. The instructions informed Ss: (a) of the nature of the communication net (which was, with minor exceptions, the same as during previous sessions), (b) that they were to solve problems having no correct or incorrect answer, but which merely called for a group decision, (c) that a unanimous decision was desirable but that they could give a minority report if they were convinced that unanimity could not be attained, and (d) that they would be given 20 minutes to discuss the problem, but could signal E by throwing their switches if agreement was reached before the end of this period. The lack of emphasis upon time is in contrast to instructions given in previous investigations. Problems were presented in counterbalanced order.

After both problems had been considered and decisions rendered, Ss were required to indicate on an 11-point scale how well they enjoyed their task in the group and how they would rate the performance of their group.

RESULTS. Of chief interest were the differences due to the communication net and to positions within nets. In addition, data were evaluated for differences due to trials (first vs. second problem) and to problems. In agreement with the results of previous studies, trials differed significantly with respect to both time and message units required to reach a decision ($p < .01$). This finding is a general one and will not be referred to again. Differences due to problems were not significant in any of the analyses performed.

There were marked differences among the groups in different communication nets in mean times required to reach a decision (16.62 min. in the star, 14.00 min. in the slash, and 9.71 min. in the comcon). The F test revealed that these differences are statistically reliable ($p < .01$). This finding is in agreement with the results obtained when the problems to be solved were of the arithmetical type, but it might be noted that the magnitudes of the differences are somewhat greater than those typically reported in earlier investigations.

There were no significant differences among positions within nets with respect to time scores. In fact, under the conditions of this experiment it would have been very surprising if such differences had been found.

Content of messages was analyzed into units by the method developed in earlier studies according to which a message unit is defined as any simple sentence or any meaningful part of a complex or compound sentence. There were no significant differences among nets in number of message units required to reach a decision (means were 28.4, 34.6, and 32.6 for the star, the slash, and the comcon, respectively). This does not agree with the findings of earlier studies, but this failure seems to be due almost entirely to the great differences in time required to reach a decision. If message units per unit time are considered, nets are ordered in the same way as in other experiments. (Mean message units per min. were 3.60, 4.95, and 7.19 for the star, the slash, and the comcon, respectively. Differences are statistically reliable [$p < .001$].)

Mean number of message units transmitted by Ss in the various positions within nets are shown in Table 1. Only the differences in the star

Table 1

Mean Number of Communication Units Transmitted by Ss in Different Positions

Nets	Positions				
	A	B	C	D	p
Star	50.8	22.8	18.1	21.8	< .01
Slash	41.6	29.6	38.3	29.0	ns
Comcon	31.5	33.3	32.8	32.6	ns

are significant, but the differences in the slash are in the same direction as that found in earlier studies. That is, Ss in the more centralized positions sent more messages than did Ss in the more peripheral positions. It is also interesting that the number of messages directed toward deviators (i.e., those who disagreed with the majority opinion) was considerably greater than the number directed toward nondeviators in equivalent positions (mean number message units received by deviators: 11.9, 19.3, and 22.7 in the star, the slash, and the comcon, respectively; by non-deviators: 9.2, 14.3, and 16.9 in the star, the slash, and the comcon, respectively). Differences between deviators and nondeviators were significant at well beyond the .01 level of confidence in each of the three nets. This finding agrees with results obtained under very different conditions by Festinger and Thibaut and by Schachter.

There were no significant differences among nets or among positions within nets either in ratings of satisfaction or in ratings of performance.

However, it is interesting that the direction of the differences in ratings of satisfaction were opposite to that found in previous investigations (mean ratings of satisfaction: 9.09, 8.86, and 8.63 for the star, the slash, and the comcon, respectively; in the star, mean ratings of satisfaction were 8.3 for Position A and 9.4 for Positions B, C, and D, where higher numbers indicate greater satisfaction). A possible explanation for this result is given in a later section.

The frequency with which individuals disagreed with the majority opinion was very small in all three nets; hence, application of statistical tests was not justified. However, it is interesting to compare the percentage of disagreements occurring in the three nets. The percentage of total opinions (decisions) which disagreed with the majority of the particular group was 18.75 in the star, 16.07 in the slash, and 9.38 in the comcon. Thus, despite the fact that Ss in the star and the slash spent more time trying to reach an agreement, the degree of unanimity actually attained was less than in the comcon.

Differences in disagreements by Ss in the various positions within nets are shown in Table 2. It can be seen that frequency of disagreement

Table 2

Percentage of Decisions Disagreed with by Ss in Different Positions

Nets	Positions			
	A	B	C	D
Star	0	31.3	25.0	18.8
Slash	7.1	28.6	7.1	21.4
Comcon	6.3	12.5	6.3	12.5

correlates rather well with the centrality of positions. In the star the most central position never disagreed with the majority opinion. Likewise the more central positions in the slash showed markedly fewer disagreements than did the more peripheral positions.

DISCUSSION. Taken together, the results given above present a reasonably consistent picture of the group process. The time required to reach a decision was longest in the star and shortest in the comcon, in agreement with earlier studies in which arithmetical problems were used. Number of message units required to reach a decision in the three nets did not differ significantly, but units transmitted per minute did. In other words, groups in the comcon reached a decision more quickly than did groups in the other two nets but did so by transmitting messages at a more rapid rate.

It has been suggested that the time differences are due entirely to the fact that in the star and in the slash the burden of writing falls mainly on one or two people; i.e., that differences are due entirely to the effects of the net upon ease of intragroup communication. Fortunately, this hypothesis can be checked rather easily. If it is true, then the rate of message transmission should be essentially the same for the S sending the greatest number of messages in each net. This is not the case; the star is significantly slower than either the slash or the comcon ($F = 6.85$, $p <$ .01). Also, it would be expected that if we selected the one S in each group who sent the greatest number of messages for that group, and then compared nets with respect to number of messages transmitted by these Ss alone, nets would differ significantly. This is not found ($F = 1.31$; $F_{.05} = 3.49$). Finally, if this hypothesis were true one would expect that time, measured from the "go" signal until the last S had thrown his switch, would correlate significantly with the greatest number of messages sent by any one S in that group. Again, the result is negative ($r = .097$; $r_{.05} =$ .396). The results of these analyses make it clear that the interrelationships of nets, decision times, and messages are not simple ones.

Another finding that requires some discussion is the relationship between net and frequency of disagreement with the majority opinion. There are two possible explanations. One is that the Ss in the more central positions were using their position to bring other members around to their own viewpoint. A second possibility is that Ss in the more central positions who held deviant opinions were subject to more direct pressure than were those in peripheral positions; this added pressure caused them to change more quickly and more frequently than peripheral deviators. The latter interpretation also explains the fact that ratings of satisfaction by Ss in different positions were not significantly different. The peripheral positions may have enjoyed being able to maintain a deviant opinion without being subjected to too much group pressure; on the other hand, Ss in the more central positions may have had their satisfaction dampened by being vulnerable to group pressure.

SUMMARY

In the experiment, groups of four persons were required to solve two human relations problems in three different communication nets: the star, the slash, and the comcon. The results were as follows: (*a*) Ss in the star required significantly more time to reach a decision than did the slash, which required more time than did the comcon; (*b*) there were no significant differences among nets in ratings of satisfaction nor in number of messages transmitted, although significantly more messages were directed toward deviators than toward nondeviators; (c) although frequencies were too small for statistical evaluation, there were more deviators in the star than in the slash, and more in the slash than in the comcon. Also, there were more deviators in peripheral positions than in more central ones.

25 The Power Variable in Communication Experiments
MAUK MULDER

INTRODUCTION

Determinants of Satisfaction

In a number of laboratory experiments on communication structures in which groups of three, four, or five subjects, interacting by means of written messages, performed group tasks, an important dependent variable has been morale or job satisfaction. . . . Bavelas interpreting Lewin's concept of "shortest path" (intended to be a dynamic concept) in a purely positional sense, developed a measure of "position centrality" in the net. In theories developed to explain satisfaction phenomena, this centrality, or other measures expressing positional characteristics, is conceived as fundamental for the job satisfaction of the group members. Several of the variables assumed to be significant determinants of satisfaction are concerned with the *immediate* effects of the structures. Examples are "availability of information" (as a result of access to information channels) and communication activity (as related to number of channels).

In our view, too much emphasis has been placed in this communication research on the positional aspect, as expressed in "channel-usage" and "access to channels" (degree of centrality), and the dynamic aspect has to a certain extent been neglected. The topological structure, characterized by invariability, determines what behaviour is *possible;* dynamic vari-

Reprinted with permission of Tavistock Publications and the author. From *Human Relations,* 13:241–257 (1960).

ables, however, determine what behaviour will actually occur. That is to say, we acknowledge that the topological "structure" (centrality) leads, *via* other variables, to satisfaction. But, especially for the prediction of satisfaction in situations different from those used in the reported studies, these other dynamic intervening variables must be identified.

In this context, the theory of Leavitt (and Shaw) on "independence of action" must be referred to. But *independence of others* is a negative, vague construct; it does not determine very precisely which action may lead to satisfaction and what kind of blocked action may lead to dissatisfaction.

In the experiments referred to above, group members in more central positions, which show a higher satisfaction, are quite distinct in certain aspects from members with a lower satisfaction: they are more active, but they also very often achieve the problem solutions themselves and pass the solutions on to other group members. We now define three constructs:

1. *Activity:* just being occupied; in the experiments this refers to the amount of communication activity per unit of time.
2. *Self-realization:* having responsibility for the completion of one's task. It may be operationally defined as the achievement of the problem solution by the person himself.
3. *The exercise of power:* determining the behaviour of another person. In the experiments this occurs when a person sends the problem solution (or essential information) to another person.

Our fundamental hypothesis is that the exercise of power is a primary determinant of satisfaction in a number of communication experiments and in general.

A further hypothesis is that both in more powerful persons and in less powerful persons there exists a *tendency toward unification (identification) with the powerful and a tendency toward separation from the less powerful*. Forming a psychological unit with the powerfuls leads to a feeling: "I am among them, I belong to them, thus a similar power position to theirs is proper for me."

The tendency toward separation from the less powerful is understood as "creating a distance": the person does not want to find himself back among the less powerful. When defining *psychological distance* between two persons as the extent of inequality existing between them, as far as a certain dimension is concerned, we hypothesize:

(i) a tendency to reduce the distance between more powerful group members and the person himself;
(ii) a tendency to increase the distance between less powerful group members and the person himself.

One point must be emphasized. The tendency to exert power will not manifest itself in all situations: when the distance between the power-persons and the person himself is too great, he will resign from striving for this goal. The preference already mentioned of less powerfuls for other less powerfuls may be an example. In such cases, the energy may be directed into other directions, for instance solidarity with other power-less group members.

HYPOTHESES AND EXPERIMENTAL DESIGN

Hypotheses

When the *exercise of power* is defined as the determination (to a certain extent) of the behaviour of another, our core hypothesis is:

A. To the extent that a person's exercise of power is greater, his satisfaction will increase.

When *self-realization* is defined as having responsibility for the completion of one's own task, the following hypothesis is formulated:

B. To the extent that a person's self-realization is greater, his satisfaction will increase.

Furthermore, hypotheses are formulated concerning the differential power positions of individuals in a group.

When we define the *psychological distance* between two persons as the extent of (psychological) inequality existing between them on a particular dimension, then the theory can be summarized as follows: there is a tendency for the individual to reduce the psychological distance to the more powerful, if this distance is not too great, and to increase the distance to the less powerful, if this distance is not too small.

The theory is formulated in the following general hypotheses:

(i) A tendency exists in the individual to reduce the psychological distance to the more powerful members of his group.
(ii) The tendency to reduce the psychological distance to the more powerful increases to the extent that this distance is smaller.
(iii) A tendency exists in the individual to increase the psychological distance to the less powerful members of his group.
(iv) The tendency to increase the psychological distance to the less powerful decreases to the extent that this distance is smaller.

The tendencies formulated in (i) and (iii) have related effects when the individual is in an in-between position (between more and less powerful persons): a move toward more powerful persons is a move away from the less powerful ones. This situation arises in our experiment, so it will often be impossible to isolate the influence of each of the separate tendencies in the resultant effect.

Derived from (i) and (iii) is the specific hypothesis:

C. A tendency exists in the individual toward relative preference for the more powerful group members.

This entails a preference, in sociometric choices, for the more powerful group members as against the less powerful.

Derived from (ii) and (iv) is the hypothesis:

D. To the extent that the distance between the more powerful and the individual is smaller, this tendency (toward relative preference for the more powerful) increases.

We expect the same "distance-increasing" and "distance-reducing" processes in the field of perception. Derived from (i), (ii), (iii), and (iv) are:

E. A tendency exists in the individual to decrease perceptually the difference in relevant qualities between more powerful group members and himself, and to increase the difference between himself and the less powerful.

By relevant qualities are meant here qualities directly related to the occupancy of power positions, for instance abilities that may give someone a "right" to claim a power position. In this hypothesis it is taken for granted that the individual does not perceive his own qualities to be better than those of more powerful, or worse than those of less powerful, group members.

F. This tendency (to decrease the perceptual distance between oneself and the more powerful and to increase the distance between oneself and the less powerful) increases to the extent that the former decreases and the latter increases.

Experimental Design

Groups of four persons solved 15 Leavitt-type problems; the subjects could not interact, however, as in Leavitt's experiment, by written communication but only by using a specially designed "intercommunicator," a telephonic send-and-receive apparatus comparable with communication systems in use on ships. Three group members were paid participants; one was the experimental subject. The variations of the self-realization (S) variable and the power (P) variable were introduced mainly through the interaction of the four group members. In SI, the subject does not devise the solution himself, but receives it (from the person in position 1); in SII he receives all information (from position 1) and then solves the problem himself.

In PI the subject is to an extreme degree powerless; in PII he has nearly complete power over two group members, who are dependent on him for receiving the solution. These manipulations are supported by some remarks during the introduction of the experimenter (S-variable) and by two remarks of paid participants during the work-period (S- and P-variables).

The two P-variations and the two S-variations combine into four conditions; in all four the (paid participant) group member in position 1 is more powerful than the subject. In PII conditions, the occupants of positions 2 or 3, and 4 are less powerful than the subject; thus the relative distance between the subject and position 1 is smaller in PII than in PI conditions.

By the use of the intercommunicator and three "stooges" it was possible to keep the sending and receiving (communication) activity per unit of time of the subjects strictly equal in the four conditions. Thus no effect in the dependent variables can be attributed to the activity variable.

The subjects were 80 recruits for the Royal Dutch Navy (20 in each condition). They were spending one day in a special camp, undergoing selection procedures for the different branches of the Navy. All were aged between nineteen years, six months, and twenty years, six months, and had attended U.L.O. schools. Their intelligence had been assessed by the means of the Raven progressive matrices test and averaged 102 (Wechsler). The experimenter by way of introduction emphasized that what Ss were about to do had nothing to do with selection. He stated that the selection procedures were finished (as they were), but that this was a piece of naval research designed to explore group cooperation in situations comparable with those on shipboard. Furthermore, they were told that they were "equals"; that we knew from their tests and other data that they had exactly the same abilities for this work.

EXPERIMENTAL RESULTS

1. Check on the Experimental Situation

(i) *Activity*

Activity is defined as the amount of communication activity (output and input) per unit of time. Through the role behaviour of the paid participants it was ensured that in all four conditions the activity was equal.

Time was also controlled by our paid participants. Mean durations in minutes of the total work session were: PISI = 92·08; PISII = 94·82; PIISI = 92·03; PIISII = 93·84. The difference per problem between PI and PII is 2 seconds; between SI and SII 9 seconds. These differences are negligible. Nor is there a subjectively felt difference. Our Ss were asked to rate the performance of their group on a scale from very bad (0) to excellent (10). The data are PISI = 6·02; PISII = 6·43; PIISI = 6·17; PIISII = 6·42. In the analysis of variance no differences appear. To summarize the activity data; there are no differences in activity between the several conditions; therefore no effect in the dependent variables can be attributed to this variable.

(ii) *The Perceived Leadership Structure*

The function of "position 1" has been mentioned above as that of sending all relevant information (in SII) or the solution (SI) to the subject. Could this difference eventually lead to different perceptions of "position 1" in SI and SII? The question was asked: "Did your group have a leader?" (if the answer was positive, S was asked to name him).

In none of the conditions did more than one subject (out of the twenty) give a negative answer to the first part of the question; to the second part, 95 percent of the respondents in all conditions named "position 1" as the leader. Thus an identical leadership structure existed in all conditions.

2. Dependent Variables: Satisfaction

(i) *Dependent Variable: Satisfaction-Scale*

Because satisfaction was the variable on which this experiment concentrated, several "measurements" of this variable have been introduced in the design. The essential measurement, applied in our earlier research, was a job-liking rating on a scale from "liked very much" (10) to "liked not so much" (0). S had to rate all group members on separate scales, in rank-sequence, first the one who had the most pleasant work, etc. In Table 1 are shown the ratings subjects give themselves.

Table 1

Means of Subject's Own Satisfaction-Rating

PISI	4·89
PISII	5·37
PIISI	7·11
PIISII	6·57

In an analysis of variance, *only the effect of the power* (P) *variable* is significant ($p < \cdot001$); the S-variable has no influence at all; the interaction (P × S) is far from significant.

(ii) *Dependent Variable: Observed Dissatisfied Remarks*

During the work session psychologically significant behaviour was scored. First, *S*s sometimes expressed *direct dissatisfaction* in their remarks to position 1, although this was *not* encouraged in the preliminary training (where the messages were rigidly formulated). Remarks were categorized as indicating dissatisfaction on account of either content or intonation.

The data are shown in Table 2.

Table 2

	PISI	PISII	PIISI	PIISII
Number of remarks	7	11	2	3
Number of persons	5	5	2	2
Total number of persons in each condition 20				

If an analysis is made of the (very small) number of persons who at least once expressed dissatisfaction in this way, a difference exists between the combined PI and PII conditions (one-tail test: $p = \cdot07$).

When the null hypothesis is tested that chances on dissatisfaction remarks are equal for each of the four conditions (a test that is not completely pure, but cannot be fully rejected), a similar relation holds (PI versus PII gives $p - \cdot045$). Ten persons of the 40 in PI made 18 dissatisfaction remarks, against 4 persons in PII, who made 5 remarks. There seems to be a somewhat stronger tendency in PI than in PII to express dissatisfaction in this way.

(iii) *Dependent Variable: Observed 'Obstructive Behaviour'*

In all four conditions it is essential that *S* sends his information to position 1; in SI the subject receives after some time the solution from position 1, in SII the subject receives all the information. It was hypothesized that the subject might express dissatisfaction by reluctance to send his own information or by not "calling" position 1. The tendency to express this behaviour is opposed by the experimenter because the time-schedule is endangered by it.

At a given moment position 1 must have available all the information. So there was a rule that, if *S* did not call upon position 1 within two minutes, the "introducer" went to the subjects' room, and his entrance was often sufficient to inspire S to call position 1. If this did not happen, after 20 seconds, combined action by the role-player and the introducer started to bring about the desired behaviour of the subjects. Since it is clear that there was in this way a strong pressure on S to limit 'waiting,' the frequency of the waiting-periods is very significant behaviour in itself. This behaviour can result from unclarity of the situation, which we may expect at the beginning of the session. For this reason the data for the period after the third problem were *a priori* chosen as the more important ones. When an analysis is made of the number of persons who exhibit this behaviour at least once (i.e., waiting more than one minute), SI and SII do not show a difference; but PI versus PII gives $\cdot 001 < p < \cdot 01$. Again, the analysis of the frequency of these acts confirms this result. The frequency after the third problem for PI versus PII is significantly different from a chance distribution: PI versus PII gives $\cdot 01 < p < \cdot 05$ (one-tail test). The S-variable has no effect.

Table 3

Obstructive Behaviour

	PISI	PISII	PIISI	PIISII
Total number of waiting periods	6	11	2	2
Idem after third problem	4	10	2	0
Number of persons	6	7	1	1
Idem, after third problem	4	6	1	0

To summarize, 10 of the 40 subjects in PI show this behaviour (delay in sending information to position 1) after the third problem 14 times, whereas one of the 40 PII-subjects did so twice. (Three Ss, all of them in PI, waited longer than 2·5 minutes.) The conclusion is that in the PI conditions a stronger tendency exists in the Ss to display obstructive behaviour, although such a manifestation is extremely difficult in our experimental situation. This phenomenon is *psychologically* very significant: the results of this direct, non-verbal behaviour, which is interpreted as satisfaction behaviour, confirm the results of the other satisfaction measurements.

(iv) *Dependent Variable: The Development of Satisfaction*

Analysis of the development of satisfaction, based on a reconstruction by the subjects themselves afterwards, and on comparison of spoken answers on three very casual questions during the work-period, showed that only the PII-subjects expressed a significant increase in satisfaction during the work-period (p-values respectively $< \cdot01$ and $< \cdot02$ with Sign Test and Chi-square for changes).

3. Importance of Position

A brief reference must be made to the results of the following measurement of importance: "How do you rate the importance of the position of each of the members of your group?" Each member is rated on a separate scale from unimportant (0) to important (10). The scales are together on one page of the booklet. Ss are not asked to rank the group members, but this nevertheless occurs implicitly. This question is introduced as bearing upon "a kind of work-division." Pressure is brought upon S not to rate all members alike. The self-ratings do not lead to significant differences. However, the pressure brought upon Ss to differentiate in their ratings has the effect that significant differences are found upon analysis of the *relation* of an individual's self-ratings with his ratings of positions 2 or 3, and 4. In Table 4 are reported the self-ratings of the subjects, *minus* his average rating of positions 2 or 3, and 4 (position 1 is not included here).

Table 4

"Importance of Position"
Self-Rating Minus Rating
of 2 or 3 and 4

PISI	$-0 \cdot 97$
PISII	$+0 \cdot 13$
PIISI	$+0 \cdot 93$
PIISII	$+2 \cdot 07$

Analysis of variance leads to significant effects between PI and PII ($p < \cdot001$) and between SI and SII ($\cdot01 < p < \cdot05$).

It may be assumed that clues for rating oneself as being more important than positions 2 or 3, and 4 are furnished by the PII variation and by the SII variation. (In a detailed analysis it appeared that in SII the subject perceived that they were solving the problem themselves, *whereas positions 2 or 3 and 4 were not.*) Essential in our context is, that even where those "relative" importance differences exist, we did not find differences in the four reported satisfaction differences.

4. Behaviour Toward Others in the Power Structure

(i) "Choice Processes"

Now follow data on the behaviour of our Ss as directed toward other group members more or less powerful than themselves. The person in position 1, the leader, is in all conditions more powerful than S himself, whereas S is more powerful than the others (positions 2 or 3, and 4) in PII-conditions. A series of sociometric questions was asked: "With which of the members of this group would you most prefer to go for a bicycle ride? Whom would you prefer least? With whom would you most prefer to go on a camping trip? Whom would you prefer least? With whom would you most prefer to be in the same branch? Whom would you prefer least?" At least one number in each space has to be filled out: from the pilot study it appeared that otherwise no rejecting response was ever given, so the question was introduced in this form, although it made analysis more difficult. In Table 5 the positive $(+)$ and negative $(-)$ choices are given for the leader (position 1) and the others (positions 2 or 3, and 4).

Table 5

Results of Sociometric Question
(Last Sub-Question)

	Choices of position 1		Choices of others	
	+	−	+	−
PISI	10	6	14	17
PISII	15	3	9	21
PIISI	16	2	4	20
PIISII	16	1	5	20
All conditions	57	12	32	78

In these results the tendency to make positive choices of position 1 cannot be isolated from the tendency to make negative choices of the others. The choice process here is clearly "relative": preference for one means less preference (rejection) for another.

Analysis of the data shows a far more positive attitude toward position 1 than toward the others. The difference between positive and negative choices on position 1 is large and very significant $(\cdot00001 < p < \cdot0001)$. Another way of presenting the data is that there are significantly more negative choices of the others than positive choices $(\cdot0001 < p < \cdot001)$.

When conditions are tested against each other, there is a difference (Table 5) in 'choices of others' between PI and PII: in PI 23 choices are positive, against 38 negative; in PII 9 choices are positive, 40 negative. The difference between PI and PII is significant $(\cdot01 < p < \cdot02)$. The S-variable has no effect. The choices of position 1 can be used in another way for analysis of these data by determining the number of Ss who made positive choices of position 1 *exclusively*.

Table 6

Number of Times That Only Position 1 Is Positively Chosen

PISI	7 (total = 20)
PISII	11 (total = 20)
PIISI	16 (total = 20)
PIISII	14 (total = 19)

In PI 18 subjects of the total 40 made a positive choice on position 1 exclusively, in PII 30 did so (against 9 who did not). In PII the difference is significant ($\cdot01 < p < \cdot02$). The difference between PI and PII is also significant ($\cdot001 < p < \cdot002$). SI and SII do not differ.

To summarize the results of the choice process:

1. There exists a strong tendency in the direction of a relative preference for more powerful persons in one's group.
2. This tendency to have a relative preference for powerful persons is stronger when the subjects themselves are in a more powerful position (in PII conditions).

(ii) Perception Processes

The intention was to determine how S compared his own abilities with those of the other group members. Perception of the abilities of the more powerful and less powerful group members was measured in the following questions:

"Could each of the others have done your work as well? Who could have? Who could not?" (All three other persons have to be mentioned, but each may be placed in one of the two spaces.)

Table 7

"Perception of Abilities"

	Opinion about position 1		Opinion about others (2, 3, and 4)	
	+	−	+	−
PISI	18	2	38	2
PISII	19	1	35	5
PIISI	18	1	31	8
PIISII	17	0	28	10
	72	4	132	25

Three analyses will be reported: first it can be stated that many more positive than negative choices are made; both the distribution of positive and negative choices on position 1 and that on others differ significantly from a chance distribution (chances on plus and minus are even), p-values being far lower than ·00001. In the second analysis it appears that the opinions about position 1 are more positive than those about positions 2 or 3, and 4 ($·01 < p < ·02$). In the third analysis differences between conditions are tested. In the "perception of the others" PII is significantly more negative than PI ($·01 < p < ·02$), and SI versus SII does not lead to significance.

The perception of position 1 is positive, at least to the degree that there are no differences between conditions in those data. But, again, a sharper analysis is possible by determining the number of subjects that make only a positive choice on position 1. These data are conceived as indices of a more meaningful 'positivity' toward position 1, but it is evident that these data are not completely absolute; it is a positivity toward position 1 that is dependent on negativity toward the others.

In PISI this is 0 (of 20), PISII = 1 (of 20), PIISI = 4 (of 20), and PIISII = 3 (of 19). Comparison of PI and PII gives (using Fisher's exact method) $p = ·027$.

To summarize the results of the perception processes:

1. When an individual judges the abilities of others in connection with his own work, his perception of the more powerful group members is more positive than his perception of the less powerful persons.
2. This tendency is stronger to the extent that the individual himself is more powerful.

With regard to conclusion 2, it is held that one of the two component tendencies, the tendency to perceive the less powerful persons more negatively, has been isolated and separately demonstrated. We may state, too, that the positive perception of the more powerful persons is—to a certain degree—demonstrated separately.

DISCUSSION

Determinants of Satisfaction

At the beginning of this paper it was asked what kinds of action satisfy the individuals in task-performing groups. Two provisional answers referred to self-realization and the exercise of power.

Self-realization is defined as having individual responsibility for the completion of one's task. In a number of industrial studies satisfaction seems to be related to responsibility for one's own task-completion. However, clear isolation from *social* variables such as 'doing important things for the total group,' prestige, competition, etc., is difficult to guarantee in the situations typical of industrial research.

The *opinions of respondents themselves* on their job satisfaction must, in particular, be considered with much critical reserve. Idealistic distortion must be expected here.

Thus it is not surprising that the empirical results are not clear, and it seemed justified to investigate in this experiment the hypothesis that completion of one's task (achievement of the solution of a problem) leads to satisfaction.

The result was not positive: no satisfaction effect of self-realization could be demonstrated. This is remarkable because, as we have seen, the "importance" measurement differentiated between SI and SII conditions. To explore self-realization and its connection with 'social' motivation further research in controlled situations is needed.

It is noteworthy that in our experiment a clear difference exists in "availability of information" between SI and SII conditions. This difference should result, according to Leavitt and Shaw, in a satisfaction difference, but it fails to do so.

The cultural taboo with regard to exercise of "power" has led to a neglect of this variable in empirical research. Our intention in this experiment was to demonstrate that the exercise of power *per se* leads to satisfaction not only through such variables as increase of status, more pleasant activity, or other concomitant gains, but in itself.

The experimental data allow for definite conclusions. Satisfaction is measured in a job-liking scale, in certain measurements designed to trace the development of satisfaction, in direct observation of negative remarks, and in observation of purely obstructive behaviour. The results are consistent: PII subjects show more satisfaction than subjects in PI conditions. This is a striking fact, because the subject in the PII conditions has power over two other group members, but has a similar power-relation to a "leader" as the two others have toward him. In this sense, he himself is also completely *dependent* but, notwithstanding this dependency, the power variable has a strong effect on satisfaction.

There is no reason to believe that the satisfaction differences between PI and PII could be explained by status differences: the importance measurement differentiates between PI and PII, but also between SI and SII, where we find no satisfaction differences. This is in agreement with a result of a study by Trow, in which higher satisfaction was not based on *a priori* perception of high status.

Our conclusion is that the exercise of power appears to be in general a primary determinant of the person's satisfaction and also that the satisfaction of more central persons and key men in the communication structure experiments by Leavitt, Shaw, and Guetzkow & Simon, is a function of exercise of power.

In a recent study, Trow suggests that "autonomy" may be considered as mediating the relationship between centrality and satisfaction reported in Leavitt's study. Autonomy (referring to access to task-relevant information) is related by Trow to Leavitt's "answer-getting potential," which he defines as 'the degree to which a person achieves his own problem solutions' and in which he emphasizes self-sufficiency.

Our experimental data have made it evident that it is not "making the answers" (S-variable) but "passing-the-answers" (P-variable) that determines satisfaction.

In Trow's experiment the essential point seems to be that the autonomy of S allows him to make decisions through which he can avoid a waste of time; consequently the group can proceed faster. Furthermore, the group goal is to finish the task in as short a time as possible. So S in the autonomy conditions co-ordinates his own activity with that of others and, by doing so, contributes in an essential way to the movement of his group towards the group goal. This autonomy, then, includes more than mere self-sufficiency; it has a 'social' character in that it includes decision-making, which affects the total group.

Behaviour Toward Others in a Power Structure

This behaviour has been explored in a number of studies. Lippitt *et al.*, hypothesizing less rational behaviour as identification, restrict themselves to the behaviour of the less powerful person toward the more powerful ones. The substitute-locomotion theory (Festinger) is also restricted to the behaviour of the less powerful persons; certain communication processes are interpreted as locomotion to the goal on a level of irreality.

We consider certain preferences or rejections and certain communication and perception phenomena as manifestations of a striving for power. The theory includes behaviour of less powerful members toward more powerful ones and the reverse: a tendency toward identification with the powerful, and a tendency toward separation from the less powerful.

Using the concept of "psychological distance," we hypothesize a tendency in the individual to reduce the psychological distance to the more powerful group members, and a tendency to increase the distance to the less powerful. These tendencies could be demonstrated in our experiment in patterns of "preference and rejection" and in "perception of others" (communication processes are not investigated). Also we hypothesize that the tendency to reduce the distance to the more powerful increases to the extent that this distance is smaller; and that the tendency to increase the distance to the less powerful decreases to the extent that this distance is smaller.

These hypotheses were also confirmed in our experiment.

This result may explain those of Thibaut and Kelley, where no preference for the more powerful persons exists in the less powerful ones. When the distance between the more powerful persons and the person himself becomes too great, the preference decreases.

The difference between our theory of power-distance reduction and the ego-defensiveness theory, is as follows. According to the ego-defensiveness theory, subjects behave as they do (e.g. show preference for the powerful) in order to defend themselves against their power and to reduce their own feelings of uneasiness. Therefore the expectation should be that the less powerful the individual is in relation to the powerful, the stronger should be his feeling of uneasiness; and, consequently, the more strongly should ego-defensive tendencies manifest themselves in preferences for the powerful. Furthermore, the more powerful the individual is in relation to the power persons, the less urgent is the preference-behaviour, explained by the ego-defensiveness theory as reducing his uneasiness.

However, as we have already seen, the factual data do not confirm this expectation, but demonstrate the opposite. This can be satisfactorily explained by our theory, in which the preferences expressed by our experimental subjects for the more powerful are interpreted as manifesting a striving for more power; whereas in the ego-defensiveness theory these preferences are explained in terms of the individual's 'acquiescence' in being less powerful, and of his adaptation to this power relation.

But if the distance between the individual and the power person is *too* great, the individual renounces this goal and, consequently, the preference for the more powerful decreases.

In the same way, we interpret the behaviour toward the less powerful not as acquiescence in the existing power relation but as an attempt to put distance between oneself and them. A very relevant point in our data is the strong relation that appears to exist between choice and power data. The "tendencies for relative preference" mentioned in Section 4 are clearly a function of power (and not a function of the rated "relative importance of position," see Table 4).

Our theory of 'power-distance' is in agreement with the theories of substitute locomotion, contagious behavior, and ego-defensiveness, each of which throws light on certain behaviour phenomena. All these theories, however, still have a character of 'openness,' and the specification of conditions is by no means completed.

SUMMARY

This paper describes an experimental study of motivation, connected with the exercise of power and self-realization. The exercise of power (determining the behaviour of another) leads to satisfaction; self-realization, operationally restricted to completing one's own task, does not.

Behaviour toward other group members, both more and less powerful, is explained in terms of a "power-distance" theory. There appears to be a tendency, on the one hand, towards reducing distance between oneself and the more powerful, provided that the distance is not initially too great; and, on the other hand, to creating distance between oneself and the less powerful, provided that the distance is not initially too small.

Noise: Signal and Semantic

INTRODUCTION   So far we have assumed that when a signal goes from one point to another in a network the signal does not change. We have assumed full fidelity in the system of communication. In practice, however, there is always some change in the signal, some distortion, and this distortion is called noise. Both the mathematical and the social psychological theories of communication recognize the presence of noise, and this is one of the points where the two theories converge.

Donald E. Broadbent in "Attention and the Perception of Speech" shows that people often receive many sets of signals at the same time. This interference among the signals often creates noise and makes it difficult to recover any message. He shows how "when the listener is thoroughly familiar with a situation so that he knows to within a small number of alternatives what each message will be, he can comprehend two simultaneous messages. But when one or both messages are drawn from a large number of possibilities, the filter in the brain lets only one message come through."

Filtering noise out is a task not only for individual brains but also for the small social groups of the preceding set of selections. George A. Heise and George A. Miller in "Problem Solving by Small Groups Using Various Communication Nets" replicate some of the Leavitt-type experiments adding the further control of the signal to noise ratio. Members of their experimental groups communicate through microphones and earphones, while white noise, "a shishing sound," is introduced into their electronic network. They find that errors in communication increase with noise but at different rates for different kinds of networks and different kinds of tasks.

Josiah Macy, Jr., Lee S. Christie, and R. Duncan Luce go even further in "Coding Noise in a Task-Oriented Group." Instead of introducing white noise they introduce coding noise. This noise arises from ambiguity: the members of their small communication networks had to "interpret descriptions of colors that are not easy to describe." They find that differently organized networks differ in their ability to filter out such noise. Some networks have more built-in redundancy with which they overcome noise.

What Macy, Christie, and Luce call ambiguity or coding noise, Stanley Schachter and Harvey Burdick call cognitive unclarity. In "A Field Experiment on Rumor Transmission and Distortion" they test the effect of cognitive unclarity on the transmission of information in a natural group rather than an experimental laboratory group. They find little distortion with cognitive uncertainty; instead they find that the transmission of information—of rumor—depends on the importance of the subject.

John R. Kirk and George D. Talbot in "The Distortion of Information" find there are three kinds of noise in human communication generally: stretch distortion; fog distortion; and mirage distortion. They illustrate each kind from a wide range of communicational media and show how we can correct for each. Their selection leads from syntactics to semantics.

26 Attention and the Perception of Speech
DONALD E. BROADBENT

Paying attention—and not paying attention—are surely two of the most important abilities of human beings. Yet in spite of their crucial role in learning and in a host of other intelligent activities, psychologists for many years did not consider them proper topics of study. Attention seemed a subjective quality, associated historically with the introspective method of investigation. That method tends to give inconsistent results and so fell into disrepute among experimental psychologists. Correspondingly, most respectable theorists failed to make use of any concept resembling attention; and, since research in psychology tends to be dominated by theory, there was little experimentation along lines that might have revived the idea.

In the past 10 years, however, the concept of attention has begun to force itself on the attention of psychologists in various ways. One is through studies of the efficiency of control systems such as those concerned with the regulation of air traffic at airports. A major cause of failure in these systems is that the human operator has too much information to handle simultaneously, or that he reacts to an unimportant signal when he should be dealing with an important one. These problems require some understanding of phenomena that would commonly be described under the heading of "attention." There is now accumulating a wide variety of experimental results that clarify these phenomena, although the larger part of the work remains to be done. In this article I shall describe some of the research on attention to spoken messages.

One of the earliest findings, and one that agrees with everyday experience, is that it is harder to understand two messages arriving simultaneously than two messages arriving one after the other. One might be tempted to explain this as a purely physical interference between the two stimuli; for example, the louder passages of one message might drown out the softer passages of the other and vice versa, rendering them both unintelligible. Actually the matter is not so simple. By recording the messages on tape and playing them for different subjects instructed to respond in different ways, the intelligibility is shown to depend on psychological factors. Specifically, either message becomes understandable if the listener is instructed to ignore the other. But the two messages together cannot both be understood, even though the necessary information is available to the ear. Another way of making the same point is to insert the words of one message into spaces between the words from the other: "Oh God say save can our you gracious see Queen." Each message is hard to understand, but each word is spoken separately and is fully audible. The difficulty evidently lies inside the nervous system, which somehow prevents an adequate response to signals that are "heard" satisfactorily.

Further experiments demonstrate that comprehension improves if the two messages differ in certain physical characteristics. For instance, it is better if a man speaks one message and a woman speaks the other; or if the loudspeaker removes the lower tones from one voice but not the other. Spatial separation of the two voices gives the best result of all. The different messages should not come through the same loudspeaker or even from separate speakers mounted one above the other; the two speakers should be separated as far as possible from each other in the horizontal plane. Interestingly enough, a listener also comprehends simultaneous spoken messages better when they come from a stereophonic system than when they are played over a single loudspeaker. (This effect, rather than the doubtful gain in realism, is for many people the main advantage of stereophonic high-fidelity systems: the listener can pay attention to different musical instruments played at the same time.)

Physical distinctions are most helpful in promoting understanding when one message has no importance for the listener and does not have to be answered. It would seem that the differences allow the brain to filter the incoming sounds and select some for response while ignoring others.

The need to throw away part of the available information can perhaps be understood by comparing the brain with man-made communication systems. Engineers nowadays talk of capacity for transmitting information, by which they mean the number of equally probable messages of which one can be sent in a specified time. Suppose, for example, that two complicated military plans have been prepared and an order is to be sent to carry out one of them. A simple communication system consisting of a red and a green lamp can transmit the message with maximum efficiency by the lighting of a single lamp. If there were four plans instead of two, however, it would be impossible to give the order by lighting one of the two lamps no matter how simple each plan might be. Either there must be more lamps or more time is needed for sending the order. In the most efficient code for two lamps, two successive flashes of the red lamp would mean one plan, a red flash followed by a green flash would mean another, and so on. One of four possible messages can be transmitted with two lamps, but only by taking two units of time. With eight possible messages the code would call for three flashes of the two lamps, taking three units of time; 16 possible messages would require four flashes, and so forth.

Although the human brain has far more than the two states represented by the red and the green lamp, the number of its possible states is presumably limited. One would expect, then, that there is a limit to the number of different possibilities among which it can distinguish in a given time. Indeed, a number of experiments suggest a close parallel with the two lamp system: in many cases a man's attention time in responding to one of several possible signals increases by an equal amount every time the number of possible signals is doubled. Since there is a maximum speed at which one signal can be distinguished from others, the brain limits the number of possibilities being considered at any one time by selecting only part of the information reaching the ears. Therefore the degree of difficulty in dealing with two simultaneous spoken messages depends on the number of other messages that might have arrived instead of the two that did arrive. If only a few other messages are possible, the two messages together may not exceed the capacity of the brain and the listener may understand both. On the other hand, if each message is drawn from a very large range of possibilities, it may be all the listener can do to respond appropriately to one of them.

Several studies support these conclusions. John C. Webster and his associates at the U.S. Navy Electronics Laboratory in San Diego, California, observed that control-tower operators in San Diego could sometimes identify two aircraft call signs arriving at the same time but could understand only one of the two messages that followed. The call signs penetrated because the operators knew pretty well which aircraft might call. They did not know what the pilots would say.

An experiment at the Applied Psychology Research Unit in Cambridge, England, required a listener to answer a rapid series of questions while pressing a key in response to an intermittent buzzer. The interference produced by the buzzer in the ability to answer questions increased after the subject had been told that he would also have to respond to a bell. Even when the bell did not ring, the subject found the questions harder to answer than when he was expecting only the buzzer.

These results help to explain why a person can sometimes listen to two things at once and sometimes cannot pay attention to more than one.

When the listener is thoroughly familiar with a situation, so that he knows to within a small number of alternatives what each message will be, he can comprehend two simultaneous messages. But when one or both messages are drawn from a large number of possibilities, the filter in the brain lets only one message come through.

How does the filter work? As yet the answer is not known. Enough is known, however, about the physical characteristics of speech and the physiology of hearing to make possible some reasonable speculation. Human speech is produced by the combined action of the vocal cords and the vocal tract, which consists of the cavities of the throat, mouth and nose. Taut vocal cords produce a buzz when air is forced through them. The buzz consists of brief pulses, or puffs of air, at the rate of 100 or more per second, each pulse containing energy at many frequencies. These pulses excite into vibration the air in the cavities of the throat, nose and mouth. The cavities can be tuned to different frequencies by changing the position of the tongue, cheeks, jaw and lips. What emerges is a train of waves that contains a particular group of frequencies and is pulsed about 100 times per second. Each pulse starts out at full strength and decays rapidly until the sound energy is renewed by the next one.

Many vowel sounds contain waves at two or more widely separated frequencies. For example, when the greatest energy is at 375 and 1,700 cycles per second, the vowel sound in the word "bit" is produced; frequencies of 450 and 1,700 cycles per second give the vowel in "bet." (These figures apply to a typical male voice. In the voices of women and children the whole range of frequencies may be higher but the listener takes this into account.) On reaching the ear, the sounds stimulate sense organs arranged along the basilar membrane in the cochlea. Low frequencies stimulate organs at one end of the membrane; high frequencies affect those at the other end. A complex sound made up several frequencies energizes several different regions of the basilar membrane. Each sense organ on the membrane connects with particular nerve fibers going to the brain; thus the word "bit" stimulates one combination of fibers and the word "bet" another combination.

If both words reach the ear simultaneously, both combinations of fibers would come into play and the brain would have the problem of deciding which belong together. It might seem then that two or more voices would produce so much confusion in the ear that the brain could not select one voice for special attention. Of course, certain obvious features help distinguish one speaker from another: accent, rate of speaking, loudness or softness. But one cannot make use of these features until one knows which frequencies belong to which voice. Thus the problem remains:

How does the brain manage to focus attention on one voice? Studies of the artificial generation of speech sounds have begun to throw some light on this problem.

Peter Ladefoged of the University of Edinburgh and I have been experimenting with a device that was developed by Walter Lawrence of the Signals Research Development Establishment in England. Our version of the apparatus sends a series of electrical pulses (analogous to pulses from the vocal cords) through two filter circuits, each of which passes primarily one frequency. The waves from one filter circuit, which are like those from the largest human speech cavity, are mixed with waves from the other, which imitate the frequencies produced by the second largest cavity. Together the two wave trains are heard as quite acceptable vowel sounds that can be changed by tuning the filters to different frequencies. Varying the pulse rate used to excite the filters alters the apparent pitch or intonation of the "speech": it rises with faster pulse rates and falls with slower ones.

When the same pulses excite both filters, a listener hears the output as readily identifiable vowel sounds. This is true even when the low frequency is fed into one ear and the high frequency into the other. But if the two filters are pulsed at slightly different rates, the "speech" becomes unacceptable and listeners say that they are hearing two sounds coming from two sources rather than a single vowel sound.

Other experiments on the fusion of sounds at the two ears, conducted by Colin Cherry and his colleagues at the Imperial College of Science and Technology in London, also support the idea that when the rate of pulsing, or modulation, is the same for two sounds, the hearer perceives them as one sound. It seems reasonable to suppose, therefore, that a man can listen to one person and ignore another primarily by selecting from the mass of sounds entering his ears all those frequencies that are being modulated at the same rate. Since it is most unlikely that the vocal cords of two speakers would vibrate at exactly the same rate at any moment, modulation would almost always provide an important (if not the sole) means of separating a pair of voices.

It is now a generally accepted principle of neurophysiology that messages traveling along a particular nerve can differ either by involving different nerve fibers or by producing a different number of impulses per second in the fibers. High-frequency and low-frequency sounds stimulate different fibers. It may be that the rate at which the sounds are pulsed controls the rate of firing of the fibers. If so, the brain could pick out one voice from others by focusing its attention on all auditory nerve fibers that are firing at the same rate.

A further indication of the importance of modulation is that it, rather than the frequency of the waves being modulated, seems under certain conditions to determine the pitch of a voice. This can be demonstrated with the artificial speech generator. A filter tuned to, say, 3,000 cycles per second is pulsed at the rate of 100 cycles per second. A listener is asked to match the pitch of the sound with either of two simple sound waves, one at 100 cycles per second and the other at 3,000. Usually he selects the 100-cycle sound.

The selection mechanism that has been described is still hypothetical, but I believe that something much like it must exist. There can be no doubt, however, that it is not the only basis for auditory attention. Several experiments have served to make this clear. In one, a listener is equipped with earphones that feed one voice into the right ear and another voice into the left. Normally the subject has no difficulty in understanding the message entering one ear and ignoring the other. But under certain conditions sound from the ear being ignored can break into consciousness. For example, Neville Moray of the University of Oxford has demonstrated that a man fully occupied in listening to speech entering one ear will hear his own name in the other ear even though he remains quite unresponsive to any other word in that ear. Under similar circumstances Anne T. Treisman of the University of Oxford has found that speech entering the rejected ear can break through to the subject's attention if it consists of words that would probably follow the words that have just been heard by the ear that is receiving attention. In these cases the content of the speech has taken precedence over its physical characteristics.

How the brain focuses attention on meaning or content is as yet an almost complete mystery. One thing is clear. If the method proposed for choosing between voices is correct, there must be two attention mechanisms. Selection on the basis of content involves examining a stimulus for its possible appropriateness to a particular set of responses rather than for the presence or absence of a physical marker. At one moment, for example, a person might be ready to write down any of the digits one through nine and highly unready to write anything else, or indeed to respond in any other way. If he hears a sound from any direction or in any voice that can be interpreted as the name of one of the digits, he will respond by writing it down; only if the sound cannot be so interpreted will he not respond. At another time he might be ready to write down letters of the alphabet but not numbers, and so on.

Both types of attention are now the subject of intensive research. The next few years should yield more definite clues to the nature of each and at least a tentative answer to the question of whether or not they depend on different mechanisms.

27 Problem Solving by Small Groups Using Various Communication Nets

GEORGE A. HEISE

and GEORGE A. MILLER

The present experiment is similar in many respects to Leavitt's, although the control of the situation is carried still further. Each S is required to reach a solution of the problem. The necessary information is divided equally among the Ss. Speech, instead of written messages, is the method of communication between group members. However, the content of the messages an S can send is restricted and suitable for quantification. The intelligibility of the speech was controlled during a test by controlling the relative intensities of the speech and the noise. These controls permit determination of the dependent variable, group performance, as a function of the independent variables: (1) group organization, (2) intelligibility of the message, and (3) type of problem.

APPARATUS AND PROCEDURE

Nets

The communication nets were set up as follows. Three Ss were located in three adjoining rooms. Each S had a microphone, amplifier, and earphones. Listening was binaural except when a listener was connected to two talkers; then the listener heard one talker in one earphone and one in the other. The five nets tested are shown schematically in Figure 1. The direction of the arrows indicates the channel from talker to listener. A

Figure 1. The five nets. The arrows indicate the direction of communication from talker to listener.

Reprinted with permission of the American Psychological Association and the authors. From *Journal of Abnormal and Social Psychology*, 46:327–331 (1951).

two-headed arrow signifies two-way communication. The nets will be referred to by number, 1 to 5. The subjects will be referred to by letter, *A*, *B*, or *C*, according to the positions indicated in Figure 1. All the channels were free of distortion, and passed frequencies from 200 to 7000 cps.

Noise

Random noise is a shishing sound that has all frequencies of vibration present at equal intensities. Because of the similarity to a white light that has all wave lengths present, such a sound is often called white noise. White noise is a very effective masking sound. This noise was introduced in equal amounts into all the channels. Some noise was always present during the tests in order to mask any airborne sounds that passed directly through the walls.

The intelligibility of speech in the presence of noise is a function of the relative intensities of the speech and the noise, and is independent of their absolute levels over a wide range. In order to control the amount of external stress introduced, the speech-to-noise ratio was set to a given value by adjusting the intensity of the noise. Each *S* was given a voltmeter that indicated the intensity of the electrical signal generated by his voice. This meter was used to monitor the speech signal at a constant level (approximately 80 db re 0.0002 dyne/cm² at the listener's earphones). Use of the meter counteracted the natural tendency of talkers to raise their voices as more noise is introduced. In this way the likelihood of errors could be controlled by the experimenter. Preliminary tests showed that 85 percent of the monosyllabic words (from a memorized list of 256) could be received correctly at a speech-to-noise ratio of +6 db, 66 percent at −2 db, and 24 percent at −10 db.

Problems

The problems were of three kinds. Problems used in Experiment I called for a comparatively stereotyped and unimaginative exchange of isolated words. The problems in Experiment II provided more opportunity for initiative in the construction of sentences. Experiment III was based on a kind of anagram problem. These problems are described in more detail in the discussions of the three experiments.

SUMMARY

The performance of a three-man group was studied for five different communication nets, three signal-to-noise ratios, and three kinds of tasks.

The first type of problem was a simple reassembling of a list of standard words. The second type consisted in the construction of a sentence, the words of which had been distributed among the group members. The third type required the group to form anagrams.

For the first type of problem, comparative group efficiency, measured in terms of time or number of words required to complete the task, could be predicted from the net structure. A closed chain in which only one-way communication was possible between any two persons was by far the least efficient; an open chain, which allowed two-way communication between any two adjacent individuals, was intermediate; a closed chain where all members talked and listened to all other members was most efficient. The second type of problem was less rigidly structured and placed a higher premium on the coordination of the group activity. The results were generally similar to those for the first type of problem, except that the open chain, which had a man in a central coordinating position, replaced the two-way closed chain as most efficient. The anagram problem did not require communication; under these conditions there was no large difference among the nets.

Lowering the signal-to-noise ratio introduced errors and increased the time and number of words required to complete the task. For the first two types of problems the stress of noise accentuated the differences between the systems and emphasized the inefficiency of the one-way closed chain. The third problem, where communication was a luxury, was solved equally well over all nets; noise did not accentuate differences.

The performance of a small group depends upon the channels of communication open to its members, the task the group must handle, and the stress under which they work.

28 | Coding Noise in a Task-Oriented Group
JOSIAH MACY, JR., LEE S. CHRISTIE, and R. DUNCAN LUCE

The existing experimental studies of small task-oriented groups have generally employed noise-free communication, in the sense of information theory. One exception is the work of Heise and Miller in which measured amounts of acoustic noise were

Reprinted with permission of the American Psychological Association and the authors. From *Journal of Abnormal and Social Psychology*, 48:401–409 (1953).

introduced into the telephone network connecting the members of a small group. The experiments reported here investigate the effects of semantic or coding noise on the performance of small task-oriented groups. In this case, the transmission of information along the transmission channel was noise free, but the coding and decoding processes were ambiguous. The ambiguity arose from the necessity for the subjects (Ss) to write and to interpret descriptions of colors that are not easy to describe. The term *coding noise* is used to refer to this ambiguity, as explained below in detail.

METHOD

Apparatus

A round table partitioned into five S compartments, similar to that described by Leavitt, was used. From each compartment to every other one were slots sufficiently large to receive the 8 by 1½-inch message cards used by the Ss. Each S was identified throughout the experiment by the color of the cards on which he wrote his messages. The communication network to be studied was imposed by physically blocking the slots not to be used. The table differed from Leavitt's in that the answer signal switches were removed and for them were substituted rubber tubes running from each S's compartment to E's station.

Procedure

The Ss were told prior to entering the experimental room that at the start of each trial they would open a box containing five colored marbles; that only one color of marble would be in everyone's box; and that their task was to determine this color by written communication on cards sent through the allowed channels. When an S knew the answer, he was instructed that he was to drop the corresponding marble down the tube in his compartment. If he wished to change his answer before the end of a trial, he could drop a second marble as a correction but the trial would end when each of the five Ss had dropped at least one marble.

The Ss were then taken to the experimental room, seated at the table, and after a brief check to insure familiarity with the apparatus, the trials started. No talking was permitted after the trials began. The groups were run for 30 successive trials—the marbles used on the first 15 trials were drawn from a set of six different plain, solid colors, easy to distinguish and to describe. At the sixteenth trial and thereafter, the marbles used were from a set of six cloudy, mottled, indistinct colors. They were still easy to distinguish if they could be directly compared, but it was difficult to describe each one clearly and unambiguously.

The experimental program was divided into two parts, with a time lapse of about nine months between parts. In Part I, four groups of five Ss, volunteer M.I.T. undergraduates, were run on each of three networks—star, chain, and circle. In Part II, four groups of five Ss, enlisted military personnel from Fort Devens and the First Naval District Receiving Station, were run on each of three networks—circle, pinwheel, and star. (See Figure 1 for diagrams of the networks.) Each S participated in only one

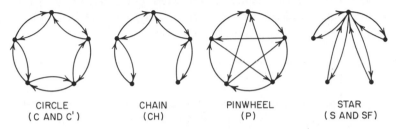

| CIRCLE | CHAIN | PINWHEEL | STAR |
| (C AND C') | (CH) | (P) | (S AND SF) |

Figure 1. Communication networks used in Part I and Part II.

experimental run. The experimental procedures in Parts I and II were as nearly identical as it was possible to make them, with the exception of the star groups of Part II. This will be discussed below.

Data Record

The data obtained consisted of a record of the marbles dropped by each man, the time to complete each trial, and the messages sent, sorted as to sender by color and as to receiver by position at the table to which they were sent.

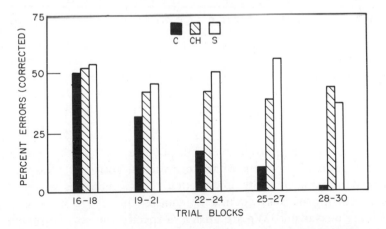

Figure 2. Corrected mean percentage errors for experimental groups in Part I.

Data on time for each trial and number of messages used showed the same relative differences between networks as previously reported for such experiments by Leavitt.

An examination of the raw data suggested that during the last 16 trials the groups had more difficulty obtaining the correct answer when certain colors were held in common than when other colors were held in common. The raw error data were therefore corrected so that all colors had the same relative error frequency, and these corrected errors are plotted in Figures 2 and 3. Every time an S ended a trial with a wrong marble as his final answer, this was counted as one error.

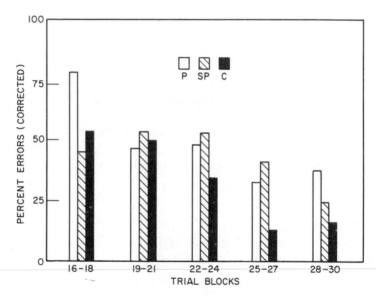

Figure 3. Corrected mean percentage errors for experimental groups in Part II.

RESULTS

Measurement of Coding Noise

It would be most appropriate at this point to measure the coding noise in this experiment in terms of the conditional entropies of information theory. However, to apply information theory measures to the coding noise occurring in this experiment requires knowledge of several facts which are unavailable. We are unable to specify the set of symbols an S would use to describe a given color marble, and, more important, we have no way of observing the transformations from the given set of marbles to the messages describing them, nor the corresponding mental transformations on the part of the receiver from the symbols of the received messages to the possible set of six marbles. Consequently, although we may discuss the noise in this experiment in terms of the concepts of information theory in a qualitative manner, we are unable to arrive at the usual quantitative measures. Nevertheless, a numerical measure is needed, and it may be achieved in an approximate manner by considering more closely the characteristics of the noise occurring in the experiment.

Since noise is fundamentally a question of uncertainty, any single valued measure of the amount of uncertainty in an experiment can be expected to be monotonically related to the noise. In this experiment, the uncertainty arose largely from different Ss' applying the same name to different marbles, with the result that comparing the marble color names used by each S to describe the marbles he had at the trial led to several possible answers or, in some cases, to a single incorrect answer. Specifically, during the first 15 trials the groups generally learned to refer to each marble by a single color name, such as "red," "black," etc. After the sixteenth trial, even though the marbles used were mottled and streaked, often with more than one color, or with shades of one color, this behavior persisted. The Ss usually attempted to use one-word color names, such as "amber," "aqua," or in some cases compound words such as "light-green" or "blue-green," to describe the marbles. These considerations led to the following procedure which was used to calculate this uncertainty (referred to as the "ambiguity," or marbles per name, and denoted by A). For each trial, the message cards sent by any S were examined, and in all cases in which a definite assignment of names to marbles could be made, on the basis of E's knowledge of the marbles in each man's box, this information was tabulated.

From these results for all five Ss for that trial, lists of names which had been used to describe each marble were compiled with the frequency of occurrence of each, and the weighted average of the number of marbles referred to by a name was calculated. This procedure was followed for all the groups run, for trials 16 to 30. These values were corrected as follows: If a given name was used to describe two different marbles on trials $i - 1$ and $i + 1$, but specific evidence for this confusion could not be found during trial i, it was assumed to be present on the strength of its occurrence before and after trial i. From these corrected values of A, an average value was computed for each network during each block of three trials.

Redundancy as a Mechanism for Reducing Errors

Since certain networks manage to achieve a reduction in the ambiguity, and hence in their error level, one is led to inquire about the mechanism of this effect. This problem may also be approached by an application of the concepts of information theory, extended to fit this case.

In the conventional case of signals transmitted along a channel, accurate transmission in the presence of noise is achieved at the expense of transmission rate by the introduction of redundancy. Since the noise here is semantic noise, we shall have to look for semantic redundancy, i.e., duplication in the coding scheme. In our case, these duplications, if they exist, will take the form of synonyms, or alternate descriptions of a given marble. We shall show that these duplications do exist and that they are used to overcome the noise.

Since the noise present in this experiment is semantic noise, and is measured by ambiguity A, the effect of the use of redundancy to overcome the noise and insure accurate transmission of the message will be to reduce or eliminate the apparent ambiguity or uncertainty present, and with channel noise the introduction of redundancy in the coding does not this will be reflected in a decrease in the measured value of A. In a sense, this case is not an exact parallel to the usual case of channel noise, since with channel noise the introduction of redundancy in the coding does not remove the noise, but merely removes the errors caused by the noise. Hence, in the channel-noise case, the redundancy must be maintained at a high level in order to insure accuracy. This is not the case with semantic or coding noise, for once the uncertainty in the coding operations has been eliminated, the redundancy may then be reduced without impairing the accuracy of the transmissions. However, it may also be thought of as having the constant character of channel noise by considering the effect of memory. Once the redundant coding has been used, and the errors reduced thereby, we may assume that the receiver remembers the synonyms used for a given symbol in the redundant code, and that in future messages these synonyms or alternate codes are understood even though not physically present. If the effect of this understood or remembered redundancy is assumed, we may describe the system as one with constant noise but with the effect of the noise overcome by the redundant coding, just as in the channel-noise case. In this description the redundancy is in two parts and that part attributable to memory does not appear in the transmitted message. Therefore, the total redundancy can remain high while the external redundancy drops. A decision on whether this is in fact the case will have to be the subject of a separate experiment, because we have data only on the external redundancy.

To detect semantic redundancy, we use a method analogous to that previously used to calculate ambiguity. In any one group, at any one trial, six names are sufficient to identify the six marbles. By tabulating from the message cards the names used by the group to describe a given marble, we obtained a record of synonyms or alternate codings used in each trial by each group. This tabulation was corrected for the ambiguity of some of the names used, on the basis that a synonym which was also applied to two other marbles should not be counted as a separate synonym for each, so the tabulation was weighted according to the ambiguity of each term. The table was also corrected for missing data—i.e., for a synonym which was used before and after a given trial, but evidence for the use of which could not be found with certainty during the trial. From these tabulations the average number of names used by each group during each trial was calculated, and from these figures the average number of extra names—that is, the number of names used beyond the necessary six—was calculated. These values were then averaged over all the groups run on a given network, and over blocks of three trials apiece, as previously. The average number of extra names used is called the redundancy R, and is tabulated in Figure 4 for the different networks, by blocks of three

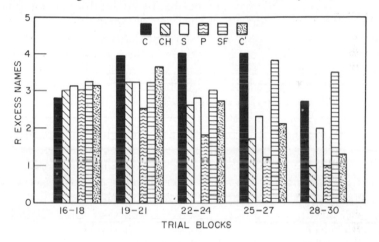

Figure 4.   Redundancy as a function of trials, all groups.

trials. Figure 4 supports the hypothesis that redundancy is used to overcome the errors due to semantic noise. Comparing Figure 4 with Figures 2 and 3, we see that those networks which reduced their error count show a rise in the redundancy subsequent to trial 16, and the reduction in errors always comes after this rise.

The Effect of the Communication Network

It has been implicit in the discussion that the amount of redundancy, and hence the error reduction, is a function of the network. For example, the circle successfully achieved error reduction, whereas the chain and the star did not. Several conjectures arose from the results of Part I, and

Part II was carried out as a preliminary attempt to verify these conjectures.

With regard to error reduction, two aspects of the communication network seem important: (a) that there are sufficient interconnections for each S to realize that the group makes errors, and (b) that there are sufficient interconnections (possibly different from those of a) for the Ss to be able to correct the errors, once they are aware of them. The type of connections necessary for (a) are those that will allow, with fairly high frequency, an S to receive what purports to be the same information via two or more routes. If there is noise, then it is unlikely that a piece of information will travel two different routes to a given person and arrive there as the same symbol. Thus, in this class of network, one or more Ss are very liable to receive two different symbols which purport to refer to the same marble, and this will certainly suggest to him that an error is being made. He may not be able to do anything about it during that trial, but in succeeding trials he can attempt to find ways to avoid further errors. Observe that the chain and the star are not in this class, since it is comparatively difficult for Ss in these networks to know that errors are being made. On the other hand, the circle is in this class.

With regard to the second condition, it is in principle sufficient that each person be connected in the network to each other person; however, it is subjectively obvious that error correction between a and b is difficult if every message from a to b must pass through a third person c. This causes difficulty in asking questions of the sort, "What do you mean by aqua?", which are vital to the creation of redundancy. Thus we might suppose that symmetric communication channels are necessary to error reduction, assuming the existence of errors is known.

So, we consider two properties, the possibility of error feedback and symmetric channels. The circle has both, and the star only the latter. This suggested that we run a case having only the former, and pinwheel (P) was elected for this purpose. It has no symmetric channels, and, clearly, it has as much possibility of error feedback as the circle. Since we were not sure that these two factors take everything into account, we elected to run more star cases, but, in contrast to Part I, to give the Ss the following information at the end of each trial: the number of errors made, and the number of different marbles dropped in error. These are the SF (star with feedback) groups of Part II. It is clear that this is at least as much information as the Ss in circle groups would have, so that any difference between the circle and SF groups favoring the former is conservative. Finally, we ran the circle groups (C') again in order to have a control group, since the Ss in Part I were M.I.T. students and in Part II military personnel.

The experimental results have been presented in Figure 3. First, let us look at the control group. The behavior is qualitatively the same as the Part I circles, simply displaced to the right. Presumably this results from differences between the two classes of *S*s in intelligence or motivation or both. We see that the pinwheel groups begin with a very large error count and reduce it to a level indistinguishable from the star and chain groups. This certainly suggests error knowledge, as expected, and some error correction through the threee-step feedback loops, but by no means the degree of error correction achieved in the circle groups. Finally the SF groups do begin error correction in a fashion not unlike the circle, but markedly displaced to the right. As we pointed out, this is a conservative difference, so we cannot claim the performance of the SF groups is the same as that of the circle.

It must be concluded that though error feedback and symmetric channels are necessary to good error reduction, there is at least one other factor of importance. Observe that in the star the entire process of noise reduction must be located at the central position. The other *S*s contribute to this process, but only in a passive way, e.g., answering questions from the center man. In the case of both the circle and pinwheel it is possible for each *S* to participate actively in the noise reduction process, and that process may be carried out in comparatively small steps and either the entire group establish a common code, or each pair or trio of persons arrive at its own private code. If this conjecture is valid, we are simply observing a time delay due to job complexity at the center position of the star, with the same two basic mechanisms operating as we pointed out earlier.

We may summarize our knowledge as Table 1.

Table 1

Qualitative Summary of Network Factors and Error Reduction

Network	Error Feedback	Highly Central Position	Symmetric Channels	Error Performance
Circle	Yes	No	All	Learns fast. Good error reduction.
Star	No	Yes	All	No learning. No error reduction.
Chain	Slight	Yes	All	No learning. No error reduction.
Pinwheel	Yes	No	None	Some initial learning. Poor error reduction.
Star with Feedback	Yes	Yes	All	Slow learning. Fair error reduction.

In conclusion, it should be pointed out that though we feel these factors to be important they are not stated with the precision we would like nor are they established with the definiteness we would like. It must be kept in mind that these experiments did not employ enough groups in each category to be conclusive. In addition, since the original experimental design was for quite another purpose, estimates and approximations were necessary in the analysis. As this seems an important area, we propose to redesign the experiment and carry out a more complete analysis in the near future.

SUMMARY AND CONCLUSIONS

An experiment involving task-oriented groups of five Ss, requiring for problem solution the use of descriptions of similarly colored marbles, was analyzed in terms of the concepts of information theory. The errors made by the group were shown to be well predicted by a measure of the semantic noise in the coding-decoding process, and the use of redundant coding to reduce the number of errors was demonstrated. Differences in behavior of groups using different communication networks was examined, and several properties of the communication network which play important roles in determining this behavior were discussed. The application of information theory to this type of group experiment, and its extension to the problem of communication which is semantically noisy, was shown to be a valid and useful method for analyzing such experiments.

---

29 | A Field Experiment on Rumor Transmission and Distortion
STANLEY SCHACHTER
and HARVEY BURDICK

Rumor is usually characterized as an unreliable, sometimes wildly distorted form of communication which spreads rapidly and mysteriously to almost all available members of a population. The conception of distortion and exaggeration as characteristic of such forms of communication arises largely from generalization of

Reprinted with permission of the American Psychological Association and the authors. From *Journal of Abnormal and Social Psychology*, 50:363–371 (1955).

findings in studies of perception and memory using the technique of serial reproduction. The impression of widespread and rapid diffusion is, with the exception of numbers of dramatic anecdotes, relatively undocumented, for there have been few studies of the spread of rumor.

The results of the few systematic studies which have been published are peculiarly at variance with the conception of rumor outlined above. In Table 1 the results of four such studies are outlined. In the first three of these studies, rumors were planted and then by means of systematic interviewing or participant observation of the relevant population, it was possible to make reasonably accurate estimates of the extent of rumor spread. For the 13 planted rumors reported in these three papers, an aver-

Table 1

Rumor Spread in Four Studies of Rumor

Study	Number of Rumors	Population × No. of Rumors	Percentage of Population Per Rumor Who Heard Rumor	Percentage of Population Per Rumor Who Told Rumor
Back et al.	9	55 × 9	5.9	4.2
Festinger, Schachter, and Back	2	100 × 2	5.1	2.5
Schall, Levy, and Tresselt	2	10 × 2	0	0
Festinger, Cartwright, et al.	1	100 × 1	59.0	21.2

age of only 5 percent of the relevant population per rumor actually heard the rumor. An average of about 3 percent per rumor is reported as having told the rumor. In addition, the authors are familiar with two other studies using planted rumors; these have remained unpublished because of complete failure of the rumors to spread. The present paper is prompted, in part, by sheer exasperation at the growing number of such abortive studies.

Whether such results should be attributed to experimental failure or accepted as evidence that our notions about rumor are much exaggerated is equivocal. Comparison of these studies with reports of spontaneously arising rumors is difficult, for so few of the studies concerned with spontaneous rumors present any accurate estimate of the extent of rumor spread. One exception is the study of Festinger, Cartwright, et al. (item 4 in Table 1) of a spontaneous rumor concerning communist activity in a housing project. Fifty-nine percent of the interviewed population reported having heard the rumor, 21 percent reported having told the rumor—considerably greater percentages than those reported in any of the studies employing planted rumors. However, since this single study was conducted specifically because the authors' attention was drawn to an already widespread rumor, it is impossible to make any guesses as to the extent to which such results may be typical of spontaneously arising rumors.

The limited data available on rumor distortion are similarly at odds with current expectations. In the two studies listed in Table 1 in which the senior author participated, and is, therefore, familiar with data not reported in the published papers, there was almost no evidence of any distortion or modification of the planted rumors. In the Festinger, Cartwright, *et al.* study, rumor spread was tested by a recognition question which made it impossible, of course, to evaluate distortion.

Such results as these are so puzzlingly at odds with current notions of the nature of rumor that one is forced to examine critically the studies here reviewed as well as to reexamine our current conceptions of rumor. We will consider first the problem of the spread of rumor and reserve for consideration in a later section of this paper the problem of rumor distortion.

In an attempt to formalize the conditions of rumor spread, Allport and Postman propose as "the basic law of rumor" that "the amount of rumor in circulation will vary with the importance of the subject to the individuals concerned times the ambiguity of the evidence pertaining to the topic at issue." A similar proposition is the "principle of cognitive unclarity" by Festinger, Cartwright, *et al.* "Rumors will tend to arise in situations where cognitive regions especially relevant to immediate behavior are largely unstructured." Both formulations agree in identifying cognitive unclarity or ambiguity and importance or relevance as key determinants of the origin and spread of rumor. The latter formulation is somewhat more specific in its treatment of the "importance" variable, relating it to areas with relevance for immediate behavior. We shall use the term in this sense.

It is probably wise, too, to make explicit what is undoubtedly implicit in both formulations—that the state of cognitive unclarity about an important issue be common to all or a major part of the population under consideration. Our apparent insistence on this factor arises from consideration of the pattern of communication which rumor customarily follows. In most social communication there is a back and forth exchange between two or more people and little further relaying of the contents of such conversations. The form of communication called rumor is characterized by a chain pattern of communication. A communicates an item to B, B communicates the item to C, C to D, and so on. In such a pattern, possession of the item of information seems to create a force to communicate it further. If one presumes that one kind of situation giving rise to such forces to communicate may be characterized by cognitive unclarity about an important issue, it seems clear that these conditions must hold for all or a large portion of the group in order that the rumor spreads. Otherwise, this chain pattern of communication will be quickly interrupted and, unless there are particularly persistent rumor-mongers involved, there will be little spread of the rumor.

Though none of the studies outlined in Table 1 attempted a direct test of the relationship of unclarity and importance to rumor spread, the technique employed in almost all of these studies assumed an acceptance of these hypotheses concerning the determinants of rumor spread. Usually the experimenters attempted to identify areas which seemed important and about which there may have been some ambiguity and then to plant rumors relevant to these areas. Since none of these studies collected evidence which would allow proper evaluation of the extent to which these conditions were satisfied, it would seem a fruitless sort of post-mortem to examine the details of these studies in terms of the postulated determinants of rumor spread.

Rather than attempt to explain such failures of rumor spread in terms of a conceptualization which is still largely untested, it would seem more worthwhile to proceed to a direct test of the conceptualization. The present study is a field experiment designed to test some of these ideas of the determinants of rumor spread. A situation which plausibly can be described as involving cognitive unclarity about an important issue is experimentally manipulated and rumors relating to the issue are systematically planted.

METHOD

DESIGN. There were three experimental conditions: (a) The "cognitive unclarity-rumor" (CU R) condition A situation of cognitive unclarity was manipulated, and a rumor was planted. (b) The "cognitive unclarity" (CU) condition—a situation of cognitive unclarity was manipulated and no rumor was planted. (c) The "rumor" (R) condition—a rumor was planted, but no situation of cognitive unclarity was created.

Six classes containing a total of 96 students were involved in the study. Two classes were assigned to each experimental condition so that in each condition there was one of the older three classes and one of the younger three classes.

PRODUCING A SITUATION OF COGNITIVE UNCLARITY. On the day of the study, between 8:25 and 8:35, the principal of the school went into four different classrooms. In each class, she interrupted the work, stood in front of the class, pointed a finger at one girl, and announced, "Miss K., would you get your hat, coat, and books, please, and come with me. You will be gone for the rest of the day." Then, without a word, she and the girl walked out of the room together. Such an action was completely unprecedented in the experience of the girls. To insure that the event remained a complete mystery, the entire staff of the school had been instructed to reply to any questions about the event that "they knew nothing about it."

The girls taken from each of the four classes had been selected on the basis of their sociometric status and their academic and disciplinary records. All four girls were matched on these three criteria. They were chosen so as to fall between the fiftieth and seventy-fifth percentile in grade average and in the number of sociometric choices they received from their classmates. In addition, none of the girls had a disciplinary record. These girls, then, were fairly average members of their classes, reasonably popular and with fair grades. None of them knew anything about the study before they were taken from class.

Was the manipulation effective in producing the desired constellation of variables? As part of the standard data-collecting procedure, the teachers in the school had all been instructed to keep a record of all questions addressed to them about the manipulation. They were asked to record who spoke to them, when, and the content of the question or remark. There were 62 girls in the four classes from which the principal had removed one student. The teachers reported a total of 198 questions, plus the report of one harried teacher, unable to keep up with the curiosity of the girls, that "everyone in the class asked me what had happened" and of another that "half the class asked questions." Virtually every girl in the classes affected made inquiries of one or more of her teachers and almost all questions were of the sort "What happened to Miss K?" "Why did the principal take Miss K. out of class?" "What's going on?" etc. We assume from the nature of these questions, which were largely expressions of curiosity, puzzlement, and attempts to get information, that the manipulation did produce a state of cognitive unclarity common to all or most of the girls involved. Evidence relevant to the importance variable will be presented in a later section.

PLANTING THE RUMOR. The rumor was planted with two girls from each of four different classes. Two of these classes were from the four in which the situation of cognitive unclarity was produced; in the remaining two classes there had been no such manipulation. The eight girls with whom the rumor was planted were also matched in terms of their sociometric, academic, and disciplinary records.

A day or two before the study took place, various teachers made appointments for 8:15 on the morning of the study to see each of the eight girls with whom the rumor was to be planted. Ostensibly, the purpose of these appointments was to discuss academic progress, next year's program, etc. This was routine procedure. Each of the interviews followed an identical pattern. After six or seven minutes of discussing the matter for which the appointment had presumably been arranged, and immediately before terminating the interview, each teacher said, "By the way, some examinations have been taken from the office. Do you happen to know anything about this?" No such thing had taken place and, of course, all of the girls interviewed denied any knowledge of the affair. The interview was timed so that each of the girls returned to her classroom before the principal entered any of the rooms.

The rumor planted in this way was intentionally chosen so as not to be an immediate explanation for the "cognitive unclarity" manipulation. It could, however, be readily linked to the morning's events as a tentative sort of explanation. It seemed preferable to entrust the planting of the rumor to teachers rather than making confederates of a number of girls and thereby imposing on them the difficult job of maintaining a standard pattern of behavior throughout the day. It seems a reasonable hunch that a clearly explanatory rumor originating from an authority figure, such as a teacher, would tend to inhibit the kind of speculation from which new rumors arise.

DATA COLLECTED. Three types of data were collected:

1. Sociometric data: Three weeks before the study took place all of the girls involved answered a sociometric questionnaire. The school was planning a school fair for which the girls were to work together at planning exhibits, running shows, etc. The sociometric questionnaire was linked to this affair and read: "As you know, we are hoping to hold the school fair early in the fall. We would like you to work with girls you enjoy being with. If you will list your two best friends we will try to arrange it."

2. Teachers' observations: as previously mentioned, all of the teachers kept a record of comments addressed to them concerning the manipulation.

3. Standardized interview: At two o'clock in the afternoon, toward the end of the school day, a team of 20 interviewers took over the school lunchroom in order to interview all of the girls involved in the study. The interviewing schedule was so arranged that an entire class was interviewed at the same time in order to prevent any communication among the girls about the nature of the interview. The classes were scheduled and brought down to the interview room in a fashion which prevented any communication among classes.

The interview was a standardized, open-end instrument designed to get information about what the girls had heard about the situation created by the cognitive unclarity manipulation, with whom they had talked about this, whether or not they had heard the planted rumor, from whom they had heard it, and to whom they had told it, and how much time they had spent discussing all of these matters during the day.

At the end of the day, after all of the girls had been interviewed, a general assembly was called for all of the classes involved in the study. The study was explained in complete detail at this gathering. The four girls who had been taken from their classes (and who had spent the day, in the company of the principal, on a tour of the University of Minnesota campus) returned to school in time for the assembly and were the heroines of the next two days.

RESULTS

1. *Knowledge of the rumor and the cognitive unclarity manipulation.* Table 2 presents data on the percentage of girls who in their interviews

Table 2

Knowledge of the Rumor and the Cognitive Unclarity Manipulation

Condition	N	Percent Knowing of CU Manipulation	Percent Knowing Rumor
CU-R1	18	100	100
CU-R2	15	100	100
CU-R1 + CU-R2	33	100	100
CU1	18	94	100
CU2	11	100	100
CU1 + CU2	29	97	100
R1	18	94	94
R2	16	100	100
R1 + R2	34	97	100

reported that they had heard the planted rumor and the percentage of girls indicating that they knew that the principal had removed girls from their classroom. In this and in several of the following tables, data are reported for each of the classes individually as well as for the two classes in each condition combined. Thus, the symbol CU-R1 stands for one of the two classes in the CU-R condition, CU-R2 for the other class in this condition, and so on. The symbol CU-R1 + CU-R2 stands for the two classes in the condition combined.

It is clear from Table 2 that virtually every girl had heard the planted rumor. Only one of the 96 girls interviewed reported that she had not heard the rumor. In terms just of having heard the rumor, there are no differences between condition. Similarly, almost all of the girls, including those in the R condition, were aware that girls had been taken out of their classes. Only two girls reported that they knew nothing about this. Eighty-five percent of the girls interviewed linked the planted rumor, in some fashion, to the manipulation.

Clearly, there had been considerable communication not only within classes but between classes. The CU girls had all heard the planted rumor. Almost all of the R girls were aware that the principal had removed girls from other classes. The unexpected volume and generality of communication make it necessary to recharacterize the three experimental conditions.

The fact that the planted rumor is widely known in both the CU-R and the CU conditions essentially reduces these two to the same condition —a situation of cognitive unclarity about an important issue, with a widely spread, planted rumor. The R condition is recharacterized as a state of cognitive unclarity about a relatively unimportant issue. Though all of the girls in this condition are aware that for some mysterious reason the principal has taken girls out of other classes, they have almost no sociometric connections with these girls. They are familiar with the faces, but indifferent to the girls. Though the manipulation poses the possibility of real changes in the relationship between the girls removed from class and their immediate classmates, no such problems exist for girls in the R condition.

Several sources of data support this recharacterization of the R condition. Previously, inferences were made about the success of the attempt to create a cognitively unclear situation from the *nature* of the questions asked the teachers. Tentative inferences relating to the importance variable may be drawn from the *number* of such questions. Virtually all subjects in all conditions knew about the cognitive unclarity manipulation. Presumably only those girls who seriously cared about the event would have attempted to glean information from the teachers. The teachers reported well over 200 questions from the 62 girls in the CU-R and CU conditions. They reported only one question from the 34 girls in the R condition.

The amount of time the girls spent speculating and discussing the manipulation may also be considered as an indication of the importance of the event. In their interviews, after they had indicated that they were aware of the manipulation and had discussed it, the girls were asked, "Could you say just how much time you've spent talking about this today? Try to make an accurate guess." Girls in the CU-R and CU conditions estimated an average of almost one hour and forty minutes, girls in the R condition estimated an average of twenty minutes. The difference is significant at better than the .001 level of confidence.[1]

Clearly these last two bits of data must be qualified by the fact that girls in the R condition necessarily learned of the events of the cognitive unclarity manipulation somewhat later than the girls in the other conditions and consequently had less time to discuss and ask questions of the teachers. However, the interviews indicate that almost all of the girls in the R condition had learned of this event by the 10:15 morning recess. Since previous to this time the girls were free to communicate to one another and to the teachers only in the two five-minute periods between classes, it is clear that this factor alone cannot account for the major differences between conditions.

Supporting evidence free of this time factor can be derived from the indications of saliency of issue in the standardized interviews with each girl. The interview was so constructed that the first question relevant to the manipulation of cognitive unclarity was a recall question and the following questions were recognition questions. After a few icebreaker questions the girl was asked: "In most schools things are pretty much the same from day to day, but sometimes things do happen that are out of the ordinary. Would you say that anything unusual happened today?" If in response to this question she failed to mention the experimental manipulation, she was asked, "Some of the other girl's we've spoken to have told us that this morning some girls were called out of class by the principal. Have you heard anything about this? What have you heard?" It is assumed that the cognitive unclarity manipulation is more salient and more important for those girls who mention it on the recall question than for those who first mention it on the recognition question. Ninety-three percent of the girls in the CU-R condition mentioned the incident in answer to the recall question; 76 percent of the girls in the CU condition mentioned it to the recall question; and only 26 percent of girls in the R condition responded to the recall question by describing this event.

Such evidence supports the recharacterization of the experimental conditions. The three conditions are characterized by an equal degree of cog-

---

[1] It could, of course, be argued that rather than indicating that the issue was unimportant in the R condition, the number of questions to the teachers and the amount of time spent talking might indicate that there was less cognitive unclarity in the R condition. Such might indeed be the case if girls in the R condition were either (a) more prone to link the rumor to the manipulation and to believe that the girls taken from class had stolen the examinations or, (b) had some other generally accepted and credited explanation for the manipulation. The data reveal, however, that there are no between-condition differences in the extent to which the rumor is linked to the manipulation or in the degree to which it is believed that the planted rumor conclusively explains why the girls were removed from class. Further, the great majority of Ss in the R condition indicated in their interviews that they had no real idea as to why the girls had been taken from class.

nitive unclarity, for the event was the same mystery to all the girls. The issue involved, however, was relatively unimportant to the R condition classes and extremely important to the CU-R and the CU classes.

2. *Transmission of the planted rumor.* Our conceptualization suggests that the force to communicate a relevant rumor should vary with the degree of importance of the issue concerning which there is ambiguity. It should be anticipated then that there will be far more transmission and discussion of the rumor in the CU-R and CU conditions than in the R condition. Table 3 presents the relevant data.

The data in Table 3 are derived from the responses of the girls to the

Table 3

Mean Number of Subjects to Whom Communications Concerning the Rumor Were Initiated

Condition	N	Mean No. of Girls to Whom Rumor Was Transmitted
CU-R1	16	3.19
CU-R2	13	2.46
CU-R1 + CU-R2	29	2.86
CU1	18	2.22
CU2	11	2.36
CU1 + CU2	29	2.28
R1	16	1.30
R2	14	.79
R1 + R2	30	1.10

interview questions concerning their knowledge of the rumor, from whom they had heard it, and to whom they had communicated it. The figures reported are the averages, for each class and condition, of the number of different girls to whom each girl is reported as *initiating* a communication concerning the rumor. There is an average of more than twice as many transmissions of the rumor in both the CU-R or CU conditions than in the R condition. The difference between CU-R and R conditions is significant at better than the .01 level of confidence; between CU and R conditions at the .03 level of confidence. There is no significant difference between CU-R and CU conditions.

Transmission of the rumor was widespread in CU-R and CU classes and relatively restricted in the R condition classes. Seventy-eight percent of the girls in CU-R and CU conditions initiated one or more communications concerning the rumor; only 40 percent of the girls in the R condition did so. Since we know that virtually all of the girls heard the rumor, it would seem that knowledge of the rumor creates far stronger forces to communicate and discuss it when the issue to which it is relevant is important than when it is unimportant. Some caution, however, must be observed in weighing this interpretation. It was previously suggested that the dramatic nature of the manipulation probably produced surprise and excitement as well as a state of cognitive unclarity. It would seem a reasonable guess that such factors would operate more strongly for the girls who were immediate witnesses of the event than for those girls who heard about the incident but were not present. The CU-R and CU conditions, then, may differ from the R condition not only in the importance of the event, but in the effects produced by being witness to the manipulation. Though we do believe that importance is the crucial variable in accounting for the differences between conditions, it is clear that, within the present design, this conclusion must be tempered by the existence of these additional factors.

It is to be expected, too, that the importance of the issue varied within class and condition. For some girls the issue may have been extremely important and for others trivial. One criterion for distinguishing among the girls on this dimension would be the nature of their relationship to the girls who are taken out of class by the principal. Plausibly, this should be a more important event for those who are good friends of the girl removed from class than for those who are not, and the friends should be expected to communicate the rumor more.

Since almost all sociometric choices were within class, the following means are based on just the four classes in the CU-R and CU conditions. Girls who on their sociometric have given one of their choices to the girl taken out of their class by the principal initiated communications concerning the rumor to an average of 3.10 different girls. Girls who did not make this sociometric choice initiated only 2.00 communications of the rumor. This difference is significant by t test at the .05 level of confidence.

3. *Origin of new rumors.* The same factors which promote the spread of the planted rumor should presumably stimulate the kind of speculation and guesswork from which new rumors arise and it should be anticipated that there will be greater diversity and circulation of new rumors in those conditions where the issue is most important. Relevant evidence is presented in Table 4.

In column 3 of Table 4 are reported the percentages of girls in each of the classes who in their interviews reported that they discussed some rumor related to the cognitive unclarity manipulation other than the planted rumor. Some 70 percent of the girls in the CU-R and CU conditions reported discussing other rumors; less than 15 percent of the girls in the R condition did so. The difference between either CU-R or CU

Table 4

The Prevalence and Variety of New Rumors

Condition	N	Percentage of Girls Reporting New Rumors	Number of Different Rumors
CU-R1	18	72.2	16
CU-R2	15	80.0	15
CU-R1 + CU-R2	33	75.8	
CU1	18	72.2	14
CU2	11	54.6	5
CU1 + CU2	29	65.5	
R1	18	5.6	1
R2	16	25.0	2
R1 + R2	34	14.7	

condition and R condition is significant at better than the .001 level of confidence. The difference between CU-R and CU conditions is not significant. Clearly the greater the importance of the issue, the greater the circulation of new rumors.

Not only is there greater circulation of rumors other than the planted rumor in the two high importance conditions but there is greater diversity of new rumors as well. In column 4 of Table 4 are listed the number of different rumors in circulation in each of the classes. There is an average of over 12 different rumors per class reported in the CU-R and CU conditions and of 1.5 different rumors per class in the two R condition classes.

In terms of our previous reasoning it might be anticipated that "good friends" would tend to circulate new rumors more than would those girls who do not choose sociometrically the girls taken out of class by the principal. Though friends circulated an average of 1.55 new rumors and nonfriends an average of 1.32, a slightly smaller proportion of friends transmitted such new rumors. Sixty-eight percent of friends reported discussing rumors other than the planted rumor and 74 percent of .the nonfriends did so. Neither of these differences is significant.

There is, however, a difference between these two groups in the kind of rumor which they report having discussed. It is possible to categorize the various rumors circulated in terms of the optimism or pessimism of the explanation offered for the removal of the girl from class. Some of these rumors were distinctly favorable to this girl, e.g., "She's a great beauty and has been invited to tea at the principal's house." Other rumors were more unfavorable, "She's being disciplined for going to a wild party last weekend." Still other rumors were neutral in tone, "She's going to attend a lecture." Table 5 presents the percentage of each type of rumor

Table 5

Friendship and New Rumors

Group	N	Number of Times New Rumors Transmitted	Percentage of New Rumors Which Were:		
			Favorable	Neutral	Unfavorable
Friends	31	48	52	19	29
Nonfriends	31	41	34	10	56

transmitted by friends and nonfriends. Of the total number of rumors transmitted by friends 52 percent are favorable and 29 percent unfavorable. Nonfriends transmitted 34 percent favorable rumors and 56 percent unfavorable. Of the friends who did transmit rumors 76.2 percent transmitted one or more favorable rumors. Of nonfriends who transmitted rumors, 47.8 percent transmitted one or more favorable rumors. This difference is significant at close to the .10 level of confidence. Though there is no difference between friends and nonfriends in the extent to which they transmit rumors other than the planted rumor, there is a tendency for friends to transmit predominantly favorable rumors and for nonfriends to transmit predominantly unfavorable rumors.

DISTORTION OF THE PLANTED RUMOR. The interview of each girl was examined for indications of distortion of the planted rumor. In no one of the 96 interviews is there any indication of distortion. In every case, the planted rumor was reported to the interviewer in essentially the form in which it was originally planted with no instance of embellishment or variation. Though many new and bizarre rumors did spring up, the planted rumor itself came through a day's discussion intact. This finding is consistent with the results of two of the studies discussed in the introduction to this paper where also there was no indication of distortion of the planted rumors. Caplow, too, in a study of rumors in war reports "the veracity of rumors did not decline noticeably during transmittal." Though he notes the existence of tendencies to distortion, his major impression is that of a marked lack of distortion.

Such findings, of course, are in direct contrast to the widespread impression of rumor as an unreliable and sometimes fantastically distorted form of communication. These results suggest that experiments such as those of Bartlett and Allport and Postman are questionable laboratory paradigms of the field situation of rumor transmission. This is not meant, in any way, to question the results of these laboratory and classroom experiments as such, but to suggest that the results of these studies are not immediately applicable to field situations in which rumor transmission is a voluntarily initiated action subject to a variety of corrective tendencies, rather than an experimentally induced communication with no possibility of correcting exaggerations, distortions, or omissions during the course of transmission.

Caplow in discussing the discrepancy between his findings and those reported in the Allport and Postman experiments suggests two mechanisms by which distortion may be eliminated or prevented during the course of transmission of a rumor. (a) "A rumor is usually heard more than once, and usually transmitted more than once by each individual in the channel. This re-circulation tends to eliminate variation. . . ." (b) Persons associated with previous inaccuracies or exaggerations tend to be excluded from the developing channels of rumor transmission.

Other factors which may account for the differences between the field studies discussed and the Allport-Postman experiments are: (a) The complexity of the material transmitted. In the laboratory experiments, the material transmitted is customarily the content of highly detailed and complicated pictures or stories. In the field studies the planted rumors have usually been relatively simple, uncomplicated, and with a minimum of irrelevant detail. Plausibly, the process of leveling (the omission of details in serial reproduction) will be most apparent when highly detailed and complicated material is transmitted.

(b) The nature of the force to communicate. In the laboratory experiments, subjects communicate the contents of picture or story only to follow the experimenter's instructions. In the field studies, subjects communicate only on their own initiative. Presumably, subjects will transmit a rumor on their own initiative only when the content of the rumor is of some interest to them. Higham in a study using the technique of serial reproduction has maintained that there is less distortion when subjects are ego-involved and interested in the content of their communication.

SUMMARY

Current notions of the determinants of rumor spread and distortion were tested in a field experiment. It has been hypothesized that rumors will spread when there is (a) a state of cognitive unclarity about (b) an important issue which is (c) common to all or most members of a group. Evidence is presented indicating that under conditions of widespread cognitive unclarity there is far more transmission of a planted rumor and far more speculation involving new rumors when the issue is important than when it is relatively unimportant.

In distinct contrast to expectations created by studies using the technique of serial reproduction, there is absolutely no indication of distortion of the planted rumor. Several factors are suggested which may account for this difference between laboratory and field situations.

30 The Distortion of Information
JOHN R. KIRK
and GEORGE D. TALBOT

It has occurred to us that distortion of information may be of three fundamentally different kinds. We shall call them (1) systematic or stretch distortion—SD, (2) fog distortion—FD, and (3) mirage distortion—MD.

When we think of information we think almost automatically of books, newspapers, radio, and television—information in the conventional codes of natural language. The concepts we shall develop have a more general bearing. We are concerned with *transduction*—the transfer of information from one conducting medium to another, as from a violin string to the air, the air to the ear, or from the ear to the auditory cortex, and the anomalies that may arise in these transfers. To be sure, it is again a more complicated case of transduction when a newspaper reporter conveys information to his editor, and the editor to the printer, and the printed page to the ultimate purchaser of a newspaper, but of particular interest to us are those information transfers involved in *perception* and *conception*. These we picture as being operationally similar and lying at different ranges along a single continuum. The same three kinds of information-distortion which we believe to afflict perception we also believe to afflict conception. All three are rife, too, in interpersonal communications. But let us here exhibit for the reader a simple sample of each:

1. Astronomer Maskelyne fired his assistant, Kinnebrooke, because the latter was clearly incompetent. Charged with clocking upper transits of certain reference stars, Kinnebrooke consistently clocked them "late."

Reprinted with permission of the publisher and the authors. From *ETC*, 17:5–27 (1959).

2. Philosopher Aristotle changed his mind because, this time, he bowed to empirical procedure. Convinced that all life comes from life, he tested this conviction through careful observation of a pond. The pond was new and fed from fresh rains, and Aristotle "saw" that it harbored no living thing. Yet, after a few days in the winds and under the sun, the pond was teeming. Life, concluded Aristotle, may generate spontaneously.

3. Prime Minister Chamberlain held out hope because he was used to the way that Englishmen honor their contracts. He was wooed by a wish, blinded by anxiety. Only a little *Lebensraum* in Czechoslovakia and the western front could keep it quiet. This, anyway, he "inferred" from Hitler's words. So, he promised "peace in our time" and made the Munich Pact and opened Poland to mass murder.

Each of these men availed himself of a sensory channel of communication. Each was victimized by a distortion of information. Even in ancient times, just such defects in the transmission of messages prompted Plato to repudiate the senses. As he put it: so long as we seek to learn what's what by consulting the channels of sense we are as prisoners in a cave, so shackled that we see on the cave's far wall only faint and flickering shadows of outer-world events. Plato was not a champion of "the extensional orientatión," and his influence was such that two millennia passed before his theory of knowledge was swept into the backwash of scientific advance.

When we read that we perceive the world "as through a glass, darkly" or "through the narrow slits of sense," we are mindful that Plato's cave-simile lives on; and when the Great Bookies of our time contend that all subsequent science and philosophy are a footnote to Plato, we concede a superficial sense in which they are right. But this footnote tells us that "the extensional orientation," while neither automatically nor even easily mastered, is ultimately rewarding. To attain it is first to do battle with the distortion of information. It is again to look upon the face of an enemy that intimidated Heraclitus.

In drawing up our "intelligence estimate" of the "enemy capabilities" we recognize three groups of "combatants," three classes of "distortion." Against these we believe three somewhat different "battle strategies" may prove effective.

The astronomers, both Maskelyne and Kinnebrooke, paid a price for *systematic* or *stretch* distortion. Aristotle was alienated from the facts of life by *fog* distortion. A *mirage* fooled Mr. Chamberlain. We hope all this is not too obvious at the moment, or we would have little motive for moving on. And while no transfer of information may ever be entirely free from any one of these three effects, we shall, for ease of exposition, discuss them separately.

I. STRETCH DISTORTION

The anamorphic lens used in photographing "cinemascope" motion pictures generates a simple case of systematic, or stretch, distortion (SD). (See Figure 1.) The camera lens so stretches the image that, on the film,

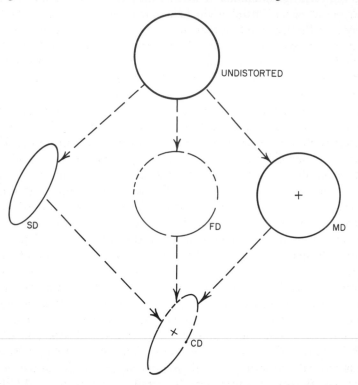

Figure 1. Diagram shows different kinds of distortion afflicting a circle. SD is *systematic* or *stretch* distortion; no information is lost. FD is *fog* distortion; information is lost. MD is *mirage* distortion; spurious information is we see the effect of all three species added. In CD (combined distortions)

everything looks oddly tall and thin, somewhat Modiglianish. Significantly, if we now project this "distorted" image through the same lens, the image will be fattened enough to assume "proper" proportions. In SD no information is lost. Rather, it is changed or recorded in an orderly or systematic way. Distortions of this kind are like the distortions a rubber sheet might undergo, so long as it is not torn. Thus, SD can be eliminated or "corrected for" by the application of a rule specifying the appropriate "topological transformation." We all know a number of simple rules of this sort. A man who *always* tells lies gives his listeners no trouble. They realize that he speaks a different language. And they soon learn a simple and reliable rule of translation: attach "not" to his main verbs. They thereby convert the liar into an oracle.

Sometimes SD is useful even when it goes "uncorrected." Some auto rear-view mirrors are cylindrically convex so that the driver may scan at a glance far more than a "flat-mirror-glimpse" of the territory behind him. Again, he sees images which are tall and thin, and they require "getting used to." As a communication channel, the cylindrical mirror's capacity for conveying optical information may be commensurate with that of the flat mirror. Still, for the *purpose* of safe driving, the "distorting" mirror may prove more valuable; its image is a map of familiar territory but with unusual "projection" for a special purpose. Once it is "got used to" it packs a greater amount of *telically pertinent* information. Similarly, the concave shaving mirror "distorts" for a purpose. That it "distorts" is eloquently testified by the scarred face of the man who has been using it for only a short time.

The reader will have realized that "getting used to" SD has operational consequences similar to "correcting for" it, and this re-education involves more than mere long-suffering exposure. The atonality of Stravinsky's most recent output or the perversity of Picasso's *Guernica* are not "got used to" until one first gets an inkling of the purposes these "devices" are intended to serve. Once one appreciates the purposes, and that they are well-served, the "devices" cease to seem artificial—they become a part of the natural "undistorted" language.

We must conclude that whether a message is appraised as distorted or undistorted will depend upon the purposes to which we relate it. This is to say that *the "distortion" concept applies in a precise way only to pertinent information, and the latter should always be goal-indexed.* What is automatically judged "undistorted" is what automatically serves our purposes. As pornography, Duchamp's *Nude Descending the Staircase* is quite hopelessly "distorted." Likewise, a map may fail as an object of art, may grievously violate the prevailing esthetic canons and yet lead to reliable predictions and so be, as indexed to the latter goal, "undistorted." Conversely, even a "representational" landscape may wound a cartographer's sensibility; and the move of modernist painters in various "non-representational" directions reminds us not to confuse cognitive with esthetic aims, though often these may be synergic.

In the language of the laboratory, SD is called "determinate error," and the label suggests that lab technicians have ways of dealing with the difficulty. Suppose that some event is recorded through several communication channels and that at no two of these are the output pattern of information "the same." If a "rule of recoding" can be applied to the information collected at one receiver so that the result "agrees" faithfully with the information collected at another receiver, then we say that SD *exists between* these channels. No sleep is lost over which of these supplies the "undistorted" or "true" picture and which the "aberrant." The lab technician chooses one channel as basic and calibrates the other systems in the language of the chosen system. The choice, of course, is not utterly arbitrary. It may be made on the basis of ease of understanding, on technical manipulability, or other species of convenience. The choice is calculated to maximize the pertinent information.

In natural language SD exists between such statements as "Tom is taller than Bill" and "Bill is shorter than Tom"; here, the "rule of recoding" is a simple rule of relational logic. Grantedly, the SD here is small. Most of us would say that these statements are two different maps of the same territory and that it is a matter of no consequence which one we use. Since we have "got used to" reading each kind of map we do not find one a "distortion" of the other. The creative writer may be sensitive to the fact that for some readers, these two maps carry a slightly different emotional freight. If the writer wants Tom to be the target of empathy and admiration, he will use the first statement; the second would appear a slight "distortion" of his intent. If he wants initial sympathy bestowed on Bill, he will choose the second statement; the first would then prove a bit "distortive."

There is an approximate logical equivalence, too, between such remarks as "When I gaze into your eyes time stops" and "Your face would stop a clock," but here no special talent is required to determine which version is apt to be the more successful communication. The last example clarifies the fact that messages in SD with each other by virtue of one "rule of recoding" (a logical rule, say) may not be in SD with reference to another rule (here, a psychological one), for various rules are justified with respect to purposes which may be disparate. The "distortive" aspect of SD reflects implicit and often unconscious use of an appropriate "rule of recoding."

Again, rules of logic establish SD between "If there is no radiation in the neighborhood, the Geiger counter will not click," Either the Geiger counter will not click or there is radiation in the neighborhood," and "Unless there is radiation in the neighborhood, the Geiger counter will not click." We have found that "distortion" between these statements is alarmingly large; they are often not recognized as "saying the same thing." Among different readers, tests show a startling lack of consensus about the ways in which any one of such statements can be legitimately "transformed." When the truth-functional connectives which strew technical orders and instructions are so disparately understood, it is small wonder to us that new-built buildings crumble, bridges break, and rockets refuse to leave their launching pads. A practical prophylaxis against this type of communication collapse is, in part, increased acquaintance with modern logic. Logic, as a discipline, can be helpfully construed as training in the preparation and interpretation of several different types of projection of natural language maps of any possible territory, the "projections" being chosen wtih cognitive and technological purposes in mind. Logic's pay-off in the language classroom, particularly at the undergraduate level, is primarily the preservation of syntactical flexibility, even its encouragement, while eliminating the "distortion" of information engendered by mere syntactical anarchy. It is a means for partly "calibrating" the members of a linguistic community so that they can communicate and work together creatively rather than at cross purposes.

A physical law may "recode" a natural language map. Logic is insufficient to establish SD between "The freight car has a gravitational mass of ten tons" and "The freight car has an inertial mass of ten tons." Yet, Einstein was able to draft a rule (the "principle of equivalence") which faithfully transforms statements of the first sort into those of the second without change in truth-value. More precisely, on the basis of the suspicious but "unaccountable" fact that the gravitational and inertial masses of a body are always proportional, Einstein "accounted" for the "unaccountable" by treating any statement about accelerated motion as in SD with some statement about gravitation and *vice versa*. This suggested the making of some maps which nobody had got around to making before. In these, light underwent deflection in gravitative fields—a phenomenon which obligingly cropped up in the territory of the solar eclipse of March 29, 1919, and in all subsequent ones.

Which reminds us: during the last four centuries much philosophic heat was engendered and some human flesh burned over rival geocentric and heliocentric maps of the universe. True, the detailed difference between the classic Ptolemaic and Copernican models was *not* an *exact* specimen of SD. Ptolemy could not have accounted for the phases of Venus, for example. Copernicus could have, if he had known about them. But all the froth, and what did Bruno in, was no such matter of detail. It *was* the much "bigger" matter of whether Earth is motionless and at the center of the universe (as befits God's "footstool") or whether the Sun is. This tremendous issue General Relativity shows to be one arising from SD and, thus, no issue at all. We know now that for every geocentric map there is a cognitively equivalent heliocentric map, and *vice versa*. The difference is one of code, not of content—at least, not of cognitive content.

II. FOG DISTORTION

Fog distortion (FD) is easier to describe, less easy to dispel. In FD, information is lost, masked out, "fogged" over, because of the inability of the transducer to respond to the smallest or largest differences in the input. A snapshot of a pastoral scene will show neither the bacteria on a bush nor the full brilliance of the sun. Germs are details too fine for the resolving power of the lens and the coarseness of the film grain; the ordinary light of the sun is far too bright for a film to record along with all the other contrasts. Low FD is what hi-fi is all about. The crisp transient response, the span of all audible frequencies, the full dynamic range in volume—these are some of the ways in which hi-fi is high.

If everybody's hearing or seeing or sensing were equally impaired, would we know it? In one sense not, and what we did not know would not "hurt" us, would not cause the feeling of frustration at missing what others get. None of our acquaintance bemoans his inability to see radio waves, for here everyone's impairment is complete.

But in another less subjective sense we *do* sometimes know what it is that we miss. We know, for example, that our unaided eyes cannot see viruses. Danger may lurk in things unsensed. And in the last movement of his last symphony Tschaikowsky writes for stereo sound, though no stereo recording that we know of has as yet exploited the fact. In the unsense, unsuspected beauties may reside. Thus there are both cognitive and esthetic reasons why we should be interested in being able to reduce FD. We can be frustrated even when we lack the feeling of frustration.

It should not be concluded, however, that FD is always bad. As we shall see, a moderate amount of FD has been helpful, at times, to science. And an artist may choose to reduce his "alphabet," may want us to focus our attention on a smaller-than-usual amount of pertinent information, and may, thus, "fog" the rest. Nor should it be inferred from the above examples that FD afflicts only micro-details. Perhaps you remember the cartoon. An anthropologist has pitched his tent, unknowingly, in the center of a huge footprint. He then remarks to a colleague, "You know, there's a superstition among the natives that a giant monster inhabits this place." FD thus works at the other end of the magnitude scale. The astronomer's inability to tell at a glance whether distant galaxies are distributed randomly through space, and the social scientist's processing of a plethora of data to verify a "fact" already recognized by less tutored laymen, are more serious cases in point.

In the laboratory, FD raises its fuzzy head as *random error*, and technicians find it not possible to "correct for" FD in any straight-forward way—what has been lost is lost. Yet, there are some strategies for dealing with the loss. First, we can make inferences to fill the "holes" in our data. Given a part of a dinosaur skeleton, the paleontologist "reconstructs" through inductive techniques what time and decay have "fogged." The cosmographer, using the data of the Hale telescope on Palomar Mountain, supplemented by that of vaster and more recent radio telescopes, assumes he has studied a statistically fair sample of the universe-at-large; he then deduces the shape and size of space-time. Even our own perceptory apparatus stops up "holes" in much the same way. The eye does not "see" what falls on that spot of the retina where the optic nerve is attached, but into this "blind spot" is interpolated the hue and texture of the surrounding image. We know that such interpolation is sometimes "false"—inductive inferences can "go wrong."

A second and more direct strategy for dealing with loss is the technological improvement in our methods for recording events. Lenses can be made "sharper" and "brighter," loudspeakers more powerful and sensitive, cyclotrons more penetrating, words more precise, and pigments purer.

Diction, too, is hurt by "fog." As language evolves, many words lose their earlier univocality and precision, and as vagueness proves *sometimes* convenient, many people pursue it finally as an end-in-itself. Distinctions get lost—for example, the earlier "nice" one between "smell" and "stink," or the more recent and not-quite-so-nice one between "hep" and "hip." And, once, we had a reasonably clear notion of what *aggression* was. To be sure, as the special sciences and trades coin new and well-defined technical terms, this "degradation" of language is balanced by a countertendency. But FD infiltrates language and our conceptualizing in still more subtle ways. Because of FD we not only do not see the trees for the forest but, often, cannot see the forest for the trees. We need the cross-classification concepts encouraged by non-aristotelian semantics; these relate "in the large" many things which would otherwise seem distant and disconnected. We require "reducing glasses" just as much as "magnifying glasses." In the interests of a better science of man, perhaps we need the former even more.

According to an old saying, "The wisdom of the age is sufficient unto the needs thereof." Thus, Newtonian mechanics was sufficient unto the needs of those whose FD was no less than that prevailing in 1850. The theories suggested by data distorted by a particular level of FD are likely to be tested by data at a roughly similar level, if the suggesting and testing occur in one and the same period of technological development. So, for a theory to be valuable, its predictive content need only be slightly more distorted than were the original suggestive data.

In pushing forward the frontiers of firm knowledge, our observational (i.e., perceptual, plus recording systems in SD) and conceptual apparatus should be yoked, at least loosely, in a symbiotic relationship. Too sudden an advance in our techniques for dispersing "fog" is apt to disclose a lag in our conceptualizing, and the shock of this disclosure may sometimes retard the growth of theory. At the present time, for example, physicists are still reeling from the downfall of parity in weak interactions.

III. MIRAGE DISTORTION

In mirage distortion (MD) we see something that "isn't there." Far from withholding information from us, MD gives us extra, unwanted information. That is, it *should* be unwanted. But we concede that there are many people who desire the "mirages" with which they are afflicted. It *should* be unwanted because it is likely to be construed *mistakenly* as pertinent information, thus introducing error into predictions. On a television variety show we may see "snow" drifting down over the dancing girls, and we may mistake an electromagnetic disturbance for the big budget.

Note that MD typically involves FD also, for the "false" or "impertinent" information replaces, blots out, "fogs" the "true" or "pertinent" information. The prototype of MD is the classical mirage itself. But it should not be thought that MD is limited to the visual or, even, the perceptual. We can also *conceive* "something" that "isn't there"—we can spin false theories. Often the false theories that we spin are outcomes of MD which has been "transferred" along the perception-conception continuum from the former pole to the latter.

It is instructive to understand how mirages (literal ones) delayed man's acceptance of the roundness of his home planet. The size and shape of Earth were estimated by Eratosthenes in the second century B.C. He came within fifty miles of the correct circumference! Two hundred years earlier, Empedocles hit upon the right explanation of lunar eclipses and, there witnessing the curvature of Earth's shadow, must have guessed Earth's shape. And people of ages past, living near seaports, are used to the way that ships, outward bound, disappear hull first and mast last. Yet, as late as the sixteenth century there were scholars who held out for Earth's flatness. That "seeing is believing" is a peculiarly modern wisp of "commonsense." Its analog in ancient times, as attested by Thomas the Doubter, was to the effect that "touching is believing." Once the hot and arid areas of Earth were opened to exploration, desert travelers were tantalized by clear but distant pools which, upon closer scrutiny, vanished. This gave point to the teaching that *whatever is seen at a distance is not to be entirely trusted.* And since all the ancient evidence for Earth's curvature involved such "distant vision," it was automatically suspect.

In the raw perceptions of everyday life little MD occurs. Our perceptual apparatus is genetically "designed" to filter out MD which would be apt to occur at threshold intensities. The retina of the human eye, for example, is theoretically sensitive enough to record even one quantum of visible light, but some neurological "fair sampler" intervenes so that something like six or seven quanta are absorbed before a neural impulse winds its way to the visual cortex. There is a similar loudness threshold. Were the human ear any more sensitive than it is, it would register the "white noise" of the Brownian movement of colloidal particles in the liquids of the semicircular canals. Evolution has "ordained" that anything sensible worth attending to can afford payments of certain threshold numbers of action-quanta.

Evolution is not omniscient, however, hence human beings are interested in lowering the levels, here and there, of FD. Nor is evolution omnipotent, hence some MD gets through the genetic barriers. In even quite "normal" people the nervous system will present, now and then, minor "mirages." We will "hear" a noise or word, "see" a flash of light, "feel" a fall, uncoordinated with anything in the "outside" world. Certain drugs will amplify these "mirages" into sustained hallucinations.

The world of the mentally ill is filled with MD at various ranges of the perception-conception continuum—even without benefit of drugs; the psychotherapist might do well to investigate the principles governing the distortion of information. Much of Sigmund Freud's psychoanalytic theory, for example, can be thought of as the formulation of "rules of recoding" for exhibiting SD between minor MD in infantile experience and somehow amplified MD in adult experience, conceptualizing, and evaluation.

The way to combat MD is to understand its source, its cause. Once the meteorology and optics of mirages were understood, mirages no longer mystified. The new knowledge even made them predictable to a degree, and hence largely ignorable. If we know a little about the physics of radio broadcasting and hear static on the amplitude-modulated signal, we know better than to "refer" this to the activities of the studio sound-effects man; if, on the other hand, we encounter crackles and pops on a frequency-modulated broadcast we may conclude that we have caught a cereal commercial. Understanding, of this depth and sophistication, is a powerful thing. It can make short shrift of MD.

Unfortunately, the discovery of general principles is hard work. It requires the construction of complex explanatory inductions. Most of us are too lazy for that; thus we deal with MD by making simple statistical-inductions-by-enumeration. We allow ourselves, thereby, to be "taken in" by MD for awhile. Gradually we begin to recognize and classify that information which has been persistently misleading and so learn to ignore it. Such crude "classification" we then think of as an "explanation." We once tried to interest a little boy in the physical theory underlying radio. "Why," we asked him, "does that little box with the knobs on it give forth music and words? How is such magic possible?" The little boy looked searchingly at us to see whether we were sick and replied, "Because it's a radio, stupid!" The ancients, too, "got used to" their desert mirages, and were then less misled by them, and so had decreasing interest in studying and explaining them.

Most of us are "lazy" in this way, and our modern eyes and ears "freeze" or "crystalize" the results of this "laziness" in our everyday perceptions. Our devices for filtering MD from our perceptions operate by Korzybskian *signal-reactions*. The neurological hook-ups are relatively inflexible, fixed, "frozen." It is for this reason that the transactional psychologists have been able to play upon our signal-reactions and "conjure up" MD at the level of raw perception; thus, the "trapezoidal window" persists in its "oscillation" even when we "know" it is rotating.

When, in our conceptualizing, we take the easy statistical-inductions-by-enumeration road, we are making our cerebral cortices mimic the signal reaction patterns of our basic perceptual equipment. Thus, you hear people say that no war will ever destroy humanity because no war ever has! Korzybski has foretold the foolishness of this sort of extrapolation. While signal reactions at the perceptual pole of the continuum filter all but a little MD from our experience, signal reactions in the conceptual range engender and amplify MD.

In the preceding section we remarked that one of the strategies for dealing with FD is the making of inductive inferences to fill "holes" in our data. But any inductive inference *can* go wrong. The going wrong of *these* "interpolative" or "extrapolative" inductions is the primary source of the most troublesome MD. The inductions which led to "the phlogiston theory" of combustion, or to "the ether theory" of the propagation of light, "explained" the immediate observations but put out "false" leads to delay men in their comprehension of nature. For millennia after Aristotle made his fateful decision concerning the spontaneous generation of living things, experiments were conducted which substantiated Aristotle's claim. Thus, FD may lead to MD which may lead, in a widening feed-back oscillation, again to FD, etc. This awful possibility justifies priority reduction of FD even at the expense of temporary inconvenience to our pet conceptual schemes.

Scientists know "mirages" as *artifacts*. The object of experimental study is some signal-source, but extra signals spawned in the channel between source and receiver are likely mistakenly to be "referred" to the source. (Amputees sometimes complain that a toe on their missing foot aches. Physicians term this "referred pain.") Such extra signals are artifacts, MD. In teletype circuits, in telegraphy, in electronic computers, and in the translation of ancient documents, MD is not negligibly rare, but the built-in redundance of such source messages makes the "mirages" easier to spot. When scientists speak half-mystically of "the uniformity of nature" they express a hope that messages from signal-sources in nature-at-large will have an obligingly similar redundance. To be prepared for a possible dashing of such hopes, some philosophers of science have recently been able to give their blessings to statistical techniques *which presuppose no redundance in nature-at-large*. We look to these as man's best means for ridding the cognitive enterprise of MD.

The neurological and biochemical correlates of the emotions are not yet well-understood. But it has long been folk wisdom that sentiments and emotions can "slant" a person's thinking. This, too, is MD. Within the last decade psychologists have learned that strong wants, strong inhibitions, and strong fears and anxieties can distort even a person's raw perceptions. It has been recognized for centuries, however, that such emotions may invade even the relatively flexible and enlightened area of *symbol-responses* and influence our conceptions and predictions. People so prone were characterized by William James as "tender-minded."

This emotional source of MD, a common one in everyday life, may be called "obliquity." *Obliquity* is a disease of optimists, pessimists, and manic-depressives. It is the tendency to construe the desirability or undesirability of some state-of-affairs *as evidence* of the existence of that state of affairs. An optimist, like the late Mr. Chamberlain, chronically puts his trust in desirability. The pessimist is convinced that the undesirable is more likely to happen. The manic-depressive vacillates wildly from one extreme to the other. Our myriad slight obliquities, of which we are largely unconscious, are what make such famous projective tests as the Thematic Apperception Test and the Rorschach work as well as they do. They may serve to alleviate the *feeling* of frustration and so enhance our *subjective* security. But in the context of accurate prediction and searching explanation, obliquities are toxic and can gnaw away, like termites, at the foundation of our *objective* security. For, except in special cases (like Merton's self-fulfilling or self-defeating prophecies), what we *wish* to be true, or *fear* might be true, manages to exist quite independently of our sentiments about the matter. Under the influence of obliquity, we approach the truth, calculate the future, at best *obliquely*, and at the cost of some delay. And the cost may be prohibitive. Mr. Chamberlain lies under stone in a small and shadowed section of Westminster Abbey. His obliquity made many other graves, marked not nearly so well.

Little has been said so far concerning the dynamic relationships among our three fundamental species of the distortion of information. It seems to us that there is much work here to be done, and preferably within a rigorous mathematical framework, that perhaps of information theory.

MD is what the information theorist or communication engineer calls "noise" in *typical* applications of the theory. Are the phenomena of SD and FD derivable as entities distinct from "noise" in information theory? We are uncertain of the answer here. Perhaps an *atypical* application of the theory would permit the concept "noise" to embrace all three of our species of distortion. Perhaps, too, these alternatives are not mutually exclusive. Each may be possible.

Our purpose has been to enlist the interest and talents of those involved in communication, in international relations, in psychotherapy, and in the social sciences, in the hope that something we have said here will suggest new lines of thought and new experiments.

The epistemologist may note that the ancient and honorable dualism between "appearance" and "reality" was dissolved, in our treatment, into "degrees of distortion" among our three species. If an ontologist objects that we may have dealt with "appearances" therewith but ignored "reality," we can add only this: it is better to have "holes" in our knowledge than to camouflage our ignorance with "mirages." We cannot say, therefore, what "reality" is in the traditional, ultimate, absolutistic sense of that word unless, *à la* Charles Peirce, we suggest that it is what human understanding would approach as a limit after indefinitely prolonged scientific inquiry. We prefer to speak of "undistorted information." Any and all information may be legitimately construed as undistorted if none of it gives us trouble. When we *are* in trouble, it is best to apply our arsenal of strategies for coping with the distortion of information. It is best *not* because trouble necessarily *implies* such distortion. It is best not *merely* because we have inductive evidence that when troubles occur we can usually abate them by treating some information as though it were distorted. It is best, rather, because employment of the strategies entails the making of inductive inferences. These latter, applied in sustained fashion, are in a restricted but important sense "self-corrective." If knowledge be a cure for the trouble, then inductive procedures will cure the trouble through accretion of further relevant knowledge.

Nevertheless, in this dawning Age of Space, we might helpfully alert ourselves to the exotic ways such knowledge might be coded. We can imagine a Martian scientist who, let us say, suffers from "mirages" in his tactile sense but has never found reason to doubt his eyes. Such a Martian, upon discovering that a "straight" stick "bends" when placed in water, might succeed in fashioning a tissue of information recording this observation and lacking FD and MD both for him and for us Terrans. In brief, he might maintain that the stick "really" bends but that the fickle sense of touch makes it still "appear" straight. The *remainder* of his physics, we are sure, would prove immensely complicated and incon-venient to us men of Earth. But we are convinced, also, that were the Martian the Einstein of his planet, the *whole* of his physics might suffer, at worst, only SD with respect to our own.

VIII

Feedback and Control

INTRODUCTION   In a communication network a signal goes from point A to point B with more or less fidelity. It also goes from point B back to A with more or less fidelity. The signals sent out are often sent back in order to control what is sent out. In human communication particularly, the signal A sends to B is largely determined by the signal B sends back to A. A can also anticipate B's reaction; A can even react to his own output himself. This is feedback. Feedback serves to control and correct the signals fed forward. It serves to realign all the signals within the network to one another. It makes A and B truly interacting members of a communication system.

Arnold Tustin in "Feedback" gives a general introduction to this basic principle of cybernetics. He shows how feedback is the basic mechanism of automatic control in thermostats, guided missiles, and also in physiology and economics. Then W. T. Powers, R. K. Clark, and R. L. McFarland formulate a rigorous theory of feedback as the basis of a general theory of human behavior. "A General Feedback Theory of Human Behavior" introduces the concepts of open and closed systems, lower and higher orders of systems, positive and negative feedback, and of entropy and negentropy. The concept of system is itself a second order of relationships: that is, a system is a set of interrelated relationships. These relationships are controlled by feedback. Consider, for example, the very complex feedback involved when two people try simultaneously to trace identical freehand figures with crayons on opposite sides of a glass window. Feedback controls are even more complicated in the "co-orientations" that we considered in the social psychological theory of human communication.

Harold J. Leavitt and Ronald A. H. Mueller conducted experiments to investigate this kind of feedback between a sender and receiver. "Some Effects of Feedback on Communication" reports how they controlled for different kinds of feedback signals—visual and verbal—and for four different amounts of feedback, from zero to full (free). They found that full feedback has the greatest effect on communication. It increases the accuracy with which information is transmitted, and it "seems to permit the participants to learn a mutual language, which language once learned may obviate the necessity for further feedback."

Seymour Rosenberg and Robert L. Hall conducted further experiments which distinguished different kinds of human feedback not only in amount or quantity but in origin: feedback of the sender's own response, of his teammate's response, or of both responses. They found, among other things, that in human communication the least significant feedback is the response from the teammate; self response and combined response are more important controls of the signals sent. Moreover, "The Effects of Different Feedback Conditions upon Performance in Dyadic Teams" is concerned explicitly with the simplest kind of human networks: the two man group. We need additional research on feedback in larger human groups.

31

Feedback
ARNOLD TUSTIN

For hundreds of years a few examples of true automatic control systems have been known. A very early one was the arrangement on windmills of a device to keep their sails always facing into the wind. It consisted simply of a miniature windmill which could rotate the whole mill to face in any direction. The small mill's sails were at right angles to the main ones, and whenever the latter faced in the wrong direction, the wind caught the small sails and rotated the mill to the correct position. With steam power came other automatic mechanisms: the engine-governor, and then the steering servo-engine on ships, which operated the rudder in correspondence with movements of the helm. These devices, and a few others such as simple voltage regulators, constituted man's achievement in automatic control up to about 20 years ago.

In the past two decades necessity, in the form of increasingly acute problems arising in our ever more complex technology, has given birth to new families of such devices. Chemical plants needed regulators of temperature and flow; air warfare called for rapid and precise control of searchlights and anti-aircraft guns; radio required circuits which would give accurate amplification of signals.

Thus the modern science of automatic control has been fed by streams from many sources. At first, it now seems surprising to recall, no connection between these various developments was recognized. Yet all control and regulating systems depend on common principles. As soon as this was realized, progress became much more rapid. Today the design of controls for a modern boiler or a guided missile, for example, is based largely on principles first developed in the design of radio amplifiers.

Indeed, studies of the behavior of automatic control systems give us new insight into a wide variety of happenings in nature and in human affairs. The notions that engineers have evolved from these studies are useful aids in understanding how a man stands upright without toppling over, how the human heart beats, why our economic system suffers from slumps and booms, why the rabbit population in parts of Canada regularly fluctuates between scarcity and abundance.

The chief purpose of this article is to make clear the common pattern that underlies all these and many other varied phenomena. This common pattern is the existence of feedback, or—to express the same thing rather more generally—interdependence.

We should not be able to live at all, still less to design complex control systems, if we did not recognize that there are regularities in the relationship between events—what we call "cause and effect." When the room is warmer, the thermometer on the wall reads higher. We do not expect to make the room warmer by pushing up the mercury in the thermometer. But now consider the case when the instrument on the wall is not a simple thermometer but a thermostat, contrived so that as its reading goes above a chosen setting, the fuel supply to the furnace is progressively reduced, and, conversely, as its reading falls below that setting, the fuel flow is increased. This is an example of a familiar control system. Not only does the reading of the thermometer depend on the warmth of the room, but the warmth of the room also depends on the reading of the thermometer. The two quantities are interdependent. Each is a cause, and each an effect, of the other. In such cases we have a closed chain or sequence—what engineers call a "closed loop."

In analyzing engineering and scientific problems it is very illuminating to sketch out first the scheme of dependence and see how the various quantities involved in the problem are determined by one another and by disturbances from outside the system. Such a diagram enables one to tell at a glance whether a system is an open or a closed one. This is an important distinction, because a closed system possesses several significant properties. Not only can it act as a regulator, but it is capable of various "self-excitatory" types of behavior—like a kitten chasing its own tail.

The now-popular name for this process is "feedback." In the case of the thermostat, the thermometer's information about the room temperature is fed back to open or close the valve, which in turn controls the temperature. Not all automatic control systems are of the closed-loop type. For example, one might put the thermometer outside in the open air, and connect it to work the fuel valve through a specially shaped cam, so that the outside temperature regulates the fuel flow. In this open-sequence system the room temperature has no effect; there is no feedback. The control compensates only that disturbance of room temperature caused by variation of the outdoor temperature. Such a system is not necessarily a bad or useless system; it might work very well under some circumstances. But it has two obvious shortcomings. Firstly, it is a "calibrated" system; that is to say, its correct working would require careful preliminary testing and special shaping of the cam to suit each particular application. Secondly, it could not deal with any but standard conditions. A day that was windy as well as cold would not get more fuel on that account.

The feedback type of control avoids these shortcomings. It goes directly to the quantity to be controlled, and it corrects indiscriminately for all kinds of disturbance. Nor does it require calibration for each special condition.

Feedback control, unlike open-sequence control, can never work without *some* error, for the error is depended upon to bring about the correction. The objective is to make the error as small as possible. This is subject to certain limitations, which we must now consider.

The principle of control by feedback is quite general. The quantities that it may control are of the most varied kinds, ranging from the frequency of a national electric-power grid to the degree of anesthesia of a patient under surgical operation. Control is exercised by negative feedback, which is to say that the information fed back is the amount of departure from the desired condition.

Any quantity may be subjected to control if three conditions are met. First, the required changes must be controllable by some physical means, a regulating organ. Second, the controlled quantity must be measurable, or at least comparable with some standard; in other words, there must be a measuring device. Third, both regulation and measurement must be rapid enough for the job in hand.

As an example, take one of the simplest and commonest of industrial requirements: to control the rate of flow of liquid along a pipe. As the regulating organ we can use a throttle valve, and as the measuring device, some form of flowmeter. A signal from the flowmeter, telling the actual rate of flow through the pipe, goes to the "controller"; there it is compared with a setting giving the required rate of flow. The amount and direction of "error," *i.e.*, deviation from this setting, is then transmitted to the throttle valve as an operating signal to bring about adjustment in the required direction.

In flow-control systems the signals are usually in the form of variations in air pressure, by which the flowmeter measures the rate of flow of the liquid. The pressure is transmitted through a small-bore pipe to the controller, which is essentially a balance piston. The difference between this received pressure and the setting regulates the air pressure in another pipeline that goes to the regulating valve.

Signals of this kind are slow, and difficulties arise as the system becomes complex. When many controls are concentrated at a central point, as is often the case, the air-pipes that transmit the signals may have to be hundreds of feet long, and pressure changes at one end reach the other only after delays of some seconds. Meanwhile the error may have become large. The time-delay often creates another problem: overcorrection of the error, which causes the system to oscillate about the required value instead of settling down.

For further light on the principles involved in control systems let us consider the example of the automatic gundirector. In this problem a massive gun must be turned with great precision to angles indicated by a fly-power pointer on a clock-dial some hundreds of feet away. When the pointer moves, the gun must turn correspondingly. The quantity to be controlled is the angle of the gun. The reference quantity is the angle of the clock-dial pointer. What is needed is a feedback loop which constantly compares the gun angle with the pointer angle and arranges matters so that if the gun angle is too small, the gun is driven forward, and if it is too large, the gun is driven back.

The key element in this case is some device which will detect the error of angular alignment between two shafts remote from each other, and which does not require more force than is available at the fly-power transmitter shaft. There are several kinds of electrical elements that will serve such a purpose. The one usually selected is a pair of the miniature alternating-current machines known as selsyns. The two selsyns, connected respectively to the transmitter shaft and the gun, provide an electrical signal proportional to the error of alignment. The signal is amplified and fed to a generator which in turn feeds a motor that drives the gun.

This gives the main lines of a practicable scheme, but if a system were built as just described, it would fail. The gun's inertia would carry it past the position of correct alignment; the new error would then cause the controller to swing it back, and the gun would hunt back and forth without ever settling down.

This oscillatory behavior, maintained by "self-excitation," is one of the principal limitations of feedback control. It is the chief enemy of the control-system designer, and the key to progress has been the finding of various simple means to prevent oscillation. Since oscillation is a very general phenomenon, it is worth while to look at the mechanism in detail, for what we learn about oscillation in man-made control systems may suggest means of inhibiting oscillations of other kinds—such as economic booms and slumps, or periodic swarms of locusts.

Consider any case in which a quantity that we shall call the output depends on another quantity we shall call the input. If the input quantity oscillates in value, then the output quantity also will oscillate, not simultaneously or necessarily in the same way, but with the same frequency. Usually in physical systems the output oscillation lags behind the input. For example, if one is boiling water and turns the gas slowly up and down, the amount of steam increases and decreases the same number of times per minute, but the maximum amount of steam in each cycle must come rather later than the maximum application of heat, because of the time required for heating. If the first output quantity in turn affects some further quantity, the variation of this second quantity in the sequence will usually lag still more, and so on. The lag (as a proportion of one oscillation) also usually increases with frequency—the faster the input is varied, the farther behind the output falls.

Now suppose that in a feedback system some quantity in the closed loop is oscillating. This causes the successive quantities around the loop to oscillate also. But the loop comes around to the original quantity, and we have here the mechanism by which an oscillation may maintain itself. To see how this can happen, we must remember that with the feedback negative, the motion it causes would be opposite to the original motion, if it were not for the lags. It is only when the lags add up to just half a cycle that the feedback maintains the assumed motion. Thus any system with negative feedback will maintain a continuous oscillation when disturbed if (a) the time-delays in response at some frequency add up to half a period of oscillation, and (b) the feedback effect is sufficiently large at this frequency.

In a linear system, that is, roughly speaking, a system in which effects are directly proportional to causes, there are three possible results. If the feedback, at the frequency for which the lag is half a period, is equal in strength to the original oscillation, there will be a continuous steady oscillation which just sustains itself. If the feedback is greater than the oscillation at that frequency, the oscillation builds up; if it is smaller, the oscillation will die away.

This situation is of critical importance for the designer of control systems. On the one hand, to make the control accurate, one must increase the feedback; on the other, such an increase may accentuate any small oscillation. The control breaks into an increasing oscillation and becomes useless.

To escape from the dilemma the designer can do several things. Firstly, he may minimize the time-lag by using electronic tubes or, at higher power levels, the new varieties of quick-response direct-current machines. By dividing the power amplification among a multiplicity of stages, these special generators have a smaller lag than conventional generators. The lag is by no means negligible, however.

Secondly, and this was a major advance in the development of control systems, the designer can use special elements that introduce a time-lead, anticipating the time-lag. Such devices, called phase-advancers, are often based on the properties of electric capacitors, because alternating current in a capacitor circuit leads the voltage applied to it.

Thirdly, the designer can introduce other feedbacks besides the main one, so designed as to reduce time-lag. Modern achievements in automatic control are based on the use of combinations of such devices to obtain both accuracy and stability.

So far we have been treating these systems as if they were entirely linear. A system is said to be linear when all effects are strictly proportional to causes. For example, the current through a resistor is proportional to the voltage applied to it; the resistor is therefore a linear element. The same does not apply to a rectifier or electronic tube. These are non-linear elements.

None of the elements used in control systems gives proportional or linear dependence over all ranges. Even a resistor will burn out if the current is too high. Many elements, however, are linear over the range in which they are required to work. And when the range of variation is small enough, most elements will behave in an approximately linear fashion, simply because a very small bit of a curved graph does not differ significantly from a straight line.

We have seen that linear closed-sequence systems are delightfully simple to understand and—even more important—very easy to handle in exact mathematical terms. Because of this, most introductory accounts of control systems either brazenly or furtively assume that all such systems are linear. This gives the rather wrong impression that the principles so deduced may have little application to real, non-linear, systems. In practice, however, most of the characteristic behavior of control systems is affected only in detail by the non-linear nature of the dependences. It is essential to be clear that non-linear systems are not excluded from feedback control. Unless the departures from linearity are large or of special kinds, most of what has been said applies with minor changes to non-linear systems.

Long before man existed, evolution hit upon the need for anti-oscillating features in feedback control and incorporated them in the body mechanisms of the animal world. Signals in the animal body are transmitted by trains of pulses along nerve fibers. When a sensory organ is stimulated, the stimulus will produce pulses at a greater rate if it is increasing than if it is decreasing. The maximum response, or output signal, occurs before the maximum of the stimulus. This is just the anticipatory type of effect (the time-lead) that is required for high-accuracy control. Physiologists now believe that the anticipatory response has evolved in the nervous system for, at least in part, the same reason that man wants it in his control mechanisms—to avoid overshooting and oscillation. Precisely what feature of the structure of the nerve mechanism gives this remarkable property is not yet fully understood.

Fascinating examples of the consequences of interdependence arise in the fluctuations of animal populations in a given territory. These interactions are sometimes extremely complicated. Charles Darwin invoked such a scheme to explain why there are more bumblebees near towns. His explanation was that near towns there are more cats; this means fewer field mice, and field mice are the chief ravagers of bees' nests. Hence near towns bees enjoy more safety.

The interdependence of animal species sometimes produces a periodic oscillation. Just to show how this can happen, and leaving out complications that are always present in an actual situation, consider a territory inhabited by rabbits and lynxes, the rabbits being the chief food of the lynxes. When rabbits are abundant, the lynx population will increase. But as the lynxes become abundant, the rabbit population falls, because more rabbits are caught. Then as the rabbits diminish, the lynxes go hungry and decline. The result is a self-maintaining oscillation, sustained by negative feedback with a time-delay.

The periodic booms and slumps in economic activity stand out as a major example of oscillatory behavior due to feedback. In 1935 the economist John Maynard Keynes gave the first adequate and satisfying account of the essential mechanisms on which the general level of economic activity depends. Although Keynes did not use the terminology of control-system theory, his account fits precisely the same now-familiar pattern.

Keynes' starting point was the simple notion that the level of economic activity depends on the rate at which goods are bought. He took the essential further step of distinguishing two kinds of buying—of consumption goods and of capital goods. The latter is the same thing as the rate of investment. The money available to buy all these goods is not automatically provided by the wages and profits disbursed in making them, because normally some of this money is saved. The system would therefore run down and stop if it were not for the constant injection of extra demand in the form of new investment. Therefore the level of economic activity and employment depends on the rate of investment. This is the first dependence. The rate of investment itself, however, depends on the expectation of profit, and this in turn depends on the trend, present and expected, of economic activity. Thus not only does economic activity depend on the rate of investment, but the rate of investment depends on economic activity.

Modern theories of the business cycle aim to explain in detail the nature of these dependences and their characteristic non-linearities. This clarification of the mechanisms at work immediately suggests many ways in which, by proper timing of investment expenditure, by more rational business forecasting, and so on, a stable level of optimal economic activity may be achieved in the near future. The day when it can unequivocally be said that slumps belong to the past will certainly be the beginning of a brighter chapter in human history.

The examples of feedback given here are merely a few selected to illustrate general principles. In this article on "theory" I should like to touch on a further point: some ways in which the properties of automatic control systems or other complex feedback systems may be investigated in detail, and their performance perfected.

Purely mathematical methods are remarkably powerful when the system happens to be linear. Sets of linear differential equations are the happy hunting ground of mathematicians. They can turn the equations into a variety of equivalent forms, and generally play tunes on them. For the more general class of non-linear systems, the situation is quite different. There exact determination of the types of motion implied by a set of dependences is usually very laborious or practically impossible.

To determine the behavior of such complex systems two principal kinds of machines are being used. The first is the "analogue" computer. The forms of this type of computer are varied, but they all share a common principle: some system of physical elements is set up with relationships analogous to those existing in the system to be investigated, and the interdependence among them is then worked out in proportional terms. The second kind of aid is the new high-speed digital computer. In this type of machine the quantities are represented by numbers rather than by physical equivalents. The implications of the equations involved are explored by means of arithmetical operations on these numbers. The great speed of operation of these modern machines makes possible calculations that could not be attempted by human computers because of the time required.

The theory of control systems is now so well understood that, with such modern aids, the behavior of even extremely complex systems can be largely predicted in advance. Although this is a new branch of science, it is already in a state that ensures rapid further progress.

At the commencement of this account of control systems it was necessary to assume that the human mind can distinguish "cause" and "effect" and describe the regularities of nature in these terms. It may be fitting to conclude by suggesting that the concepts reviewed are not without relevance to the grandest of all problems of science and philosophy: the nature of the human mind and the significance of our forms of perception of what we call reality.

In much of the animal world, behavior is controlled by reflexes and instinct mechanisms in direct response to the stimulus of the immediate situation. In man and the higher animals the operation of what we are subjectively aware of as the "mind" provides a more flexible and effective control of behavior. It is not at present known whether these conscious phenomena involve potentialities of matter other than those we study in physics. They may well do so, and we must not beg this question in the absence of evidence.

Whatever the nature of the means or medium involved, the function of the central nervous system in the higher animals is clear. It is to provide a biologically more effective control of behavior under a combination of inner and environmental stimuli. An inner analogue or simulation of relevant aspects of the external world, which we are aware of as our idea of the environment, controls our responses, superseding mere instinct or reflex reaction. The world is still with us when we shut our eyes, and we use the "play of ideas" to predict the consequences of action. Thus our activity is adjusted more elaborately and advantageously to the circumstances in which we find ourselves.

This situation is strikingly similar in principle (though immensely more complex) to the introduction of a predictor in the control of a gun, for all predictors are essentially analogues of the external situation. The function of mind is to predict, and to adjust behavior accordingly. It operates like an analogue computer fed by sensory clues.

It is not surprising, therefore, that man sees the external world in terms of cause and effect. The distinction is largely subjective. "Cause" is what might conceivably be manipulated. "Effect" is what might conceivably be purposed.

Man is far from understanding himself, but it may turn out that his understanding of automatic control is one small further step toward that end.

32 | A General Feedback Theory of Human Behavior
W. T. POWERS, R. K. CLARK,
R. I. McFARLAND

FUNDAMENTAL DEFINITIONS

We will often employ the term "system" in this paper. Much work has been done on general systems theory, but we have found that for our purposes we have needed to formulate our own concepts, for convenience in discussing later ideas.

A system, as we use the term, is a collection of functions (not, as is often proposed, a collection of variables). A function is a relationship among several variables, and a variable is a combination of two classes of percept. Thus, to define "system," we start by defining "percept."

A percept is the basic unit of experience. It is that "bit" of perception which is self-evident to us, like the intensity of a light, or the taste of salt.

A variable is always a combination of two classes of percept. One class contains percepts which do not vary; by these percepts we keep track of the "identity" of the variable. The other class contains percepts which do change; these percepts carry the information about the "magnitude" of the variable. "Magnitude" is used here in its most general sense, including the meanings of "intensity," "size," or any other word for the general class of variable attributes.

A function is the direct relationship between any two or more variables. We shall uniformly imply by this term a stable relationship, which does not alter its form over reasonable periods of time. Since the variables we shall be talking about are assumed to correspond to physical events, we will always assume that whatever functional relationship is seen among variables is imposed by the operation of some physical "devise," such as a neural network or a muscle or a chemical reaction. We shall sometimes represent these functions as mathematical expressions, in which case they are to be taken as idealized representations of some physically-occurring relationship.

Reprinted with permission of the publisher and the authors. From *Perceptual and Motor Skills*, 11:71–88 (1960).

A system is a set of functions interrelated in a special way. Given a set of variables and the physical devices which relate them in pairs or larger groups, we can define the environment of the system as all those variables and functions not included within the set chosen as our system.

THE BASIC FEEDBACK CONTROL SYSTEM

There are two major classes of feedback in common knowledge. One is the type which is wholly internal to a system, involving closed loops which do not cross the input or output boundaries of the system, and the other is the type in which the feedback path exits through the output boundary, passes through the environment (with attendant modification of the information) and reenters at the input boundary, the rest of the loop being completed within the system. Both types of feedback can exist simultaneously, but only the external type is unequivocally perceivable as a feedback loop by an external observer. The behavior of any system with internal feedback could be simulated exactly by another system with no internal loops, so such internal loops cannot be firmly identified by external observations.

We will be primarily concerned with externally connected feedback loops. Since we will be attempting to build a model of human behavior, we will regularly assume, unless special circumstances dictate otherwise, that the sense of the feedback is negative; this is, indeed, necessary if a feedback control-system is to exist. The meaning of the term "negative feedback" will become apparent as we discuss the operation of the general control system.

The general control system consists of three functions plus an environment function, and five variables. We will discuss these in order from the input boundary, through the system to the output boundary, and through the environment back to the input boundary.

The input boundary consists of a function we call the Feedback Function, abbreviated F in equations. The environmental variable which is the input to this function we call v_e (which may represent, remember, many variables). The output variables of this function we call the feedback signal, "f," reserving, as we shall do consistently, the term "signal" for variables inside the system. The feedback signal is some function of v_e, the form of the function being determined by the properties of the input device. Mathematically, the relationship would be written

$$f = F(v_e).$$

The next function is the Comparator Function (C), which receives both the feedback signal f and a reference-signal, symbolized as "r." The

Comparator Function subtracts f from r and its output signal is called the error-signal, "e," representing the discrepancy between f and r.

The function at the output boundary we call the Output Function, (O), which receives the error signal as its input signal and produces the output-signal (or variable), "o." This would be written

$$o \quad O(e) = O(r\text{-}f).$$

The Comparator Function is often only implicit in the operation of the output function, some devices being capable of responding directly to the difference between two input signals. For clarity we shall usually speak of the Comparator as a separate function and the error signal, e, as a real signal inside the system.

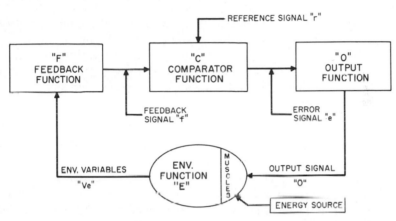

Figure 1. Feedback control system, general form.

The output variable o is the input variable to the Environment Function, (E), which in turn produces as an output variable (or set of variables) v_e, the input to the system. Thus, the loop is completed: see Figure 1. We would write

$$v_e = E(o).$$

For this system to be a control-system, it is necessary that for any error signal, the operation of all the various functions be such as to tend to bring f closer to r (in other words, to reduce the magnitude of the error signal). This is exactly what is meant by "negative feedback." If the environment offers no resistance at all to the output, so that o is capable of altering v_e to any desired extent, then the system will come to equilibrium with the feedback signal equal to the reference-signal. If the reference-signal is altered by some (unnamed) agency, the system will automatically respond to the ensuing error-signal by bringing f to the same (new) magnitude as r, thus erasing the error-signal and simultaneously reducing the output of the system to zero. For a system in this kind of environment, it can be shown that under all conditions within the operating range of the various functions, the feedback signal will be caused by the actions of the system to "track" a slowly changing reference-signal. Thus, the reference-signal is the obvious means by which the system can be controlled.

In an environment which resists the output efforts of the system, or which introduces arbitrary disturbances into v_e, the system will still come to equilibrium, but an error-signal of nonzero magnitude will exist at equilibrium; this error-signal (or the discrepancy between f and r) will be just sufficient to maintain the output function at the right level of activity to keep equilibrium. In a reasonably efficient feedback control system, the error will be only a small fraction of the total magnitude of the reference-signal; the feedback signal will still be maintained to a reasonable approximation "at the reference-level." Only when environmental disturbances cause some signal in the system to exceed the level its associated devices can handle would we expect to find any appreciable discrepancy between f and r.

AGGREGATES OF FEEDBACK CONTROL SYSTEMS

Let us consider a collection of functions in an extensive system (which may in some cases prove to be more than one system). As we have already noted, some of these functions will be members of the input boundary, others of the output boundary, imposing relationships between system and environmental variables, in one direction or the other.

Some of the boundary functions will be found to form feedback control-systems (in pairs, one input system and one output system) with perhaps some intermediate function within the total system. All such boundary feedback systems will classify as first-order systems. In the human being, these boundary systems correspond largely to what have been unfortunately labelled as the "spinal reflexes." The spinal reflex systems are fairly efficient control-systems having proprioceptive inputs and motor outputs and receiving reference-signals both in the output function (muscle-bundle) and in a comparator function (ventral horncells). Indeed, these first-order systems almost monopolize the output facilities of the organism. There are input functions, however, which are not part of these control-loops.

Idealizing from this neurological hint, we will restrict our model so that all its output boundary functions belong to first-order control systems, and none are controlled directly and exclusively by "higher" systems. We allow some input functions to generate signals within the system which are not part of first-order control-loops.

In the human systems, it is the rule that many first-order systems affect the same variables in the local environment and thus affect each others' input variables v_e. It will be common, then, that many first-order systems will act as environmental disturbances on the inputs of other first-order systems. These disturbances will be corrected, or at least resisted, by each local system, and chaos will obviously result if reference signals are not properly coordinated.

We can now select out of all the remaining functions in our system those which form second-order control systems to perform this coordination. These control-systems will receive not only the output signals from some of the "unused" first-order input functions, but will also receive as inputs the same variables which serve as feedback signals in the first-order system [in the human system, it is well-known that the proprioception feedback signals in the first-order spinal loops (and peripheral nerves in the cranium) divide, one branch going to more central systems].

Thus, if we wished we could now define a second-order input and output boundary; crossing the input boundary will be all or most of the signals generated by first-order feedback functions, whether involved in the first-order loops or not, and crossing the output boundary will be a set of output signals which enter the first-order systems. These signals cannot be considered as adding to the outputs of the first-order systems, because feedback systems tend to go into violent conflict if their outputs are tied together, thus inactivating those systems (the theory of conflict will be discussed later). The only feasible control-point is the reference-signals of the lower-order systems; therefore, in our model we identify (for the time being) the output signals of second-order systems with the reference-signals of first-order systems. To put it graphically, the output of a second order system is not a muscular force, but a goal toward which first-order systems automatically adjust their input signals (proprioceptive sensations). Thus, the second-order system acts, so to speak, by specifying for the first-order system the kind of sensation it is to seek; the first-order system adjusts its output until its input signals match as closely as possible, in the given environment, the "example" given by the reference-signal, thus (quite incidentally) producing environmental effects which an external observer could see.

This viewpoint is extremely important to understand: in all the feedback systems we will discuss, it is of no concern at all to the feedback system what actual effects are produced in the environment. The system reacts only to the signals injected into it by its feedback function, and for any one system nothing else exists. Even when we speak of systems which deal in human interrelationships, these complex systems not only do not "care" about what is actually going on in the "real" environment, they cannot even know what is going on "out there." They perform the sole function of bringing their feedback signals, the only reality they can perceive, to some reference-level, the only goal they know. If we were discussing servomechanisms, such anthropomorphisms would be unnecessary, but when we are talking of the very systems in which we live, now and always, which we must employ even to think, anthropomorphism is an essential ingredient of understanding.

It is evident now that we could go on defining successively higher orders of control until we had exhausted our collection of functions. We would then find all the sub-systems, each a feedback control system, arranged in a hierarchy (or many overlapping hierarchies) in which a system of any one order perceives an environment made up of the feedback signals of the systems in the next lower order, and which acts to change that environment by producing output signals which are the reference-signals of the same lower-order systems. This structure is exactly the basic organization of our model. A model of this type could be constructed (ignoring practical difficulties) which would reproduce any kind of human behavior that did not involve changing the form of any functions or adding new systems to the structure: the model thus far is intended as a model of those human systems which produce learned behavior, after learning has taken place. This model, being built entirely of feedback control systems, is inherently capable of maintaining dynamic equilibrium (error-signals small, but not necessarily a physically static system) in the presence of a wide variety of environments, both familiar and strange. It is "adaptive" to the extent that it can cope with a large variety of new environmental configurations, but it cannot do a thing about an environment which changes its properties (summed up as the E-function in Fig. 1). We still lack something to account for non-rote learning, for that requires altering the structure of the system, not merely its information content.

THE NEGENTROPY SYSTEM

We borrow the term "negentropy" from information theorists to refer to the process of decreasing entropy in a local system (at the expense, of course, of increasing entropy elsewhere), which process has been identified by some with an increase of organization within a system. We conceive of the central nervous system as being a collection of neurones forming a complex and largely random network, which can have its effective structure altered by activating and inactivating connections within the net to produce networks with semi-permanent and well-defined functions, which to human beings would appear less random.

The processes which alter the connections within the basic bed of "uncommitted neurones" (McCulloch's term) to form the various orders of feedback control must themselves represent the working of a system which is not the result of learning, but which is present and active from birth or before. This system may be physically indistinguishable from the resulting learned systems (perhaps it is implicit in the "random" connections in the "unorganized" neurones), but it is functionally quite different. Its output must be complicated and must extend throughout the CNS, because systems which have been learned are apparently subject to further modifications or additions. Rather than attempt to postulate what the nature of this output must be, we will define it simply in terms of what it must do.

The output of the N-system, we hypothesize, results in the following kinds of events. (1) Uncommitted neurones in physically suitable regions become tentatively organized to process a number of feedback signals from the highest existing order of control (which in the beginning may be first order). (2) Other uncommitted neurones likewise undergo tentative organizations which generate signals serving as reference-signals for the next lower order of system. (3) These tentative organizations of input and output can occur at a variable rate. (4) When a particular organization has occurred often enough within a collection of uncommitted neurones, the organization tends to persist, and the input and output functions of a new order of control system have been formed (as Hebb and others have suggested).

Thus, we have identified the output variable of the N-system as "the processes which alter organization in uncommitted neurones" (as well as in existing systems). The magnitude of this variable we postulate to be measured by the rate at which new organizations are formed one after the other.

The changing organizations occurring in potential output functions will result in a continuous alteration of the reference-signals in the momentary highest-order systems; this results in observable trial-and-error behavior, which shows some organization owing to the existing hierarchy. The continuing reorganization occurring in the new input function does not have such externally-observable results, but is subjectively recognized as a kind of trial-and-error effort to perceive new patterns, a common experience in a learning situation which includes what we experience as tentative formulation of hypotheses. The "hypotheses" here should be thought of as tentative definitions of new variables, which may or may not prove to repeat themselves in experience, depending on the organization of lower-order perceptual functions and the properties and nature of the environment.

The input variables which affect the input boundary of the N-system we call "intrinsic"; we suppose these to be a set of sensory signals which are measures of a set of physiological states, including but not necessarily limited to the ones commonly associated with the "drives." When these variables are each at some certain critical level, the organism is operating optimally, as far as the N-system is concerned. There may be many effects, such as those due to radiation damage, which are deleterious to the organism, but which are not directly represented by intrinsic signals.

The N-system we assume to be a feedback control system which is organized to maintain the intrinsic signals at particular reference-levels. These reference-levels may be set by neural signals (as, perhaps, for sex or hunger signals) or they may be determined by the physical properties of the N-system functions. In either case, the reference-"signals" must be genetically determined, not determined by experience, for the N-system must be a complete control system (which implies reference-signals in existence) before any learned system can be developed. When all intrinsic reference-levels are satisfied by their respective signals, we say the organism is in its intrinsic state.

The overall operation of the N-system is thus very easy to describe (see Figure 2). If some event occurs which makes one or more of the

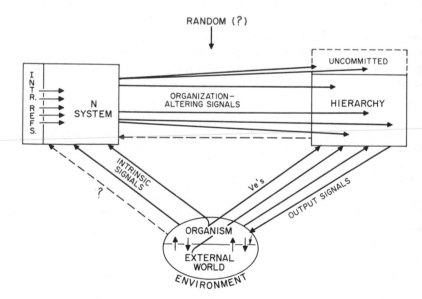

Figure 2.   Overall organization in model.

intrinsic signals depart from its reference-level, the N-system produces an output signal proportional (as a first approximation) to the error. Since the output signal has been defined as a rate of reorganization of neural networks, the net result is to establish a certain rate of attempting to learn.

We would say "rate of learning" except that whether or not anything can be learned by reorganization depends to an important degree on the nature of the environment. If the reader will keep in mind this hedge, we will after all use the more convenient expression "rate of learning."

Simply put, the rate of learning is approximately proportional to the intrinsic error signal, and this is a fundamental property of the human organism.

A particular organization will become a stable learned feedback system not because there is anything that "tells" the system to stop reorganizing, but because the lower-order systems and the environment are such that this particular organization produces behavior which results in a lessening of the intrinsic error, thus slowing or halting the reorganization process. If the same organization proves to have an intrinsic-error-reducing effect several times, then reorganization will stop with the new higher-order system in approximately the same form several times, and we suppose that this will cause the organization to tend to persist, or even to become a semi-permanent part of the hierarchy of learned systems. This kind of learning has many evolutionary advantages; for one, a new system will not be fixed for every chance arrangement of the environment, but only for situations which tend to repeat. Another advantage is that while reorganization will stop with the new system in approximately the same form as before, there will tend to be differences in detail, so that the "noise level" is reduced, much as one eliminates irrelevant variations from planetary photographs by superimposing many negatives to form a composite print.

MODIFICATIONS OF THE BASIC FEEDBACK UNIT

Our model so far has many properties like those of human beings, but we are lacking several important ingredients (at least!). The model has no memory for past experiences, it cannot use past information in present actions, and it is incapable of imagining (which we defined as the ability to perceive sensory events generated internally rather than generated by present-time interactions at the input boundary of the whole system). As we consider them, memory and imagination are fundamentally related.

To see how we propose to introduce the function of memory, refer to Figure 3. A new block has been added labelled "R," which stands for the recording function. We assume that there is a recording function associated with every individual feedback subsystem (associated functionally, not necessarily in space).

This recording function has an input which is the same feedback signal used in the local feedback loop and sent to higher-order systems. The

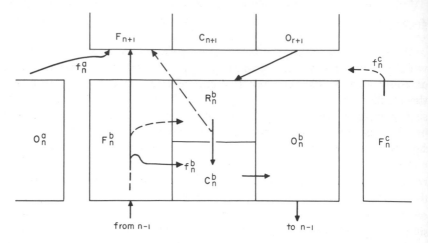

Figure 3.   Relationships among orders.

function R receives this signal and by some means neither we nor anyone else understands, records the information carried by it. The result is a set of recordings which may be permanent or which might have some finite half-life. (There is no present way to tell whether forgetting is due to fading of the recordings or to failure of the recovery apparatus.)

The recording function has the further property that when it is selectively stimulated by a signal external to the local system, it will produce a signal which is a facsimile of the signal that was recorded. This reproduced signal carries the same information, or some significant portion of it, that the original feedback signal carried. To all intents, it is a sensory signal, but one arising from a past event rather than a present one. Current experiments in brain stimulation tend strongly to support this view of memory.

It will be noticed that the signal from a higher-order system in Figure 3 no longer serves directly as the reference-signal for the pictured system. Rather, the higher-order output signal stimulates a memory-trace in R, which in turn produces a signal that is used as a reference-signal in the associated subsystem. Thus, the reference-signals which control a given feedback unit are examples of its own past sensory signals, and one could now express the task of the control system as being that of reproducing in present-time experience some previously-experienced perceptual field, or portion thereof. To some degree new perceptual fields could be demanded and brought about by stimulation of combinations of memory-traces. Rote learning could occur in the form of new recordings and hence an enlarged repertoire of reference-signals.

SUMMARY

What has been presented so far is a model, a collection of functions which handle signals, arranged into a hierarchical structure and composed of elementary feedback control-systems of the external-loop type. For the feedback systems of any one order of control, the environment consists of a set of feedback signals, the same ones used in the control-loops of the next lower order; this environment is controlled by means of signals sent into the lower-order recording functions.

This set of systems is controlled by signals from higher orders or from random reorganizations of potential higher-order output functions in the bed of uncommitted neurones; such control signals stimulate the recording functions in the controlled system so as to give rise to reference signals, reproductions of past feedback signals produced by the local feedback functions.

The rate at which reorganizations take place in this hierarchy is proportional to the degree of intrinsic error existing in the N-system, which is a feedback control-system of the external-loop type concerned with maintaining a set of intrinsic variables at their genetically-determined reference-levels; the function of the N-system is to maintain the organism in its intrinsic state, or as near to it as possible. The output action of the N-system is conceived of as essentially random.

While we have made occasional reference to psychological or neurological properties of human beings as a means of making certain points more acceptable, this portion of the paper has been primarily concerned with presenting the structure of our model, not its application to understanding human behavior.

The operation of this model can be summed up perhaps more clearly in plain language. A system at a given order has goals given to it by higher-order systems. These goals are in the form of perceptual images of past experiences or combinations of past experiences. The system acts to make its present perceptual field match the goal-field as nearly as possible. It does not act directly on the external world, but on the only environment with which it is in immediate contact, the set of next-lower-order systems. Its action is that of selecting and stimulating goals for lower-order systems; it is capable of perceiving the signals (either feedback or reference) resulting from its selection, so a set of lower-order signals can be specified which, if achieved, would be interpreted by the system's own feedback function as the required magnitude of perceptual variable.

Only first-order systems act directly on the (non-CNS) environment.

Some Effects of Feedback
on Communication
HAROLD J. LEAVITT
and RONALD A. H. MUELLER

INTRODUCTION

The experiments reported here are concerned with the transmission of information from person A to person or persons B. Our problem deals with only one of the many relevant variables, the variable of feedback. The question becomes: how is the transmission of information from A to B influenced by the return of information from B to A? It is apparently taken for granted in industry, in the lecture hall, and in radio that it is both possible and efficient to transmit information from A to B without simultaneous feedback from B to A. On the other hand, the information theories of the cyberneticists and, to some extent, trial and error concepts in learning theory suggest that for A to hit successfully some target, B, requires that A be constantly informed of A's own progress. The servo-mechanism needs a sensory system that is capable of transmitting cues about the errors of its own motor system. The human being learning some motor skill apparently utilizes the same process. But when the human being (A) seeks to transmit information to another human being (B), A's own sensory system is hardly an adequate source of information *unless* B takes some action which will help A to keep informed of A's own progress. If A were trying to hit B with a brick, A's eyes combined with an inactive B would probably be adequate to permit A to hit his target after several trials. But if A seeks to hit B with information, he will probably be more successful if B helps to provide some cues which A's own sensory system cannot pick up directly. In other words, where communication between A and B is the goal, feedback, in the form of verbal or expressive language, should make for greater effectiveness.

If we take the human memory mechanism into account, we need not require that there be *contemporaneous* feedback between A and B. It may not even be necessary that there be any feedback from B_2 if feedback

Reprinted with permission of Tavistock Publications and the authors. From *Human Relations*, 4:401–410 (1951).

from a similar B_1 has already occurred. The practice sessions of the past may have provided enough feedback to permit one to hit his present target accurately. Language, for example, may be thought of as a tool originally learned with feedback, but currently useful in a multitude of situations without simultaneous feedback to help us at least to get within range of our targets. But if the material to be communicated is relatively new and relatively precise, previously learned language may not be enough. Accurate transmission may require some additional contemporaneous feedback.

In addition to this hypothesis that contemporaneous feedback should increase the accuracy of transmission of information from A to B, is the hypothesis that the completion of the AB circuit produces other effects on the AB relationship. Feedback from both A and B can increase the certainty of B that he is getting the intended information, and the certainty of A that he is getting it across. This increase in certainty, assuming motivated participants, should have some effect on feelings of frustration or achievement and, hence, on the feelings of hostility or security that pervade the relationship.

Our purpose, then, in these experiments is to try to test these hypotheses; to try to determine experimentally the effects of feedback (or the absence of feedback) on certain kinds of A to B communications.

EXPERIMENT I

What Are the Effects of Progressive Levels of Feedback?

We chose as our material-to-be-communicated in these experiments a series of geometric patterns. The patterns were all composed of six equal rectangular elements, but the relationships of the elements to one another differed from pattern to pattern (see Figure 1 (A) for sample pattern).

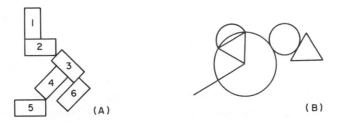

Figure 1. Sample problems. (A) Sample of problems used in Experiment I. (B) Sample of problems used in Experiment II.

A's (the instructor's) job was to describe orally one of these abstract patterns to the members of his class as accurately as possible, accuracy to be measured from the students' reproductions of the described (but unseen) patterns.

Two instructors were used, and four groups of students (total student N = 80), with each instructor describing four patterns to each student group. There were four conditions of feedback: 1. *Zero feedback* in which instructors sat behind a movable blackboard to describe the patterns. No questions or noises were permitted from the students. 2. The *visible audience* condition in which students and instructor could see one another but no speaking by students was allowed. 3. A *yes-no* condition in which the visible audience was permitted to say only yes or no in response to questions from the instructor. And 4. a *free feedback* situation in which students were permitted to ask questions, interrupt, etc.

With the use of a kind of Latin Square arrangement it was possible then to have each instructor use each condition of feedback in a different order. (See Table 1.)

Table 1

Design of Experiment 1

Pattern No.	1	2	3	4		5	6	7	8
Class 1:	zero	V–A	Y–N	free		zero	V–A	Y–N	free
		(Instructor X)					(Instructor Y)		
Class 2:	V–A	Y–N	free	zero		V–A	Y–N	free	zero
		(Instructor Y)					(Instructor X)		
Class 3:	Y–N	free	zero	V–A		Y–N	free	zero	V–A
		(Instructor X)					(Instructor Y)		
Class 4:	free	zero	V–A	Y–N		free	zero	V–A	Y–N
		(Instructor Y)					(Instructor X)		

Besides reproducing the test patterns, students were asked to estimate their confidence in the correctness of their answers and, after the last pattern, to indicate the feedback condition they found most comfortable. We also timed the description of each pattern.

All students were given the same instructions at the beginning of the class period. They were told that the experiment was a test of their ability to understand instructions, and that they were to work as rapidly and as accurately as possible. Both instructors had had some previous experience in describing similar patterns, and both had participated in the construction of the test patterns.

Students' papers were scored for accuracy on a scale from 0 to 6. A particular rectangular element was scored correct if it bore the correct relationship to the preceding element. The first element was scored correct if it was correctly oriented on the page.

Results:

1. ACCURACY. The mean accuracy score for *all* patterns increased steadily from *zero* to *free feedback*. With *zero feedback* the mean was 4·7 out of a possible 6. The range of means for the eight different patterns given under this condition was 3·1 to 5·9. Under the *visible audience* condition the mean score was 5·3 with a range from 4·5 to 5·9. Under the *yes-no* condition the mean score was 5·5, the range 5·0 to 5·8. With *free feedback* the mean was 5·6 and the range 5·1 to 6·0.

2. CONFIDENCE LEVEL. Students' estimates of their own accuracy correlated closely with actual accuracy. For all patterns the mean confidence levels were: *zero feedback*, 4·6; *visible audience*, 5·3; *yes-no*, 5·6; *free feedback*, 5·5. No effects of experience could be detected. There was a tendency to favor one instructor for the *free feedback* situation and the other for all others. These differences were slight and may indicate a differential skill on the part of the instructors in handling the different feedback conditions.

3. TIME. The mean time required to give instructions under the four conditions were: *zero feedback*, 229 seconds; *visible audience*, 249 seconds; *yes-no*, 316 seconds; *free feedback*, 363 seconds. Any decrease in time with experience is once again obscured by differences in difficulty. No clear-cut differences between instructors were apparent.

4. OTHER OBSERVATIONS. Both instructors noticed some rather interesting behavior under certain conditions. When using *free feedback*, both found that on some occasions the students utilized their opportunities to speak by speaking aggressively and with hostility. There were comments like: "That's impossible"; "Are you purposely trying to foul us up?"; "You said left, it has to be right"; and so on. These comments even flowed on to students' papers, when they wrote beside their patterns such comments as: "The teacher made mistakes on this one, I didn't." These hostile reactions seemed to occur only when the *free feedback* condition *followed* other conditions. Both instructors noticed too that their *free feedback* experience stood them in good stead in the *zero feedback* situations. A student in the *free feedback* situation might say, "Oh, it looks like an L." In the next use of that pattern the instructors would find themselves saying, "It looks like an L."

Commentary

Although these data indicate that *free feedback* does yield more accurate results than the other conditions, some new questions arise. Can it not be argued that the *free feedback* method is more effective simply because it requires more time? Would the time required decrease if *free feedback* were used continuously? Does the *free feedback* method always put the teacher on the spot? Will he be attacked for his errors or lack of knowledge? Though free feedback may be helpful at first, is it of any use after the student and the teacher have had an opportunity to straighten out their language difficulties? Can the teacher improve just as much after a series of experiences without feedback as after a series with feedback? Can we show continuous improvement in the course of several trials without feedback?

EXPERIMENT II

Feedback versus No Feedback

In an attempt to answer some of these questions we designed another series of experiments that seemed to permit the most efficient use of our limited supply of instructors and students. The purpose of these experiments was to compare the two extreme conditions, *free feedback* and *zero feedback*, over a longer series of trials.

Method

Using eight new geometric patterns, all made up of six elements (see Figure 1 (B), we selected ten instructors and ten separate groups of students, the groups ranging in size from six to twenty-four. Five of the instructors were members of the English Department at the Institute, one taught German, one economics, and three psychology. Four of the classes were speech classes, six were general psychology. For *three* pairs of instructors the procedure was as follows:

Instructor *A* faced class *A* with four patterns in sequence and *zero feedback*. Then instructor *B* faced class *A* with four new patterns in sequence and *free feedback*. Instructor *A* then faced class *B* with his original four patterns and *free feedback*. Then instructor *B* faced class *B* with his original four patterns and *zero feedback*. For the other two pairs of instructors the procedure was reversed, instructor *A* beginning with free feedback.

We again asked for confidence levels, from both the students and instructors.

Results:

1. OVERALL. The results of this experiment bear out the trend of the first. The mean student accuracy score for all *zero feedback* trials was 5·2 of a possible 6; the mean with *feedback* was 5·9. These means represent the students of ten instructors. The ranges for individual instructors were, with *zero feedback*, 3·8 to 5·8; with *free feedback*, 5·6 to 6·0. This difference between these means is significant at the 1 percent level.

In students' confidence in their results, the data again correlate closely with accuracy. The mean for *zero feedback* is 5·0 with a range from 3·5 to 5·7, while for *free feedback* the mean is 5·8 and the range 5·4 to 6·0. These differences are also significant.

In terms of time required to describe each pattern, *free feedback* remains a more time-consuming process. The average time for *zero feedback* is 166 seconds with a range from 60 to 273. For *free feedback* the average time is 284 seconds with a range of 193 to 423. These differences too are significant.

Finally in our measure of teacher confidence, means were 4·5 with *zero feedback* and 5·0 with *free feedback*, with respective ranges of 2·5 to 5·5 and 4·5 to 5·8. In all cases instructors were *less* confident than their students.

In every case individual instructors changed in the same direction as the means. Every instructor got better results with feedback than without, and every instructor took longer with feedback than without.

2. EFFECTS OF EXPERIENCE. In Figure 2 are shown curves representing the changes in accuracy from pattern to pattern. Each instructor, you will recall, described four patterns in sequence under conditions of *zero feedback* and then *free feedback*.

From these accuracy curves one can see that *free feedback* starts at almost the maximum level and stays there. *Zero feedback* changes in the direction of greater accuracy from trial to trial.

As far as time (Figure 3) is concerned, the reverse is true. *Zero feedback* remains more or less constant, while *free feedback* time *declines progressively*.

There is at least one other way of analyzing the data that provides some rather interesting results. Our experimental design supplied us with data for all combinations of (a) inexperienced (with these patterns) and experienced instructors, and (b) inexperienced and experienced classes, working (c) with and without feedback. The data broken down this way

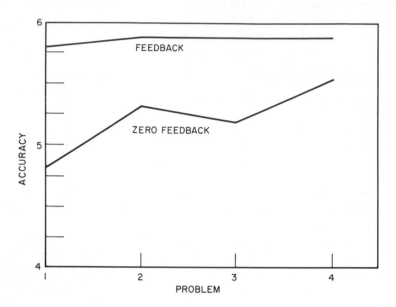

Figure 2.   Accuracy—each point represents the mean of 10 groups.

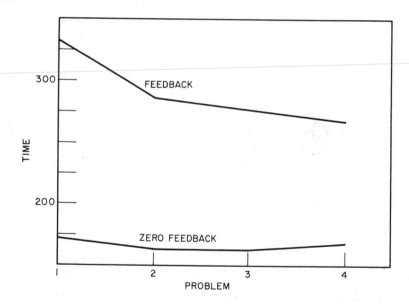

Figure 3.   Time—each point represents the mean of 10 groups.

indicate that instructors' experience is the most significant factor present. Differences between experienced and inexperienced instructors are always greater than between experienced and inexperienced classes. This difference holds for *zero feedback* only, since with *free feedback* there are no perceptible differences among any of the different conditions.

3. OTHER OBSERVATIONS. One of our hypotheses in these experiments centered on the effects of feedback on the relationship between sender and receiver. We have no quantitative data that are relevant to this hypothesis, but we do have some observations that were astonishing in their consistency. These observations amounted to this. When an instructor faced a new class with *free feedback*, he got fairly rational feedback. That is, the students asked questions or asked for elaboration or repetition of a point. But when an instructor faced a class that had just been exposed to a *zero feedback* session, the instructor got an attack. The students asked lots of questions, but with barbs and implications about the instructor's (in)ability to do his job. The new instructor had innocently opened Pandora's box. This hostility did not last through more than one or two patterns, nor did it prevent the majority of students from expressing a preference for the *free feedback* method.

Commentary

In a sense these experiments demonstrate the obvious. When a receiver *B* is free to ask questions he can get a better understanding of what the sender *A* is trying to communicate. Moreover, with *free feedback* both the sender and the receiver can feel, correctly, more confident that they have respectively sent and received accurately. *Free feedback* requires more time, but there is some evidence that this time differential decreases with increased understanding between the sender and the receiver. Apparently the use of continuing *free feedback* could lead directly back into *zero feedback*, for once the common areas of misunderstanding have been clarified, contemporaneous feedback will no longer be necessary.

Apparently it is possible to improve communication skill with minimal feedback. The fourth *zero feedback* pattern is almost always more accurately sent than the first. This improvement can perhaps be thought of as a kind of personal feedback in which the instructor's own words are utilized to help him to increase his own effectiveness in the future. Much of it is no doubt empathetic, the instructor imagining himself in the receiver's place and correcting his sending as a consequence. Some of the improvement, however, may come from feedback which our experimental barriers failed to block out; feedback in the form of noises, sighs, shuffling of chairs. We do not know from these experiments whether or not an instructor using *zero feedback* could eventually reach the *free feedback* level of accuracy and confidence, but it is clear that under our experimental conditions he can improve over his own original *zero feedback* level.

Besides the findings about the direct effects of feedback, the data raise some questions about indirect effects. We observed in both experiments that *free feedback* after *zero feedback* is accompanied by hostility. This hostility was apparently an effect of the *zero feedback* experience. It lasts only through one or two *free feedback* trials. Why should this be so? We believe that the mechanism centers around the notion of "certainty." In our attempts to satisfy our needs we must be as certain as possible that we are successful. Uncertainty is frustrating. Without feedback uncertainty is prevalent.

In the same vein we noted that instructors' confidence is lower than students' confidence. We suggest that the instructor can be satisfied only by knowing that the receiver is getting the proper information. But the receiver can be satisfied by comparing his own work with the sender's directions. The receiver then has more information available against which to check his own progress toward his goal. Hence he can be more certain of his progress. But the sender is not sure of what the receiver is receiving. He can get *some* information with feedback, but almost none but his own empathy without feedback. Hence his certainty and confidence are low. These differential feelings of certainty, adequacy, and hostility seem to us to be the most significant differentials between our *free feedback* and *zero feedback* systems.

SUMMARY AND CONCLUSIONS

Since the scope of this research has been limited by the utilization of one kind of problem, one kind of sender-receiver situation, and a relatively short series of experiences, our conclusions must be severely circumscribed.

To summarize, we found that, within narrow limits: 1. A completion of the circuit between sender and receiver (feedback) increases the accuracy with which information is transmitted. 2. Feedback also increases receiver and sender confidence in what they have accomplished. 3. The cost of feedback is time. But the difference in time between *free feedback* and *zero feedback* appears to decrease. 4. A sender and a receiver can improve without what we have defined as feedback experience. 5. *Free feedback* experience improves subsequent *zero feedback* trials measurably. 6. Sender experience contributes more than receiver experience to improved accuracy of communication. 7. *Zero feedback* engenders some hostility in the receiver that becomes clearly perceptible when the situation *changes* from *zero* to *free feedback*. This hostility is short-lived, lasting through only one or two *free feedback* trials. 8. *Zero feedback* engenders doubt in the sender.

These findings support the hypothesis that *free feedback* is an aid to accuracy in interpersonal communication. *Free feedback* seems to permit the participants to learn a mutual language, which language once learned may obviate the necessity for further feedback.

The findings also support the hypothesis that the presence or absence of feedback affects the sender-receiver relationship. *Zero feedback* is accompanied by low confidence and hostility; *free feedback* is accompanied by high confidence and amity.

34 | The Effects of Different Social Feedback Conditions upon Performance in Dyadic Teams

SEYMOUR ROSENBERG and ROBERT L. HALL

In the present study, one of three types of feedback stimuli was presented to a group member following a response. They are: (a) information based upon the error magnitude of the subject's own response only, termed "direct" values. This type of feedback stimulus is typically used in individual learning studies to differentiate a particular range of response magnitudes; (b) information that combines in a simple additive function the error magnitudes of both the subject's own response and that of his teammate, termed "confounded" values; (c) information based upon the error magnitude of a teammate's response only, termed "other's" values. These three feedback conditions may be viewed as comprising two extremes and an intermediate point of a continuum, which specifies the fractional weight given to a subject's response relative to the fractional weight given to his teammate's response in the feedback stimulus to the *subject*. The feedback value to the subject is "direct" when his response weight in the feedback is 1.0 and his teammate's response weight is 0.0 (one extreme of the continuum). The subject's feedback value is "other's" when his own response weight in his feedback is 0.0 and his teammate's is 1.00 (other

Reprinted with permission of the American Psychological Association and the authors. From *Journal of Abnormal and Social Psychology*, 57:271–277 (1958).

extreme of the continuum). The subject's feedback value is "confounded" when his feedback values contain nonzero weighing of both his own and his teammate's response. The present paper will describe the effects of these feedback conditions upon individual and team measures, and upon changes in these measures over a series of discrete trials.

The stimulus event following a response has been variously termed: feedback, knowledge of performance, knowledge of results, reinforcement, terminating stimulus, etc. There is little disagreement about the importance of such general parameters of this stimulus event as its frequency and periodicity, coarseness of measurement, delay, manner of presentation, type and amount of informational error, number of trials, etc. However, these parameters have been studied almost exclusively in experiments using individual subjects. Since there has been very little systematic attempt either to determine the values of such parameters particularly relevant to interpersonal settings, or to formulate variables unique to these settings, the research to date is incomplete or, at best, difficult to apply to interpersonal settings. The application or extension of parameters to interpersonal contexts presents a number of interesting and novel problems. For example, when a stimulus event following a response by Person A is some joint function of his behavior and that of a Person B, it is difficult to specify in quantified terms the stimulation of A from knowledge obtained in individual research and, further, to specify changes in stimulus parameters that occur over time. In attempting to apply current knowledge to interpersonal settings, the investigator may also encounter the need to formulate novel variables. For example, one class of variables unique to interpersonal settings is variations in the mathematical function that expresses the way the responses of Persons A and B are combined to produce a stimulus event to one or both persons. Distributional variables of any sort, i.e., combinations of treatments of group members, are also novel. Neither in social psychology nor in learning psychology has there been any systematic experimental analysis of social and learning variables simultaneously. This study is one of the early experiments in such a program.

METHOD

SUBJECTS. The subjects (Ss) were 54 male Air Force basic trainees whose modal age was about 17 years. They were assigned as a unit for use as Ss in psychological research. Ss from such units were excluded from the experiment if their Armed Forces Qualification Test (AFQT) score was below the 65th percentile rank, which is roughly equivalent to a Stanford Binet IQ of 108. Ss were used in pairs, randomly assembled.

APPARATUS. The two Ss were seated in identical adjacent booths. The walls of the booth were sufficiently high so that Ss could not see each other. One wall of each booth consisted of the panel and table. Each S faced a separate panel. A micrometer was mounted behind the shield so that the knob at the beginning of each trial projected ¼ inch from the face of the panel. The S could touch only the knob portion of the micrometer. He could turn the knob by reaching under the shield, but he received no visual cues nor special tactual cues from the knob to indicate the amount it was turned. The knob could only be turned to the left. The experimenter (E), seated on the other side of the panel, could read the micrometer scale, which is a linear measure of the amount the knob is turned. Also, on the panel in front of each S, there was a linear scale extending from zero in the center to 80 in each direction, indicating "size of error." A movable pointer above the scale displayed a score to the S after each trial. The scale was concealed by a hinged shield during the Ss' response period and the feedback delay period. The scale also contained "off the scale" marks at each end. At the center of the scale an interval of 10 units was marked off by two red lines and was labeled "try to get pointer within red lines for good score." No cues were present on the scale to indicate whether error scores to the left of zero on the scale indicated too large or too small a response magnitude. For counterbalancing, excessive response magnitudes were shown to the left of zero for half of the Ss and to the right of zero for the other half of the Ss.

PROCEDURE. Each pair of Ss was given the same instructions, followed by 50 response-feedback trials. Each member of a pair was independently assigned to one of the three feedback conditions for all 50 trials. To satisfy a convenient analysis of variance design to be described later, certain restrictions were imposed upon the numbers of Ss assigned to each condition.

After the two Ss were seated in adjacent booths, a few minutes were spent by the E "setting them at ease." The identical panels, one for each S, were then put in place. The following tape-recorded instructions were played:

The Air Force needs to know more about how well people can do certain tasks. The experiment in which you are to take part is a study of just one such task. It is a simple task of turning a knob the right amount. Listen carefully to these instructions and the experimenter will point out things as they are mentioned. For this experiment a panel will be placed beside each of you. On the front of the panel you see a shield and underneath the shield, where you cannot see it, is a small knob. Do not look under the shield. You are expected to work without seeing the knob. Your job is to learn to turn your knob just the right amount. You will have a number of chances to do this. To help you, you will be shown, after each trial, the error in the score that you made. Your error score will be shown you on the scoreboard at the top of your panel. The movable pointer, which is moving now, tells you how much you missed. To make a *good* score, try each time to get the pointer within the two red lines. Always turn your knob to the left as shown by the small sign tacked on your panel. A buzzer will be used to tell you when to start and stop. The buzzer sounds like this. [Buzzer is sounded.] When the buzzer starts, you start to make your setting. As soon as you have made the setting you think is correct, take your hand away from the knob. When the buzzer stops, you must take your hand away whether you are finished making your setting or not. You will find that you have plenty of time without rushing. A few seconds after the buzzer stops you will be shown on your scoreboard the error in the setting you just made. Shortly after that, you will hear the buzzer again. This means that you are to start again and try once more to make a good score. After each trial your knob is set back by us. Each time the buzzer starts, you start over and try again to make a good score. Now we are ready to start. Do not touch your knob until you hear the buzzer.

It should be noted that the Ss were give no cues that they might be working as a team. They did not talk to each other. To control for inadvertent cues by E to Ss in different treatments, each pair of Ss was assigned to one of the treatments only *after* Ss were seated in the closed booths and instructed.

The procedure for one complete trial consisted of three automatically timed phases: (*a*) a response period of eight seconds, indicated to the Ss by a mild buzzer, during which the knob could be turned; (*b*) a delay of eight seconds during which E recorded response magnitude and moved the scale pointer (still concealed from each S) to its appropriate value for that trial; (*c*) exposure of the pointer position to the S by lifting the hinged shield. During this interval the micrometer was reset by E to its original position. The shield was lowered after 5–10 seconds and the response interval for a new trial was started.

Response magnitude for each S during each trial was read by the E directly from the micrometer scale. Twenty-five scale units equals one complete knob rotation. Where an S was receiving "direct" feedback (his response magnitude only), a perfect score (goal score) was 100 micrometer units (four knob turns). Where an S was receiving "confounded" feedback (the combination of his own and his teammate's response magnitude), a score to the S was computed by averaging the response magnitudes of the two persons. An average of 100 units was a perfect score. An S receiving "other's" feedback (his teammate's response magnitude) received a perfect score when his teammate made four knob turns or 100 micrometer units.

MEASUREMENT AND STATISTICAL DESIGN. Three measures were computed for each trial and transformed to logarithms to reduce skewness: (*a*) "individual accuracy," $A_t = \log(|X - 100| + 1)$, where X is response magnitude, in micrometer units of one S; (b) "team accuracy," $A_t = \log (|X + Y - 200| + 1)$, where X and Y are response magnitudes of the two Ss in micrometer units; (c) "response (role) differentiation," $D_t = \log (|X - Y| + 1)$.

Each of the three measures was subjected to a similar analysis of variance. The design consists of three rows corresponding to the three feedback conditions to which one S could be assigned and three columns corresponding to the same three feedback conditions to which his teammate could be assigned. Thus, there are nine row-column cells. Three pairs of Ss were assigned to each of these nine cells (combinations of feedback conditions). Fifty trials constitutes a third criterion of classification in the analysis.

For the A_i measure, one member of each dyad was randomly selected. Data from the second member were not analyzed. Thus, the same team is never represented twice in the analysis of A_i. Two analyses of variance of A_i were also avoided because of the complex experimental dependency between the two Ss in most of the combinations of feedback conditions. The rows represent the feedback condition of the member whose A_i is contained in the cell. The columns represent the condition of his partner.

When either team measure (A_t or D_t) is used in this statistical design, row and column classifications bear the same relationship to the dependent variable, i.e., represent the feedback condition for one of the team members. Put in another way, the row variable is exactly the same as the column variable. In such a design, combinations of experimental conditions on one side of one of the diagonals are also found on the other side of that diagonal. Data must be arbitrarily distributed between cell-pairs whose conditions are the same.

Two orthogonal polynomial components were extracted from interaction effects containing trials. The components were the "linear" and "quadratic" and were used to test the presence of differential rates of development of a measure with trials. These components supplement the test for over-all trials effects since the latter is too general a test of trend and fails to distinguish simple trend types.

RESULTS

Analyses of variance of the three measures are summarized in Table 1. Note that row and column effects are pooled in the analysis of A_t and D_t since the effects tested are the same. For A_i, the effects refer to two different operations with respect to the dependent variable, i.e., an S's response measure classified by his own feedback conditions (rows) and that of his partner (columns).

Table 1

Summary of the Statistical Analyses of the Three Response Measures

Source	df of Each Analysis	Individual Accuracy $A_i = \log(|X-100|+1)$ Mean Sq.	F	Team Accuracy $A_t = \log(|X-200|+1)$ Mean Sq.	F	Differentiation $D_t = \log(X-Y)+1$ Mean Sq.	F	Error Term for F
1. Teams	26	83009		70602		59782		
A. Rows (Feedback cond.)	2	620276	17.32***	174340 ⎫	5.46**	209026 ⎫	3.46*	1D
B. Columns (Feedback cond.)	2	10784	.30	284080 ⎭		121978 ⎭		1D
C. Rows × Columns	4	63434	1.77	40915	.98	7984	.17	
D. Within Cells	18	35817		41952		47799		
2. Trials	49	2312		4102		3041		
3. Teams × Trials	1274	1405		1559		1559		
A. Rows × Trials	98	2089	1.54**	1242	1.09[a]	1439	.89[a]	3D
a. Linear	2	22418	4.51*	3854	2.38	16513	.92	3Da
b. Quadratic	2	10372	4.19*	4438	1.56	2452	1.09	3Db
c. Residual	94	1480	1.18	1119	.90	1097	.87	3Dc
B. Columns × Trials	98	1025	.75	2120	—[a]	1515	—[a]	3D
a. Linear	2	1274	.26	35148	—[a]	5046	—[a]	3Da
b. Quadratic	2	500	.20	5582	—[a]	6890	—[a]	3Db
c. Residual	94	1031	.82	1343	—[a]	1325	—[a]	3Dc
C. Rows × Columns × Trials	196	1463	1.08	1486	.96	1448	.87	3D
a. Linear	2	6751	1.36	7806	.95	9863	.84	3Da
b. Quadratic	2	10263	4.15*	2706	.84	6140	1.43	3Db
c. Residual	94	1163	.92	1326	.97	1169	.84	3Dc
D. Within Cells × Trials	882	1358		1548		1660		
a. Linear	18	4966		8201		11753		
b. Quadratic	18	2473		3212		4280		
c. Residual	846	1258		1371		1389		

[a] For each of the two team measures, A_t and D_t, rows and columns mean squares refer to exactly the same effects. Therefore, these two sources of variance were pooled within each analysis of variance and a single F ratio computed. The same procedure was adapted for the "rows × trials" and "column × trials" variances. Note that the numerator of such Fs has associated with it four df.

*P < .05; **P < .01; ***P < .001.

In the case of A_i, different feedback conditions of the Ss result in significant differences in average level of his accuracy over the 50 trials (row effects), in over-all trend differences (interaction of rows with trials), and in linear and quadratic trend components. Figure 2(A) illustrates these

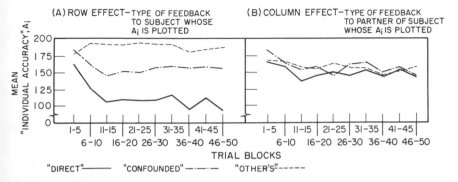

Figure 1. Differences among groups of Ss in their mean A_i as a result of differences in: (A) *their own feedback* conditions; (B) feedback conditions of *their partners.*

differences. Note that on the ordinate, the smaller A_i values are associated with greater accuracy, and that on the abscissa the trials are grouped in sets of five. The graph points up a rather simple positive relationship between individual accuracy and contribution of the S to his own feedback. In striking contrast, different feedback conditions of S's partner (column effects) do not result in any significant differences in Ss' accuracy. This is apparent from Figure 1(B) which illustrates no consistent divergencies among groups. Figures 1(A) and 1(B) would not illustrate the presence of any unique effects produced by particular combinations of an S's condition and that of his partner, if any existed. For example, if the combination of "other's–other's" conditions resulted in an exaggerated degree of inaccuracy for S (over and above that accounted for by the main effects), these graphs would fail to show this effect. However, such an effect would be reflected in "rows × columns" and/or "rows × columns × trials" interactions in the A_i analysis. The results in Table 1 fail to support, with any statistical significance, the presence of such combinatorial effects except in the isolated instances of a quadratic component in Source 3C.

An examination of both team measures, A_t and D_t, reveals a rather consistent picture. For both measures, differences in the feedback conditions yield significant differences on the average of the 50 trials (Sources: Sum of 1A and 1B). Differences in trend, however, are not revealed (Sources: Sum of 3A and 3B) unless one is willing to use a more liberal

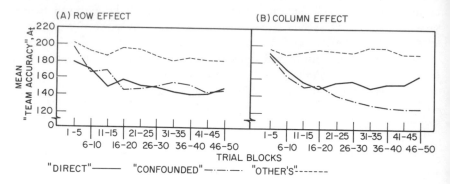

Figure 2. Differences among groups of subject-pairs in their mean A_t as a result of differences in feedback conditions to: (A) one member of the pair; (B) the second member of the pair.

confidence level (or another error term) as a basis for rejecting null hypothesis. In the case of A_t, the F value of 2.38 for linear differences in trend falls between the .05 and .10 levels. Figures 2(A) and 2(B) illustrate the A_t data for rows and columns, respectively, and do suggest the existence of trend differences among conditions. The "replication" between row effects and column effects does not appear to be perfect, but no reversals are apparent. It is interesting to note, in Figure 2(B), that confounded feedback results in somewhat better team accuracy than direct feedback to each S. Figures 3(A) and 3(B) present for rows and columns,

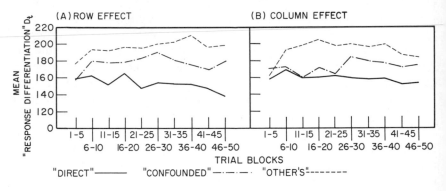

Figure 3. Differences among groups of subject-pairs in their mean D_t as a result of differences in feedback conditions to: (A) one member of the pair; (B) the second member of the pair.

respectively, the D_t measure, the ordinate indicating the mean magnitude of difference between teammates' responses. "Replication" is again somewhat imperfect although no serious contradictions are apparent. Teams containing an S who received as feedback only his teammate's response showed greatest D_t, while teams with an S receiving "direct" feedback-showed the least D_t.

Finally, it is again important to note that Figures 2 and 3 would not illustrate unique effects in A_t and D_t produced by particular combinations of feedback conditions to which pairs of Ss were exposed. However, the analyses of the two team measures in Table 1 fail to support the statistical significance of any such combinational effects since none of the "rows $\times$ columns" or "rows $\times$ columns $\times$ trials" interactions are significant. Team accuracy and response differentiation values (as quantified in this study) are apparently determinable from an additive weighting of each of the two feedback conditions of the Ss.

DISCUSSION

As noted previously, the three feedback conditions in the study can be viewed as points on a continuum. The continuum is describable as the proportion of contribution of an S's own response to his feedback, relative to the contribution of his teammate's response. The continuum may be expressed as the ratio of the weights accorded responses of the two Ss in a simple weighted average; that is, the size of the ratio, k_1/k_2, in the simple function:

$$\text{Feedback} = k_1 X + k_2 Y - G$$

where X and Y are response magnitudes of two Ss, G is goal score, and $k_1 + k_2 = 1$. The three feedback conditions would then be expressed:

a. Feedback $= (1)(X) + (0)(Y) - 100 = X - 100$, for Subject X, or Feedback $= (0)(X) + (1)(Y) - 100 = Y - 100$, for Subject Y, in "direct" feedback.

b. Feedback $= (.5)(X) + (.5)(Y) - 100 = .5X + .5Y - 100$ for both Ss, in "confounded" feedback.

c. Feedback $= (0)(X) + (1)(Y) - 100 = Y - 100$, for Subject X, or Feedback $= (1)(X) + (0)(Y) - 100 = X - 100$, for Subject Y, in "other's" feedback.

The findings concerning A_t (individual accuracy) are rather simply summarized in terms of its relation to the k_1/k_2 ratio. Both average magnitude and rate of development of A_i are related monotonically to the magnitude of k_1/k_2 where k_1 and k_2 are the constants applied to the feedback function of the S. No relationship was found between A_i of an S and the k_1/k_2 ratio of his teammate's feedback function.

The use of this ratio to summarize succinctly the relationships discovered early in this research program imply little about its future utility. A more articulated theory may not use this variable. One could also describe, for example, the feedback conditions along a continuum or continua which express the "quality of the feedback." Quality of feedback may refer to the size *and* consistency of the covariance between feedback values and the response magnitudes of an S (i.e., reliability of feedback as a measure of response magnitude). The correlation coefficient may be used as a measure of this covariance, although more comprehensive measurement techniques are probably required. Quality of feedback may also refer to any constant difference in magnitude between a feedback value and a response value. In other words, quality is reduced by both variable and constant errors in the feedback. It may be noted that "quality of feedback" is oriented toward individual feedback. Such an orientation points up, however, a number of interesting feedback variables that are likely to arise in interpersonal settings. For example, there is some reason to expect that the quality of feedback to an S may change systematically with time. In confounded feedback, the variable error in the feedback with respect to the response probably decreases with time (as each S "learns"), but constant errors stabilize. Individual learning experiments have generally tended to maintain such conditions constant over trials rather than to systematically vary them. An interesting exception occurs where a response is being gradually molded or differentiated. Here the R-S relationship is manipulated as a function of trials (or a joint function of trials and response adequacy).

The two team measures, especially A_t, do not bear the same relationships with the feedback condition as does A_i. Indeed, differential trend effects are difficult to establish at all except through the use of liberal confidence levels. The difference in average value of A_t among the three feedback conditions are highly significant, however, and are worthy of comment because of an apparent difference in result as compared with A_i. Confounded feedback to a team member appears to result in at least as accurate, and possibly more accurate, team performance than direct feedback. This finding, if valid, points up an interesting phenomenon about distribution of feedback to teams where a group product rather than an individual product is the criterion. Since the task is one which permits compensation by one team member for difficult-to-extinguish constant errors of the second, dyads, *on the average*, would yield superior group products. The D_t findings attest to a greater difference in response magnitude between team members in confounded feedback than in direct feedback. This difference persists over trials and is consistent with the above hypothesis but does not obviate other explanations. Indeed, another tenable hypothesis is that the feedback values displayed to an S are much finer (more detailed) than he can discriminate kinesthetically. The inappropriate detail then acts as "noise" in the feedback producing response variability. In the confounded feedback condition, the feedback values (although as detailed as in direct feedback) are less variable from trial to trial than in direct feedback, since the former are based on an average of two response magnitudes. Ss, in turn, may respond with less variability *about the goal score* from trial to trial. Further study of the phenomenon would be necessary both to replicate the differences in the A_t found in the present study and to examine intentionally the hypotheses stated here.

The D_t measure, aside from corroborating the hypothesis above, has special interest for social psychologists. The response distribution in an interpersonal relationship receives considerable attention under such headings as role, role differentiation, role distribution, etc. The D_t measure is a considerable simplification of the usual role differentiation measures, but seems to represent the same type of measurement operation. The simplicity stems from the fact that a single response class (i.e., a single dimension of behavior) is used in this study. The analysis of the D_t measure under different feedback conditions points up a rather novel independent variable for social psychology. Response or role differentiation, D_t, bears the same simple relationship to the k_1/k_2 ratio as does A_i. The trend relationships are not as apparent, however.

The D_t measure also has some interesting implications for team reassemblies or team-member interchangeability. Conditions, whether they be feedback or other, which minimize the D_t value would appear to provide greatest flexibility for team reassemblies since teammates who respond similarly can be reassembled with a minimum of training. Teams requiring differentiation among a number of response classes for effective performance may require other feedback conditions.

SUMMARY

Knowledge of results (feedback) available to an individual working in a team may be a measure of: (*a*) his own response only, (*b*) a combination of his own and a teammate's response, (*c*) a teammate's response only. Each teammate may receive any of these three types of feedback.

The independent variable consisted of these three conditions of feedback in all six combinations. Ss were used in pairs, and each pair was given 50 trials on a simple knob-turning task with one of these combinations of feedback conditions. A total of 27 pairs of Ss was used in the study.

Three response measures were analyzed: (*a*) individual response accuracy, (*b*) team accuracy, (*c*) response (role) differentiation between team members. Analyses revealed significant differences between feedback conditions on each of these measures. Teams containing an S who received as feedback only his teammate's response showed poorest individual and team accuracy and greatest response differentiation. Differences among conditions in trend were consistently significant only for the individual accuracy measure. Learning rate on this measure was best when an S received information about his own response only and poorest when information consisted only of his teammate's response.

CHAPTER IX

Redundancy and Equilibrium

INTRODUCTION   Redundancy, like feed-
back, improves the accuracy with which signals are transmitted. Feedback
is an error correcting mechanism that can overcome noise. Redundancy is
the repetition of a signal that also helps overcome noise. Feedback and
redundancy are, however, more significantly related to one another because they both maintain the stability and equilibrium of a communication system.

If the same signal is simply repeated over and over again, the redundancy is 100 percent. There is no variability or indeterminacy at this
high degree of redundancy. The receiver can predict with confidence
what the next signal will be. This means, as we have seen earlier, that the
signal has no surprise value and carries no new information. There is too
much redundancy for communication. Zero percent redundancy leaves
the receiver with sheer unpredictability: the next signal can be anything. At this low degree of redundancy the receiver cannot tell what is
noise and what is information. The fact is that communication requires
a balance between the predictable and the unpredictable. It requires some
equilibrium and stability. And this is true of human behavior in general.

Benjamin N. Colby's "Behavioral Redundancy" demonstrates how this
balance between order and disorder is a prerequisite for any meaningful
human behavior. He posits "that life in general, like language, seeks an
equilibrium of about 50 percent redundancy . . . Without some sort of
homeostatic or 'pendulum' principle in which deviations from the mid-
point are checked and reversed before getting out of hand in either
direction, life would not be possible." On the basis of his analysis we can
hypothesize, among other things, that some kinds of communication net-

works are more redundant than others, and that some are more stable than others.

The brain is a communicational network not wholly different from human groups in its processes of storing and transmitting information and in maintaining its equilibrium. Some of the principles that W. Ross Ashby presents in "The Application of Cybernetics to Psychiatry" have heuristic value for the analysis of social networks. For example, "when a whole system is composed of a number of subsystems, the one that tends to dominate is the one that is least stable . . . and . . . a whole can rest at some state, be in 'equilibrium,' only when every one of its parts rests at its component of that state."

Like the brain and the small social group, the city is also a communicational system. Karl W. Deutsch writing "On Social Communication and the Metropolis" shows that the city generally features a tremendous number of signals. While there may be a high degree of redundancy in the signals of a small town, the many signals of the metropolis are more likely to interfere with one another, to become noisy, and to need filtering. There is in fact a communicational overload in the metropolis which threatens the equilibrium of the metropolis.

Stability in a communicational system does not require that the system be static and unchanging. Mervyn L. Cadwallader in "The Cybernetic Analysis of Change in Complex Social Organizations" regards large-scale formal organizations like corporations, armies, and churches as communicational networks, and they are fully stable only if any changeless redundancy in their output is corrected by feedback from the environment.

These four selections on redundancy and equilibrium not only conclude the analysis of syntactics but also point to the range of application of the foregoing syntactic analyses as a whole. These applications range from the communicational structures within neurophysiological systems to the communicational structures within large cities.

35 Behavioral Redundancy
BENJAMIN N. COLBY

Equilibriums of various kinds at work in the brain and measurable in electrical units will most likely be among the first stepping stones to more generally defined, scaled equilibrium principles of human behavior. Other contributions in this direction may come when the intricacies of endocrinology and other biological homeostatic tendencies can be linked adequately to outside environmental events in scaled, quantitative terms. Before that time comes general equilibrium theories in the behavioral sciences can rarely be more than heuristic. But this does not deny the value of heuristic hypotheses. This is illustrated in the following description of how an equilibrium theory of redundancy can be useful for studying cultural and personal value systems.

Man dislikes venturing away from the relatively safe order of the known into any sort of new order less understood at the outset. This is an underlying tendency of human behavior long recognized both generally and particularly. Clyde Kluckhohn pointed out the great extent of this tendency when he said, "Most men most of the time, dread both spontaneity and change in most of their activities." Certainly the more regular, understandable, and predictable man's environment becomes, the more he is freed to do those things not strictly concerned with his mere animal existence. It is to his interest to avoid the disruption change may bring. Predictability of tomorrow's events and of what people may do or think is of paramount importance.

But there are other trends in the opposite direction which temper the dread of the unexpected. These are trends toward disorganization, toward the unknown, and toward experimental innovations. They have been discussed under many rubrics—the creative desire at one extreme and the destructive urge at the other. Freud's conception of the instincts, notably the death instincts can be included here.

Reprinted with permission of the Mental Health Research Institute and the author. From *Behavioral Science*, 3:317–322 (1958).

The formative process, the trend in man which moves toward organization usually predominates when this organization gives man power over his environment. But curiously enough the opposing, often irrational force which tends to destroy that organization and break up thought-structures does not run counter to man's ultimate objectives—preservation and comfort. It is vital to them. When man loses control over some part of his environment, he has to seek new methods and organizations to re-adapt himself. Before this is possible the old habits and organizations which now are useless must be eliminated. Here is where the destructive force functions. Without it, man's methods of environmental control would be too rigid, his freedom of choice would be dangerously restricted and the feedback mechanism so necessary to adjustment would be paralyzed. For predictability to be constantly maintained at a high level of efficiency, value systems must be changeable, must always be in process. Man's inner disorganizing force thus is always at work, even to some extent in periods of easy living, when the environment is adequately controlled. By maintaining some sort of equilibrium between order and disorder or rigidity and fluidity he can stay at peak adjustment.

In addition to the functional working of these basic tendencies there appears to be a complementary balancing mechanism which responds in a reverse manner to environmental circumstances. Simply stated, in times of easy, predictable living man may seek out the unexpected as a relief from boredom; while in times of chaos man may flee from it, grasping at the slightest remaining straw of certitude before making any creative effort to reformulate the problems besetting him.

The process of constant reformulation, reassessment, and affirmation of value structures regulated by the movement either toward or away from organization does not always result in increased accuracy—at least by standards of science. Some value systems have to meet needs other than environmental exigencies. Such is the case when man seeks a cosmic or religious "understanding." Realism in myths and rituals, for example, is often only an ancillary criterion. But in spite of empirical inconsistencies, myths and rituals provide order and form in those regions of human concern otherwise most disordered and bewildering. In this area particularly, the formative process moves at a slow rate and thought-structure is rather rigid.

When man is not faced with the exigencies of his environment—as is the case in sleep, or other situations provoking imaginal productions—structure yields its rigidity and there is greater spontaneity in mental process. Experiences of unrelated endogenous images represent man's extreme penetration point of that disordered, unstructured world in which it is impossible to remain for greatly prolonged periods.

Summarizing thus far, the processes involving myth, ritual, and endogenous images are probably linked with homeostatic or equilibrium systems from which the balance between order and disorder discussed in this paper has been inferred.

Analogies are fraught with difficulties, particularly in the behavioral sciences; but there is one special example from linguistic and communication studies that should be mentioned here, for it may have closer connections to our problem than those of mere analogy. It has been found that languages have about 50 percent redundancy—where half the phonemes in a message are the result of free choice and half of them are determined by the statistical structure of the language. Greenberg, Osgood, and Saporta have shown that over a period of time, though the redundancy of language varies slightly, it always remains near 50 percent. Using the material of Llorach the redundancy of Spanish was calculated for four periods in Spanish linguistic history. The results from classic Latin through to Modern Spanish were respectively, 51.2, 43.7, 52.5 and 49.1 percent. The process resembles the swinging of a pendulum or the maintenance of an equilibrium centering on 50 percent redundancy.

Direct connections between this phenomenon and other types of human behavior have not been established. But for all present purposes and with the exception of the time dimension, it is perhaps easier to think in terms of such a principle. *One may say then that life in general, like language, seeks an equilibrium of about 50 percent redundancy—an equilibrium between the new (unexpected) and the old (predictable); between disorganization and organization.* Without some sort of homeostatic or "pendulum" principle in which deviations from the midpoint are checked and reversed before getting out of hand in either direction, life would not be possible. Only by maintaining the proper equilibrium can growth occur.

The two concepts of organization and disorganization can each be subdivided into an active and passive aspect. The active aspect of organization is man's striving to create form. The passive aspect is his desire to repose in that form which has already been created. These two aspects are similar to such dichotomies as creativity and culture, or freedom and determinism. Man's desire to repose in that form which has already been created, the passive aspect, is merely the desire of all men for a stable culture and society, in which there is a minimum of new and unexpected things. On the other hand, the active, creative desire is his rebellion against his culture—in its confining elements.

The active aspect of disorganization is the disorganization which takes place prior to a better and more adjusted organization. The passive aspect of disorganization may represent an innate need for novelty. An input of new, unexpected information probably functions to prevent the atrophy of adjustment mechanisms within the individual.

It will be recalled that in imaginal productions of the human mind unrelated, endogenous images were described as representative of a low redundancy situation, while imagination in a mythical or ritual context was considered to be highly redundant. The relationships are actually not nearly so simple. Imaginal productions involve a whole network of relations of entirely different qualities. One of the most important of these relationships is that between the mind and kinesthetic inputs. Recent experiments by Lilly and by Hebb have shown that the relative presence or absence of physical stimulation has a direct bearing on the image-producing processes within the brain. At McGill University subjects cut off from sensory stimulation have found it difficult to carry on organized, directed thinking for any sustained period. Experiments by Lilly at Bethesda have shown the same thing. After prolonged absence of sensory stimulation mental patterns apparently move from random thoughts and images to fullflown three-dimensional visual phenomena.

These developments point to an inner biological need. They reflect important relationships between imaginary or symbolic processes (whether of a fantastic or rational nature) and the sensory physiology of the body. It is quite possible that the physiological states or conditions which must be maintained depend in part on those processes which in humans have developed into imaginal and symbolic functions.

In view of these considerations, the work on human value orientations being carried out by Charles Morris has a very special interest. Morris has been working with 13 one-paragraph descriptions of value orientations or "Ways of Life" which are similar to philosophical or religious attitudes. Way number One is a description of the Apollonian orientation to life, Way number Three, the Christian, number Seven, the Maitreyan, and so on. These thirteen descriptions are read by subjects and ranked according to the subject's order of preference. At an early stage in his analysis, Morris placed his value orientations into three basic categories, and emphasis on sensory or external stimulation can be seen to have an important part in at least two of them:

Dependence was characterized as a need "for easy compliance with the world. The person depends, hangs on the physical and social world, is receptive to it, belongs to it, does not retreat from it or attempt to make it over, wishes sustenance, wishes a dependable world." Dominance was put in terms of "the need to be dominant in a situation (which is not necessarily to need to be domineering). Not a dependable world but a controllable world, a world in which effort is efficacious, a world in which one can initiate changes and lead them to a desired eventuation. The need is for power over persons and things, the excitement of overcoming, the sense of domination." Of detachment it was said: "It is a movement away from excessive external stimulation, away from demanding pushing world. A movement toward the inner man. Not comfort is wanted, not power, but awareness of oneself. Not involvement in the world, but the world at a safe distance. That one may listen to the self, protect the self, savor the self, live with heightened consciousness."

The person with dependency leanings will place greater emphasis on sensory stimulation. He is bound to the outer world through the senses. On the other hand, introversion or detachment is due to dissatisfaction with the confining, redundant outside social world. As the introvert moves further from the mid-point of redundancy his actions tend to be of an increasingly mental nature providing release from tactual kinesthetic and other sensory stimulation. In Morris' words, it is "a movement toward the inner man." Dominance stresses, above all, action, and it is at the mid-point of behavioral redundancy that action is most predominant. This is the point toward which adjustment tends to concentrate, the adjustment process itself consisting primarily of the active aspects of organization and disorganization. Dominant people usually stress action, particularly if they have a strong physique and are high in social orientation.

We might ask, how is it that some individuals apparently crave a great deal of security through close adherence to cultural norms and commonplaces while others may tend toward a position of extreme idiosyncrasy or deviance, if some sort of middle position between the two is vitally necessary? The answer undoubtedly lies in the complexity and multidimensionality of the problem which we have up to now pictured as a simple, general equilibrium process. For expositional purposes we shall refer to the general model as that of "behavioral redundancy." Behavioral redundancy may function as a governor of a substantial number of more specific redundancy equilibriums which are weighted and balanced differently among individuals according to physiological and anatomical differences, as well as to differences in experiential history. A person may balance high redundancy from one area with low redundancy from another. A deviant in a social group may demonstrate little need for a high redundancy of behavior in cultural and may compensate for this with some other type of redundancy not immediately apparent to others of his social groups.

The formulation of value systems is just one aspect of the formulation of redundancy systems, but as values provide a kind of programming for the individual or a code of conduct, it is easier to visualize behavioral redundancy in a value pattern framework. Returning to Morris' thirteen Ways of Life, it may be seen that these Ways must result either in a certain amount of redundancy (expectedness or organization) for the individual, or in the means for him to create it. The following list of the thirteen Ways is our own characterization of them in the interest of brevity. Tentatively listed opposite each one is the type of redundancy or expectedness which it promises to provide:

Way	Expectedness (or means of control)
1. Apollonian	Unchanged order
2. Independence	Inner order
3. Sympathy and love	Golden Rule
4. Dionysian	Conformance to social situation
5. Group participation, no privacy	Cohesion of the ever-present group
6. Practicality and action, master changing conditions	Effectiveness of practicality and action
7. Eclectic—action, enjoyment, contemplation	Confidence in adaptability and method
8. Comfort—friends, food, relaxation	Catering of others, familiarity of surroundings
9. Receptivity, wait	Trust
10. Stoic control, denial of comfort	Inner order
11. Inner life, meditation	Power over imagination
12. Adventure, power manipulation, accomplishment	Self-confidence in abilities
13. Let oneself be used, devotion and confidence	Determinism

Value structures as we tend to see them now may not always balance at the midpoint of redundancy. They may intermesh with redundancy patterns in "traits" which are psychologically more peripheral, or "motives" which are more central and profound. The kind of redundancy involved must be defined. To see how the placement of values varies according to the kind of redundancy involved, the following examples will be useful: Referring to Morris' earlier categories of Dependence and Detachment, a continuum of social redundancy can be set up. In this continuum, the movement toward people and the establishment of rigid forms of social usage and roles represent the high redundancy end of the continuum, and the movement away from people represents the low end. Movement toward people would be Morris' "Dependence" and movement away from people would be his "Detachment." The relative or rank positions of the thirteen Ways on this continuum are shown in Figure 1.

Detachment	Dependence
2—11—10—9—6—7—12—1—3—4—13—5—8	
Low	High
Redundancy	Redundancy

FIGURE 1. An ordinal scale showing positions of the thirteen ways on a continuum from low to high redundancy.

Many different types of redundancy continua can be set up in this manner. On another level, some of Morris' thirteen Ways allow more variation and experimentation with values themselves while others are more rigid. In Figure 2 these Ways are shown on a variation continuum:

Wide Variance	Narrow Variance
2—4—7—11—12—6—8—9—5—3—1—10—13	
Low	High
Redundancy	Redundancy

FIGURE 2. An ordinal scale showing positions of the thirteen ways on a continuum from low redundancy to high redundancy according to the degree of variance from rigid or normal values that is allowed by each way.

To introduce another dimension, the balancing of the redundancy pendulum cross-cuts the concepts of structure and process. A low redundancy in structure may balance a high redundancy in process, and vice versa. A high effectiveness in methodology can supply needed self-assurance in the fact of structural chaos, while a well-defined structural organization can provide a feeling of safety and assurance when effective methodology is lacking.

An illustration of very high structural redundancy and the consequent lack of redundancy in process can be found in the Trobrianders who are context-bound in cultural patterns of extreme rigidity. Dorothy Lee says, "Within the pattern, the Trobriander feels safe and acts with assurance. Away from home, he likes to reproduce known previous order, even physically." On the other side, Lee's description of United States culture is an excellent illustration of redundancy in process: "for members of our culture, value lies ideally in change, in moving away from the established pattern; and safety is insured through scientific prediction, not exact experience."

It is of course possible for emphasis on redundancy of structure or process to approach extreme positions before adjustments take place. Even during unfavorable ecological conditions the disorganization or discarding of ineffective value patterns may be so strongly resisted as to endanger the cohesion of the group. Such has been the case with the Texan homesteaders described by Vogt. These Texans or "Okies" who did not emigrate all the way to California as did the others, were probably more tenacious of their old value patterns which, in F. Kluckhohn's categories, especially emphasized orientations toward the future, mastery over nature, and individualism. Such orientations in behavioral redundancy terms stress process too highly and apparently are not an effective value combination for their particular situation. The "Homesteaders" are rapidly losing members from their settlement in New Mexico, and Vogt predicts the eventual disappearance of the community. It is interesting that a nearby Mormon town represents a highly successful adjustment which, with regard to the ecological circumstances, does not have such an apparently unbalanced emphasis on values of process.

Generally speaking, it is not unreasonable to assume that the low redundancy area of a culture can be detected where there is a large degree of variation through time and situation. Values found in the low redundancy area of a culture, because of their variation, require a greater amount of conscious consideration by the members of that culture. Hence they tend to be more explicit than the other type which, due to high redundancy, provides the basis of common assumptions and understandings—the results of which may or may not be immediately evident to the outside observer. Those values which are less redundant in a culture thus tend to be values of the individual—values which he himself selects, sometimes consciously, sometimes not. These individual value selections can never be entirely free ones, for they must balance somehow with the more redundant, often more implicit, values of his culture.

Thus to arrive at the universal values which Kluckhohn and others are concerned with, it may be profitable to study the range of idiosyncratic values found among individual members of a culture. If laws can be discovered which explain and predict the direction of change of these less redundant, idiosyncratic values over time and in various situations, one may find an important key to the study of the universal values against which these idiosyncratic values have to adjust or balance. This will undoubtedly be of crucial importance for predicting the direction of over-all cultural change.

36 | The Application of Cybernetics to Psychiatry
W. ROSS ASHBY

Cybernetics can hardly fail to interest the scientifically minded psychiatrist for it studies just those functions that are peculiarly "of the brain." It asks such questions as: how much information has the brain received?, what combinations did the signal

Reprinted with permission of the British Journal of Psychiatry and the author From *Journal of Mental Science*, 100:114–124 (1954).

form?, what memories are relevant?, what pattern of action will be adaptive? It studies switching, co-ordination, and integration—processes to which all the other cerebral processes are subsidiary. I propose, therefore, to review those branches of cybernetics that are likely to be applicable in practice, ignoring those branches, however attractive, that have no immediate prospect of application.

In one other aspect I shall have to ask your co-operation. Cybernetics uses, basically, the methods and concepts of physics. These concepts have the great advantage of being precise and, above all, free from ambiguity; but they have the initial disadvantage of treating biological matters from a point of view rather different from that used traditionally. To master the subject, therefore, one has to learn to translate one's concepts from the familiar psychological to the unfamiliar physical. For this reason I shall have to ask you to see some of the old facts from a new angle. I hope to show that the new angle is worth achieving, for some subjects that previously possessed only obscure and ill-defined concepts can now attain an altogether new standard of objectivity and precision.

Perhaps the most fundamental advance made by cybernetics has been the discovery of exactly what is meant by a "machine." I don't want to start a discussion of whether the brain is "only" a machine, for that would lead us astray. But we do, as practical people, often study the mechanistic *aspect* of the brain; and so long as we are studying that aspect we must, if we are not to contradict ourselves, use concepts that are appropriate. Until a few years ago, no one quite knew what the word "machine" implied. We knew intuitively that *some* limitation was implied, but no one knew what; and much rather aimless argumentation raged round the question whether a machine could, or could not, show certain forms of behaviour. The matter is now much clearer. We know that the essential feature of a machine is that, as a physical system, it is closed to "variation," that is, to information and noise. It is becoming evident that "information" is to complex machines what "energy" is to ordinary physical systems. When the concept of "energy" achieved full accuracy, just about a century ago, almost every branch of physics benefited and great advances followed rapidly. It is not impossible that the concept of information may be equally fertile in the study of complex mechanisms and the brain.

Some of the elementary applications of cybernetics to psychiatry are now well known and my reference to them can be brief. Well known, for instance, is the importance of feedback, that is of circularity in action, and of stability. Such matters must inevitably concern the psychiatrist; for whoever deals with such highly dynamic systems as human beings will always find that questions of stability are of high importance. There are plenty of interesting topics here. There is not time for me to develop the subject fully, so I will merely pick on one or two facets of the subject for illustration. Take, for instance, the question: can a system be "over"-stable? The answer is undoubtedly "yes." The over-stable system is in general too rigid, responding to the events around it with insufficient amplitude. If the over-stability occurs in some *portion* of a dynamic system, then it tends to lose its effect over the other parts and to become functionally *less* effective in the whole action. This is due to the fundamental law that when a whole system is composed of a number of subsystems, the one that tends to dominate is the one that is *least* stable, the one that is nearest to instability. This statement is capable of mathematical proof and holds over all mechanisms, whether built of cogs, or neurones, or relays. As a simple illustration, consider the relations between a flock of sheep and the dog that guides them. The flock is driven this way or that by the dog's movements; and equally the dog's movements are determined, perhaps through a shepherd, by the way the flock moves; so flock and dog form a whole, with feedback between the two parts. Now, regarded simply as a physical variable, the flock is undoubtedly the *more* stable in its movements than the dog. To see that this is so, examine their respective tracks after they have gone past. We shall find that each small deviation of the flock's direction has evoked a much larger deviation of the dog's, for he goes far out to drive the flock back. Thus, in their movements, the dog is an amplifier, the flock a diminisher. The dog is thus the *less* stable; and it is the dog that determines the direction of the whole. *The one nearest to instability rules.*

Another example is given sometimes by a family with a neurotic member; for the neurotic member may keep the whole family in a ferment while the more normal members are inconspicuous. And the same principle must apply in the brain, where, if any part or subsystem should become less than normally stable it will exert more than the normal degree of influence on the brain's activities. Conversely, should any part become excessively stable, that part will be unable to co-operate adequately in the activity of the whole. *Stability*, then, *can be excessive; its penalty is loss of control.*

The opposite fault, instability, is, of course, well known. What is not always appreciated is that the conditions under which instability appears are often sharply bounded and critical even in a system in which every part varies continuously. So if some factor affects stability, and there are few that do not, we should not assume that a slow and continuous variation of this factor will necessarily produce a slow and continuous change in the system's behaviour: on the contrary, *every dynamic system is potentially explosive*—that is, likely to develop a runaway. The conditions that this will develop are usually bounded sharply. So we would expect the change from stability to instability to be sudden, and out of proportion to the small change in the evoking conditions. These facts are true universally, and are quite independent of the particular details of the particular mechanism. They are equally true whether the mechanism is electronic, or neuronic, or hydraulic, or composed of cogs and rods. They are therefore necessarily true of the brain.

More can be added. Once a runaway has started, a mere holding of the external conditions constant is, in general, insufficient to stop the runaway. Even a return of the external conditions to the values that originally gave stability will usually be insufficient. Usually a runaway can be stopped only by a gross change of other variables. The approach of instability is often heralded by some form of oscillation. Observation of this may enable us to predict that instability is developing; it may enable us to take steps for its prevention. These facts should surely find application in psychiatry.

So far I have considered the brain only as a single, complete, mechanism; but cybernetics has forced us to consider the type of mechanism that might be called "statistical": that is, a machine composed of parts each of which is an ordinary, determinate component, but a machine in which the components are so many that a vast amount of minor variation occurs and in which the assembly is so large that much of it is also arranged at random. Such a system has a good deal of internal freedom, and its behaviour will show laws that are valid only statistically: we can say what it will *probably* do but not what it *will* do. It will be law-abiding in its general tendencies but not in its details. The cerebral cortex may well be such a system.

We are, in fact, beginning to realize that the simple little neuronic structures that we used to imagine in the cortex, with one neuron doing this, and another doing that, with, in the very "complicated" forms, a third intervening, are ludicrously inadequate. They don't give even a first approximation to the real state of affairs. The modern calculating machine has taught us to think much bigger, though the largest of these is far below the mammalian brain in complexity. I cannot do better here than quote Lashley, who is describing our present knowledge and ideas:

". . . theories of neuron interaction must be couched, not in terms of the activity of individual cells but in terms of mass relations among the cells. Even the simplest bit of behavior requires the integrated action of millions of neurons; . . . I have come to believe that almost every nerve cell in the cerebral cortex may be excited in every activity. . . . Differential behavior is determined by the combinations of cells acting together rather than by cells which participate only in particular bits of behavior. The same neurons which maintain the memory traces and participate in the revival of a memory are also involved, in different combinations, in thousands of other memories and acts."

Lashley's picture is, in my opinion, far more realistic than any yet proposed. It recognizes that while there are systems like the typewriter, in which each part is of the same order of size as the whole, there are also systems, such as that of Great Britain, regarded as an economic machine, in which the parts are almost invisible when viewed against the whole. It recognizes, in neuro-physiology, that even a minor action by a person is the outcome of almost uncountable neuronic activities in almost unimaginable complexity. Have I exaggerated a little?—there's no harm in that: at the moment our chief danger is that we will go on thinking too small, hanging on too tenaciously to our old habits. To-day, a resolute megalomania is a virtue; for we *will* have to change our ways of thinking about the brain—the new concepts are too big to be obtained from the old by a mere modification.

To show how profoundly the new views affect our thinking about the brain I will take as example the storage of memory and the question of its localization. (I say the "storage" of memory, for memory in all its aspects is too large a subject to be discussed now.) The word "memory" is often used to refer to the power of the *reproduction* of learned material: can the subject repeat the nonsense-syllables he learned yesterday, or can the patient repeat a text learned at school? This power of reproduction seems to be something of a by-product of the brain's activity: the not very intelligent parrot can do it quite well, and the magnetic tape-recorder can do it so much better than the human being that evidently the brain uses some essentially different method. More important in the brain, though less obvious, is the type of memory shown when a certain behaviour that has changed persists in its changed form. "Once a bicycle-rider, always a bicycle-rider"; so long as the skill persists, the person is showing memory, though he may perhaps be quite unable to recapture the feelings he had in the days before he could ride. This is a memory that shows in action rather than in recitation. It is often unconscious.

A good deal is now known about what sort of physical basis such a memory must have. Let me take the points in turn.

Its physical basis must be quantitatively suitable: it must have sufficient capacity. This capacity is measurable; and no mechanism of capacity K can carry a memory of information-content greater than K. Now an adult's memory capacity is very, very roughly about a thousand million units, so whatever the physical basis may be, it must be capable of providing that capacity.

In what material form is this capacity to be provided? In answering, we must remember that most elementary components, whether mechanical, or neuronic, or physico-chemical, carry only a unit or two on each component. Thus a reverberating neuronic circuit, that can be either at rest or fully excited, can carry only one unit, one *bit*. Suppose that our brains did in fact use such circuits for carrying our memories, and that an average circuit was composed of three cells. It would then follow, by simple arithmetic, that about a third of all our cortical cells would have no function other than to be set once and then to remain unchanged. This would be most wasteful and inefficient.

For this, and for similar reasons, a number of workers have examined the possibility that memory might be carried on much smaller structures, on the ultramicroscopic, or even on the molecular. Though there is as yet no certainty, physical considerations make it likely, in the opinions of Pauling and of von Foerster, that the essential change in memory occurs on structures of about ten to forty Ångstrom units, a size that would allow millions to occur in every nerve cell.

Is there anything against this? Before we reject the suggestion off-hand we should remember that the gene has about this size. The resemblance may not be as accidental as it seems, for any memory-basis in the brain has to subserve a function that is strikingly similar to that required of the gene during evolution and embryogenesis. Each has to be stable over long periods of time, and each has to be able to change to at least one other state. Each, too, has to be able to affect the processes that go on around it without itself being destroyed by them. From the point of view of information and control, the genes are simply the first message the mother gives the child: they are the memory-basis, in the mechanisms of heredity, for the information which one generation passes on to the next. Since the functions are so similar, we should not be surprised if their underlying physico-chemical bases prove to be similar.

We are thus led to a view of the brain whose memory-traces are: very small in size; scattered profusely over the cortex; and far too numerous to be arranged and controlled individually. We are thus forced to reconsider the questions of what we mean by the "localization" of such traces. When a system is small and simple, the localization of function within it is also simple. Thus, when I press down the key of the letter "S" on a typewriter, I can see that the typewriter's response among the levers is sharply limited to a certain few. These levers "belong" to "S" in a way that the other levers do not. "S" is here clearly and unambiguously localized. When, however, the system becomes very large, so that the component parts are incomparably smaller than the whole, this simplicity disappears. Thus, suppose we were to ask, is Britain's brewing industry localized? Two answers are possible. If we ask the exciseman he will reply: Every building in my district either is or is not in the brewing industry; of course brewing is localized. On the other hand, if we ask the geographer he will reply: No county in England contains the brewing industry; brewing in England is not localized. So the exciseman and the geographer hold exactly opposite views, and both of course are right. What allows this difference is that in a large system, such as a country or a cortex, the properties of the whole can be very different from those of the parts.

What this means in the cortex is that it is quite possible to have traces that are localized in the sense that each individual trace exists in some definite place in the brain, and that are also not localized in the sense that the whole set of them are not collected together in a small, anatomically recognizable region. This is what the modern statistical view of the cortex implies. It implies that the memory-traces that underlie each reaction are multiple, probably very much so, and that the individual traces are scattered over the cortex as widely and with as little apparent order as the industries of England are scattered over the counties.

This possibility was considered by Lashley as far back as 1929. He rejected it at the time, not because it was incompatible with the experimental and clinical facts, but because it seemed bound to lead, in the cortex, to chaos. For consider what this localization implies: there will be free intermingling of all the groups of memory-traces belonging to all the learned reactions, and this intermingling will take place in a network of neurons that is, histologically, rich in cross connections. Lashley was not alone in thinking that such a network could end only in chaos. Nevertheless, there is evidence, which I have given in *Design for a Brain*, to show that suitably arranged corrective feedback is capable of ensuring automatically that the patterns that develop are not chaotic but orderly and integrated.

We have now come to that process that is most peculiarly "of the brain" and of particular interest to the psychiatrist: the process of integration. What does it mean, in purely objective terms?

Sometimes we use it descriptively, as when we say, after a pianist has played a piece of music correctly, that the various movements of his fingers were integrated. This aspect of integration can now be defined with full objectivity and precision. Sommerhoff, in his *Analytical Biology*, and I have come independently not only to the same opinion but to the same definition. We find that in any activity variables can be divided into the essential and the nonessential, and that in all cases the presence or absence of integration corresponds to whether the essential variables are or are not held within given limits. So far no exception to this rule has been found.

The word "integration" can also be used to refer to the success with which a number of parts are joined or related to form a whole so that the whole produces some desired behaviour. How the component parts of the nervous system are modified during learning so that the whole shall produce integrated rather than chaotic behaviour has been a major problem in physiological psychology. As Sommerhoff puts it: "The fundamental problem . . . is to discover how the behaviour of myriads of blind, stupid, and, by inclination, chaotic atoms can obey the laws of physics and chemistry, and at the same time become integrated into organic wholes and into activities of . . . purpose-like character."

The principles that govern the self-integrating mechanism are now well known, and prove to be essentially simple and straight-forward. Of course, the machine that embodies them has to be a little unusual, but not more so than any other machine that undertakes a special job. Let me sketch the method.

It depends on the fundamental law, true for all mechanisms, that a whole can rest at some state, be "in equilibrium," only when every one of its parts rests at its component of that state. This means, more picturesquely, that every part has, as it were, a power of veto, and that the whole can be in equilibrium only if every part is in equilibrium in respect of its own conditions. So if one part is built to allow equilibrium only when the other parts achieve certain conditions, then the *whole* will behave as if hunting for those conditions. In the living organism, the method would imply that there would have to be a certain basic structural form and a certain basic method of functioning.

The basic problem (see Figure 1) is as follows: There is an environment

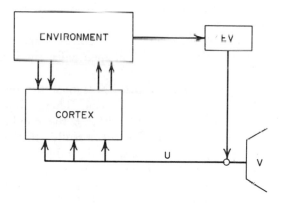

Figure 1.

and, interacting with it through receptors and effectors, a cerebral cortex. The environment has some action, for good or evil, on the organism's essential variables (E.V.), which must, if the organism is to survive, be kept within certain "physiological" limits. The cortex has various possible modes of behaviour, and the organism's problem is to find, given a particular environment, a mode of behaviour that shall so act on the environment as to make it keep the essential variables within their limits—satisfy the organism's basic needs. This can be achieved automatically if, and only if, E.V. (in the Figure) allows some random variation from a source V to pass along U to the cortex, the relation being such 'that the variation shall be allowed to pass when, and only when, E.V. is outside its proper limits—not conversely. The system is then, like the homeostat, self-integrating.

Some further identifications between this purely functional diagram and the nervous system's anatomy can now be made. Cortex and environment have already been marked. What of the essential variables E.V.? At present their localization in the brain is not known with certainty, and further research will be necessary; but it is obvious that sites worth considering would be the medulla and the hypothalamus. Enough is known to make these sites by far the most likely. The site of V is not important, for Brownian movement would provide an excellent source of the variation required, which, you will notice, need not be in any way systematic or specially designed. So V could be small, perhaps even of molecular size. It won't be found until specially looked for. The channel U, however, must be quite large, for it must carry V's effects over most of the cortex. One thinks naturally of a tract like the mammillo-thalamic, that goes on to project over the cingulate gyrus, and one thinks too of the periventricular fibres that go to the dorso-medial nucleus of the thalamus and on to the frontal cortex; but these matters are not yet settled; they offer an exceptional opportunity to any worker who likes relating the functional and the anatomical.

So much for the modern view on how the cortex adapts to the environment. Next we can consider what will happen when the mechanism goes wrong.

For simplicity, we can consider first the limits that determine what values the essential variables E.V. will seek. These limits are set by heredity, and should correspond, in health, to the conditions that the organism must achieve if it is to live successfully. If they are set by heredity at a wrong value the organism will actively seek that wrong value, perhaps to its own destruction. Such an abnormality will, of course, not be common, for it would be eventually lethal and subject to rapid elimination under natural selection. Such does, however, occur, from time to time. A child is sometimes born congenitally devoid of the normal reflexes that protect him against injury: he is unable to feel pain, and he injures himself seriously and incessantly. Such a child, studied scientifically, should show some abnormality at the site of E.V. The mental defective who is self-mutilating, too, may be abnormal in the same way, and anatomical and histological studies of such cases should be most instructive.

Another abnormality that would spoil the power of adaptation is failure along the tract U. Along this channel comes the flow of variation that will force the patterns in the main cortical network to change when it is behaving in a non-adaptive manner. U can be at fault by transmitting either too little or too much. If transmitting too little, say by being cut by a tumour, or by a destruction of V, we would find that the cortex would be unable to change from one way of behaving to another. Having made a wrong action it would tend to persist in it, and we would remark that it was lacking in originality and initiative. Contrast this with what would happen if U was to carry too much variation from V. Now we would see just the opposite: a restless system ever on the change, actively trying one new behaviour after another, changing merely for the sake of change. The two types remind one somewhat of melancholia and mania, though whether these psychoses are really due to such a fault must be left for future research. The investigation should not be unduly difficult, for both the site of the abnormality and its effects on behaviour are rigorously predictable.

Another prediction that can be made with some confidence comes from the fact that the cerebral cortex is large and that any particular action depends on the sum, or average, of a large number of elements. In such a case, the accuracy of the action taken will depend, by a well known statistical theorem, on the *number* of the elements contributing. If the number should become diminished we would expect to see the error increase, and the amount of increase can be predicted. We would expect a gross cerebral lesion, not to abolish the learned reactions totally but to lead to an increased error in all the activities shown, so that, for instance, the patient's writing would become more shaky, his aim with a shot-gun more erratic, and his judgment more capricious. The prediction approximates to what is commonly seen, but here again research is necessary if the matter is to be tested stringently.

At this point I would like, if I could, to say something about how this new knowledge can help towards the development of more active and efficient methods of psychotherapy. Unfortunately, as you can see, this advance from the mechanistic basis of brain function has a long way to go before it can develop concepts and complexities adequate to represent, or to explain, the complexities of human neurosis. Nevertheless, there are some aspects of this work that seem encouraging. For instance, the psychoanalyst cannot, I think, be other than interested when he hears that this work strongly suggests that all cortical adaptations occur only on a basis, and under the direction, of more primitive and simpler forces. The forces, represented in the Figure by the essential variables E.V., are affected by the external world, the environment, only by being moved into, or out of, the normal physiological state. They receive no detailed information about the environment and they undertake no detailed activity, leaving the details to the cortex: They simply allow or disallow. Do the essential variables, seen by the mechanist, correspond to the basic instinctual forces seen by the psychoanalyst? This work is too recent for me to hazard an opinion, but it seems to me that a study of the relations between these two concepts might well lead to advances in both sciences.

Another possible application to psychotherapy is given by certain recent work in cybernetics which has shown the fundamental importance in any complex mechanism of those combinations that are "self-locking," that is to say, of those combinations that, once formed, are no longer accessible to the influences that would unlock them again. We might, in order to have a definite example, call this the "problem of the oyster": the oyster, on receipt of signals of danger can shut quickly, but, being shut, cannot receive signals of safety. So every oyster tends to be self-locking in the shut condition. Oysters have long since evolved methods for getting themselves open again, but such a power does not exist generally. Often such a self-locking property leads to serious disorganization. The circulating disorder of the calculating machine is of this type, and it seems not impossible that the psychoanalytic "complex," as a portion of the psychic structure that is not accessible to those influences that would modify or re-educate it, may be of this type. I need not go further into the matter now: what I want to make clear is that the methods of cybernetics may be applicable here, and may be able to help in the task of breaking up the unyielding complex. Here is a field that might well attract the research worker who would like to develop psychoanalysis by making its basic concepts less metaphysical and more biological. Cybernetics offers the possibility of a psychology that recognizes to the full the richness and complexity of Man's strivings, while being based on concepts that share the objectivity and precision of physics. You will see that I do not regard psychoanalysis and cybernetics as being in the least incompatible.

Finally, I would like to discuss a possibility which seems to me to offer the best hope of all of understanding the aetiology of the psychoses, especially that of the so-called "functional" psychoses. Up to this point we have been considering the behaviour, normal and abnormal, of the basic adapting mechanism shown in the Figure. Such a mechanism, however, almost inevitably requires ancillary mechanisms, working to maintain the main system in a condition of optimal efficiency. We know, of course, quite a lot about the brain's optimal conditions in the elementary variables of oxygen supply, pH, ionic conditions, and so on; but we know as yet only a little of its more complex and subtle needs. These may show in a variety of ways not obviously related to the disturbances that their vagaries may cause. It is very likely that ancillary mechanisms will not only exist but will also be somewhat complex, for the cortex has not one but several optima, with different working conditions corresponding to different situations. Thus on one occasion the cortex may have to deal with a sudden and brief, but very dangerous, emergency, with speed of action as its most desirable quality. On another occasion it may have to deal with a mild, long drawn out difficulty for which the most desirable quality is the ability to handle relationships of great complexity. On yet another occasion its optimal action may be simply to leave well alone; and on another occasion its optimal action may be to attack with the utmost violence. Each style of behaviour corresponds to a "temperament"; and the cortex must be able, on different occasions, to act with different temperaments. The change from one temperament to another must, in a mechanistic brain, be due to the change in value of some parameter. We see therefore that the brain, if it is to be well equipped with a variety of temperaments, must possess ancillary mechanisms capable of setting the parameters of its action to a variety of values. This deduction is not surprising, for it has long been known that the autonomic has two main styles of behaviour—the sympathetic, adjusted for vigorous action, and the parasympathetic, adjusted for rest and digestion. The body thus has an ancillary mechanism, the autonomic, that can adjust it to either of two optima. Is it not likely that the cortex itself should have its own ancillary mechanisms, suited to its own needs?

If this were so, we would expect these ancillary mechanisms to have their own faults and disorders, especially since the human brain is, on the evolutionary scale, a recent development. Suppose, then, that one of these ancillary mechanisms became faulty while the cortex itself remained healthy: we can predict something of what we would see in the patient's behaviour. We would see that the *details* of the patient's behaviour were essentially normal, for the details were determined by an essentially normal cortex; but we would find that the general tenor was essentially abnormal, a caricature of some recognizable temperament. In other illnesses we sometimes see similar caricatures; in exophthalmic goitre, for instance, we can trace the characteristic, though distorted, pattern of the person who is alarmed and alert. In disorders of the cortex's own ancillary mechanisms we would similarly see caricatures of the common temperaments. Thus we might see the healthy person's ability to think along new and original lines exaggerated to the incomprehensible bizarreness of the schizophrenic. We might see the healthy person's ability to think at great speed in an emergency exaggerated and distorted to the ideational flight of the maniac. We might see the ability to take things calmly exaggerated to the inertia of the melancholic. We might see the healthy person's power of pursuing an end tenaciously exaggerated to the unshakeable delusion of the paranoiac. I need not give further examples, for I wish only to illustrate my point; much more research will be necessary if these possibilities are to be explored thoroughly.

Cybernetics is not more than a few years old, and its application to psychology and psychiatry has hardly begun. Most of the workers who use cybernetics are applying it to communication engineering and to calculating machines; those who are applying it to the living brain are few. But they have the advantage that the field is new, almost completely unexplored, so that worthwhile discoveries are to be won fairly easily. For this reason I would like to take this opportunity of recommending the subject to those of you who are interested in research. Don't think that cybernetics demands a highly sophisticated technique; Wiener's book, though magnificent in many ways, has given a most misleading suggestion in this respect. In fact, as a new branch of science, cybernetics starts almost from first principles, and what is needed for its application to the living brain is not so much an elaborate technique as a power of seeing the stale old psychological and physiological problems from a new angle.

37 | On Social Communication and the Metropolis
KARL W. DEUTSCH

Any metropolis can be thought of as a huge engine of communication, a device to enlarge the range and reduce the cost of individual and social choices. In the familiar telephone switchboard, the choices consist of many different lines. Plugging in the wires to connect any two lines is an act of commitment, since it implies foregoing the making of other connections. The concentration of available outlets on the switchboard permits a wider range of alternative choices than would prevail under any more dispersed arrangement. It also imposes less stringent conditions of compatibility. The limits for the potentially useful size of a switchboard are fixed by the capacity of the type of switching and control equipment available.

Reprinted with permission of *Daedalus*, Journal of the American Academy of Arts and Sciences, and with permission of George Braziller, Inc. and of the author. From *Daedalus*, Vol. 90, No. 1, *The Future Metropolis*, pp. 99–110 (1961).

The facilities of the metropolis for transport and communication are the equivalent of the switchboard. The units of commitment are not necessarily telephone calls but more often face-to-face meetings and transactions. For any participant to enter into any one transaction usually will exclude other transactions. Every transaction thus implies a commitment. The facilities available for making choices and commitments will then limit the useful size of a metropolis.

CONTACT CHOICES: THE PRODUCT OF CITIES

From this perspective, the performance of a metropolis could be measured in terms of the average number of contact choices which it offers to its inhabitants within, say, one hour of round-trip commuting time, at the prevailing levels of effort and equipment. Efficiency in cities, as in other organizations, differs from effectiveness. Effectiveness is the probability of carrying out a given type of performance, regardless of cost, while efficiency consists in low cost for a given performance. The more persons or services available to a city dweller within a round trip of one hour, the more effective would be his city or metropolitan area, and the cheaper the cost of maintaining a metropolis area; and the cheaper the cost of maintaining a metropolis that places, say, 1,000,000 people and 50,000 public and private institutions, firms or service points within a given commuting radius, the more efficient the metropolis could be said to be. The effectiveness of a metropolis could be measured in contact choices within one hour of travel time, while the efficiency of the same city would be measured by the ratio of such choices to some unit of cost. How many choices will $100 per capita buy for the residents of city X? As in many problems of design, one criterion cannot entirely override another. Some increases in effectiveness may have to be sought even at the price of rising costs, and some gains in efficiency may be worth some concessions in performance.

According to this view, the essential performance of the metropolis is in the enhancement of the range and number of such choices, and the basic cost is the maintenance of a system of facilities that makes a wide range of choices possible. One might ask: how many choices can an individual buy at a cost he can afford—and how many such choices on the average can the community buy for different groups of people, at prices it can afford? For each type of city and for each type of communication and transport system, it might then be possible to sketch demand and cost curves based either on the best available knowledge, or on prevailing practice.

Large cities, of course, serve many other functions. They offer playgrounds for children, lanes for lovers, shelter for residents and transients. But houses, playgrounds, and lovers' lanes are found in villages as well, and so sometimes are factories, power stations, mills, inns, manor houses and castles. Almost any one kind of installation found in a metropolis can also be found in the countryside. It is the multiplicity of different facilities and of persons, and the wide choice of potential quick contacts among them, that makes the metropolis what it is. And this essential character applies to large cities in underdeveloped as well as in advanced countries.

This general function of the metropolis is facilitated by its geographic location at some nodal point in a larger transportation network. The more the arteries that intersect at the site of the city, the greater the opportunities the city has to facilitate a wide range of choice. Again, the larger the city, the more diversified its industries, repair shops, and service installations—hospitals, research institutes, libraries, and labor exchanges—the wider the range of possible choices among them. The larger, the more diversified, the more highly skilled and educated the population, the greater the range of available personal choice either with respect to organizations or to opportunities in the world of culture, recreation and the arts.

In terms of economics, particularly in regard to the location of industrial enterprises, many of these considerations appear as external economies, actual or expected. Roads, port and rail connections, municipal services, the supply of skilled and unskilled labor, and the availability of high-level professional and scientific talent—all appear as so many potential factors of production, and some of them may even appear as free goods, against which no additional items of cost need to be budgeted. As will be evident later, the expectation may not be an altogether realistic one: the effective attractions of the area for new industries may lead after a time lag of some years or decades to substantial problems of congestion and overload. Yet locating in or near a great city is not only an exercise in economic rationality. Often the decision is made in intuitive and human terms; and most often perhaps the economic reasoning and the human preferences for location may seem to reinforce one another. Both tend to seek a widening range of choice at low, or at least tolerable, costs of choosing; and just this is the special advantage of the city. The rising proportions of industrial staff whose jobs are oriented to communication, service or professional functions may reinforce this attraction.

The power of the metropolis as an engine of communication is thus attested indirectly by its power of attraction over people. Though this power has an economic component, in the aggregate it is far more than economic. "How ya gonna keep 'em down on the farm, after they've seen Paree?" asked an old song; and the sociologists and anthropologists of the 1940's and 1950's have been reporting the vast attraction of urban areas in

Asia and Africa to former villagers, far beyond any immediate economic or social push. They are held even in the squalor of the shanty towns and *bidonvilles*. If freedom is the opportunity to choose, then the metropolis, in so far as it is an engine for facilitating choice, is also one of liberation. This liberation may be physical, in terms of the visits, the meetings, the sights now possible, or psychological and vicarious, in terms of the choices and experiences which can now be made in the imagination. In either case, it is a liberation whose reality and whose social, political, and psychological relevance cannot be doubted.

COMMUNICATION OVERLOAD: THE DISEASE OF CITIES

People come to large cities because there, among other reasons, they find a wider range of choice within their individual limitations than they are likely to find anywhere else. Inevitably this means that every metropolis must offer each of its residents enough freedom for a wide range of choises to be significant to them; and this also means enough freedom so that serious problems of peak loads and of recurrent, possibly growing, overloads are imposed on the city's many but limited facilities. Recurrent overloads are thus not an alien disturbance intruding into the even functioning of the metropolis. They are, on the contrary, an ever possible result of the essential nature of the metropolis as a device for facilitating a wider range of free choices.

To put it differently, the likelihood of such overloads is a result of the probability of coincidences in human choices and behavior under conditions of freedom. These overloads are not only the occasional loads, for which reserve capacities must be provided, but also the regular rush-hour loads, the result of relatively synchronized hours for work and recreation which in turn permit a larger range of choices than staggered hours would.

Despite their origin, however, recurrent overloads will tend to paralyze many functions, and eventually to blight the very structure of a metropolis. It is for good reason that waiting-line theory has become a fast growing field in operations research and social science. Taken together, increasing overloads of this kind reduce or destroy many attractions of the metropolis as well as the economic value of many of the capital investments in it.

Even in the absence of such overloads, the very effectiveness of a metropolis may produce subtle changes in its culture and in the cast of mind of its residents. A wider range of relevant choices implies ordinarily an additional burden on those who are choosing. Some years ago, Clifton Fadiman wrote a thoughtful article "The Decline of Attention" in modern, and especially American culture. Since then Richard Meier has written of "attention overload" and of the "communication-saturated" society as characteristic problems of modern—and thus particularly of urban and metropolitan—culture. These, too, are overloads in communication, but they occur not in streets and telephone lines but within the minds and nervous systems of people.

To increase the range of visible and relevant choices that confront a person usually means to increase the opportunity cost of whatever course he may eventually choose. Whatever he does will necessarily imply foregoing something else that also has appeared relevant and in a sense attractive. The wider the range of relevant choices we put before a person of limited physical and psychic resources and capabilities, the more acute and pressing we make his problem of economy in allocating his own time, attention and resources; and if he has been raised in a "conscientious" culture, such as the American or Northwest European, we are quite likely also to have increased his vague but nagging sense of self-doubt and misgiving as to whether he has made the best choice, and thus the best use, of his opportunities.

Cities therefore may produce a pervasive condition of communications overload. Whereas villagers thirst for gossip, city dwellers with more ample choices may crave privacy. But the internal communications overload of other people makes them less receptive to our needs. Their limited attention or their real need for privacy may tend to exclude us, and in the midst of crowds of neighbors we may experience persistent loneliness. Such loneliness, inflicted on us by others, is the obverse of our own need for privacy; and our own limited capabilities for concentration, attention, and responsiveness will make both their and our loneliness less likely to be overcome.

What people cannot overcome, they may try to gloss over. The poets and the social scientists—both critics of our culture—have catalogued the many rituals of self-deception that men practice: the reading of mass media that purvey illusions of "inside information" to the millions commonly excluded from it; the fancy dress of conformity which they don, from ivy league dress to the black leather jackets of youth gangs, or beatnik beards and sandals. Even these foibles that convey a sense of belonging, of identity, should be seen in perspective. People indulge in them, not necessarily because they are more shallow or stupid than their forebears in a village or small town, but because the commitments the metropolis imposes—of greater freedom, wider choices, greater burdens on their attentions and their powers of response—have temporarily become too much for them.

This temporary overburdening may be particularly acute for newcomers from some radically different cultural background. Then the

effects of psychological uprooting through contact with the wider opportunities of metropolitan life are superimposed on the effects of the shock
of a new culture and the weakening of the traditional bonds of family
and familiar authority.

Communication overloads may be reduced through effective cues for
orientation. Consider, for example, the practice of the old city builders,
who placed the most important structures of visual attraction, such as
cathedrals, palaces, or monuments, at the nodal points in the street network of the city. The nodal points, as the term is used here, were those
located at the main intersections of the city's traffic flow, and hence most
often observed as the city's landmarks, and they were also those points
most useful for orientation. The experience of visual beauty in a place of
visual usefulness was thus often an inevitable part of a city dweller's daily
coming and going. It is perhaps not too fanciful to surmise that this combined experience of perception and clarity of orientation in such cities as
London, Paris, Bern, Cologne or Prague contributed, and still contributes
to the charm of those cities and to the feeling of their inhabitants that
they were members of a deep and rich culture. Bridges can fulfill a similar
orienting function: the San Francisco Bay Bridge and the Golden Gate
Bridge come readily to mind, together with the Embarcadero Tower of
the old ferry building, visible for a long distance along the major artery of
Market Street.

In many modern metropolitan areas, however, these conditions are no
long fulfilled. Major intersections in many American cities are often
adorned with gasoline stations or car lots, with flimsy, low, shop buildings
with large neon signs. At the same time, many of the largest, most expen-
sive, and sometimes most impressive constructions are put on side lots,
well away from the main intersections, as for example Rockefeller
Center, the Lever and Seagram buildings, the United Nations building or
the Museum of Modern Art in New York City. In Boston, the John Han-
cock building, tallest and most monumental in the city, is tucked away
on a side street. Many of our visible landmarks are only of very limited
help in orientation, and are best seen from afar or by special visit. At the
same time, many of the major intersections passed daily by most of us are
either nondescript or appallingly ugly and give subtle but depressing
impressions of disorientation, tiredness, or tension.

Such crucial traffic points cannot be easily abandoned. When elegant
entertainment and shopping shifted from the central intersection of Times
Square to the area of Rockefeller Center, the old subway system became
less convenient to users of the Center, who have to make their way there
and back by foot, bus, or taxi and who thus have increased congestion.
This contrast between the changing fashions in regard to neighborhoods
and the unchanging nature of fixed intersections in a major traffic network

helps to make the market mechanism such an unsatisfactory instrument for the development of these crucial sites.

Overloads on some of the public and private services available in an urban area may sometimes be reinforced in their effects by a shrinking, or even an atrophy, of these services. Services vulnerable to this kind of process include service and repair shops, stockrooms, and parts depots, hospitals and clinics, libraries and museums. Many of the services of these institutions might be needed on Saturdays, in some cases, as is true of the cultural institutions, or on Sundays, or often for many hours on each work day. Institutions such as supermarkets and suburban shopping centers provide such longer hours of service, but many others do not, and some now curtail the amount of service previously offered. Much of this situation seems caused by rising labor costs, by fixed budgets, by the rising cost of able managers for small or middle-sized undertakings, or by the difficulty of dividing units of managerial effort so as to obtain management for some extra hours daily or weekly, and perhaps by some subtle development in American metropolitan areas that makes the personnel in service industries prefer shorter hours to more pay. This may be a rational choice, but it may become less so if too much of the new leisure is frittered away in waiting for delayed services. An increase in staff, with additional compensation for staggered hours (already practiced in suburban supermarkets), might be one approach an affluent society could well explore. In any case, free-market forces alone seem unlikely to overcome the persistent gap between the rising need for services in metropolitan areas and the actual volume of services rendered.

SUBURBS: AN ESCAPE FROM OVERLOADS

In the congested metropolis, a major effect of the cumulative overloads on communications, transport, and other urban amenities is frustration. Withdrawal to a suburb offers partial surcease. Taxes play a role in these frustrations. The late Justice Holmes once said he did not mind paying taxes, for this was the way he bought civilization; but exasperated city dwellers may flee to the suburbs from a metropolis where so much tax money buys so little in civilized living. The remedy is not to lower the urban tax cost as such but to improve the quality of metropolitan government and metropolitan living by attacking the whole range of overloads. Several lines for such an attack have been proposed, but most are proposals for escape. When put into practice they have not been markedly successful. For example, the shift in population to dormitory suburbs around the old cities has produced mounting burdens on commuting. A farther shift to some twenty-five or fifty miles from the city would make commuting prohibitive for many; whereas some men have been able to afford the financial and physical costs, their wives have found themselves marooned in a more or less rural environment, deprived of most of the choices and opportunities that make city life attractive.

The schemes for satellite towns are more far-reaching: each would be near the city, with separate though limited facilities for employment, shopping, services, and entertainment. Some towns of this kind have been built, but in Britain, at least, they have proved less popular than expected. Still more far-reaching schemes for decentralization would break up the large cities altogether in favor of a wide scattering of major factories and administrative offices over much greater regions. Such a proposal would require a heavy reliance on medium- and long-distance transport and on telecommunications, as well as the acceptance of rural (or nearly rural) isolation.

All these schemes are unsatisfactory in the same fundamental respect. For escape from the frustrations of the metropolis, they would sacrifice the primary purpose of the large city—a wider range of choice with a low cost. The search for more effective ways of dealing with urban problems cannot ignore this basic function of a metropolis, it must rather be the starting point.

A STRATEGY OF SEARCH FOR SOLUTIONS

The concept of a metropolis as a device for facilitating choice in communications can contribute first of all to answering some general questions, from which one may proceed to more specific surmises and to ways in which both the tentative general answers and the specific surmises can be tested. The first questions might be these: what is the usual ratio of the cost of transport and communication facilities to the cost of shelter? how does this ratio change for different types of cities? how is it influenced by an increase in the scale of a city, as measured by its total population?

There are several ways of exploring this inquiry; they should give us interchangeable indices of the same underlying fact. The proportion of communication costs to shelter costs could be measured in terms of the ratio of total capital investment in communication and transport facilities to the total capital investment in shelter. Or it could be measured in terms of the ratio of current expenditure of communication and transport to current expenditure on shelter; or in terms of the ratio of total manpower employed in communication and transport to the manpower employed in the construction and maintenance of shelter. Doubtless, a range of further indicators of this kind for related ratios might be developed, but those already given should serve amply to illustrate the point.

One could also study the ratios of some appropriate nonmonetary indicators, such as the physical proportions of certain relevant facilities. The known ratio of the area of land that is devoted to streets in a city to the land area devoted to dwellings and gardens could perhaps be used more effectively within the context of the other ratios noted above.

Other types of large-scale organization could be studied. As taller skyscrapers are built, what is the change in the ratio of space devoted to elevator shafts to the total volume of the building? As corporations grow bigger, what is the ratio of telephone calls and written messages to some measure of the total volume of company activities? Such questions are aimed not merely at promoting speculation but also at suggesting a surmise to be tested: as the size and functions of a city grow, the proportion of resources devoted to transport and communications may have to grow faster, or at least as fast, if increasing overloads are to be avoided. It may be that some lag may produce no ill effects. Then the crucial question would be: what lag in the growth of such facilities is acceptable? Research may disclose a range of acceptable or desirable proportions for investment in such facilities and thus offer a potentially useful tool to planners.

What would life be like in an otherwise normal metropolis if its transport and communication facilities had been deliberately somewhat overdeveloped by present-day standards? Suppose its streets and intersections were hardly ever jammed, its parking spaces rarely unavailable, its public transport frequent, rapid, clean and uncrowded, its telephone lines usually free, with quickly available connections? If this sounds too much like utopia, it might still be asked: how much improvement in well-being in a city could be purchased by how large an investment in drastically improved transport and communication?

Some years ago, Sigfried Giedion drew attention to the late nineteenth-century shift to the pavilion system in large exhibitions, away from the earlier practice of centralizing all major exhibits in one giant building of the Crystal Palace type. Giedion suggested that, as the exhibitions and the crowds of visitors grew larger, they gave rise to intolerable demands for more corridors to keep the crowds moving. The solution devised was to break up the exhibition into scattered pavilions, and to let the visitors make their way from one to another across the network of footpaths or across the open ground. People preferred to walk hundreds of yards in the open to the next pavilion rather than push their way for dozens of yards along some crowded corridor or hall. The principle may be relevant perhaps to the metropolis and the problems of urban decentralization.

Again, the question of cost arises. The shift to the pavilion system made the visitors themselves responsible for keeping dry and warm, a cost previously borne by the management of the single central hall. When a shift occurs from a compact city to a spreading network of suburbs, costs are also shifted from the city government to suburban families, who must now maintain one or two cars and pay toll rates for most of their telephone calls. In addition, there is now the financial, physical, and nervous cost of commuting. The decisive factor is the increase in delay in arriving and in the danger and tension. The ten or twelve miles between Wellesley and Boston may require twenty-five to thirty minutes with light traffic and good weather, in bad weather or dense traffic, forty-five minutes or more; and there are perhaps a hundred intersections. Over an adequate expressway the same trip might take fifteen to twenty minutes, with less tension and fatigue. A radial and peripheral system of improved expressways, permitting safe traveling speeds of seventy miles an hour—assuming corresponding improvements in the safety features of cars—would permit a city to double its effective radius and quadruple its potential area of integration. Our road experts have told us that "speed kills" if resorted to at the wrong time and place. But our city planners might well remind us that delays, too, can kill when their cumulative burden is added over a long period to an intensive working day.

Safe speed is not cheap. It cannot be achieved except by planned investment under public guidance. But it could do much to humanize life in our cities. The day may come when a profession of specialized expediters may watch over the smooth and quick flow of traffic and communication in our metropolitan areas, to identify and remove bottlenecks and overloads before their effects become cumulative and choking.

The same considerations apply even more strongly to public transportation. Improved and publicly subsidized rail transport—on the ground and underground—offers perhaps some of the most promising opportunities to combine high speed in mass transportation with safety at tolerable cost. The old-style commuting trains that take forty minutes for twenty miles not only exhaust their passengers but also drive more and more people to the somewhat faster highways. A drastic improvement in the speed and caliber of public transportation might relieve the pressure on the road system. Similarly, an extension of local telephone call rates to the entire suburban area—on the analogy of the successful principle of uniform postal rates—might reduce some of the need to travel back and forth and thus further reduce the pressure on the transport system. Still another step might be the partial staggering of service hours, so that more stores and service facilities would be available for more hours daily, thus reducing the peak loads when all stores open or close. Rotating assignments and staggered hours might require more employees, but it might pay off in higher profits for the stores and in greater freedom for the community.

None of these improvements would be cheap, and none easy to achieve.

Such improvements, however, might be a key factor in rehabilitating our metropolitan areas. What is needed is a realistic analysis of the problem of peak loads and of the rising capital requirements for transport and communication. Only a substantial investment in transportation and communications can make metropolitan decentralization practicable, and only a substantial strengthening of public control over strategic land sites can restore beauty to our cities. Ways will have to be found to let planners use the powers of the community to guide urban growth toward a clear and pleasing pattern of new and old landmarks where people can once again feel well-oriented, exhilarated, and at home.

The various lines of research suggested in these pages have a common origin and a common goal. Our inquiry has centered on the function of a metropolis in aiding its residents in their choices and in their search for responses. The ranges and costs of such choices and responses are basic to our analysis. Proportionately accelerated investment in communications, together with an improved knowledge of the general order of magnitude of these proportions, suggests a possible approach to urban decentralization. It also points up the need for greater clarity and beauty in our cities, and perhaps also for more responsive government, capable of integrating a wider range of metropolitan and suburban services, if the expanded metropolis is to become a genuine home for its people.

38 | The Cybernetic Analysis of Change in Complex Social Organizations
MERVYN L. CADWALLADER

In the view of the general agreement about the fundamental role of communication in human life, it might be assumed that any major breakthrough in the scientific study of communication phenomena would be hailed as an event of considerable significance for sociology. This has, indeed, occurred, but with the rapid development of information and cybernetic theory, most sociologists have remained unaware of it.

Cybernetic theory has been extensively applied in electronics, telecommunications, automation, and neurology. Some first attempts at the

Reprinted with permission of the University of Chicago Press and the author. From *The American Journal of Sociology,* 65:154–157 (1959).

application of cybernetics in experimental psychology are reported in *Information Theory in Psychology*. Communication theory has been slower in gaining attention among the social scientists interested in large social systems. The pioneers include economist Kenneth E. Boulding and electrical engineer Arnold Tustin, who have suggested a variety of empirical applications to the problems of economic analysis. Karl W. Deutsch has undertaken a cybernetic analysis of the emergence of nationalism in political communities. The work of these men demonstrates that cybernetics can be employed as a theoretical system in social analysis. The present essay sketches how some of the concepts and principles of cybernetics might be used in the analysis of change in formal social organizations.

THE ULTRASTABLE SYSTEM. The fundamental theme of cybernetics is always regulation and control in open systems. It is concerned with homeostasis in organisms and the steady states of social organizations. Its orientation is the source of considerable misunderstanding because many of the sociologists who are interested in the subject of social change object to the use of all concepts of equilibrium, homeostasis, or stability, arguing that to include such ideas as a central part of social theory is to preclude the possibility of dealing with change. They seem to believe that stability and change are not only contradictory ideas but that the processes themselves are totally incompatible. The difficulty here is not merely semantic: some kinds of stability do negate certain kinds of change. What has been overlooked is that at least one category of stability depends upon and is the consequence of change. Just this kind of stability is of prime interest to cybernetics.

An open system, whether social or biological, in a changing environment either changes or perishes. In such a case the only avenue to survival is change. The capacity to persist through a change of structure and behavior has been called "ultrastability." If a complex social organization is to survive critical changes in its environment, it can do so only by changing its structure and behavior. That Great Britain has survived through medieval, mercantile, and capitalist periods means that as a national state it has ultrastability. Any industrial corporation, such as International Business Machines or General Electric, that has survived the last fifty years of social change in the United States has done so through a process of self-transformation and not through the continuation of original organizational and operational patterns. Therefore, the concept of ultrastability will aid in distinguishing between systems that achieve stability under specific constant conditions and those that can learn or evolve new structures and behavior so as to remain stable under changing conditions. The latter is the focus here.

Another way of expressing the above is to say that some classes of open systems adapt to a fluctuating environment through processes of learning and innovation. There is nothing new in such a statement if the reference is to biological organisms. The novelty here lies in the proposal that complex formal social organizations, such as industrial corporations, armies, churches, and so on, be regarded as learning and innovating systems. Or, to put it another way, large-scale formal organizations are treated as open problem-solving systems, studied with a variety of theoretical problem-solving models, i.e., as learning and innovating systems.

By common convention we are used to thinking in terms of individual human beings as inventing or innovating, but not of social groups. But it is valid to talk about innovations produced by a social organization taken as a whole, and this is not to deny the fact of individual innovation. Any such system capable of purposeful problem-solving behavior and of learning from the past and innovating for the future is an ultrastable system.

CYBERNETICS AND THE ANALYSIS OF ULTRASTABLE ORGANIZATIONS. From the point of view of cybernetics, any large scale formal social organization is a communication network. It is assumed that these can display learning and innovative behavior if they possess certain necessary facilities (structure) and certain necessary rules of operation (content).

First, consider the structure of the system—as it might be represented in the language of cybernetics. Any social organization that is to change through learning and innovation, that is, to be ultrastable, must contain certain very specific feedback mechanisms, a certain variety of information, and certain kinds of input, channel, storage, and decision-making facilities. This can be stated in the form of an axiomatic proposition: that complexity of purposeful behavior is a function of the complexity of the communication components or parts of the system. More specifically, every open system behaving purposefully does so by virtue of a flow of factual and operational information through receptors, channels, selectors, feedback loops, and effectors. Every open system whose purposeful behavior is predictive, and this is essential to ultrastability, must also have mechanisms for the selective storage and recall of information; it must have memory. Does the social organization under scrutiny behave purposefully, does it solve problems, and does it forecast future events? If the answers are in the affirmative, then one must find in it certain kinds of communications, information, and control mechanisms.

In addition to the requisite structural components mentioned above, the communication net must contain or acquire information that makes learning and innovating behavior possible. This is a "program." That is to say, it must acquire or discover rules of behavior, instructions regarding internal mechanisms and processes—all of which will result in performance to be identified as learning, problem-solving, and innovating.

Innovation by any system is subject to the limitations and possibilities established by the quantity and variety of information present in it at a particular time and by the information available to it from the environment. Something cannot be created from nothing, much less something new. Therefore the range of possible new combinations that may be formed by an innovating system depends upon the possible range of output, the range of available information stored in the memory, and the operating rules (program) governing the analysis and synthesis of the flow of information within the system. In order to innovate, the system must be able to analyze information, that is, it must separate it into constituent parts. In a social system this is a consequence of certain explicit operating rules about what can and should be done, by whom, when, and why.

The utilization by a system of a particular part of its fund of information as an output for the solution of an environmental problem is not usually determined by pure chance, unless the system, in dealing with a totally unfamiliar situation, is trying completely random outputs. In the long run there must emerge an organization of the trial process in any open system capable of storing information about past behavior. Purposeful and predictive behavior depends upon memory, whether the system is organismic or social. Continuing behavior is modified by the results of specific acts. This is one kind of negative feedback and one which introduces a bias into the program of the system which changes the probabilities of various kinds of future acts in terms of present and past successes and failures.

If the problem-solving output of the system is organized solely in terms of past successes and failures, a point would be reached in its development at which it would not try anything new: all obstacles would be attacked with the techniques which had already proved successful. Innovation depends, therefore, on preventing such a freezing of the behavior of the system in old patterns. This is accomplished in a variety of ways. "Mistakes" in the identification, analysis, and synthesis of information may be the source of novel behavior. The loss of information (forgetting) about the past countermands the freezing process, to some extent, in all open systems complex enough to learn. In addition, the program of the system may contain specific instructions preventing the synthesis of all information into old familiar patterns and explicitly supporting certain kinds and amounts of novel action. Whenever novel behavior is successful, a negative feedback of information reinforces the creation and use of novelty. Not only will the system innovate, but it will remember that the act of innovating enabled it to circumvent obstacles and reach its goals. It will have discovered that a technique which worked in the past can be improved upon. Finally, in doing so, the system will have achieved the state of ultrastability which, for an open system, is the optimum road to survival.

THE ELEMENTS OF A MODEL, EMPIRICAL INDICATORS, AND SAMPLE HYPOTHESES. One of the main tasks which a theoretical model performs for the scientist is the selection of relevant variables and significant hypotheses from the infinite number of possibilities. A cybernetic model would focus the investigator's attention on such things as the following: (1) the quantity and variety of information stored in the system; (2) the structure of the communication network; (3) the pattern of the subsystems within the whole; (4) the number, location, and function of negative feedback loops in the system and the amount of time-lag in them; (5) the nature of the system's memory facility; (6) the operating rules, or program determining the system's structure and behavior.

The operating rules of the system and its subsystems are always numerous. Relevant for the present problem are (1) rules or instructions determining range of input; (2) rules responsible for the routing of the information through the network; (3) rules about the identification, analysis, and classification of information; (4) priority rules for input, analysis, storage, and output; (5) rules governing the feedback mechanisms; (6) instructions for storage in the system's memory; (7) rules regarding the synthesis of information for the output of the system—especially those concerned with the matter of usual or novel output.

It is now possible to suggest a few cybernetic propositions determining the presence, absence, and nature of innovative processes in complex communications systems. For example, it can be said that: (1) the rate of innovation is a function of the rules organizing the problem-solving trials (output) of the system; (2) the capacity for innovation cannot exceed the capacity for variety or available variety of information; (3) the rate of innovation is a function of the quantity and variety of information; (4) a facility, mechanism, or rule for forgetting or disrupting organizing patterns of a high probability must be present; (5) the rate of change for the system will increase with an increase in the rate of change of the environment (input). That is, the changes in the variety of the inputs must force changes in the variety of the outputs or the system will fail to achieve "ultrastability."

While no exact mathematical relationship between the elements of such a system has been specified, it is assumed that this is possible in principle but that its realization must wait for the results of actual experimentation and field tests. The use of mathematical devices for the measurement of information and the representation of networks will be a necessary and crucial first step in research programs designed to test hypotheses derived from the above theory. Research might be carried out along the following lines: (1) the volume of mail, telegrams, telephone calls, and memos could be sampled at input terminals, output terminals, and at crucial points in the network; (2) the volume of printed and written materials stored in the libraries and files of the system could be measured; (3) tracer messages would enable the observer to map channel connections, one-way couplings, two-way couplings, and to locate relatively independent subsystems; (4) the time taken by regular or tracer messages to move through a feedback loop would give information on time-lag; (5) the many techniques already in use by the social scientist for measuring values and attitudes will be useful tools for the detection and measurement of implicit operating rules. The techniques of content analysis could be put to use for the abstraction of critical operating rules contained in the official documents of the formal organization, in order to isolate and index those parts of the program of the system which constrain and determine the range, routing, identification, analysis, storage, priority, feedback, and synthesis of information. Above all else, the rules supporting the synthesis and use of unusual as against usual patterns of action would be of special concern in a description and analysis of the ultrastable system in the process of change, or of a system with a certain potential for purposeful change.

PART **3**

Semantics

CHAPTER X

Code and Culture

INTRODUCTION   While signals are the most fully analyzed and understood components of communication, meanings are the least known and the least analyzed. This is partly due to the difference between signals and meanings. Meanings are more complex and less objective. While signals can be recorded on film and tape, meanings are often unrecordable. They are essentially psychological and cultural.

F. G. Lounsbury in "The Varieties of Meaning" provides a theoretical introduction by showing how the syntactic, semantic, and pragmatic aspects of communication are each integral to the concept of meaning. In short, semantic analysis alone is meaningless. Lounsbury proposes four dimensions for the analysis of meaning, four axes that run through semantic space. The first is the situational-behavioral which determines whether the meaning is conveyed by the context of the signal or the reactions to the signal. The second is the linguistic-extralinguistic that determines whether the meaning is conveyed by words or by some other aspect of communication. The third is the intraorganismic-extraorganismic that determines whether the meaning derives from outside the individual (cognitive) or inside him (covert or affective). And finally, there is the general-particular that determines whether the meaning is conveyed by the type or the token. Semantics has more dimensions than syntactics, and we are not always agreed on which dimensions to use. The other three selections in this chapter all emphasize the situational-behavioral dimension.

Gregory Bateson in his "Information, Codification, and Metacommunication" analyzes the encoding and decoding of meanings. Coding is the process of translating between meanings and signals, and Bateson shows that it involves a psychological perception of configurations, the gestalt of the situation-behavior. Coding is meaning making, and meanings are configurational. Coding is also decision making, choosing between a figure and ground in a gestalt, and these choices involve evaluations and values. Much of our everyday communication is not a simple and direct coding of meanings, however, but is metacommunication instead, in which the meaning that is coded is simply that some communication is going on. This is a thoroughly situation-behavior dimension of meaning.

Basil Bernstein provides a more specific illustration and analysis of this dimension. He shows that meaning is embedded in a social system, and that different social systems can generate quite different codes of meaning. In a social system based on a great deal of intimacy and little social distance, meanings do not have to be made explicit. In such a system there is little noise and little need for redundancy. But in another social system, one with greater social distance, meanings do have to be made more explicit. Bernstein's "Elaborated and Restricted Codes" demonstrates the situation-behavior matrix of these codes of meaning in England, and shows how the meaning is always related to the situation.

With an even more specific and less theoretical case study, Leonard Schatzman and Anselm Strauss show how the semantic orientations in middle-class communication are quite different from those of the lower class. "Social Class and Modes of Communication" shows how the perspectives, imagery, and general framework of transmitted meanings differ from one class to another. Members of different social classes report on an event in different ways. Actually they have perceived different configurations, and in a sense they have not seen the same event. Therefore they also differ in how they code what they have seen.

The situation-behavior dimension is the cultural dimension, the dimension of this chapter. This chapter also considers meaning from the point of view of giving meaning, of coding. The chapter after this one considers the cognitive-affective dimension.

The Varieties of Meaning

39 | ## F. G. LOUNSBURY

Speech events, from the standpoint of behavioral analysis, have a dual character. In behavior sequences they occur on the one hand as *responses* to antecedent stimuli, and they may be studied and analysed as such. But they serve on the other hand also as *stimuli* which elicit or in part determine subsequent behavioral responses, and they may be viewed in this role and analysed accordingly. We may diagram thus:

$$S \rightarrow R(\text{ling.})$$

$$S(\text{ling.}) \rightarrow R$$

The full study of language cannot ignore either of these two roles of the speech act, although of course it is quite legitimate to concentrate on them one at a time or to introduce a division of labor in their study.

The linguistic response, by virtue of its acoustic consequences and/or its kinesthetic properties, becomes also a linguistic stimulus, either to another individual (a hearer) or to the same individual (the speaker himself). The above diagrams may then be connected, showing the mediational function of speech in social and in individual behavior:

$$S \rightarrow R(\text{ling.}) = S(\text{ling.}) \rightarrow R$$

Speech events are always links in a chain; they are parts of a behavioral concatenation which continues—with interruptions and rests, to be sure, and sometimes overtly but sometimes only internally—throughout the life of an individual or even throughout the history of a speech community. Antecedents and consequences of speech events are relevant data for the study of these events themselves.

Reprinted with permission of the Georgetown University Institute of Languages and Linguistics. From *Georgetown University Monograph Series on Languages and Linguistics*, 8:158–164 (1955).

This mediate position of the speech act—its position as a link in a behavioral chain, and its dual character both as a response to antecedent stimuli and as a stimulus to succeeding responses—has been recognized by philosophers, linguists and psychologists and has shaped the development of the general theories of signs.

Charles Morris, following C. S. Peirce, distinguishes three aspects of semiosis: the semantic, the pragmatic, and the syntactic. The study of semantics, as defined by Morris, has as its focus the relations of signs to things signified. Pursued systematically, this leads to the study of the relations between signs-as-responses and the properties of the stimulus situations which elicit them. The study of pragmatics, in this framework, is concerned with the relations between signs-as-stimuli and the responses which they elicit. Syntactics, finally, is concerned with the relations of signs to signs within a system of signs. If the study of language is placed against this framework, it is seen that Morris's "syntactics" coincides nicely with our "structural linguistics," that his "semantics" applies to certain varieties of referential meaning, and that his "pragmatics" may cover many things ranging from the study of connotative meaning to ethnology.

Leonard Bloomfield implicitly recognized similar distinctions when he gave his definition of "the *meaning* of a linguistic form" as "the situation in which the speaker utters it and the response which it calls forth in the hearer."

The meaning of a linguistic form, or of any sign, in its broadest sense is taken to be the total relevant context of the linguistic or other sign. In the case of animal sign behavior under experimental laboratory conditions such total relevant context may not be too difficult to ascertain, for the antecedent situational contexts are controlled, and the "relevant" responses are limited by behaviorist definition to the immediate overt and observable. In human sign behavior, however, including the all-important case of language, such conditions do not prevail. The situational contexts which give meaning to signs are not under the investigator's control. Neither can the "relevant" responses be defined narrowly as the overt and observable. Nor can the time boundaries of the relevant context be constrained to the immediately preceding and following periods of observation. The broad conception of meaning, then, is not directly usable.

There is no better discussion of these problems than that given by Bloomfield in Chapter 9 of his *Language*. Bloomfield has solved the dilemma presented by the complexity and elusiveness of meaning insofar as it pertains to the work of the structural linguist. The dependence of structural linguistics (i.e., of "syntactics," or sign-to-sign relationships in Morris's terms) upon questions of meaning was seen to be minimal, and at the few points of real dependence Bloomfield's well-known "fundamental assumption of linguistics" and an accompanying simple operation fill the linguist's needs. These do not, of course, give any aid to the student of meaning, whom Bloomfield felt, as a linguist, he was not in a position to advise. The real problems of meaning were seen to fall mainly within the domains of other sciences.

It is not to be expected that any one approach to the study of meaning will be capable of dealing with it in all of its aspects or in all of its complexity. It is readily apparent, moreover, that the various writers on this subject are often referring to quite different things when they use the term. "Meaning" to a psychologist is not the same as it is to a lexicographer. It is not the same thing to an ethnologist as it is to a linguist. To each of these specialists, and to still others—to the language teacher, to the literary critic, and to the philosopher, it presents widely varying aspects. Further, the techniques for the description of meaning are as various as the aspects it presents. For the most part their development is lopsided, the emphasis being in some cases on very practical matters to the neglect of theory, while in other cases it is on theoretical system building, to the neglect of practical method.

We shall attempt to sketch here a tentative framework for discriminating among a number of varieties of meaning, or of phenomena called "meaning" in the technical literature of some of our disciplines.

If we start from our broadest definition of the meaning of a form, namely, the total relevant context of the form, we may make a first dichotomy between the stimulus-bearing parts of this context and the response portions of it. The former may be called *situational meaning* and the latter *behavioral meaning*.

A second dichotomy may be made between the linguistic portions and the nonlinguistic or extralinguistic portions of the total context. Accordingly we may distinguish between *linguistic meaning* and *extralinguistic meaning*. This dichotomy cuts across the first one, inasmuch as any stimulus situation which calls forth a particular linguistic form may contain both nonlinguistic and linguistic parts, and also since any further responses may be in part linguistic and in part nonlinguistic. Or we may look at it in another way. Of the linguistic context surrounding a given form, a part may be antecedent and a part may be subsequent. Due to the phenomenon of linguistic structure, the occurrence of the form in question is partly determined by the antecedent portions of the linguistic context and by antecedent anticipations of a few parts of the subsequent linguistic context. These portions of the linguistic context, then, are "situational" as already defined. Further, and again due to the facts of linguistic structure, the occurrence of the given form exercises some conditioning effects upon the portions of the linguistic context which follow. These portions are "behavioral" in the sense previously defined.

The intersection of these two dichotomizations must yield four sub-varieties of meaning. Morris's trichotomy of "semantic," "syntactic," and "pragmatic" corresponds to these in the following way. The distinction between the syntactic on the one hand, and the semantic and pragmatic together on the other hand, corresponds to our distinction between linguistic and extra linguistic meanings. The further distinction between the semantic and the pragmatic seems to fall along the same lines as that between our extralinguistic-situational and our extralinguistic-behavioral varieties of meaning.

A third dichotomy recognizes that phenomena internal to the organism of an individual speaker or hearer constitute an important part of the "meaning" of a linguistic form. It distinguishes between the internal and the external stimuli which determine the occurrence of a given linguistic response. Further, it distinguishes between the covert and the overt responses which may be made to a given linguistic stimulus. The "meanings" dichotomized by this criterion may be referred to as *intraorganismic* and *extraorganismic* meanings respectively. The internal stimuli and the internal or covert responses are largely inaccessible to observation. One of the goals of the psychology of language, however, is to learn as much as possible about these internal states which accompany and constitute a part of language behavior. The methods are partly inference from the analysis of overt behavior, partly the use of electrical devices which register continuous records of certain changes in internal states, and partly, of course, judicious use of introspective data.

Undoubtedly the simple dichotomy of internal vs. external to the behaving organism is overly crude. Among the intraorganismic varieties of meaning a further important distinction could be made according to whether their locus is cortical or somatic. Accordingly one might distinguish between *cognitive meaning* and certain other varieties whose locus is somatic. The former are inferable, at best, from circumstantial evidence of a linguistic nature. The latter can be indicated, and to some extent measured, by the use of appropriate apparatus.

The dichotomies previously drawn intersect with the present ones. Thus, the situational and behavioral distinctions are applicable to the category of cognitive meaning, as are also the linguistic and extralinguistic distinctions. The linguistic vs. extralinguistic dichotomy, when applied to the internal situations and response of somatic locus, yields important subvarieties. On the one hand we have the covert speech or subliminal articulations which accompany and facilitate thought. On the other hand we have the physiological states, particularly of viscera and of skin which are associated both in the response role and in the stimulus role with speech as well as with other forms of behavior. When these somatic phenomena are associated with the occurrence of any given linguistic form—either as part of the stimulus situation which elicits it, or as part of the total response which is made to it—they constitute parts of the "meaning" of that form. The one variety, which has the organs of speech as its locus, may be referred to as *covert linguistic meaning*. The other variety, of locus elsewhere in the body, may be referred to as *affective meaning*. Both varieties are known to us from introspection, and they have been verified as well through the employment of specially designed laboratory machinery.

The handling of the data of meaning presents problems of classification similar to those encountered in handling the data of linguistic form. In phonemics these currently find recognition in the terms "phoneme," "allophone," and "defining features of the phoneme." Similar distinctions are made in morphemics and also in what might analogously be termed "tagmemics." These are the distinctions of (a) a given class, (b) any particular member of the class, and (c) the "essential," or "distinctive," or "defining" features of the class. In semantics, similar distinctions have been made. Peirce's "type" and "token" represent, respectively, a class, and any particular member of the class. Morris's "designatum" and "denotatum" represent the same distinctions, and his "semantical rule," or "significatum," corresponds to the third distinction, that of the defining features of the class. Bloomfield's "distinctive meaning," or "linguistic meaning" as he alternatively termed it, made this same third distinction and corresponds to Morris's significatum. Morris used his terms only for the semantic aspects of meaning, i.e. for what we have here called situational meanings. It would be preferable now to choose terms of wider application, as it may prove necessary to extend similar distinctions into the pragmatic or behavioral aspects of meaning. We shall therefore speak instead of the *particular meanings*, the *generalized meanings*, and the *abstract meaning* of a form. These terms correspond to Morris's denotata, designatum, and significatum, respectively, but unlike these, they may be applied to behavioral as well as to situational meanings.

We have made distinctions of four kinds, or in four dimensions of difference among varieties of meaning:

1. Situational *vs.* behavioral
2. Linguistic *vs.* extralinguistic
3. Extraorganismic *vs.* intraorganismic (and within the latter cognitive *vs.* affective and covert linguistic)
4. Particular *vs.* generalized *vs.* abstracted

Distinctions of each kind intersect those of the other kinds. Our purpose, however, is not to arrive at some final number of pigeonholes for the varieties of meaning which the product of these differentiations would yield. Rather, it is to call attention to some of the ways in which the uses of the term *meaning* have differed. Different writers, representing different scientific and scholarly interests, have often focused on quite different phenomena within this field, while yet applying the same general term, "meaning," to all. If difficulties in communication have ensued, it is not to be wondered at. A second reason for drawing these distinctions is that we feel that the study of meaning is not quite so hopeless a task as a generation of descriptive linguists has assumed it to be. A preliminary dissection of the phenomenon, however tentative its lines may be, may help in the formulation of research problems and in the interpretation of their results. In particular, it may help us to relate the results of one line of investigation to those of other lines of investigation.

40 Information, Codification, and Metacommunication
GREGORY BATESON

The basic principles upon which information is codified in the brain or mind of human beings are still unknown, but from the external characteristics of human beings and from what communications engineers can tell us, certain generalities are clear.

First, codification must, in the nature of the case, be systematic. Whatever objects or events or ideas internal to the individual represent certain external objects or events, there must be a systematic relationship between the internal and the external, otherwise the information would not be useful. The engineer's term for nonsystematic elements in codification is "noise"; in the presence of too many such random elements there would be no possibility of "decodification"—that is, no possibility of steering the individual's actions in regard to external events. (Strictly there is, of course, no "decodification." Information codified in the form of, for example, neural impulses may guide the organism in its verbal utterances or in action. But these types of output are again codifications or transformations of the neural showers. The information is never translated back into the actual objects to which it refers.)

Second, it is evident that the codification must be such that relationships are preserved. While it is impossible for a man to have inside him-

Reprinted with permission of W. W. Norton & Company, Inc., and the author. From Jurgen Ruesch, M.D., and Gregory Bateson, *Communication: The Social Matrix of Psychiatry*, pp. 168–186 and 212–214. Copyright 1951 by W. W. Norton & Company, Inc.

self a tree corresponding to the external tree that he perceives, it is possible to have internal objects or events so related to each other that their relations reflect relationships between parts of the external tree. Obviously very profound transformations occur in any codification—and indeed, codification is transformation in the mathematical sense of the word. We may expect, for example, to find in some cases that spatial relations in the external world will be represented by temporal relations in the processes of mind: when the eye scans an object, the shape of the object is certainly transformed into a temporal sequence of impulses in the optic nerve. And in other cases, temporal sequences will be represented as spatial relations in the brain: a memory of past sequences must surely be so codified. But whatever the transformations of codification, information is merely lost unless relations among external events are systematically translated into other relations among the events and processes of the mind.

Further, engineers are able to describe several known possible varieties of codification, with which we can compare and contrast what seems to happen in human beings. Broadly there are three important kinds, all of which possibly occur in human mental processes. All three types of codification are also exemplified by various sorts of electronic machinery, and the mechanical examples will be cited to give a more vivid idea of what is meant by codification.

First, there is what the engineers call "digital" codification. This is the method used in the ordinary desk calculating machine, which is made up of interlocking cogs and is essentially a counting mechanism which counts the teeth of the cogs and how many times they rotate in complex interaction. In this type of codification the input already differs very profoundly from the external events about which the machine is "thinking." In fact, for such machines it is necessary to have a human being who will codify the external events in terms of their arithmetical *relations* and feed this codification into the machine in an appropriate manner which defines what problem the machine is to solve.

Second, there is the type of calculating machine which the engineers call "analogic." In these machines the external events about which the machine is to think are represented in the machine by a recognizable model. For example, a wind tunnel is a thinking machine of this kind. In such machines changes in the external system can be represented by corresponding changes in the internal model, and the results of such changes can then be observed. Whether any analogic mechanisms exist in the human central nervous system is exceedingly doubtful, but subjectively we think that we form images of the external world, and these images seem to aid us in our thinking. The nature of these conscious images is, however, obscure, and in any case it is difficult to imagine the operation of any true analogic model in a system such as the central nervous system, which has no moving parts. Apart from the central nervous system, however, there is a possibility that the whole moving body may be used as an analogic component. It is probable, for example, that some people empathize the emotions of others by kinesthetic imitation. In this type of thinking, the body would be an experimental analogue, a model, which copies changes in the other person, and the conclusions from such experimental copying would be derived by the more digital central nervous system which receives proprioceptive cues. It is also certain that human beings often use parts of the external world as analogic models to aid them in solving their own internal problems. Indeed, many patients use the psychotherapist in this way.

Third, there are a few machines which are capable of codifying information in units comparable to what the psychologists call Gestalten. An example of such a machine is the recently invented device which reads aloud from printed matter. The machine recognizes the twenty-six letters and makes a different sound for each letter. Further, it recognizes these letters in spite of minor differences between different sorts and sizes of type font, and it also recognizes the same letter regardless of where its image falls upon the screen. In sum, the machine must allow for lateral or vertical displacement on a "retina" and for slight rotational displacement. In achieving this recognition, the machine is doing something very closely comparable to that recognition of Gestalten whereby a human being knows that a square is a square even though it may be of almost any size and presented at any angle. The essential characteristic of such machines is that they can identify formal relations between objects or events in the external world and classify groups of such events according to certain formal categories. A message denoting the presence or absence of an event which fits a certain formal category is then transmitted, possibly by a single signal within the machine. This last possibility of summarizing a complex message in a single "pip" is the advantage which Gestalt codification provides. An enormous economy of communication within the machine can thus be achieved.

A fundamental difference between codification by Gestalten and enumerative digital codification can be illustrated by contrasting codification which occurs in the type of machine which will transmit a half-tone block picture over wire with the type of codification in the process which we call vision. The machine transmits billions of messages. Each message is the presence or absence of a "pip," such presence or absence denoting the presence or absence of a dot in the original half-tone block. The machine is in no way concerned with what the picture represents. On the other hand, a human being looking at such a picture sees it as representing a man, a tree, or what not. The shower of impulses originating in the retina and traveling in the optic nerve is in some ways not unlike the shower of pips transmitted by the machine, but in the brain this neural shower impinges upon a network which has the characteristic of being able to discriminate formal relations within the shower—these formal relations being, in fact, related to those which exist in the original picture. The human being is thus able to categorize large areas of the picture in terms of Gestalten.

The existence of Gestalt processes in human thinking seems to be the circumstance which makes us believe that we are able to think about concrete objects, not merely about relationships. And this belief is further fortified by our use of language, in which substantives and verbs always stand for externally perceived Gestalten. When, however, it is realized that the recognition of Gestalten depends upon the formal relations among external events, then it is evident that thinking in terms of "things" is secondary—an epiphenomenon which conceals the deeper truth that we still think only in terms of relationships. We may summarize the external relationships by constructing Gestalten in our minds, but still it is the relationships in the afferent neural showers which provide the basis for our Gestalten.

The same general truth—that all knowledge of external events is derived from the relationships between them—is recognizable in the fact that to achieve more accurate perception, a human being will always resort to change in the relationship between himself and the external object. If he is inspecting a rough spot on some surface by means of touch, he moves his finger over the spot, thus creating a shower of neural impulses with definite sequential structure, from which he can derive the static shape and other characteristics of the thing investigated. To judge the weight of an object we heft it in the hand, and to inspect a seen object with care we move our eyes in such a way that the image of the object moves across the fovea. In this sense, our initial sensory data are always "first derivatives," statements about *differences* which exist among external objects or statements about *changes* which occur either in them or in our relationship to them. Objects and circumstances which remain absolutely constant relative to the observer, unchanged either by his own movement or by external events, are in general difficult and perhaps always impossible to perceive. What we perceive easily is difference and change—and difference is a relationship.

The Gestalt psychologists have stressed the relations between "figure" and "ground," and while we are not concerned here with the detailed elaboration of Gestalt theory, it is necessary to stress one broad characteristic of the figure-ground phenomenon which must be allowed for in any attempts we may make to understand the codification which occurs in human mental processes. In all figure-ground phenomena, it seems that the perceiver uses the fact that certain end organs are *not* stimulated as a datum for achieving a fuller understanding of those impulses which come from end organs which are stimulated. A human subject, if he places his hand in a closed illuminated box, can tell from neural impulses of warmth or pain originating in his hand that there is illumination, but he cannot decide whether the light comes from a small bright source, or is a general illumination of the box. With his retina, on the other hand, he can immediately tell the difference between general illumination and a small source of light. He does this by combining in the brain the information that certain end organs have been stimulated with the information that certain others were *not*, or were less stimulated. Similarly, as was noted above, in the transmission of a half-tone block the *absence* of pips on wire at a specific moment can be a signal denoting the absence of a dot on the picture. (The mechanical system could as easily have been set up so that the absence of a pip in the wire would denote the presence of a dot in the picture, etc.) This ability of the human brain to use the *absence* of certain afferent impulses in the interpretation of those impulses which do arrive, seems to be a primary condition of the figure-ground phenomenon. We may see the ability to distinguish between general illumination and a small source of light as an elementary form of Gestalt perception.

Further, it would seem that in creating Gestalten the perceiver rules out as irrelevant "ground" a great many impulses which actually impinge upon end organs. The construction of Gestalten would seem to depend upon something like inhibition—a partial negation of certain impulses—which permits the perceiver to attend to those matters which he perceives as "figures."

One of the characteristics of codified information follows from what has been said above, especially from the discussion of the figure-ground hypothesis. This is the fact that information is always *multiplicative*. Every piece of information has the characteristic that it makes a positive assertion and at the same time makes a denial of the opposite of that assertion. The very simplest perception that we can imagine, upon which, for example, the tropisms of protozoa are presumably based, must still tell the organism that there is light in that direction and not light in that other direction. Many pieces of information may be more complex than this, but always the elementary unit of information must contain at least this double aspect of asserting one truth and denying some often undefined opposite. From this it follows that when we have two such "bits" of information the gamut of possible external events to which the information may refer is reduced not to a half, but to a quarter, of the original range; similarly three "bits" of information will restrict the possible gamut of external events to an eighth.

The multiplicative nature of information is illustrated by the game of

Twenty Questions. The questioner in this game must, in twenty questions, identify what object the respondent has in mind. The respondent can only answer the questions with "yes" or "no." Every question answered segments the possible range of objects which the respondent might have in mind, and if the questioner plans his questions correctly, in twenty questions he can determine among something over a million objects which one it is that the respondent has in mind ($2^{20} = 1,048,576$). The questioner structures the possible universe of objects with a ramifying system of questions which is what we would call a "codification system," and a very brief trial of the game will give the reader an idea of the difficulties which occur in communication when the two persons do not have precisely similar codification systems—i.e., when the respondent misunderstands the questions. If the game is played strictly according to the rules, there is almost no way of correcting such misunderstandings: the questioner can hardly detect what has happened.

CODIFICATION AND VALUE

Briefly, what we here attempt to argue is that the system of codification and the system of values are aspects of the same central phenomena. The precise relation between the notions of value and information has exercised Occidental philosophers for two thousand years, and a final formulation is not to be expected in this book. It is necessary, however, to strive to make our position clear If we are to study the clash and transmission of values.

We examine first some of the resemblances which seem to link value with codification:

1. The value system and the codification system are alike in that each is a system ramifying through the total world of the individual. The value system, as organized in terms of preference, constitutes a network in which certain items are selected and others passed over or rejected, and this network embraces everything in life. Similarly, it was pointed out in regard to the codification system that all events and objects which present themselves are in some degree classified into the complex system of Gestalten which is the human codification system.

2. A further resemblance springs from the fact that both in the case of codification and in the case of value, the negated class is usually undefined. In the case of preference, a man will say that he likes this or that but will often omit to define the alternatives to which this or that is preferred. Alternatively he may say that he dislikes such and such and will omit to state what he would like better. Similarly in the codification of information human beings discard the ground and observe the figure. People

will say that the figure has "meaning" for them; and that that which is preferred or that which is disliked has value as against an undefined background of alternatives.

3. It is well known that the network of value partially determines the network of perception. This is best illustrated by the experiments of Adalbert Ames, Jr., in which a person is made to act in a situation in which he is subject to an optical illusion—i.e., perceives a false Gestalt. Even though he is aware of the illusion, it is almost impossible for him to correct his action except by many repeated trials. Gradually he learns to correct for the shape which he knows to be real, even though, at first, he cannot see that the objects have this shape. As he achieves correction, his image of the objects changes and he begins to see them as they really are—that is, he begins to form an image such that, acting in terms of that image, he will achieve his goal. It is also evident that perception determines values: as we see things, so we act. But equally the success or failure of our action will determine our later vision. It is evident too that much of the change which in psychotherapy seems to be change in the patient's system of values seems, subjectively to that patient, to be a change in the way he perceives things. Action would seem to be the middle term in which perception and value meet.

4. It is well known that wish and perception partially coincide. Indeed this discovery is one of Freud's greatest contributions. Not only does every human being tend to see in the external world (and in himself) that which he wishes to be the case; but having seen in the external world something even disastrous, he must still wish his information to be true. He must act in terms of what he knows—good or evil—and when he acts he will meet with frustration and pain if things are not as he "knows" them to be. Therefore he must, in a certain sense, wish them to be as he "knows" they are.

5. The preceding paragraph brings up a matter of great theoretical importance: the problem of the relation between the concept "information" and the concept "negative entropy." Wiener has argued that these two concepts are synonymous; and this statement, in the opinion of the writers, marks the greatest single shift in human thinking since the days of Plato and Aristotle, because it unites the natural and social sciences and finally resolves the problems of teleology and the body-mind dichotomy which Occidental thought has inherited from classical Athens. The concept of entropy and the Second Law of Thermodynamics which defines this concept are, however, hazy in the minds of many social scientists, and therefore some explanation is necessary.

(a) According to the Second Law of Thermodynamics, any system of objects in a state from which work can be obtained will tend to change away from this state if random events are allowed to occur. The classic instance is the case of molecules of gas sorted into two containers according to their velocity (i.e., temperature). For such a system, Carnot pointed out, the "available energy" of the system is a function of the difference of temperature between the gas in the two containers. He also pointed out that such available energy—i.e., "negative entropy"—will be diminished either if the system is made to do work or if random events are allowed to occur such as a mixing of the molecules. The system will change toward a more random or probable state—i.e., toward "entropy."

(b) It is evident that Carnot and the engineers generally were applying their own value system as engineers when they enunciated these generalizations. To them "available energy" was a desideratum in the cylinders of heat engines.

(c) The probability law will, however, apply in all cases, and is not restricted to instances in which the sorting is by temperature; or to instances from which physical work can be obtained. If, for example, a pack of cards is in any state which we call "sorted," any shuffling of the pack will probably upset this arrangement.

(d) Wiener points out that the whole range of entropy phenomena is inevitably related to the fact of our knowing or not knowing what state the system is in. If nobody knows how the cards lie in the pack, it is to all intents and purposes a shuffled pack. Indeed, this ignorance is all that can be achieved by shuffling.

(e) From this it follows that the "system" which is really referred to in statements about sorting and negative entropy includes the speaker, whose information and value systems are thus inextricably involved in every such statement which he makes.

6. The relation between information and value becomes still more evident when we consider the asking of questions and other forms of seeking information. We may compare the seeking of information with the seeking of values. In the seeking of values it is clear that what happens is that a man sets out to "trick" the Second Law of Thermodynamics. He endeavors to interfere with the "natural" or random course of events, so that some otherwise improbable outcome will be achieved. For his breakfast, he achieves an arrangement of bacon and eggs, side by side, upon a plate; and in achieving this improbability he is aided by other men who will sort out the appropriate pigs in some distant market and interfere with the natural juxtaposition of hens and eggs. Similarly in his courtship, he will endeavor to make a particular girl fall in love with him—and prevent her from behaving in a random manner. Briefly, in value seeking he is achieving a coincidence or congruence between something in his head—an idea of what breakfast should be—and something external, an actual arrangement of eggs and bacon. He achieves this

coincidence by altering the external objects and events. In contrast, when he is seeking information, he is again trying to achieve a congruence between "something in his head" and the external world; but now he attempts to do this by altering what is in his head.

Negative entropy, value, and information, are in fact alike in so far as the system to which these notions refer is the man plus environment, and in so far as, both in seeking information and in seeking values, the man is trying to establish an otherwise improbable congruence between ideas and events.

7. From what has been said above, it would be natural for the reader to ask a question somewhat as follows: "If the value system and the system of codification of information are really only aspects of the same central phenomenon, then how would you translate statements in terms of the one into statements in terms of the other?" Indeed, only by an adequate answer to this question can we make clear what we here mean by the two "aspects" of the system. We now attempt this:

Whatever communication we consider, be it the transmission of impulses in a neural system or the transmission of words in a conversation, it is evident that every message in transit has two sorts of "meaning." On the one hand, the message is a statement or report about events at a previous moment, and on the other hand it is a command—a cause or stimulus for events at a later moment. Consider the case of three neurons, A, B, and C, in series, so that the firing of A leads to the firing of B, and the firing of B leads to the firing of C. Even in this extremely simple case, the message transmitted by B has the two sorts of meanings referred to above. On the one hand it can be regarded as a "report" to the effect that A fired at a previous moment; and on the other hand it is a "command" or cause for C's later firing. The same thing is true of all verbal communication, and indeed of all communication whatsoever. When A speaks to B, whatever words he uses will have these two aspects: they will tell B about A, conveying information about some perception or knowledge which A has; and they will be a cause or basis for B's later action. In the case of language, however, the presence of these two meanings may be obscured by syntax. A's words may have the syntax of command, which will partly obscure their report aspects. For example, A may say "Halt!" and B may obey the command ignoring the informational aspects—e.g., the fact that A's words indicate some perception or other mental process of which his command is an indication. Or A's words may have the syntax of report, and B may fail to notice that this report has influenced him in a certain direction.

This double aspect of all communication is, of course, a commonplace of the psychiatric interview and is indeed the basis of a large part of all differences between the content of consciousness and the unconscious.

The patient is continually aware of only one aspect of what he is saying—whether it be the "report" or the "command"—and the psychiatrist is continually calling his attention to that aspect which he would prefer not to recognize. Conversely, the psychiatrist is not infrequently and often deliberately influencing the patient by comments and interpretations which have the appearance of report but which in fact exert influence upon the patient. Be that as it may, from the point of view of the present study, we state flatly that all communication has this duality of aspect and note that it remains important to investigate which of these aspects is perceived by the selective awareness of therapist and patient respectively in the given context.

Returning now to the question of translating statements about the codification of information into statements about the value system, it seems that this translation contains exactly the same type of difficulty that would be presented by the task of translating the report aspect of A's message into its command aspect. This difficulty may be summarized in the following form: that the translation is impossible unless we have total knowledge of B's psychological mechanism. If A says that the cat is on the mat, the observer can predict B's responses to this news only in so far as he knows B's psychic habits, especially his evaluation of cats and mats and the inhibitions which may prevent him from acting as he would like to act.

Into the above discussion, a fallacy has been allowed to creep. The question was how to translate statements about A's codification system into statements about A's value system; but for this question has been substituted a different question of predicting what will be the stimulus or command content of A's message as received by B. In the analogy, we have compared the integrated individual who both perceives and acts to a relationship involving two individuals, one (A) who perceives, codifies, and transmits information, and another (B) who acts upon this information. Any such comparison is clearly fallacious. Indeed, it is our thesis that precisely this fallacy is involved in all attempts to distinguish between the value system of an individual and his codification system. All attempts to translate from one system to another will inevitably lead to some fallacy of this order. They lead to describing the individual as though he were two separate persons, a perceiver and an active agent.

Let us therefore now attempt to put the two halves of the individual together. We may say that he perceives, and we may say that he acts as a result of his perception, but these two statements are really insepa-rable. Our only data about his codification of external events are derived from his reactions (introspective reports being only a special case among other reactions). His reactions are, in fact, a further stage of codifica-tion, another complex transformation derived from the original events.

Two steps of codification or transformation have occurred between external events and the individual's reaction to these events, and the observer has access only to the "product" (in the mathematical sense) of the two steps when superimposed. From this product it is impossible to arrive at any knowledge of either stage as a separate process. If the individual studied makes evident mistakes in his reaction to external events —as the patient often does—the observer has absolutely no means of knowing wherein the error lies. The subject may have "perceived" the events wrongly, or he may have translated correct perceptions into wrong actions: but which of these errors has occurred the external observer cannot tell. The question is unanswerable and therefore unreal.

8. This, then, would be our conclusion in regard to the nature of the relationship between codification and evaluation—that these two processes may occur separately, but that for the purposes of all scientific discussion they must be treated as a single process and studied through the complex characteristics of the relation between input (i.e., stimulus) and output (i.e., reaction) of the individual.

9. But there is also this point: that, whether or not it is realistic to separate two aspects of the single process, human beings in Occidental cultures do really talk and act as though these processes were separable. Right or wrong, the idea that value and codification are different phenomena modifies behavior and the events of therapy. Human beings in their interaction in therapy and in daily life draw inferences about each other's values and motivations, phrasing these inferences (so far as they phrase them at all) in terms of value and perception—i.e., in terms which presume a division in what, according to the present argument, should be grouped under a single heading of "codification-evaluation." In a later section we shall argue that it is specifically these inferences that are crucial to therapeutic change.

10. Lastly, a word must be said about consciousness, not to solve the ancient problems presented by this strange subjective datum but rather to indicate how those problems are related to the conceptual scheme which is here offered. Whatever may be the mechanistic or spiritual base of the phenomenon, it is certainly a special case of codification and reductive simplification of information about certain parts of the wider psychic life. It is, of course, true that the presence of consciousness denotes an extraordinary complication of the psyche, and many specifically human problems and maladjustments arise from this mirroring of a part of the total psyche in the field of consciousness. But still the fact seems clear that the content of consciousness is an extreme reduction, derived from the total rich continuum of psychic events. Every such reduction is a transformation or codification in the same sense in which the terms are here used and, as in all other cases of codification, the nature of the

transformation is not itself subject to direct introspection or voluntary control. This, indeed, is the point which we wish to stress: that while the (possibly illusory) sense of free will is closely bound up with the subjective experience of consciousness, the process by which items are selected for focusing in the mirror of consciousness is itself an unconscious process, not, at any given moment, subject to any exercise of the will. Over time, an individual can "train himself" to various sorts of special awareness, and to this extent he can modify the codification of ideas entering consciousness. But at a given instant, the determinism of that instant is seemingly complete.

Many schools of therapy operate upon the premise that therapeutic change is actually a change in the scope and content of consciousness, and the matter is therefore important to the present study. For present purposes, however, the problem of such changes is rephrased as follows: We assume that the person who "trains himself" does so as a result of past experience—especially interpersonal experience—which has determined his ability and motivation to undertake such changes. Such changes occur in therapy, and we must ask therefore about the interpersonal events and contexts of therapy which motivate and facilitate these changes. In brief, the introduction of consciousness as a concept will not profoundly modify the type of question which is here studied.

SELECTIVE AND PROGRESSIONAL INTEGRATION

Certain characteristics of the total codification-evaluation process will now be considered, in such a way as to pose questions about changes in this process—such changes being, according to our hypothesis, essential to therapy.

Broadly, there seem to be two sorts of process within the general area of codification-evaluation. These may be contrasted by considering two extreme examples. The first process we shall call decision by selective integration, and we shall exemplify it by a man's making a choice among a number of objects. To make this choice, he recognizes the specific objects as apples, oranges, pears, etc., and he knows from past experience which he likes and what actions and gratifications will be involved in eating the various sorts. If there is an unknown fruit among them, this too will be categorized as "unknown," and this category will have positive or negative value, determined by past experience. In this process of selective integration, the man categorizes and evaluates alternatives according to impressions derived from past experience, equating and differentiating elements of the unique present according to his experience with other elements in his unique past.

In contrast, an entirely different process of decision seems to occur in, for example, an extemporizing dancer. For any given movement within a sequence of movements, it is evident that some type of selection occurs which is different from the choice of a fruit of a given species. The dancer's choice is influenced to a much greater extent by the ongoing characteristics of his sequence of action, and even, perhaps, by the ongoing dancing of a partner. This second type of decision we shall call decision by progressional integration, and we shall amplify the example by saying that the phenomenon is not confined to activities involving rapid physical movement, though the movement of the dancer is a convenient model to characterize the state of any person whose actions involve relatively rapid complex movement in "psychological space." It seems that this type of progressional integration is especially characteristic for action sequences in which the component acts are imperfectly differentiated and categorized, and in which speed of decision is important.

Both the selective and progressional processes are probably present in some degree in every human decision. The man who is choosing fruit is in part influenced by the ongoing sequences of his own metabolism, by his preference for certain sequences of taste, and by the intricacies of ongoing courtesy between himself and any other person present. To this extent he acts on a progressional integration. Correspondingly, the dancer may envisage alternatives of action (including the alternative of ceasing to dance), and he may introspectively believe that he is choosing among these categories. In general, it seems that the selective and progressional phenomena may occur each within a frame defined by the other: After he has decided to eat a certain fruit, the details of the act of eating may be progressively determined within the framework of the selective decision. And conversely, in ongoing decisions involving long spans of time it is common for an individual to act selectively at every step and to discover that he has gradually made a major decision (e.g., the choice of a profession) by some progressional process.

It is clear, too, that persons differ in the relative importance of these two processes. Some will try to act selectively in contexts where the time relations of the actions would seem to demand progressional integration; while others will let themselves be guided by a progressional psychological *élan* even in contexts where the alternatives could have been more conventionally evaluated in categories. From a therapeutic point of view, it is important that certain types of patients benefit by learning to categorize the universe, while others must learn to act more freely in terms of progressional integration.

It also seems that cultures differ in the extent to which individuals within a given culture live according to one mode or another; and that cultures may differ in the relationship between these modes. In Balinese culture, for example, where the character structure of the individual seems to be codified in kinesthetic terms and feelings rather than in terms of the zonal modalities, it is conspicuous that categories of selective integration are necessary to enable any individual to determine what type of progressional action sequence he should follow. The selective categories of the social organization, in Balinese culture, are the major premises, within the terms of which the individual may behave with a very free progressional integration. He must know the caste of the individual whom he is talking to before he can talk at all. He must know the nature of the context in which he finds himself at the moment, but once these categories are determined, he is free to act in terms of a progressional spontaneity which many Occidentals envy. Occidental cultures seem often to promote a compulsive·categorization of the details of behavior, while leaving the individual a greater freedom to act in terms of progressional integration in regard to the wider decisions. These generalizations are, however, liable to be reversed or modified from individual to individual.

Man lives by those propositions whose validity is a function of his belief in them.

Two sorts of propositions of this kind were mentioned above. First, the propositions about codification. Such a statement as "The word 'cat' stands for a certain small mammal" is not either true or false. Its truth depends upon agreement between the speakers that it be true. In terms of such agreement they understand each other: or where disagreement occurs they will meet with misunderstanding. And this statement about the word "cat" is only one of a vast category of statements about codification, which category ranges all the way from the conventions of local phonetics up through the conventions of vocabulary to the conventions of syntax; and the same category will include the conventions of timing, pitch, emphasis, tone of voice, and all the other modalities of verbal and nonverbal communication, since all communication involves codification and these are the conventions of codification.

In addition, the preceding section contained statements about metacommunication; and this category of statements is a larger genus within which the statements about codification are to be included as a subcategory. When A communicates with B, the mere act of communicating can carry the implicit statement "we are communicating." In fact, this may be the most important message that is sent and received. The wisecracks of American adolescents and the smoother but no less stylized conversations of adults are only occasionally concerned with the giving and receiving of objective information; mostly, the conversations of leisure hours exist because people need to know that they are in touch with one another. They may ask questions which superficially seem to be about matters of impersonal fact—"Will it rain?" "What is in today's war news?"—but the speaker's interest is focused on the fact of communication with another human being. With comparative strangers, we "make conversation" rather than accept the message which would be implicit in silence—the message, "We are *not* communicating." It seems that this message would provoke anxiety because it implies rejection; perhaps also because the message itself is explosive with paradox. If two persons exchange this message, are they communicating?

Many sorts of games are of interest in this connection. An implicit message which is exchanged at bridge tables and on tennis courts is the affirmed agreement between the players as to the rules and goals. By participating in the game, they affirm the fact of communication, and by competing, they affirm the fact of shared value premises.

Similarly, every courtesy term between persons, every inflection of voice denoting respect or contempt, condescension or dependency, is a statement about the relationship between the two persons. Such messages are carried on the stream of verbal communication, and all these messages and their codification determine such matters as role and status, whose truth and stability depend upon implicit or explicit agreement between the persons that the relationship is as indicated. Moreover, all cues which define status and role are metacommunicative, since the recipient of any message is guided in his interpretation of that message and in his resulting action by his view of the relative roles and status between himself and the speaker.

It appears, then, that within the larger genus of metacommunicative propositions, it is possible to recognize at least two subcategories—the propositions about codification and the propositions about interpersonal relationship. It is certain, however, that overlapping frequently occurs between these subcategories and that a very small shift in emphasis or interpretation will cause a given proposition to appear to shift from one subcategory to the other. This shifting character is due to two circumstances: (a) that statements about relationship must still be codified; and (b), that every statement in a given codification is an implicit affirmation of this codification and is therefore in some degree metacommunicative. (When I say, "I see the cat," I am implicitly affirming the proposition that the word "cat" stands for that which I see.) The shifting relation between the propositions of codification and the propositions of human relationship can be illustrated by the following example: The statement "A policeman carries a nightstick as a badge of authority" contains both the statement of status and the statement of how this status is codified; the same example will serve to emphasize that all interpersonal actions are, in some degree, messages. When the policeman uses his nightstick, he is asserting his status in a particular relationship to a particular offender.

41 Elaborated and Restricted Codes: Their Social Origins and Some Consequences
BASIL BERNSTEIN

INTRODUCTION

This paper represents an attempt to discuss some aspects of the inter-relationships between social structure, forms of speech, and the subsequent regulation of behavior. The practical context of the enquiry is the differential response to educational opportunity made by children from different social classes. It has become abundantly clear that the determinants of this response are complex and that the response encapsulates the effects of socialization. The problem requires specification of the sociological processes which control the way the developing child relates himself to his environment. It requires an understanding of how certain areas of experience are differentiated, made specific and stabilized, so that which is relevant to the functioning of the social structure becomes relevant for the child. What seems to be needed is the development of a theory of social learning which would indicate what in the environment is available for learning, the conditions of learning, the constraints on subsequent learning, and the major reinforcing process.

The behavioral implications of the physical and social environment are transmitted in some way to the child. What is the major channel for such transmissions? What are the principles which regulate such transmissions? What are the psychological consequences and how are these stabilized in the developing child? What factors are responsible for variations in the principles which regulate the transmissions? The socio-linguistic approach used here is a limited attempt to provide some kind of answer to these questions.

The general framework of the argument will be given first. This will be followed by a detailed analysis of two general linguistic codes. Towards the end of the paper, some variants of the codes will be very crudely associated with social class.

Reprinted with permission of the publisher and the author. From J. J. Gumperz and D. Hymes, eds., "The Ethnography of Communication," *American Anthropologist Special Publication*, 66(2), 55–69 (1964).

In order to make a distinction between language and speech, a simple view of language has been adopted. Only two levels of language will be distinguished. The first level consists of the formal elements which may be used for the purposes of organization. These are relational elements and syntactic devices. There are rules regulating the use of such elements. This level is referred to as structure. Language may be looked at from this point of view, in terms of the range of structural alternatives or options which may be used for the purposes of organization. The second level consists of words which have objective reference or can be given objective reference. This level is called vocabulary. From the point of view of vocabulary, language may be considered as the totality of meanings evoked by the words which carry objective reference. Putting the two levels together, it could be said that language represents the world of the possible. On the one hand, it contains a finite set of options and the rules of their regulation at the structural level and a set of options at the level of vocabulary. Language then represents the totality of options and the attendant rules for doing things with words. It symbolizes what can be done.

Speech, on the other hand, is constrained by the circumstances of the moment, by the dictate of a local social relation and so symbolizes not what can be done, but what *is* done with different degrees of frequency. Speech indicates which options at the structural and vocabulary level are taken up. Between language in the sense defined and speech is social structure. The particular form a social relationship takes acts selectively on what is said. In terms of this approach, the form the social relationship takes regulates the options which speakers select at both the structural and vocabulary levels. Inasmuch as the social relationship does this, then it may establish for the speakers specific principles of choice: coding principles. These specific principles of choice, the canons which regulate selections, entail from the point of view of the speakers and listeners planning procedures which guide the speakers in the preparation of their speech and which guide the listeners in the reception of speech.

Changes in the form of the social relationship, it will be argued, act selectively upon principles of selection. Changes in the form of the social relationship can affect the planning procedures an individual uses in the preparation of his speech and it can affect the orientation of the listener. Different forms of social relationships may generate quite different speech systems or linguistic codes by affecting the planning procedures. These different speech systems or codes may create for their speakers different orders of significance. The experience of the speakers may then be transformed by what is made significant or relevant by the different speech systems. This is a sociological argument, because the speech system is taken as a consequence of the form of the social relationship, or, put more generally, is a quality of the social structure. The social structure becomes the independent variable. There are important psychological implications. The speech system or linguistic code, itself a function of the social structure, marks out selectively for the individual what is relevant in the environment. The experience of the individual is transformed by the learning which is generated by his own apparently voluntary acts of speech.

Summarizing the argument, the following is obtained. Different social structures may generate different speech systems or linguistic codes. The latter entail for the individual specific principles of choice which regulate the selections he makes from the totality of options represented by a given language. The principles of choice originally elicit, progressively strengthen, and finally stabilize the planning procedures an individual uses in the preparation of his speech and guide his orientation to the speech of others. What he actually says, from a developmental perspective, transforms him in the act of saying.

As the child learns his speech, or in the terms used here, learns specific codes which regulate his verbal acts, he learns the requirements of his social structure. The social structure becomes the substratum of his experience essentially through the effects of the linguistic process. The identity of the social structure, it is thought, is transmitted to the child essentially through the implications of the linguistic code which the social structure itself generates. From this point of view, every time the child speaks or listens, the social structure of which he is part is reinforced and his social identity is constrained. The social structure becomes for the developing child his psychological reality by the shaping of his acts of speech. Underlying the general pattern of the child's speech are, it is held, critical sets of choices, preferences for some alternatives rather than for others, which develop and are stabilized through time and which eventually come to play an important role in the regulation of intellectual, social and affective orientation. Children who have access to different speech systems or linguistic codes, by virtue of their position in the class structure, may adopt quite different intellectual and social procedures which may be only tenuously related to their purely psychological abilities.

ELABORATED AND RESTRICTED LINGUISTIC CODES

A start may be made by putting the following questions, although the answers are bound to be both limited and inadequate.

1. What kinds of social relations generate what kinds of speech systems?

2. What kinds of principles or planning procedures control the speech systems?

3. What kinds of relationships in the environment do these planning procedures both give access to and stabilize?

Two general coding systems will be distinguished. These systems will be defined in terms of the kinds of options speakers take up in order to organize what they have to say. These speech systems or linguistic codes are *not* defined in terms of vocabulary. If it is difficult to predict the syntactic options or alternatives a speaker uses to organize his meanings over a representative range of speech, this system of speech will be called an elaborated code. In the case of an elaborated code, the speaker will select from a wide range of syntactic alternatives and so it will not be easy to make an accurate assessment of the organizing elements he uses at any one time. However, with a restricted code, the range of alternatives, syntactic alternatives, is considerably reduced and so it is much more likely that prediction is possible. In the case of a restricted code, the vocabulary will be drawn from a narrow range but because the vocabulary is drawn from a narrow range, this in itself is no indication that the code is a restricted one.

If a speaker is oriented towards using an elaborated code, then the code through its planning procedures will facilitate the speaker in his attempt to put into words his purposes, his discrete intent, his unique experience in a verbally explicit form. If a speaker is moving towards a restricted code, then this code, through its planning procedures, will *not* facilitate the verbal expansion of the individual's discrete intent. In the case of an elaborated code, the speech system requires a higher level of verbal planning for the preparation of speech than in the case of a restricted code. It will be argued that the general behavior elicited from speakers by these two codes is directed towards different dimensions of significance. The events in the environment which take on significance when the codes are used are different, whether the events be social, intellectual, or emotional. These two codes, elaborated and restricted, it will be argued, are generated by particular forms of social relationships. They do not necessarily develop as a result of the speaker's innate intelligence. The level at which a speaker operates a particular code may well be a function of his native ability, but the *orientation* is entirely a matter of the sociological constraints acting upon the speaker.

I want first to examine some variants of a restricted code which exemplify the social characteristics of this code. These variants represent ideal cases and so they will be referred to as examples of the pure form of a restricted code. These variants all have one major common attribute: the verbal component of the message, given the social context, is highly predictable. Because the verbal component of the message is highly predictable, it necessarily follows that this must also be the case for the syntactic alternatives. Prediction refers to an ability of an observer who knows the code. In the case of the variants to be discussed, both observers and speakers share the ability to make the same level of prediction. Thus these variants can be subsumed under the general title of restricted code, as a special case of lexicon prediction.

RESTRICTED CODE (LEXICON PREDICTION)

A distinction will be made between the verbal component of the message and the extraverbal components. The verbal channel in this paper refers only to the transmission of words. The extraverbal channels include messages transmitted through the expressive associates of the words (intonation, etc.), and messages transmitted through gesture, physical set, and facial modifications. In the first variant of the ideal case, the messages transmitted through all channels (verbal and extraverbal) approach maximal redundancy from the perspective of both transmitter and receiver. This variant will occur where the organization and selection of all signals is bound by rigid and extensive prescriptions. The social relations will be of an ascribed status form, located usually, but not always, in religious, legal, and military social structures. The status relations are such that the area of discretion available to the incumbents is severely reduced, with the consequence that few options exist through which the incumbents may signal their discrete intent. The individual is transformed into a cultural agent. In these social relations, if discrete intent is signaled, that is, if the messages depart from maximal redundancy, then such messages are likely to be evaluated by the receiver(s) as violations, as profane.

The second variant of the ideal case of a restricted code is one where there is considerably less redundancy in the messages carried through the extraverbal channels, while the verbal channel carries messages approaching maximal redundancy. Consider the case of a mother telling her child stories which both know by heart—"And little Red Riding Hood went into the woods" ritualistic pause, "and what do you think happened?" ritualistic question. . . . This is another social relationship which constrains the options available to the incumbents of the statuses for the transmission of difference, or for the transmission of discrete intent. If the mother wishes to transmit her discrete experience or her uniqueness, she is unable to do this by varying her verbal selections. She can do it only by varying the messages transmitted through the *extraverbal channels;* through changes in muscular tension if she is holding the child, changes in facial set, gesture, or intonation. The verbal component of the messages

ensures that ascribed status aspects of the social relation are made salient
or the saliency of ascribed status aspects of the relation generates the
characteristics of the order of communication. Notice that in this variant,
the code defines the channels through which new information will be
transmitted. New information will be made available *through the extraverbal channels. Interpersonal* aspects of this social relation will be regulated by the encoding and decoding of messages passing through the
extraverbal channels. The code symbolizes and reinforces the form of the
social relation and controls the channel through which new learning is
made available. The mutual intents of mother and child are transmitted
through extraverbal channels, and these channels are likely to become
objects of special perceptual activity.

The third variant refers to an order of communication where the verbal
component approaches maximal redundancy, but where the extraverbal
channels permit messages of a relatively much lower order of prediction.
If this is the case, then it is very likely that the extraverbal channels will
become objects of special perceptual activity, as both transmitter and
receiver will signal their discrete experience through the agency of such
channels. There are many examples of this variant. I shall give only one.
Consider a dance hall downtown. A boy asks a girl to dance. They have
never met before. Although the precise nature of their initial communications will vary, it is suggested that they will take this form from the point
of view of the boy.

> "Do you come here often?"
> "Bit crowded-n'it?"
> "S'nice floor?"
> "Band's alright/dead/with it."

Clearly there are many examples of such routines. It is suggested that the
exchange of social routines approaching maximal redundancy occurs in
those social relationships where the participants have low predictability
about each other's discrete intent. The routine establishes predictability
at a high level of consensus. The consensus is obtained by making the
status aspect of the social relation salient. In fact, the form of the social
relation at this point is one of ascribed status, as in the other two cases
previously discussed. What is said is impersonal in the sense that the
verbal component comes prepacked. Interpersonal aspects of the relation
will be again transmitted through the extraverbal channels, and these will
again become objects of special perceptual activity. How the social relation develops will depend upon the decoding of extraverbal messages, as
these will carry new information which refers to the discrete intent of the
participants. Further, this variant of a restricted code affords the possibility of deferred commitment to the relation. Whether the relation will

shift from one of status to an interpersonal form regulated by speech will depend upon the decoding of extraverbal messages. This variant differs from the preceding two in terms of a greater use of potential options available in the extraverbal channels. It is suggested that the preliminaries to oriental bargaining relationships also exemplify this variant of a restricted code (lexicon prediction).

In all the three variants of a restricted code (lexicon prediction), the following interrelated characteristics may be found. Clearly, the social contents and function of these variants greatly differ. Attention has been drawn only to very general characteristics of the code.

1. The status aspect of the social relation is salient.

2. New information is made available through extraverbal channels and these channels will become objects of special perceptual activity.

3. Discrete intent can only be transmitted through variations in the extraverbal signals.

4. The code reinforces the form of the social relation by restricting the verbal signaling of differences.

RESTRICTED CODE (HIGH STRUCTURAL PREDICTION)

In this form, which is empirically the most general, only the syntactic alternatives taken up to organize meaning across a representative range of speech carry high predictability. In the case of a restricted code (lexicon prediction), it was argued that the controls on lexicon selection and syntactic organization were functions of social assumptions common to the speakers. These assumptions, translated behaviorally, refer to prescriptions inhering in the relative statuses the speakers are filling. It was noted that the speech refracted through these prescriptions did not permit the signaling of discrete intent. In the case of a restricted code (structural prediction) the options available for verbal and extraverbal messages are very much greater than in the case of a restricted code (lexicon prediction). The constraint exists essentially at the syntactic level. The range of syntactic alternatives used in this code is reduced and therefore the alternatives are relatively predictable. The lexicon, however, is likely to be drawn from a narrow range; but the fact that the lexicon is drawn from a narrow range is no criterion for deciding whether the code is restricted.

What is responsible for the simplification of the structure, the narrowing of the lexicon range, and the consequent constraint on the *verbal* elaboration of unique experience? It is suggested that the code is a function of a specific form of social relation. In the case of a restricted code (structural prediction), the speech is played out against a backdrop of assumptions common to the speakers, against a set of closely shared interests and identifications, against a system of shared expectations; in short, it presupposes a local cultural identity which reduces the need for the speakers to elaborate their intent verbally and to make it explicit. In one sentence the extent to which the intent of the other person may be taken for granted, the more likely that the structure of the speech will be simplified and the vocabulary drawn from a narrow range.

Concretely, a restricted code (structural prediction) will arise in closed communities like prisons, combat units of the armed service, criminal subcultures, and also in peer groups of children and adolescents and between married couples of long standing. In fact, the code will develop wherever the form of the social relation is based upon some extensive set of closely shared identifications, self-consciously held by the members. It is important to note that the use of specialist terms does not of itself indicate a restricted code (structural prediction). (For the sake of simplicity the term restricted code will be used for this speech system unless the context requires greater precision.)

I would like to examine in some detail the characteristics of this code. Consider a group of boys at a street corner, or a group of close friends in a bar, or a courting couple. I suggested that if one were observing these relationships, one would be struck by the following:

1. The observer would be eavesdropping on inclusive relationships, and so he would be struck by the measure of his own exclusion. He might have difficulty at first in following the speech as it would tend to be fast, fluent, relatively unpaused, and so the articulatory clues would be reduced.

2. On the other hand, if he could write down the sequences, he might be surprised to find that they would be relatively impersonal. If intent does not have to be verbalized and made explicit, if much can be assumed and taken for granted, there is no need to use a level of verbal planning which requires careful selection and fine discriminations. Consequently, he could expect that there would be a reduction in the number of qualifiers, a simple verbal stem limited to the active voice. There might be an increase in some personal pronouns like "you" and "they," and a reduction in others like the self-reference pronoun "I." He might find, over and above idiosyncratic use, a greater frequency of terminal sequences like "isn't it," "wouldn't they," "you know," "you see," etc. In other words, he might expect a reduction in the use of those elements which facilitate the verbal transmission of discrete experience and the speech would emphasize the communality of the speakers. This does not mean that there would be no differences between the speakers, only that the differences would be transmitted in a particular way. The verbal meanings would be condensed, but the amount of speech would still be considerable. The change would be in quality, not quantity.

3. He might notice the vitality of the speech and this vitality would serve an important function. The burden of changes in meaning would be carried through the extraverbal component of the communication. The "how" of the communication would be important rather than the "what." The discrete intent of the speakers, the "I" of the speakers, would be transmitted not through varying their verbal selections, but through varying the expressive features of the communication, through changes in gesture, physical set, intonation, facial modification.

4. He might also notice that the speech sequences, from his point of view, would tend to be dislocated—disjunctive. There might well be logical gaps in the flow of meaning. The speakers would not be worried because they could take much for granted. The connecting devices in the speech might not clarify the logical organization of meaning. In fact, the observer might find that the meanings were strung together rather like beads on a string rather than being logically ordered.

5. Finally, the content of the speech is likely, but not necessarily, to be concrete, narrative and descriptive, rather than analytical or abstract. If the speech moved in the direction of the abstract, it would be likely that the propositions would not be fully developed, relying on sequences like "you see," "you know," "wouldn't it" to bridge points of uncertainty.

Putting all this together, an observer might be struck by the fact that the speech in these social relationships was fast, fluent, with reduced articulatory clues, the meanings might be discontinuous, dislocated, condensed and local, but the quantity of speech might not be affected, that there would be a low level of vocabulary and syntactic selection, and that the "how" rather than the "what" of the communication would be important. *The unique meaning of the person would tend to be implicit.*

In fact, the sequence might have the same *general* form as this:

It's all according like well those youths and that if they get with
gangs and that they most
they most
have a bit of a lark around and
say it goes wrong
and that and they probably knock some off I think they do it just to be a
bit big you know
getting publicity here and there.

Verbal I.Q. average
(lower working-class)
Transcript of a tape-recorded discussion

The point I want to make is that a restricted code is available to *all* members of society as the social conditions which generate it are universal. But it may be that a considerable section of our society has access only to this code by virtue of the implications of class background. I am suggesting that there is relatively high probability of finding children limited to this code among sections of the lower working-class population. On this argument, the general form of their speech is not substandard English but is related to and shares a similar social origin with the restricted code I have just outlined. It is a special case—a case where children can use one and only one speech system. What this code makes relevant to them, the learning generated by apparently spontaneous acts of speech, is not appropriate for their formal educational experience. But only from this point of view is it inappropriate.

A restricted code (structural prediction) shares the general social characteristics of the variants of a restricted code (lexicon prediction). It is perhaps somewhat less misleading to say that it is on the same dimension but at the opposite end. It limits the verbal signaling of discrete intent; the extraverbal signals become important bearers of changes in meaning and so tend to become the objects of special perceptual activity. *The status aspect of the social relation is salient with a consequent reduction in role discretion.* The code is a facility for the transmission of global, concrete, descriptive, narrative statements in which discrete intent is unlikely to be raised to the level of elaboration and so made explicit.

ELABORATE CODES (LOW STRUCTURAL PREDICTION)

I shall consider finally the nature of an elaborated code, its regulatory function and its social origin. Restricted codes can be considered status-oriented speech systems. The codes reinforce the form of the social relation, by limiting the verbal signaling of personal difference. The forms of an elaborated code are quantitatively and qualitatively different from the codes so far discussed. An elaborated code was defined in terms of the difficulty of predicting the syntactic alternatives taken up to organize meaning across a representative range of speech. This difficulty arises because an extensive range of syntactic alternatives is available within this code and therefore the probability of which alternatives will at any one time be taken up is low. This code, through its planning procedures, allows the speaker to elaborate verbally and to make explicit his discrete intent. An elaborated code, or at least an orientation towards this code, will develop to the extent that the discrete intent of the other person may *not* be taken for granted. Inasmuch as the other person's intent may not be taken for granted, then the speaker is forced to expand and elaborate his meanings, with the consequence that he chooses more carefully among syntactic and vocabulary options.

Now to the extent a speaker does this his sequences will carry *verbally* the elaboration of his experience. The potential discrepancy between speakers in expectations, in nuances of interests, generates in them a tension to select from their linguistic resources a verbal arrangement which closely specifies a given referent. Meanings which are discrete and local to the speaker are cut so that they are intelligible to the listener. The condition of the listener, unlike the case of a restricted code, will be taken into account in the preparation of the speech. In terms of what is transmitted *verbally* rather than what is transmitted *extraverbally*, an elaborated code encourages the speaker to focus upon the other person as an experience different from his own. An elaborated code is *person* rather than status oriented.

In the case of a restricted code, what is transmitted *verbally* refers to the other person in terms of his status or local group membership. What is *said* reflects the form of the social relation and its basis of shared assumptions. Speakers using a restricted code are dependent upon these shared assumptions. The mutually held range of identifications defines the area of common intent and so the range of the code. The dependency underpinning the social relation generating an elaborated code is not of this order. With an elaborated code, the listener is dependent upon the *verbal elaboration of meaning*. In restricted codes, to varying degrees, the extraverbal channels become objects of special perceptual activity; in elaborated codes it is the verbal channel.

It is important to consider differences in the role relations which these codes presuppose.

The form of the social relation which generates an elaborated code is such that a range of discretion must inhere in the role if it is to be produced at all. Further, the speaker's social history must have included practice and training for the role. These role relations receive less support from shared expectations. The orientation of the speaker is based upon the expectation of psychological difference—his own and that of others. Individuated speech released through an elaborated code presupposes a history of a particular role relation if it is to be both prepared *and* delivered appropriately. The range of discretion which must necessarily inhere in the role involves the speaker in a measure of social isolation. He may be differentiated from his social group as a figure is differentiated from its ground. The role relations which presuppose a restricted code are quite different. The range of discretion of the role is confined to the area of common intent and, therefore, the role receives explicit support from the status components of the relationship. Looked at from another point of view, control on the role is mediated through a restricted self-editing process as far as the *verbal* messages are concerned. Although it is going too far to argue that the role relations of a restricted code orient its speakers to seeking affirmation, confirmation, or similarity, it is likely that role strain results from persistent attempts to signal discrete intent in a verbally elaborated form. This source of role strain in restricted code relationships is precisely the role relationship appropriate for an elaborated code.

These codes are translations of different forms of social relations or even qualities of different social structures; thus, different orientations, different ranges of discretion, different forms of dependency, and different sources of strain inhere in the respective roles. Thus speakers limited to a restricted code may be unable to manage the role requirements which are necessary for the production of an elaborated code. Conversely, it is possible that an individual limited to an elaborated code cannot switch codes because of an inability to switch roles.

An elaborated code generated originally by the form of the social relation becomes a facility for transmitting individuated verbal responses. As far as any one speaker is concerned, he is not aware of a speech system or code, but the planning procedures which he is using both in the preparation of his speech and in the receiving of speech are creating one. These planning procedures promote a relatively higher level of structural organization and vocabulary selection than in the case of a restricted code. What is then made available for learning by an elaborated code is of a different order from what is made available in the case of a restricted code. The learning generated by these speech systems is quite different, whether it be social, intellectual, or affective. From a developmental perspective, an elaborated code user comes to perceive language as a set of theoretical possibilities available for the transmission of unique experience. The concept of self, unlike the concept of self of a speaker limited to a restricted code, will be verbally differentiated, so that it becomes in its own right the object of special perceptual activity. In the case of a speaker limited to a restricted code the concept of self will tend to be refracted through the implications of the status arrangements. Here there is no problem of self, *because the problem is not relevant*.

The preparation and delivery of relatively explicit meaning is the major purpose of an elaborated code. This affects the manner of delivery. The speech of a restricted code, it was argued above, would be delivered in a fast, fluent, relatively unpaused style with reduced articulatory clues. The speech controlled by an elaborated code will be punctuated by relatively frequent pauses and longer hesitations. A specific monitoring, or self-editing, system initially generates the code. The time dimension underlying the planning process producing an elaborated code tends to be longer than the time dimension underlying the planning process producing a restricted code. The delay between impulse and verbal signal is mediated through an extensive self-editing process in the case of an elaborated code. If a speaker is limited to a restricted code, then a specific planning or monitoring system develops and becomes progressively strengthened. These differences in the time dimension inhering in the planning processes of the two codes will have a number of psychological consequences, which cannot be developed here.

As a child learns an elaborated code, he learns to scan a particular syntax, to receive and transmit a particular pattern of meaning, to develop a particular planning process and *very early learns to orient towards the verbal channel*. He learns to manage the role requirements necessary for the effective production of the code. He becomes aware of a certain order of relationships (intellectual, social, and emotional) in his environment and his experience is transformed by these relations. As the code, through its planning procedures, becomes established, the developing child voluntarily through his acts of speech generates these relations. He comes to perceive language as a set of theoretical possibilities for the presentation of his discrete experience to others. An elaborated code through its regulation, induces developmentally in its speakers an expectation of separateness and difference from others. It points to the possibilities inherent in a complex conceptual hierarchy for the organization of experience.

It is possible to distinguish two modes of an elaborated code. One mode facilitates relations between *persons* and the second facilitates relations between *objects*. These two modes of an elaborated code would, in principle, differentiate different ranges of experiences and would presuppose different role relations. Although there is little time to develop this distinction, it might have some relevance to the present problems of C. P. Snow's two cultures.

A child *limited* to a restricted code will tend to develop essentially through the regulation inherent in the code. For such a child, speech does not become an object of special perceptual activity, neither does a theoretical attitude develop towards the structural possibilities of sentence organization. The speech is epitomized by a low level and limiting syntactic organization and there is little motivation or orientation toward increasing vocabulary. This code becomes a facility for transmitting and receiving concrete, global, descriptive, narrative statements involving a relatively low level of conceptualization. The planning processes which generate the speech involve a relatively short time dimension and, thus, a reduced self-editing function. Extraverbal channels tend to become the agencies through which discrete intent is signaled and so these extraverbal channels early become objects of special perceptual activity. It is a status-oriented code and elicits and progressively strengthens a relatively undifferentiated adherence to the normative arrangements of a local social structure. The verbal channel promotes the transmission of social rather than individual symbols. As the child learns a restricted code, he learns to control a particular role relation, and code switching may be hampered by the role requirements of a restricted code. Finally, an individual limited to a restricted code will tend to mediate an elaborated code through the regulation of his own. Clearly one code is not better than another; each possesses its own esthetic, its own possibilities. Society, however, may place different values on the orders of experience elicited, maintained, and progressively strengthened through the different coding systems.

The orientation towards these codes, elaborated and restricted, may be independent of the psychology of the child, independent of his native ability, although the *level* at which a code is used will undoubtedly reflect purely psychological and physiological attributes. The orientation toward these codes may be governed entirely by the form of the social relation, or more generally by the quality of the social structure. The intellectual and social procedures by which individuals relate themselves to their environment may be very much a question of their speech models within the family and the codes these speech models use.

Finally, I should like to draw attention to the relations between social class and the two coding systems. The subcultural implications of social class give rise to discrete socialization procedures. The different normative systems create different family role systems operating with different modes of social control. It is considered that the normative systems associated with the middle-class and associated strata are likely to give rise to the modes of an elaborated code while that associated with some sections of the working class is likely to create individuals limited to a restricted code. Clearly, social class is an extremely crude index for the codes, and more specific conditions for their emergence have been given in this paper. Variations in behavior found within groups who fall within a particular class (defined in terms of occupation and education) within a mobile society are often very great. It is possible to locate the two codes more precisely by considering the orientation of the family role system, the mode of social control, and the resultant verbal feedback. Variations in the orientation of the family role system can be linked to the external social network of the family and to occupational roles. It is not possible to do more than mention the possibilities of these more sensitive indices.

Very broadly, then, children socialized within middle-class and associated strata can be expected to possess *both* an elaborated and a restricted code while children socialized within some sections of the working-class strata, particularly the lower working-class, can be expected to be *limited* to a restricted code. As a child progresses through a school it becomes critical for him to possess, or at least to be oriented toward, an elaborated code if he is to succeed.

Some research specific to this thesis based upon small samples of subjects and speech does indicate that middle-class and working-class subjects aged fifteen years, male, matched for average verbal I.Q., differ in their coding orientation in the predicted direction. This research further indicates that differences in the time dimension of the planning processes inhering in the respective codes are also in the predicted direction. It is important to repeat that these results are based upon small samples. Further research has shown that middle-class and working-class subjects, male, at two age levels, matched for average verbal and average nonverbal I.Q., operated with the predicted codes in a sample of representative written work. This study also showed a relation between levels of abstraction and the use of the respective codes.

There is also firm evidence showing a relative deterioration in verbal I.Q. between the ages of eight and eleven years and between eleven and fifteen years for working-class children when compared with middle-class children between the same ages. Other research shows clearly that the verbal I.Q. scores of working-class subjects, particularly lower working-class, are likely to be severely depressed in relation to their scores at the higher ranges of a nonverbal test. This deterioration in verbal I.Q., discrepancy between verbal and nonverbal I.Q. tests and failure to profit from formal education on the part of working-class children, particularly those of lower working-class origins, is thought to be closely related to the control on types of learning induced by a restricted code. The relative backwardness of some working-class children may well be a form of culturally induced backwardness transmitted to the child through the implications of the linguistic process. The code the child brings to the school symbolizes his social identity. It relates him to his kin and to his local social relations. The code orients the child progressively to a pattern of relationships which constitute for the child his psychological reality and this reality is reinforced every time he speaks.

CONCLUSION

An attempt has been made to show how two general coding systems and their variants are elicited by the structure of social relations. The dimensions of relevance created by the different coding systems have been explored. Although the main burden of the paper has been to examine broad social class affiliations of the codes and to indicate briefly their socializing and formal educational consequences, it is tentatively thought that the theory might well have a more general application. Elaborated and restricted codes and their variants should be found in any social structure where their originating conditions exist. The definitions should, in principle be capable of application to a range of languages although in any one case elaboration and restriction will be relative.

42 Social Class and Modes of Communication
LEONARD SCHATZMAN
and ANSELM STRAUSS

Common assumptions suggest that there may be important differences in the thought and communication of
social classes. Men live in an environment which is mediated through
symbols. By naming, identifying, and classifying, the world's objects and
events are perceived and handled. Order is imposed through conceptual
organization, and this organization embodies not just anybody's rules but
the grammatical, logical, and communicative canons of groups. Communication proceeds in terms of social requirements for comprehension,
and so does "inner conversation" or thought. Both reasoning and speech
meet requirements of criticism, judgment, appreciation, and control. Communication across group boundaries runs the danger—aside from sheer
language difficulties—of being blocked by differential rules for the ordering of speech and thought.

If these assumptions are correct, it follows that there should be observable differences in communication according to social class and that
these differences should not be merely matters of degree of preciseness,
elaboration, vocabulary, and literary style. It follows also that the modes
of thought should be revealed by modes of speaking.

Our data are the interview protocols gathered from participants in a
disaster. The documents, transcribed from tape, contain a wealth of local
speech. Respondents had been given a relatively free hand in reporting
their experiences, and the interviews averaged twenty-nine pages. These
seemed admirably suited to a study of differences between social classes
in modes of communication and in the organization of perception and
thought. We used them also to explore the hypothesis that substantial
intraclass differences in the organization of stories and accounts existed;
hence low-class respondents might fail to satisfy the interviewer's canons
of communication.

Approximately 340 interviews were available, representing random
sampling of several communities ravaged by a tornado. Cases were selected by extreme position on educational and income continuums. Interviewees were designated as "lower" if education did not go beyond

Reprinted with permission of the University of Chicago Press and the authors.
From *The American Journal of Sociology*, 60:329–338 (1955).

grammar school and if the annual family income was less than two thousand dollars. The "upper" group consisted of persons with one or more
years of college education and annual incomes in excess of four thousand
dollars. These extremes were purposely chosen for maximum socioeconomic contrast and because it seemed probable that nothing beyond formal or ritual communication would occur between these groups.

Cases were further limited by the following criteria: age (twenty-one
to sixty-five years), race (white only), residence (native of Arkansas and
more than three years in the community), proximity (either in the
disaster area or close by), good co-operation in interview (as rated by
interviewer), and less than eight probes per page (to avoid a rigid ques-
tion-answer style with consequent structuring of interview by the interviewer's questions). The use of these criteria yielded ten upper-group
cases, which were then matched randomly with ten from the lower group.

DIFFERENCES BETWEEN CLASSES

Differences between the lower and upper groups were striking; and,
once the nature of the difference was grasped, it was astonishing how
quickly a characteristic organization of communication could be detected
and described from a reading of even a few paragraphs of an interview.
The difference is not simply the failure or success—of lower and upper
groups, respectively—in communicating clearly and in sufficient detail for
the interviewer's purposes. Nor does the difference merely involve correctness or elaborateness of grammar or use of a more precise or colorful
vocabulary The difference is a considerable disparity in (a) the number
and kinds of perspectives utilized in communication; (b) the ability to
take the listener's role; (c) the handling of classifications; and (d) the
frameworks and stylistic devices which order and implement the communication.

PERSPECTIVE OR CENTERING

By perspective or centering is meant the standpoint from which a
description is made. Perspectives may vary in number and scope. The
flexibility with which one shifts from perspective to perspective during
communication may vary also.

LOWER CLASS. Almost without exception any description offered by a
lower-class respondent is a description as seen through his *own* eyes; he
offers his own perceptions and images directly to the listener. His best
performance is a straight, direct narrative of events as he saw and experi-

enced them. He often locates himself clearly in time and place and indicates by various connective devices a rough progression of events in relation to his activities. But the developmental progression is only in relation to himself. Other persons and their acts come into his narrative more or less as he encountered them. In the clearest interviews other actors are given specific spatial and temporal location, and sometimes the relationships among them or between them and himself are clearly designated.

The speaker's images vary considerably in clarity but are always his own. Although he may occasionally repeat the stories of other persons, he does not tell the story as though he were the other person reconstructing events and feelings. He may describe another person's act and the motive for it, with regard to himself, but this is the extent of his role-taking—he does not assume the role of another toward still others, except occasionally in an implicit fashion: "Some people was helping other people who was hurt." This limitation is especially pronounced when the behavior of more than two or three persons is being described and related. Here the description becomes confused: At best the speaker reports some reactions, but no clear picture of interaction emerges. The interaction either is not noticed or is implicitly present in the communication ("We run over there to see about them, and they was alright"). Even with careful probing the situation is not clarified much further. The most unintelligible speakers thoroughly confound the interviewer who tries to follow images, acts, persons, and events which seem to come out of nowhere and disappear without warning.

MIDDLE CLASS. The middle class can equal the best performance of the lower class in communicating and elaborating a direct description. However, description is not confined to so narrow a perspective. It may be given from any of several standpoints: for instance, another person, a class of persons, an organization, an organizational role, even the whole town. The middle-class speaker may describe the behavior of others, including classes of others, from their standpoints rather than from his, and he may include sequences of acts as others saw them. Even descriptions of the speaker's own behavior often are portrayed from other points of view.

CORRESPONDENCE OF IMAGERY BETWEEN SPEAKER AND LISTENER

Individuals vary in their ability to see the necessity for mediating linguistically between their own imagery and that of their listeners. The speaker must know the limits within which he may assume a correspondence of imagery. When the context of the item under discussion is in physical view of both, or is shared because of similarity of past experience, or is implicitly present by virtue of a history of former interaction, the problem of context is largely solved. But when the context is neither so provided nor offered by the speaker, the listener is confronted with knotty problems of interpretation. In the accounts of the most unintelligible respondents we found dream-like sets of images with few connective, qualifying, explanatory, or other context-providing devices. Thus, the interviewer was hard pressed to make sense of the account and was forced to probe at every turn lest the speaker figuratively run away with the situation. The respondents were willing and often eager to tell their stories, but intention to communicate does not always bring about clear communication. The latter involves, among other requirements, an ability to hear one's words as others hear them.

LOWER CLASS. Lower-class persons displayed a relative insensitivity to disparities in perspective. At best, the respondent corrected himself on the exact time at which he performed an act or became aware that his listener was not present at the scene and so located objects and events for him. On occasion he reached a state of other-consciousness: "You can't imagine if you wasn't there what it was like." However, his assumption of a correspondence in imagery is notable. There is much surnaming of persons without genuine identification, and often terms like "we" and "they" are used without clear referents. The speaker seldom anticipates responses to his communication and seems to feel little need to explain particular features of his account. He seldom qualifies an utterance, presumably because he takes for granted that his perceptions represent reality and are shared by all who were present. Since he is apt to take so much for granted, his narrative lacks depth and richness and contains almost no qualifications and few genuine illustrations. The hearer very often is confronted with a descriptive fragment that supposedly represents a more complete story. The speaker may then add phrases like "and stuff like that" or "and everything." Such phrasing is not genuine summation but a substitute for detail and abstraction. Summary statements are virtually absent, since they signify that speakers are sensitive to the needs of listeners. Certain phrases that appear to be summaries—such as "That's all I know" and "That's the way it was"—merely indicate that the speaker's knowledge is exhausted. Other summarylike phraseologies, like "It was pitiful," appear to be asides, reflective of self-feeling or emotion rather than résumés of preceding detail.

MIDDLE CLASS. The middle-class respondent also makes certain assumptions about the correspondence of the other's images with his own. Nevertheless, in contrast with the lower group, he recognizes much more fully that imagery may be diverse and that context must be provided. Hence he uses many devices to supply context and to clarify meaning. He qualifies, summarizes, and sets the stage with rich introductory material, expands themes, frequently illustrates, anticipates disbelief, meticulously locates and identifies places and persons—all with great complexity of detail. He depends less on saying "You know"; he insists upon explaining if he realizes that a point lacks plausibility or force. Hence he rarely fails to locate an image, or series of images, in time or place. Frequent use of qualification is especially noteworthy. This indicates not only multiple centering but a very great sensitivity to listeners, actual and potential—including the speaker himself.

In short, the middle-class respondent has what might be called "communication control," at least in such a semiformal situation as the interview. Figuratively, he stands between his own images and the hearer and says, "Let me introduce you to what I saw and know." It is as though he were directing a movie, having at his command several cameras focused at different perspectives, shooting and carefully controlling the effect. By contrast, the lower-class respondent seems himself more like a single camera which unreels the scene to the audience. In the very telling of his story he is more apt to lose himself in his imagery. The middle-class person—by virtue, we would presume, of his greater sensitivity to his listener—stands more outside his experience. He does not so much tell you what he saw as fashion a story about what he saw. The story may be accurate in varying degrees, although, in so far as it is an organized account, it has both the virtues and the defects of organization. The comparative accuracies of middle- and lower-class accounts are not relevant here; the greater objectivity of the former merely reflects greater distance between narrator and event.

In organizing his account, the middle-class respondent displays parallel consciousness of the other and himself. He can stop midstream, take another direction, and, in general, exert great control over the course of his communication. The lower-class respondent seems to have much less foresight, appearing to control only how much he will say to the interviewer, or whether he will say it at all, although presumably he must have some stylistic controls not readily observable by a middle-class reader.

CLASSIFICATIONS AND CLASSIFICATORY RELATIONS

LOWER CLASS. Respondents make reference mainly to the acts and persons of particular people, often designating them by proper or family names. This makes for fairly clear denotation and description, but only as long as the account is confined to the experiences of specific individuals. There comes a point when the interviewer wishes to obtain information about classes of persons and entire organizations as well as how they impinged upon the respondent, and here the lower-class respondent becomes relatively or even wholly inarticulate. At worst he cannot talk about categories of people or acts because, apparently, he does not think readily in terms of classes. Questions about organizations, such as the Red Cross, are converted into concrete terms, and he talks about the Red Cross "helping people" and "people helping other people" with no more than the crudest awareness of how organizational activities interlock. At most the respondent categorizes only in a rudimentary fashion: "Some people were running; other people were looking in the houses." The interviewer receives a sketchy and impressionistic picture. Some idea is conveyed of the confusion that followed upon the tornado, but the organizing of description is very poor. The respondent may mention classes in contrasting juxtaposition (rich and poor, hurt and not-hurt), or list groups of easily perceived, contrasting actions, but he does not otherwise spell out relations between these classes. Neither does he describe a scene systematically in terms of classes that are explicitly or clearly related, a performance which would involve a shifting of viewpoint.

It is apparent that the speakers think mainly in particularistic or concrete terms. Certainly classificatory thought must exist among many or all the respondents; but, in communicating to the interviewer, class terms are rudimentary or absent and class relations implicit: relationships are not spelled out or are left vague. Genuine illustrations are almost totally lacking, either because these require classifications or because we—as middle-class observers—do not recognize that certain details are meant to imply classes.

MIDDLE CLASS. Middle-class speech is richly interlarded with classificatory terms, especially when the narrator is talking about what he saw rather than about himself. Typically, when he describes what other persons are doing, he classifies actions and persons and more often than not explicitly relates class to class. Often his descriptions are artistically organized around what various categories of persons were doing or experiencing. When an illustration is offered, it is clear that the speaker means it to stand for a general category. Relief and other civic organizations are conceived as sets or classes of co-ordinated roles and actions; some persons couch their whole account of the disaster events in organizational terms, hardly deigning to give proper names or personal accounts. In short, concrete imagery in middle-class communication is dwarfed or overshadowed by the prevalence and richness of conceptual terminology. Organization of speech around classifications comes readily, and undoubtedly the speaker is barely conscious of it. It is part and parcel of his formal and informal education. This is not to claim that middle-class persons always think with and use classificatory terms, for doubtless this is not true. Indeed, it may be that the interview exacts from them highly conceptualized descriptions. Nonetheless, we conclude that, in general, the thought and speech of middle-class persons is less concrete than that of the lower group.

ORGANIZING FRAMEWORKS AND STYLISTIC DEVICES

One of the requirements of communication is that utterances be organized. The principle of organization need not be stated explicitly by the speaker or recognized by the listener. Organizing frames can be of various sorts. Thus an ordering of the respondents' description is often set by the interviewer's question, or the speaker may set his own framework ("There is one thing you should know about this"). The frame can be established jointly by both interviewer and respondent, as when the former asks an open-ended question within whose very broad limits the respondent orders his description in ways that strike him as appropriate or interesting. The respondent, indeed, may organize his account much as though he were telling a special kind of story or drama, using the interviewer's questions as hardly more than general cues to what is required. The great number of events, incidents, and images which must be conveyed to the listener may be handled haphazardly, neatly, dramatically, or sequentially; but, if they are to be communicated at all, they must be ordered somehow. Stylistic devices accompany and implement these organizing frames, and the lower and upper groups use them in somewhat different ways.

LOWER CLASS. The interviewer's opening question, "Tell me your story of the tornado," invites the respondent to play an active role in organizing his account; and this he sometimes does. However, with the exception of one person who gave a headlong personal narrative, the respondents did not give long, well-organized, or tightly knit pictures of what happened to them during and after the tornado. This kind of general depiction either did not occur to them or did not strike them as appropriate.

The frames utilized are more segmental or limited in scope than those used by the middle class. They appear to be of several kinds and their centering is personal. One is the personal narrative, with events, acts, images, persons, and places receiving sequential ordering. Stylistic devices further this kind of organization: for instance, crude temporal connectives like "then," "and," and "so" and the reporting of images or events as they are recollected or as they appear in the narrative progression. Asides may specify relationships of kinship or the individuals' location in space. But, unless the line of narrative is compelling to the speaker, he is likely to wander off into detail about a particular incident, where the incident in turn then provides a framework for mentioning further events. Likewise, when a question from the interviewer breaks into the narrative, it may set the stage for an answer composed of a number of images or an incident. Often one incident becomes the trigger for another, and, although some logical or temporal connection between them may exist for the speaker, this can scarcely be perceived by the interviewer. Hence the respondent is likely to move out of frames quickly. The great danger of probes and requests for elaboration is that the speaker will get far away from the life-line of his narrative—and frequently far away from the interviewer's question. As recompènse the interviewer may garner useful and unexpectedly rich information from the digressions, although often he needs to probe this material further to bring it into context. General questions are especially likely to divert the speaker, since they suggest only loose frames; or he may answer in general, diffuse, or blurred terms which assume either that the listener was there too or that he will put meaningful content into the words. If a question is asked that concerns abstract classes or is "above" the respondent—a query, say, about relief organizations—then very general answers or concrete listing of images or triggering of images are especially noticeable. When the interviewer probes in an effort to get some elaboration of an occurrence or an expansion of idea, he commonly meets with little more than repetition or with a kind of "buckshot" listing of images or incidents which is supposed to fill out the desired picture. The lack of much genuine elaboration is probably related to the inability to report from multiple perspectives.

One requirement of the interview is that it yield a fairly comprehensive account of the respondent's actions and perceptions. With the lower-class respondent the interviewer, as a rule, must work very hard at building a comprehensive frame directly into the interview. This he does by forcing many subframes upon the respondent. He asks many questions about exact time sequence, placement and identification of persons, expansion of detail, and the like. Especially must he ask pointed questions about the relations of various personages appearing in the account. Left to his own devices, the respondent may give a fairly straightforward narrative or competently reconstruct incidents that seem only partially connected with each other or with his narrative. But the respondent seldom voluntarily gives both linear and cross-sectional pictures.

The devices used to implement communication are rather difficult to isolate, perhaps because we are middle class ourselves. Among the devices most readily observable are the use of crude chronological notations (e.g., "then, . . . and then"), the juxtaposing or direct contrasting of classes (e.g., rich and poor), and the serial locating of events. But the elaborate devices that characterize middle-class interviews are strikingly absent.

MIDDLE CLASS. Without exception middle-class respondents imposed over-all frames of their own upon the entire interview. Although very sensitive generally to the needs of the interviewer, they made the account their own. This is evidenced sometimes from the very outset; many respondents give a lengthy picture in answer to the interviewer's invitation, "Tell me your story." The organizing frame may yield a fluid narrative that engulfs self and others in dense detail; it may give a relatively static but rich picture of a community in distress; or, by dramatic and stage-setting devices, it may show a complicated web of relationships in dramatic motion. The entire town may be taken as the frame of reference and its story portrayed in time and space.

Besides the master-frame, the middle-class respondent utilizes many subsidiary frames. Like the lower-class person, he may take off from a question. But, in doing so—especially where the question gives latitude by its generality or abstractness—he is likely to give an answer organized around a subframe which orders his selection and arrangement of items. He may even shift from one image to another, but rarely are these left unrelated to the question which initially provoked them. He is much more likely also to elaborate than to repeat or merely to give a scattered series of percepts.

One prerequisite for the elaboration of a theme is an ability to depart from it while yet holding it in mind. Because he incorporates multiple perspectives, the respondent can add long asides, discuss the parallel acts of other persons in relation to himself, make varied comparisons for the enrichment of detail and comprehension—and then can return to the original point and proceed from there. Often he does this after first preparing his listener for the departure and concludes the circuit with a summary statement or a transitional phrase like "well—anyhow" that marks the end of the digression.

The stylistic devices utilized by any respondent are many and varied. But each speaker uses some devices more frequently than others, since certain ones are more or less appropriate to given frames. There is no point in spelling out the whole range of devices; they are of the sort used in any clear detailed narrative and effective exposition. If the respondent is pressed to the limit of his ability in explaining a complex point or describing a complicated scene, he calls into play resources that are of immensely high order. Sometimes a seemingly simple device will turn out on closer inspection to demand a sophisticated handling of communication—for instance, the frequent and orderly asides that break into exposition or narrative and serve with great economy to add pertinent detail.

INTRACLASS DIFFERENCES

MIDDLE CLASS. Although all middle-class accounts were informative, there were considerable differences of construction among them. The frames utilized by any respondent are multiple, but respondents tend to use either a frame emphasizing sequence, human drama, and personal incident or one stressing interlocking classes of civic acts. Each orientation is implemented by somewhat different stylistic techniques. There are of course different ways of narrating; thus one can dwell more upon conditions for activity than upon the acts themselves. Similarly, accounts focused upon town organization vary in such matters as the scope of description and the degree of emphasis upon temporal sequence. Both frameworks are interchangeable, and their use is a function either of the speaker's habitual orientation or of his definition of the interview situation rather than of his ability to use one or the other mode.

LOWER CLASS. Lower-class persons can best be distinguished in terms of ability to meet the minimum requirements of the interview. Some literally cannot tell a straight story or describe a simple incident coherently. At the other extreme we find an adequate self-focused narrative, with considerable detail tightly tied to sequential action, including retrospective observation about the narrator's facts as he develops them. Midway between these extremes are the people who can tell portions of narrative but are easily distracted: either an image suggests some other image, or the interviewer asks a question focusing interest and concentration elsewhere than upon the narrative or he calls for some expansion of detail. Then the interviewer must remind the speaker of the break in narrative. The interviewer constantly must be on the *qui vive* to keep the story going and to fill in gaps.

In the best accounts, also, competent description is handled by linking a variety of perceptions to the narrative. Images then appear to the listener to be in context and thus are fairly comprehensible. At the other extreme, images and incidents are free-floating. Probing improved the quality of this sort of interview but slightly. More frequently, the interviewer was confronted with fragments of the narrative and its related imagery. Then he had to piece together the general lineaments of the story by a barrage of probes: "Who?" "When?" "Where?" Even then the reader of these interviews will come across stray images and be hard pressed to fit them into the context. Competence in recounting narrative generally is accompanied by competence in making understandable departures from the narrative itself, and, lacking both skills, some lower-class respondents gave quite baffling and unintelligible reports. The best accounts are moderately clear, although subject to all the limitations already discussed.

DISCUSSION

Only if the situation in which the respondent spoke is carefully taken into account will we be on safe ground in interpreting class differences. Consider, first, the probable meaning of the interview for the middle-class respondents. Although the interviewer is a stranger, an outsider, he is a well-spoken, educated person. He is seeking information on behalf of some organization, hence his questioning not only has sanction but sets the stage for both a certain freedom of speech and an obligation to give fairly full information. The respondent may never before have been interviewed by a research organization, but he has often talked lengthily, fairly freely, and responsibly to organizational representatives. At the very least he has had some experience in talking to educated strangers. We may also suppose that the middle-class style of living often compels him to be very careful not to be misunderstood. So he becomes relatively sensitive to communication *per se* and to communication with others who may not exactly share his viewpoints or frames of reference.

Communication with such an audience requires alertness, no less to the meanings of one's own speech than to the possible intent of the other's. Role-taking may be inaccurate, often, but it is markedly active. Assessing and anticipating reactions to what he has said or is about to say, the individual develops flexible and ingenious ways of correcting, qualifying, making more plausible, explaining, rephrasing—in short, he assumes multiple perspectives and communicates in terms of them. A variety of perspectives implies a variety of ways of ordering or framing detail. Moreover, he is able to classify and to relate classes explicitly, which is but another way of saying that he is educated to assume multiple perspectives of rather wide scope.

It would certainly be too much to claim that middle-class persons always react so sensitively. Communication is often routinized, and much of it transpires between and among those who know each other so well or share so much in common that they need not be subtle. Nor is sensitive role-taking called forth in so-called "expressive behavior," as when hurling invective or yelling during a ball game. With the proviso that much middle-class speech is uttered under such conditions, it seems safe enough to say that people of this stratum can, if required, handle the more complex and consciously organized discourse. In addition to skill and perspicacity, this kind of discourse requires a person who can subtly keep a listener at a distance while yet keeping him in some degree informed.

Consider now, even at risk of overstating the case, how the interview appears to the lower group. The interviewer is of higher social class than the respondent, so that the interview is a "conversation between the classes." It is entirely probable that more effort and ability are demanded by cross-class conversation of this sort than between middle-class respondent and middle-class interviewer. It is not surprising that the interviewer is often baffled and that the respondent frequently misinterprets what is wanted. But misunderstanding and misinterpretation are only part of the story.

Cross-class communication, while not rare, probably is fairly formalized or routinized. The communicants know the ritual steps by heart, and can assume much in the way of supporting context for phrase and gesture. The lower-class person in these Arkansas towns infrequently meets a middle-class person in a situation anything like the interview. Here he must talk at great length to a stranger about personal experiences, as well as recall for his listener a tremendous number of details. Presumably he is accustomed to talking about such matters and in such detail only to listeners with whom he shares a great deal of experience and symbolism, so that he need not be very self-conscious about communicative technique. He can, as a rule, safely assume that words, phrases, and gestures are assigned approximately similar meanings by his listeners. But this is not so in the interview or, indeed, in any situation where class converses with class in nontraditional modes.

There still remains the question of whether the descriptions of perceptions and experiences given by the lower-class respondent are merely inadequate or whether this is the way he truly saw and experienced. Does his speech accurately reflect customary "concrete" modes of thought and perception, or is it that he perceives in abstract and classificatory terms, and from multiple perspectives, but is unable to convey his perceptions? Unless one assumes that, when talking in familiar vein to familiar audiences, speech and gesture incorporate multiple perspectives, which is, as we have already indicated, improbable, one concludes that speech does in some sense reflect thought. The reader is perhaps best left at this point to draw his own conclusions, although we shall press upon him certain additional evidence and interpretation arising from examination of the interviews.

In any situation calling for a description of human activities it is necessary to utilize motivational terminology, either explicitly or implicitly, in the very namings of acts. In the speech of those who recognize few disparities of imagery between themselves and their listeners, explicit motivational terms are sparse. The frequent use among the lower class of the expression "of course" followed by something like "They went up to see about their folks" implies that it is almost needless to say what "they" did, much less to give the reason for the act. The motive ("to see about") is implicit and terminal, requiring neither elaboration nor explanation. Where motives are explicit ("They was needin' help, so we went on up there"), they are often gratuitous and could just as well have been omitted. All this is related to preceding discussions of single centering and assumed correspondence of imagery. To the speaker it was quite clear why people did what they did. There was no need to question or to elaborate on the grounds for acts. Under probing the respondent did very little better: he used motivational terms but within a quite narrow range. The terms he used ordinarily reflected kinship obligations, concern for property, humanitarian ("help") sentiments, and action from motives of curiosity ("We went down to see"). Such a phrase as "I suppose I went to her house because I wanted reassurance" would rarely occur.

Middle-class persons exhibit familiarity with a host of distinct "reasons" for performing particular acts. Their richness in thinking allows activities to be defined and described in a great variety of ways. Here, indeed, is an instrument for breaking down diffuse images ("They was runnin' all over") into classes of acts and events. The middle-class person is able to do this, for one thing, because he possesses an abstract motivational terminology. Then, too, the fine and subtle distinctions for rationalizing behavior require devices for insuring that they will be grasped by the hearer. In a real sense the need to explain behavior can be linked with the need to communicate well—to give a rational account as well as to be objective. Hence, there is a constant flow of qualifying and generalizing terms linked with motivational phraseology ("I don't know why, but it could be he felt there was no alternative . . .").

It is not surprising to find the middle class as familiar with elements of social structure as with individual behavior. Assuredly, this familiarity rests not only upon contact with institutions but upon the capacity to perceive and talk about abstract classes of acts. The lower-class person, on the other hand, appears to have only rudimentary notions of organizational structure—at least of relief and emergency agencies. Extended contact with representatives of them, no doubt, would familiarize him not only with organizations but with thinking in organizational, or abstract, terms. The propensity of the lower class to state concretely the activities of relief organizations corroborates the observation of Warner that the lowest strata have little knowledge or "feel" for the social structures of their communities. It also suggests the difficulty of conveying to them relatively abstract information through formal media of communication.

It may be that rural townspeople of the lower class are not typical of the national or urban low strata. This raises the question—vital to urban sociology but to which currently there is no adequate answer—of whether pockets of rural-minded folk cannot live encapsulated in the city and, indeed, whether lower-class persons have much opportunity to absorb middle-class culture without themselves beginning the route upward, those remaining behind remaining less urban.

CHAPTER **XI**

Meaning and Categories

INTRODUCTION   There are many differ-
ent ways of coding, of labeling and ticketing meanings. Each label and
ticket is a category, and there are many kinds of categories. These differences in ways and categories are the dimensions of semantics, the
parameters or axes of meaning in general. The preceding chapter considered what Lounsbury called the situation-behavior dimension of meaning. This chapter analyzes what he called the cognitive-affective dimension.

Charles E. Osgood in his "Studies on the Generality of Affective
Meaning Systems" measures meanings using a scaling technique called
"the semantic differential." He measures the position of words in semantic space, by which he means their position on three sets of scales.
The first of these scales is the evaluative dimension which ranks the
meaning of a word along a pleasant to unpleasant axis. The second dimension is potency which scales meanings along a strong to weak axis. The
third dimension is activity which scales meanings along an active to
passive axis. He tests whether the scalar position of a word (and its
equivalent in other languages) differs from culture to culture. He tests, in
fact, what is often called the hypothesis of linguistic relativity. Osgood
and his associates find that there is "considerable generality in semantic
space across people" but not across concepts.

"The Communication of Emotional Meaning" by Joel R. Davitz summarizes a broader group of experiments which examine the decoding of
affective meanings from verbal signals and also from such nonverbal
signals as facial expressions. Davitz and his associates follow Osgood's
tridimensional analyses—evaluative, potency, and activity—and find that

emotional meanings are decodable from words and from other cues and indexes. People can label and categorize these meanings clearly and appropriately.

But much of our meaning does not come from isolated and single words and cues. Meanings are generally given in configurations of many cues, all given at the same time. When two pictures are the same except for different captions under them, we can decode quite different meanings from the two pictures. When two dramatic scenes on television are the same except for the accompanying music, we can again decode quite different meanings. Percy H. Tannenbaum's "The Indexing Process in Communication" integrates the results of experimental data to show how such meanings are decoded and what those meanings are. He shows that a message is seldom given in isolated bits of meaning, but more often in a configuration of many cues.

Fundamentally, these dimensions and cues of meaning represent ways in which behavior and experience is organized and classified. John B. Carroll and Joseph B. Casagrande in "The Function of Language Classifications in Behavior" test whether these classifications differ in different cultures. Like Osgood, they test the hypothesis of linguistic relativity. They ask to what extent speakers of Hopi, Navaho, and English use different categories. They find that the unique form of a language, the configuration of its syntax, has a "potential influence" on the kinds of meanings a people perceive, and on the kinds they learn.

Joshua R. Fishman provides a summary of the coding and categories in semantics by reexamining the hypothesis of linguistic relativity. "A Systematization of the Whorfian Hypothesis" surveys and integrates the studies of this hypothesis and establishes a double dichotomy. The first is a behavioral dichotomy between linguistic and nonlinguistic behavior: Does nonverbal behavior vary with verbal behavior? In other words, are the categories of our language reflected in our technology, social organization, and religion? The second dichotomy is between the semantic and the structural parts of language: Does the vocabulary vary with the grammar? And do both of these vary in the same way with nonverbal behavior? Fishman proposes that we test not for the relativity of all meanings, but for only one part of the problem, such as semantic and verbal meaning.

43

Studies on the Generality of Affective Meaning Systems

CHARLES E. OSGOOD

LEARNING THEORY AND MEASUREMENT MODELS

The upper portion of Figure 1 gives the paradigm considered essential for the formation of symbolic, meaningful processes. Significates ($\dot{S}$), such as the object APPLE, are assumed to elicit a complex pattern of total behavior (R_T), including automatic as well as skeletal reactions. When some other stimulus, as a potential sign $\boxed{S}$, such as visual perception of the object APPLE or auditory perception of the word "apple," accompanies or antedates the significate, it is assumed that this new stimulus becomes conditioned to some distinctive portion of the total object reaction, this portion coming to function in behavior as *a representational mediation process* (r_m). This process is representational because it is part of the very same behavior that the thing signified produces, hence its symbolic, semantic property; it is a mediation process by virtue of the fact that the self-stimulation it produces (s_m) can become associated with a variety of overt, adaptive acts (R_X) which "take account of" the thing signified. Psychological meaning is identified with such representational mediation processes, and linguistic responses, as a subset of R_X, would seem to offer the most elaborate and discriminative possibilities for measuring meaning. However, in order to attain comparability and objectivity, it is necessary to devise a representative sample of scaled linguistic responses.

Now let me ask you to do the impossible—to imagine a space of some unknown number of dimensions; the center portion of this figure will help through at least three. This will be our hypothetical *semantic space*, and we may explore it by analogy with the more familiar color space. Like all self-respecting spaces, this one has an origin, which we define as com-

Reprinted with permission of the American Psychological Association and the author. From *American Psychologist*, 17:10–28 (1962).

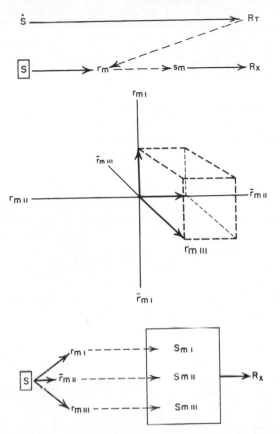

Figure 1. The mediation model (A) and its suggested coordination with the measurement model (B and C).

plete "meaninglessness" (cf., the neutral grey of the color space). If we locate a sign as a point in this space, then its meaning could be represented by a vector from the origin to that point: the length of the vector would index the "meaningfulness" of the sign (cf., saturation in the color space) and its direction would index the "semantic quality" of the sign (cf., hue and brightness in the color space). Furthermore, distance between the endpoints of any two vectors in this semantic space should index the "meaningful similarity" of the signs thus represented. The central and lower portions of this figure suggest a coordination between learning theory and measurement models—namely, that vector direction in the measurement space is coordinate with which alternatives among a set of bipolar representational mediators are elicited by the sign and vector length is coordinate with how intensely these reactions are elicited.

But to talk about "direction" in any space we need some reference coordinates. One more analogy with the color space will prove useful to us: Just as complementary colors are defined as points equidistant and in opposite directions from the origin in the color space, which when mixed together in equal proportions cancel each other out to neutral grey, so may we conceive of *verbal opposites* as defining straight lines through the origin of the semantic space and canceling each other out to meaninglessness when "mixed." Imagine now a whole set of different straight-line "cuts" through the space, each defined by a pair of opposites: We might have a subject indicate his "meaning" of a concept by a series of binary decisions—it is *beautiful* (not ugly), *soft* (not hard), *quick* (not slow) and so on. If these cuts were orthogonal, and hence independent of each other—a whopping big assumption that demands justification, of course—then each binary decision would reduce uncertainty about the location of the concept by half. Or, if each straight-line cut were scaled into seven discriminable steps, as we have done in our work, then each decision would reduce uncertainty of location by 6/7ths, and only three orthogonal cuts would yield a space of 343 regions.

But we still have the problem of reference coordinates. Is the up-down, north-south, and east-west of the semantic space to be completely arbitrary, or is there some "natural," built-in structuring of the space analogous to the gravitational and magnetic determinants of geophysical space? This question is an empirical one, and the logical tool is some variant of factor analysis. We need to take a large and representative sample of dimensions defined by verbal opposites, determine their inter-correlations when used in judging the meanings of a representative sample of concepts, and then see if they fall into "natural" clusters or factors that can serve as reference coordinates. And since it is only through replication in the same domain that factor analysis becomes a hypothesis-testing device, we need to make repeated analyses using different subjects, concepts, and methods, being particularly careful that the rules for successive samplings of scales are independent of the factor structures found in previous analyses. Table 1 presents the results of three out of some 10 or more general factor analyses we have made on American subjects during the past decade. The scales shown for the three factors in order of magnitude under each analysis are the seven having the highest loadings, and they are typical of all the analyses we have done using either a broad sample of concepts or no concepts at all. An *evaluative factor*, which we identify as the attitudinal component of meaning, is characterized by scales like *good-bad, pleasant-unpleasant,* and *positive-negative;* what we call a *potency factor*, orthogonal to evaluation, is characterized by scales like *strong-weak, heavy-light,* and *hard-soft;* what we call the *activity factor*, independent of both evaluation and potency, is characterized by scales like *fast-slow, active-passive,* and *excitable-calm.*

Table 1

Reproducibility of Three Major Factors

Frequency-of-Usage Sampling Graphic Method (rotated) 20 Concepts/ 50 Scales	Frequency-of-Usage Sampling Forced-Choice Method No Concepts/ Same Scales	Logically Exhaustive Sampling Graphic Method (standard) 20 Concepts/76 (300) Scales
good—bad	delicate—rugged	good—bad
nice—awful	nice—awful	harmonious—dissonant
beautiful—ugly	clean—dirty	successful—unsuccessful
honest—dishonest	pleasant—unpleasant	beautiful—ugly
fragrant—foul	fragrant—foul	wise—foolish
fair—unfair	smooth—rough	positive—negative
sweet—sour	good—bad	kind—cruel
strong—weak	strong—weak	hard—soft
large—small	large—small	masculine—feminine
heavy—light	heavy—light	severe—lenient
rugged—delicate	active—passive	strong—weak
hard—soft	brave—cowardly	tenacious—yielding
bass—treble	thick—thin	heavy—light
deep—shallow	deep—shallow	serious—humorous
fast—slow	sharp—dull	fast—slow
active—passive	fast—slow	active—passive
sharp—dull	treble—bass	excitable—calm
hot—cold	active—passive	rash—cautious
angular—rounded	bright—dark	heretical—orthodox
ferocious—peaceful	young—old	competitive—cooperative
tense—relaxed	high—low	ornate—plain

The problem for the present paper concerns *the generality of this semantic factor system,* both across the people doing the judging and across the concepts being judged. Is the evaluation-potency-activity system merely the lowest common denominator that averages out of many diverse individual systems or is it shared? Is it limited to Americans speaking the English language, or is it shared by all humans regardless of language and culture? Is there interaction between the semantic scales and the particular concepts being judged, such that we need different "semantic differentials" for different concept classes? To anticipate our general conclusions a bit, we will find that this factor system does seem quite stable across people but quite unstable across concept classes, and I will want to offer some speculations about the "whys" of this result.

However, before presenting the relevant studies, a methodological note is in order: As indicated in Figure 2, our kind of data represents *a three-*

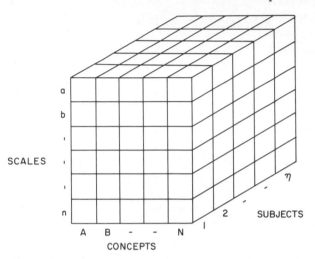

Figure 2. The cube of data generated when η subjects judge N concepts against n scales.

way correlational and factorial problem rather than the more usual two-way problem of subjects-by-tests. That is to say, when η subjects judge N concepts against n scales, a cube of data is generated within which there are three potentially independent sources of variation in factor structure— scales, subjects, and concepts. This situation presents some complications but also some opportunities. For example, we can do separate correlational and factorial analyses for single subjects (e.g., correlating scales across concepts) or we can do the same for single concepts (e.g., correlating scales across subjects); we can collapse the cube by averaging over either all subjects or all concepts or over subsets of subjects or concepts; we can correlate subjects over both scales and concepts, and then factor the subjects to determine their similarities and differences in the judgmental task.

SPECULATIONS ON THE "WHY" OF GENERALITY ACROSS PEOPLE

The evidence to date, then, indicates considerable generality in semantic space across people, both within and between language—culture groups. The dominant factors of *evaluation, potency,* and *activity* that keep appearing certainly have a response-like character, reflecting the ways we can react to meaningful events rather than the ways we can receive them. But these major factors also seem to have an *affective* as well as a response-like character.

Let me speculate a bit further and suggest that the highly generalized nature of the affective reaction system—the fact that it is independent of any particular sensory modality, yet participates with all of them—is at once the mathematical reason why *evaluation, potency,* and *activity* tend to appear as dominant factors and the psychological basis for synesthesia and metaphor. It is *because* such diverse sensory experiences as a *white* circle (rather than a black), a *straight* line (rather than crooked), a *rising melody* (rather than a falling one), a *sweet* taste (rather than a sour one), *a caressing* touch (rather than an irritating scratch) can all share a common affective meaning that one can easily and lawfully translate from one modality into another in synesthesia and metaphor. This is also the basis for the high interscale communalities which determine the nature and orientation of general factors. Speculating still further, I would suggest that this meaning system is intimately related to the nonspecific projection systems from the hypothalamic, reticular, or limbic systems and their cortical connections in the frontal lobes—both are gross, nondiscriminative, but highly generalizable systems, and both are associated with the affective, purposive and motivational dynamics of the organism.

GENERALITY ACROSS CONCEPTS

Now, let us flip the coin over and ask about the generality of semantic factor structures across the concepts being judged. You will recall that the cube of data generated when a group of subjects judges a sample of concepts against a set of scales makes it feasible to compute separate correlation matrices for each concept "slice" (i.e., *r*'s based on interscale cross-products over subjects) and factorize such matrices. In what we refer to as our "Thesaurus Study"—because the adjectival scales were sampled from that source on a rational, representative basis—20 different concepts, like FOREIGNER, KNIFE, MODERN ART, DEBATE, and HOSPITAL, were judged against 76 scales by 100 college subjects.

Now, imagine the 20 separate correlation matrices for the different concepts lined up as a deck; if we go through the deck at the point of intersection of a particular pair of scales (e.g., of *sober-drunk* vs. *mature-youthful*), we will isolate 20 *r*'s, one for each concept. If scale relations were reasonably constant over concepts, then we would expect only minor variations within such rows of correlations—but this proved *not* to be the case. Corresponding *r*'s were found to vary as much as from

+ .60 to − .60 in the same row. A couple of examples will serve to suggest what is happening: *sober* goes with *youthful* for the concept DAWN, but with *mature* for the concept UNITED NATIONS; *pleasurable* goes with *feminine* for the concept MOTHER, but with *masculine* for the concept ADLAI STEVENSON. It would appear that the nature of concept being judged exercises a *denotative restriction* on scale meaning—I will come back to this point. What about the correspondence of factors derived from such single-concept matrices? Here the picture is better: something identifiable as an *evaluative* factor appeared for each concept, and it was usually the first in order of magnitude; something identifiable as a *potency* (or *dynamism*) factor appeared for all but two concepts; but other factors varied among what we call *activity*, *stability* and *receptivity* in most inconsistent ways.

This instability of scale relations and factors across concepts contrasts sharply with the stability we have found across people. This shows up most clearly in several studies where both types of generality can be compared. In a study on the 1952 election, conducted by George Suci, separate analyses were made for three types of voters, Stevenson Certains, Eisenhower Certains, and Taft Certains, judging the same 20 politically relevant concepts against the same set of 10 scales. Although, as would be expected, these different voter groups differed markedly in their meanings (localizations in the factor space) of such concepts as TRUMAN, SEN. MCCARTHY, and FEDERAL SPENDING, their scale factor systems were almost identical—but for these political concepts the three usually independent factors of evaluation, potency, and activity were fused into a single, dominant factor describable as *benevolent dynamism* vs. *malevolent insipidity*.

SPECULATIONS ON THE "WHY" OF CONCEPT/SCALE INTERACTION

The preceding evidence as a whole forces us to the conclusion that *there is a significant interaction between concepts and scales in the process of semantic judgment*. Where are the implications of this? From the standpoint of the practice of semantic measurement, this means that there is no such entity as "*The* Semantic Differential," with a rigidly defined set of factors—except perhaps in the sense of a common denominator from which more specific instruments are to be derived. For significant concept classes we will therefore want to develop specific instruments, and for the important class of personality concepts we have already done some work. From the standpoint of the theory of language and cognition, this conclusion invites fresh speculation about the principles that may govern such concept/scale interaction—and a whole host of new experiments. Here we are just beginning, and I will close this paper with some of our speculations on the matter.

I start with the credible notion of an affective mediating system which is biologically determined and capable of some limited number of gross, bipolar discriminations. This is the system the semantic differential technique is assumed to tap primarily; I have referred to the aspect of meaning indexed as *connotative*. But there is another aspect of the meaning of signs which I refer to as *denotative:* This is the elaborate set of essentially arbitrary correlations between nonlinguistic and linguistic events, e.g., between the visual perception of APPLE object and vocalizing the word "apple." I assume that these correlations are mediated by the sensory and motor discrimination systems of the brain—regions where lesions produce various types of aphasia. Both of these biological systems —the affective energizing system and the sensory-motor discrimination system—are integrated in ordinary behavior, as we know, and I think integration of the same systems in language behavior is one of the reasons for concept/scale interaction.

I have been criticized for this usage of the terms "connotation" and "denotation" by a number of linguists, psycholinguists, and philosophers, but I think the distinction and perhaps even the usage is justified. If I were to ask you the question, Is a BABY *large* or *small?*, you would undoubtedly say "small." And if I were to ask, Is a railroad SPIKE *large* or *small?*, you would probably say "large." Within the class of human organisms, a baby *is* "a small one," and within the class of nails a spike *is* "a large one." I think the semantic differential technique is one which tends to draw out these connotations of signs; it is a procedure in which a single stimulus is judged successively against a series of different scales. In all other psychophysical methods with which I am familiar, even the so-called "absolute judgment" methods, a series of different stimuli are judged successively against a single scale—e.g., in judging weights, in scaling the loudness of tones, and so forth—and I think this judgmental situation tends to draw out the denotative meaning of scales. Note that if I ask you, Is a BABY *larger* or *smaller* than a SPIKE?, you immediately say "larger," now disregarding the within-class connotations of these objects. We have just begun a series of experiments comparing these two methods of "absolute judgment," and I believe we will be able to demonstrate that many of the standard phenomena of the traditional method, such as "anchoring effects," do not appear in the semantic differential procedure.

What has all this to do with concept/scale interaction? I think the semantic differential is subject to what might be called *denotative contamination*. Most adjectival scale terms have variable denotative meanings as well as their affective connotation. Particular concepts exert a selective limitation upon scale meanings, drawing forth a denotative usage of some and the connotation of others. The denotation of *masculine-*

feminine is elicited by the concept ADLAI STEVENSON while its potency connotation is elicited by the concept DYNAMO; a denotation of the scale *hot-cold* is tapped by the concept LAVA, whereas its activity connotation is tapped by concepts like JAZZ and FESTIVAL. It is clear that if certain scales are denotatively relevant to a certain class of concepts, they will tend to fall out of the general affective factors with which they usually correlate. I am hopeful that comparisons between the two psychophysical methods mentioned above—the traditional method eliciting denotative judgments and the semantic-differential method eliciting connotative judgments—will enable us to disentangle these two confounded processes.

Another cause of concept/scale interaction is what might be called *factorial coalescence.* The general factors we obtain with large and diverse sets of concepts presumably indicate the major ways in which the affective representational system *can* make discriminations. However, it may be characteristic of certain classes of concepts that two or more of these potentially independent factors just simply are correlated, and hence coalesce mathematically. But what is the dynamism that produces such correlations? I think it is a special instance of *cognitive interaction*, a phenomenon studied by Heider as "imbalance," by Festinger as "dissonance," and by Tannenbaum and myself as "incongruity." Our own studies—on attitude change, on word mixture and on facial fusion—are most directly relevant, because we have dealt with change in meaning of the interacting elements as one of the resolutions of cognitive stress. The basic notion is this: whenever two or more signs are presented near-simultaneously, the representational mediating reactions characteristic for each must interact and reach a compromise—this is because the affective meaning system is capable of assuming only one "posture" at a time; the congruity hypothesis states that, in such interactions and independently on each factor, the change in meaning for each sign is inversely proportional to its initial polarization or intensity—that is to say, the more intensely meaningful signs are modified less.

What has all *this* to do with concept/scale interaction? In the process of making semantic-differential judgments, a subject first looks at, and then "keeps in mind," the concept being judged; then he goes down the page, looking at each scale term and delivering his check mark. Now suppose we are judging a concept like MOTHER, which has an intense evaluative meaning—to whatever extent a scale has some evaluative loading itself, its affective meaning should become momentarily *more* evaluative, and in correlational terms this means a rotation in the semantic space toward the evaluative factor. To generalize, this should mean that each concept, or concept class, will tend to produce rotation of scales toward its own characteristic attribute in the semantic space. Thus, if *potency* is a dominant attribute of the concept class ATHLETES, then *good-bad* should rotate toward increased correlation with *strong-weak* and de-creased correlation with *kind-cruel*, whereas *active-passive* should shift toward *strong-weak* and away from *excitable-calm*—all such rotations tending to produce a coalescent "dynamism" factor. By measuring the meanings of an experimental set of both concepts and scale terms, we should be able to predict from the congruity formula the direction and magnitude of scale rotation in the process of judgment—this is another study we have on the planning boards.

44 | The Communication of Emotional Meaning
JOEL R. DAVITZ

Emotional meanings can be communicated accurately in a variety of nonverbal media. This is the basic propo-sition upon which our research rests, and it is supported by all our work. Vocal communication has been the principal focus of our attention; but we have also studied facial, musical, and graphic modes of expression. In each instance, the accuracy with which emotional meanings were com-municated far exceeded chance expectation. Individuals indeed differ in their ability to communicate, but notwithstanding these individual differ-ences, our results demonstrate incontrovertibly that nonverbal, emotional communication is a stable, measurable phenomenon.

Although most of our research has been concerned with nonverbal media, we also have investigated metaphorical statements as an indirect, verbal means of emotional expression. Metaphors convey emotional mean-ings more accurately than any nonverbal mode we have thus far studied, but in many respects, the results obtained in our study of metaphors parallel those obtained with nonverbal techniques. Thus, our conclu-sions are based principally on investigations of nonverbal expressions, with at least tentative evidence that these conclusions might be generalized to some forms of verbal communication.

From *The Communication of Emotional Meaning*, edited by Joel R. Davitz, pp. 177–191. Copyright © 1964, McGraw-Hill, Inc. Used by permission of McGraw-Hill Book Company and the author.

Having established the fact that emotional communication occurs both in verbal and nonverbal media, we explored individual differences in various aspects of the communication process. Much of our research was designed to account for individual differences in ability to receive and understand emotional messages; this ability was thought of in terms of emotional sensitivity. Problems in transmitting emotional messages were studied separately in terms of expressiveness, although we recognized that transmitting and receiving messages in any communication process are inextricably interrelated. Finally, we focused some of our research on perceived characteristics of the message in relation to the meanings conveyed. Our findings will therefore be reviewed under three broad headings: (1) Problems of Sensitivity; (2) The Message and its Emotional Meaning; and (3) Problems of Expressiveness.

Problems of Sensitivity

A large part of our research focused on problems of emotional sensitivity. We have found marked individual differences in ability to understand emotional messages expressed in vocal, facial, musical, graphic, and metaphorical modes of communication. The range of individual differences does not seem to be greater in any particular mode of communication, nor does the stability of behavior differ markedly from one mode to another. In all media, people differ in ability to identify the meanings expressed, individuals varying from performances at about chance level of expectation to nearly perfect accuracy. But regardless of the individual's level of performance, behavior on any given test of sensitivity tends to be internally consistent and remarkably stable over time.

In most of our research, emotional sensitivity was defined operationally by the total number of items correctly identified on any given instrument. This scoring procedure, similar to that followed in most intelligence tests, was based on the assumption that emotional sensitivity like intelligence, can best be measured by responses to a variety of items encompassing various emotional meanings expressed by several different persons. For example, our measure of sensitivity to vocal expression was based on an overall estimate of accuracy of response to eight emotional meanings expressed by a number of different speakers.

In addition to an overall estimate of accuracy, we also investigated the kinds of items correctly identified and the kinds of errors made in identification. Both variables were found to be stable characteristics of an individual's response to emotional stimuli. A person who correctly identifies an emotional expression on one occasion is likely to identify that expression correctly on a second occasion. Similarly, a person who makes one kind of error when first confronted with an emotional expression tends to make the identical error when he again encounters that emotional expression. Thus, people who mistake joy for anger, or anger for joy, are consistent over time in the nature of their erroneous responses.

Another aspect of the general response to emotional stimuli deserves brief mention; that is, the tendency to selectively attend, or inattend, to emotional meanings. Blau called this variable "affect attention," and found, in his sample of blind and sighted adolescents, a wide range of differences along this dimension of behavior. For some people, and perhaps in some situations, the emotional meaning of a message is of primary importance; whereas other people consciously recognize emotional meanings only when instructed to do so. Despite these differences in awareness, it seems reasonable to assume that emotional meanings influence the total response to any communication regardless of whether or not the respondent is aware of the emotional meanings conveyed. The tendency to attend to affective meanings, however, is not necessarily related to emotional sensitivity. Blau found that among blind subjects there was indeed a rather high relationship between his measures of affect attention and emotional sensitivity ($r = .52$, $p < .01$); but among his sighted subjects these two variables were found to be independent. The relation between affect attention and emotional sensitivity, therefore, is a function of other variables, one of which appears to be blindness. On the basis of present evidence, we cannot generalize about the effect of handicap in other sensory modalities, but the results obtained thus far clearly call for further exploration of affect attention as an important dimension of behavior in the communication of emotional meanings.

In summary, then, stable individual differences have been found in the following aspects of receiving emotional messages: (1) overall sensitivity to emotional expressions, measured in terms of accuracy of identification; (2) the kinds of emotional expressions correctly identified; (3) the specific nature of erroneous responses; and (4) the degree to which individuals attend to the emotional meanings of a total communication.

Measures of sensitivity in the several nonverbal modes we've studied are positively interrelated. Beldoch, for example, found statistically significant intercorrelations among abilities measured by vocal, graphic, and musical tests of communications; Davitz and Mattis found a similiar relation between abilities measured in vocal and facial modes of expression. Thus, a person who is accurate in identifying the emotional meaning of vocal expressions also tends to be accurate in identifying facial, graphic, and musical expressions. Emotional sensitivity to nonverbal stimuli, therefore, seems to be a function of some general factor that accounts for the common variance among a variety of manifestly different measures.

The intercorrelations among measures in various nonverbal modes, however, tend to be low, though statistically significant. For any two modes of communication, our data show that approximately 10 to 35 per cent of the common variance can be accounted for by some general factor of sensitivity. Thus, while abilities in the several nonverbal modes are undoubtedly related to each other, individuals also show special sensitivities to specific modes of expression. Although as a group, persons who are accurate in one nonverbal mode are generally more accurate in another mode, some persons within the group may be particularly sensitive to vocal expressions, for example, and relatively insensitive to facial expressions.

The argument for a general factor of sensitivity, therefore, is somewhat mitigated by the relatively low intercorrelations we have obtained. However, we have also obtained evidence that sensitivity is related to other aspects of the total communication process. Levy found that sensitivity, expressiveness, and self-understanding are positively interrelated. That is, people who are accurate in identifying the emotional expressions *of* others are more effective in expressing emotional meanings *to* others. They are also more accurate in identifying the meanings of their own expressions. These interrelations were investigated only in the vocal mode of communication, but for this mode at least, the positive relation between transmitting and receiving emotional messages is unequivocal.

In conjunction with our findings about the positive interrelations among sensitivities in various nonverbal modes of communication, the positive relation between expressiveness and sensitivity lends further credence to the assumption that a general factor partially accounts for the variance in a variety of manifestly different behaviors. In a subsequent section, we shall offer one possible interpretation of this general factor.

Sensitivity to verbal expressions, as measured by the accuracy of identifying the meaning of metaphorical expressions, is positively related to performance on the vocal test of emotional expression, but independent of sensitivity to facial expression. Thus, a person who accurately identifies the meaning of metaphors also tends to be accurate in identifying the meaning of vocal expressions, but he may be relatively insensitive to the meaning of facial expressions. Verbal intelligence is correlated with ability on both the metaphorical and vocal tests, but even when verbal intelligence is controlled, the correlation between scores on these two tests of sensitivity remains statistically significant. In most interpersonal situations, emotional meanings are expressed simultaneously in vocal and verbal modes, and undoubtedly these simultaneous expressions interact in the communication process. We are currently investigating the nature of this interaction, but at the present time can only note that sensitivity to meanings conveyed verbally is positively related to sensitivity in a mode by which verbal content typically is expressed.

Emotional sensitivity develops chronologically, beginning at least as early as age five and continuing to increase progressively with both chronological and mental age. Dimitrovsky found chronological increments in sensitivity through age twelve, and Blau's observations suggest continued growth throughout early adolescence. Beyond these age limits, our observations are not sufficiently systematic to permit generalization over the life span, but we suspect that some form of emotional sensitivity occurs even earlier than five years old and begins to taper off, probably as a function of losses in perceptual acuity, at about age forty. Many observers have reported that even very young infants show gross differential responses to strong stimuli, but one cannot equate this kind of response with the labeling behavior measured in our research. It is probably more appropriate to consider the infant's gross reactions as a developmental precursor of subsequent emotional sensitivity as we have operationally defined it, since the types of labeling responses required in our tests depend upon acquisition of fairly complex, symbolic skills. With further refinement of our measurement techniques, perhaps we might obtain reliable estimates of sensitivity below age five. Even at age five, however, most children perform beyond chance expectation in recognizing vocal expressions, and there are stable individual differences in sensitivity at all age levels thus far tested. Our evidence also suggests that consistency of performance over time increases with age, five-year-olds being least consistent from time to time, and twelve-year-olds performing at about the same level of consistency as adult samples.

Beginning at about age six, girls develop more rapidly than boys do, at least in so far as our measure of sensitivity to vocal expression is concerned. This sex difference in sensitivity was not found in our adult samples; presumably, therefore, the factors that influence differential development of boys and girls during childhood are mitigated by subsequent learning or maturation during adolescence. The question of sex differences nevertheless remains unresolved. Many of our adult samples were obtained from a college population and as other research suggests, similarities between male and female college students in a variable like emotional sensitivity may not be representative of the general population. Moreover, the children studied by Dimitrovsky differed in socioeconomic status from the samples of adults studied in most of our other research; therefore, Dimitrovsky's finding of sex differences in children remains to be explored more fully with adults from a wider socioeconomic and educational range than we have thus far sampled.

We have found no consistent evidence of personality correlates of emotional sensitivity, operationally defining these personality variables in terms of paper and pencil measures obtained from psychologically normal adults. These measures include a description of self-concept based on

Gough's 300-item Adjective Check List, the Guilford-Zimmerman Temperament Survey, the Allport-Vernon-Lindzey Study of Values, the Edwards Personal Preference Schedule, the Psychaesthenia and Hysteria scales of the MMPI, and the Dogmatism and Opinionation scales developed by Rokeach. Although certainly not conclusive, our preliminary evidence using projective techniques as a source of personality information is not promising. The data, therefore, compel us to conclude that personality variables, as we have measured them, are independent of overall estimates of emotional sensitivity.

Perhaps our most interesting lead in this area comes from the study of errors in identification, for it seems likely that personality factors, if they operate at all in the communication process, influence the errors made in judgment rather than overall sensitivity. A person with high aggressive needs, for example, generally might be sensitive or insensitive to relatively obvious expressions of various emotional meanings regardless of his aggressive needs; but in instances of more subtle emotional expression, when the discrimination involved is relatively more difficult, and the response less "stimulus-bound," the person's aggressive needs might very well play an important role in determining the nature of his erroneous response. In this sense, one might view some of the more subtle and difficult items of emotional expression as stimuli for projective behavior, focusing primarily on an analysis of errors instead of total accuracy in the investigation of personality correlates. This hypothesis, however, is not supported by any systematic data we've obtained and is suggested only for further exploration.

Outside the normal range, we have found that schizophrenic persons, in comparison to nonschizophrenic control subjects, are less sensitive to emotional communication. This relative insensitivity cannot be accounted for by decreased motivation or attention, as measured by performance on a nonemotional control task, but the basis of the schizophrenic person's deficit is not evident from our research. We have also obtained preliminary evidence that specific psychotic subgroups (paranoid versus nonparanoid) differ from each other in the kinds of errors they make in identifying emotional expressions, and both subgroups, in turn, differ from a normal control group. At this stage of our research, however, we are not sure that these findings contribute to the understanding of schizophrenia or psychosis in general, and we have not been able to account for the schizophrenic's lower performance in terms of the various kinds of deficit usually associated with schizophrenia. We can only report that schizophrenics differ from nonschizophrenics in various aspects of emotional communication.

In contrast to our research concerned with personality variables, we have obtained consistent evidence in support of perceptual and cognitive correlates of emotional sensitivity. Among the variables related to sensitivity as measured by the vocal test are: verbal intelligence; abstract symbolic ability; knowledge of vocal characteristics of emotional expression; ability to discriminate pitch, loudness, time, and timbre of auditory stimuli; and ability to distinguish figure from ground in a visual perception task. The intercorrelations among these variables are low, indicating a relatively independent contribution of each variable to the total response of identifying emotional expressions. Inspection of the scatter plots suggests that a minimal level of ability in each of several perceptual and cognitive dimensions is required for successful performance on the emotional identification task, but high ability in any single dimension does not, in itself, result in greater sensitivity. Thus, emotional sensitivity is multidetermined, requiring a variety of perceptual and cognitive abilities, each contributing a necessary but not sufficient factor to the total sensitivity response. A deaf person obviously cannot be very sensitive to vocal expressions simply because he cannot hear the auditory cues involved, but extremely high auditory acuity does not in itself guarantee emotional sensitivity. Similarly, without sufficient abstract symbolic ability, a person is severely handicapped in performing the rather complex symbolic task involved in identifying emotional meanings. But symbolic ability is only a necessary, and not sufficient, basis for sensitivity. We have undoubtedly failed to identify all the perceptual and cognitive variables which contribute to emotional sensitivity. Perhaps other psychological factors, such as interest and motivation, contribute to the total sensitivity response. Nonetheless, our data strongly support an interpretation of emotional sensitivity primarily in terms of perceptual and cognitive processes.

In order to be sensitive to meanings expressed in a given mode, obviously one must be capable of perceiving stimuli in that mode of communication. A major sensory defect, therefore, precludes emotional sensitivity in the particular mode affected. There is a prevalent folklore belief, however, that sensory deficit in one modality is accompanied by heightened, compensatory acuity in another modality. This belief is the basis for a common assumption that blind persons, for example, are particularly accurate in identifying auditory cues.

Although we have found that auditory acuity is not in itself a sufficient basis for sensitivity to vocal expressions of emotion, it seemed reasonable to assume that increased auditory acuity is positively related to emotional sensitivity tested in the vocal mode of expression. Blau investigated this assumption in his study of blind and sighted adolescents. Contradicting usual assumptions about the blind, Blau found they were no more accurate than sighted control subjects in identifying everyday sounds. Moreover, while blind adolescents, in comparison to a comparable sample of sighted control subjects, pay more attention to the emotional aspects of vocal communication, they are indeed *less* accurate in identifying the emotional meanings expressed. We cannot as yet account for this lower sensitivity among the blind, but our results clearly demonstrate that compensation in terms of increased emotional sensitivity in nonhandicapped modes is not an inevitable consequence of sensory deficit.

Finally, in the area of receiving or understanding emotional messages, we have obtained some evidence about the effect of training. The evidence is indeed slight, and provides only a global picture of short-term training experience; nevertheless, the results support the hypothesis that training increases sensitivity. We do not know the particular aspects of training which are most effective, and we cannot define the generality of effects produced. But we do know that practice in expressing and receiving emotional communications results in higher scores on a subsequent test of sensitivity. In a sense, this vague, tentative conclusion is an interesting commentary on the course of one's research, reflecting the changes that occur, usually without awareness, as one develops a line of investigation. At the very beginning, our primary interest in emotional communication arose from problems in training, specifically, the problem of training student therapists in the task of recognizing emotional meanings expressed by their clients. However, we have completed only one small study directly concerned with this problem, and can only report that training seems to have a positive effect. Having accumulated other information relevant to the total communication process, perhaps we can return to the original training problem with greater insight and technical skill.

The Message and Its Emotional Meaning

In comparison to the amount of work concerned with problems of sensitivity, proportionately less of our research has been focused on the emotional message itself and the meaning it conveys. For the most part, what we know in this area concerns vocal communication, and systematic knowledge even about this mode of expression is limited.

Perhaps our most fortunate hunch in exploring problems of meaning in relation to characteristics of the vocal message was the choice of Osgood's tridimensional scheme as a basis for describing meaning. Thus, we began with three dimensions of emotional meaning, valence, activity, and strength, and searched for correlates of these dimensions in terms of characteristics of the vocal message perceived as auditory cues. Investigating only the more obvious auditory characteristics of speech, we found that the activity dimension of meaning accounted for much of the variance in rate, volume, pitch, and timbre of vocal expressions. Emotions characterized subjectively as "active" tend to be expressed by a fast rate of speech, high volume or loudness, high pitch, and blaring timbre. In direct contrast, relatively "passive" emotions are expressed by a slower rate of speech, lower volume, lower pitch, and more resonant timbre. These vocal characteristics, of course, are physically related to each other in the production of speech, and in this sense, the correlations between activity and each auditory characteristic are not independent of each other.

The findings in regard to the activity dimension are remarkably consistent, but valence and strength have no such simple correlates in the vocal message. Thus, while the relatively obvious auditory characteristics of a vocal message are accounted for by the activity dimension of emotional meaning, it would seem likely that valence and strength are communicated by more subtle aspects of speech, such as changes in rhythm, inflection, and enunciation.

We cannot confidently generalize these findings to other modes of expression, though informal observations tend to support our findings in the vocal area. For example, in the graphic mode, expressions of a subjectively active feeling, such as anger, almost always involve much more movement than expressions of a passive feeling, such as boredom; similarly, in metaphorical expressions, items concerned with active feelings such as anger (e.g. stamping) and joy (e.g. dancing) typically involve greater movement than items which express a passive feeling such as sadness (e.g. lying down). Activity, therefore, seems to be a major determinant of the form of emotional expression, regardless of the mode of communication.

These findings are related to the types of errors most frequently made in identification. Erroneous responses, by and large, tend to be similar to the intended meaning in terms of activity level. For example, two active emotions, such as anger and joy, are frequently mistaken for each other in the vocal mode; but expressions of two unpleasant emotions, such as anger and sadness, or two strong emotions, such as love and joy, are rarely confused for one another. Once again, our research evidence is based on vocal communication, but our observations about other modes of communication are consistent with these findings.

We have not developed an extensive dictionary of vocal cues associated with each kind of emotional meaning. In this respect, our work with metaphors has been most successful. With only five categories of emotional meaning, anger, anxiety, joy, love, and sadness, a tripart division of characteristics in terms of situational cues, conventional expressive behaviors, and words with primarily subjective, connotative meanings was comprehensive enough to account for almost all the metaphors obtained.

Anxiety, for example, was typically expressed by metaphors describing a situation of threatening hostility, expressive behaviors such as trembling, or by words such as "fragmentation and instability," which presumably refer to subjective experiences associated with anxiety. Metaphors of sadness typically describe situations of loss or hostility that has occurred in the past, expressive behaviors such as crying, or words such as "dark and hollow."

This attempt at objective analysis of one kind of verbal expression represents only a beginning and has several obvious limitations. Many verbal statements in everyday communication contain cues associated with more than one dimension of emotional meaning, and, as yet, we have no objective way of determining the "figure" and "ground" of emotional communications. Moreover, our dictionary of metaphors probably would not be effective in objectively translating the emotional meanings of subtle, literary metaphors whose referents may be highly personal and primarily subjective. Nevertheless, with these limitations in mind, plus awareness of the fact that we studied only five categories of emotional meaning, the tridimensional categorization of verbal characteristics may serve as something of a model for further research along this line of investigation.

One of the most intriguing, and in some ways, disturbing findings of our research concerns the rate of emitting various kinds of responses in identifying emotional expressions. We generally assumed a chance level of emitting each category of meaning in a given list of emotional categories. Thus, if we presented a list of emotions comprised of anger, joy, love, and sadness, we assumed that by chance each emotional meaning would be emitted a quarter of the time. But Dimitrovsky's findings with children clearly contradict this assumption, for in her sample, anger and sadness responses were emitted far more frequently than either joy or love. This does not affect the validity of our assumption that by chance one would expect a quarter of the items to be identified correctly, but it does suggest, for future research, a more careful investigation of the base line of response for each kind of emotional meaning. It also poses the problem of accounting for children's extraordinarily high rate of emitting unpleasant emotional meanings in response to adult vocal expressions. Although the specific vocal instrument used by Dimitrovsky has not been used in studies of adults, data have been obtained with similar tests, and we have found that normal adults generally do *not* emit a larger proportion of responses with unpleasant, rather than pleasant, emotional meaning. Thus, Dimitrovsky's finding seems to be particularly characteristic of children responding to adult voices. In light of these results, one wonders if anger and sadness indeed characterize the world of emotional meanings in which many children live?

Problems of Expressiveness

Of the several aspects of communication, we have devoted least attention to problems of expressiveness. Levitt's study has been our only major investigation focused directly on the expressive function in the communication process.

Paralleling our findings about sensitivity, Levitt found that abilities to express vocally and facially are positively related. The relationship, however, is not high, accounting for only a small part of the variance in each mode of expression. These results are especially interesting in the light of results obtained in several other studies: (1) Levy's finding that expressing and receiving emotional messages are positively related; (2) Beldoch's finding that sensitivities in three modes of communication are positively interrelated; and (3) Davitz and Mattis's finding that sensitivities to vocal and facial expressions are positively related. Considered together, these researches form a chain of findings that suggest a general factor underlying a wide range of behaviors involved in various aspects of the total communication process.

In most typical instances of everyday communication, emotional meanings are simultaneously expressed in more than one mode. We assumed that expression in two modes (facial plus vocal) would be more effective than expression in either mode taken singly. However, this assumption was not supported; information from two modes of expression does not necessarily result in more accurate communication. Probably the specific modes involved determine whether or not communication is aided or impeded by dual channels of information operating simultaneously. Our own research has thus far considered only two nonverbal modes of simultaneous expression; a study of verbal plus nonverbal information might very well provide quite different results.

The general problem of determining *who* expresses most effectively to *whom* remains virtually untouched. In contradiction to our expectations, we did *not* find that homogeneity of native language among speakers and listeners was related to accuracy of their nonverbal, vocal communication. In fact, our most important cross-cultural finding is the remarkable accuracy with which speakers and listeners from different cultures communicate with each other in a nonverbal mode. This suggests a fairly high degree of similarity in vocal expression across cultures, regardless of obvious differences in verbal communication. But these results are only suggestive because of the small sample studied to date.

Finally, we have obtained some evidence about the relation of interpersonal compatibility to emotional communication. Once again, these suggestions are based on preliminary findings, but the data clearly contradict the assumption that interpersonal sensitivity is linearly related to compatibility.

Methodological Comments

At this point, it might be useful to describe in some detail a paradigm of our general research method, for our findings and the ideas they suggest are inevitably a function of our method of investigation. Because a great deal of our research involved vocal communication, this paradigm will be described primarily in terms of vocal expression; however, our general procedures were the same for all modes of communication.

We typically began with a list of emotional meanings to be expressed. Sometimes, as in Levitt's study, the list of meanings had some previous empirical basis, but in most instances, we merely chose emotional meanings which seemed to be clearly different from each other. These meanings were not the same from study to study, in one sense reflecting a looseness in our method, but in another sense, providing, inadvertently I confess, a basis for generalizing our findings across different categories of emotional meaning.

On some occasions we presented the speaker with a situation related to each emotional meaning to help the speaker simulate the particular emotion to be expressed. At other times, we merely presented the speaker with a list of emotions and asked him to express each one as effectively as he could. Without any formal data, I can only report that the more detailed situational descriptions of each emotional category did not result in consistently superior communication. In fact, there seemed to be almost no difference between the results obtained by the two methods.

At any rate, at the very beginning of our method we departed from the reality of everyday communication, for we relied on experimental instructions rather than on actual emotional states as a basis for inducing emotional expressions. Thus, subjects spoke *as if* they were angry or happy, probably rarely experiencing actual anger or happiness during the research procedure. It was possible, of course, that this artificiality of inducing emotional expression might have mitigated the validity of our generalizations about everyday emotional communication, but the substantial number of consistent findings that make "psychological sense" would seem to provide ample evidence for the validity of our techniques.

Each speaker recited standard verbal content with the intent of expressing a variety of emotional meanings. We chose the content-standard technique as the least undesirable of several methods we tried. Reciting the alphabet or saying nonsense syllables seemed to introduce an extraneous factor that complicated, rather than simplified, our investigations. We have subsequently realized that the verbal content we've used may very well have influenced the communication process; we are therefore currently studying the interaction between verbal and nonverbal variables in emotional expression. But for the most part, I believe it is safe to assume that most of the variance in our vocal test is a function of nonverbal rather than verbal factors.

Each vocal expression was tape recorded, and our next step was to identify those items which communicated each emotional meaning. The term "communicate" has been used in a variety of ways by different writers, but for our purposes we needed an operational definition that would permit us to decide concretely that one item *did* communicate a given emotional meaning and another did not. Of course, such a definition must be reasonable in relation to other usages of the term, but we also recognized that whatever definition we chose, it would in some respects be arbitrary and open to question. In everyday conversation, despite individual differences in understanding the meaning of many words, one usually assumes that he is communicating with another person unless he perceives fairly strong evidence to the contrary; in our research, we could not make such an assumption. Therefore, recognizing the arbitrariness of our decision, we defined communication in terms of two specific criteria; we said that vocal expression communicated a given emotional meaning if (1) a plurality of listeners agreed with the intent of the speaker and (2) the number of "correct" responses in the plurality exceeded chance expectation at the .01 level. With this definition we undoubtedly obscured patterns of communication involving special sensitivities of some listeners in response to particular speakers; that is, I might communicate accurately with another person unusually sensitive to my expressions despite the fact that no one else would agree with that person's interpretation of my intended emotional meaning. But our primary concern was not with these kinds of unusual interpersonal sensitivity, but rather, with more common and conventional patterns of communication.

In defining communication, we also had to define "meaning." The meaning of any sign or symbol can be defined in terms of some behavioral response, and just as there are many aspects of behavior, there are many kinds of meaning. We chose a "labeling," or "naming," response on the assumption that the label a listener applied to a vocal expression realistically defined the meaning that expression had for him. If the listener's response agreed with the speaker's intent, we said that the listener was "sensitive to" or "understood" the speaker. In this respect, our research method paralleled everyday communication in so far as labeling behavior is commonly associated with understanding or meaning. But our technique differed from usual interpersonal communication in that the listener was always given a list of emotional names from which to choose his response, and he was required to limit his choice to one category of meaning contained in the list. This certainly differs from the typical everyday situation in which a listener has no explicit list of labels from which to choose his response. At this point, our problem was similar to the psychometric issue of essay versus objective tests, on the one hand, we wanted some standardization of responses to assure reliability of scoring, but on the other hand, we also wanted to achieve a reasonable degree of verisimilitude in respect to everyday communication. Our choice of an objective form of response assured us of scoring reliability, and we can only argue for the verisimilitude of our tests on the basis of the results obtained.

45 | The Indexing Process in Communication
PERCY H. TANNENBAUM

From a broad viewpoint, we may conceive of two major classifications of variables that are operative in a given communication message having some effect, intended or otherwise. There are, on the one hand, factors in the recipients of the message which may enhance or limit its effectiveness. A variety of such audience variables has been studied, but we still lack adequate measures to explore many of the presumably critical factors.

The other major classification consists of factors in the message itself. Obviously the content of a message will determine, to an extent, its effects. But what is the effective content? One obvious answer is to regard the *total* message as the single gross stimulus input into a communication situation, and to attribute any measurable effect of the communication to that single entity, as such. This has been the approach that has characterized most of the hundreds of studies that have demonstrated communication effects of one kind or another. There has been little attention to the distinctive components of this stimulus pattern.

Some investigations of content analysis represent a certain degree of refinement from this gross approach. Here the focus is usually on the determination of the relative frequencies of arbitrarily-established con-

Reprinted with permission of the publisher and the author. From *The Public Opinion Quarterly*, 19:292–302 (1955).

tent categories, or in the isolation of basic themes or appeals. But in most studies of this kind, the causal relationship between content categories and effects is more often assumed than demonstrated.

The notion of an indexing process in communication effects is an outgrowth of regarding the communication message as a set of distinctive stimulus elements—of individual signs or cues usually (e.g., language), but not necessarily (e.g., pictorial communication), arranged in a sequential order of some kind. The nature of the basic message unit—is it the morpheme, the word, the phrase, the sentence, etc.?—remains undecided at present and is the undefined term of the system. This issue, however, is a vital one in communication theory and will ultimately have to be resolved. For our purposes here it is sufficient to make the assumption of the message being a *set* (in mathematical set theory terminology) of such undefined elements.

An *index* is considered to be a single such stimulus element or a stimulus complex that may serve to predispose a particular interpretation or meaning of the total stimulus pattern or of some segment of this stimulus pattern other than itself. Or, continuing the set theory analogy further, an index is a subset of the total message set; more precisely, it is a *proper subset*, in that it may be composed of one or more of the elements, but is never all of them. In a given communication message, then, there may be one or more such subsets which may or may not overlap (or intersect) one another, depending on the conditions of membership imposed.

One way in which an index may influence the effects of a communication is, of course, in terms of *attracting attention* to that message. If a particular cue or cue combination within the total message structure somehow raises the threshold of attention for that message and guides its selection over other messages, then it has served to influence its potentiality for effect. This is particularly true of the *mass* communication situation. Schramm has referred to this aspect of the indexing process as follows: "Communications is a buyer's market. Far more stimuli come to us than we are able to attend to. . . . There is good reason to think that we scan our communication environment like an index, selecting among cues and concentrating our attention on the signs associated with the cues that specially attract us. . . . For example, we habitually listen to a newscast a a relatively low level of attention until a cue word or phrase awakens our attention and invites us to respond to a group of signs associated with the cue."

This illustration stems directly from one of Schramm's own studies. He found that the presence of the name of a well-known person—in this case, a popular campus athlete—in association with a particular radio newscast item significantly enhanced the recall of that item. Moreover, some sort of generalization effect seemed to exist: items closely adjacent to the name-linked one were recalled significantly more frequently than when the name cue was absent.

Another way in which an index may function is in influencing the *decoding* the message. An incoming stimulus pattern impinges on and interacts with the predisposing, subjective factors within the recipient of the communication. The result of such integration of the message complex within the subjective frame of reference of the individual is the precipitation of the meaning of that message for that person. This internal activity also serves to mediate any responses the individual may make to the message in that it provides the distinctive self-stimulation for such responses. ·If a particular message segment influences this central perceptual process in some way, it has then served as an index.

In the nomenclature of perception, the focus of inquiry here is whether the part can influence the perception of the whole, or, in some cases, whether it can influence the perception of another of the parts. As a problem in perception this is not novel. The literature of traditional perception abounds with examples of this, as does that of the more contemporary "new look" perception.

VERBAL INDICES

There is considerable evidence for the influence of verbal indices on perception. Asch found that the simple substitution of the word "cold" for "warm" in a list of eight descriptive adjectives significantly altered the impression of the personality these adjectives were supposed to describe. And there is further evidence for the operation of the warm-cold variable as an index. Several experiments have shown that the verbal applied to an ambiguous design in many cases determined the nature of the reproduction of that design. Following another line of study, Farnsworth and Beaumont demonstrated that aesthetic evaluation of paintings was significantly affected by a statement of their commercial value. Not least, the study in rumor transmission by Allport and Postman contains abundant evidence of the role of both verbal and non-verbal parts on the perception of the whole.

THE NEWSPAPER HEADLINE. In an experiment by Tannenbaum, two stories were planted in a regular front page of a college daily. Three different headlines, each emphasizing a separate segment of the story, were presented to different groups of subjects with the main body of the story held constant. One story, for example, dealt with a report of a day's proceedings in a murder trial, with one headline indicating innocence of the defendant, one guilt, and the third non-committal.

Differential effects of the headline, in reply to a question regarding the innocence or guilt of the defendant, were significant beyond the 5 percent level. On the other story, the headline effect was significant at the .15 level. It was also shown that the effect of the headline was inversely related to the extent to which the story was read—i.e., the more thorough the reading, the less the effect of the headline *per se,* and vice-versa.

THE NEWSCAST "LEAD." Tannenbaum and Kerrick repeated the headline experiment in the form of a radio newscast. A regular newscast was written from the front-page stories, including the two experimental items. Three variations of the newscast were recorded, the variable being the introductory statement or "lead" to the experimental stories. Here again, differences in the effect of the "lead" index were significant beyond the 5 percent level. No significant effect was noted on the second story, but this can be attributed to the fact that we were dealing with well-structured attitudes that were not susceptible to change.

PICTURE CAPTIONS. Can slightly different captions alter the meaning of the same accompanying pictorial material? Using Osgood's semantic differential technique as the measuring device, this problem was investigated with five selected pictures of the Thematic Apperception Test. Each picture was presented in three variations: without a caption, with a caption loading the meaning in one direction, and with a caption loading the meaning in the opposite direction.

The results showed a significant index effect of the two opposing captions. On the direction of loading on the intended scales (e.g., toward *happy* in the case of a picture captioned AT THE STATION: REUNION, and toward *sad* when the caption was AT THE STATION: PARTING). Moreover, the effect of the caption generalized to other scales so that the total interpretation was congruent with the aspect made explicit in the caption. In some instances where the caption was quite opposite to the basic content of the picture, the effect was sufficient to cause a shift in judgment in the direction of the caption.

THE WORD "BUT." In another study in verbal indexing, the effect of a single word—the common conjunction "but"—immersed in a stream of conversation was studied. A tape recording was made of two individuals discussing the use of radio for adult educational purposes. The script was written in this manner: One discussant would make a point, then the second discussant would say something of the order of: "I agree with you BUT . . .", and would then proceed to make essentially the same point but in somewhat different words. In this manner the discussion went back and forth—first one person making a point, and then the other indicating agreement, adding the word "but," and proceeding to make the same point with a different vocabulary.

Two recordings of this conversation were made. One was left intact and the other was edited so that all the "but's" were deleted. The two recordings, then, were identical except for the absence or presence of the index word. Two groups of subjects were exposed to the respective tapes, and, following exposure, were asked a series of questions relating to the content. The main question for purposes of analysis was: "Is it your opinion that the discussants agreed with each other or that they disagreed?" A Chi-square analysis of the replies indicated a significant difference between the two groups beyond the 5 percent level, with the index word "but" apparently creating a predisposition of disagreement.

NON-VERBAL INDICES

Most people exposed to an undergraduate psychology course are well acquainted with the common optical illusions to be found in most texts—e.g., the Müller-Lyer, Poggendorf and Zöllner illusions. These are prime examples of the effect of non-verbal indices in visual perception. Similarly, the more recent experiments in social perception contain evidence of non-verbal indexing. Bruner and Postman found that the presence of differently-valued symbols (a swastika, a dollar sign, and an abstract geometric design) drawn on identically-sized discs influenced the perceived size of those discs. In the same way, the studies of Ansbacher and of Bruner and Goodman on the perceived size of postage stamps and coins, respectively, can be considered as cases of indexing.

POLITICAL SYMBOLS. As part of a study in pictorial symbolism, the effect of commonly-used political symbols on judgments of various animal drawings was investigated. The animals dealt with were the bear, eagle, lion, donkey, and elephant. To various groups of subjects the following modes of presentation were offered for each animal for judgment on the semantic differential: (a) drawing of the animal itself (e.g., plain drawing of the bear); (b) drawing of the animal in a typical non-political situation (e.g., a dancing bear); and (c) political cartoon of the animal (e.g., the Russian bear, with the hammer-and-sickle symbol clearly indicated on his chest). In addition, subjects rated the orthographic forms of the symbol and the thing symbolized—e.g., the word "bear" and the word "Russia."

The results clearly indicate significant differences between the profiles of judgment for the three forms of pictorial representation. And, whereas judgments of the non-political symbols showed some evidence of compromise (e.g., judgments of the dancing bear shifted from those of the plain drawing of the bear only on those scales of the semantic differential appropriate to the stereotyped situation), judgments of the political drawings showed no such compromise, differing on almost all of the ten scales from those of the other two stimulus situations. Indeed, the profile of the political cartoon of the bear was almost identical with that for the word "Russia." It is to be noted that subjects were asked to judge the *total* drawing.

COLOR. Can different colors significantly alter the judgments of articles with which they are associated? A latin-square analysis of variance design was set up in which five nationally-advertised products (a shirt, ice cream, rug, automobile, and cake) and a control (color spot)—making six objects of judgment—were judged by six groups of subjects against 20 bi-polar scales of the semantic differential. Subjects were instructed to rate the *products* only. The same design was applied to four different conditions of color-usage—intense (80 percent saturation) color in product, pale (20 percent saturation) color in product, intense color in background, and pale color in background. Separate analyses were conducted for each scale under each condition.

The findings of this study can be summarized as follows: (a) Using the product-color interaction as the error term, *F*-values between colors were significant for several of the non-evaluative descriptive scales such as warm-cool, heavy-light, rough-smooth, flimsy-sturdy, and exciting-dull, and only for the condition of intense color on product; using the less stringent error term of within-cells variance, several additional scales, still non-evaluative ones, showed significant color effects. (b) Particularly on the evaluative scales (e.g., good-bad, tasty-distasteful, etc.) the color-product interaction was the significant factor, indicating the importance of selecting appropriate, culturally-accepted colors to go with particular advertised products. (c) Pastel colors, both in the product and background, elicited small but consistently more favorable judgments.

MUSIC. A recently-completed experiment indicates that background music can have a significant effect on the impact of dramatic material presented over television. Three conditions of presentation of a one-act play were used: the stage presentation, a one-camera kinescope recording made at the same time as the stage presentation with the single camera situated on the center aisle of the theatre, and a two-camera studio presentation utilizing all the techniques of TV production, including close-ups, super-imposed images, etc. Six groups of subjects were employed—three groups for the conditions indicated, and another three groups where an appropriate musical background score was *added* to the presentation. Subjects were asked to rate the play, as such, on ten selected scales of the semantic differential.

The results indicate that the musical index was not effective on the evaluative judgments, but that it exercised a significant effect over all three conditions of presentation in terms of judgments of the strength or potency of the drama and along an active-passive continuum. For the particular play and the particular music used, the music background effect was one of making the play appear stronger and more active. No significant interaction between the music and the presentation was indicated.

DISCUSSION

It is apparent from the foregoing results that what we have referred to as the indexing process is a general phenomenon that may be operative in many kinds of communication situations. In each of the seven experimental studies reported, the manipulation of a single index under conditions of single communication exposures produced significant effects on the judgments of the total message. These findings are somewhat spectacular in themselves. They are even more so when we consider the implications they hold for the more common communication situations where we have repeated exposures to similar, related messages, each accompanied by a number of cues pointing in the same direction. Under such conditions, the cumulative index effects may completely dominate the interpretation of the communication.

What is the mechanism by which an index exercises its influence on the perception of message, and thus on their effects? As part of the general body of perception theory, this is still an unresolved issue. Similarly, lacking a precise knowledge of the dynamics of the communication process, it is impossible to give a complete account of the functioning of the indexing process in communication.

However, within the domain of the communication studies reported here, there are certain aspects of its operation that become evident. To begin with, an index does not achieve its status as an index merely by virtue of being a part—even a highly-structured part—of the total stimulus content and structure. It is effective as an index to the extent, first, that it has meaning for the recipient of the message. In other words, it is the significance or meaning that the communicatee attributes to the particular message segment—and not its mere existence as a message segment—that is of importance. And, second, it is the way in which the communicatee then integrates his meaning of this one segment into his interpretation of the total message that promotes its influence. It is not the communicator's or the experimenter's decision that determines what is and what is not an index. It is the communicatee's or subject's meaning and consequent utilization thereof that is the critical factor. It follows, then, that if two individuals have different meanings of the particular message part under consideration, the functioning of this part as an index will differ in kind if not in extent. Similarly, if one individual utilizes this part in his final interpretation of the message more than the other, then the difference will be in extent.

In a sense, most message parts may be considered as indices, since it is reasonable to assume that the final interpretation of a communication is a result of the integration of the meanings and significances of its individual units. But the notion of an indexing process, as advanced here, is that some parts may *exercise an inordinate effect* in this integrative process, and that their "contribution" to the final meaning may be out of all proportion to that of the other parts. It is when a message part exercises such excessive influence that we refer to it as an index.

For analytic purposes, the indexing process may be conveniently considered within the general framework of Osgood's mediation theory. Figure 1 represents a symbolic model. The cues of the message (S_1, S_2

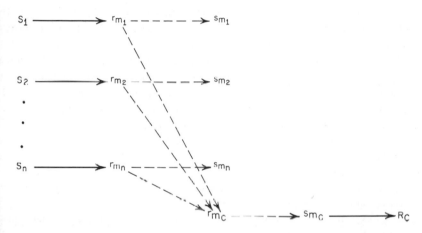

Figure 1. Symbolic account of the development of the significance of a communication.

. . . S_n) each elicit mediational processes (r_m — — — $\rightarrow$ S_m) within the individual exposed to them, according to previous experience. Each of these mediation processes represents, at this level, the meaning or significance of that cue for that individual. Within the context of a communication message, the mediating reactions (r_m) of the cues may be further thought of as becoming integrated into a higher-order mediating reaction to the communication per se. This mediating reaction (r_{mc}) produces a distinctive pattern of self-stimulation (S_{mc}) which is at once the awareness or significance of the message and a necessary condition for evoking appropriate responses (R_c), such as, e.g., ratings on an attitude scale in a typical experimental situation.

Thus, this central mediation process represents a distinct psychological state of the individual at a given time. As outlined above, this state is the representation of the meaning of the message—i.e., how it is decoded by its recipient. On the encoding side, it represents the intentions of the communicator.

The particular mediating reaction thus elicited is obviously only one of a number of such available reactions. In other words, just as there may be a number of different meanings of a single sign or cue, there are also a number of different significances within a mature individual's repetoire for the particular message. That is, the particular r_{mc} elicited is only one of a number of such possible mediating reactions, each of which has associated with it its own distinctive pattern of self-stimulation, and thus may lead to differential meanings and responses. This set of possible reactions may be thought of as belonging to a *hierarchy*. The specific reaction that, for some reason or other, goes to the top of the hierarchy in a given communication situation, is the one that is responsible for the specific meaning attributed to that message, or for the way in which it is perceived.

Within this general paradigm, presented here all too briefly, the indexing process may be operationally stated: A message part serving as an index is one which selectively sensitizes a particular perception of the message by channeling a particular mediating reaction to the top of the hierarchy. To put it another way, the hierarchy may be considered as a set of possible reactions each with a certain probability of occurrence at a given time. An index serves to raise the probability of one of these reactions occurring over all others. In Figure 1, each of the cues shown tend to produce a single mediating reaction to the communication. Let us suppose, however, that another in this set of message cues, say S_k, exercises a more profound effect than the other cues combined, and leads to the evoking of a different mediating reaction to the communication (r_{mck}) which has a higher probability of occurrence. This mediating reaction will produce its own stimulation (S_{mck}) and will thus lead to a different response. We then speak of S_k as an index.

This analysis still fails to define the mechanism by which an index influences the probabilities or how it channels a particular reaction to the top of the hierarchy. It is the writer's contention that the mechanics of this process rest in the neurophysiological system of the individual and will ultimately have to be accounted for on that microscopic level of analysis. For example, it may well be that in the case of sequentially-organized messages where the index appears at the beginning of the message—e.g., the "lead" in the radio newscast study—the operation of the index may be accounted for on the basis of a *stimulus trace* persisting through time in the central nervous system. Such a notion is entirely plausible, but for the present is only speculative.

46

The Function of Language Classifications in Behavior
JOHN B. CARROLL
and JOSEPH B. CASAGRANDE

More than fifty years ago George Santayana wrote in his essay *The Sense of Beauty:* "Grammar, philosophically studied, is akin to the deepest metaphysics, because in revealing the constitution of speech, it reveals the constitution of thought and the hierarchy of those categories by which we conceive the world." The world of experience is characterized by a logic that deals with continua; our experiences present themselves to us in almost limitless variations and shadings; and there are no boundaries between the parts of experience except those which are created by our perceptions.

If a language is to be used for efficient person-to-person communication about the world of experience, it must operate with a logic that deals with discrete entities—a logic of criteriality which distinguishes experiences on certain arbitrary and agreed-upon terms. When we give proper names to individual persons, pet animals, and geographical locations, we are responding to an extreme need for discreteness and specific differentiation, but most of the time we are well satisfied to convey our experiences by means of a relatively small number (a few thousand, say) of general categories into which we learn to fit them. As a first approximation we may regard each word of a language like English as the name of a category of experience. *horse, petunia, he, ecstasy, reprimand, green, very,* and *nevertheless* are all categories of experience. Not all categories of experience are symbolized by discrete words; some are represented by grammatical phenomena such as are indicated in the following contrasts: *horse v. horses's; petunia v. petunias; he v. him; ecstasy v. ecstatic; reprimand v. reprimanded; green v. greener; the very old man v. the very idea;* and the classic *dog bites man v. man bites dog.*

If we agree that the categories of a language are "arbitrary" in the sense that they could be replaced by other, equally acceptable ways of categorizing experience, we could begin to inquire to what extent the several thousand languages of the world have similar categories. How many languages have a distinct, generic term for *horse?* How many lan-

From *Readings in Social Psychology,* 3d ed., edited by E. E. Maccoby, T. M. Newcomb, and E. L. Hartley, pp. 18–31. Copyright © 1958 by Holt, Rinehart and Winston, Inc.

guages have only a term for what we would call *quadruped*, applying it alike to horses, dogs, wolves, giraffes and adding appropriate qualifying terms? Are there languages which have no generic term for *horse* but only terms for particular breeds and conditions of horses? (We are told that Arabic is such a language.) Or let us take a grammatical problem: do all languages distinguish singular and plural? (No, Chinese does not.) Are there languages which have *more* levels of grammatical number than our two? (Yes; some languages have four "numbers," singular, dual, trial, and plural.) Investigations along these lines are not to be undertaken lightly, for they require an immense sophistication in the techniques of linguistic science. We can nevertheless predict the major outlines of the results. There would be many semantic areas of remarkable (though rarely complete) uniformity among languages, while other areas would tend to show considerable diversity. The linguist Morris Swadesh has surveyed a wide variety of languages in an effort to arrive at a list of concepts for which one would be fairly sure to find a distinct word or word-like form in every language. His final list of 100 such concepts includes things like: personal pronouns: *I, thou, we, he, ye, they;* position and movement: *come, sit, give, fly, stand, hold, fall, swim;* natural objects and phenomena: *ice, salt, star, sun, wind;* descriptives: *old, dry, good, new, warm, rotten, cold;* miscellaneous: *name, other, not, burn, blow, freeze, swell, road, kill.* But even in observing this apparent uniformity, we must not be misled into thinking that there are exact semantic correspondences between languages. English *horse*, French *cheval*, and German *Pferd* may have different ranges of application and different semantic overtones; the measurement of such differences is a problem beyond the scope of this paper. Further, we can find rather obvious lacks of correspondence when we look at the different ranges of meaning covered by the English *proceed* v. French *procéder* ("to proceed" but also "to behave or conduct oneself"), or English *experience v.* French *expérience* ("experience" but also "experiment"). It would appear that the categories of one language are sometimes "untranslatable" into another language; even if we ignore such problems as finding the difference between the English and the Russian concepts of democracy, there remain such cases as German *Gemütlichkeit* and French *acharnement* which are presumably incapable of exact rendering in English. Even such a simple concept as that represented by the word *too* is extremely clumsy to express in Amharic, the official language of Ethiopia. In the realm of grammar, Edward Sapir's classic work *Language* will suggest the extent to which languages differ among themselves in grammatical concepts. Although Sapir felt that "no language wholly fails to distinguish noun and verb," his writings suggest that there are few basic concepts which universally find expression in the grammatical structures of languages. This is not to say that there are grammatical concepts which *cannot* be expressed in all languages; in general, any grammatical concept found in one language can be expressed somehow in every language, even if the expression is a little awkward or periphrastic. Languages do differ remarkably, however, in the grammatical concepts which are mandatory: for example, the use of the singular-plural distinction is said to be mandatory in English but completely optional in Chinese. If someone says "I'm going out to hunt bear," he is dispensing with the singular-plural distinction and talking in the pattern of Chinese—which happens to be convenient because he does not know whether he will bag one bear or more than one.

The real question for the social psychologist is this: Is the behavior of a person (aside from his language behavior) a function of the language he happens to speak? Granted that languages differ in the ways we have described, what effects will these differences have on the way a person thinks, the way he deals with other people, or the way he deals with his environment?

The notion that language makes an important difference in behavior has a long history, beginning with the writings of the German philologist W. von Humboldt more than a century ago. In more recent times, the linguist Benjamin Lee Whorf has been the chief exponent of what he termed "linguistic relativity":

. . . the background linguistic system (in other words, the grammar) of each language is not merely a reproducing instrument for voicing ideas but rather is itself the shaper of ideas, the program and guide for the individual's mental activity, for his analysis of impressions, for his synthesis of his mental stock in trade. Formulation of ideas is not an independent process, strictly rational in the old sense, but is part of a particular grammar and differs, from slightly to greatly, between different grammars.

The linguistic relativity hypothesis is a special case of the culture-personality theory. Substituting terms in Smith, Bruner, and White's précis of culture-personality theory, we may express it this way: Each language creates a special plight to which the individual must adjust. The human plight is in no sense universal save in this fact: that however different the language may be, it has certain common problems with which to deal—time, space, quantity, action, state, etc. But each language handles these problems differently and develops special ways of communicating. These ways of communicating create special needs, special responses, and lead to the development of special modes of thinking.

The alternative to the linguistic relativity hypothesis would be a statement that the behavior of a person is not a function of the language he happens to speak or be speaking, that his modes of categorizing experience and dealing with his world operate independently of language, that language is simply a way of communicating something which is in every way prior to its codification in language.

This paper reports two experiments designed to explore, in a preliminary way, to what extent and under what conditions the linguistic relativity hypothesis can be accepted.

In order to find evidence to support the linguistic relativity hypothesis it is not sufficient merely to point to differences between languages and assume that users of those languages have correspondingly different mental experiences; if we are not to be guilty of circular inference, it is necessary to show some correspondence between the presence or absence of a certain linguistic phenomenon and the presence or absence of a certain kind of "nonlinguistic" response. This being the case, we must be clear as to what we mean by a nonlinguistic response. Unfortunately, it is extremely difficult to define this rigorously. We might be tempted to do so by saying that a nonlinguistic response is one which can be elicited without the intervention of any symbolic system, but as soon as we realize that the bells, buzzers, lights, levers, and food pellets through which we elicit the behavior of dogs and rats may be regarded as symbolic systems, this definition would serve to exclude large classes of responses which we would still like to call "nonlinguistic." When we come to examine the actual behaviors used in our experiments, we will find that their "nonlinguistic" character resides in the fact that they are neutral, as it were, with respect to the *special* symbolic systems against which they are being tested. For example, in the second experiment to be presented, a child is asked to tell whether a blue rope "goes best with" a blue stick or a yellow rope. Now, by appropriate reinforcement techniques, we could teach the child always to choose on the basis of form or always to choose on the basis of color, and we could do this without using English or Navaho or any other special symbolic systems. Suppose, again, we were studying differences in the arithmetical abilities of children who had learned the decimal system and of children who had learned only the system of Roman numerals. The arithmetical behavior being studied is analogous to our "nonlinguistic" behavior because it is *neutral* to any one special system of arithmetical symbolism in the sense that it is *possible* to operate in either system, though not necessarily with the same efficiency.

As Brown and Lenneberg have suggested, two approaches present themselves for the testing of the linguistic relativity hypothesis. Brown and Lenneberg used the first of these—an *intralinguistic* approach which, capitalizing on the fact that the speakers of a given language manifest differences in their knowledge and use of that language, attempts to show that these differences are correlated with certain other behaviors. In both experiments reported here, we have used the second approach—an *inter-*

linguistic design in which nonlinguistic behaviors of speakers of two different languages are compared. Use of this second approach entails an advantage and a danger: it may become possible to select linguistic features in two languages which are strikingly and fundamentally different, but it becomes difficult to assure oneself that any observed behavioral correlates are *not* due to irrelevant factors such as dissimilar cultural backgrounds and experiences.

EXPERIMENT I

In the Hopi language, still spoken in the pueblos of northeastern Arizona, the semantic domains of verbs for various kinds of physical activities have structures quite different from the corresponding domains in English. In speaking of *breaking*, the Hopi must use verbs depending upon whether there is one fission or many fissions (a distinction not unlike that between "break" and "shatter"). He uses the same verb for *spilling* and for *pouring*, but must use a different verb depending upon whether the material being spilled or poured is liquid or nonliquid. He can use the same verb in speaking of denting an object like a fender and in speaking of pressing a doorbell. The question posed in this experiment was whether these linguistic features would show corresponding features of nonlinguistic behavior in speakers of Hopi when contrasted with speakers of English. The "nonlinguistic" behavior chosen for study was that of sorting or classifying pictures of the actions represented by verbs of breaking, spilling, pressing, and similar physical activities.

Method. Line drawings were prepared, representing various physical actions such as falling, breaking, dropping, etc. These drawings were then assembled in sets of three, or triads, in such a way that, on the basis of comparative linguistic analysis, it could be hypothesized that in each triad native speakers of Hopi would tend to put a different pair of pictures together as contrasted with native speakers of English.

The test was administered individually to 14 Hopi adults (age range 24 to over 66) who were known to be fluent speakers of Hopi. All could speak English with varying degrees of competence, but regarded themselves as more fluent in Hopi. The test was also administered to 28 "Anglos" (as they are called in the Southwest) consisting of 12 adults of comparable degree of education in a rural New England community and 16 graduate students at Harvard University.

The test was introduced as an experiment in "how we think" and started with six pretest items, of which the first is shown as Figure 1. The three pictures were presented as physically separated photographs which could be shuffled and arranged at the will of the subject, who was asked simply

FIGURE 1   FIGURE 2

FIGURE 3   FIGURE 4

Figures 1, 2, 3, and 4.   Sample items from Experiment I.

to decide which two of the three pictures went together. The subjects had no difficulty in seeing that the two pictures of *falling* objects went together. The remaining five pretest items were designed to reveal whether the subjects understood the task and to make it clear that they were to respond on the basis of the action or type of action represented rather than incidental features of any objects depicted. The test proper consisted of 17 "critical" items and five "control" items about which no linguistic hypothesis was formulated. (We shall omit further discussion of the control items because they showed no interesting differences between Hopis and Anglos.)

The subjects were also asked to tell why their choices went together. No suggestion was given that the experiment had anything to do with language, and most of the Hopis responded in English. Occasionally, however, subjects volunteered that it seemed to "work better" to "think in Hopi," and gave their verbalizations in Hopi. The results, therefore, consist not only of the choices made by the subjects but also (except for three or four cases) the stated reasons for the choices.

RESULTS. The nature of the results and some of the problems in their interpretation may be first illustrated by presenting data for one of the "critical" items in detail. The pictures for Item 20 are presented in Figure 2.

The linguistic basis for this item resides in the fact that in Hopi there is a verb *'u'ta* which means "to close an opening," and this is the verb normally used for placing covers on open boxes, closing lids, closing holes in tubes or walls, etc., in contrast, placing a cover on something for protection against dust or damage is represented by the verbs *na:kwapna* or *nönöma*. In English, however, we tend to use *cover* regardless of whether we are covering an opening or not, and we tend to reserve *close* for the situation where an opening can be more or less exactly fitted with a lid or other special stoppage (also for special cases like *closing a book*). On this basis it was hypothesized that Hopis would tend to put together pictures *A* and *C*, while Anglos would tend to put together pictures *B* and *C*.

In presenting this item to Anglo subjects, it was necessary to explain (without mentioning or suggesting the verbs "cover" or "close") that in picture *C* a woman was placing a wicker plaque over a box of food (the traditional Hopi "piki" corn bread).

Table 1 shows the number of subjects in various classifications making each of three possible groupings, together with a classification of the reasons for these choices.

The small numbers of cases make statistical significance testing diffi- cult if not impossible, but even if we are to make a statistical test, it must be recognized that a given response may mean different things. Thus, at least three Hopis put pictures *A* and *C* together on the ground that both show *'u'ta* "closing an opening," but to at least four Anglos pictures *A* and *C* go together because they show boxes. The most striking result here is the fact that Hopis tend *not* to put pictures *B* and *C* together, while Anglos, particularly educated ones, show a strong tendency to do so. Only four out of 14 Hopis put pictures *B* and *C* together, while 11 out of 16 college-educated Anglos did so. We can look at the reasons for the choices more closely. Only four out of the 14 Hopis mentioned any kind

Table 1

Choices and Reasons for Choices for the Item of Figure 2

Group	"Hopi" response: A and C combined	"English" response: B and C combined	Neutral: A and B combined
14 Hopi adults	3 Both 'u'ta 1 Neither is na: kwapna 1 Both are boxes 1 Both holding the lid 2 (Not given) (N = 8)	2 Both covering 2 (Not given) (N = 4)	1 Both will be tightly covered 1 Both being covered (N = 2)
12 Rural Anglos	4 Both are boxes 2 Both covering with lids (N = 6)	4 Both covering, v. closing or shutting (N = 4)	1 Both covering 1 Both more familiar (N = 2)
16 Graduate students	1 Putting on a flat cover 3 (Not given) (N = 4)	8 Both covering, v. closing or shutting 1 Both putting on top 1 Both "dealing with entire structure" 1 (Not given) (N = 11)	1 Both (customarily) "used and covered" v. one-time covering (N = 1)

of "covering" in giving their reasons (whatever their choice), while 17 out of 28 Anglos did—a result significant below the 10-percent level.

Although limited, these results suggest that speakers of Hopi tend to organize their perceptions of situations such as those pictured in Figure 1 in terms of "closing openings" instead of "putting covers on things."

There were several other critical items showing results tending to favor our hypothesis. For the pictures of Figure 3, it was expected that Hopis would tend to pair A and C because both represent the action called *lelu̇wi*, "to apply or spread over a surface," while Anglos would pair B and C because they both show "painting." (Hopi has a word for painting, but its use is restricted to cases where one paints a picture or a design, as distinct from covering a surface with paint.) Six of the 14 Hopis paired A and C, while only four of all 28 Anglos did so; of these four, two paired on the basis of the fact that both showed the use of a tool versus the use of one's hands; the significance of this result is at just below the 5-percent level by Fisher's test. Actually, a more striking result was unanticipated: Anglos had a strong tendency to pair either *B* and *C* or *A* and *B* because they felt both members of these pairs represented "decorating" versus mere painting or covering. "Artistic creation" was also mentioned as a basis for these choices.

Another item showing interesting results is shown in Figure 4. As has been mentioned, "spilling" (accidentally) and "pouring" (intentionally) are not distinguished in Hopi; there is a way of translating the idea of "accidentally" but this is handled as a separate expression instead of being built into the verb, as in English. Hopi uses slightly different forms for pouring: *wehekna*, "to pour liquid," and *wa:hokna*, "to pour sand, gravel, or other nonliquid loose things," but the form for dropping something is entirely different: *po:sna*. We found that eight out of 14 Hopis (57 percent) paired pictures *A* and *C*, consonant with the linguistic forms; these figures contrast with the finding that only seven out of 28 Anglos, or 25 percent, made this pairing. The probability of chance occurrence of a result as extreme as this, determined by the χ^2 test with continuity-correction, is less than 10 percent. At least 16 of the 20 Anglos who paired pictures *B* and *C* explained that there was unintentional, accidental action in both of them, while only two Hopis drew attention to this accidental character of the action. Instead, Hopis rarely seemed concerned about whether the man in picture *A* *meant* to pour out the peaches, while Anglos frequently queried the experimenter about this.

Admitting the results from all 17 "critical" items as evidence, we present in Table 2 a summary to show the extent to which our hypotheses were favored by the data. There is probably not a truly significant difference between the 29 percent representing the tendency of the Hopi subjects to make the expected "Hopi" response of pairing pictures *A* and *C* and the 22.6 percent and 24.0 percent, values for the two Anglo groups, but the trend is at least one of those tantalizingly modest ones which can be characterized only as being "in the predicted direction."

Upon re-examination of the purely linguistic data and consideration of certain unanticipated difficulties which had arisen in the subjects' interpretations of the drawings, it was possible to weed out five items which had gone sour, so to speak, leaving 12 critical items for which the results are presented in the lower part of Table 2. Here we see a sturdier trend in favor of our general hypothesis, although the results are still far from striking. It is not really legitimate to treat Table 2 as a contingency table and apply a χ^2 test, because the events represented there are not necessarily independent; were we to assume that all the choices are independent, however, and were we then to apply a χ^2 test to the lower part of Table 2, we would find that the probability of this χ^2 being exceeded by chance would be less than .01.

The results encourage us to think that not only do we have a promising

Table 2

Total Frequency of Pairing

		"Hopi" response: A and C	"Anglo" response: B and C	Neutral: A and B	Total
17 "critical items"	14 Hopi	69 (29.0%)	126 (52.9%)	43 (18.1%)	238
	12 Rural Anglos	46 (22.6)	119 (58.3)	39 (19.1)	204
	16 Educated Anglos	65 (24.0)	156 (57.5)	50 (18.5)	271
12 "critical items" with "good hypotheses"	14 Hopi	57 (34.0)	80 (47.6)	31 (18.4)	168
	12 Rural Anglos	31 (21.5)	85 (59.0)	28 (19.5)	144
	16 Educated Anglos	36 (18.8)	122 (63.9)	33 (17.3)	191

technique for studying the linguistic relativity hypothesis, but we also have an indication that in further and more extensive trials of this method we may obtain greater assurances that language categories influence at least one variety of nonlinguistic behavior. Several suggestions towards improvement of the experimental methodology may be offered: (1) drawings should be given extensive pretests to insure that they are interpreted similarly by all subjects; (2) the experiment should utilize contrasting groups of monolinguals (rather than bilinguals as we had to use here); and (3) subjects should be asked to choose which of two pictures, A or B, go best with a fixed third picture, C. (This procedure is used in Experiment II).

EXPERIMENT II

This second experiment was an attempt to show that behavior can be influenced by a grammatical phenomenon as well as a purely lexical or semantic phenomenon.

It is obligatory in the Navaho language, when using verbs of *handling*, to employ a particular one of a set of verbal forms according to the shape or some other essential attribute of the object about which one is speaking. Thus, if I ask you in Navaho to hand me an object, I must use the appropriate verb stem depending on the nature of the object. If it is a long flexible object such as a piece of string, I must say *šanléh;* if it is a long rigid object such as a stick, I must say *šaníįįh;* if it is a flat flexible material such as a paper or cloth, I must say *šanitcóós,* and so on.

The groups of words in Navaho which together regularly take one or another of these verb stems, say the family of words for all long, rigid objects, carry no linguistic marker of their class membership. They comprise what Whorf has called a *covert class,* as distinguished from an *overt class* such as gender in Latin with the familiar *—us, —i, —a, —ae* case and number suffixes. Nor, in the absence of native grammarians, are there any terms in Navaho for these categories themselves. This like many another grammatical rule operates well below the level of conscious awareness. Although most Navaho-speaking children, even at the age of three or four, used these forms unerringly, they were unable to tell why they used a particular form with any particular object. Even though a child could not name an object, or may not have seen one like it before, in most cases he used the correct verb form according to the nature of the object.

Because of this obligatory categorization of objects in Navaho, it seemed reasonable that Navaho-speaking children would learn to discriminate the "form" attributes of objects at an earlier age than their English-speaking compeers. The finding of American and European psychologists that children tend first to distinguish objects on the basis of size and color might—at least at the level of verbal facility in dealing with these variables—be partly an artifact of the particular language they use. The hypothesis was, then, that this feature of the Navaho language would affect the relative potency, or order of emergence of such concepts as color, size, shape or form, and number in the Navaho-speaking child, as compared with English-speaking Navaho children of the same age, and that Navaho-speaking children would be more inclined than the latter to perceive formal similarities between objects.

This hypothesis was tested using a variety of experimental materials and several different procedures, of which only one will be reported here. Although the test was expressly adapted to Navaho, the design as well as the basic hypothesis could be extended to other languages since nearly all languages have obligatory categories.

The procedure whose results we will report here was called Ambiguous Sets and was actually interposed between several other procedures well after the child had become accustomed to the experimental situation.

METHOD. Ten pairs of objects (colored wooden blocks, sticks, and pieces of rope) were used, each of which differed significantly in two respects, e.g., color and size, color and shape, size and shape, or shape and Navaho verb-form classification. These pairs of objects were arranged before the child, one pair at a time. After being presented with a pair of objects, the child was shown a third object similar to each member of the pair in only one of the two relevant characteristics, but of course matching neither, and was asked to tell the experimenter which of the pair went best with the object shown to him. For example, one of the pairs consisted of a yellow stick and a piece of blue rope of comparable size. The child was then shown a yellow rope, and the basis of his choice could be either color or the Navaho verb-form classification—since different verbal forms are used for a length of rope and a stick. The ten sets of objects were presented in the alphabetical order of the letters shown in Table 3, with the exception that the first set presented was set O, and the last was set P.

The subjects were 135 Navaho children ranging from three to about ten years of age, drawn from the vicinity of Fort Defiance and Window Rock, Arizona, on the Navaho reservation. On the basis of a bilingualism test and other criteria of language dominance, the 135 subjects were divided into five groups: monolingual in Navaho, Navaho-predominant, balanced bilingual, English-predominant, and English monolingual. For purposes of statistical analysis Navaho monolinguals and Navaho-predominants were grouped together (59 subjects), as were the English monolinguals and English-predominants (43). The remaining 33 subjects were classed as "balanced bilinguals" and this group included a number of individuals whose language status was dubious.

The experiment was conducted in Navaho or, with appropriate modifications in the instructions, in English, as indicated. An interpreter was used with Navaho-speaking children, although the experimenter was able to give instructions in Navaho for some of the procedures used. Most of the testing was done in the children's homes—usually Navaho hogans of the traditional sort—and in the presence of parents, grandparents, siblings, and other interested and very curious onlookers.

Although the establishment of contrasting groups of Navaho children on the basis of language dominance was regarded as providing adequate control, a supplementary control group was obtained by testing 47 white American middle-class children in the Boston metropolitan area, with an age range roughly comparable to that of the Navaho children.

RESULTS. The children were not at all baffled by the ambiguity inherent in the task; their choices were invariably made with little or no hesitation.

The data were analyzed both item by item and by age. In considering the results, shown in Table 3, it must be remembered that it was our hypothesis that Navaho-dominant children would be more likely to make their choices on the basis of similarity in shape and verb-stem classifica-

Table 3

Results of the "Ambiguous Sets" Experiment

Set	Attributes Contrasted	Objects in Set			Percent of "a" Choices			
		Comparison Model	Alternative Choices (a)	(b)	Navaho-Dominant Navahos (N = 59)	English-Dominant Navahos (N = 43)	P*	White American Children (N = 47)
O	Verb-stem, color	blue rope	yellow rope	blue stick	70.7	39.5	<.01	83.0
P	"	yellow rope	blue rope	yellow stick	70.7	39.5	<.01	80.7
H	"	blue stick	yellow stick	blue cylinder	71.2	44.2	<.01	76.6
N	"	blue stick	yellow stick	blue oblong block	72.4	44.2	<.01	82.9
I	shape, size	small blue cube	medium blue cube	small blue sphere	79.2	60.5	<.05	72.4
L	" "	small blue cylinder	large blue cylinder	small blue oblong	59.4	44.2	>.10	82.9
K	shape, color	medium blue cube	medium white cube	medium blue pyramid	45.7	39.5	>.10	70.2
G	size, color	medium blue cube	medium yellow cube	small blue cube	21.0	23.2	>.10	74.4
J	" "	medium blue cube	medium white cube	large blue cube	15.2	14.0	>.10	55.3
M	" "	medium blue cube	medium black cube	small blue cube	59.3	30.2	<.01	74.4

* This is the probability that χ^2 as obtained in a 2 × 2 table comparing the two groups of Navahos would be equalled or exceeded under the hypothesis of no difference.

tion than on the basis of size or color. Thus, for the first seven sets listed in Table 3, we would expect the Navaho-dominant children to choose the object listed under (a), the "Navaho choice." This prediction is borne out by the data, for the differences between the two groups of Navaho children are all in the expected direction, and five are significant (by a two-tailed χ^2 test) at better than the 5-percent level. The most striking differences come for those sets of objects that involve a contrast embodied in the Navaho system of verbal categories: sets O and P where the contrast is between color and material and verb stem, and sets H and N where the contrast is between color and verb stem, material being the same, comparing objects of the long-rigid class, and of the so-called "round object" class. The less striking differences involve contrasts which are not formally recognized in Navaho grammar since the same verb stem is used in talking about the cubes and pyramids of set K.

In sets G, J, and M our hypothesis would not lead us to predict any difference between the groups; they may be regarded as control items. Both groups of children show a marked preference for color rather than size in sets G and J. Set M shows a significant difference between the two Navaho groups, possibly explicable on the basis of the greater potency of color for the English-dominant children, the contrast of the blue and yellow of set G and the blue and white of set J being more marked than that between the black and dark blue of set M.

Table 4 shows that there are important and consistent developmental

Table 4

Percent of "a" Choices in the First Seven Sets, by Age Level

Age	Navaho-Dominant Navahos		English-Dominant Navahos		White American Children	
	N*	Percent	N*	Percent	N*	Percent
3 }	14	64	7	33	{ 8	45
4 }					10	69
5	13	57	9	38	10	91
6	12	64	5	34	8	93
7	9	71	9	36	4	100
8	6	74	5	49	5	83
9–10	5	81	8	75	2	93

* Note that this N is the number of cases yielding data; each case contributes seven responses, and the percentages are computed on the basis of the total number of responses.

trends for the seven critical sets involving the contrast between shape or verb form and color—a trend which gives added significance to the differences between the Navaho-dominant and English-dominant groups noted above, since the Navaho-dominant children averaged almost a year younger. In both the Navaho groups (the data for white Americans will be discussed below) the trend is toward the increasing perceptual saliency of shape or form, as compared with color, with increasing age. The curve starts lower and remains lower for English-dominant Navaho children, although it rises rather rapidly after the age of seven. Navaho children stay ahead of their English-speaking age mates, although the two curves tend to converge as age increases.

Thus far discussion has been restricted to the results for two contrasting groups of Navaho children. These groups had been established in the hope that maximum possible control would be gained over the variables of race, culture, and environment which might affect the results. All the children tested were from the same rather small area on the Navaho reservation; the parents of nearly every child were both Navaho, except for the few cases in which one of the parents was a member of some other American Indian tribe. To be sure, the cultural variable could be only imperfectly controlled—the English-dominant children were almost inevitably more acculturated to the local variant of white American culture than were the Navaho-dominant children, but certanly the culture contrast is not as great as between Navaho-speaking children and English-speaking white children, say, from the Eastern United States. However, we may well ask how the performance of these Navaho children compares with that of children speaking English or another language on the same or a comparable test. In an experiment closely similar in materials and procedures to the one reported here, Clara Brian and Florence Goodenough found a marked preference for color over form for American children aged three to six. At age three years six months, 33.6 percent of choices were for form over color; at age four, 24.7 percent for form over color; and at age four years six months, 36 percent (as compared with 64 percent for Navaho-dominant children in this age group and 33 percent for English-dominant children of the same age group). The Brian and Goodenough results are also in substantial agreement with those of Alice Descœudres working with French-speaking children more than 40 years ago.

When we compare our Navaho results with those obtained for 47 white American children in the Boston area, we find that the responses of the white American children are more similar to those for the Navaho-dominant children than for the English-dominant children; as we may see from the last column of Table 3, they consistently tend to choose object "a" on the basis of form or shape in preference to color and size. The white children today, however, can hardly be considered a fair control group for the Indian children, for their cultural background of experiences with forms and colors is enormously different. Early and continued practice with toys of the formboard variety is likely to impress the white American child with the importance of form and size as contrasted with a "secondary" quality like color. Further, social class is known to be correlated with tendency to choose form over color, and our white American children tended to be from the upper middle class. Nevertheless, it is interesting to observe in Table 4 that the white American children show the same developmental trend as either group of Navaho children. As a matter of fact, at the earliest age level, the three- and four-year-old Navaho-dominant children outstrip their white American age mates in preferring form to color.

If we consider only the two groups over which we have exercised the maximum control over the variables we presume to be relevant, the Navaho-dominant and English-dominant Navaho children, we have shown that language patterning seems to be correlated with a tendency to match objects on the basis of form rather than color or size. When we also consider the data from white American children, as well as the age trends, we may amend our hypothesis in possibly the following form: The tendency of a child to match objects on the basis of form or material rather than size or color increases with age and may be enhanced by either of two kinds of experiences: (a) learning to speak a language, like Navaho, which because of the central role played by form and material in its grammatical structure, requires the learner to make certain discriminations of form and material in the earlier stages of language learning in order to make himself understood at all; or (b) practice with toys and other objects involving the fitting of forms and shapes, and the resultant greater reinforcement received from form-matching. If our results are accepted as supporting this revised hypothesis, they indicate, we believe, that the potential influence of linguistic patterning on cognitive functioning and on the conceptual development of the child, as he is inducted by his language into the world of experience, is a fruitful area for further study.

47

A Systematization of the Whorfian Hypothesis
JOSHUA A. FISHMAN

When Whorf says that "there is a precarious dependence of all we know upon linguistic tools which themselves are largely unknown or unnoticed," he hits all of us where it hurts most—at the foundations of our certainty in our scientific findings and in our everyday decisions. When he attacks the view that grammars are "merely norms of conventional and social correctness" and claims that they are, instead, the cement out of which we fashion experience, we feel that he must either be pointing at an unnoticed and potentially dangerous popular fallacy or tilting at nonexistent windmills. When he says that "we cut up nature—organize it into concepts—and ascribe significances as we do . . . largely because of the . . . absolutely obligatory . . . patterns of our [own] language," he stirs in us both our ethnocentric group-pride as well as our universalistic anti-ethnocentrism. In short, Whorf (like Freud) impugns our objectivity and rationality. It is not surprising then that recent years have seen many logical as well as not a few experimental efforts to evaluate and re-evaluate both the conceptual and the empirical grounds upon which the Whorfian hypothesis rests.

LEVEL 1. LINGUISTIC CODIFIABILITY AND CULTURAL REFLECTIONS (THE FIRST LANGUAGE-LANGUAGE LEVEL)

The weakest level of the Whorfian hypothesis (in the sense of being least pretentious or least novel) is that which provides evidence that languages differ "in the same ways" as the general cultures or surrounding environments of their speakers differ. Evidence along these lines has long been provided by ethnologists and folklorists, and its fragmentary and belated presentation by Whorfians can hardly be considered as either a serious contribution to the social sciences generally or as a substantiation of higher levels of the Whorfian hypothesis specifically.

From the point of view of the language data presented at this first level

Reprinted with permission of the Mental Health Research Institute and the author. From *Behavioral Science*, 5:323–339 (1960).

of argumentation, it is not the grammatical structure as such that is under consideration but, rather, the lexical store or the so-called "semantic structure." Actually, that which is dealt with at this level might be referred to in present-day terms as contrasts in *codifiability*. Language X has a single term for phenomenon *x*, whereas language *Y* either has no term at all (and therefore refers to the phenomenon under consideration —if at all—only via a relative circumlocution) or it has three terms, y_1, y_2, and y_3, all within the same area of reference. As a result, it is much *easier* to refer to certain phenomena or to certain nuances of meaning in certain languages than in others. Thus, codifiability is also related to the question of translatability and to "what gets lost" in translation from one language to another.

Admittedly Whorf's examples are largely drawn from American Indian languages (and contrasted with American English), and the implication is therefore strong that we are not only dealing with groups whose languages differ markedly but whose lives and outlooks also differ greatly. Nevertheless, at *this* level of analysis, Whorf (and others even more frequently than he) does not take pains to relate linguistic factors to non-linguistic ones, but merely presents an enchanting catalog of codifiability differences. English has separate words for "pilot," "fly (n.)," and "airplane," but Hopi has only one. Eskimo has many words for different kinds of "snow" but English has only two. On the other hand, Aztec has only one basic word for our separate words "cold," "ice," and "snow." We have one word for "water," whereas Hopi has two, depending on whether the water is stationary or in motion. English has such words as "speed" and "rapid," whereas Hopi has no real equivalents for them and normally renders them by "very" or "intense" plus a verb of motion. English has separate terms for "blue" and "green" but only one term for all intensities of "black" short of "gray." Navaho, on the contrary, does not have separate highly codeable terms for "blue" and "green" but does have two terms for different kinds of "black." English has the generic term "horse" but Arabic has only scores of different terms for different breeds or conditions of horses. The kinship terminology in some languages is certainly vastly different (and in certain respects both more refined and more gross) than it is in English. In all of these cases, it is not difficult to relate the codifiability differences to gross cultural differences. Obviously, Eskimos are more interested in snow, and Arabs in horses, than are most English speakers. Obvious, also, is the fact that these codifiability differences help speakers of certain languages to be more easily aware of certain aspects of their environment and to communicate more easily about them. This, essentially, was the lesson we learned from Bartlett's early work on remembering. In this sense, then, their languages structure their verbal behavior in a non-trivial way and ostensibly also structure their pre-verbal conceptualizations as well.

LEVEL 2. LINGUISTIC CODIFIABILITY AND BEHAVIORAL CONCOMITANTS

At the second level of analysis of the Whorfian hypothesis, we leave behind the limitations of *inference* from codifiability in language to ease of formulation or expression via language. That is to say, we leave behind the *language-language behavior* level for the level in which *language-nonlanguage behavior* becomes of paramount interest to us. That this is a necessary direction for our inquiry to take has been recognized by Carroll and Casagrande:

In order to find evidence to support the linguistic relativity hypothesis it is not sufficient merely to point to differences between languages and to assume that users of these languages have correspondingly different mental experiences. If we are not to be guilty of circular inference, it is necessary to show some correspondence between the presence or absence of a certain linguistic phenomenon and the presence or absence of a certain kind of non-linguistic response.

Note that the above quotation merely refers to "*a certain linguistic phenomenon*" rather than restricting the *type* of linguistic phenomenon that requires attention. The hallmark of the second level is that the "predictor" variables seem once more to be of the lexical or semantic codifiability type (and in this respect similar to Level 1, discussed above), whereas the "criterion variables" are of the non-linguistic behavior type (and in this respect different from, and an advance over, those encountered at Level 1). Thus far, there have been only a very few studies which strike me as operating at this level of analysis. The earliest one by far is that of Lehmann who demonstrated that identifying a different number with each of nine different shades of gray was of substantial help in behaviorally discriminating between these shades of gray. In essence, then, the numbers functioned as verbal labels. The availability (codifiability) of such labels for some Ss resulted in much better discrimination-identification of the shades of gray than that which obtained in other Ss who had to perform the same discrimination-identification task without being provided with such labels.

Some exceptionally interesting and sophisticated work with the codifiability concept in the color area has more recently been reported by Brown and Lenneberg and by Lenneberg alone. These investigators have shown that culturally encoded colors (i.e., colors that can be named with a single word) require a shorter response latency when they need to be named than do colors that are not culturally encoded (i.e., that require a phrase—often an individually formulated phrase—in order to be described). At this point, their evidence pertains to Level 1 that we have previously discussed. In addition, these investigators have gone on to show that the more highly codified colors are more readily recognized or remembered when they must be selected from among many colors after a period of delay subsequent to their original presentation. This finding was replicated among speakers of English and speakers of Zuni, although somewhat different segments of the color spectrum were highly codeable for the two groups of Ss. The investigators summarize their findings to this point as follows:

> It is suggested that there may be general laws relating codability to cognitive processes. All cultures could conform to these laws although they differ among themselves in the values the variables assume in particular regions of experience.

Going on from this original statement, Lenneberg has further refined its experimental underpinnings by showing that the *learning* of color-nonsense syllable associations was predictably easier or harder as the learning task involved color categories that varied in degree from the ones that were most commonly recognized by his English-speaking Ss. He therefore concluded that "there is good evidence that the shape of word frequency distributions over stimulus continua regulates the ease with which a person learns to use a word correctly." This conclusion should be as applicable to original language learning as it is to second and to artificial language learning, for it basically pertains not to language usage per se but to concept formation as such.

The color continuum seems to be a particularly fortunate area in which to study codifiability-cognition phenomena precisely because it is a real continuum. As such, no "objective" breaks occur in it and it is a matter of cultural or sub-cultural consensus as to just which breaks are recognized, just where on the spectrum they are located, and how much of a range they include. The demonstration that these various codifiability considerations influence recognition, recall, and learning has been most fortunately executed. Lenneberg and Brown are also alert to the fact that at this level it is perfectly acceptable to work with intralinguistic designs rather than to necessarily utilize the interlinguistic designs in terms of which the Whorfian hypothesis is most frequently approached. What is easily codifiable, and the specific range and content of easily codeable categories, does depend on the particular language under consideration. It also depends on the particular experiences of subgroups of speakers. As a result, contrasts in rate, ease or accuracy of various cognitive functions should be (and are) demonstrable both intralinguistically and interlinguistically as a function of codeability norms. Intralinguistic codifiability-cognition differentials in various natural population groupings should be of particular interest to students of social stratification.

Brown and Lenneberg have conducted their work with a conscious awareness of the Whorfian hypothesis and how it must be further specified or delimited. On the other hand, there have been other investigators who have also worked in the language-behavior domain at this level without any particular awareness of the Whorfian hypothesis as such. If the organizational framework here being advanced has been insightfully developed, it should nevertheless be possible to subsume their findings within it. In fact, it may turn out that within the context of the Whorfian hypothesis these other studies will obtain a new coherence and provocativeness.

The only study at this level that is directly inspired by the Whorfian hypothesis while utilizing an *interlinguistic* design is the one which Carroll and Casagrande refer to as "Experiment I."

LEVEL 3. LINGUISTIC STRUCTURE AND ITS CULTURAL CONCOMITANTS

When we turn our attention from the second to the third and fourth levels of the Whorfian hypothesis, we progress from lexical differences and so-called "semantic structure" to the more "formal" and systematized grammatical differences to which linguists have most usually pointed when considering the structure of a language or structural differences between languages. There is some evidence that although Whorf and others may, at times, have reverted to lower levels of presentation and documentation they, nevertheless, did associate linguistic relativity in its most pervasive sense with structural (i.e., grammatical) rather than merely with lexical aspects of language. This is suggested by such formulations as Sapir's that meanings are "not so much discovered in experience as imposed upon it, because of the tyrannical hold that linguistic *form* has upon our orientation to the world." Somewhat more forcefully stated is Whorf's claim that "the world is presented in a kaleidoscopic flux of impressions which has to be organized . . . largely by the linguistic *systems* in our minds." More forceful still—and there are a large number of possible quotations of this kind—is Whorf's statement that

. . . the background linguistic system (in other words, the grammar) of each language is not merely a reproducing instrument for voicing ideas, but rather is itself the shaper of ideas, the program and guide for the individual's mental activity, for his analysis of impressions, for his synthesis of his mental stock in trade. Formulation of ideas is not an independent process, strictly rational in the old sense, but it is part of a particular grammar and differs, from slightly to greatly, between grammars.

Finally, we may offer in evidence the paraphrasings of the Whorfian hypothesis by two eminent American linguists who have been both interested in and sympathetic to this hypothesis. The first of these says simply that "It is in the attempt properly to interpret the *grammatical categories* of Hopi that Whorf best illustrates his principle of linguistic relativity." The other, as part of a more extended and systematic argument, says

Language as a whole has structure and all of its parts and subdivisions also have structure . . . [if] the rest of cultural behavior has been conditioned by language, then there must be a relationship between the *structure* of language and the *structure* of behavior.

At the third level of analysis, we once more find ourselves in a realm of rich though ambiguous anthropological and ethnological data. As was the case with Level 1, above, the direct association or chain of reasoning between grammatical structure on the one hand and "something else" (be it *Weltanschauung* or even some less embracing segment of culture or values) on the other is not explicitly stated. Often, the "something else" is not stated at all and yet there is the general implication that grammatical oddities of the type presented cannot help but be paralleled by unique ways of looking at or thinking about or reacting to the surrounding environment. Thus, one encounters such evidence as that Chinese has no singular and plural or that it has no relative clauses (which we English speakers *do* have), whereas other languages have more levels of grammatical number (including singular, dual, tri-al, and plural forms—which we English speakers do *not* have). In this vein, the cataloging of grammatical differences can continue at great length (languages that do recognize gender of nouns and those that do not, languages that have tenses and those that do not, etc.); for both anthropologists, linguists, and a variety of nonspecialists have contributed to the fund of knowledge of phenomena of this type, always with the implication that it is clearly illogical to seriously suggest that linguistic phenomena such as these would have no relationship to life, to thought, and to values.

On the other hand, there are also several investigators that *have* attempted to indicate what the "something else" might be. In contrasting Hopi with English, Whorf has pointed to such odd grammatical features in Hopi as the absence of tenses, the classification of events by duration categories such that "events of necessarily brief duration (lightning, wave, flame, meteor, puff of smoke, pulsation) cannot be anything but verbs," the presence of grammatical forms for indicating the type of validity the speaker intends to attribute to his utterance (statement of current fact, statement of fact from memory, statement of expectation, and statement of generalization or law), etc. To Whorf all of these grammatical features seemed congruent with an outlook on life that was "timeless" and ahistorical in the sense that past, present, and future are seen as a continuity of duration, experience being cumulative and unchanging for countless generations. As a result of the "timelessness" of Hopi life, it is of greater importance for Hopi speakers to distinguish between the duration of events and their certainty than to indicate when they occurred. A similarly ingenious and sensitive analysis is followed by Hoijer in connection with the Navaho verb system in which there is no clean separation between actors, their actions, and the objects of these actions. As Hoijer sees it, the Navaho verb links the actor to actions which are defined as pertaining to classes-of-beings. Thus it would appear that people merely "participate in" or "get involved in" somehow pre-existing classes of actions rather than serve as the initiators of actions. Hoijer interprets these grammatical characteristics as being consistent with the "passivity" and "fatefulness" of Navaho life and mythology in which individuals adjust to a universe that is given. Finally, in Nootka, Whorf finds a connection between the absence of noun-verb distinctions and "a monistic view of nature."

The efforts by Whorf, Hoijer, Glenn and similar scholars merit considerable respect. They must be separated in our evaluation from pseudo-serious efforts to attribute or relate the musicalness of Italians to the light, melodious nature of the Italian language, or the stodginess of Germans to the heavy, lugubrious quality of the German language, or the warm, folksiness of Eastern European Jews to the intimate emotional quality of Yiddish, etc. Superficially, the two approaches may seem similar, but the latter approach does not even have a serious structural analysis of language to recommend it. Nevertheless, the appeal of the Whorfian hypothesis for some lies precisely in the fact that it attempts to apply modern scientific methods and disciplined thought to such "old chestnuts" as the presumed "naturalness" that Hebrew (or Greek, or Latin, or Old Church Slavonic) be the language of the Bible, given its "classic ring" and its "otherworldly purity." However, with all of our admiration for those who have had the temerity as well as the ingenuity to attempt a rigorous analysis at this level, we must also recognize the limitations which are built into this approach. As many critics have pointed out, the third level of analysis has not normally sought or supplied independent confirmation of the existence of the "something else" which their grammatical data is taken to indicate. As a result, the very same grammatical designata that are said to have brought about (or merely to reflect) a given *Weltan-*

schauung are also most frequently the only data advanced to prove that such a *Weltanschauung* does indeed exist. Thus, once more, we are back at a language-language level of analysis (language structure ⟷ language-behavior-as-indication-of-world-view).

Verbal behavior may long continue as our major avenue of insight into values and motives. What we must be ever more dissatisfied with, however, are the self-selected lists of grammatical examples and the self-selected enumerations of cultures, cultural values or themes, and the evidence pertaining to the existence of such themes. In attempting to avoid these particular pitfalls, students of the Whorfian hypothesis have increasingly come to express a preference for a study design which investigates the relationship between grammatic structure on the one hand and *individual* non-linguistic behavior on the other. Although this is both a logical and a very promising solution to many of the above-mentioned problems, there is nevertheless no need to conclude at this point in our knowledge that it is the only one possible.

LEVEL 4. LINGUISTIC STRUCTURE AND ITS BEHAVIORAL CONCOMITANTS

The conceptual and methodological superiority of the fourth level of the Whorfian hypothesis is one thing. The accessibility of this level for study may well be quite another thing. It does seem that this level is in some ways the most demanding of all, for it requires detailed technical training at both the predictor and the criterion ends of the relationship to be investigated. This may be the reason why there currently appears to be only one study which might possibly be said to be an example of work at this level, although in the future we might expect it to elicit greatly increased interest among socio-linguists and social psychologists with technical linguistic training. This is the study by Carroll and Casagrande which they refer to as Experiment II. The grammatic features of interest to Carroll and Casagrande in this study are the particular verb forms required in Navaho verbs for handling materials in accord with the shape or other physical attribute (flexibility, flatness, etc.) of the object being handled. Note that Carroll and Casagrande are concerned here with distinctions in verb *forms* rather than distinctions between mere lexical absence or presence of verbs as such. Presumably it is this fact which permits us to consider Experiment II as a Level 4 study rather than as a Level 2 study. The nonlinguistic data utilized by Carroll and Casagrande are the object-classifying behaviors of their Ss when presented first with a pair of objects which differ from each other in *two* respects (e.g., color and shape) and then with a third object similar to each member of the original pair in one of the two relevant characteristics. The Ss were asked to indicate "which member of the (original) pair went best with the (third) object shown him." If the S's reaction was governed by the requirements of Navaho verbal form, he would have to select a certain one of the original set of objects.

THE DEGREE OF LINGUISTIC RELATIVITY

The fascination of the Whorfian hypothesis is in some ways compounded of both delights and horrors. We have already speculated concerning the delights. Let us now mention the horrors. The first is the *horror of helplessness*, since all of us in most walks of life and most of us in all walks of life are helplessly trapped by the language we speak. We cannot escape from it—and, even if we could flee, where would we turn but to some other language with its own blinders and its own vice-like embrace on what we think, what we perceive, and what we say. The second horror is the *horror of hopelessness*—for what hope can there be for mankind?; what hope that one group will ever understand the other?; what hope that one nation will ever fully communicate with the other? This is not the place for a full-dressed philosophical attack on these issues. Let us merely consider them from the point of view of the kinds of evidence supplied by some of the very studies we have mentioned.

The most "reassuring" facts that derive from Levels 1 and 2, the lexical and semantic codifiability levels of the Whorfian hypothesis, are that the noted non-translatability and the selective codifiability really pertain not so much to all-or-none differences between languages as to differences in relative ease or felicity of equivalent designation. Whenever we argue that there is no English word (or expression) for ——, which means so-and-so (or approximately so-and-so, or a combination of Y and Z) in English, we are partially undercutting our own argument. In the very formulation of our argument that there is "no English word (or expression) for ——" we have gone on to give an English approximation to it. This approximation may not be a very successful one but if that becomes our concern we can go through the contortions (both intellectual and gesticulational) that are required for an inching up on or a zeroing in on the non-English word or expression that we have in mind. The amount of effort involved may, at times, be quite considerable and even the final approximation may leave us dissatisfied. However, after all is said and done, this is not so different, in terms of both process and outcome, as the communication problems that we face with one another even within our *own* speech community. We can do no better than to quote Hockett's conclusions at this point, in support of what has just been said.

Languages differ not so much as to what *can* be said in them, but rather as to what it is *relatively easy* to say in them. The history of Western logic and science constitutes not so much the story of scholars hemmed in and misled by the nature of their specific languages, as the story of a long and fairly successful struggle *against* inherited linguistic limitations. Where everyday language would not serve, special sub-systems (mathematics, e.g.) were devised. However, even Aristotle's development of syllogistic notation carries within itself aspects of Greek language structure.

The impact of inherited linguistic pattern on activities is, in general, *least* important in the most practical contexts and most important in such "purely verbal" goings-on as story-telling, religion, and philosophizing. As a result, some types of literature are extremely difficult to translate accurately, let alone appealingly.

Turning now to Levels 3 and 4, where we become concerned with the imbedded structural features of a language, it seems to be important that we realize that Whorf never proposed that *all* aspects of grammatical structure must *inevitably* have direct cognitive effects. Thus, to begin with, we are faced with the task of locating those few grammatical features which might have definable but unconscious functional correlates in our unguarded behavior.

If we look to Levels 2 and 4, these being the levels in which the behavioral concomitants of linguistic features are experimentally derived, we once more must reach the conclusion that linguistic relativity, where it does exist, is not necessarily an awesomely powerful factor in cognitive functioning. The relationships that have been encountered, though clear-cut enough, seem to be neither very great nor irreversible in magnitude. The very fact that increased infant and early childhood experience with toys and objects requiring primarily a form reaction can result in a *Navaho-like classifying preference* among monolingual English-speaking children also means that other kinds of environmental experiences might very well produce an *English-like classifying preference* among monolingual Navaho-speaking children. No one has yet directly studied the success with which behaviors predicted on the basis of linguistic relativity can be counteracted by either (a) simply making Ss aware of how their language biases affect their thinking or (b) actively training Ss to counteract these biases. It may be, after all, that this is an area in which Ss can, with relatively little effort, learn how to "fake good." Furthermore, one might suspect that the impact of language *per se* on cognition and expression ought somehow to be greater and more fundamental than the impact of one or another language feature. Thus the impact of language *determinism* upon cognition ought to be more pervasive and more difficult to counteract than that of language *relativity*.

None of the foregoing should be interpreted as implying that linguistic relativity, wherever it exists, is an unimportant factor in human experience or one that deserves no particular attention except from those who are professionally committed to unravelling the unimportant in painful detail. Quite the contrary; just because it is such a seemingly innocuous factor it is very likely to go unnoticed and, therefore, requires our particular attention in order that we may appropriately provide for it.

SUMMARY AND CONCLUSIONS

The four levels of the Whorfian hypothesis that have been presented here are essentially subsumable under a double dichotomy. As Figure 1 reveals, we have essentially been dealing with two factors—one pertaining to characteristics of a given language or languages and the other pertain-

Data of Language Characteristics	Data of (Cognitive) Behavior	
	Language Data ("Cultural Themes")	Non-linguistic Data
Lexical or "Semantic" characteristics	Level 1	Level 2
Grammatical characteristics	Level 3	Level 4

Figure 1.   Schematic Systematization of the Whorfian Hypothesis

ing to behavior of the speakers of the language or languages under consideration. The first factor has been dichotomized so as to distinuish between lexical or semantic structure on the one hand (both of these being considered as codeability features) and grammatical structure on the other. The second factor has been dichotomized so as to distinguish between verbal behavior per se (frequently interpreted in terms of cultural themes or *Weltanschauungen*) and individual behavioral data which is other than verbal in nature.

In a rough way, we might say that Levels 1 and 3 are concerned with *large group phenomena* whereas Levels 2 and 4 are concerned with *individual behavior*. Whorf was aware of and interested in both kinds of data, for he held that "our linguistically determined thought world not only collaborates with our *cultural idols and ideals* but engages even our unconscious *personal reactions* in its patterns and gives them certain typical character(istic)s."

In general, Whorf is not deeply concerned with "which was first, the language patterns or the cultural norms?" He is content to conclude that "in the main they have grown up together, constantly influencing each other." Nevertheless, he does state that if these two streams are to be separated from each other for the purposes of analysis he considers language to be by far the more impervious, systematic, and rigid of the two. Thus, after a long association between culture and language, innovations in the former will have but minor impact on the latter, "whereas to inventors and innovators it (i.e., language) legislates with the decree immediate." Although Whorf is leary of the term correlation it seems most likely that he considered language structure not only as interactingly reflective of "cultural thought" but as directly formative of "individual thought." With proper cautions, the four levels of the Whorfian hypothesis that have been differentiated in this review may be seen as quite consistent with this conclusion.

Some of the characteristics, difficulties, and potentials of further empirical and theoretical study at each of the four differentiated levels have been considered. All levels can make use of both interlinguistic or intralinguistic designs, although Levels 1 and 3 most commonly employ the former—if only for purposes of contrast.

Although evidence favoring the Whorfian hypothesis exists at each level, it seems likely that linguistic relativity, though affecting some of our cognitive behavior, is nevertheless only a moderately powerful factor and a counteractable one at that. Certainly much experimental evidence has accumulated that points to a large domain of contra-Whorfian universality in connection with the relationships between *certain* structures of particular languages and *certain* cognitive behaviors of their speakers. The time might, therefore, now be ripe for putting aside attempts at grossly "proving" or "disproving" the Whorfian hypothesis and, instead, focusing on attempts to delimit more sharply the types of language structures and the types of non-linguistic behaviors that do or do not show the Whorfian effect as well as the degree and the modifiability of this involvement when it does obtain.

Because of Whorf's central role in making us aware of this phenomenon so that we may now better come to grips with it, both intellectually and practically, none can deny that he richly deserves to be characterized by his own standard for what constitutes a real scientist.

All real scientists have their eyes primarily on background phenomena in our daily lives; and yet their studies have a way of bringing out a close relation between these unsuspected realms . . . and . . . foreground activities.

PART 4

Pragmatics

CHAPTER XII

Mass Communication

INTRODUCTION Pragmatics studies the relation between signals and their effects on people. Naturally, the effect of a signal depends on its meaning, just as its meaning depends on its context and structure. Just as syntactics is the basis for semantics, semantics is the basis for pragmatics.

Like cultures, communication systems differ. They differ in signals as between Choctaw and English or between punched cards and speech. They also differ in networks and coding, as is demonstrated in Parts Two and Three of this book. Communication systems also differ in their effects because in human communication these effects are always mediated through culture. The same message in two different kinds of social organization will have two different kinds of effects. Earlier chapters that analyzed syntactics also showed in passing that different kinds of small experimental groups have different kinds of reactions to signals. This chapter analyzes the reactions and effects in large groups. It will emphasize pragmatics in the cultural context of industrial societies, that is, mass societies with mass media of communication. It will show how pragmatics in large groups is rooted in the structural syntactics of small groups.

Wilbur Schramm reviews the mathematical theory of communication and applies it to mass communication. "Information Theory and Mass Communication" applies such concepts as channel capacities and networks to the study of the mass media. This leads to such hypotheses as "the relative entropy of radio and television would be less than that of newspapers." And "take the chief newspapers of the leading cities in half a dozen countries . . . Washington has the greatest output of traffic, New

York the greatest input traffic. Moscow has the greatest degree of individual closure: that is, it is most likely to talk, if at all, to itself."

Joseph T. Klapper asks in greater detail the fundamental pragmatic question about mass communication: What are its effects? He outlines the answer in "What We Know about the Effects of Mass Communication: The Brink of Hope." He speaks of hope because his survey of recent studies shows that we are beginning to understand these effects. We have turned away from the old hypodermic theories which assumed that the mass media simply injected people with new information and orientations. Instead, modern studies recognize that mass communication "functions among and through a nexus of mediating factors and influences." This nexus is the culture of the people. In this respect our understanding of pragmatics has to go beyond the mathematical theory of communication. Klapper maintains that the mass media do not simply transmit information; most often they reinforce existing attitudes rather than convert people to new ones.

Mass communication does not make individuals change their ideas easily because ideas are not held by individuals. Instead, ideas are held by individuals in groups—in groups of friends, family groups, professional groups. In groups, individuals reinforce each other's ideas and maintain a consensus of the group as a whole. It is in groups that people maintain the coorientations described in Chapter IV. This is also the image of society that emerges from studies of the effects of mass communication. In urban settings with newspapers and television and in rural settings with county agents, face-to-face groups remain the important nexus of communication. Individuals do not read newspapers or watch television; they read and watch as couples, families, and groups. Elihu Katz's "Communication Research and the Image of Society: Convergence of Two Traditions" shows that in urban and in rural settings personal influence is more effective than the mass media to change popular opinion, particularly in the later stages of any campaign.

The receptivity to communication is determined by the expectations of groups of people. These expectations, this larger pattern, differs in modern industrial societies from those in the less industrialized areas of the world. In his "Communication Systems and Social Systems: A Statistical Exploration in History and Policy," Daniel Lerner shows that there is a high correlation between urbanization, literacy, participation in voting, stability of government, and the use of mass media. Wherever any one of these characteristics is present the others are generally present also, and wherever any one is absent the others are generally absent also. The mass media, therefore, cannot by themselves affect people and effect culture change; they have to operate as part of a general cultural setting.

48 Information Theory and Mass Communication
WILBUR SCHRAMM

It is proposed in this paper to take a brief overview of information theory itself, then to examine broadly its applicability to mass communication, and finally to look in more detail at some of the areas of mass communication in which it promises to be most helpful.

THE NATURE OF INFORMATION THEORY

A system is any part of an information chain which is capable of existing in one or more states, or in which one or more events can occur. The vibrating metal diaphragm of a telephone or a microphone is a system. So is the radio frequency amplifier circuit of a radio receiver. So is a telegraph wire. So is the air which carries the pulsations of sound waves. So is the basilar membrane of the ear. So is the optic nerve. So, in a little different sense, is the semantic system of an individual. Each of these is capable of assuming different states or playing host to different events, and each can be coupled to other systems to make a communication chain.

If information is to be transferred, systems must obviously be *coupled*. We say systems are coupled when the state of one system depends to some degree on the state of the system that adjoins it. Thus when a microphone diaphragm is depressed so as to cause a coil to cut magnetic lines of force and generate a current in a wire, those systems are coupled. When light frequencies strike the eye and cause discharges in the optic nerve, those systems are coupled. A break in the coupling will obviously prevent any information from being transferred. That is what happens when a microwave link goes out during a television broadcast, or when a student's attention wanders in class.

Reprinted with permission of the publisher and the author. From *Journalism Quarterly*, 32:131–146 (1955).

Most human communication chains contain a large number of coupled systems, and they contain one kind of system which Dr. Shannon has not primarily dealt with: the *functional*, as opposed to the *structural*, system. A functional system is one that *learns;* its states depend on its own past operation. The air that carries sound waves, or the metal diaphragm of the microphone, is a structural system. So is the sensory system of a human being. But the central nervous system, and especially the aspect of it to which we refer as the semantic system, is a functional system. It is capable of learning. It codes and decodes information on the basis of past experience. Incidentally, this is one of the pitfalls in the way of applying information theory mathematics to human communication. These are probability formulas, and if the probabilities are altered—i.e., if any learning takes place—during the experiment, the events can no longer be regarded as a stochastic process and the formula will not apply. It is therefore necessary rigidly to control the learning factor.

Systems may be either *corresponding* or *non-corresponding*. Corresponding systems are capable of existing in identical states. Thus, the sound input of the microphone and the sound output of the loudspeaker are capable of existing in identical states—therefore, corresponding. But the air and the diaphragm are not corresponding. Neither are the diaphragm and the current, or the light signal and the central nervous system.

We can now say what information theory means by *communication*. Communication occurs when two corresponding systems, coupled together through one or more non-corresponding systems, assume identical states as a result of signal transfer along the chain. Unless the sound that goes into the telephone is reproduced by the sound that comes out of the telephone at the other end of the line, we do not have communication. Unless the concept in the semantic system of Mr. A. is reproduced in the semantic system of Mr. B., communication has not taken place. Begging the question of whether a meaning as seen by one individual can ever be reproduced exactly by another individual—or whether we can test it accurately enough to be sure—we have no great difficulty in adapting this definition to our common understanding of the term communication.

But when we define *information* in terms of information theory, then we have to get used to a somewhat different approach. We can, of course, measure the "information" transmitted along a communication chain in terms of many kinds of units—letters, morphemes, phonemes, facts (if we can satisfactorily define a fact). But none of these is satisfactory for the precise needs of information theory. Information is there defined in terms of its ability to reduce the uncertainty or disorganization of a situation at the receiving end.

This brings us to the basic terms of information theory, *entropy* and

redundancy. Entropy simply means the uncertainty or disorganization of
a system; redundancy is the opposite.

Entropy is measured in terms of the information required to eliminate
the uncertainty or randomness from a situation within a system or involving two systems. Entropy will obviously be at its maximum when all
states of the system are equally probable—that is, when they occur completely at random, as when a coin is tossed.

HOW APPLICABLE IS THE THEORY?

The concepts of information theory have an insightful quality, an
intuitive sort of fit, when they are applied freely to mass communication
situations.

For one thing, it is obvious that human communication, like any other
kind of communication, is merely a chain of coupled systems (see Figure 1). In mass communication, these chains take on certain remarkable

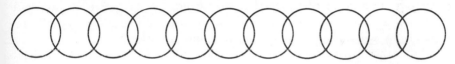

Figure 1.

characteristics. They are often very *long*. The account of a news event
in India must pass through very many coupled systems before it reaches
a reader in Indiana. Again, some of the systems have phenomenally high
rates of output compared to their input. Shannon would call them high-
gain *amplifiers*. These are the mass media, which have the power to produce many simultaneous and identical messages. Also, in this kind of
chain, we have certain networks of systems within systems. Two of
these are very important. The mass media themselves are networks of
systems coupled in a complicated way so as to do the job of decoding,
interpreting, storage and encoding which we associate with all communicators. Likewise, the individual who receives a mass media message is a
part of a network of group relationships, and the workings of this network help to determine how he responds to the message.

But each system in the mass communication chain, whatever the kind
of system, is host to a series of events which are constrained by their
environments and by each other, and therefore to a certain degree
predictable and subject to information theory measurements. Much of
the scholarly study of mass communication consists of an examination of
the constraints on these events, and discovering the dependency of events
in one of these systems on events in another system.

For example, a large part of what we call "effects" study is the comparison of events in one system with events in another. A readership study compares the events in a newspaper with the events in an individual's reading behavior. A retention study compares the events in a medium with the events in an individual's recall. And so forth. We have every reason to suspect, therefore, that a mathematical theory for studying electronic communication systems ought to have some carry-over to human communication systems.

ENTROPY AND REDUNDANCY

The term *entropy* is still strange to students of social communication, but *redundancy* is an old and familiar idea. The redundancy concept of information theory gives us no great trouble. Redundancy is a measure of certainty or predictability. In information theory, as in social communication, the more redundant a system is, the less information it is carrying in a given time. On the other hand, any language or any code without redundancy would be chaos. In many cases, increasing the redundancy will make for more efficient communication.

For example, on a noisy teletype line, it helps considerably to have certain probabilities controlling what letters follow others. If a q (in English) occurs followed by two obvious errors, the operator at the receiving end can be quite sure that the q is followed by a u and that the next letter will be another vowel. When a circuit is bad, operators arbitrarily repeat key words twice. Remember the familiar cable language—THIS IS NOT—REPEAT, NOT . . .

The amount of redundancy—using that term freely—is therefore one of the great strategy questions confronting mass communication. The most economical writing is not always the most effective writing. We could write this entire paper in the terse, economical language of mathematics, but that would not necessarily communicate most to the people who will read this paper. A newspaper reporter may choose to explain the term *photosynthesis* in twenty words, which is redundancy unnecessary to a scientist but highly necessary to a layman. There is a kind of rule of thumb, in preparing technical training materials, that two or more examples or illustrations should be given for each important rule or term. There is another rule of thumb, in broadcast commercials, that product names should be repeated three times. All these are strategy decisions, aimed at using the optimum of redundancy. And indeed, finding the optimum degree of redundancy for any given communication purpose is one of the chief problems of encoding.

Relative entropy, as we have pointed out, is merely the other side of the coin from redundancy. The lower the redundancy, the higher the relative entropy.

One of the aspects of human communication where entropy and redundancy measures have already proved their usefulness is in the study of language. Morphemes, phonemes, letters and other linguistic units obviously do not occur in a language completely at random; they are bound by certain sequential relationships, and therefore subject to measures of entropy and redundancy. We know, among other things, that the relative entropy of English is slightly less than 50 percent. Shannon has estimated, incidentally, that if the relative entropy of the language was only 20 percent—if the next letter in a sequence were, on the average, 80 percent predictable—then it would be impossible to construct interesting crossword puzzles. But if the relative entropy were 70 percent—if the structure were only 30 percent redundant—then it would be easily possible to construct *three-dimensional* crossword puzzles. This information about crossword puzzles, of course, is not intended to represent the results of modern linguistic scholarship.

Wilson Taylor's "Cloze" procedure is one of the interesting ways we have available for use in estimating the entropy or redundancy of prose. Taylor deletes every *n*th word in a passage, and asks readers to supply the missing words. The scatter of different words suggested for each of the missing terms provides a measure of the predictability of the passage to that particular audience. For example, if we present two paragraphs to the same group of 20 readers, and on the average this is the score they make.

Paragraph A

16 specify word A (correct)	
2	B
2	C

Paragraph B

6 specify word A (correct)	
4	B
4	C
3	D
1	E
1	F
1	G

—if we get this result, it is clear that the uncertainty or relative entropy of Paragraph B is considerably greater for this audience than is that of Paragraph A. Paragraph A is apparently more redundant than B. Taylor has gone into this use of information theory in his doctoral dissertation, and it is clear that the redundancy or relative entropy of a passage is closely related to its readability.

If we consider an entire mass medium as a system, then it is evident that the maximum entropy of a newspaper or a broadcasting station is immensely greater than that of a semaphor, a calling card, a personal letter or a sermon. The paper or the station has a very great freedom to do different things and produce strikingly different products. A large newspaper, like the New York *Times,* has higher maximum entropy than a smaller newspaper. If we could devise any way to make a valid comparison, I think we should find that the relative entropy of radio and television would be less than that of newspapers. If this is indeed the case, it may be that the tremendous wordage of broadcasting puts a burden on originality, and the scant feedback to a broadcasting station puts a premium on any formula which has proved popular. A successful formula is soon imitated. A popular program promptly spawns a whole family that look like it. A joke passes quickly from comedian to comedian. We might say that for comedians, joint and conditional entropy are quite low. For comic strips, relative entropy is obviously very low, and redundancy very high.

But it is also evident that no medium uses as much of the available freedom as it could. Complete freedom would mean random content. The art of being an editor or a program manager consists in no small degree of striking the right balance between predictability and uncertainty—right balance being defined as the best combination of satisfied anticipation and surprise. From time to time we have tried to quantify this amount of organization or predictability in a mass medium. One of the simpler ways to approach it is to tabulate the news sources in a paper.

The usual way we handle figures like this is by means of the statistics of central tendency—mean, standard deviation, etc. Suppose we were to handle it by information theory mathematics. If relative entropy were at a maximum, each of these news sources would be represented equally. Actually, the relative entropy of news sources in the *Times* for that day was about 52 percent. Throughout that week it hung around 50 percent, minus or plus 5. This seems quite typical of large newspapers. Four Chicago papers, two other New York papers, and the Washington *Post and Times Herald,* all were between 41 and 57 percent for the same period. The London *Times* and Paris *Figaro* were a little over 40 percent. During the same period, a radio news wire averaged about 45 percent relative entropy.

This rather remarkable order of agreement represents a pattern of constraint which, if we understood it completely, would tell us a great deal about mass media. Why do large papers, on the average, use about half the freedom open to them to represent different news sources? Availability is one reason, but the chief reason is simply that this is the editors' definition of what their clientele want, and can absorb, and *should* have, and can be given within the bounds of physical limits and custom. Information theory appears to offer us a new way to study this characteristic of the media.

THE IDEA OF NOISE

The idea of noise is another information theory concept which intuitively makes sense in the study of mass communication. Noise, as we have said, is anything in the channel other than what the communicator puts there. Noise may be competing stimuli from inside—AC hum in the radio, print visible through a thin page in a magazine, day-dreaming during a class lecture—or from outside—competing headline cues on a newspaper page, reading a book while listening to a newscast, the buzz of conversation in the library. In general, the strategy of a mass communicator is to reduce noise as much as possible in his own transmission, and to allow for expected noise in the reception. An increase in redundancy, as we have already suggested, may combat noise; a radio announcer may be well advised to repeat a highly important announcement.

The information theory formula for maximum transmission capacity in the face of noise also furnishes some guides as to what can be done. This formula is

$$W \log_2 \left(\frac{P + N}{N} \right)$$

in which W is band width, P is power of transmission, N is noise. In other words, you can approach maximum efficiency by reducing noise, increasing band width or increasing power. Two of the great problems of mass communication, of course, are to understand exactly what is meant by band width and power, for any given situation. Is the band width of a talking picture or television greater than that of a silent picture or radio? Is the band width of a sight-sound medium like television greater than that of print? You can certainly increase band width by using a high fidelity phonograph, but can you also increase it by buying time on more radio stations? Similarly, what constitutes power, in this sense, within persuasive communication? Supposedly, the nature of the arguments and the source will contribute to it. Will talking louder contribute to power, so defined? Will buying bigger ads?

To basic questions like these, information theory is unlikely to contribute except by stimulating insights, but it should be pointed out that there are formulas for calculating noise which may well prove to be useful in tests of learning and retention from mass communication, and in rumor analysis and other functions of communication chains.

COUPLING

That brings us to talk of coupling, which is another point at which information theory comes very close to our usual way of thinking about human communication. We are accustomed to think of "gatekeepers." Strictly speaking, every system that couples two other systems is a gatekeeper. But there are certain especially important gatekeepers in mass communication: the reporter walking his beat, the telegraph editor deciding on what to select from the wire, the press association wire filer deciding what stories to pass on, the commentator deciding what aspect of current life to focus on, the magazine editor deciding what parts of the environment to represent, and others. All these are subject to the stability and fidelity measures of information theory: how likely are they to pass on the information that comes to them? How faithfully are they likely to reproduce it?

Even the terms used to talk about fidelity in electronic systems sound familiar to us in light of our experience with mass communication. How much of the information do the gatekeepers *filter out?* How much *fading* and *booming* do they introduce (by changing the emphasis of the message)? How much *systematic distortion* are they responsible for (through bias)? How much *random distortion* (through carelessness or ignorance)?

The newspaper itself—if we want to consider it as a system—is a gatekeeper of the greatest importance. The daily life of a city presents itself to the paper's input. Selected bits of the daily life of the rest of the world enter the input through the telegraph desk. What comes out? What is the stability of the paper for reproducing local news as compared with national news, civic news as compared with crime news, news of one presidential candidate as compared with news of another? And what about fidelity? To what extent does the paper change its input by cutting, by rewriting, by choosing a headline which affects the meaning, by giving one story better position than another?

Think of the reporter walking his beat. Everything he sees and hears is news for someone, but he must make a selection in terms of what his editors and—supposedly—his readers want. His stability is necessarily low. But how is his fidelity? Does he get the quotes from a speech right? Does he report an accident accurately?

Or think of the receiver at the end of the mass communication chain. What stories from the *Reader's Digest*, what items from the newspaper, does he pass on to his friends? And how accurately does he represent the content? Does he reproduce the part of the content which reinforces his previous attitudes? Does he get the point of an article?

Rumor analysis is a fascinating use for the coupling concepts of information theory. What kinds of rumors encourage the stability of the chain—that is, what kinds of rumors will tend to be passed on? And what factors govern how faithfully a rumor is passed on?

Content analysis codes are subject to study for stability and fidelity. How much of the information in the measured content do they respond to? How faithfully do they reproduce it? As a matter of fact, many of the concepts of information theory are stimulating to content study. For example, the heavy redundancy of Communist propaganda shows up from almost any content study, as does the relatively low entropy of the semantic systems within which the Communist propagandist works. The close coupling of units in the Communist propaganda chain is striking. And the stability and fidelity of the Communist gatekeepers, transmitting the official line, are very high. If they are not, the Party gets a new gatekeeper.

Measures of stability and fidelity are available, in information theory, and relatively easy to use. When they are applied to a long chain—such as the one, previously referred to, which carries news from "India to Indiana" and back—it becomes apparent that the stability of the main points along the chain is quite high: that is, a bureau like London is quite likely to pass along a story that comes from New Delhi. The closer one gets to the source of news, the lower the stability, because the input is large, the output capacity relatively small. Bloomington, for example, regularly publishes about 65 local stories, but can only put two or three on the wire. Delhi, likewise, can send London only a small part of the Indian news. Chicago, on the other hand, can send out more than half the stories available. The problem in measuring the fidelity of this kind of chain is to define measurable units. Using length as one criterion, it becomes apparent that the greatest loss is near the source of news. Using rewriting as a criterion, it seems that the chief rewriting is done at the first wire points and the chief national bureaus.

CHANNEL CAPACITY

Channel capacity is another important concept which is common both to information theory and to mass communication. All channels, human, electronic or mechanical, have an upper limit on their ability to assume different states or carry different events. We can estimate, for example, the amount of information the eye is capable of transmitting to the optic nerve, and it is less than the information available to the eye, although apparently more than the semantic system can handle. We can estimate the capacity of a telephone line or a microphone, and have very good formulas for doing so. But when we consider the characteristics of a chain and recall that the chain is no stronger than its weakest link, then our chief interest turns to the channel capacity of man, who is the weakest link in most communication chains.

Perceptual experiments have told us a great deal about the ability of man to transmit information through some of his systems. In general, we can say that man's ability to handle information is faster than most mechanical systems (such as smoke signals and flags), but far slower than that of most electronic devices (e.g., the electronic computers). We still have a great deal to find out about man's capacity for handling language and pictorial information.

Many of the capacity problems of mass communications, of course, find man at the mercy of his works. The reporter who has only 30 minutes to write his story before deadline, the editor who is permitted to file only 200 words on the wire, the radio news bureau desk which has room for only 13 minutes of copy and must select from 300 stories, the editor who finds a big advertising day crowding out his news—all these are communicators suffering from capacity problems they have helped to make. It is also obvious that the channel capacity of the New York *Times* is greater than that of a small daily. But for the *Times* and its smaller brothers there is an even greater channel restriction: the reader. The reader of a daily can spend, on the average, about 40 minutes on his paper. And he reads rather slowly. Even so, he can read faster than he can listen, so to speak. A radio speaker usually stays under 150 words a minute, not because he cannot talk faster, but because he fears he will crowd the channel capacity of his listeners.

Shannon has developed a theorem for a channel with noise which is both remarkable in itself and highly meaningful for persons concerned with mass communication. His theorem says, in effect, that for rates of transmission less than the capacity of a channel it is possible to reduce noise to any desired level by improving the coding of the information to be transmitted; but that for rates of transmission greater than channel capacity it is never possible to reduce noise below the amount by which the rate of transmission exceeds channel capacity. In other words, as Wilson notes, error can be reduced as much as desired if only the rate of transmission is kept below the total capacity of the channel; but if we overload the channel, then error increases very swiftly.

Information theory thus promises us real assistance in studying the capacity of channels. For example, in a recent publication an information theory model is proposed to measure an individual's channel capacity for semantic decoding. Verbal information is to be fed the individual at increasing rates. This information consists of a group of adjectives describing an object. The receiver is asked to respond in each case by touching the corresponding object, in a group of objects, in front of him. (He has already over-learned this response, so supposedly no learning takes place during the experiment.) The time from the stimulus until the subject touches an object is taken as the total time for decoding and encoding. It is hypothesized that as the rate increases this total time will decrease until it becomes stable. As the rate increases further, the number of errors will begin to increase, until at a certain rate the time will become highly variable and the process will break down. The rate at which the total time becomes stable is taken as the optimum channel capacity, because it is there that the largest amount of accurate information is being transmitted.

This experiment has not yet been done with the accurate controls which would be required, but some striking confirmation of it comes out of experiments with retention of newscasts. Subjects were presented newscasts of increasing density but constant length—5, 10, 20, 30, 40, 50 items. The average subject's ability to recall the subject of these items leveled off vary sharply between 10 and 20. There was practically no additional learning between 20 and 30. After 20, the number of errors began to increase rather sharply. In other words, the amount of information transmitted behaved about as hypothesized above, and the resulting curve was strikingly like those typically resulting from experiments on the capacity of subjects to discriminate among stimuli.

NETWORKS

Of all the potential contributions of information theory to mass communication, perhaps the most promising is in the study of communication networks. Networks are as important in mass communication as in electronic communication. Every functional group is a communication network. The staff of a newspaper or a broadcasting station, a film production crew, the group with which a member of the mass communication audience talks over what he reads, hears and sees—all these are communication networks. The intercommunication within the network is measurable, whether it consists of conversation, print, gestures or electronic currents.

Osgood and Wilson have suggested a series of measures derived from information theory, for dealing with groups. In addition to the common entropy, redundancy, noise, fidelity and capacity measures, they suggest *traffic* (what members do the most talking, and how much talking is done?), *closure* (to what extent is the group a closed corporation?), and *congruence* (to what extent do members participate equally in the communication of the group, or to what extent are there members who are chiefly talkers and others who are chiefly listeners?). All these formulations can be dealt with mathematically. Measures like these suggest quite different and stimulating way of studying small groups, and in particular they commend themselves for use in studying the important groups within mass communication.

Suppose, for example, we want to study some part of the world news network. Suppose that we take the chief newspapers of the leading cities in half a dozen countries—for example, the United States, Great Britain, France, Germany, Italy and the Soviet Union—and tabulate for one week the stories which the papers in each city carry from the other cities in the network. This has been done in a small way, with interesting results. Washington has the greatest output traffic, New York the greatest input traffic. Moscow has the greatest degree of individual closure: that is, it is most likely to talk, if at all, to itself. Within a country, there are startling differences in the amount and distribution of input. In general there appears to be a little more organization (redundancy) in the pattern of input than in the pattern of output: that is, source entropy is higher than destination entropy. And the congruence (the correlation between source and destination frequencies of points in the network) varies markedly with political conditions and cultural relationships at a particular time.

Let us take a simpler example of group communication. Here is a record of telephone calls amongst four boys (who telephoned incessantly). The calls were tabulated at periods two months apart—20 calls while the boys were organizing a school newspaper, and 20 calls two months later, after the paper was well launched.

It is clear that the relative transitional entropy of this group became less in the two months—that is, it became better organized—and also that the congruence had changed so that increasingly one pattern could be predicted: i.e., the boys would call Mike. It seems that whereas Mike must have been the organizer at first, he became the leader later, and the other boys turned to him for advice or instructions.

This kind of result suggests the hypothesis that the entropy of communication within a functional group decreases as the group becomes more fully organized into work roles and better perceives the existence of leadership. By way of testing this and preparing the way for studying actual media staffs, some experiments have been done with groups of five journalism students who were given assignments that simulated the work of an actual newspaper staff, including reporting, reference, editing, copyreading and setting in type. All their intercommunications were

Table 1

Twenty Telephone Calls by Four Boys

A. In process of organizing a school newspaper:

	Mike	Bud	Mike T.	John	Total
Mike		4	4	2	10
Bud	3		1	2	6
Mike T.	1	1		0	2
John	1	1	0		2
Total	5	6	5	4	

B. After school newspaper had been published two months:

	Mike	Bud	Mike T.	John	Total
Mike		3	1	1	5
Bud	7		1	0	8
Mike T.	5	1		0	6
John	1	0	0		1
Total	13	4	2	1	

recorded. Not enough groups have yet been put through the procedure to reveal all the variables, but the pattern so far is very clear and interesting. Some of the groups were started on their assignments entirely unstructured—that is, no roles were assigned. In others a leader was appointed. In still others, every person was assigned a job. Inasmuch as some measure of leadership almost always appeared, regardless of assignment, participants were asked at the end whether they perceived a leader or leaders, and if so, whom? This, in general, seems to be the pattern:

(a) As the perception of leadership increases, the relative transitional entropy of communication in the group decreases—that is, it becomes easier to predict who will talk to whom.

(b) As the degree of initial organization is increased, the total amount of communication decreases and the total time required to do the job decreases.

(c) However, between the group in which a leader is appointed and the group in which all members are assigned roles, these measures change much less than between the other groups and the unstructured group. In some cases, the group in which a leader only was appointed actually finished the job more quickly than the group in which all roles were assigned. This suggests that there may be a stage in which increasing organization does not contribute to efficiency; and also, that it must make a difference who is appointed leader, even in these previously unacquainted groups.

These results are presented only to suggest that the approach is a promising one for group study, and especially for the study of the kind of functional groups that play such an important part in mass communication.

FINALLY

How can we sum up the import of all this for the study of mass communication?

Even such a brief overview as this must make it clear that information theory is suggestive and stimulating for students of human communication. It must be equally clear that the power of the theory and its stimulating analogic quality are greatly at variance with the puny quality of the mathematical examples I have been able to cite—that is, examples of the use so far made of information theory mathematics in studying mass communication. Why should this be?

The theory is now—1948, as I have said, for most of us. Its application is fringed with dangers. One of these has been indicated—the danger of working with stochastic processes in functional systems which may learn and thereby change the probabilities. It should also be said that we do not as yet know much about the sampling distributions of these entropy formulas, and it is therefore not always wise to use them for hypothesis testing and statistical inference. Finally, we must admit frankly the difficulty of bridging the gap between the formula's concept of information (which is concerned only with the number of binary choices necessary to specify an event in a system) and our concept of information in human communication (which is concerned with the relation of a fact to outside events—e.g., how "informative" is it?).

This is not to say that the transfer cannot be made. Certainly I have no intention of saying that the theory has only analogic value, and that the contribution of its mathematical tools is necessarily small. These tools seem to me to be extremely promising in the study of language, channel capacities, couplings, and network groups, if nowhere else. It will be to our advantage to explore these uses and others.

49

What We Know about the Effects of Mass Communication: The Brink of Hope

JOSEPH T. KLAPPER

Twenty years ago writers who undertook to discuss mass communication typically felt obliged to define that unfamiliar term. In the intervening years conjecture and research upon the topic, particularly in reference to the effects of mass communication, have burgeoned. The literature has reached that stage of profusion and disarray, characteristic of all burgeoning disciplines, at which researchers and research administrators speak wistfully of establishing centers where the cascading data might be sifted and stored. The field has grown to the point at which its practitioners are periodically asked by other researchers to attempt to assess the cascade, to determine whither we are tumbling, to attempt to assess, in short, "what we know about the effects of mass communication." The present paper is one attempt to partially answer that question.

The author is well aware that the possibility of bringing any order to this field is regarded in some quarters with increasing pessimism. The paper will acknowledge and document this pessimism, but it will neither condone nor share it. It will rather propose that we have come at last to the brink of hope.

THE BASES OF PESSIMISM

The pessimism is, of course, widespread and it exists both among the interested lay public and within the research fraternity.

Some degree of pessimism, or even cynicism, is surely to be expected from the lay public, whose questions we have failed to answer. Teachers, preachers, parents, and legislators have asked us a thousand times over these past fifteen years whether violence in the media produces delinquency, whether the media raise or lower public taste, and just what the media can do to the political persuasions of their audiences. To these questions we have not only failed to provide definitive answers, but we have done something worse: we have provided evidence in partial sup-

Reprinted with permission of the publisher. From *The Public Opinion Quarterly*, 21:453–474 (1957–1958).

port of every hue of every view. We have on the one hand demonstrated that people's existing tastes govern the way they use media, and on the other hand reported instances in which changed media usage was associated with apparently altered tastes. We have hedged on the crime and violence question, typically saying, "Well, probably there is no causative relationship, but there just might be a triggering effect." In reference to persuasion, we have maintained that the media are after all not so terribly powerful, and yet we have reported their impressive successes in such varied causes as promoting religious intolerance, the sale of war bonds, belief in the American Way, and disenchantment with boy scout activities. It is surely no wonder that a bewildered public should regard with cynicism a research tradition which supplies, instead of definitive answers, a plethora of relevant but inconclusive, and at times seemingly contradictory, findings.

Considerable pessimism, of a different hue, is also to be expected within the research fraternity itself. Such anomalous findings as have been cited above seemed to us at first to betoken merely the need of more penetrating and rigid research. We shaped insights into hypotheses and eagerly set up research designs in quest of the additional variables which we were sure would bring order out of chaos, and enable us to describe the process of effect with sufficient precision to diagnose and predict. But the variables emerged in such a cataract that we almost drowned. The relatively placid waters of "*who* says *what* to *whom*" were early seen to be muddied by audience predispositions, "self-selection," and selective perception. More recent studies, both in the laboratory and the social world, have documented the influence of a host of other variables, including various aspects of contextual organization; the audiences' image of the source; the simple passage of time; the group orientation of the audience member and the degree to which he values group membership; the activity of opinion leaders; the social aspects of the situation during and after exposure to the media, and the degree to which the audience member is forced to play a role; the personality pattern of the audience member, his social class, and the level of his frustration; the nature of the media in a free enterprise system, and the availability of "social mechanism[s] for implementing action drives." The list, if not endless, is at least overwhelming, and it continues to grow. Almost every aspect of the life of the audience member and the culture in which the communication occurs seems susceptible of relation to the process of communicational effect. As early as 1948, Berelson, cogitating on what was then known, came to the accurate if perhaps moody conclusion that "some kinds of *communication* on some kinds of *issues,* brought to the attention of some kinds of *people* under some kinds of *conditions* have some kinds of *effects.*" It is surely no wonder that today, after eight more years at the inexhaustible fount of variables, some researchers should feel that the formulation of any systematic description of what effects are now effected, and the predictive application of such principles, is a goal which becomes the more distant as it is the more vigorously pursued.

This paper, however, takes no such pessimistic view. It rather proposes that we already know a good deal more about communications than we thought we did, and that we are on the verge of being able to proceed toward even more abundant and more fruitful knowledge.

THE BASES OF HOPE

This optimism is based on two phenomena. The first of these is a new orientation toward the study of communication effects which has recently become conspicuous in the literature. And the second phenomenon is the emergence, from this new approach, of a few generalizations. It is proposed that these generalizations can be tied together, and tentatively developed a little further, and that when this is done the resulting set of generalizations can be extremely helpful. More specifically, they seem capable of organizing and relating a good deal of existing knowledge about the processes of communication effect, the factors involved in the process, and the direction which effects typically take. They thus provide some hope that the vast and ill-ordered array of communications research findings may be eventually molded, by these or other generalizations, into a body of organized knowledge.

This paper undertakes to cite the new orientation, to state what seem to be the emerging generalizations, and to at least suggest the extent of findings which they seem capable of ordering. In all of this, the author submits rather than asserts. He hopes to be extremely suggestive, but he cannot yet be conclusive. And if the paper bespeaks optimism, it also bespeaks the tentativeness of exploratory rather than exhaustive thought. Explicit note will in fact be taken of wide areas to which the generalizations do not seem to apply, and warnings will be sounded against the pitfalls of regarding them as all-inclusive or axiomatic.

THE PHENOMENISTIC APPROACH. The new orientation, which has of course been hitherto and variously formulated, can perhaps be described, in a confessedly oversimplified way, as a shift away from the concept of "hypodermic effect" toward an approach which might be called "situational," "phenomenistic," or "functional." It is a shift away from the tendency to regard mass communication as a necessary and sufficient cause of audience effects, toward a view of the media as influences, working amid other influences, in a total situation. The old quest of specific effects stemming directly from the communication has given way to the observation of existing conditions or changes—followed by an inquiry into the factors, including mass communication, which produced those conditions and changes, and the roles which these factors played relative to each other. In short, attempts to assess a stimulus which was presumed to work alone have given way to an assessment of the role of that stimulus in a total observed phenomenon.

Examples of the new approach are fairly numerous, although they still represent only a small proportion of current research. The so-called Elmira and Decatur studies, for example, set out to determine the critical factors in various types of observed decisions, rather than focussing exclusively on whether media did or did not have effects. McPhee, in theoretical vein, proposes that we stop seeking direct media effects on taste and inquire instead into what produces taste and how media affect that. The Rileys and Maccoby focus on the varying functions which media serve for different sorts of children, rather than inquiring whether media do or do not affect them. Some of the more laboratory-oriented researchers, in particular the Hovland school, have been conducting ingeniously designed controlled experiments in which the communicational stimulus is a constant, and various extra-communicational factors are the variables.

This new approach, which views mass media as one among a series of factors, working in patterned ways their wonders to perform, seems to the author to have made possible a series of generalizations which will now be advanced. They are submitted very gingerly. They seem to the author at once extremely generic and quite immature; they seem on the one hand to involve little that has not been said, and on the other hand to be frightfully daring. They do seem, however, to be capable of relating a good deal of data about the processes, factors, and directions of communication effects, and of doing this in such a way that findings hitherto thought anomalous or contradictory begin to look like orderly variations on a few basic themes.

EMERGING GENERALIZATIONS. The entire set of generalizations will first be presented in their bare bones, and without intervening comment. The remainder of this paper will be devoted to justifying their existence and indicating the range of data which they seem able to organize. Without further ado, then, it is proposed that we are as of now justified in making the following tentative generalizations:

1. Mass communication ordinarily does not serve as a necessary and sufficient cause of audience effects, but rather functions among and through a nexus of mediating factors and influences.

2. These mediating factors are such that they typically render mass communication a contributory agent, but not the sole cause, in a process

of reinforcing the existing conditions. (Regardless of the condition in question—be it the level of public taste, the tendency of audience members toward or away from delinquent behavior, or their vote intention—and regardless of whether the effect in question be social or individual, the media are more likely to reinforce than to change.)

3. On such occasions as mass communication does function in the service of change, one of two conditions is likely to obtain. Either:
   a. the mediating factors will be found to be inoperative, and the effect of the media direct; or
   b. the mediating factors, which normally favor reinforcement, will be found to be themselves impelling toward change.

4. There are certain residual situations in which mass communication seems to wreak direct effects, or to directly and of itself serve certain psychophysical functions.

5. The efficacy of mass communication, either as contributory agents or as agents of direct effect, is affected by various aspects of the media themselves or of the communication situation (including, for example, aspects of contextual organization, the availability of channels for overt action, etc.).

Therewith the generalizations, and herewith the application. The schemata will be applied first to the field of persuasive communication, and then, much more briefly, to the data dealing with the effects of mass communication on the levels of audience taste. The hope, in each case, is to show that the data support the generalizations, and that the generalizations in turn organize the data and suggest new avenues of logically relevant research.

THE GENERALIZATIONS APPLIED: PERSUASION

Persuasive communication here refers to those communications which are intended to evoke what Katz and Lazarsfeld have called "campaign" effects, i.e., to produce such short term opinion and attitude effects as are typically the goals of campaigns—political, civic, or institutional. Long-range phenomena, such as the building of religious values, are not here a focus of attention, nor are the marketing goals of most advertising.

REINFORCEMENT. It is by now axiomatic that persuasive communication of the sort we are discussing is far more often associated with attitude reinforcement than with conversion. The now classic *People's Choice* found reinforcement, or constancy of opinion, approximately ten times as common as conversion among Erie County respondents exposed to the presidential campaign of 1940, and a nine to one ratio was found in the more elaborate study of Elmira voters in 1948. Various other studies have attested that, in general, when the media offer fare in support of both sides of given issues, the dominant affect is stasis, or reinforcement, and the least common effect is conversion.

But we are not here proposing merely that the media are more likely to reinforce than to convert. We are also proposing, as some others have proposed before us, and as we have stated in generalization number 1, that the media typically do not wreak direct effects upon their audiences, but rather function among and through other factors or forces. And we are going slightly farther by proposing, in generalization number 2, that it is these very intervening variables themselves which tend to make mass communication a contributing agent of reinforcement as opposed to change. We shall here note only a few such variables, deliberately select- ing both from among the long familiar and the newly identified, in order to suggest the extent of findings for which this generalization seems able to account, and which, seen in this light, become logically related mani- festations of the same general phenomenon.

Audience predispositions, for example, have been recognized since the very beginnings of communications research as a controlling influence upon the effect of persuasive mass communication. A plethora of studies, some conducted in the laboratory and some in the social world, have demonstrated that such predispositions and their progeny—selective ex- posure, selective retention, and selective perception—intervene between the supply of available mass communication stimuli and the minds of the audience members. They wrap the audience member in a kind of pro- tective net, which so sifts or deflects or remolds the stimuli as to make reinforcement a far more likely effect than conversion.

Let us turn from these very old friends to newer acquaintances. Com- munications research has recently "rediscovered" *the group*. Katz and Lazarsfeld, drawing on the literature of small group research, have pro- posed, with considerable supporting evidence, that primary-type groups to which the audience member belongs may themselves function as re- inforcing agents and may influence mass communication to do likewise. People tend, for example, to belong to groups whose characteristic opinions are congenial with their own; the opinions themselves seem to be intensified, or at least made more manifest, by intra-group interaction; and the benefits, both psychological and social, of continued membership in good standing act as a deterrent against opinion change. Group- anchored norms thus serve, on a conscious or unconscious level, to mediate the effects of communications. The proposition has been em- pirically demonstrated by Kelley and Volkart, who found that, in gen- eral, persuasive communications were more likely to be rejected if they were not in accord with the norms of groups to which the audience member belonged; there were indications, furthermore, that the tendency was intensified in regard to issues more salient to the group, and among persons who particularly valued their membership. Groups are further likely to supplement the reinforcing effect by providing areas for oral dissemination. Various studies have shown that communications spread most widely among persons of homogeneous opinion, and especially among those who agree with the communication to begin with. The "rediscovered group," in short, intervenes between the media stimuli and the people who are affected, and it does so, other conditions being equal, in favor of reinforcement.

Consider another phenomenon which is now in the limelight of communication research: *opinion leadership*, or, as it is sometimes called, "the two-step flow of communication." The operation of such leadership is by definition interventive. And opinion leaders, it turns out, are usually supernormative members of the same groups to which their followers belong—i.e., persons especially familiar with and loyal to group standards and values. Their influence therefore appears more likely to be exercised in the service of continuity than of change, and it seems therefore a reasonable conjecture—although it has not, to the author's knowledge, been specifically documented—that their role in the process of communication effect is more likely to encourage reinforcement than conversion.

All the intervening phenomena which have thus far been cited pertain, in one way or another, to the audience members—to the element of *whom* in the old Lasswell formula. But the range of mediating influences is not so restricted. *The nature of mass communication* in a free enterprise society, for example, falls under this same rubric. It is surely not necessary to here rehearse in detail the old adage of how the need for holding a massive audience leads the media, particularly in their entertainment fare, to hew to the accepted, and thus to tend to resanctify the sanctified. But it should here be noted that this is to say that the demands of the socio-economic system mediate the possible effects of mass communication in the direction of social reinforcement.

Such phenomena as these lend some credence to the proposition that the media typically work among and through other forces, and that these intervening forces tend to make the media contributing agents of reinforcement. And the generalization, to which these factors lend credence, in turn serves to organize and relate the factors. Diverse though they may be, they are seen to play essentially similar roles. One is tempted to wonder if they do not constitute a definable class of forces—whether, if the process of communicational effect were reduced to symbolic formulation, they might not be severally represented as, say, Q_1, Q_2, and so forth to Q_n. The author does not propose anything so drastic. He merely notes that the generalization suggests it. It suggests, simultaneously, relevant topics for further research. *Do* opinion leaders actually function, as the generalization suggests, to render mass communication a more likely agent of reinforcement than of change? And what of all those Q's between Q_3 or Q_8 and Q_n? What other phenomena function in a similar manner and toward the same end?

We may note also that this generalization, simple though it is, not only accounts for such factors as provide its life blood. It provides as well a sort of covering shed for various bits and pieces of knowledge which have hitherto stood in discrete isolation.

Consider, for example, the phenomenon of *"monopoly propaganda"*—i.e., propaganda which is vigorously and widely pursued and nowhere opposed. Monopoly propaganda has been long recognized as widely effective, and monopoly position has been cited as a condition which virtually guarantees persuasive success. But monopoly propaganda can exist only in favor of views which already enjoy such wide sanction that no opposition of any significance exists. Viewed in the light of the generalization, monopoly position is seen not as an isolated condition of propaganda success, but as a specific combination of known factors. It is a name for the situation in which both the media and virtually all the factors which intervene between the media and the audience, or which operate co-existently with the media, approach a homogeneity of directional influence. Monopoly position is, as it were, a particular setting of the machine, and its outcome is logically predictable.

CHANGE, WITH MEDIATORS INOPERATIVE. Generalization number 3 recognizes that although the media typically function as contributory agents of reinforcement, they also function as agents of attitude change. In reference to this simple point, there is surely no need for lengthy documentation: the same studies that find reinforcement the predominant effect of campaigns typically reveal as well some small incidence of conversion, and a plethora of controlled experiments attest that media, or laboratory approximations of media, can and often do shift attitudes in the direction intended by the communicator. But the generalization further proposes—and in this it is more daring than its predecessors—that such attitude changes occur when either of two conditions obtain: when the forces which normally make for stasis or reinforcement are inoperative, or when these very same forces themselves make for change.

Let us consider first the proposition that change is likely to occur if the forces for stasis are inoperative. A set of experiments which has already been mentioned above is extremely indicative in reference to this proposition. Kelley and Volkhart, it will be recalled, found that, in general, communications opposed to group norms were likely to be rejected if the issue was particular salient to the group, and that they were more likely to be rejected by persons who particularly valued their group membership. But there is another side to the Kelley-Volkhart coin, viz., the findings that the communication opposed to group norms was more likely to be *accepted when the issue was not particularly salient* to the group, and that it was more likely to be accepted *by persons who did not particularly value their membership* in the group. Put another way, *changes were more likely to occur in those situations in which the mediating effect of the group was reduced.*

A whole slew of other findings and bits of knowledge, both old and new, and previously existing as more or less discrete axioms, seem susceptible of being viewed as essentially similar manifestations of this same set of conditions. It has long been known, for example, that although the media are relatively ineffectual in conversion, they are quite effective in forming opinions and attitudes in regard to *new issues*, particularly as these issues are the more unrelated to "existing attitude clusters." But it is precisely in reference to such issues that predispositions, selective exposure, and selective perception are least likely to exist, that group norms are least likely to pertain, that opinion leaders are least ready to lead—that the mediating forces of stasis, in short, are least likely to mediate. The intervening forces, in short, are likely to be inoperative, and the media are more likely to directly influence their audience.

Much the same explanation can be offered for the observed ability of the media to influence their audience on peripheral issues while simultaneously failing in the major mission of the moment, and the same situation probably obtains in regard to media's ability to *communicate facts or even change opinions on objective matters without producing the attitude changes* that such facts and opinions are intended to engender. It may well be that the facts and opinions are not related to the desired attitude change sufficiently strongly to call the protective mediating forces into play: the communication content is probably not recognized as necessarily relevant to the attitude, as not salient, and mediation does not occur. This interpretation, by the way, could very easily be tested.

The inverse correlation between the capability of the media to wreak attitude change and the degree to which the attitude in question is ego-involved may well be another case in point. But this paper cannot analyze and rehearse, nor has the author wholly explored, the entire range of phenomena which might be explained on the basis of the forces for stasis being inoperative. If the generalization is at all valid, it will gather such phenomena unto itself. Let it be the role of this paper to present it, to germinate as it will.

CHANGES THROUGH MEDIATORS. Let us turn now to the second part of the proposition about the conditions under which media may serve as agents of opinion change. It has been suggested that such an effect is likely when either of two conditions obtain: when the forces for stasis are inoperative—as in the cases which have just been discussed—and, secondly, when the intervening forces themselves favor change.

Let us look again, for example, at the influence of group membership and of group norms. These typically mediate the influences of mass communication in favor of reinforcement, but under certain conditions they may abet communicational influences for change.

In an ingeniously designed experiment by McKeachie, for example, communications regarding attitudes toward Negroes, and the discussion which these communications engendered, made some group members aware that they had misperceived the pertinent group norms. The great majority of such individuals showed opinion changes in the direction of the norm, which was also the direction intended by the communication. The *newly perceived norms* impelled the audience toward the communicationally recommended change.

A switch in group loyalties or in reference groups may likewise predispose an individual toward consonant opinion changes suggested by mass communication. Studies of satellite defectors, for example, suggest that persons who have lived for years as respected members of Communist society, and then fall from grace, develop a new susceptibility to Western propaganda. As their lot deteriorates, they turn their eyes and minds to the West, and their radio dials to VOA and RFE. By the time they defect they have developed a set of extremely anti-Communist and pro-Western attitudes, quite out of keeping with their previous lives, but in accord with what they regard as normative to their new refugee primary group.

Group norms, or predispositions otherwise engendered, may furthermore become dysfunctional; in learning theory terminology, the response they dictate may cease to be rewarding, or may even lead to punishment. In such situations the individual is impelled to find a new response which does provide reward, and communications recommending such a changed response are more likely to be accepted. Some such phenomenon seems to have occurred, for example, in the case of Nazi and North Korean soldiers who remained immune to American propaganda appeals while their military primary group survived, but became susceptible when the group disintegrated and adherence to its normative attitudes and conduct ceased to have survival value. The accustomed group norms in such instances had not merely become inoperative; they had become positively dysfunctional and had sensitized and predisposed their adherents to changes suggested by the media.

Personality pattern appears to be another variable which may mediate the influence of communications, and particular syndromes seem to abet change. Janis, for example, found in a laboratory study that those of his subjects "who manifested social inadequacy, inhibition of aggression, and depressive tendencies, showed the greatest opinion change" in response to persuasive communication. They appeared, as Hovland puts it, to be "predisposed to be highly influenced."

In sum, it appears that the generalization is supported by empirical data —that intervening variables which mediate the influence of mass communication, and which typically promote reinforcement, may also work for change. And again, the generalization, in turn, accounts for and orders the data on which it is based. Group membership, dysfunctional norms, and particular personality patterns can be viewed as filling similar roles in the process of communicationally stimulated opinion change. Other similarly operative variables will doubtless be identified by a continued phenomenistic approach, i.e., by the analysis of accomplished opinion changes.

The generalization furthermore serves, as did the others, to relate and explain various discrete findings and isolated bits of knowledge. It would appear to cover, for example, such hitherto unrelated phenomena as the susceptibility to persuasive appeals of persons whose primary group memberships place them under cross-pressures, and the effects of what Hovland has called "role playing."

The first case—*the susceptibility to persuasive communications of persons whose primary group membership places them under cross-pressure* —is fairly obvious. In terms of the generalization, such people can be said to be at the mercy of mediating factors which admit and assist communicational stimuli favoring both sides of the same issue. We may also observe that any attitude shift which such a person may make toward one side of the issue does not necessarily entail any reduction of the forceful mediation toward the other direction. On the basis of the generalization, we would therefore predict not only change, but inconstancy, which has in fact been found to be the case.

The effects of role playing seem another, if less obvious, example of opinion change occurring as a result of a mediating, or, in this case, a superimposed factor which in turn rendered a communication effective. Hovland reported that if persons opposed to a communication are forced to defend it, i.e., to act in a public situation as though they had accepted the recommended opinion, they become more likely actually to adopt it. The crucial element of role playing is, of course, artificially superimposed. But in any case, the entire phenomenon might be viewed as something very akin to what occurs when an old norm, or an old predisposition, ceases to lead to reward. Successful role playing in fact invests the opposing response with reward. The communication is thus given an assist by the imposition of new factors which favor change. The potentialities of this technique, incidentally, are of course appalling. The Communists have already developed and refined it and we have christened the process "brain-washing."

Various other bits of knowledge about communication effect can be viewed as related manifestations of this same general phenomenon, i.e., the phenomenon of communications inducing attitude change through the assistance of mediating factors which themselves favor change. But it is the goal of this paper to be only suggestive, rather than exhaustive or exhausting, and thus generalization number three may be here left, to suggest whatever it will.

So much, then, for the first three generalizations, which attempt to relate the processes, the factors, and the directions of effect. It is hardly germane, at this juncture, to belabor generalizations four and five. They serve only to recognize residual categories. Thus number four merely points out that some persuasive or quasi-persuasive effects do appear, at least to our present state of knowledge, to be direct. The apparently un-motivated learning of sufficiently repeated facts or slogans is a case in point. And generalization number five merely points out that the persua-sive efficacy of the media is known to be affected by numerous variables pertaining to the content, the medium itself, or the communication situa-tion—by such matters, for example, as the number and order of topics, the degree of repetition, the likelihood of distraction, the objective possibil-ities of action, and the like. The proposed schemata suggests that these variables are of a different and residual order as compared with the kind of *mediating* variables which we have just been discussing.

We have thus far been laboring to make and document three points, viz., (1) the set of generalizations is supported by our knowledge of the effects of persuasive communications; (2) the generalizations organize, or bring into logical relation, or, if you will, "predict" in an *a posteriori* sense, a large portion of that knowledge; and (3) in so ordering the data they simultaneously suggest new and logically related avenues for further research.

It is proposed that the same set of generalizations is similarly applicable to other types of communication effect. To spell this out in detail is beyond the scope of a single paper. It may be well for the sake of the argument, however, to at least suggest the applicability of the generaliza-tions to one other area, the effects of mass communication upon levels of public taste.

THE GENERALIZATIONS APPLIED: EFFECTS ON TASTE

REINFORCEMENT. It has been long known that the media do not seem to determine tastes, but rather to be used in accordance with tastes other-wise determined. The typical audience member selects from the media's varied fare those commodities which are in accord with his existing likes, and typically eschews exposure to other kinds of material. His existing likes, in turn, seem largely to derive from his primary, secondary, and reference groups, although they are not uncommonly affected by his special personality needs. Whatever their origin, they intervene between the audience member and the vast array of media fare, and between the specific content and his interpretation of it. The media stimuli are thoroughly sifted and molded, and they serve, typically, as grist for the existing mill. Put in a now familiar way, the effects of mass communication are mediated, and the media serve as contributing agents of reinforcement.

CHANGES. But the media are also associated with changes in taste. Oddly enough, little attention has been paid to the one change which occurs continually—the changing tastes of growing children. Wolf and Fiske seem to be the only researchers who explicitly noted that the pattern of development in children's comic book preferences precisely parallels the changing needs of their developing personalities, as expressed, for example, in games. And no one, to the author's knowledge, has ever pointed out that the pattern of development in comic book and TV preferences also parallels the previously characteristic patterns of development in regular reading preferences. In short, the development and its integral changes in taste are culturally wholly catholic. In terms of our present set of generalizations, this is to say that such mediating variables as personality, cultural norms, and peer group interests impel the media to function as contributory agents of taste change.

The media have also been observed, although rarely, to play a role in elevating the tastes of adults. Suchman, for example, investigated the previous habits of some 700 persons who regularly listened to classical music broadcasts, and found that in the case of 53 percent the radio had either "initiated" their interest in music or had "nursed" a mild but previously little exercised interest. But—and here is the essential point the radio had functioned in almost all of these cases not as a necessary and sufficient cause, but as an "energizing agent" or implementer of tendencies otherwise engendered. The so-called initiates had been urged to listen by friends, or in some cases fiancés, whose tastes they respected and whose good opinion they sought, or by their own belief that a taste for classical music would increase their social prestige. The mediating factors, in short, were at it again.

The literature on taste effects is relatively sparse, and seems to offer no illustration of changes which could be ascribed to the forces of stasis being inoperative. It might be conjectured that such effects occur among extreme isolates, but the possibility seems never to have been investigated.

In any case, our two generalizations which regard both reinforcement and change as essentially products of mediating factors account for virtually all of the hard data on the effect of mass communication on public taste. The generalizations furthermore suggest that the data are neither contradictory nor anomalous, but logically related. Stasis, reinforcement, developmental patterns, and individual change appear as different but understandable and predictable products of the same machines.

RESIDUAL MATTERS. There remains a certain residuum of related data and respectable conjecture for which the generalizations do not account. They do not explain why tastes in the development of which media has played a large role tend to have a sort of pseudo-character—why music lovers whose passions have been largely radio-nurtured, for example, appear to be peculiarly interested in the lives of composers and performers, and to lack real depth of musical understanding. Nor do the generalizations cover the phenomenon of media *created* pseudo-interests, about which much speculation exists. McPhee has noted, for example, that the tremendous availability of newscasts seems to have created in some people an addiction, an ardent hunger which is sated by the five-minute newscast, despite its lack of detail and regardless of its irrelevance to the addict's life and interests. McPhee notes a similar passion for big-league baseball results, even among people who have never been in a ball park nor even seen a game on TV. Meyersohn regards this sort of thing as an indication that media create their own common denominators of national taste.

We know little about this phenomenon. Perhaps it is a direct effect, or perhaps it involves mediators as yet unspotted. In any case, deeper understanding seems likely to come from what we have called the phenomenistic approach—from an inquiry into the functions which such addiction serves for the addict, and into the role of the media in creating or serving the addiction.

APPLICATION TO OTHER FIELDS

We have now considered the extent to which the proposed generalizations are applicable to existing data regarding the effects of mass communication on opinions and attitudes, and upon levels of taste. It is proposed that they are equally applicable to questions about the effects of specific types of media fare, such as fantasy or depictions of crime and violence, on the psychological orientations and behavior of the audience. In the interests of brevity, these other areas of effect will not be discussed, except to note that the classic studies, both old and new, seem particularly suggestive. The old studies of soap opera listeners by Warner and Henry and Herzog, for example, and the more recent and differently focused work of the Rileys and of Maccoby, all relate such variables as group orientation and personality needs to media use and media effects.

They speak, implicitly and explicitly, of the *functions* served by media, and of the role of the media in effects of which they are not the sole cause.

SUMMATION AND CONCLUSIONS

It is time now to look quickly back over the ground we have covered, and to evaluate the set of generalizations which have been proposed—to inquire into what they have enabled us to do, and to note their weaknesses.

On the positive side, they appear to serve three major functions:

First, as this paper has been at some pains to demonstrate, the generalizations have permitted us in some measure to organize, or to account for, a considerable number of communications research findings which have previously seemed discrete, at times anomalous, and occasionally contradictory. The author submits, tentatively and with due humility, that the schemata has in fact made possible organization of several different orders:

. . . it has enabled us to relate the *processes* of effect and the *direction* of effect, and to account for the relative incidence of reinforcement and of change.

. . . it has provided a concept of the process of effect in which both reinforcement and change are seen as related and understandable outcomes of the same general dynamic.

. . . it has enabled us to view such diverse phenomena as audience predispositions, group membership and group norms, opinion leadership, personality patterns, and the nature of the media in this society, as serving similar functions in the process of effect—as being, if you will, all of a certain order, and distinct from such other factors as the characteristics of media content.

. . . it has enabled us to view such other unrelated phenomena as monopoly propaganda, new issues, and role-playing as manifestations of the same general process—as specific combinations of known variables, the outcomes of which were predictable.

So much for the organizational capabilities of the media. But note that this organization of existing data, even within so sketchy a framework as these generalizations provide, permitted us to see gaps—to discover, for example, that certain presumed outcomes have to date been neither documented nor shown not to occur. And thus the second contribution: the generalizations seem capable of indicating avenues of needed research, which are logically related to existing knowledge. Put another way, even this simple schemata seems capable of contributing to the cumulatibility of future research findings. This is in no way to gainsay that future thought and research must inevitably change the generalizations themselves. As presently formulated, they constitute only a single tentative step forward, and their refinement or emendation seems more likely to enlarge than to reduce the area of their applicability.

Finally, it is in the extent of this applicability, coupled with the foetal nature of the generalizations, that the author finds particular bases for hope. Sketchy and imperfect as they are, these propositions regarding the process and direction of effect seem applicable to the effects of persuasive communications, to the effects of mass communication on public taste, and, though it has not here been demonstrated, to the effects of specific media fare upon the psychological orientations and overt behavior patterns of the audience. Furthermore, the mediating variables to which they point—variables such as predisposition, group membership, personality patterns and the like—seem to play essentially similar roles in all these various kinds of effect. Even if these generalizations turn out to be wholly in error—and certainly they are imperfect—they seem nevertheless sufficiently useful and sufficiently applicable to justify the faith that *some* generalizations can in due time be made.

These particular generalizations, however, do not usher in the millennium. They are imperfect, and underdeveloped; they are inadequate in scope, and in some senses they are dangerous.

They do not, for example, cover the residuum of direct effects except to note that such effects exist. They are less easy to apply, and perhaps inapplicable, to certain other broad areas of effect, such as the effect of the existence of the media on patterns of daily life, on each other, and on cultural values as a whole. We have here spoken of cultural values as a mediating factor, which in part determines media content, but certainly some sort of circular relationship must exist, and media content must in turn affect cultural values.

Such concepts suggest what is perhaps the greatest danger inherent both in these generalizations and in the approach to communications research from which they derive. And that is the tendency to go overboard in blindly minimizing the effects and potentialities of mass communication. In reaping the fruits of the discovery that mass media function amid a nexus of other influences, we must not forget that the influences nevertheless differ. Mass media of communication possess various characteristics and capabilities distinct from those of peer groups or opinion leaders. They are, after all, media of *mass* communication, which daily address tremendous cross-sections of the population with a single voice. It is neither sociologically unimportant nor insignificant that the media have rendered it possible, as Wiebe has put it, for Americans from all social strata to laugh at the same joke, nor is it insignificant that total strangers, upon first meeting, may share valid social expectations that small talk about Betty Furness or Elvis Presley will be mutually comprehensible. We must not lose sight of the peculiar characteristics of the media, nor of the likelihood that of this peculiar character there may be engendered peculiar effects.

In any case, the most fruitful path for the future seems clear enough. It is not the path of abstract theorizing, nor is it the path, which so many of us have deserted, of seeking simple and direct effects of which media are the sole and sufficient cause. It appears rather to be the path of the phenomenistic approach, which seeks to account for the known occurrence and to assess the roles of the several influences which produced it, and which attempts to see the respondents not as randomly selected individuals each exchangeable for the other, but rather as persons functioning within particular social contexts. It is likewise the path of the cumulating controlled experiments in which the multifarious extra-media factors being investigated are built into the research design. These are the paths which have brought us to what seems the verge of generalization and empirically documented theory. They are the paths which have brought us to the brink of hope.

50 | # Communication Research and the Image of Society: Convergence of Two Traditions
ELIHU KATZ

Research on mass communications has concentrated on persuasion, that is, on the ability of the mass media to influence, usually to change, opinions, attitudes, and actions in a given direction. This emphasis has led to the study of campaigns—election campaigns, marketing campaigns, campaigns to reduce racial prejudice, and the like. Although it has been traditional to treat audience studies, content analysis, and effect studies as separate areas, there is good reason to believe that all three have been motivated primarily by a concern with the effective influencing of thought and behavior in the short run.

Other fields of social research have also focused on the effectiveness of campaigns, a prominent example being the twenty-year old tradition of research by rural sociologists on the acceptance of new farm practices. Yet, despite this shared concern, the two traditions of research for many years were hardly aware of each other's existence or of their possible relevance for each other. Indeed, even now, when there is already a certain amount of interchange between them, it is not easy to conceive of two traditions that, ostensibly, seem more unrelated. Rural sociology suggests the study of traditional values, of kinship, primary relations, *Gemein-*

Reprinted with permission of the University of Chicago Press and the author. From *The American Journal of Sociology*, 65:435–440 (1959).

schaft; research on mass communications, on the other hand, is almost a symbol of urban society.

The recognition that these two traditions of research have now begun to accord each other is, in large measure, the product of a revision of the image of society implicit in research on mass communications. Thus, although the convergence now taking place has surely proceeded from both directions, this paper attempts to present the story from one side only.

COMMUNICATION RESEARCH AND THE IMAGE OF SOCIETY

Until very recently, the image of society in the minds of most students of communication was of atomized individuals, connected with the mass media but not with one another. Society—the "audience"— was conceived of as aggregates of age, sex, social class, and the like, but little thought was given to the relationships implied thereby or to more informal relationships. The point is not that the student of mass communications was unaware that members of the audience have families and friends but that he did not believe that they might affect the outcome of a campaign; informal interpersonal relations, thus, were considered irrelevant to the institutions of modern society.

What research on mass communications has learned in its three decades is that the mass media are far less potent than had been expected. A variety of studies—with the possible exception of studies of marketing campaigns—indicates that people are not easily persuaded to change their opinions and behavior. The search for the sources of resistance to change, as well as for the effective sources of influence when changes *do* occur, led to the discovery of the role of interpersonal relations. The shared values in groups of family, friends, and co-workers and the networks of communication which are their structure, the decision of their influential members to accept or resist a new idea—all these are interpersonal processes which "intervene" between the campaign in the mass media and the individual who is the ultimate target. These recent discoveries, of course, upset the traditional image of the individuated audience upon which the discipline has been based. Moreover, there is good reason to believe that the image of society in the minds of students of popular culture needs revision in other dimensions as well. But these remarks are concerned only with the discovery that the mass audience is not so atomized and disconnected as had been thought.

INTERPERSONAL RELATIONS AND MASS COMMUNICATIONS

Given the need to modify the image of the audience so as to take account of the role of interpersonal relations in the process of mass communications, researchers seem to have proceeded in three directions. First of all, studies were designed so as to characterize individuals not only by their individual attributes but also by their relationship to others. At the Bureau of Applied Social Research of Columbia University, where much of this work has gone on, a series of successive studies examined the ways in which influences from the mass media are intercepted by interpersonal networks of communication and made more or less effective thereby. These were studies of decisions of voters, of housewives to try a new kind of food, of doctors to adopt a new drug, and so on. Elsewhere, studies have focused on the relevance of such variables as relative integration among peers or membership in one kind of group rather than another. These studies are rapidly multiplying.

A second strategy is the study of small groups; indeed, a number of links have been forged between macroscopic research on the mass media and the microscopic study of interpersonal communication.

But, while research on small groups can provide many clues to a better understanding of the role of interpersonal relations in the process of mass communications, it focuses almost exclusively on what goes on *within* a group. The third strategy of research, then, was to seek leads from research concerned with the introduction of change from *outside* a social system. Here the work of the rural sociologists is of major importance. For the last two decades the latter have been inquiring into the effectiveness of campaigns to gain acceptance of new farm practices in rural communities while taking explicit account of the relevant channels of communication both outside and inside the community. Yet, despite the obvious parallel between rural and urban compaigns, it was not until after the "discovery" of interpersonal relations that the student of mass communications had occasion to "discover" rural sociology.

INTERPERSONAL RELATIONS AND RURAL COMMUNICATION

If the assumption that interpersonal relations were irrelevant was central to the research worker on mass communications, the opposite was true of the student of rural campaigns. And the reasons are quite apparent: rural sociologists never assumed, as students of mass communications had, that their respondents did not talk to each other. How could one overlook the possible relevance of farmers' contacts with one another to their response to a new and recommended farm practice? The structure of interpersonal relations, it was assumed, was no less important for channeling the flow of influence than the farm journal or the county agent.

Why did relationships among members of the audience figure so much more prominently in research on new farm practices than in research on marketing campaigns, campaigns to reduce prejudice, and the like? Consider the following explanations.

It is obvious, in the first place, that rural sociologists define their arena of research, at least in part, by contrast with the allegedly impersonal, atomized, anomic life of the city. If urban relationships are "secondary," rural life must be somewhere near the other end of the continuum. Hence primary, interpersonal relations—their location, their sizes and shapes, and their consequences—are of central concern.

Second, research on mass communications, linked as it is to research on opinions and attitudes, is derived more directly from individual psychology than sociology. Students of rural change, on the other hand, have a sociological heritage and a continuing tradition of tracing the relations of cliques, the boundaries of neighborhoods, the web of kinship and the like. Only recently has sociological theory begun to have a cumulative impact upon research on mass communications.

Rural sociologists, moreover, who study the adoption of new farm practices are, typically, in the employ of colleges of agriculture, which, in turn, are associated with state colleges and universities. The locale of operations is somewhat more circumscribed, as a result, than it is in the case of the student of urban mass media. The student of the adoption of new farm practices is not interested in, say, a respresentative national sample. Sometimes, therefore, he will interview all the farmers in a given county or a very large proportion of them, and this makes it possible to collect data on the relations among individual respondents, which, obviously, is impossible in random cross-sectional sampling where respondents are selected as "far apart" from each other as possible. By the same token, the investigator of rural communication is more a part of the situation he is studying; it is more difficult for him to overlook interpersonal influence as a variable.

Finally, a fact, related in part to the previous one, is that the rural sociologist has been primarily interested in the efficacy of the local agricultural agency's program, and, while the local agent employs the mass media as well as personal visits, demonstrations, and other techniques, his influence is plainly disproportionately effective among the more educated and those enjoying prestige in the community and considerably less so among others. Research workers soon were able to suggest, however, that the county agent's effectiveness for a majority of the population may be indirect, for the people he influences may influence others. This idea of a "two-step" flow of communication also suggested itself as a promotional idea to magazines and other vehicles of mass communications, but it was not actually studied—perhaps because it was more difficult to define operationally—until rather recently.

SOME CONSEQUENCES OF CONVERGENCE

That research on mass communications and on the diffusion and acceptance of new farm practices have "discovered" each other is increasingly evident from the references and citations in recent papers in both fields. The realization of the shared interest in the problem of campaigns—or, more accurately now, in the shared problems of diffusion—has evidently overcome academic insulation. From the point of view of students of mass communications, it took a change in the image of the audience to reveal that the two traditions were studying almost exactly the same problem.

Now that the convergence has been accomplished, however, what consequences are likely to follow? First of all, the two will be very likely to affect each other's design of research. The problem of how to take account of interpersonal relations and still preserve the representativeness of a sample is paramount in studies of mass communications, while that of rural sociologists is how to generalize from studies of neighborhoods, communities, and counties. What is more, despite their persistent concern with interpersonal relations, students of rural diffusion have never mapped the spread of a particular innovation against the sociometric structure of an entire community; paradoxically, a recent study deriving from the tradition of research on mass communications has attempted it. Clearly, both fields can contribute to the refinement of research design, and their contributions, moreover, would have implications not only for each other but for a growing number of substantive fields which are interested in tracing the spread of specific innovations through social structures. This includes the work of students of technical assistance programs, of health campaigns, of marketing behavior, of fads and fashions, and the like.

Second, the convergence has already revealed a list of parallel findings which strengthen theory in both. Several findings that seem most central are:

1. In both urban and rural settings personal influence appears to be more effective in gaining acceptance for change than are the mass media or other types of influence. A number of studies—but by no means all—have found that there is a tendency for adopters of an innovation to credit "other people" with having influenced their decisions. What is of interest, however, is not the precise ranking of the various sources of influence but the undeniable fact that interpersonal communication plays a major role in social and technical change both in the city and on the farm.

2. When decision-making is broken down into phases (e.g., becoming aware of an innovation, becoming interested in it, evaluating it, deciding to try it, etc.), the mass media appear relatively more influential in the

early informational phases, whereas personal influences are more effective in the later phases of deliberation and decision. The tendency in both traditions is no longer to look at the media as competitive but, rather, as complementary by virtue of their function in various phases of an individual's decision.

3. The earliest to accept an innovation are more likely than those who accept later to have been influenced by agricultural agencies, mass media, and other formal and/or impersonal sources, whereas the latter are more likely to be influenced by personal sources (presumably, by the former). Furthermore, the personal sources to which early adopters respond are likely to be outside their own communities, or at a greater distance, than are the personal sources influencing later adopters. The orientation of early adopters—"cosmopolitan," "secular," "urbanized," "scientific" (to choose from among the terms that have been employed)—also reveals an openness to the rational evaluation of a proposed change and a willingness for contact with the world outside their communities. Many of the studies support the notion of a "two-step" flow of communication in which innovators are influenced from outside and in which they, in turn, influence others with whom they have personal contact.

This is not to claim that there are no differences between communication in urban and rural society or that the direction of the difference between the two kinds of communities may not be essentially as originally perceived by social theorists. Nor is it claimed that all research findings are mutually compatible. Instead, the purpose of this paper is to call attention to the image of society implicit in two fields of research on communication, pointing to the influence of such images on the design of research and on "interdisciplinary" contacts, and to call attention to a few remarkably similar findings in these heretofore unrelated fields, suggesting that the study of communication will surely profit from their increasing interchange.

51 Communication Systems and Social Systems: A Statistical Exploration in History and Policy
DANIEL LERNER

People who live together in a common polity develop patterned ways of distributing information, as of distributing other commodities. These patterns of information flow interact at many points with the patterns of power, wealth, status, and other values to form a *system*, i.e., institutional variation in one is accompanied by regular and determinate variations in the others. This paper aims to determine the degree of systemic relationship between communication and other institutions in most of the societies around the world.

We have identified two main types of public communication systems—media and oral. These are differentiated according to the paradigmatic question of communication research: who says what, how, to whom? On these four variables the differences are as follows:

	Media Systems	Oral Systems
Channel	Media (Broadcast)	Oral (Point-to-Point)
Audience	Mass (Heterogeneous)	Primary (Homogeneous)
Source	Professional (Skill)	Hierarchical (Status)
Content	(Descriptive)	(Prescriptive)

Media systems have been described in detail by communication specialists. The main flow of public information is activated by a professional corps of communicators, skilled in producing descriptive messages ("news") for transmission through impersonal "media" (print, film, radio) to relatively undifferentiated mass audiences.

Oral systems we know mainly from the reports of anthropologists. Since preliterate networks are considerably more diverse than media systems (which have an "homogenizing" effect on behavioral styles) their public institutions exhibit much variation. In some oral systems, for example, power is not rigidly hierarchized. In the modal type, however, messages usually emanate from sources authorized to speak by their place

Reprinted with permission of the Mental Health Research Institute and the author. From *Behavioral Science*, 2:266–275 (1957). A revised version of the original article is printed as Chapter II in the author's *The Passing of Traditional Society*, Free Press, New York (1958).

in the social hierarchy, i.e., by status rather than skill criteria. These messages typically appear to be prescriptive rather than descriptive, i.e., announcing the regulations that are to govern audience behavior toward imminent events of community-wide interest, such as tax collections and military drafts. They are transmitted through oral channels to highly differentiated audiences, i.e., the "natural" primary groups of kinship, worship, work, or play. Each of these groups completes the diffusion pattern of an oral network by acting as a relay channel of mouth-to-ear communication within and between groups.

If we accept this terse formulation as satisfactorily differentiating the characteristics of two general models of communication systems, we come next to the problem of describing their occurrence with sufficient accuracy to discriminate consistently between media and oral systems in the observable world. Here we run into trouble, for there are few societies that give a perfect fit to either of these idealized sets of paired comparisons. For example, in Britain, where public communication approximates most closely the model of a media system, people still talk to each other about public issues. Conversely, in Saudi Arabia, which corresponds to the oral system, there is a radio station. In most societies, as we move from the ideal types into empirical data, various elements in the patterns begin to shift. Most societies in the world appear to be in some stage of transition from one pattern to the other.

We notice, however, two general features that appear to be common to all societies. First, the *direction* of change is always from oral to media system (no known case exhibits change in the reverse direction). Second, the *degree* of change in communication behavior appears to correlate significantly with other behavioral changes in the social system. These observations indicate that we are dealing with a secular trend in communication systems, a long-term process of historical change that is unilateral in direction. Moreover, this trend appears to be systemic, since it occurs interdependently with a variety of non-communication factors. From this we derive the proposition that a communication system is both index and agent of change in a total social system. Leaving aside the genetic question of causality (on the view that once the process is started, chicken and egg in fact "cause" each other), the hypothesis may be formulated in a suitable manner for testing as a correlation matrix, viz:

	Type I	Type II
Communication	media	oral
Socioeconomic	urban	rural
Political	representative	nonrepresentative
Cultural	literate	illiterate

Associated with each communication system is a "profile" of economic, political, and cultural attributes. To sharpen the differences, they are stated above in dichotomous fashion. The dogmatic character of such a formulation need trouble no one, however, for empirically we treat them as continuous variables, on which differences are calibrated. Just as there is no perfect media system, so there is no perfectly urban or perfectly representative or perfectly literate society. Our model is probabilistic, our measures are distributive, and our test of fit is correlational.

The precedure was to determine the actual degree of correlation among these indices, for all societies of the world which supplied data. These indices were defined in such fashion as to permit maximum use of the statistical data reported by UNESCO and other U.N. agencies. As the number of countries reporting varies from one index to another, our correlations apply to groups of nations ranging from 54 to 73 in number.

Each index is considered a reliable guide to the state of public participation in its "sector" as a whole. Thus the literacy index, by specifying the proportion of population which can read in one language, is considered to give a fair picture of national participation in the whole cultural sector. Also, the proportion of population actually voting in national elections indexes participation in the whole political sector. Similarly, urbanization, computed as the proportion of population living in cities over 50,000, is taken as an index of participation in the whole economic sector. While urbanization is usually taken more narrowly, as a measure only of occupational distribution, a broader interpretation can be based on previous studies showing high intercorrelations between occupational distribution, per capita income, and literacy.

These indices express degree of participation within four sectors which, in this discussion, can be taken to represent the whole social system. What they differentiate is the participant style of modern democratic societies from the nonparticipant ways of traditional hierarchic societies. By "participant style" we mean here the *frequency*, not the quality, of participation by individuals. The point is simply that *more* individuals receive and use the opportunity to participate, regardless of the "value" of their participation. Accordingly, the items selected to form the communication index also focus on frequency of participation by the general population. These items are: (*a*) circulation of daily newspapers; (*b*) number of radio receivers; (*c*) seating capacity of cinemas. Each of these items was first correlated separately with the other indices. After their separate coefficients had been determined, the three items were handled jointly as a single index. (In all cases they were expressed, for comparability between items and countries, as proportion per 1,000 population.)

TESTING THE COMMUNICATION ITEMS

Each of the three communication items was correlated with the cultural index of literacy. The coefficients, for a group of 73 self-governing countries, were as follows:

Item	Correlation with Literacy
Daily newspaper circulation	.75
Number of radio receivers	.74
Cinema seating capacity	.61

It is obvious that newspaper circulation should correlate better with literacy than does movie attendance, the enjoyment of which does not require literacy. The high correlation of radio receivers leads, for explanation, in another direction. Whereas building cinemas (in which *imported* feature films are shown) requires no advanced technology, the mass production of radio receivers does require a fair rate of industrialization on a high technological level.

The differential rate of industrialization is subsumed, up to a certain determinate point, under our index of urbanization. Having established that a high correlation exists between literacy and media, we now seek to establish that urbanization is interdependent with both. Rising production and distribution of the media usually occur only where and when there is the minimal urbanization required for modern industrial processes. By the same token, urbanization requires rising literacy for industrial participation. At a certain point, when urbanization has done its work, literacy becomes the independent variable in the process of growth and a new phase of modernization begins. But the growth of literacy itself, in this phase, soon becomes closely associated with the growth of media. The media teach literacy, and growing literacy develops the market which consumes the media product. The high coefficients correlating literacy with each of the media suggest that these may be considered as reciprocal causes and effects in a communication market whose locus can only be, at least in its historical inception, urban.

The role of cities becomes clearer if we consider the further suggestion that sheer density of population, without countervailing urbanization, tends to operate as an anti-literacy force in most societies. This appears to be so despite the fact that education is cheaper when pupils live close together and hence, other things being equal, density should be associated with greater literacy. But, in the absence of significant urbanization, other things are *not* equal—i.e., the production, distribution, and consumption of wealth are much lower. This has a direct depressing effect on all public services, notably free public education. In dense nonurban societies, where national income is relatively small, few schools are maintained by public funds; also, since per capita income is lower and less widely distributed, fewer individuals can afford to attend school. Hence, the more people there are in a given area, the smaller is the proportion being educated and the harder it is to get a rising proportion of literates among them—until they begin to be redeployed into cities. In sparsely settled lands the influence of urbanization is less marked and literacy rates will probably respond directly to rises in per capita national income. But in populous societies urbanization is the intervening variable and is crucial for the "take-off" toward increasing literacy. It appears that only when dense populations show a significant rate of urbanization do literacy rates begin to rise. The rise of literacy levels off, however, after a certain degree of urbanization is present in the society. This means that the continued growth of literacy—say, after the society has become half-literate—depends upon some factor other than the continued growth of cities.

The counter-literacy force of sheer population density is evident in the populous Asian societies, such as India and Indonesia, where significant rates of urbanization have not yet occurred. The suggested interplay of density and urbanism as factors conditioning literacy may be represented as follows:

| | | Urbanism | |
		High	Low
Density	High	High (Literacy)	Low (Literacy)
	Low	High (Literacy)	High/Low (Literacy)

To facilitate testing of these relationships between density, urbanization, and literacy, we formulated three distinct hypotheses: (a) that literacy and population density, in areas of low urbanization, vary inversely and exhibit a negative correlation; (b) that the rate of literacy increases positively as the degree of urbanization increases (whether density is low or high); (c) that when urbanization exceeds a determinate figure then literacy will be high, regardless of population density, but will no longer be raised simply by rising urbanization. (No hypothesis is offered under the fourth set of conditions, where *both* urbanization and density are *low*, the impact of rising urbanization upon literacy being indeterminate in this case.)

A more complex formulation would take these three hypotheses together and would seek to determine the triadic conditions under which monotone relations actually obtain between urbanization, density, and literacy. Here we take the simpler course of testing the pairwise relationships by correlation. Our main interest here being to establish the crucial role of urbanization in the early phase of modernizing a social system, we suggest its differential functioning under conditions of low and high density only as a lead for future investigation. In computing these correlations, population density was defined as the number of persons per square kilometer of territory, and urbanization was defined as the proportion of total population living in cities over 50,000. Correlation of literacy with population density gave us a negative coefficient of $-.60$. Inspection of the two sets of figures showed that this inverse relationship was due to the massive nonurban societies—China, India, Indonesia, Egypt, etc. This may be regarded as confirmation of the first hypothesis that sheer density of population, in areas of low urbanization, is a counter-literacy factor—as density rates increase, literacy rates tend to decrease.

Confirmation of the second hypothesis, that literacy *increases* as urbanization increases, was also clear from the coefficient of correlation between these variables: $+.64$. (It should be noted that inaccuracies in the raw statistical data tend to bias the results against this hypothesis. Density is computed by formal territorial jurisdiction rather than effective area of habitation; since the densest countries tend to have the largest "waste" areas this minimizes their actual density. Also the cutting point of 50,000 excludes many cases of genuine urbanization in the less dense and populous countries, where cities of smaller size represent a significant degree of urbanization. Hence, making the raw data more accurate would tend to raise all coefficients in the direction hypothesized.)

Our third hypothesis, that after a certain point in urbanization has been passed literacy is high regardless of other demographic variables, was made more plausible (though not completely confirmed) when we ranked all 73 countries with respect to literacy and urbanization.

Number of Countries	Literacy	Urbanization (Mean)
22	Over 80 percent	28.0 percent
4	61–80	29.2
12	41–60	25.0
13	21–40	17.0
22	Under 20	7.4

Clearly, urbanization is an important factor up to the point at which one-fourth of the population lives in cities over 50,000. The direct and monotonic relationship between literacy and urbanization (the surplus of 1.2 percent in the second row, which contains only four countries is insignificant) is clearest from the time urbanization reaches 10 percent until it passes 25 percent. Beyond this point urbanization levels off, while literacy continues to rise "independently" (in countries of extremely high *and* extremely low population density).

If we take 10 percent and 25 percent as approximate cutting points in the scale of urbanization, we are able to classify societies into three categories which also discriminate quite consistently the degree of literacy and media participation in each society. Let us designate these three categories as Modern, Transitional, Traditional, to mean the following:

	Literacy	Urbanization	Communica-tion System
Modern	Over 61 percent	Over 25 percent	Media
Transitional	21–60	10–25	Media-Oral
Traditional	Under 20	Under 10	Oral

These cutting points are somewhat arbitrary, of course, in the sense that their outcome is partly determined by the statistical input. (Had urbanization been indexed by cities over 20,000 rather than 50,000 population, for example, the upper cutting-point on this continuum might well be located at 20 percent rather than 25 percent.)

The results do enable us, however, to specify two main phases in the process of secular change toward a participant social system. The first phase, speaking summarily, is urbanization. It is the transfer of population from scattered hinterlands to urban centers that provides minimum conditions needed for "take-off" toward widespread participation. Only cities have developed the industrial complex of machines and skills which produces, among other things, newspapers and radio networks and motion pictures. In this first phase, accordingly, increases in urbanization tend in every society to be accompanied by increases in the production and availability of communication media. Once the basic industrial plant is in operation, however, the development of a participant society passes into a subsequent phase. Increasing urbanization, once having provided the initial conditions of production, no longer automatically assures equivalent increases in consumption. The need now shifts to increasing the conditions which govern consumption.

Of this next phase, literacy is both the index and agent, since literacy provides the basic skill required for operation of a media system. Only the literate produce the media contents which, as our literacy-media correlations showed, mainly the literate consume. Hence, in societies which are about 25 percent urbanized, the highest correlation of media consumption is with literacy. Here we wish to stress, in summary fashion, that by the time this modern phase gets well under way, a different social system is in operation than that which governed behavior in a society that was under 10 percent urbanized and under 40–60 percent (roughly, less than half) literate. With higher literacy and media participation comes also increasing availability and use of facilities for participation in all sectors of the social system. An index of this is political participation, which reaches its most developed expression in governance by representation. We refer here to representation that reflects popular choice between real alternatives made through an electoral mechanism that gives one equal vote to every person defined as adult ("universal suffrage").

CHAPTER **XIII**

Intercultural Communication

INTRODUCTION   Within a given culture communication has many complex effects. When communication takes place between two cultures, these effects are even more complex. When messages are transported across cultural boundaries, they are encoded in one context and decoded in another. In these intercultural situations there is little of the coorientation that is a prerequisite for communication in general. This greatly increases the possibility of misunderstanding and of unexpected reactions. This makes intercultural communication a significant illustration and testing ground for hypotheses about communication generally. Moreover, much of our communication is intercultural, as when we read a statement from ancient Athens or modern Moscow, or see a performance from Calcutta or La Paz.

Edward T. Hall and William Foote Whyte show how signals and meanings differ from culture to culture, and they show how this makes the effects of signals quite unusual when they are sent from one culture to another. "Intercultural Communication: A Guide to Men of Action" shows that when a man says anything across cultural boundaries there may be a great difference between what was intended and what was received. The word "maybe" means one thing in the United States and can hardly be translated for export. Much of the difficulty in intercultural communication is not just a matter of understanding such words, but of understanding nonverbal signals that are generally coded so automatically within a single culture that we are quite unconscious of them. The way different peoples perceive and code time and space, for example, is so automatic they are quite unaware of the categories they use. Then when they do use these categories in intercultural communication they "trip over invisible cultural ropes."

The difficulties in intercultural communication vary with the differences in social organization between the cultures and also with the content of the message communicated. S. N. Eisenstadt's "Communication Processes among Immigrants in Israel" shows how different groups of "new" immigrants from different ethnic origins have different kinds of social organization and communicational elites. European immigrants in Israel are organized quite differently from Yemenite immigrants or North African immigrants. Each of these groups must maintain communication within the group to maintain social roles, identifications, and values. Each group must also communicate with established settlers from still other ethnic origins. This often gives rise to new communicational elites that conflict with older elites. In this situation some kinds of elites are more effective with some kinds of messages in intercultural communication, and some kinds of elites change more rapidly than others.

In Samoan society the elites are very important in all kinds of communication. As Felix and Marie Keesing show, "Opinion Formation and Decision Making" is a group responsibility within a hierarchical social organization. This makes it difficult for the Samoans to understand and to accept some Western forms of communication and decision making. Western forms of voting, for example, are based on individual choice, and this is antithetical to the corporate process of making decisions in Samoa. "It is rarely possible in a hierarchical society such as Samoa to get a public expression of individual opinion or minority opinion on any issue that has been 'processed' through the elite leadership system; and any secret polling would be resented." Often we cannot ask a Samoan what he thinks. That is an ineffective question. But we can ask him what his family thinks.

In intercultural communication, as in any kind of communication, the interaction is not determined simply by the situation or the task at hand. Instead the interaction is also shaped and defined by traditional standards and traditional expectations. John W. Bennett and Robert K. McKnight analyze the communication between Japanese and Americans in the light of these "Social Norms, National Imagery, and Interpersonal Relations." The Japanese are more status conscious and think in terms of the social hierarchy, while the Americans are egalitarian and regard others more as persons than as statuses. The effects of communication between these two groups are filtered through these contrasting cultural norms.

52 | Intercultural Communication: A Guide to Men of Action
EDWARD T. HALL
and WILLIAM FOOTE WHYTE

Anyone who has travelled abroad or dealt at all extensively with non-Americans learns that punctuality is
variously interpreted. It is one thing to recognize this with the mind; to
adjust to a different kind of *appointment time* is quite another.

In Latin America, you should expect to spend hours waiting in outer
offices. If you bring your American interpretation of what constitutes
punctuality to a Latin-American office, you will fray your temper and
elevate your blood pressure. For a forty-five-minute wait is not unusual
no more unusual than a five-minute wait would be in the United
States. No insult is intended, no arbitrary pecking order is being established. If, in the United States, you would not be outraged by a five-
minute wait, you should not be outraged by the Latin-American's forty-
five-minute delay in seeing you. The time pie is differently cut, that's all.

Further, the Latin American doesn't usually schedule individual appointments to the exclusion of other appointments. The informal clock of
his upbringing ticks more slowly and he rather enjoys seeing several
people on different matters at the same time. The three-ring circus atmosphere which results, if interpreted in the American's scale of time and
propriety, seems to signal him to go away, to tell him that he is not being
properly treated, to indicate that his dignity is under attack. Not so. The
clock on the wall may look the same but it tells a different sort of time.

The cultural error may be compounded by a further miscalculation.
In the United States, a consistently tardy man is likely to be considered
undependable, and by our cultural clock this is a reasonable conclusion.
For you to judge a Latin American by your scale of time values is to risk
a major error.

Suppose you have waited forty-five minutes and there is a man in his

Reprinted with permission of the Society for Applied Anthropology and the
authors. From *Human Organization*, 19:5–12 (1960).

office, by some miracle alone in the room with you. Do you now get down to business and stop "wasting time"?

If you are not forewarned by experience or a friendly advisor, you may try to do this. And it would usually be a mistake. For, in the American culture, *discussion* is a means to an end: the deal. You try to make your point quickly, efficiently, neatly. If your purpose is to arrange some major affairs, your instinct is probably to settle the major issues first, leave the details for later, possibly for the technical people to work out.

For the Latin American, the discussion is a part of the spice of life. Just as he tends not to be overly concerned about reserving you your specific segment of time, he tends not as rigidly to separate business from non-business. He runs it all together and wants to make something of a social event out of what you, in your culture, regard as strictly business.

The Latin American is not alone in this. The Greek businessman, partly for the same and partly for different reasons, does not lean toward the "hit-and-run" school of business behavior, either. The Greek businessman adds to the social element, however, a feeling about what length of discussion time constitutes good faith. In America, we show good faith by ignoring the details. "Let's agree on the main points. The details will take care of themselves."

Not so the Greek. He signifies good will and good faith by what may seem to you an interminable discussion which includes every conceivable detail. Otherwise, you see, he cannot help but feel that the other man might be trying to pull the wool over his eyes. Our habit, in what we feel to be our relaxed and friendly way, of postponing details until later smacks the Greek between the eyes as a maneuver to flank him. Even if you can somehow convince him that this is not the case, the meeting must still go on a certain indefinite—but, by our standards, long—time or he will feel disquieted.

The American desire to get down to business and on with other things works to our disadvantage in other parts of the world, too; and not only in business. The head of a large, successful Japanese firm commented: "You Americans have a terrible weakness. We Japanese know about it and exploit it every chance we get. You are impatient. We have learned that if we just make you wait long enough, you'll agree to anything."

Whether this is literally true or not, the Japanese executive singled out a trait of American culture which most of us share and which, one may assume from the newspapers, the Russians have not overlooked, either.

By *acquaintance time* we mean how long you must know a man before you are willing to do business with him.

In the United States, if we know that a salesman represents a well-known, reputable company, and if we need his product, he may walk away from the first meeting with an order in his pocket. A few minutes conversation to decide matters of price, delivery, payment, model of product—nothing more is involved. In Central America, local custom does not permit a salesman to land in town, call on the customer and walk away with an order, no matter how badly your prospect wants and needs your product. It is traditional there that you must see your man at least three times before you can discuss the nature of your business.

Does this mean that the South American businessman does not recognize the merits of one product over another? Of course it doesn't. It is just that the weight of tradition presses him to do business within a circle of friends. If a product he needs is not available within his circle, he does not go outside it so much as he enlarges the circle itself to include a new friend who can supply the want. Apart from his cultural need to "feel right" about a new relationship, there is the logic of his business system. One of the realities of his life is that it is dangerous to enter into business with someone over whom you have no more than formal, legal "control." In the past decades, his legal system has not always been as firm as ours and he has learned through experience that he needs the sanctions implicit in the informal system of friendship.

Visiting time involves the question of who sets the time for a visit. George Coelho, a social psychologist from India, gives an illustrative case. A U.S. businessman received this invitation from an Indian businessman: "Won't you and your family come and see us? Come anytime." Several weeks later, the Indian repeated the invitation in the same words. Each time the American replied that he would certainly like to drop in—but he never did. The reason is obvious in terms of our culture. Here "come any time" is just an expression of friendliness. You are not really expected to show up unless your host proposes a specific time. In India, on the contrary, the words are meant literally—that the host is putting himself at the disposal of his guest and really expects him to come. It is the essence of politeness to leave it to the guest to set a time at his convenience. If the guest never comes, the Indian naturally assumes that he does not want to come. Such a misunderstanding can lead to a serious rift between men who are trying to do business with each other.

Time schedules present Americans with another problem in many parts of the world. Without schedules, deadlines, priorities, and timetables, we tend to feel that our country could not run at all. Not only are they essential to getting work done, but they also play an important role in the informal communication process. Deadlines indicate priorities and priorities signal the relative importance of people and the processes they control. These are all so much a part of our lives that a day hardly passes without some reference to them. "I have to be there by 6:30." "If I don't have these plans out by 5:00 they'll be useless." "I told J. B. I'd be finished by noon tomorrow and now he tells me to drop everything and get hot on the McDermott account. What do I do now?"

In our system, there are severe penalties for not completing work on time and important rewards for holding to schedules. One's integrity and reputation are at stake.

You can imagine the fundamental conflicts that arise when we attempt to do business with people who are just as strongly oriented away from time schedules as we are toward them.

The Middle Eastern peoples are a case in point. Not only is our idea of time schedules no part of Arab life but the mere mention of a deadline to an Arab is like waving a red flag in front of a bull. In his culture, your emphasis on a deadline has the emotional effect on him that his backing you into a corner and threatening you with a club would have on you.

One effect of this conflict of unconscious habit patterns is that hundreds of American-owned radio sets are lying on the shelves of Arab radio repair shops, untouched. The Americans made the serious cross-cultural error of asking to have the repair completed by a certain time.

How do you cope with this? How does the Arab get another Arab to do anything? Every culture has its own ways of bringing pressure to get results. The usual Arab way is one which Americans avoid as "bad manners." It is needling.

An Arab businessman whose car broke down explained it this way:

First, I go to the garage and tell the mechanic what is wrong with my car. I wouldn't want to give him the idea that I didn't know. After that, I leave the car and walk around the block. When I come back to the garage, I ask him if he has started to work yet. On my way home from lunch I stop in and ask him how things are going. When I go back to the office I stop by again. In the evening, I return and peer over his shoulder for a while. If I didn't keep this up, he'd be off working on someone else's car.

If you haven't been needled by an Arab, you just haven't been needled.

A PLACE FOR EVERYTHING

We say that there is a time and place for everything, but compared to other countries and cultures we give very little emphasis to place distinctions. Business is almost a universal value with us; it can be discussed almost anywhere, except perhaps in church. One can even talk business on the church steps going to and from the service. Politics is only slightly more restricted in the places appropriate for its discussion.

In other parts of the world, there are decided place restrictions on the discussion of business and politics. The American who is not conscious of the unwritten laws will offend if he abides by his own rather than by the local rules.

In India, you should not talk business when visiting a man's home. If you do, you prejudice your chances of ever working out a satisfactory business relationship.

In Latin America, although university students take an active interest in politics, tradition decrees that a politician should avoid political subjects when speaking on university grounds. A Latin American politician commented to anthropologist Allan Holmberg that neither he nor his fellow politicians would have dared attempt a political speech on the grounds of the University of San Marcos in Peru—as did Vice-President Nixon.

To complicate matters further, the student body of San Marcos, anticipating the visit, had voted that Mr. Nixon would not be welcome. The University Rector had issued no invitation, presumably because he expected what did, in fact, happen.

As a final touch, Mr. Nixon's interpreter was a man in full military uniform. In Latin American countries, some of which had recently overthrown military dictators, the symbolism of the military uniform could hardly contribute to a cordial atmosphere. Latin Americans need no reminder that the United States is a great military power.

Mr. Nixon's efforts were planned in the best traditions of our own culture; he hoped to improve relations through a direct, frank, and face-to-face discussion with students—the future leaders of their country. Unfortunately, this approach did not fit in at all with the culture of the host country. Of course, elements hostile to the United States did their best to capitalize upon this cross-cultural misunderstanding. However, even Latin Americans friendly to us, while admiring the Vice President's courage, found themselves acutely embarrassed by the behavior of their people and ours in the ensuing difficulties.

BEING COMFORTABLE IN SPACE

Like time and place, differing ideas of space hide traps for the uninformed. Without realizing it, almost any person raised in the United States is likely to give an unintended snub to a Latin American simply in the way we handle space relationships, particularly during conversations.

In North America, the "proper" distance to stand when talking to another adult male you do not know well is about two feet, at least in a formal business conversation. (Naturally at a cocktail party, the distance shrinks, but anything under eight to ten inches is likely to provoke an apology or an attempt to back up.)

To a Latin American, with his cultural traditions and habits, a distance of two feet seems to him approximately what five feet would to us. To him, we seem distant and cold. To us, he gives an impression of pushiness.

As soon as a Latin American moves close enough for him to feel comfortable, we feel uncomfortable and edge back. We once observed a conversation between a Latin and a North American which began at one end of a forty-foot hall. At intervals we noticed them again, finally at the other end of the hall. This rather amusing displacement had been accomplished by an almost continual series of small backward steps on the part of the American, trying unconsciously to reach a comfortable talking distance, and an equal closing of the gap by the Latin American as he attempted to reach his accustomed conversation space.

Americans in their offices in Latin America tend to keep their native acquaintances at our distance—not the Latin American's distance—by taking up a position behind a desk or typewriter. The barricade approach to communication is practiced even by old hands in Latin America who are completely unaware of its cultural significance. They know only that they are comfortable without realizing that the distance and equipment unconsciously make the Latin American uncomfortable.

HOW CLASS CHANNELS COMMUNICATION

We would be mistaken to regard the communication patterns which we observe around the world as no more than a miscellaneous collection of customs. The communication pattern of a given society is part of its total culture pattern and can only be understood in that context.

We cannot undertake here to relate many examples of communication behavior to the underlying culture of the country. For the businessman, it might be useful to mention the difficulties in the relationship between social levels and the problem of information feedback from lower to higher levels in industrial organizations abroad.

There is in Latin America a pattern of human relations and union-management relations quite different from that with which we are familiar in the United States. Everett Hagen of MIT has noted the heavier emphasis upon line authority and the lesser development of staff organizations in Latin-American plants when compared with North American counterparts. To a much greater extent than in the United States, the government becomes involved in the handling of all kinds of labor problems.

These differences seem to be clearly related to the culture and social organization of Latin America. We find there that society has been much more rigidly stratified than it has with us. As a corollary, we find a greater emphasis upon authority in family and the community.

This emphasis upon status and class distinction makes it very difficult for people of different status levels to express themselves freely and frankly in discussion and argument. In the past, the pattern has been for the man of lower status to express deference to his superior in any face-to-face contact. This is so even when everyone knows that the subordinate dislikes the superior. The culture of Latin America places a great premium upon keeping personal relations harmonious on the surface.

In the United States, we feel that it is not only desirable but natural to speak up to your superior, to tell the boss exactly what you think, even when you disagree with him. Of course, we do not always do this, but we think that we should, and we feel guilty if we fail to speak our minds frankly. When workers in our factories first get elected to local union office, they may find themselves quite self-conscious about speaking up to the boss and arguing grievances. Many of them, however, quickly learn to do it and enjoy the experience. American culture emphasizes the thrashing-out of differences in face-to-face contacts. It de-emphasizes the importance of status. As a result, we have built institutions for handling industrial disputes on the basis of the local situation, and we rely on direct discussion by the parties immediately involved.

In Latin America, where it is exceedingly difficult for people to express their differences face-to-face and where status differences and authority are much more strongly emphasized than here, the workers tend to look to a third party—the government—to take care of their problems. Though the workers have great difficulty in thrashing out their problems with management, they find no difficulty in telling government representatives their problems. And it is to their government that they look for an authority to settle their grievances with management.

Status and class also decide whether business will be done on an individual or a group basis.

In the United States, we are growing more and more accustomed to working as members of large organizations. Despite this, we still assume that there is no need to send a delegation to do a job that one capable man might well handle.

In some other parts of the world, the individual cannot expect to gain the respect necessary to accomplish this purpose, no matter how capable he is, unless he brings along an appropriate number of associates.

In the United States, we would rarely think it necessary or proper to call on a customer in a group. He might well be antagonized by the hard sell. In Japan—as an example—the importance of the occasion and of the man is measured by whom he takes along.

This practice goes far down in the business and government hierarchies.

Even a university professor is likely to bring one or two retainers along on academic business. Otherwise people might think that he was a nobody and that his affairs were of little moment.

Even when a group is involved in the U.S., the head man is the spokesman and sets the tone. This is not always the case in Japan. Two young Japanese once requested an older American widely respected in Tokyo to accompany them so that they could "stand on his face." He was not expected to enter into the negotiation; his function was simply to be present as an indication that their intentions were serious.

ADJUSTMENT GOES BOTH WAYS

One need not have devoted his life to a study of various cultures to see that none of them is static. All are constantly changing and one element of change is the very fact that U.S. enterprise enters a foreign field. This is inevitable and may be constructive if we know how to utilize our knowledge. The problem is for us to be aware of our impact and to learn how to induce changes skillfully.

Rather than try to answer the general question of how two cultures interact, we will consider the key problem of personnel selection and development in two particular intercultural situations, both in Latin cultures.

One U.S. company had totally different experiences with "Smith" and "Jones" in the handling of its labor relations. The local union leaders were bitterly hostile to Smith, whereas they could not praise Jones enough. These were puzzling reactions to higher management. Smith seemed a fair-minded and understanding man; it was difficult to fathom how anyone could be bitter against him. At the same time, Jones did not appear to be currying favor by his generosity in giving away the firm's assets. To management, he seemed to be just as firm a negotiator as Smith.

The explanation was found in the two men's communication characteristics. When the union leaders came in to negotiate with Smith, he would let them state their case fully and freely—without interruption, but also without comment. When they had finished, he would say, "I'm sorry. We can't do it." He would follow this blunt statement with a brief and entirely cogent explanation of his reasons for refusal. If the union leaders persisted in their arguments, Smith would paraphrase his first statement, calmly and succinctly. In either case, the discussion was over in a few minutes. The union leaders would storm out of Smith's office complaining bitterly about the cold and heartless man with whom they had to deal.

Jones handled the situation differently. His final conclusion was the same as Smith's—but he would state it only after two or three hours of discussion. Furthermore, Jones participated actively in these discussions, questioning the union leaders for more information, relating the case in question to previous cases, philosophizing about labor relations and human rights and exchanging stories about work experience. When the discussion came to an end, the union leaders would leave the office, commenting on how warmhearted and understanding he was, and how confident they were that he would help them when it was possible for him to do so. They actually seemed more satisfied with a negative decision from Jones than they did with a hard-won concession from Smith.

This was clearly a case where the personality of Jones happened to match certain discernible requirements of the Latin American culture. It was happenstance in this case that Jones worked out and Smith did not, for by American standards both were top-flight men. Since a talent for the kind of negotiation that the Latin American considers graceful and acceptable can hardly be developed in a grown man (or perhaps even in a young one), the basic problem is one of personnel selection in terms of the culture where the candidate is to work.

The second case is more complicated because it involves much deeper intercultural adjustments. The management of the parent U.S. company concerned had learned—as have the directors of most large firms with good-sized installations overseas—that one cannot afford to have all of the top and middle-management positions manned by North Americans. It is necessary to advance nationals up the overseas-management ladder as rapidly as their abilities permit. So the nationals have to learn not only the technical aspects of their jobs but also how to function at higher levels in the organization.

Latin culture emphasizes authority in the home, church, and community. Within the organization this produces a built-in hesitancy about speaking up to one's superiors. The initiative, the acceptance of responsibility which we value in our organizations had to be stimulated. How could it be done?

We observed one management man who had done a remarkable job of building up these very qualities in his general foremen and foremen. To begin with, he stimulated informal contacts between himself and these men through social events to which the men and their wives came. He saw to it that his senior North American assistants and their wives were also present. Knowing the language, he mixed freely with all. At the plant, he circulated about, dropped in not to inspect or check up, but to joke and to break down the great barrier that existed in the local traditions between authority and the subordinates.

Next, he developed a pattern of three-level meetings. At the top, he himself, the superintendents, and the general foremen. At the middle level, the superintendents, general foremen, and foremen. Then the general foremen, foremen, and workers.

At the top level meeting, the American management chief set the pattern of encouraging his subordinates to challenge his own ideas, to come up with original thoughts. When his superintendents (also North Americans) disagreed with him, he made it clear that they were to state their objections fully. At first, the general foreman looked surprised and uneasy. They noted, however, that the senior men who argued with the boss were encouraged and praised. Timorously, with great hesitation, they began to add their own suggestions. As time went on, they more and more accepted the new convention and pitched in without inhibition.

The idea of challenging the boss with constructive new ideas gradually filtered down to the second and third level meetings. It took a lot of time and gentle handling, but out of this approach grew an extraordinary morale. The native general foremen and foremen developed new pride in themselves, accepted new responsibilities, even reached out for more. They began to work to improve their capacities and to look forward to moving up in the hierarchy.

53 Communication Processes among Immigrants in Israel
S. N. EISENSTADT

The study here reported, part of a larger research project on the absorption of new immigrants in Israel, is mainly concerned with two interdependent problems: (1) the place of the process of communication within the social structure, and (2) the conditions under which this process is effective or ineffective. The basic assumption of our investigation is that in order to ascertain what kinds of communications influence different types of people under different social and psychological conditions, it is first necessary to locate the place and structure of the process of communication within the social system in which these people participate. Of special importance from this point of view are the types of social roles and persons—the "leaders" or "influentials"—who perform specific functions as transmitters of communication within the social system. We have tried to follow up some of the conclusions and insights of former studies, especially those of Lazarsfeld and associates and of Merton, which indicated the importance of

Reprinted with permission of the publisher and the author. From *The Public Opinion Quarterly*, 16:42–58 (1952).

analyzing different status-positions, persons, and personal relations as loci and channels of communication within different social groups.

This report is based mainly on investigations conducted in four immigrant settlements: two agricultural cooperative settlements, one semi-urban, and one urban settlement. While comparative data have been gathered from a much wider sample, the present analysis is based on 250 families, coming from the following countries and regions: 60 from Yugoslavia, 65 from Yemen, 85 from North Africa, and 40 from Eastern and Central Europe. Almost all of these families settled in more or less compact, ethnically homogenous clusters (except for the European families which were not dispersed).

The field-work was carried out from October, 1949, to November, 1950, and dealt mainly with "new" immigrants; i.e., those who had arrived after the establishment of the State of Israel. At the time our field work was completed, the average "new" immigrant had been in Israel for approximately 19 months.

COMMUNICATIONS TO WHICH THE IMMIGRANTS WERE EXPOSED

The main types of communications to which the immigrants were exposed may be distinguished by content, since in all of them both oral and written media were used.

(1) Communications related to the economic sphere. The main purpose of these was (a) to direct the immigrants to the different working opportunities, housing and relief facilities, etc., available to them, and (b) to impress upon them their own duties in these areas. These communications emanated from the main absorbing agencies: the Absorption Department of the Jewish Agency and the Labour Exchange. It is quite obvious that these types of communication were among the first, the most constant, and most permanent to which the immigrants were exposed.

(2) Cultural and educational communications. The main purposes here were to induce the immigrants (a) to send their children to the different types of schools and to participate in the social life of the school (parents' committees, etc.), (b) to study the Hebrew language in evening classes, and (c) to participate in different cultural activities (lectures, folk-dances, festivals, etc.). This type of communication came mainly from the different civic authorities responsible for dealing with the new immigrants, and also to some extent from representatives of different political parties. In this category we may also include the various recreational mass media, especially motion pictures, which were provided for the immigrants, usually by private persons or proprietors.

(3) Political communication and propaganda. The central purposes of these communications were (a) to instruct the immigrants in their basic

civic rights and duties, particularly in the realm of local government (this aspect was very strongly emphasized in the agricultural cooperative settlements), and (b) to induce them to enroll in the various political parties. While the civic authorities were still active in this field, the most important part was played by the party representatives.

THE EFFECTIVENESS OF COMMUNICATIONS

The extent of the immigrants' exposure to these different types of communication may be seen from the fact that when asked whether they had received any "economic" communications, or heard or knew of them, all of the immigrants answered affirmatively. The exposure figure was 85 percent for the "cultural" communications, and 80 percent in the "political" category. But to what extent were these different kinds of communication successful? In order to be able to answer this question, we must first distinguish between two main aspects of communication effects.

The effectiveness of any communication can best be judged by the number of immigrants who have undertaken to perform new roles and to participate permanently in different activities and organizations. These new roles have two principal aspects. The first is primarily a technical one involving some minimal orientations connected with role performance (such as the routine of applying for work, keeping and signing different relief papers, etc.). The second aspect may be called the fully institutional one: the performance of all the activities connected with a specific role and a full understanding of its institutional meaning. In regard to work, for example, such an understanding would entail willingness to learn new skills and to participate intelligently with supervisors and fellow-workers. It is obvious that the first aspect can be learned and performed without the second—at least for some time. This distinction is of great importance in our study because (a) every communication which purports to direct behavior must necessarily touch both of these aspects, and (b) the effectiveness of communications differed greatly with respect to them.

In the primary situation of absorption, the technical aspects had an essentially compulsory character; without learning them, the immigrants could not satisfy their minimal basic needs. The technical aspect was more prominent in the economic fields (and to some extent also in the educational field) than in the cultural and political areas. In all these fields, however, it was found that the immigrants learned the technical requirements of their roles much sooner and more fully than they learned the institutional ones. Many of them stopped at the technical level. They themselves would emphasize the necessity of mastering these aspects in order to satisfy their basic needs. This connection was quite clear to them, but the meaning and importance of their institutional roles were not. The distribution of effective communications in different spheres among different types of immigrants is shown in Table 1. The data clearly demonstrate the greater effectiveness of communications relating to technical role performance.

Table 1

Percentage of Immigrants (by Countries of Origin) Affected by Communications in Different Spheres

Country of origin	Economic Sphere		Cultural Sphere			Political Sphere	
	Tech. Comm.	Insti. Comm.	Tech. Comm.	Insti. Comm.	Recrea- tion	Tech. Comm.	Insti. Comm.
I. At the end of 6 months							
Yemen	70	50	25	20	5	25	25
Yugoslavia	85	60	65	55	40	75	60
North Africa	75	45	40	25	25	45	35
Central & Eastern Europe	85	60	70	45	45	75	45
II. At the end of 12 months							
Yemen	85	65	45	40	15	50	45
Yugoslavia	95	80	80	70	45	90	85
North Africa	90	55	45	35	45	60	50
Central & Eastern Europe	90	60	75	55	55	70	50

The table also suggests that although the effectiveness of communication is not equally distributed among different cultural and ethnic groups, these differences in themselves cannot account for the differences in effectiveness. At this stage we must look for more dynamic and specific causes in the conditions under which effectiveness may vary.

THE PROCESS OF TRANSMISSION OF COMMUNICATION: THE PLACE OF THE "ELITES"

The first condition analyzed was the process of transmission of communication from various officials, propagandists, and leaders to the immigrants. Three main types of transmission may be distinguished: (1) direct, impersonal appeals to the whole group of immigrants in meetings, or through newspapers, proclamations, and the like; (2) personal appeal to a specific individual or small group by an official; (3) transmission of communication through communal leaders of different types.

From Table 2 it can be seen that the most effective way of transmitting communication is through communal leaders, while formal, impersonal contact is least effective. What is the exact role of these leaders in the communications process? The main explanations were given by the immigrants themselves when asked for their reactions to different communicative efforts. They emphasized that these leaders (or, as we may more accurately call them, "elites") serve for them as main transmitters of communication relating to the "wider" aspects and problems of the social structure. They are the main communicators of the system's ultimate values and problems, and only those communications which are transmitted through them are fully accepted by the immigrants. As one immigrant put it: "I have heard about these things which the party-man told us when they tried to make us join their party. But in all these things we know that we have to rely on our teachers and rabbis as they understand these things much better than we do; and if they would have thought it right, they would have told us themselves." Or, to take another example: "We have joined in these cultural activities mainly because the chairman of our organization and *A* (a leading intellectual-teacher in a settlement) have talked about it with us and have persuaded us that it is good and worthwhile. In all these matters we rely very much on them and we would heed them much more than any stranger." This emphasis on the role of elites as transmitters of communications was stressed in either a positive or a negative way by about 75 percent of the immigrants in our sample.

Table 2

Effectiveness of Communications (in Percentage of People Affected by Them), According to Channels of Transmission

	6 Months	12 Months
Formal, impersonal	10	15
Personal appeal from official to immigrant	25	35
Through leaders (elites)	65	55
	100%	105%

The transmission of communications through the elites, however, is not in itself sufficient to assure its effectiveness; this can be clearly seen from Table 2. Some other conditions are necessary to assure effectiveness of communication. Among these conditions two seem to be of greatest importance: first, the way in which the communication is transmitted from the elites to the immigrants; and second, the extent of the elites' agreement with the communication transmitted to them. As for the first condition, it was established that the effectiveness of communication is dependent on its transmission from the elites in more or less face-to-face relations of essentially a primary character. We have carefully investigated those cases where the communication through the elites was not effective; in about 60 percent of them it was found that either the elites tried to transmit the communication in a formal, impersonal way in which the element of authority prevailed, or that the immigrants themselves were not prepared to maintain personal relations with the elites. Communication is effective only insofar as it is transmitted in a more direct, personal way in which the element of authority is intermingled with primary relations and identifications. About 65 percent of our interviewees stressed the point (with different degrees of insight) that their acceptance of their elites' guidance and communication is dependent on its being transmitted in this way. "We do not want only to hear orders from far-away people, even if they are very wise and know everything. Our rabbis know that the best way is to gather all of us in the synagogue and to tell us all about it and to explain it to us. Otherwise, we do not listen. . . ." "Our secretary has of late acquired the habit of telling us what to do—in important matters and not only in some minor details—by putting written notices on the board and just telling us that this is the right thing to do, that he knows it better. It is quite possible that he knows it better, but in this way he will not get anything. . . . We want to understand, and the best way is to have an open talk about everything, whenever it is important. . . ." The infusion of primary personal elements into the hierarchal elite-non-elite relationship is, then, of crucial importance in the maintenance of effective institutional communications. Although no full analysis has been attempted here, the data seem to indicate that the maintenance of personal relations is a more basic condition for the effectiveness of communications than transmission through elites, and that the latter must be built on the former. This does not apply, however, to merely technical communications or to those based solely on compulsion.

The remaining cases of non-effective communication transmitted through the elites were due to the second factor; namely, the elites' lack of agreement with the content and purpose of communication transmitted to them. Whenever such consensus was lacking, the elites would block the further transmission of a communication either by simply ignoring it, or by using their own influence to counteract its impact on the immigrants. Significantly enough, most of these cases occurred in the cultural field where the elites (especially the traditional elites) had definite orientations which quite often were incompatible with those offered by the representatives of the absorbing social system. The same situation existed for some time within the modern recreational field; communications in this area had little effect on traditional elites or on those coming from regions where most of the types of entertainment (principally American films) were alien. The extent of such incompatibility was much smaller within both the economic and the political fields, although it also existed here. Within these fields, the elites' failure to transmit a communication was usually due more to apathy and lack of active interest than to active disagreement and incompatibility.

CULTURAL DIFFERENCES

While this general orientation existed within all the immigrant ethnic groups, some very important differences can be discerned in the exact structuring of the elites' communicative function. In the more traditional groups, like the Yemenites (and to some extent also the North African Jews), there was a relatively small differentiation between different leaders and elites, and the traditional religious, and economic elite enjoyed a virtual monopoly of communication. The only distinction was that the economic elite was more concerned with relations with the "outside world" than the religious elite.

Among the different groups of European immigrants, however, there existed a greater differentiation between elites. This differentiation had a double aspect. On the one hand, the difference between functional specialists and general "communal leaders" (or between the monomorphic and polymorphic types, to use Merton's nomenclature) is clearly discernible. On the other hand, a greater emphasis evolves, especially in the second type, between those whose activities are mainly oriented to the immediate community and those who concentrate on broader country-wide affairs.

The same distinctions affect the process of communication transmission by the elites. While the insistence on personal relations (which do not exclude, however, some degree of differential allocation of authority) exists in both cultural types, the social situations in which they occur differ to a very great extent. Within the traditional groups, they are mostly confined to traditionally defined situations which are specifically constructed as focal-points of communication-transmission. Some of the most outstanding examples are: (1) the daily, or more usually, weekly (Sabbath) gatherings in the synagogue in which the traditional elites expound their views on different matters almost ex-cathedra, and answer questions directed towards them; (2) the juridical meetings of the elites in which they act as arbitration (traditional) judges; and (3) the meetings in traditional schools. The extent of informal, spontaneous groupings and discussions in which elites and non-elites participate is usually very small; they are usually restricted to pure non-elite membership, and they do not have the same influence in regard to wider problems as they have in the more ritually prescribed situations.

Within the modern groups the situation is different. The range of clearly prescribed situations in which communication transmission takes place is usually confined to general meetings of a settlement, and the like. The number of more informal occasional groupings and discussions in which all may participate and which may be initiated by non-elite members, is much larger than it is in the traditional groups, where there is very little discussion among members after the elites have transmitted communications. At the same time, the functional differentiation within the elite also gives rise to a more specifically "professional" communication and advice-taking, usually confined to some definite technical problems.

CHANGES IN THE EFFECTIVENESS OF COMMUNICATION: THE CAUSES

Hitherto we have analyzed the communication process without accounting for the changes in communication effectiveness over a period of time. The analysis of these changes is of interest not only as an indicator of trends in public opinion, but also, and perhaps mainly, because it can throw some light on the basis and reasons for the elites' specific position within the communication process. We indicated earlier the importance of this position without explaining it thoroughly. Our problem here is why, and under what conditions do the elites succeed in preserving their focal position as communicators? The analysis of trends of change can help us to solve this problem.

The changes which took place in the second half of our investigation can be summarized in the following way: (1) There was a constant increase in the efficacy of technical communication. (2) There was a constant increase in the efficacy of communication which reached the immigrants not through their own leaders but through personal contacts with officials, teachers, and through some new persons from their own midst aspiring to positions of leadership. (3) There was an increase in the effective exposure to recreational mass communication, especially in the urban and semi-urban centers. (4) The increase in effectiveness of communication occurred in all fields, but mainly in the political and cultural areas.

Our analysis is mainly focused on the last three changes and is based on interviews and observations of those people who disattached themselves, as it were, from their former elites and developed a greater predisposition to receive the communication transmitted to them from representatives of the absorbing social system. What were the causes of this development? When asked about their reasons for disattaching themselves from their former elites, the immigrants answered in a great variety of ways and pointed out various practical difficulties. Interwoven through their answers, however, were some main themes which reflected the immigrants' social definition of these difficulties.

(1) *Growing disillusionment about the elites' ability to assure them of various amenities and rights accruing to them in the new social system.* This disillusionment is usually felt first in the economic field and only gradually extends to the other areas. It gives rise to scepticism in the immigrants' reception of elite-transmitted communications, for these communications are not effective in orienting them to their new roles. While in the first stages this disillusionment is confined mainly to the technical aspects, its scope increases gradually so as to reflect on the elites' standing within the entire social system.

(2) *Doubts as to the elites' prestige-positions within the new social system.* This is closely related to the first theme. As one immigrant put it: "In our place they were really very important and honored as they knew everything about our tradition, how to arrange things, the right ways to behave. But here it changes, it is otherwise. . . . They do not always understand this and they cannot help us in getting our way here. That is why I became interested in the new (political) organizations and frequent these meetings. The organizers are here really important people and know how to advise you, and so some of us are going there." This point of view was emphasized in about 60 percent of the interviews.

(3) *Disillusionment with the elites' ability to interpret the new social system and its values to the immigrants.* This is, of course, closely related to the second objection, but it emphasizes another aspect of the problem: "We are often bewildered here and they confuse us only more. They do not understand how one should arrange things here, why it is different here, what the most important things are in the State and among people. They speak as if we were still in Algiers, without trying to understand the organization here. Our instructor, however, and some of the people from X (a nearby settlement) show a much greater understanding of all these problems. Because of this, we do not listen any longer to these confusing explanations of the old people and associate much more with these people from X, and some of the organizers. It is true that we do not like everything they do, but I think it is much more sensible to listen to them and then to judge. . . ." This theme was emphasized by a somewhat greater percentage of interviewees, about 70 percent. All these themes seem to converge into the following two common foci which are stressed and emphasized to a much larger extent, and which come out especially in critical situations.

(4) *The feeling that attachment to the old elites blocks their achievement of full status within the new society.* This, together with the next theme, are the most powerful motivations responsible for changes in re-

sponsiveness to communication. These themes were emphasized in various forms and with different depths of insight in about 85 percent of the interviews:

They want to remain as in the old days, but this is not good here. If we shall do it here, we shall remain strangers. Nobody will really pay attention to us, or honor us.

If we do not change quickly and do not listen to these old people, we shall always remain at the bottom . . . unimportant people. . . .

(5) *The loss of a feeling of participation in the new social system and of belongingness to it as a result of clinging to the old elites.* "Lately I began to feel that whenever I meet the old leader, whenever they try to explain things to us, to organize us, I live in our imaginary world, a world of yesterday. I feel they really do not belong here. They are trying to keep us in our old life. But I feel that we really belong to the new life here, and that they are real obstructions on our way here. Whenever they talk to us, I have the feeling of being taken out of this new country, of not belonging here. I try not to get in touch with them, but to go on a new way."

The changes in the process of communication and in its transmitters have not in most cases affected its formal structure. Whenever a change occurred, it resulted in the replacement of one type of leader and transmitter of communication by another type or types; only rarely has it resulted in the lack of development of personal relations with any leaders whatsoever. In about 40 cases, most of them from urban and semi-urban centers such development did take place. It is interesting to note that these are the families within which most of the increased participation in the modern mass media of entertainment took place. Most of these families were members of traditional and semi-traditional groups to whom this kind of recreation is entirely alien. Some came from Europe. Among all of them, however, a definite increase in this direction took place. The interviews, and also some direct observations, suggest that a very powerful motive for vicarious identification and for anonymous, non-institutional participation in recreational situations was responsible for this increase. The longing for some sort of identification and participation was very often related to feelings of complete loss of effective social contacts, of disillusionment with old ways coupled with inability to find social and psychological security within the new setting or to communicate within it: "You ask me why I go so often to the motion pictures. I do not know . . . I do not really understand them, but we feel very lonely here. We do not always understand the people around us. . . . In the cinema it is different. We are all alike, it is pleasant there, so many people, all enjoying it, and we enjoy it also, being together. No, we do not know most of the people, perhaps it would be good to know them . . . but at least the pictures are nice and it is nice to see them."

Although the number of cases is very small and our conclusions are necessarily very tentative, the relation between the loss of institutionally-patterned personal communication with elites (and, consequently, of a feeling of social participation) and the exposure to the mass media of recreation is very suggestive.

CONCLUSIONS

We may now attempt to summarize some of the main conclusions of this study: All the following propositions should be seen as tentative ones and in need of further elaboration and amplification. They relate mainly to the functions that the processes of communication fulfill both within (and for) the social system, and for the individuals who participate in that system. Most of the explicit conclusions of our study relate to the second problem, but some more implicit conclusions can also be drawn in relation to the first. Although most of the conclusions are couched in sociological terms, they do not assume that the more frequently used psychological approach is not relevant. In our view both approaches are complementary and the problem of communication can be understood only through their interpenetration.

(1) One of the main functions of communication within the social system is to maintain effective performance of social roles inherent in it, to assure full social participation within its various spheres, and to maintain the members' identification with its ultimate values and symbols.

(2) The process of communication is therefore conducted within specific channels and through specific persons whose positions within the social system are structured in such a way as to maximize the degree of fulfillment of these functions. Among the channels, two are most important: (a) close, primary, interpersonal relations in which basic mutual identifications are maintained; and (b) persons and agencies in positions of leadership who perform roles of elites within different spheres of the social system. The incumbents of these positions (and those aspiring to these positions) originate and transmit communications and manipulate symbols to other members of the system—particularly symbols related to the performance of social roles and behavior and to identification with the ultimate values and main symbols of the system.

(3) The specific structuring of these functions differs from one social system to another according to its principles of authority, system of values, functional specialization and division of labor. Within most social systems, however, ritual and festive situations serve as foci of intensive

communication in which the ultimate values of the social system are mediated to its members.

(4) The individual is most receptive to those communications which help him to satisfy various needs, and specifically to perform different status-conferring roles.

(5) The effectiveness of any communication directed to the performance of roles, etc., is therefore dependent on:

(a) its positive function in conferring and maintaining status aspirations and identifications (i.e., being compatible with the status images and aspirations of the receivers of communication).

(b) its being originated by prestige-bearing elites or mediated through them.

(c) its being compatible with the cultural orientations and social interests of the elites.

(d) its being transmitted by the elites in personal primary relations which are interwoven within the structure of hierarchy between the elites and non-elites.

(e) its being assimilated through personal interaction in primary groups and relations.

(6) The effectiveness of any communication or communication system is minimized whenever there exists no compatibility between the various conditions mentioned under (5).

(7) The security of the elites' position as transmitters of effective communication is dependent on their ability to perform, through the process of communication, the following functions for the non-elite members: (a) to help them in achieving and maintaining their various statuses within the social structure; (b) to mediate to them successfully the broader problems and ultimate values of the social system; (c) to enhance their prestige aspirations through identification with bearers of prestige; and (d) to enhance their feeling of participation and belongingness to the social system and their understanding of its working.

(8) Whenever the elites cannot perform these functions, the effectiveness of their communication is minimized and the non-elite members become predisposed to receive communication from other persons or groups aspiring to elite-status.

(9) Whenever the contact between elite and non-elite members is severed without any personal relation with new elites being established, the non-elite members become predisposed to participation in media which confer on them vicarious identification and anonymous participation in the social system. The most outstanding example of such media are the mass-communication media of modern society.

54 Opinion Formation and Decision-Making
FELIX MAXWELL KEESING
and MARIE MARGARET KEESING

In orally transmitted cultures such as that of Samoa, communication processes especially among elite persons may come to have something of the character of an "art" or "game." In the traditional setting, at least, virtually the whole gamut of situations and problems which individuals may be called on to face have occurred more or less regularly, and solutions for them tend to be institutionalized in the forms of patterned behavior. With the content of communication in the sense of the range of actions and expectations rather fixed, the techniques of communication themselves have become a focus of interest.

Many observers have made this point directly or inferentially: "Samoan leaders delight in talking"; "Samoans loved discussion for its own sake"; "What is enjoyed and sought is not the decision but the prolonged drama of the *fono* proceedings." "A speaker is applauded not for what he says but for his control of the nuances of the speaking art." The analogy of a "game" particularly brings out the fact that deliberation and negotiation have a recognized set of rules and objectives—the "ideal" behavior; but interest moves beyond the "basic strokes" which all must master to the purposeful breaking of the "correct" order by those with virtuosity. Within the defined bounds there exists in "real" behavior many kinds of variability in the communication processes: the graceful performance of what is expected; the high pressure competition; the exciting gambit; the trick play; the daring maneuver; the disguised stroke; the dangerous edge beyond which essential rules are infringed. Tensions here may bring open breaks, so that the individual may suffer ignominious failure or more or less serious penalties. The communication "arts" provide an area of life in which the Samoans move with such certainty that it is as "normative" to deviate as to conform, and pleasure, excitement, and honor tend to march with virtuosity in deviation.

The question inevitably arises as to how far the Samoan communication techniques prove efficient or inefficient in the face of modern acculturation conditions and needs. All kinds of new problems have arisen

Reprinted from *Elite Communication in Samoa: A Study in Leadership*, pp. 91–129, by Felix M. Keesing and Marie M. Keesing with the permission of the publishers, Stanford University Press. © Copyright 1956 by the Board of Trustees of the Leland Stanford Junior University.

which have required realistic decisions. Samoan councils have been faced with new tasks and constitutional procedures especially by government edict. Samoan leaders have had to negotiate with Europeans having very different communication techniques, e.g., "Roberts' rules of order," much more emphasis on the decision-making objective, "democratic" representation, voting. With increasing self-government they have become participants along with Europeans in Western-type assemblies. How far, then, has it been possible to reconcile Samoan and Western communication behaviors?

"Messages" leading to opinion formation may originate, in Samoa as elsewhere, from any point where a problem occurs. The matter may be gossiped about or otherwise talked about, opinions formed, and stands taken, at the level of the ordinary people if it is not a concern subject to elite notice and judgment.

Local elite persons are likely to hear of problems under discussion. They will object if in their judgment any issue has an elite angle and is not brought to their attention. Inversely they will push the matter aside if they think it is not appropriate to their status.

An issue brought to the attention of an elite person may be such that he can render a personal decision outright. This, however, is very much the exception rather than the rule. It would be one of the usually few matters over which, by individual right, or by deliberately delegated authority, he already commands an absolute power (*pule*): say, disposal of a specific piece of land or of the products of certain trees, or directing a work party to undertake a given task. In the overwhelming number of instances the elite person would have to initiate a group deliberative process: this means, in Samoa, meetings of appropriate assemblies, usually of the *fono* or "council" type.

Reference of a problem to the appropriate group or groups assumes very great importance. As noted earlier a titleholder is essentially a responsible group representative. His "voice" is correspondingly a group voice. He must therefore correctly consult back to his adherent supporters as well as deal with his peers or superiors. In earlier discussions we set out the formal and informal organizations or "collectivities" which might provide "voices" in a traditional deliberation process: the household, close kin, and community assemblies and the supravillage elite or *matai* assemblies of extended family, regional, and "all Samoa" character. Which deliberating group would be appropriate to handling a given problem is defined by tradition and custom: one involving the roles of untitled persons would, for example, be dealt with in household consultations or the interested community-level council. Concerns of the extended family units such as the naming of a major titleholder would call for joint deliberations by the various kin branches. Distinctive elite concerns, such as the naming of a spokesman from one council level to a higher council level would touch the sub-elite groupings lightly if at all.

Whether or not, in a given problem situation, all adherents of a given titleholder are actually consulted, the weight of their support is nevertheless ideally always there as a generalized "voice," back of his personal "voice." *In principle, adherents of an elite person share a collective responsibility, which implies in turn the right to be consulted and so to exercise at least an indirect control over the titleholder.* Samoan elite representation involves one "voice" or vote per power bloc (i.e., the adherent group), not one to each individual person as such.

In the sections which follow, therefore, it must never be forgotten that each elite member, in speaking publicly, has by implication his group back of him. For his part the titleholder can never afford to neglect the fact that the power to make or unmake his authority lies with his adherents. He as an individual is bearing the title and role with their consent, and if he fails to carry these with dignity, honor, and satisfaction in his supporters' eyes he can be rendered powerless, replaced, and even banished or otherwise punished. At all levels the titleholder who loses the support of his group is liable to repudiation, even though in practice this seems to have very low incidence. Having this support he may engage in conduct which the outside observer might judge as being "authoritarian," "arbitrary," even overbearing, and yet continue to receive respect, veneration, and service.

The sensitivity of the elite person to the group he represents tends to be a paramount factor in shaping his public positions. At the village-council level this is not so significant as at higher organizational levels. The interests of the community and its constituent households and their close kin groups tend strongly to coincide with those of the titleholders in the village council. In wider consultations, however, the elite person is not only likely to put the interest of his own community and immediate kin adherents first, but indeed has virtually a duty to do so. Only slowly, and with constant likelihood of conflicts, are wider sensitivities and loyalties gaining in balance—a problem of course not confined to Samoa.

The adherent group is here spoken of as if it were an entity. But where higher or senior titles are involved, a great array of adherent "voices" may have to be channeled in to make a single "voice." The item under consideration may be passed up and down, back and forth, through a number of echelons ranging from the "grass root" non-elite views at a variety of household, close kin, and community levels over Samoa, through village councils and perhaps several levels of *matai* councils representative of village, district, or great kin aggregations. Less formal consultations of many kinds may also take place depending on idiosyncratic and other variables. This is quite comparable with the process in a government office or business where a memorandum may not only have to be "cleared" across a number of established desks, but also requires informal conferences of line and staff character.

The elite person is also sensitive to the opinions of those of equal or higher authority. Emphasis has been laid to this point upon consultation "downward" to the hierarchically lower adherent group. The elite person, with the rare exception of the titleholders in supreme authority, is also likely to have to consult "outward" to peers or near peers, and "upward" on matters of serious importance to the titleholders of higher rank within the kin group or geographic alignment. As a chief put it: "The respected traditional habit of this country . . . is to refer matters to other posts of dignity." Even where authority has definitely been delegated to the lower ranking person or status position this may often be considered wise. A lower ranking titleholder can hardly afford the risk of finding himself aligned against a person of equal or higher authority with whom he has interlocking relationships. In a matter of serious ramifications he might want to consult a number of higher titleholders. Such "voices" might be brought into play directly or kept behind the scenes. In the latter case their existence is likely to be well known and taken into account in any deliberation process.

Certain resemblances between such deliberative processes, and forms of elite communication in Western society are obvious. The following propositions might be postulated as appearing to have considerable common application:

1. *Elite decisions tend to involve group responsibility rather than individual responsibility.*
2. *Elite decisions tend to be made only after problems have been brought into sharpest possible focus, usually in multiple consultations at a variety of hierarchical levels.*
3. *To be effective the views of an elite person, or a decision made by an elite group, must have marshaled behind it a weight of support from the adherent, the peer, and the superior groups concerned.*
4. *An understanding of elite decisions calls for analysis of all the "voices" involved, with their inherent rights and responsibilities.*

A broad but significant illustration of the way traditional systems can dispense with formal distinctions and divisions of function is the lack of a stimulus among the Samoans to separate the legislative, executive, and judicial facets of decision-making. The same elite leader or council moves easily across the arc of deliberation in all these spheres. In the modern setting, the government authorities have been unable, despite efforts, to separate clearly the powers of a district representative as between legislative and executive authority, and find it difficult enough to keep him from those judicial spheres which have been assigned to judges, the more so as he freely exercises these facets of authority in his own Samoan spheres. Even in American Samoa, with the strong official emphasis on the American values involved in the separation of these responsibilities, progress is exceedingly slow in getting such a system understood and practiced. In elections of 1955, however, the American governor declared that no district executive official could be a candidate for legislative office; Samoan leaders holding such posts, and hitherto used to sitting in the legislature, were thus forced to make a choice. The problem specialist, sitting eight hours a day in his office, waiting for the social system to feed him technical business, is still a rare and mainly a very recent phenomenon in the Samoan setting.

Voting, in the broad sense of giving the "franchise" or "universal suffrage" to Samoan adults at large has only very recently been considered as a feasible possibility. It is significant that the Samoan term *palota*, a "vote," Samoanized from the English word "ballot," is one of the few modern political concepts for which an indigenous Samoan term does not appear to have emerged, adapted as necessary, into standardized usage. Discussion has centered particularly on the issue as to whether representatives at the higher levels might be elected at large "by popular vote" instead of by a hierarchy of representatives on behalf of the mass base of adherent groups. This, to many observers who want "democracy" in Samoa, has been the missing element. While the election principle could hardly involve at this time in Samoan history the naming of a "royal" *Fautua* to his governmental post—Western Samoa is in the British tradition—is it not reasonable, they ask, for membership in regular legislative bodies and for some representative executive posts to be subject to general suffrage?

Western-style "voting" has been introduced selectively into modern governmental bodies in which Samoan leaders participate, as in the Western Samoa Legislative Assembly, the *Fono* of *Faipule* (Advisory Council of Representatives), and in both houses of the legislature in American Samoa. Samoans have also long seen the general franchise and secret ballot exercised in each territory: in Western Samoa by the resident Europeans (i.e., mainly part-Samoans) in electing five members to the Legislative Assembly, and in American Samoa in providing representation for the small resident group not living within the *matai* system. Religious denominational assemblies, too, including some attended abroad by elite leaders, are settings in which Western-style voting is observed.

Something of a critical "tip-over" point in the acculturation responses is currently occurring here in both territories, at least in elite levels of "voice" consolidation under government auspices. Coincident with the revisions, from 1948 on, of the structures and powers of the central governmental bodies in Western Samoa under stress of the self-government movement, Samoan leaders have started voluntarily to experiment not only with "equal voting" but also with the "secret ballot." Samoan districts have in some instances tried out an election system in naming their Representatives to the *Fono* of *Faipules* instead of using the Samoan method of talking through to a unanimous name. In this case, however, the majority-minority decisions were limited to elite electors and not subject to the general franchise.

Samoan political leaders appear particularly anxious currently to conform to Western political techniques as a public indication of their preparedness for self-government. It may be expected, therefore, that in official settings open or secret voting will become rather rapidly established in essentially the same spheres as in Western parliamentary procedures. In Samoan-style deliberations, however, the traditional methods of selecting representatives and otherwise equating opinions are likely to predominate for a long time, though with a few modern embellishments which creep in today in some situations such as asking for a show of hands rather than depending on speeches to reveal the various stands.

It may be expected, therefore, that long after equality in voting becomes accepted for territorial political purposes, the elite leadership pattern of traditional Samoa will hold strongly. Particularly is this apt to be so in the matter of nominations to higher positions subject to election. In Western Samoa, the non-elite Samoan is not very likely in the near future to have his voting choice widened beyond the elite personnel who would in the traditional order be eligible for the positions concerned. In American Samoa, however, this pattern is already loosening, as has been seen, in the case of personnel elected to the lower House of Representatives, and this could influence longer-term development among the younger generation in Western Samoa.

Where a united stand is taken by an elite group it is often crucial to try to ascertain how far this represents genuine agreement or merely a public front of agreement. Government authorities throughout modern Samoan history, for example, have often been puzzled as to how to gauge the strength, genuineness, and potential permanence of apparently unanimous decisions by Samoan leaders, and how to estimate what undercover opposition might exist. Were they hearing a well-established opinion, or that of dominating leaders only? How firm or brittle was the agreement? How potentially powerful were any submerged contrary voices? These problems are still valid, and are significant for many other societies besides Samoa.

Elite negotiation is likely to be strongly oriented toward producing a public show of at least immediate unanimity. Obviously, in Samoa as elsewhere, there is much at stake, where elite persons enter into formal consultations, besides the problems at issue: the solidarity of their own groups, the issues of "peaceful coexistence," the prestige of the negotiators. An appropriate Samoan saying is: *ne'i te'a ma le fainga,* "do not be far from the basket (when a group netting party is fishing)," i.e., in an important enterprise, be where opinion accumulates, as fish are driven by the nets into the giant basket at the head of the drive.

Elite opinion formation, therefore, is likely to involve every possible effort to delay or avoid a public position which aligns a majority against a minority. For this reason discussions and negotiations are likely to go on and on, in and out of formal meetings, until by suasion, compromise, or downright weariness, at least an outward appearance of unanimity is forthcoming, if only by a formal polite bowing to the prestige of the superior titleholder. Samoan custom is here buttressed by Christian principle; Samoans will often say that it is the brotherly duty of all to go as far as possible to come to agreement. Not to do so in the intimate setting of the village and the kinship group may result in divisions and factions that tend to persist for generations, with corresponding loss of power and loss of pleasant associations for all the people concerned. Under old-time Samoan conditions, the impasse of a majority-minority situation might easily pass from verbal disagreement to open fighting and war.

A number of corollary propositions arise from the analysis in this chapter of the interplay of individual and group "voices." An obvious point is that elite persons, called on to formulate opinion, need time for proper consultation with the group or groups they represent. As an extension of an earlier discussion it may be said that *elite persons are rarely in a position to make "spot" decisions in the fields of their responsibility.*

This fact is surprisingly little realized by government officials and others in such areas. Too often they expect outright answers on new problems from an elite assembly during its session. They assume or imply that the representatives have the authority delegated to them on such specifics, or are in a position to exercise arbitrary authority.

A general implication which shows clearly in the discussion to this point is the great difficulty of gauging Samoan public opinion in the sense of mass opinion: what is on view is likely to be always the formal opinion as processed through elite formulation mechanisms. Particularly difficult, and in some respects perhaps impossible, is the application of communication measurement techniques established in research on Western societies.

It is rarely possible in a hierarchical society such as Samoa to get a public expression of individual opinion or minority opinion on any issue that has been "processed" through the elite leadership system; and any secret polling would be resented. Elite subjects must be dealt with through elite channels. Thus, of Samoans who have testified before the various government investigatory bodies on political affairs in each territory, only a handful have expressed points of view that differed from the standard patterns as voiced by the leaders, and these in virtually every case were individuals who have lived outside of Samoa, and who were markedly deviant in Samoan terms.

Outsiders who are used to a ready formulation of individual judgment find particularly disconcerting the wall of inhibition here. It is a rare, socially deviant individual even among the elite who would be prepared to express his personal opinion outside the proper communication channels on any issue that has been or is due to be "processed," through the group leadership system. For a non-elite person to yield a considered personal judgment in this way to an outsider would be virtually unthinkable. In such a milieu an opinion poller can obviously have thin pickings only, and random sampling response techniques on any public question would be ruled out. Should a subject of elite concern be raised it would be passed off in some polite way or the interrogator referred to the appropriate titled person.

An investigator needing information must obviously go to the persons who not only command it but also have the right to impart it, i.e., a purposive and controlled rather than a random type of sampling. In the case of elite matters, this would be to the appropriate chief or orator at the highest level of authorized communication. This is one of the main techniques of the ethnologist in handling his informant samples: going to elite leaders on elite topics, to specialists on their own expert data, to women, and even to children on appropriate concerns.

55 Social Norms, National Imagery, and Interpersonal Relations
JOHN W. BENNETT and ROBERT K. McKNIGHT

Intercultural experience can be seen to include two important phases: first, the experience of learning from the host society and its institutions; and second, the application of this learning after the visitor's return home. In this chapter we shall examine the texture of interpersonal relations among Japanese and Americans dur-

Reprinted with permission of the publisher and the authors. From *In Search of Identity: The Japanese Overseas Scholar in America and Japan* by John W. Bennett, Herbert Passin, and Robert K. McKnight, pp. 225–239. The University of Minnesota Press, Minneapolis. © Copyright 1958 by the University of Minnesota.

ing the sojourn, with special reference to the manner in which the images of nations and conceptions of social position combine to affect communication and learning. We do not imply that learning is non-existent if communication is restricted, because obviously learning of some kind takes place even through mere visual observation of a society. Our goal is to show that the Japanese student and his American host are not free agents in the interaction process: they enter the engagement with culturally conditioned conceptions and expectations which influence communication and learning.

But these influences are not entirely the consequence of unique patterns of behavior assimilated in the family or in the rituals of the culture. They are also based upon interpretations of the events of international history, as these interpretations have resulted in the formation of a stereotype about the behavior of the members of other nations. Thus we have noted that in any society there exist generally accepted definitions of specific historical contacts between it and other nations; common evaluations of the prestige and national character of other peoples; and common understandings (for example, "social distance" ratings) about the appropriate kinds or patterns of interaction between members of its own and other national groups.

The person moving to a new society not only brings these common understandings with him, but he may also feel a need to test and perhaps adjust his images and interpretations of historical contacts, national character, and appropriate social postures. Since many goals of the incoming person are to be met through the medium of interpersonal relations, the intricacies of this learning and adjustmental process constitute one of the major theoretical and practical problems in the study of intercultural experience.

A CULTURAL MODEL OF INTERACTION

We shall first construct a model of interaction between Japanese students and Americans with the help of two sets of data: first, the major norms or principles of interpersonal relations of Japanese and American culture; and second, the reciprocal status relationships of the two peoples when considered in the roles of typical "nationals" of their countries. Together these two sets of data will permit us to describe some fundamental "givens" for interaction between Americans and Japanese. Our model of interaction is based upon two sources of information: available studies of Japanese and American patterns of social behavior and attitudes toward intercultural relations; and observation and recording of behavior and attitudes of our subjects and Americans with whom they associated.

Japanese Interpersonal Norms

Numerous studies by social scientists of national character or culture have appeared in recent years, initially as a response to the need for knowledge of enemy countries in World War II. Most of these studies have asked a substantive question: what is the *nature* of the behavior shared by all, or a majority, of the members of a national society? Once this shared behavior is "discovered," its written description becomes an outline of the national culture of that country. This approach has been extensively criticized on the grounds that the behavior of the members of any complex society is so variable that any attempt to describe the shared items results in superficial generalization. Critics have also pointed out that descriptions of national cultures frequently consist of statements of norms only, and do not denote actual behavior.

At this point in the account of our own research it is necessary to raise questions about the nature of national cultures. However, we shall not attempt to claim that our answers to these will be valid for all members of the Japanese nation. We do claim validity for our own subjects and are also willing to guess that much of what we say will apply to the majority of Japanese men who were socialized in prewar and wartime Japan in families of the middle and upper income brackets. We shall not claim that our subjects necessarily behaved in the manner suggested, for the description itself pertains to norms or principles and not to behavior. In a subsequent section we shall provide a description and analysis of the behavior of our subjects with reference to these norms.

This procedure implies the concept of a "cultural model": essentially a highly generalized description of principles, shared by a large number of people and maintained in the form of personal values. To some degree these principles or norms constitute guides or rules for behavior: sometimes followed literally, sometimes not, but always available as a generalized protocol for use by the individual in finding his way through social relationships and in judging the acts of others.

The first half of the model we shall construct pertains to the patterns of interpersonal relations in the two societies, Japan and America. We recognize that as representatives of the class of modern industrial nations, these two countries have cultures very similar in many respects. The Japanese are, in fact, often called the "Americans of the Orient," a phrase referring to their industrious orientation toward life and nature; their interest in mass-cultural pursuits like baseball; and their success with capitalist enterprise in a collectivist world. Similarities in all these areas are a fact—but it is equally apparent that some significant differences have existed in other aspects of social life in the two countries. Among these differences the norms and patterns of interpersonal behavior are probably the greatest. Thus, while a Japanese and an American may share an interest in baseball which brings them closer together than either one might be to a member of some other nation, the two may differ so widely in their habits of behavior in social situations that communication between them may be seriously impeded.

Studies of Japanese social norms by Ruth Benedict and others have revealed the following general features: articulate codification of the norms; strong tendencies toward a face-to-face, or "primary group" type of intimacy; an emphasis upon hierarchical status positions; concern for the importance of status; relative permanence of status once established; and "behavioral reserve" or discipline. These will be discussed in order.

ARTICULATE CODIFICATION OF RULES. During the long Tokugawa period of centralized feudalism, Japanese patterns of interpersonal behavior underwent an elaborate institutionalization. The Shogunate attempted to fix the position of each class with respect to the others and established written rules of behavior for its members. The family system had developed historically along patrilineal lines, and during Tokugawa times such patterns of relations between kin were proclaimed as an official social code. After the Meiji Restoration, the *samurai* class in control of the nation maintained these formalized rules and even elevated them to the status of an idealized spiritual expression of the Japanese ethos. The reason for this enhancement of the Tokugawa code after the Restoration lay in the need to preserve and strengthen national discipline and unity as a practical policy in industrialization and other aspects of modernization. Thus, Japan moved into her modern era in possession of a system of rules of social behavior based on feudal and familial principles.

It is necessary to note that this system of codified rules was consistently adhered to in actual behavior by only a minority of the population: the *samurai* and nobility. The remainder of the population followed the rules in part, or only in "public" situations where the pressure for conformity was strong. In the decades subsequent to the Restoration a generalized version of the code was adopted by the developing business and official classes, and this is the situation which continues to prevail in Japan today (although since the Occupation a considerable liberalization of social behavior can be found in all classes and groups). Since the student subjects of the research project were persons from upper- and middle-class groups socialized in prewar and wartime Japan, we can use the gross aspects of this social code as a backdrop for the interpretation of their behavior.

The strength and the influence of this code were enhanced further by the fact that up to the period of the Occupation, no large migration to Japan of Westerners had occurred. In this situation relatively few Japanese were presented with the need to learn the modes of interaction of other societies—particularly the more "open" type of the Western nations. This isolation was intensified during the militarist-nationalist epoch of the 1930s and 1940s, in which the social code was given renewed emphasis as a counter-measure against liberal trends. The codified norms—*on* or ascribed obligation; *giri* or contractual obligation; *chu* or loyalty to one's superior; *ninjo* or humane sensibility; and *enryo* or modesty and reserve in the presence of the superior—were incorporated in the school curriculum as ethical doctrine, and exemplified in a multitude of cultural expressions.

PRIMARY ASSOCIATIVE QUALITIES. An important aspect of Japanese social norms may be described in Western sociological terms as that of "primary association." Emphasis upon personal qualities, obligations between subordinate and superior, and distinctions based on age or sibling birth-order are features suited to the atmosphere of a small, highly interactive social group, like the family or a feudal manor. It goes without saying that in the modern mass society of Japan these rules have not always been observed, but the fact is that to an extraordinary degree the Japanese have succeeded in organizing present-day society into small, cell-like groupings, in which highly personalized relationships are governed by an explicit code of behavior. Even in impersonal situations, as in labor organizations, rules of this primary associative type have been used at least symbolically as models for interaction and responsibility.

HIERARCHY. If Japanese social norms present an image of society in the character of a primary group, it is at least a hierarchically organized primary group—one in which there are explicit gradations of status from superior to inferior. The family is ideally organized on patrilineal-patriarchal principles, with the father as dominant, the eldest son superordinate to the younger, and so on. Primogeniture was the law of the land until the Occupation period, and, even though no longer so, it is still followed in a great many cases.

Japanese business firms, government bureaus, and many universities and schools are organized in ways reminiscent of this familial model; or their organization may be more closely related historically to feudal or lord-vassal principles. In such cases the employee and the employer, chief and underling, or teacher and pupil occupy positions which carry with them defined and ascribed rights and duties, in which the superior generally occupies a paternalistic and authoritarian role. The term *sensei* means teacher, or mentor, but its wide application to people outside of the teaching profession suggests its connotation of benevolent but stern authority and superiority. Likewise the term *oyabun* ("parent-status" or "parent-surrogate"), while strictly appropriate only for certain types of economic groups, is often applied to any highly paternalistic superior.

CONCERN FOR STATUS. All this would imply, of course, very considerable preoccupation with matters of social status. It is necessary or at least desirable for every Japanese to know his own status in the interaction situation, since it is in status that one finds the cues for reciprocal behavior. To put this in sociological terms, there exists a very close tie between status and role: the role behavior expected of one in a given status position is clearly defined and there are relatively few permitted alternatives or variations from the pattern (when alternatives are present, they, too, are often very clearly defined). Thus the behavior of a person of a given status in a social relationship, can constitute familiar and unmistakable cues for the appropriate behavior of a person of another status.

Concern with status is evidenced further by the incorporation into the Japanese language of a multitude of forms expressing varying degrees of politeness, levels of formality and respect, and subservience or dominance. This type of language dramatizes status differences between persons by the use of such devices as honorific suffixes, special verb endings, and differing pronouns. To mention only the most commonly used forms for designating the second person singular, there are *anata, omae, kimi, kisama,* and *temai*. The proper use of each of these forms depends upon the relative status of the speaker and the particular situation in which the conversatoin or interaction takes place. Status in language depends upon age, sex, and class differences, as well as on the degree of intimacy and the extent of formal obligation existing between those communicating.

RELATIVE PERMANENCE OF STATUS. Once status positions are clearly defined, the parties holding these statuses are expected to occupy them for very long periods—often throughout life. A superior, for example one's professor, retains strong symbolic hierarchical precedence throughout the life of both parties, even when the student has become a professional equal in productivity, rank, and pay. Subtle changes in status of course occur, and we do not wish to make too sweeping a generalization. However, as compared with the fluid patterns typical of Western society, Japanese society possesses considerably more orderly and predictable allocations of status—or at least the expectations of this.

BEHAVIORAL RESERVE AND DISCIPLINE. A "tight" social organization based on concern with status and hierarchy is by necessity one in which social behavior tends to be governed more by norms, or public expectancies, and less by free or idiosyncratic response to a given situation. At the same time, a system of this kind requires institutional outlets in the event that obligations, duties, status relationships, and the like, for one reason or another, may be unclear or not yet defined. The Japanese have utilized, for this purpose, the concept of *enryo*, loosely translatable as "hesitance" or "reserve." The development of this pattern in Japanese culture is of particular importance for our problem here.

The original meaning of *enryo* pertained to the behavior of the subordinate in hierarchical status relations. The subordinate was expected to show compliant obsequiousness toward the superior: he should hold his temper, check any aggressive response to frustration (and of course, bide his time). This pattern of behavior may be manifested by Japanese when they interact with persons of their own or any society whom they regard as superior in status. Whenever the presumption is that a superior person occupies the "alter" status, *enryo* is likely to be observed by "ego."

Now, as Japan entered the stage of industrialization, with its expanded opportunities for individual enterprise and mobility (a process still under way), social situations became more complicated, more ambiguous, and more violative of the traditional rules and behavioral prescriptions. Since at the same time the basic hierarchical, primary-group character of the norms prevailed, there emerged strong needs for adjustive behavior. *Enryo* became the escape-hatch: in the new ambiguity, behavioral reserve and noncommitment became the frequent alternative, and the Japanese manifested such withdrawn, unresponsive behavior in the event that a particular interpersonal situation lacked clear designation of the statuses of ego and alter. Much the same situation holds when the Japanese is overseas. Here, too, his behavior is frequently characterized by *enryo*— often concealing confusion and embarrassment over his ignorance of the social rules of the foreign society. Thus the "shyness" or reserved behavior often found in Japanese on the American campus can be due either to the fact that the Japanese views Americans, or certain Americans, as superior people; or to the fact that he is simply not sure how to behave in American social situations, regardless of status. The rule goes, when status is unclear, it is safest to retreat into *enryo*. This form of response is most typical of persons socialized in prewar and wartime Japan; the postwar generation, many of whom have grown up in the more liberal atmosphere of the Occupation and after, are much more tolerant of ambiguity.

Japanese and American Patterns of Social Behavior

We may now view these normative patterns from a comparative cultural perspective. A detailed description of the American norms will not be required, since it may be presumed that the reader has sufficient familiarity with them. We shall select those American rules of interpersonal behavior that are "opposites" to the Japanese patterns just described. In a later section we shall discuss cases of similarity.

There is among Americans a tendency toward an initial egalitarian response on the part of "ego": two persons are presumed to be equal unless proven otherwise. (The Japanese norms contain an opposite premise: when status is vague, inequality is expected.) In practice this egalitarian principle in American interpersonal behavior leads to what the Japanese might perceive as fluidity and unpredictability of behavior in interaction, and highly variable or at least less apparent concern for status. Things like wealth, public versus private situations, and a host of other features may all, in the American case, influence the behavior of ego and alter in ways which are not subject to predictable codification. Allowance is made continually for subtle changes in roles of those interacting, with a strain toward equalization if hierarchical differences appear. Thus, while in social situations the Japanese may find it difficult to communicate unless status differences are clear, the American, in view of his egalitarian preference, may point to and actually experience status difference as a source of interpersonal tension and difficulty in communication. Thus the Japanese may see the free flow of communication as enhanced by clear status understandings; the American may view it instead as requiring maximal intimacy and freedom of expression.

Finally, reserve or discipline is in some cases much less apparent in American social behavior. Initially, outward display of feelings is encouraged, and reserve may develop after status differences are recognized. Once again the Japanese may proceed on an approximately opposite principle: behavioral freedom and expressivity become a potentiality after statuses are clearly differentiated—especially when equality is achieved— but not before. Moreover, even when statuses are clear to the Japanese participants in social relations, interaction often continues to be hesitant and guarded. (Important institutionalized exceptions to the general rule of avoidance are found in the frank behavior tolerated in *sake* parties, behavior of the male guest and his geisha partner, and a few others.)

In American interpersonal behavior the patterns of tact, obsequiousness, and other forms of retiring behavior are seen continually, but they are often much more situational and idiosyncratic. Americans lack a concept with the generalized cultural meaning of *enryo;* reserve may be a useful form of behavior for some people, but not others, or in some situations; it may be associated with status differences, or it may not. And when this reserve is associated with status positions (and in the presence of hierarchical patterns generally), Americans are likely to express attitudes of guilt or regret, or are likely to conceal the existence of such patterns by verbally reaffirming egalitarian principles. Moreover, some American normative attitudes frown on "manipulative" tendencies; frankness, openness, and humility are valued highly, if not always observed.

Quotations from interviews with student subjects (sojourners and returnees) may serve to indicate the Japanese perspective on their own and the American patterns of interpersonal behavior.

Q.: What did you like about America that you didn't about Japan?
A.: Well, it's hard to give concrete examples, but mainly I was satisfied with what you might call the smartness of life—the modernness of things. And also the simplicity and frankness of life. You don't have to worry about *gimu-giri-on* [obligations] over there . . . In the United States you have to visit relatives too, but such visits are more personal, more real—more meaningful. Here in Japan they are for the sake of *giri* and righteousness and all that stuff.
Q.: Could you define the term "Americanized" as it is used by Japanese students?
A.: Well, to be Americanized means to be indifferent to social position—indifferent to social formality—such as in formal greetings. It concerns points about how one acts socially.
This is about human relations—it didn't surprise me but it did impress me very much to find that relations with others are always on an equal plane in the U.S. In Japan I automatically used polite language with seniors so that this just seemed natural—and if I used polite words in Japan I didn't necessarily feel that this was feudalistic—though some do. At first in the U.S. when young people, like high school students, talked to me as an equal, I felt conflicted, or in the dormitory it surprised me to see a boy of 20 talk to a man of 45 as an equal.
In Japan, my father and some of my superiors often told me that my attitude toward superiors and seniors was too rude. Here, though, my attitude doesn't seem rude—at least it doesn't appear as rude as I was afraid it would. It is easier to get along with people in America, because for one thing, Americans are not so class conscious and not so sensitive about things like status. In Japan, my conduct to superiors seemed rude, but the same behavior isn't rude here. For instance here it is all right simply to say "hello" to teachers, while in Japan I would be expected to say *"ohayo gozaimasu"* [polite form of "good morning"] with a deep bow. In Japan I did things like this only when I really respected somebody.
A main problem with me is the problem of *enryo*, or what you call modesty. Even in life in America you have to be modest, but in a different way from the so-called Japanese *enryo*. But the trouble is that I don't know when and where we have to show *enryo* in American life. You never can be sure.
The good thing about associating with Americans is that you can be friendly in a light manner. Not so in Japan. Japanese are nosey in other peoples' business—they rumor, gossip. It gives you a crowded feeling, after you get back. Of course in Japan friendships are usually deep—it is good to have a real friend to lean on—you know where you stand with your friends; it is the opposite of light associations.
I have few American friends—those I have are usually Americans who have been to Japan. I think the reason is that my character is somewhat backward.

I don't try to speak first, but let the other fellow open up. Those who have been to Japan know about this and speak first, and that makes it easier to start an association.

From the information on contrasting cultural norm and cue systems supplied thus far, it is possible to predict in a general way that when a Japanese interacts with an American, certain blockages to communication and to the correct assessment of status behavior may occur. Japanese are likely to confront Americans with unstated assumptions concerning status differences, while the American may be inclined to accept the Japanese at face value—that is, as a *person*, not a *status*. In the resulting confusion it may be anticipated that the Japanese will retreat into what he calls *enryo*, since this form of behavior involving attenuated communication is appropriate toward persons of unclear or superior status.

The National Status Image

For reasons usually found in the cultural background of the peoples concerned, and in the historical relations of nations, there is a tendency on the part of some to view other nations and peoples much as one would view persons in a hierarchically oriented social group. Modernization, which brings an increased need for knowledge of other peoples, has brought as well a strong sense of competition—a desire to know where one stands, or where one's nation stands relative to other nations in technological and other areas of development. This desire to know one's position and the tendency to view other nations hierarchically are probably found to some degree in all modern societies, but may be exaggerated among those nations that are in the middle ranks in the competitive race for modernization—and particularly in those societies which have incorporated into their own culture a strong hierarchical conception of status. Thus, in societies with hierarchical patterns, there will occur certain established techniques which are defined as appropriate for governing behavior toward the nationals of countries judged either to be higher or lower than that of the actor. On the other hand, for societies with egalitarian ideals of social relations, while there may be a tendency in the national popular ideology to view other nations hierarchically in terms of power and progress, there will be no ready behavioral pattern to follow toward individual members of these other societies. Ideally, regardless of national origin, individuals will be considered as "human beings," theoretically equal. Such theoretical equality is often violated in practice, of course, but the violations are based not on systematic hierarchical conceptions, but on transitory and situationally determined attitudes.

The Japanese tendency to locate other nations on a hierarchical scale is well known, and is observable even at the level of formal diplomatic interchange. With respect to the Japanese attitude toward the United States, the tendency toward a superordinate status percept is very strong —although qualified and even reversed in certain contexts (American arts and literature have been viewed as of questionable merit, for example) and in certain historical periods. The historical basis for this generally high-status percept may be found in America's historic role in the opening of Japan; in the use of America as a model for much of Japan's modernization; and in the participation and guidance of the United States in reform and reconstruction during the Occupation. America, though not always a country for which the Japanese feel great affection, has come to be a symbol of many of Japan's aspirations, as well as a "tutor" whom the "pupil" must eventually excel (or even conquer). Therefore, whatever the specific affectual response, we have found that the Japanese student subjects often perceived America as deserving of respect or at least respect-avoidance (*enryo*), and were further inclined to project this image onto the American individual. Evidence of these views available in our research data is sampled at the end of this section, in the form of quotations from interviews.

Within tolerable limits of generality, America may be specified as a society in which egalitarian interpersonal relationships are the ideal pattern and, in tendency at least, the predominant pattern of behavior. But in the United States, especially as the country emerges from political isolation, there also has appeared a tendency to rate other nations in a rough hierarchical order. Thus, some European nations in the spheres of art, literature, and the manufacture of sports cars would be acclaimed by many Americans as superior, and Americans are increasingly concerned about their technological position *vis-à-vis* Russia. However, this tendency to rate other nations hierarchically does not automatically translate itself into code of behavior for Americans to follow toward the people of other countries, as is the case for many Japanese. It may leave the social situation a little confused for the Americans, but in the background of thinking for many individual Americans is the notion that in social relations people should be treated initially as equals.

The Cultural Model of Interaction

When a person from a national society with hierarchical tendencies encounters a person from a society with egalitarian tendencies, and moreover when the country of the latter is generally "high" in the estimation of the former, the idealized paradigm as shown in Figure 1 would be approximated. In this diagram, X, the person from a country with egalitarian views, behaves toward Y, the person from a hierarchically oriented country, as if he occupied the same "level"; that is, in equalitarian

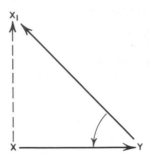

Figure 1.

terms. But Y perceives X in a high-status position X_1, "above" X's image of his own status in the relationship. Since from Y's point of view X does not behave as he "ought" to—he behaves as an equal rather than as a superior—Y may be expected to feel confusion and disorientation. The confusion can be resolved readily only by Y's assuming an equal status with X, or by X's assuming the position X_1 assigned to him by Y; i.e., either by closing or by validating the "arc of status-cue confusion" shown by the arrow.

The reader will note that in effect we have already substituted "average American" for X, and "average Japanese" for Y. We have found that the diagram has been meaningful as an ideal model for the analysis of inter-action patterns between Japanese and Americans. In many cases the conditions denoted by the diagram were actually found: Americans do behave toward Japanese as equals, while the Japanese perceive the Americans as, and in some cases expect them to behave like, superiors. In this ideal situation since the Japanese is generally not able to respond as an equal, and since withdrawal and distant respect are proper behavior both for interaction with superiors and for interaction in situations where status is ambiguous, he simply retires into *enryo* and communication is impaired. This model does much to explain what many educators and foreign student counsellors have come to feel as "typical" behavior of the shy, embarrassed Japanese student on the American campus.

A revealing interchange on the matter of status imagery by some twelve Japanese sojourner students was recorded during a two-hour group discussion planned by the project but not attended by Americans. A translation of part of this interchange follows.

M: As I see it, Japanese think of Americans as nobility. So, it is hard to ac-cept invitations because of the status difference.

K: I don't agree fully. Americans are not nobility to us, but they do have a higher social status, so that it is hard to accept invitations. But there is a "category" of persons who are known and placed as "foreign students," and we can take advantage of this general foreign student status and go to American homes and places.

N: During foreign student orientation we came and went as we desired as "foreign students." But here, as an individual person, I have felt it necessary to return invitations which are extended to me, and this I find very difficult since I have no income and must return the invitation in a manner suited to the status of the person.

M: Only if the invitation is from Americans who we can accept as status equals to us should it be returned. . . . American table manners are difficult to learn, and it is a problem similar to that encountered by anyone who attempts to enter a higher social class in Japan. . . . Japanese just can't stand on an equal footing with Americans. . . . I wouldn't want an American janitor to see my house in Japan. It is so miserable.

N: Why? That seems extreme.

M: Because I have social aspirations. I am a "climber." A Japanese house in Tokyo is too dirty to invite an American to—for example, could I invite him to use my poor bathroom? (General laughter)

At a later point in the discussion, the following emerged:

Mrs. N: I have watched American movies in Japan and in the United States I have seen American men—and they all look like Robert Taylor. No Japanese men look like Robert Taylor.

M: Again I say it is not a matter of beauty, but one of status.

Mrs. N: No, it is not status—not calculation of economic worth or anything —but of beauty. Americans are more beautiful—they look nicer than Japanese.

U: It is the same in other things. Americans look nice, for example, during an oral examination in college. They look more attractive. Japanese look down, crushed, ugly.

At a still later point, one of the discussants embarked on a long monologue on the ramifications of the status problem. Part of this monologue runs as follows:

A high-status Japanese man going out with American girls knows something of what he must do—for example, he must be polite—but he does not know the language so he can be no competition to American men, who will be superior. In an emergency, for example, the Japanese male regresses to Japanese behavior. Great Japanese professors are embarrassed for the first few months in the United States because they can't even beat American college juniors in social behavior or expression of ideas. They don't know the language, they feel inferior. These people, forgetting that they were unable to defeat America, become highly antagonistic to the United States. . . . They reason that Japan must be superior, not inferior to the United States, because they are unable to master it. While in America, of course, they may write home about their wonderful times and experiences—to hide their real feelings. Actually while they are in the U.S. they feel as though they were *nothing*.

Some quotations from two different interviews with another subject:

Before I came to the States, I expected that whatever I would do in the U.S. would be observed by Americans and would become their source of knowledge of Japan and the Japanese. So I thought I had to be careful. In the dormitory, there is a Nisei boy from whom I ask advice about my manners and clothing. I asked him to tell me any time when my body smells or my clothing is dirty. I, as a Japanese, want to look nice to Americans. . . .
. . . In general, I think I do less talking than the others in my courses. I'm always afraid that if I raise questions along the lines of *Japanese* thinking about the subject—or simply from my own way of looking at something—it might raise some question on the part of the others. When talking to a professor I can talk quite freely, but not in class. I am self-conscious.

These specimen quotations help to show that quite frequently the perspective of many Japanese students toward America has some of the qualities of the triangular model of interaction. Regardless of how our Japanese subjects may have behaved, or learned to behave, they harbored, as a picture in the back of their minds, an image of the Americans as people a notch or two "above" Japan and the Japanese. Thus even while a Japanese may "look down" on what he calls "American materialism," he may "in the back of his mind" continue to "look up" to the United States and its people as a whole, as a "generalized other." Our cultural model of interaction is thus felt to be a very fundamental and highly generalized component of imagery, as well as a very generalized way of describing the behavior of Japanese and Americans in certain typical interactive situations.

Quite obviously the model, taken by itself, would be a very poor instrument of prediction of the actual behavior of a particular Japanese with Americans. It is apparent that there would have to be a considerable knowledge of situational variability, amount of social learning, and many other factors before all the major variants of Japanese social behavior in America with respect to status could be understood. While there is no need to seek complete predictability of individual behavior, some attempt may be made to show how the social behavior of the Japanese subjects of research did vary in actual social situations in America, and to see if these variants followed a consistent pattern.

A Selective Bibliography
for Further Reading

ACKOFF, RUSSELL L., 1958, Towards a Behavioral Theory of Communication, *Management Science*, 4:218–234.

ADAMS, RICHARD N., and JACK J. PREISS, eds., 1960, *Human Organization Research*. Homewood, Ill.: Dorsey.

ASHBY, W. ROSS, 1952, *Design for a Brain*. New York: Wiley.

ATTNEAVE, FRED, 1959, *Applications of Information Theory to Psychology*. New York: Holt, Rinehart and Winston, Inc.

AYER, A. J. and others, 1955, *Studies in Communication*. London: Secker & Warburg.

BACK, K. W., 1951, Influence Through Social Communication, *Journal of Abnormal and Social Psychology*, 46:9–23.

———, 1962, Social Research as a Communication System. *Social Forces*, 41:61–68.

BALES, ROBERT F., 1950, *Interaction Process Analysis*. Reading, Mass.: Addison-Wesley.

———, F. L. STRODTBECK, T. M. MILLS, and MARY ROSEBOROUGH, 1951, Channels of Communication in Small Groups, *American Sociological Review*, 16:461–468.

BAR-HILLEL, YEHOSHUA, 1964, *Language and Information*. Reading, Mass.: Addison-Wesley.

BAVELAS, ALEX, 1950, Communication Patterns in Task-Oriented Groups, *Journal of the Acoustical Society of America*, 22:725–730.

BEER, STAFFORD, 1959, *Cybernetics and Management*. London: English Universities Press.

BERELSON, BERNARD, 1952, *Content Analysis in Communication Research*. New York: Free Press.

———, 1959, The State of Communication Research, *Public Opinion Quarterly*, 23:1–6.

———, and MORRIS JANOWITZ, 1953, *Reader in Public Opinion and Communication*. New York: Free Press.

BERLO, DAVID K., 1960, *The Process of Communication*. New York: Holt, Rinehart and Winston.

BERG, J., 1955, Cooperation without Communication and Observation, *Journal of Social Psychology*, 4:287–296.

BERNE, ERIC, 1953, Concerning the Nature of Communication, *Psychiatric Quarterly*, 27:185–198.

BERNSTEIN, BASIL, 1960, Language and Social Class, *British Journal of Sociology*, 11:271–276.

———, 1962, Linguistic Codes, Hesitation Phenomena and Intelligence. *Language and Speech*, 5:31–46.

BERTALANFFY, L. VON, 1951, Problems of General System Theory, *Human Biology*, 23:302–312.

BIRDWHISTELL, RAY L., 1952, *Introduction to Kinesics*. Washington, D.C.: Department of State, Foreign Service Institute.

BLACK, MAX, 1962, *Models and Metaphors*. Ithaca, N.Y.: Cornell University Press.

BLAU, PETER M., 1960, A Theory of Social Integration, *American Journal of Sociology*, 65:545–556.

BOSSARD, JAMES H. S., ELEANOR S. BOLL, and WINOGENE P. SANGER, 1950, Some Neglected Areas in Family Life Study, *Annals of the American Academy of Political and Social Science*, 272:68–76.

BRILLOUIN, L., 1956, *Science and Information Theory*. New York: Academic Press.

BROADBENT, DONALD E., 1958, *Perception and Communication*. New York: Pergamon.

BROWN, ROGER W., 1958, *Words and Things*. New York: Free Press.

BURKE, KENNETH, 1962, What Are the Signs of What, *Anthropological Linguistics*, 4 (6):1–23.

CARNAP, R., 1955, Meaning and Synonymy in Natural Languages, *Philosophical Studies*, 7:33–47.

CARROLL, JOHN B., 1953, *The Study of Language*. Cambridge, Mass.: Harvard University Press.

———, 1958. Communication Theory, Linguistics, and Psycholinguistics. *Review of Educational Research*, 28:79–88.

———, 1959, An Operational Analysis of Language Behavior, *Anthropological Linguistics*, 1:37–54.

CARTIER, FRANCIS A., and K. A. HARWOOD, 1953, On the Definition of Communication. *Journal of Communication*, 3:1–10.

CARTWRIGHT, DORWIN, and ALVIN ZANDER, eds., 1953, *Group Dynamics*. New York: Harper & Row.

CHAPPLE, E. D., 1949, The Interaction Chronograph, *Personnel*, 25:295–307.

CHERRY, COLIN, 1957, *On Human Communication*. Cambridge, Mass.: Technology Press of MIT., and New York: Wiley.

CHOMSKY, NOAM, 1957, *Syntactic Structures*. The Hague: Mouton.

CLELAND, C. L., 1960. Characteristics of Social Systems within Which Selected Types of Information Are Transmitted. *Rural Sociology*. 25:212–218.

COHEN, A. M., W. G. BENNIS, and G. H. WOLKON, 1962, The Effects of Changes in Communication Networks on the Behavior of Problem Solving Groups. *Sociometry*, 25:177–196.

COHEN, A. R., 1958, Upward Communication in Experimentally Created Hierarchies, *Human Relations*, 11:41–53.

COHEN, MARCEL, 1956, Social and Linguistic Structure, *Diogenes*, 15:38–47.

CONKLIN, HAROLD C., 1959, Linguistic Play in Its Cultural Context, *Language*, 35:631–636.

COOK, P. H., 1951, An Examination of the Notion of Communication in Industry, *Occupational Psychology*, 25:1–14.

CRIDER, DONALD B., 1956–1957, Cybernetics: A Review of What It Means and Some of Its Implications in Psychiatry, *Neuropsychiatry*, 4:35–58.

CROWLEY, THOMAS H., *et al.*, 1962, *Modern Communication*. New York: Columbia University Press.

DAVISON, W. PHILLIPS, 1959–1960, On the Effects of Communication, *Public Opinion Quarterly*, 23:343–360.

DAVITZ, JOEL R., and LOIS JEAN DAVITZ, 1959, The Communication of Feeling by Content-Free Speech, *Journal of Communication*, 9:6–13.

——, 1961, Nonverbal Vocal Communication of Feeling, *Journal of Communication*, 11:81–86.

DeFLEUR, MELVIN L., and OTTO N. LARSEN, 1958, *The Flow of Information*. New York: Harper & Row.

DEUTSCH, F., 1952, Analytic Posturology, *Psychoanalytic Quarterly*, 21:196–214.

DEUTSCH, KARL W., 1952, Communication Theory and Social Science, *American Journal of Orthopsychiatry*, 22:469–483.

——, 1952, On Communication Models in the Social Sciences, *Public Opinion Quarterly*, 16:356–380.

DEXTER, LEWIS ANTHONY, and DAVID MANNING WHITE, eds., 1964, *People, Society, and Mass Communications*. New York: Free Press.

DE YOUNG, J. E., and C. L. HUNT, 1962, Communication Channels and Functional Literacy in the Philippine Barrio, *Journal of Asian Studies*, 22:67–77.

DOOB, LEONARD W., 1961, *Communication in Africa*. New Haven, Conn.: Yale University Press.

DUNCAN, HUGH DALZIEL, 1962, *Communication and the Social Order*. New York: Bedminster.

EISENSTADT, S. N., 1955, Communications Systems and Social Structure, *Public Opinion Quarterly*, 19:153–167.

FAIRBANKS, G., 1954, A Theory of the Speech Organism as a Servosystem, *Journal of Speech and Hearing Disorders*, 19:133–139.

FEARING, FRANKLIN, 1953, Toward a Psychological Theory of Human Communication, *Journal of Personality*, 22:71–88.

FESTINGER, LEON, 1950, Informal Social Communication, *Psychological Review*, 57:271–282.

——, 1957, *A Theory of Cognitive Dissonance*. New York: Harper & Row.

FIRTH, J. R., 1957, *Papers in Linguistics 1934–1951*. New York: Oxford.

FISCHER, JOHN L., 1958, Social Influences in the Choice of a Linguistic Variant, *Word*, 14:47–56.

FODOR, JERRY A., and JERROLD J. KATZ, eds., 1964, *The Structure of Language*. Englewood Cliffs, N.J.: Prentice-Hall.

FOERSTER, H. VON, MARGARET MEAD, and H. L. TEUBER, 1949–1957, *Transactions of Conferences on Cybernetics*, 5 vols. New York: Josiah Macy Jr. Foundation.

GARVIN, PAUL L., ed., 1963, *Natural Language and the Computer*. New York: McGraw-Hill.

GERBER, GEORGE, 1956, Toward a General Model of Communication, *Audio-Visual Communication Review*, 4:3–11.

GLEASON, H. A., JR., 1961, *An Introduction to Descriptive Linguistics*, rev. ed., New York: Holt, Rinehart and Winston, Inc.

GOETZINGER, C., and M. VALENTINE, 1964, Problems in Executive Interpersonal Communication, *Personnel Administration*, 27:24–29.

GOFFMAN, ERVING, 1959, *The Presentation of Self in Everyday Life*. New York: Doubleday.

———, 1961, *Encounters: Two Studies in the Sociology of Interaction*. Indianapolis: Bobbs-Merrill.

GOODENOUGH, WARD H., 1956, Componential Analysis and the Study of Meaning, *Language*, 32:195–216.

GREENBERG, JOSEPH H., 1957, *Essays in Linguistics*. Chicago: University of Chicago Press.

GROOTAERS, W. A., 1952, Language Behavior of an Individual During One Day, *Orbis*, 1:126–129.

GUETZKOW, HAROLD, and WILLIAM R. DILL, 1957, Factors in the Organizational Development of Task Oriented Groups, *Sociometry*, 20:175–204.

GUGENHEIM, F., 1961, Application of Communications Analysis to Studying Staff Utilization, *Journal of Educational Sociology*, 35:79–90.

GUILBAUD, G. T., 1959, *What Is Cybernetics?* New York: Grove.

HALL, EDWARD T., 1955, The Anthropology of Manners, *Scientific American*, 192:84–90.

———, 1959, *The Silent Language*. New York: Doubleday.

———, 1960, The Silent Language in Overseas Business, *Harvard Business Review*, 38:87–96.

HARE, A. PAUL, 1962, *Handbook of Small Group Research*. New York: Free Press.

———, EDGAR F. BORGATTA, and ROBERT F. BALES, eds., 1955, *Small Groups*. New York: Knopf.

HARRAH, DAVID, 1963, *Communication: A Logical Model*. Cambridge, Mass.: The MIT Press.

HARRIS, ZELLIG S., 1952, Discourse Analysis, *Language*, 28:1–31.

HEINICKE, CHRISTOPH, and ROBERT F. BALES, 1953, Developmental Trends in the Structure of Small Groups, *Sociometry*, 16:7–38.

HENLE, PAUL, ed., 1958, *Language, Thought, and Culture*. Ann Arbor, Mich.: University of Michigan Press.

HERDAN, G., 1964, *Quantitative Linguistics*. London: Butterworth.

HJELMSLEV, LOUIS, 1961, *Prolegomena to a Theory of Language*. Madison, Wis.: University of Wisconsin Press.

HOCKETT, CHARLES F., 1958, *A Course in Modern Linguistics*. New York: Macmillan.

———, 1960, The Origin of Speech, *Scientific American*, 203 (3):89–96.

HOIJER, HARRY, ed., 1954, *Language in Culture*. Chicago: University of Chicago Press.

HOVLAND, CARL I., IRVING L. JANIS, and HAROLD H. KELLEY, 1953, *Communication and Persuasion*. New Haven, Conn.: Yale University.

HYMAN, H. H., and P. B. SHEATSLEY, 1947, Some Reasons Why Information Campaigns Fail, *Public Opinion Quarterly*, 11:412–423.

HYMES, DELL H., 1962, "The Ethnography of Speaking" in *Anthropology and Human Behavior*, edited by Thomas Gladwin and William C. Sturtevant. Washington, D.C.: Anthropological Society of Washington, pp. 13–53.

——, ed., 1964, *Language in Culture and Society*. New York: Harper & Row.

JACKSON, WILLIS, ed., 1953, *Communication Theory*. New York: Academic Press.

JACOBSON, EUGENE, ROBERT L. KAHN, FLOYD C. MANN, and NANCY C. MORSE, eds., 1951, Human Relations Research in Large Organizations, *Journal of Social Issues*, 7:1–74.

JAKOBSON, ROMAN, C. GUNNAR M. FANT, and MORRIS HALLE, 1952, *Preliminaries to Speech Analysis*. Cambridge, Mass.: Massachusetts Institute of Technology, Acoustics Laboratory, Technical Report 13.

JANIS, IRVING L., and CARL I. HOVLAND, 1959, *Personality and Persuasability*. New Haven, Conn.: Yale University Press.

JOHNSON, F. CRAIG, and GEORGE R. KLARE, 1961, General Models of Communication Research, *Journal of Communication*, 11:13–26.

——, and GEORGE R. KLARE, 1962, Feedback: Principles and Analogies, *Journal of Communication*, 12:150–159.

JOOS, MARTIN, ed., 1957, *Readings in Linguistics*. Washington, D.C.: American Council of Learned Societies.

KATZ, ELIHU, 1957, The Two-Step Flow of Communication, *Public Opinion Quarterly*, 21:61–78.

——, and PAUL F. LAZARSFELD, 1955, *Personal Influence: The Part Played by People in the Flow of Mass Communication*. New York: Free Press.

KELLEY, HAROLD H., 1951, Communications in Experimentally Created Hierarchies, *Human Relations*, 4:39–56.

KENT, ALLEN, 1962, *Textbook on Mechanized Information Retrieval*. New York: Wiley.

KEPHART, W. M. A., 1950, A Quantitative Analysis of Intragroup Relationships, *American Journal of Sociology*, 60:544–549.

KJELDERGAARD, PAUL M., 1961, The Psychology of Language, *Review of Educational Research*, 31:119–129.

KLAPPER, JOSEPH T., 1960, *The Effects of Mass Communication*. New York: Free Press.

LANZETTA, JOHN T., and THORNTON B. RODY, 1957, Group Learning and Communication as a Function of Task and Structure "Demands," *Journal of Abnormal and Social Psychology*, 55:121–131.

LARSEN, OTTO N., and RICHARD J. HILL, 1958, Social Structure and Interpersonal Communication, *American Journal of Sociology*, 63:497–505.

LEAVITT, HAROLD J., 1958, *Managerial Psychology*. Chicago: University of Chicago Press.

LENNEBERG, ERIC H., and JOHN M. ROBERTS, 1956, The Language of Experience, *International Journal of American Linguistics*, Memoir 13.

LEVI-STRAUSS, CLAUDE, 1951, Language and the Analysis of Social Laws, *American Anthropologist*, 53:155–163.

——, ROMAN JAKOBSON, C. F. VOEGELIN, and THOMAS A. SEBEOK, 1953, Results of the Conference of Anthropologists and Linguists, *International Journal of American Linguistics*, Memoir 8.

LORGE, IRVING, and HERBERT SOLOMON, 1955, Two Models of Group Behavior in the Solution of Eureka-Type Problems, *Psychometrika*, 20:139–148.

LUCE, R. DUNCAN, and H. RAIFFA, 1957, *Games and Decisions*. New York: Wiley.

LURIA, A. R., 1961, *The Role of Speech in the Regulation of Normal and Abnormal Behavior*. London: Pergamon.

MACCOBY, ELEANOR, T. H. NEWCOMB, and E. L. HARTLEY, eds., 1958, *Readings in Social Psychology*, 3d ed., New York: Holt, Rinehart and Winston, Inc.

MACRAE, DONALD G., 1951, Cybernetics and Social Science, *British Journal of Sociology*, 2:135–149.

MACKAY, DONALD M., 1950, Quantal Aspects of Scientific Information Theory, *Philosophical Magazine*, 41:289–311.

———, 1956, Towards an Information Flow Model of Human Behaviour, *British Journal of Psychology*, 47:30–43.

———, 1961, Operational Aspects of Some Fundamental Concepts of Human Communication, *Journal of Communication*, 11:183–189.

MAIER, N. R. F., *et. al.*, 1959, *Communication in Organization*. Ann Arbor, Mich.: University of Michigan, Foundation for Research in Human Behavior.

MARCH, JAMES G., and HERBERT A. SIMON, 1958, *Organizations*. New York: Wiley.

MARSCHAK, JACOB, 1955, Elements for a Theory of Teams, *Management Science*, 1:127–137.

McINTOSH, ANGUS, 1961, Patterns and Ranges. *Language*, 37:325–337.

MEIER, RICHARD L., 1956, Communication and Social Change, *Behavioral Science*, 1:43–59.

MILLER, GEORGE A., 1951, *Language and Communication*. New York: McGraw-Hill.

———, 1956, The Magical Number Seven, Plus or Minus Two: Some Limits on Our Capacity for Processing Information, *Psychological Review*, 63:81–97.

———, 1962, Some Psychological Studies of Grammar, *American Psychologist*, 17:748–762.

MULDER, MAUK, 1960, Communication Structure, Decision Structure and Group Performance, *Sociometry*, 23:1–14.

MURPHY, GARDNER, 1961, Toward a Field Theory of Communication, *Journal of Communication*, 11:196–201.

NAFZIGER, RALPH O., and DAVID MANNING WHITE, eds., 1963, *Introduction to Mass Communication Research*. Baton Rouge, La.: Louisiana State University Press.

NOKES, PETER, 1961, Feedback as an Explanatory Device in the Study of Certain Interpersonal and Institutional Processes, *Human Relations*, 14:381–387.

OETTINGER, A. G., 1960, *Automatic Language Translation*. Cambridge, Mass.: Harvard University Press.

OSGOOD, CHARLES E., and THOMAS A. SEBEOK, eds., 1954, Psycholinguistics, a Survey of Theory and Research Problems, *International Journal of American Linguistics, Memoir 10*.

———, GEORGE J. SUCI, and PERCY H. TANNENBAUM, 1957, *The Measurement of Meaning*. Urbana, Ill.: University of Illinois.

———, and K. V. WILSON, 1961, *Some Terms and Associated Measures for Talking About Human Communication*. Urbana, Ill.: University of Illinois, Institute of Communication Research.

PIERCE, J. R., 1961, *Symbols, Signals and Noise*. New York: Harper & Row.

PIKE, KENNETH L., 1959, Language as Particle, Wave, and Field, *The Texas Quarterly*, 2 (2):37–54.

PITTENGER, ROBERT E., CHARLES F. HOCKETT, and JOHN J. DANEHY, 1960, *The First Five Minutes*. Ithaca, N.Y.: Martineau.

POLANSKY, NORMAN, RONALD LIPITT, and FRITZ REDL, 1950, An Investigation of Behavioral Contagion in Groups, *Human Relations*, 3:319–348.

Pool, Ithiel de Sola, ed., 1959, *Trends in Content Analysis*. Urbana, Ill.: University of Illinois.

Postal, P., 1964, *Constituent Structure: A Study of Contemporary Models of Syntactic Description*. Bloomington, Ind.: Indiana University Press, and The Hague: Mouton.

Pye, Lucian, ed., 1963, *Communication and Political Development*. Princeton, N.J.: Princeton University.

Quine, Willard Van Orman, 1960, *Word and Object*. Cambridge, Mass.: The MIT Press, and New York: Wiley.

Redfield, Charles E., 1958, *Communication in Management*, rev. ed., Chicago: University of Chicago Press.

Riecken, Henry W., 1958, The Effect of Talkativeness on Ability to Influence Group Solutions to Problems, *Sociometry*, 21:309–321.

Riley, John W., Jr., and Matilda White Riley, 1959, Mass Communication and the Social System, in *Sociology Today: Problems and Prospects*, edited by Robert K. Merton, Leonard Broom, and Leonard S. Cottrell, Jr. New York: Basic Books, pp. 537–578.

Rosenblith, Walter A., ed., 1961, *Sensory Communication*. Cambridge, Mass.: MIT, and New York: Wiley.

Rubenstein, Albert H., 1953, Problems in the Measurement of Interpersonal Communication in an Ongoing Situation, *Sociometry*, 16:78–100.

Ruesch, Jurgen, 1952, The Therapeutic Process from the Point of View of Communication Theory, *American Journal of Orthopsychiatry*, 22:690–701.

———, and Weldon Kees, 1956, *Nonverbal Communication*. Berkeley and Los Angeles: University of California Press.

Saporta, Sol, ed., 1961, *Psycholinguistics*. New York: Holt, Rinehart and Winston, Inc.

Schachter, Stanley, 1951, Deviation, Rejection, and Communication, *Journal of Abnormal and Social Psychology*, 46:190–207.

Scher, Jordan M., 1959, Two Disruptions of the Communication Zone: A Discussion of Action and Role Playing Techniques, *Group Psychotherapy*, 12:127–133.

Schramm, Wilbur, ed., 1960, *Mass Communication*, 2d ed. Urbana, Ill.: University of Illinois Press.

———, ed., 1963, *The Science of Human Communications*. New York: Basic Books.

Sebeok, Thomas A., Alfred S. Hayes, and Mary Catherine Bateson, eds., 1964, *Approaches to Semiotics*. The Hague: Mouton.

Shannon, Claude E., and Warren Weaver, 1949, *The Mathematical Theory of Communication*. Urbana, Ill.: University of Illinois Press.

Shaw, Marvin E., 1954, Some Effects of Unequal Distribution of Information Upon Group Performance in Various Communication Nets, *Journal of Abnormal and Social Psychology*, 49:547–553.

———, 1955, A Comparison of Two Types of Leadership in Various Communication Nets, *Journal of Abnormal and Social Psychology*, 50:127–134.

———, and Gerald H. Rothschild, 1956, Some Effects of Prolonged Experience in Communication Nets, *Journal of Applied Psychology*. 40:281–286.

Skinner, B. F., 1957, *Verbal Behavior*. New York: Appleton-Century-Crofts.

Starkweather, John A., 1956, The Communication-Value of Content-Free Speech, *American Journal of Psychology*, 69:121–123.

————, 1961, Vocal Communication of Personality and Human Feelings, *Journal of Communication*, 11:63–72.

STEPHAN, F. F., 1952, The Relative Rate of Communication between Members of Small Groups, *American Sociological Review*, 17:598–608.

TAYLOR, DONALD W., and WILLIAM L. FAUST, 1952, Twenty Questions: Efficiency in Problem Solving as a Function of Size of Group, *Journal of Experimental Psychology*, 44:360–368.

————, PAUL C. BERRY, and CLIFFORD H. BLOCK, 1958, Does Group Participation When Using Brainstorming Facilitate or Inhibit Creative Thinking?, *Administrative Science Quarterly*, 3:23–47.

THAYER, LEE O., 1963, On Theory Building in Communication: Some Conceptual Problems, *Journal of Communication*, 13:217–235.

THIBAUT, JOHN W., and COULES, J., 1952, The Role of Communication in the Reduction of Interpersonal Hostility, *Journal of Abnormal and Social Psychology*, 47:770–777.

————, and HAROLD H. KELLEY, 1959, *The Social Psychology of Groups*. New York: Wiley.

TODA, M., and Y. TAKADA, 1958, Studies of Information Processing Behavior, *Psychologica*, 1:265–274.

TRAGER, GEORGE L., 1958, Paralanguage: A First Approximation, *Studies in Linguistics*, 13:1–12.

————, 1959, The Systematization of the Whorf Hypothesis, *Anthropological Linguistics*, 1:31–35.

ULMANN, STEPHEN, 1962, *Semantics: An Introduction to the Science of Meaning*. New York: Barnes & Noble.

VERPLANCK, WILLIAM S., 1955, The Control of the Content of Conversation: Reinforcement of Statements of Opinion, *Journal of Abnormal and Social Psychology*, 51:668–676.

WAGER, L. WESLEY, 1962, Channels of Interpersonal and Mass Communication in an Organizational Setting, *Sociological Inquiry*, 32:88–107.

WALSTER, ELAINE, and LEON FESTINGER, 1962, The Effectiveness of "Overheard" Persuasive Communications, *Journal of Abnormal and Social Psychology*, 65:395–402.

WALTON, E., 1963, Study of Organizational Communication System, *Personnel Administration*, 26:46–49.

WATERMAN, J. T., 1957, Benjamin Lee Whorf and Linguistic Field Theory, *Southwestern Journal of Anthropology*, 13:201–211.

WEINREICH, URIEL, 1963, "On the Semantic Structure of Language" in *Universals of Language* edited by Joseph Greenberg. Cambridge, Mass.: The MIT Press, pp. 114–171.

WELLS, RULON, 1957, A Mathematical Approach to Meaning, *Cahiers Ferdinand de Saussure*, 15:117–137.

WHITE, LESLIE A., 1962, Symboling: A Kind of Behavior, *Journal of Psychology*, 53:311–317.

WHITEHORN, JOHN C., 1958, "Problems of Communication between Physicians and Schizophrenic Patients," in *Psychopathology of Communication*, edited by Paul H. Hoch and Joseph Zubin. New York and London: Grune & Stratton.

WHORF, BENJAMIN LEE, 1956, *Language, Thought, and Reality: Selected Writings of Benjamin Lee Whorf*, edited by John B. Carroll. New York: Wiley.

WIENER, NORBERT, 1950, Speech, Language, and Learning, *Journal of the Acoustical Society of America*, 22:696–697.

———, 1950, *The Human Use of Human Beings*. Boston: Houghton Mifflin.

———, 1961, *Cybernetics*, 2d ed., Cambridge: The MIT Press, and New York: Wiley.

WITTGENSTEIN, LUDWIG, 1953, *Philosophical Investigations*. New York: Macmillan.

ZIFF, PAUL, 1960, *Semantic Analysis*. Ithaca, N.Y.: Cornell University Press.

Index